BIOGRAPHICAL DICTIONARY OF CHRISTIAN THEOLOGIANS

BIOGRAPHICAL DICTIONARY OF CHRISTIAN THEOLOGIANS

EDITED BY Patrick W. Carey
AND Joseph T. Lienhard

GREENWOOD PRESS
Westport, Connecticut • London

Library of Congress Cataloging-in-Publication Data

Biographical dictionary of Christian theologians / edited by Patrick
W. Carey and Joseph T. Lienhard.
   p. cm.
  Includes bibliographical references and index.
  ISBN 0–313–29649–9 (alk. paper)
  1. Theologians—Biography Dictionaries. I. Carey, Patrick W.,
1940– . II. Lienhard, Joseph T.
  BR95.B575 2000
  230'.092'2—dc21   99–22143
  [B]

British Library Cataloguing in Publication Data is available.

Library of Congress Catalog Card Number: 99–22143
ISBN: 0–313–29649–9

First published in 2000

Greenwood Press, 88 Post Road West, Westport, CT 06881
An imprint of Greenwood Publishing Group, Inc.
www.greenwood.com

Printed in the United States of America

The paper used in this book complies with the
Permanent Paper Standard issued by the National
Information Standards Organization (Z39.48–1984).

10 9 8 7 6 5 4 3 2 1

CONTENTS

PREFACE

The *Biographical Dictionary of Christian Theologians* is meant to be a practical work of reference. Its goal is to provide readers with a concise introduction to the lives and thought of more than 450 Christian theologians. Whenever possible, articles first sketch the theologian's education and career and then provide a concise summary of that theologian's major works and contributions to theology. A short bibliography of primary and secondary works concludes each article. The articles are meant to be descriptive, rather than argumentative or polemical, in their presentations of the theological traditions that have emerged in almost 2,000 years of Christian history.

Articles follow a format first used in Henry Warner Bowden's *Dictionary of American Religious Biography* (Greenwood Press, 1977; 2d ed. 1993). A standard format was the goal for each entry; but in some cases, limited information made uniformity impossible. Accuracy was, of course, the primary goal of authors and editors; but limitations of space made it impossible to deal with subtle problems of dating or complexities of interpretation. Whenever possible, each entry supplies the theologian's date and place of birth and death, and a brief account of his or her education and career. There follows a summary of the theologian's most important contributions to theology. The entry ends with a short bibliography, divided into two parts. Part A lists the most important editions of primary works—that is, the theologian's own writings. Part B lists secondary works, which are modern studies of the theologian's thought and influence. For most articles, Part B of the bibliography is restricted to about six entries, which are biographies or systematic interpretative studies. Each article also has the author's name supplied. A list of contributors, with their academic positions, is found at the end of the volume.

Entries are restricted to Christian theologians who died before 1994, when this project was begun. Moreover, "theologian" is here understood in a fairly restricted sense: those whose work was primarily in systematic and spiritual theology, or historians of the Christian Church whose work was primarily theological in orientation. The editors have excluded exegetes, canon lawyers, and philosophers of religion such as René Descartes, Immanuel Kant, and Georg Hegel. In other words, entries were restricted to those whose work was primarily the result of a study of Scripture and tradition. Within these limits, the editors tried to choose the most important and representative theologians from the Catholic, Orthodox, and Protestant traditions and, especially in treating the post-Reformation period, gave particular attention to theologians of the English-speaking world. When a theologian's name is mentioned within an article not about that theologian, an asterisk is placed beside the name to indicate an entry in this volume.

The length of each entry was determined by the editors' perception of each theologian's importance to the development of Christian theological traditions. The longest entries comprise 2,000 words; such entries are limited to such crucial theologians as St. Augustine, Thomas Aquinas, Martin Luther, John Calvin, Karl Barth, and Karl Rahner. The shortest entries are 250 words long.

The primary readership that the editors had in mind was graduate students in a master's degree program in theology. The volume is intended to give such students a first orientation to the great theologians of the Christian tradition. The editors hope, of course, that the volume might also be useful to clergy and others who are interested in the Christian theological tradition, to advanced scholars who seek some brief note on an unfamiliar theologian, and to any reader who seeks an introduction to the life and works of theologians who have influenced thought and culture.

In carrying out this project, Joseph T. Lienhard was responsible for selecting and editing entries on theologians from the pre-Reformation era, and Patrick W. Carey for those from the post-Reformation period. Both consulted with experts in various historical periods as they prepared the list of entries, and invited many scholars to contribute articles. Many scholars contributed their time and talent to the preparation of this volume; whatever success and value it has will largely be due to their generosity and their willing cooperation with the editors.

ACKNOWLEDGMENTS

The editors of this volume thank our many contributors, whose expertise on various theologians contributed so much to the quality of the entire project. No project like the present one could be completed without the helpful assistance of the interlibrary loan officials at Fordham and Marquette and the research librarians who over the years proved eminently helpful in locating rare resources for us. We also want to thank our research assistants, Carl F. Baechle and Stephen M. Hildebrand, for the pre-Reformation theologians and Ian Christopher Levy, Anne Slakey, and Jeffrey W. Barbeau for the post-Reformation theologians. All five assistants played a major role in ensuring consistency of format, checking resources, typing corrections, and proofreading the entries. Anyone who has had the aid of graduate research assistants knows the value they bring to projects like this. Finally, we thank Greenwood Press, and especially Dr. George F. Butler, associate editor, for inviting us to organize and edit this volume. We appreciate in particular the patience with the long delay in getting this volume ready for publication.

ABBREVIATIONS

AAP	*Annals of the American Pulpit*, 9 vols. (New York, 1857–69; 1969)
ACO	*Acta Conciliorum Oecumenicorum*
ACW	Ancient Christian Writers
AHC	*Annuarium Historiae Conciliorum*
ANF	Ante-Nicene Fathers
BBKL	*Biographische-Bibliographische Kirchen Lexicon*
Catholicisme	*Catholicisme, hier, aujourd' hui et demain*
CCCM	Corpus Christianorum continuatio mediaevalis
CCSG	Corpus Christianorum series graeca
CCSL	Corpus Christianorum series latina
CH	*Church History*
ChP	*Christliche Philosophie im katholischen. Denken des 19. und 20. Jahrhunderts*
CPG	*Clavis Patrum Graecorum*
CPL	*Clavis Patrum Latinorum*
CSCO	Corpus Scriptorum Christianorum Orientalium
CSEL	Corpus Scriptorum Ecclesiasticorum Latinorum
CWS	Classics of Western Spirituality
DAB	*Dictionary of American Biography*, 20 vols. (New York, 1928–37; four supplements 1944–74)
DACB	*Dictionary of American Catholic Biography*, ed. John J. Delany (New York, 1984)

DAH	*Dictionary of the American Hierarchy* (New York, 1940)
DARB	*Dictionary of American Religious Biography*, 2d ed., rev. (Westport, Conn., 1993)
DCA	*Dictionary of Christianity in America*, ed. Daniel G. Reid et al. (Downers Grove, Ill., 1990)
DDC	*Dictionnaire du droit canonique*
DHGE	*Dictionnaire d'histoire et de géographie ecclésiastiques*
DMA	*Dictionary of the Middle Ages*
DNB	*Dictionary of National Biography*, 22 vols. (London, 1959–60)
DS	Heinrich Joseph Denzinger and Adolfus Schönmetzer, *Enchiridion Symbolorum Definitionum et Declarationum de rebus fidei et morum* (Würzburg, 1854; 36th ed. Barcelona, 1976)
DSAM	*Dictionnaire de spiritualité ascétique et mystique*
DTC	*Dictionnaire de théologie catholique*
ECatt	*Enciclopedia Cattolica*
EEC	*Encyclopedia of the Early Church*
EKL	*Evangelishes Kirkenlexikon*, 5 vols. (Göttingen, 1985–)
EncPh	*Encyclopedia of Philosophy*
ER	*Encyclopedia of Religion*, ed. Mircea Eliade et al., 16 vols. (New York, 1987)
EThL	*Ephemerides Theologicae Lovanienses*
FC	Fathers of the Church
GCS	Die griechischen christlichen Schriftsteller der ersten [drei] Jahrhunderte
GOTR	*Greek Orthodox Theological Review*
HDOC	*Historical Dictionary of the Orthodox Church*, ed. Michael Prokuret et al. (Lanham, Md., 1996)
HE	*Historia ecclesiastica*
HERE	*Hasting's Encyclopedia of Religion and Ethics*
HTR	*Harvard Theological Review*
Hurter	*Nomenclator literarius theologiae catholicae*
JECS	*Journal of Early Christian Studies*
JEH	*Journal of Ecclesiastical History*
JR	*Journal of Religion*
JTS	*Journal of Theological Studies*
Koch	Ludovicus Koch, *Jesuiten-Lexikon: Die Gesellschaft Jesu, Einst und Jetzt* (Paderborn, 1934)
KThD	*Katholische Theologen Deutschlands im 19. Jahrhundert*, ed. H. Fries and G. Schwaiger, 3 vols. (Munich, 1975)
LCC	Library of Christian Classics

LCL	Loeb Classical Library
LThK²	*Lexikon für Theologie und Kirche*, 2d ed. (1957–1965)
LThK³	*Lexikon für Theologie und Kirche*, 3rd ed. (in progress)
MGH	Monumenta Germaniae Historica
NAW	*Notable American Women, 1607–1950*, ed. Edward T. James et al., 3 vols. (Cambridge, Mass., 1971)
NCAB	*National Cyclopedia of American Biography*
NCE	*New Catholic Encyclopedia*, 15 vols., 3 supplementary vols.
NDB	*Neue Deutsche Biographie* (Berlin, 1953–)
NPNF	Nicene and Post-Nicene Fathers
NYT	*New York Times*
OC	Orientalia Christiana
ODB	*Oxford Dictionary of Byzantium*, 3 vols. (New York, 1991)
ODCC	*Oxford Dictionary of the Christian Church*, 3rd rev. ed. (Oxford, 1997)
OEncR	*Oxford Encyclopedia of the Reformation*
Patrology	Johannes Quasten, *Patrology*, 4 vols.
PG	Patrologia Graeca
PL	Patrologia Latina
PLS	Patrologiae Latinae Supplementum
PO	Patrologia Orientalis
PRE	*Realenzyclopädie für protestantische Theologie*
RechScRel	*Recherches de science religieuse*
RevScRel	*Revue des sciences religieuses*
RGG	*Religion in Geschichte und Gegenwart*
RHE	*Revue d'histoire ecclésiastique*
RHPhR	*Revue d'histoire et de philosophie religieuses*
RSPhTh	*Revue des sciences philosophiques et théologiques*
RTAM	*Recherches de théologie ancienne et médiévale*
SC	Sources Chrétiennes
SH	*New Schaaf-Herzog Encylopedia of Religious Knowledge*, ed. Samuel M. Jackson et al., 12 vols. (New York, 1908–12; Grand Rapids, Mich., 1949–50)
Sommervogel	*Bibliothèque de la compagnie de Jesus*, 11 vols. (Brussels-Paris, 1890–1932)
StPatr	*Studia Patristica*
SVTQ	*St. Vladimir's Theological Quarterly*
ThSt	*Theological Studies*
TRE	*Theologische Realenzyklopädie*

TU	Texte und Untersuchungen zur Geschichte der altchristlichen Literatur
VC	*Vigiliae Christianae*
ZKG	*Zeitschrift für Kirchengeschichte*
ZKTh	*Zeitschrift für katholische Theologie*

Biographies

A

ABBOTT, LYMAN (18 December 1835, Roxbury, Mass.–22 October 1922, New York, N.Y.). *Education*: B.A., New York Univ., 1853; New York bar exam, 1856. *Career*: practiced law, 1853–59; ordained Congregationalist minister, Farmington, Maine, 1860; minister, Terre Haute, Ind., 1860–65; secretary of American Freedmen's Union Commission, 1865–69; minister, New York, N.Y., 1865–69, and Plymouth Church, Brooklyn, N.Y., 1888–99; editor, *Illustrated Christian Weekly*, 1871–76, *Christian Union*, 1876–93, and *Outlook*, 1893–1922.

Abbott was a pastor who popularized a liberal evangelical Reformed theology and a form of social Christianity that influenced a number of American businessmen and industrialists during the progressive era of American history. Central to his theological thought was the idea that God resided in the human soul and that the Christian task was to open the individual to the indwelling power of God leading the Christian toward a conversion experience that would socialize the human character and ultimately lead to the reconstruction of the social order.

Like a number of liberal American Protestant theologians, he was open to Darwinian thought and biblical criticism. In fact, he tried to accommodate Christian teachings on inspiration, salvation, ecclesiology, and society to evolutionary modes of thought.

Bibliography

A. *The Evolution of Christianity* (Boston, 1892); *Christianity and Social Problems* (Boston, 1896; New York, 1970); *Theology of an Evolutionist* (New York, 1897); *What Christianity Means to Me: A Spiritual Autobiography* (New York, 1918).

B. DAB 1:24–25; DARB 3–4; NCAB 1:473; NYT 23 October 1922, 1; SH 1:7; Ira

V. Brown, *Lyman Abbott: Christian Evolutionist* (Cambridge, Mass., 1953; Westport, Conn., 1970); Edward Wagenknecht, "Lyman Abbott: The Life of God in the Soul of Man," in *Ambassadors for Christ: Seven American Preachers* (New York, 1972), 214–48.

Patrick W. Carey

ABELARD, PETER (1079, Le Pallet, Brittany—1142, Cluny). *Education*: studied dialectic at Loches under Roscelin of Compiègne, and at Paris under William of Champeaux, 1094–1106; attended Anselm's* school of theology at Laon, 1114. *Career*: taught at Melun and Corbeil, 1106–8; taught at Paris and Melun, 1108–14; lectured on Ezechiel at Laon, 1114; returned to teach at Paris, 1115–18; entered Benedictine order at St. Denis, near Paris, 1118; transferred to Maisoncelle, 1120; condemned at Soissons, 1121; enforced retirement to St. Médard, 1121; return to St. Denis, followed by flight to Provins, return, and founding of the Paraclete, 1122; abbot of St. Gildas de Ruys, Brittany, 1125–32; taught at Paris, 1134–40; attacked by Bernard of Clairvaux,* 1140; condemned at Sens, appeal and journey to Rome, 1141.

The outlines of Abelard's life to around 1134 are exceptionally well known from the *Historia calamitatum* (*Story of My Adversities*), for although its authenticity as Abelard's work has been questioned, its accuracy as regards the events of his life is not in doubt. Eldest son of the knight Berengar of Le Pallet in Brittany, he relinquished his inheritance to become a wandering scholar or, in his own words, a freelance knight of Minerva. At Melun, he clashed with the nominalist master Roscelin of Compiègne on the question whether universals have real existence, then went on to confute the realist William of Champeaux at Paris. While teaching logic at Melun, Corbeil, and Paris, he developed a moderate conceptualism, in many respects anticipating the Aristotelian solution, which would become available in Latin by the mid-twelfth century. At his mother Lucia's request, he returned in 1113 to Brittany to assist his parents with their retirement into the religious life. Returning to France, he attended Anselm of Laon's lectures on Sacred Scripture. Disillusioned by Anselm's pedantic style, Abelard claimed that with the help of a single commentary on the text any literate person could equal or surpass the master. Challenged by his fellow students to prove his contention, he gave two lectures on one of the more obscure passages in Ezekiel, and was expelled from the school for his temerity. He returned to Paris and founded his own school on the Left Bank, at Mont Ste. Geneviève. Successful but bored, he embarked on an affair with Heloise, niece of Fulbert, a canon of the cathedral. She became pregnant with a son, whom they named Astralabe. Despite an attempt by Abelard to reconcile Fulbert with the offer of a secret marriage, Fulbert hired men to attack and castrate Abelard for his misdeed. Fleeing in shame from the notoriety, Abelard entered the Benedictine community of St. Denis, after placing Heloise as a nun in the convent at Argenteuil, where she had been raised.

Abelard earned the dislike of his fellow monks at St. Denis by denouncing their worldliness and casting doubt on the monastery's claim to have been founded by Dionysius the Areopagite.* His first theological work, *Theologia "summi boni"* (*Theology of the "Highest Good"*), a treatise on the unity and trinity of God, aroused suspicion among his colleagues and was ultimately condemned at the Council of Soissons in 1121. Some of the accusations were: that Abelard denied the consubstantiality of the Holy Spirit with the Father, that he identified the Holy Spirit with the *anima mundi*, or world soul, and that he attributed power to the Father, wisdom to the Son, and goodness to the Holy Spirit in such a way as to deny that all three Persons possessed these attributes in the one divine nature. After a hearing in which he was denied opportunity to speak in his own defense and was compelled to burn his book with his own hands, he was immured at the monastery of St. Médard. Within a year the abbot at St. Denis allowed him to return, then to found a hermitage at Nogent-sur-Seine, called the Paraclete. His students flocked to hear him teach again, so that the buildings at the Paraclete had to be enlarged to accommodate their numbers.

In 1125, Abelard was named abbot of the monastery of St. Gildas de Ruys on the coast of Brittany, where his attempts to bring Cluniac reforms to a remote and primitive Celtic community met with such hostility that he was forced to flee for his life back to France. During his absence, the nuns at Argenteuil, where Heloise was now abbess, had been expropriated by the monastery of St. Denis, which owned the convent's land. Turning to Abelard for assistance, she was granted the Paraclete, secured its approval by Pope Innocent II, and continued to rely on Abelard for direction of the community.

After his return to France, Abelard resumed teaching in Paris. He enlarged and rewrote the three short books of the *Theologia "summi boni"* in five unwieldy new books as the *Theologia "christiana."* Dissatisfied, he made further additions and changes, ultimately formulating a completely new outline for the work. The result was called the *Theologia "scholarium,"* and survives in various redactions in six manuscripts. One of these, the longest, is printed as *Introductio ad theologiam* (PL 178). The new *theologiae*, like the first, were constructed in three books. Of these, the first salvaged portions of book one of the *Theologia "summi boni,"* prefacing them with a new introductory statement about faith, charity, and the sacraments, while the second comprised principally books two and three of the *Theologia "summi boni,"* including Abelard's series of logically argued objections and responses in defense of the trinitarian faith. A third and final book represented mostly new material, although based on ideas sketched in book five of the *Theologia "christiana."*

The late 1130s were Abelard's most productive period; he composed *Ethica*, the commentary on Romans, and the *Sic et Non* for his students at the cathedral school of Notre Dame, as well as the *Rule*, the *Hymnarius*, the *Problemata Heloissae* and the commentary on Gn 1 and 2 for the Paraclete. In 1140, at the instigation of William of St. Thierry,* Bernard of Clairvaux launched a new investigation into Abelard's works, which culminated in Abelard's condemnation at the Council of Sens in 1141. Abelard appealed unsuccessfully to Pope

Eugenius III, then set out for Rome to plead his case. He was taken ill at Cluny and, unable to continue his journey, accepted the hospitality of Peter the Venerable until his death in 1142. There is some controversy as to whether his *Dialogus inter philosophum, Judaeum et Christianum* was written during this final year at Cluny, or in the 1130s.

Abelard introduced into scholastic Latin the word *theologia* as a general term for systematic inquiry into the divine nature. His own series of theologies were essentially treatises on the unity and trinity of God, intended to offer a rational account of the doctrine of the Trinity and to suggest that some dim notion of it had existed not only in the Old Testament but even in some of the pre-Christian Greek and Roman philosophers. In his revisions, he nuanced the apparent appropriation of power to the Father, wisdom to the Son, and goodness to the Holy Spirit, so as to make clear that these attributes belong to all three persons in the one divine nature. Ultimately, his trinitarian language would be adapted by Hugh of St. Victor* and Peter Lombard* for their theological textbooks, thereby entering the mainstream of scholastic usage. Similarly, his compilation of apparently contradictory texts from Scripture and the Fathers in the *Sic et Non* is not to be understood as a rationalistic attack on tradition, but as a sourcebook for training his students in the reconciliation of conflicting authorities, a basic component of the scholastic method. In the introduction, he listed a series of principles for theological interpretation of texts. Apparent contradictions in the sources may result from the interpreter's failure to understand the text, from scribal error or a translator's mistake, a change in the sense of the words used, or an actual change of opinion by the original author. The student must also bear in mind that Sacred Scripture was written under the inspiration of the Holy Spirit, so that the exegete would do well to pray for guidance from the Spirit when attempting an interpretation. Lastly, he is advised, with a tag from Aristotle, that to learn the truth, he must question everything.

Abelard's commentaries on Romans and on Gn 1 and 2 approach the text on the literal level, carefully analyzing language and authorial intention, with the occasional excursus into theological questions raised by the text. One of the more famous of these is his excursus on Rom 3:19–26, where he asks how we are reconciled to God by the death of his Son, and in response develops his distinctive theory of the Atonement. Rejecting both the ransom theory, by which Christ is understood to have freed us from bondage to the devil, and the Anselmian satisfaction theory, he finds the key to Christ's saving work in the implications of Jn 15:13, "Greater love has no man than to lay down his life for his friends." Redemption from sin is the deeper love for God in us which is the effect of Christ's gift of grace, displayed in his willingness to die for us. The theory's weakness lies in Abelard's failure to make clear whether our love for God is a subjective human response or results from the activity of the Holy Spirit.

Common to many of Abelard's works is the quest for adequate definitions of good and evil. In his *Ethica*, he works out a definition of sin as intention, namely deliberate contempt of God, instead of locating sin in the deed or even in the act of will by which the deed was committed. Thus, the crucifiers of Christ, who acted in the conviction that they were obeying God, could not be held to have sinned, an opinion for which Abelard was later attacked by Bernard of Clairvaux. Original sin, meanwhile, is the inherited punishment, and not the guilt, of Adam's fall. Similar themes are explored in his *Dialogus*, a work less concerned with actual differences among Christians, Jews, and philosophers (identifiable perhaps with contemporary Muslims, but more probably with Cicero or the Platonists) than with defining the supreme good, supreme evil, and the merely indifferent. Ultimately, the supreme good is identified as God, and the supreme evil as a life lived in hatred or contempt of God. An example of the merely indifferent is found in the newborn human creature which, although good as a product of God's good creation, has exercised itself neither in virtue nor in vice, so that it is morally neutral. Commenting on Gn 1:31, Abelard approaches the problem of physical evil, again from the point of view of intention, although in this case he argues for the goodness of all creatures insofar as they conform to God's good intention, although some (such as the rebel angels) have become evil by their own choice, while others (such as venomous plants or animals) are evil only if misused by human beings.

Ultimately, Abelard's most enduring contribution to the history of theology may lie in his relationship with Heloise and the convent of the Paraclete. His *Hymnarius Paraclitensis* contains hymns and sequences still in use in both Catholic and Protestant worship. The *Problemata Heloissae* touch on practical issues in religious life, some of which are still current. Finally, the correspondence between the lovers continues to move its readers in every generation. It is a testimony to the success of their joint efforts that the Paraclete earned the admiration of both Bernard of Clairvaux and Peter the Venerable of Cluny, and survived as a convent for women until the French Revolution.

Bibliography

A.   PL 178; *Petrus Abaelardus philosophische Schriften*, ed. B. Geyer (Münster, 1919–27); *Peter Abelard's Theologia "summi boni,"* ed. H. Ostlender (Münster, 1939); *The Story of Abelard's Adversities*, ed. and trans. J. T. Muckle (Toronto, 1954); *Historia calamitatum*, ed. J. Monfrin (Paris, 1959); *Petri Abaelardi Opera theologica*, vols. 1–2, ed. Eligius M. Buytaert; vol. 3, ed. Eligius M. Buytaert and Constant J. Mews, CCCM 11–13 (Turnhout, 1969–87); *Dialogus inter philosophum, Judaeum et Christianum*, ed. R. Thomas (Stuttgart and Bad Cannstatt, 1970); *Dialectica*, ed. L. M. De Rijk, 2 vols. (New York, 1970); *Ethics*, ed. and trans. David Luscombe (Oxford, 1971); *The Letters of Abelard and Heloise*, trans. Betty Radice (Harmondsworth, 1974); *Hymnarius Paraclitensis*, ed. J. Szövérffy, 2 vols. (Albany, N.Y., 1975); *Sic et Non*, ed. Blanche Boyer and Richard McKeon (Chicago, 1976–77); *A Dialogue of a Philosopher with a Jew, and a Christian*, trans. Pierre J. Payer (Toronto, 1979); *The Hymns of Abelard in English Verse*, trans. Jane Patricia (Lanham, Md., 1986).

B.   DMA 1:16–20; LThK³ 1:9–10; NCE 1:15–17; ODCC 3–4; TRE 1:7–17; Charlotte Charrier, *Heloise dans l'histoire et dans la légende* (Paris, 1933); David Luscombe, *The*

School of Peter Abelard (New York, 1969); Jean Jolivet, *Abelard, ou la philosophie dans la langage* (Paris, 1970); Leif Grane, *Peter Abelard: Philosophy and Christianity in the Middle Ages* (New York, 1970); Peter Dronke, *Abelard and Heloise in Medieval Testimonies* (Glasgow, 1976).

Wanda Zemler-Cizewski

ADAM, KARL (22 October 1876, Pursruck in Oberpfalz–1 April 1966, Tübingen, Germany). *Education*: studied at Regensburg Sem., 1894–1900; Ph.D. in historical and systematic theology, Univ. of Munich, 1904; habilitation, 1908. *Career*: ordained priest, 1900; instructor, Univ. of Munich, 1908–17; professor of moral theology, Univ. of Strasbourg, 1917–18; professor of theology, Regensburg Sem., 1918–19; professor of theology, Univ. of Tübingen, 1919–49; professor emeritus, 1949–66.

Adam was a pioneer in the renewal of Catholic theology in the first half of the twentieth century and thereby prepared the way for the Second Vatican Council. In particular, he introduced Catholics around the world to the notion of the church as community and also raised their awareness of the humanity of Jesus Christ.

Adam initially wrote on the Latin Fathers, especially on Tertullian* and Augustine.* In his historical theology, he was guided by the work of Ignatius Döllinger,* Joseph Schnitzer, and Albert Ehrhard and, as a result, was viewed with suspicion by the Vatican's Holy Office.

At the University of Tübingen, Adam turned to systematic theology. In his analysis of the act of Christian faith, he used the phenomenological method of Max Scheler to describe the experience of Christian belief and its objective referent, God. Then, building on the work of the Catholic Tübingen School, especially of J. S. Drey,* J. A. Möhler,* and J. Kuhn,* Adam explained that the church is primarily a community, indeed the "mystical body of Christ" (1 Cor 10:17–18; 1 Cor 15:44; Rom 12:5). In fashioning this ecclesiology, Adam deliberately presented an alternative, on the one hand, to the First Vatican Council's notion of the church as an institution, "a true society," and, on the other hand, to liberal Protestantism's view (e.g., of Friedrich Heiler*) that the church is a complex of opposites.

Beginning in the 1920s, Adam developed a kerygmatic Christology, for he found unsatisfactory both the abstract, deductive Christology of neoscholasticism and "the life-of-Jesus research" of Adolf Harnack.* In this endeavor, Adam crafted an imaginative or narrative presentation on Jesus Christ, derived from Judeo-Christian Scripture and shaped by the doctrine of the Council of Chalcedon (A.D. 451) as well as by the neoromanticism that was dominant in Germany between the world wars. In contrast to the implicit monophysitism of much Catholic thought at the time, Adam stressed that Jesus Christ was/is a full human being, indeed "our brother." This emphasis contributed to the christological renewal in the second half of the twentieth century, for example, in the writings of K. Rahner,* E. Schillebeeckx, H. Küng, and W. Kasper. Throughout the 1920s, in response to directives from Rome's Holy Office, Adam revised his books in order to avoid the Vatican's censure.

In 1933, although not a Nazi, Adam briefly and naively highlighted how Adolf Hitler seemingly espoused some values (e.g., family and national heritage) consonant with Catholicism. He retracted this view in January 1934. After the war, Adam was one of the first Catholic theologians in Germany to contribute to the ecumenical movement.

Bibliography

A. *Der Kirchenbegriff Tertullians* (Paderborn, 1907); *The Spirit of Catholicism* (Augsburg, 1924; New York, 1929); *Christ Our Brother* (Regensburg, 1926; New York, 1931); *The Son of God* (Augsburg, 1933; New York, 1934); *One and Holy* (Düsseldorf, 1948; New York, 1951); *The Christ of Faith* (Düsseldorf, 1954; New York, 1957); bibliography in *Abhandlungen über Theologie und Kirche: Festgabe für Karl Adam*, ed. M. Reding (Dusseldorf, 1952).

B. LThK³ 1:141–42; ODCC 69; Jakob Laubach, ''Karl Adam,'' in *Theologians of Our Time*, ed. Leonhard Reinisch (Munich, 1960; Notre Dame, Ind., 1964), 92–108; Walter Kasper, ''Karl Adam,'' *Theologische Quartalschrift* 156 (1976): 251–58; Hans Kreidler, *Eine Theologie des Glaubens* (Mainz, 1988); Robert A. Krieg, *Karl Adam* (Notre Dame, Ind., 1992).

Robert A. Krieg

AFANASSIEFF, NIKOLAS N. (4 September 1893/94, Odessa–4 December 1966, New York, N.Y.). *Education*: mathematics and medicine, Univ. of Novorossisk, 1916–20; Ph.D., Univ. of Belgrade, 1921–27. *Career*: school teacher, Yugoslav Macedonia, 1927–30; lecturer in patristic history, St. Sergius Orthodox Theological Institute, Paris, 1930–32; chair of canon law, St. Sergius, 1932–41; ordained priest, Paris, 1940; priest in Tunis, 1941–47; professor, St. Sergius, Paris, 1947–66.

Afanassieff was yet another of the singularly brilliant number of emigré Russian theologians gathered in Paris (see also G. Florovsky,* S. Bulgakov, and N. V. Lossky*) whose work contributed significantly to both Eastern Orthodox thought and to Christian scholarship worldwide. His own contribution lay in his elaboration of the concept of ''eucharistic ecclesiology.'' He sought to derive both the nature and theology of the church from the eucharistic assembly where, as he wrote, the whole church of Christ is present complete. From the ''logic of the Eucharist,'' too, comes the development of the ecclesiastical ministries, the orders of clergy and laity, whose present form Afanassieff was content to see as the result of centuries of evolution. Although he was a professor of canon law, he remained sceptical all his life about the benefits of ''law and order,'' that is, the institutional and societal aspects of ecclesiastical life and history. For him, the church was always first and primarily the epiphany of the new age in Christ manifested through the Spirit in the Eucharist. His work was enormously influential on such later Orthodox theologians as A. Schmemann,* J. Meyendorff,* D. Staniloae,* and J. Zizioulas, though the latter three in particular were concerned to respond to and correct the one-sidedness in his thought that refused to take the church's institutional forms too seriously, in particular the episcopal office and its ministry of unity.

Bibliography

A. *L'Eglise du Saint-Esprit*, trans. Marianne Drobot (Paris, 1975); "The Church Which Presides in Love," in *The Primacy of Peter*, ed. John Meyendorff (London, 1963), 57–110.

B. HDOC 21–22; LThK³ 1:188; Aidan Nichols, *Theology in the Russian Diaspora: Church, Fathers, Eucharist in Nikolai Afanassieff* (Cambridge, 1989).

Alexander Golitzin

ALAN OF LILLE (ca. 1114/20, Lille, France–1202, Cîteaux). *Career*: perhaps lived and taught in Paris and Chartres 1157–70, in Montpellier 1171–85; perhaps returned to Paris; entered Cîteaux around 1202.

Alan's works include philosophy, theology (written during his years in Paris), polemics, sermons, spiritual writings, poetry and canon law; his *De arte sive de articulis fidei catholicae*, although incomplete, was original and similar to the *Sententiae* of Peter Lombard*, which eventually eclipsed Alan's work; *Questiones disputatae* and *Theologicae regulae* broke new ground in theological discourse; a moral work, *Liber parabolarum*, was a series of proverbs on moral conduct; the epic *Anticlaudianus* treated nature's attempt to create a perfect man, written with a style and breadth that inspired Dante and Chaucer; the polemic *Contra haereticos* attacked Waldensians, Albigensians, Jews, and Saracens. Influenced by Boethius,* Alan developed a concise style in his theological works. He quoted or paraphrased a thesis from dogmatic or moral theology and followed it with a brief, clear exposition. In his philosophical works, he was able to synthesize a style from Plato, Aristotle, and the church fathers. This style led him to be accused of pantheism and undue theological rationalism, but such criticism ignores his firm grounding in Christian orthodoxy. Alan of Lille is venerated within the Cistercian order and was known as the "Universal Doctor" among his contemporaries, a reference to his almost encyclopedic erudition.

Bibliography

A. PL 210; *Anticlaudianus*, ed. Robert Bossuat (Paris, 1955).

B. DMA 1:119–20; LThK³ 1:315–16; NCE 1:239–40; ODCC 16; TRE 2:155–60; Albert Dupuis, *Alain de Lille* (Lille, 1859).

Thomas S. Ferguson

ALBERT THE GREAT, Albertus Magnus, Albertus de Lauing, Albertus Theutonicus, Albertus Coloniensis; *doctor universalis* (ca. 1200, Lauingen, Bavaria–1284, Cologne). *Education*: studied in Padua, 1223; novitiate and theological studies presumably in Cologne; baccalaureate, Univ. of Paris. *Career*: entered the Dominican order, perhaps in 1223 or possibly 1229; teacher, Dominican houses in Germany; *magister theologiae*, Univ. of Paris, 1246–48; founded and taught at *studium generale*, Cologne, 1248–54, 1257–60; provincial of the Dominican province of Germany, 1254–57; bishop of Regensburg, 1260–61; resigned episcopate, 1261; resided in Italy, 1261–63; papal nuncio to the German-speaking countries and Bohemia, 1263; scholarly work in Germany, spending his final years in Cologne, 1263–84.

Albert's numerous writings, highly influential throughout the Middle Ages, encompass almost all the knowledge of his time, thus giving rise to the title *doctor universalis*. His early works include *De natura boni* (before his studies in Paris) and *De bono* (of the Paris period); the summas *De sacramentis*, *De incarnatione*, *De resurrectione*, *De IV coaequaevis*, *De homine* (the last two known over centuries under the title *Summa de creaturis*); a commentary on Peter Lombard's* *Sentences*, with many *quaestiones* added; and the *Quaestiones theologicae*. While in Cologne (1248–52) he wrote commentaries on all the works of Psuedo-Dionysius the Areopagite,* including, in contrast to Aquinas, the *Mystical Theology*. Albert began his enormous project of an exhaustive exposition of classical philosophy, paraphrased in understandable Latin, in Cologne with the commentary on the *Nicomachean Ethics* (the first commentary on this work in the West) and ended in the sixties with the treatments of metaphysics, ethics and politics. Albert freely added his own *digressiones* to his commentaries. By including works of other authors in his commentary he filled out areas missing in Aristotle's own books. The commentaries on Porphyry and Boethius,* the *De sex principiis*, the pseudo-Aristotelian *De vegetabilibus* and *De causis*, as well as (perhaps) on Euclid's *Elements*, also belong to this series. The commentaries on biblical books (prophets, Job, gospels), composed presumably in the sixties, represent a further genre. Albert's principal late writings are *De sacrificio missae*, *De corpore Domini*, and the incomplete *Summa de mirabili scientia Dei* (*Summa theologiae*). There also exist sermons and brief responses to particular questions, for example, *De unitate intellectus* (*contra Averroistas*), *De fato*, *De XV problematibus*, and the *Problemata determinata*. Inauthentic are the following works, attributed to Albert in the past: the Mariological writings *De laudibus beatae Mariae virginis*, *Mariale* and *Biblia mariana*; the commentaries on the Psalms and John's Apocalypse; *De adhaerendo Deo*; *Paradisus animae sive de virtutibus*; several writings on alchemy or magic (e.g. *Semita recta*, *De secretis mulierum* and probably *Speculum astronomiae*). The *Philosophia pauperum* and *Summa naturalium* were not written by Albert but contain extensive excerpts from authentic works of his.

Albert's contributions lie not so much in theology as in philosophy and natural science, especially in botany, zoology, and mineralogy, where he gave full recognition to experimental methods. He defended the independence of philosophy from theology. He was primarily responsible, despite adamant opposition, for the acceptance of Aristotle within Christianity. In important questions like the teaching on the *rationes seminales* or illumination, he supported Aristotelianism against the traditional Augustinianism. Albert defined theology primarily as a practical and affective science *secundum pietatem* (i.e., directed toward the attainment of eternal happiness). By creating the notion of the *lumen gloriae*, which became classical, he achieved a synthesis of two previously antagonistic positions on the question whether God himself, or merely divine "theophanies," is the content of eternal life.

Although no theologian of the Middle Ages enjoyed greater prestige, Albert did not inaugurate a school. His theology was soon overshadowed by that of his pupil Thomas Aquinas.*

Bibliography

A.   The edition by August Borgnet and Emil Borgnet (Paris, 1890–99) is incomplete and unreliable. A critical edition, *Alberti Magni opera omnia*, is in progress (Cologne, 1951–).

B.   DMA 1:126–30; LThK³ 1:337–39; NCE 1:254–58; ODCC 34–35; TRE 2:177–84; Georg Wieland, *Untersuchungen zum Seinsbegriff im Metaphysik-Kommentar Alberts des Grossen* (Münster, 1972; 2d ed. 1992); *Albert the Great: Commemorative Essays*, ed. Francis J. Kovach and Robert W. Shahan (Norman, Okla., 1980); *Albertus Magnus— Doctor universalis 1280/1980*, ed. Gerbert Meyer and Albert Zimmermann (Mainz, 1980); *Albertus Magnus and the Sciences*, ed. James A. Weisheipl (Toronto, 1980); Ingrid Craemer-Ruegenberg, *Albertus Magnus* (Munich, 1980); *Albert der Grosse. Seine Zeit, sein Werk, seine Wirkung*, ed. Albert Zimmermann (New York, 1981); Beroald Thomassen, *Metaphysik als Lebensform. Untersuchungen zur Grundlegung der Metaphysik im Metaphysik-Kommentar Alberts des Grossen* (Münster, 1985).

William J. Hoye

ALCUIN (ca. 730, Northumbria–804). Cultural adviser to Charlemagne and guiding spirit of the Carolingian revival of letters, Alcuin was educated in the cathedral school of York, famous for its library of Christian and classical sources alike. Succeeding his teacher Aelbert as master, he led the school to even greater prominence until, traveling to Rome to obtain the pallium for his new archbishop Eanbald, he met Charlemagne at Parma (781), and Charlemagne invited him to enter his service. Having received permission from both king and archbishop, Alcuin went to Aachen, where he organized the palace school and library as a place for both scholars and students, a kind of informal academy. He gave his associates nicknames from biblical and classical antiquity (Charlemagne was "David"; Theodulph, "Pindar"; Alcuin, "Flaccus") and educated students in the *trivium* and *quadrivium* of the liberal arts. In 796 Charlemagne appointed Alcuin abbot of St. Martin's at Tours, whose school, library, and scriptorium Alcuin established as one of the greatest in Europe, this time with the help of former students from York. Alcuin died at St. Martin's, still only a deacon from his days at York. His students went on to found schools of their own (Leidrad at Lyons; Rabanus Maurus* at Fulda; Theodulf* at Orléans).

Alcuin's works include educational dialogues (on grammar, dialectic, rhetoric, spelling), poems (including the long historical poem *On the Bishops, Kings, and*

Saints of York) and inscriptions, philosophical writings on the soul and on moral subjects, and a voluminous correspondence.

Alcuin's theological accomplishments include a recension of the Vulgate, a revision of the Roman lectionary in use in Gaul, a Sacramentary and votive Masses, hagiography, and biblical exegesis. His greatest challenge as a theologian was Spanish adoptionism, and his several treatises, written over the last decade of his life against Elipandus, archbishop of Toledo, and Felix, bishop of Urgel in the Carolingian Spanish March, represent a growth in theological and especially Christological sophistication through the careful reading of patristic and conciliar texts.

Alcuin's most influential work was his treatise *On the Faith of the Holy and Undivided Trinity*, a short summary of Catholic faith in three books, copied in every century until the advent of printing and then published in several editions. Wholly unoriginal in one sense, it skillfully organizes and weaves together paraphrases and verbatim citations (all unacknowledged) from the Fathers into an original synthesis that acquires enormous power from its succinct systematic character. Although not directed specifically against the adoptionists, it was in a way Alcuin's most perfect anti-adoptionist treatise, since it defends the logic of an orthodox Christology by showing its context in the whole of the system of faith.

Bibliography

A.   Collected works, including the *Vita Alcuini*, in PL 100–101; *Letters* in MGH *Epistolae* 4.1–481; 5.643–45; *Poems* in MGH *Poetae Latini* 1.160–351; 2.690–93; 4.903–10, 1128; 6.159.

B.   BBKL 1:118–19; DMA 1:142–43; NCE 1:279–80; ODCC 35–36; TRE 2:266–76; SH 1:111–12; Eleanor Shipley Duckett, *Alcuin, Friend of Charlemagne* (New York, 1951); Gerald Ellard, *Master Alcuin, Liturgist* (Chicago, 1956); Bonifatius Fischer, *Die Alkuin Bibel* (Freiburg, 1957); D. Bullough, "Alcuin and the Kingdom of Heaven," in *Carolingian Essays*, ed. Uta-Renate Blumenthal (Washington, D.C., 1983); John C. Cavadini, "The Sources and Theology of Alcuin's *De fide* . . . ," *Traditio* 46 (1991): 123–46; idem, *The Last Christology of the West* (Philadelphia, 1993).

John C. Cavadini

ALEXANDER, ARCHIBALD (17 April 1772, Lexington, Va.–22 October 1851, Princeton, N.J.). *Education*: studied with William Graham at Liberty Hall, 1790–91. *Career*: itinerant evangelist, Va., 1792–94; ordained minister, Hanover, Va., 1794; pastor, Briery and Cub Creek, Va., 1794–98; president, Hampden-Sydney Coll., 1797–1807; pastor, Philadelphia, Pa., 1807–12; professor of theology, Princeton Sem., 1812–51.

Alexander was the first professor of theology at Princeton Seminary. Against Deists on the one hand and "enthusiasts" on the other, he taught that the Bible is the objective rule of faith and practice, which the believer must study inductively. While his employment of induction and his insistence upon the reasonableness of the Christian religion lent a rationalistic flavor to his writings, he was in fact an "experimental" Calvinist who argued that genuine religious experience and true theological knowledge were the result of "the impression of divine truth on the mind, by the energy of the Holy Spirit." As the founder of the Princeton tradition, Alexander articulated the themes that reigned at Princeton until its reorganization in 1929. As such, he is the progenitor of the Princeton Theology, a theology devoted to the Reformed faith and characterized by the blending of "vital piety" with "sound theological learning."

Bibliography

A. *Evidences of the Authenticity, Inspiration, and Canonical Authority of the Holy Scriptures* (Philadelphia, 1826); *Thoughts on Religious Experience* (Philadelphia, 1841).

B. DAB 1:162–63; DARB 13–14; NCAB 2:22; NCE 1:299; SH 1:121–22; James Alexander, *The Life of Archibald Alexander* (New York, 1854); Andrew Hoffecker, *Piety and the Princeton Theologians* (Phillipsburg, N.J., 1981); David Calhoun, *Princeton Seminary*, 2 vols. (Edinburgh, 1994–96).

Paul Helseth

ALEXANDER OF HALES, *doctor irrefragabilis* (ca. 1185, Hales, Shropshire, England–21 August 1245, Paris). Alexander left his birthplace to study philosophy and theology in Paris where he became a *magister regens* in the faculty of arts in 1210, and later in the faculty of theology. He was the first to use Peter Lombard's* *Sentences* as the basic textbook for teaching theology. On the occasion of the university's conflict with the city in 1239–40, he left Paris in protest, going to Angers. After a brief time spent at the papal curia and in England in 1231/32, he returned to Paris. In 1235 he entered the Franciscan order, thus giving the Franciscans their first chair (*magister regens*) at the university. In 1245 he participated in the Council of Lyons. He was engaged by Henry III of England as a diplomat to the French king.

Alexander is regarded as the founder of the early Franciscan school of theology. His thought is traditional, relying primarily on Augustine,* John of Damascus* and Pseudo-Dionysius the Areopagite.* He presupposed the compatibility of philosophy and theology, without however explicitating his position on their relationship as intensely as later theologians did. He was among the first scholastics to reflect on the conception of theology as a science in the Aristotelian sense. He alludes to proofs of God's existence, but hardly developed them. Alexander maintained that creation in time can be known not only by faith but also by pure reason and criticized pagan philosophers for not having discovered this truth. He found analogies for the triune God throughout creation, thus establishing nature as a path back to the triune Creator. He maintained that human beings are free in both will and intellect, so that they may choose the morally good. He seems to have been the initiator of a tract on the topic of synderesis. One of his disputed questions treats the notion of conscience.

Alexander's *Summa*, which to a great extent is simply a compilation by various collaborators, notably John of La Rochelle, was completed after his death under the supervision of William of Militona.

Bibliography

A. *Quaestiones Disputatae "Antequam Esset Frater,"* 3 vols. (Quaracchi, 1960); *Summa Theologica,* 4 vols. (books 1–3, Quaracchi, 1924–48; book 4 can be found in the edition published in Cologne in 1622); *Glossa in Quatuor Libros Sententiarum Petri,* 4 vols. (Quaracchi, 1951–57).

B. DMA 1:148; LThK³ 1:362–63; NCE 1:296–97; ODCC 39; TRE 2:245–48; Adrian Fuerst, *A Historical Study of the Doctrine of the Omnipresence of God* (Washington, D.C., 1951); Elisabeth Gössmann, *Metaphysik und Heilsgeschichte. Eine theologische Untersuchung der Summa Halensis* (Munich, 1964); Meldon Wass, *The Infinite God and the "Summa fratris Alexandri"* (Chicago, 1964); Walter H. Principe, *Alexander of Hales' Theology of the Hypostatic Union* (Toronto, 1967).

William J. Hoye

ALPHONSUS MARIA DI LIGUORI (29 September 1696, Marianella near Naples–1 August 1787, Pagani near Salerno, Italy). *Education*: Univ. of Naples, 1708–17; doctor of civil and ecclesiastical laws, Univ. of Naples, 1717; theological studies at his home in Marianella, 1723–25. *Career*: lay evangelist, near Naples, 1724–25; ordained priest, 1726; evangelist, Naples countryside, 1726–32; founder, Congregation of the Most Holy Savior, 1732 (approved by Pope Benedict XIV in 1749 as the Congregation of the Most Holy Redeemer, the Redemptorists); bishop of Sant' Agata dei Goti, province of Beneventum, 1762–75; retired to Pagani, 1775–87.

Liguori was an eighteenth-century pastoral theologian whose primary aim was to promote the love of God for humanity. As a lay and clerical evangelist in the countryside around Naples, as a founder of a religious order, as a bishop, and as a moral theologian, Liguori sought practical ways of assisting people and priests to respond to the love of God. In the Enlightenment era he was on the side of the pietists, revivalists, and religious reformers who sought to enhance and deepen the religious life of his generation—a generation he believed to be affected by religious indifference, materialist and rationalist philosophies, Enlightened despots, and by unbelief on the one hand and rigorous Jansenist spirituality and ineffective pastoral programs on the other.

Between 1728 and 1778 Liguori wrote 111 works, mostly texts of ascetical and moral theology. His writings focused primarily upon the art and substance of preaching, asceticism and devotionalism (particularly devotion to Mary and to the eucharistic presence of Christ), basic Christian doctrine and apologetics, and the moral direction of consciences through the confessional.

Liguori's written works on preaching and parish missions directed missionaries to adapt their sermons to the concrete situations of the people and to emphasize the love of God as the principal motive for conversion of heart and mind. He did not originate the idea of giving popular parish missions as a means of the salvation of souls, but he was innovative in calling for a periodic renewal of parish missions for the ongoing conversion and sanctification of the people.

Liguori also promoted devotion to the Virgin Mary. His *Glories of Mary* (1750) was a popular devotional text that accepted the teaching on the Immaculate Conception of Mary and the idea that Mary directly cooperated in the redemption of the world, which was effected by the death and resurrection of Jesus. It was proper, therefore, to call her a co-redemptress and a mediatrix of grace. Liguori's emphasis upon Mary, much criticized by Protestants and some Catholics who thought he overemphasized the role of Mary, contributed much to the rise of Marian devotions and the Marian dogma of the Immaculate Conception in the nineteenth century.

In his ascetical and spiritual theology Liguori tried to counter the rigors of the Jansenist view of grace, salvation, and predestination. His point of departure was the love of God for all of humanity. In opposition to the Jansenists he supported frequent communion and asserted that God offers every person the possibility of salvation and sanctification. His spirituality, too, was Christocentric, emphasizing the love of Christ, manifested in the Incarnation, passion, death, and resurrection, as was evident in his *Pratica di amar Gesù* (1768).

His doctrinal, dogmatic, and apologetical works, which he wrote primarily during his episcopate, served the pastoral purpose of confirming the common faith of the church in opposition to attacks from unbelievers and rationalists. In a typical eighteenth-century Catholic fashion he developed for unbelievers and materialists proofs for the existence of God and the spirituality of the soul, for theists reasons for the necessity of a revealed religion and the truth of the Christian religion, and for Christians separated from Rome arguments for the Catholic Church as the only church of Christ, emphasizing in particular, in opposition to Febronius,* the supreme and infallible authority of the pope—another doctrine that would be taken up in the nineteenth century and defined at the Vatican Council (1870).

More than one-third of Liguori's published works were in moral theology, an area where he had his greatest theological influence. His moral writings were attempts to discover the will of God in the practical circumstances of daily living. His greatest accomplishment was his *Theologia moralis* (the definitive three-volume edition of which was published in 1779), a textbook intended to direct priests in cases of conscience in the confessional. The text tried to avoid the laxity of the probabilists and the rigorousness (tutorism) of the Jansenists. His own moral system has become known as equiprobabilism, a middle course between probabilism (the moral system that held that when there is question solely of the lawfulness or unlawfulness of an action, it is permissible to follow a solidly probable opinion in favor of liberty even though the opposing view is more probable) and probabiliorism (the moral system that held that it is not lawful to act on the less safe opinion unless it is more probable than the safe opinion). Like the probabilists he wanted confessors to leave room for personal liberty and the decision of conscience. But, unlike the probabilists, he believed it was lawful to act on the less safe opinion (among moralists) when it is equally probable with the safe opinion, and that it is not lawful to follow the less safe opinion when the safe opinion is notably and certainly more probable.

Liguori's spiritual and moral theology greatly influenced Catholic developments in the nineteenth century through his Redemptorist followers and through his republished texts. His reputation for holiness and sound teaching was officially acknowledged in the nineteenth and twentieth centuries. He was beatified in 1816, canonized in 1839, declared a doctor of the church in 1871, and made patron saint of confessors and moralists in 1950.

Bibliography

A.   *Opere Ascetiche*, ed. F. Delerue et al. (Rome, 1933–); *Opera dogmatica*, 2 vols. (Rome, 1903); *Lettere*, ed. P. Kuntz, 3 vols. (Rome, 1887–90); *Theologia moralis* (1753–55, and many subsequent eds.), critical ed. L. Gaudé, 4 vols. (Rome, 1905–12; repr. 1953); *Complete Works*, ed. Eugene Grimm, 22 vols. (New York, 1886–97; 2d ed. of vols. 1–5, 12, Brooklyn, N.Y., 1926–28); *The Way of Saint Alphonsus*, ed. B. Ulanov (London, 1961).

B.   DHGE 2:715–33; DSAM 1:357–89; Ecatt 1:864–73; LThK³ 1:387–89; NCE 1: 336–41; ODCC 45–46; TRE 21:199–202; A. M. Tannoia, *Della vita ed instituo del venerabile Alfonso Maria Liguori*, 3 vols. (Naples, 1798–1802), ET in 5 vols. (London, 1848–49); Théodule Rey-Mermet, *Le Saint du siècle des Lumières, Alfonso de Liguori (1696–1787)* (Paris, 1982; 2d. ed 1987); idem., *La Morale selon Saint Alphonse de Liguori* (Paris, 1987); François Bourdeau, Jean Delumeau et al., *Alphonse de Liguori, pasteur et docteur* (Paris, 1987); *Alphonso M. de Liguori e la Società Civile del suo tempo*, ed. Pompeo Giannantonio (Florence, 1990); Frederick M. Jones, *Alphonsus de Liguori: The Saint of Bourbon Naples, 1696–1787* (Dublin, 1992).

Patrick W. Carey

ALTHAUS, PAUL AUGUST WILHELM HERMANN (4 February 1888, Hannover-Obershagen, Germany–18 May 1966, Erlangen, Germany). *Education*: studied at Univ. of Tübingen, Univ. of Göttingen, Preachers' Sem., Hannover-Erichsburg, 1909–14. *Career*: lecturer, Univ. of Göttingen, 1914; Lutheran military chaplain in Lódz, German-partitioned Poland, 1914–18; assistant professor, Univ. of Rostock, 1919–25; professor of systematic theology, Univ. of Erlangen, 1925–66; president of the Luther Society, 1927–58.

Althaus was an authority on the theology of Martin Luther* and the Reformation. Althaus is most remembered as an interpreter of Martin Luther. His Luther is neither the idealistic German liberator of the German-Christians nor is he the late-medieval mystic shaped mostly by the nominalism of Gabriel Biel* and his successors. Althaus portrays Luther as a theologian and priest who, with great courage, creativity, and daring, steered a true course between a moribund papacy on the one hand and radical fanaticism on the other. Like his constant model and muse, Althaus refused to give in to a wholehearted radicalism of the right or left, looking always toward the middle for answers requiring thought and discernment in order to be understood. His basic political conservatism and his publicly uncritical stance toward the National Socialist regime on most points left him open to the criticism of complicity in or indifference toward the Nazi terror.

Though initially a strong public supporter of Adolf Hitler's New Germany, Althaus grew cool toward the church's political expression of National Socialism in the German-Christian movement and became privately bitter toward the totalitarian state he had originally accepted. From about 1927 Althaus was openly sympathetic toward the National Socialist German Workers' Party and was a member of the theologically conservative *Christlich-Deutsche Bewegung* ("Christian-German Movement"). His brief flirtation with the pro-Nazi and anti-Jewish German-Christians was motivated among other things by his royalist sympathies and his opposition to the social democracy imposed on Germany by the socialist and communist conspirators who had started the revolution of 1918–19 and had given the nation the Weimar Republic. A paternal monarch-figure to lead Germany out of chaos at home and back to a place of dignity and respect among nations was needed, according to this view.

Although Althaus had mild National Socialist and German-Christian leanings, he publicly resigned from the "Christian-German" wing of the conservative German-Christian movement in November of 1933. This was in response to a speech made in the Berlin Sports Palace on the occasion of a national German Christian rally in which the speaker called for elimination of the Old Testament, the Pauline Epistles, and other "Jewish elements" from the biblical canon. In 1934 Althaus wrote and spoke against the German-Christian movement and the National Socialist and radical German-Christian fiction that a peculiarly "Germanic" form of religion had been transmitted to Luther through the Rhenish Mystics. He was also subtly critical of the National Socialist state overstepping its bounds in relations with the church. He did not, however, join the ranks of the nascent *Bekennende Kirche* ("Confessing Church") of Reformed theologians such as Karl Barth.* In 1937, in fact, he published two political essays in which he argued for the validity of a morally responsible totalitarian state and the right and obligation of such a state to protect its interests through war if need be.

Bibliography

A. *Christus und die deutsche Seele* (Gütersloh, 1934); *Die deutsche Stunde der Kirche*, 3d ed. (Göttingen, 1934); *Evangelium und Leben: Gesammelte Vorträge* (Gütersloh, 1927); *Kirche und Staat nach lutherischer Lehre* (Leipzig, 1935); *Politisches Christentum: Ein Wort über die Thüringer "Deutschen Christen,"* 2d ed. (Leipzig, 1935); *Theologie der Ordnungen*, 2d ed. (Gütersloh, 1935); *The Theology of Martin Luther*, trans. Robert C. Schultz (Philadelphia, 1966).

B. LThK³ 1:467; TRE 2:329–36; "Althaus, Paul August Wilhelm Hermann," in *The Lutheran Cyclopedia*, rev. ed. Erwin L. Lueker (St. Louis, Mo., 1975), 22; James A. Zabel, *Nazism and the Pastors. A Study of the Ideas of Three Deutsche Christen Groups*

(Missoula, Mont., 1976); Robert P. Ericksen, *Theologians under Hitler: Gerhard Kittel, Paul Althaus, Emanuel Hirsch* (New Haven, Conn., 1985).

                                                                    Guy C. Carter

AMBROSE OF MILAN, Aurelius Ambrosius (ca. 338–397). Born into the Roman aristocracy, Ambrose had no intentions of pursuing an episcopal career. Like his brother Satyrus, he was trained in law, and was appointed provincial governor (*consularis*) of northern Italy. When Auxentius, the "Arian" bishop of Milan, died in 374, Ambrose entered the city basilica in order to quell disturbances over the choice of a successor. His success in doing so incited popular enthusiasm to elect him as bishop. Ambrose came from a Christian family but, typical of those who wielded civic or military authority, had not been baptized nor "brought up nor trained from childhood in the bosom of the church," as he wrote. His very lack of ecclesiastical qualification or theological training made him amenable to a crowd divided over trinitarian doctrine. Within a week, Ambrose was baptized and hurried through the lower orders to the office of bishop, hardly satisfying conciliar canons, which forbade the ordination of neophytes.

Once installed as bishop, Ambrose ostensibly continued to follow the neutral religious policies of Valentinian I, which preserved an uneasy peace in Milan. In the meantime, the new bishop discharged his pastoral obligations by addressing himself to the study of Scripture and Latin and Greek theology. His works on major themes and characters in Genesis reveal an influence of Philonic exegesis as well as familiarity with Origen* and Basil of Caesarea.*

Ambrose also wrote several small treatises on virginity, defending the divine calling of the virgin as a living martyr to the elite households of Milan. Ambrose later proposed Mary's pre- and post-partum virginity as a model for young women.

Ambrose's entry into doctrinal controversy began with his response to accusations of heresy made against him by anti-Nicenes in Milan. He defended the Nicene creed unambiguously as the only standard of orthodox Christianity. In *On the Faith* Ambrose attacked his Homoian opponents as Arians, using the same kinds of polemical arguments employed against Arius* a half century before, namely, that they taught that the Son is created and unlike the Father in substance. Ambrose declared that the divine nature is common to the Father, Son, and Holy Spirit: "We confess Father and Son and Holy Spirit with the result that the fullness of divinity and unity of power exist in perfect Trinity." In fact, there are no attributes of the Father that the divine nature of Christ does not share. The unity (*unum*) of the Father and Son is affirmed to the extent that there is no multiplicity (*multiplex*) because they are *indifferens*. From this position Ambrose would never deviate.

Ambrose's attempts to secure the emperor Gratian's political support for the pro-Nicene cause did not succeed until just before the council of Aquileia (381), where he managed the deposition of two Homoian prelates and other lesser clergy on the grounds of heresy. Even so, Ambrose's two other major theological treatises, *On the Holy Spirit* and *On the Incarnation of the Lord*, reveal that the struggle with anti-Nicene theology was not fully over. The latter treatise demonstrates a marked progression in Ambrose's understanding of his opponents. Ambrose argued for the complete separation of the divine and human natures in Christ in order to avoid any tendency to diminish the fully divine status of the incarnate Son.

Ambrose was not so much an original thinker as a passionate pleader and organizer. Whether opposing anti-Nicenes or aristocratic pagans such as Q. Aurelius Symmachus, against whom he effectively stifled all attempts to restore the Altar of Victory, Ambrose was a master at utilizing social and political resources to gain the upper hand. His active building program in Milan and promotion of martyr cults established an undisputed hegemony for pro-Nicene orthodoxy and for his memory.

Bibliography

A.   CPL 123–68; Patrology 4:144–79.

B.   DMA 1:230–32; EEC 1:28–29; LThK³ 1:495–97; NCE 1:72–75; ODCC 49–50; TRE 2:362–86; J. R. Palanque, *Saint Ambroise et l'Empire romain. Contribution à l'histoire des rapports de l'église et de l'état à la fin du quatrième siècle* (Paris, 1933); F. Homes Dudden, *The Life and Times of Saint Ambrose*, 2 vols. (Oxford, 1935); Angelo Paredi, *Saint Ambrose: His Life and Times*, trans. M. J. Costelloe (Notre Dame, Ind., 1964); Y.-M. Duval, ed., *Ambroise de Milan. XVIᵉ centenaire de son élection episcopale* (Paris, 1974); Neil McLynn, "The 'Apology' of Palladius: Nature and Purpose," JTS 42 (1992): 52–76; idem, *Ambrose of Milan: Church and Court in a Christian Capital* (Berkeley, Calif., 1994); Christoph Markschies, *Ambrosius von Mailand und die Trinitätstheologie* (Tübingen, 1995); D. H. Williams, *Ambrose of Milan and the End of the Nicene-Arian Conflicts* (New York, 1995); idem, "Polemics and Politics in Ambrose of Milan's *De fide*," JTS 46 (1995): 519–31.

Daniel H. Williams

AMES, WILLIAM (1576, Ipswich, England–14 November, 1633, Rotterdam, Holland). *Education*: A.B., Christ Coll., Univ. of Cambridge, 1607; fellow, Christ Coll., 1608–10. *Career*: minister, Holland, 1610; chaplain, British community of the Hague, 1611–19; consultant, Synod of Dort, 1618–19; overseer of the burse, Univ. of Leyden, 1619–22; professor of theology, Univ. of Franeker, 1622–30; minister, independent congregation in Rotterdam, 1630–33.

Ames was an English Puritan theologian who had an imposing influence upon the theological tradition of seventeenth and early eighteenth century New England theologians. As a young man he was significantly influenced by the Puritan theologian William Perkins (1558–1602) who taught at Christ College, Cambridge. His explicit and vocal nonconformist positions prevented him from obtaining any opportunities for educational and ministerial advancement in the Anglican Church in the early seventeenth century and, therefore, he left England in 1610 for the more open religious atmosphere in Holland, where he was appointed a minister and theologian. In Holland, moreover, he reasserted his op-position to the Roman remnants in the Church of England and to the Arminian party that was developing within the Reformed Church in Holland. He became, in fact, a consultant to the moderator at the Synod of Dort (1618–19), clearly identifying him with the opposition to Arminian notions of predestination, grace, and human freedom.

His most important and influential work in theology, *The Marrow of Theology* (the first complete edition published in 1627), demonstrated clearly the influence of Peter Ramus' (1515–72) method of ordering a subject of knowledge by de-fining all terms carefully, arranging all materials into dichotomies (each defined again), and moving from universal principles to specifics. The *Marrow* was a kind of summa of Reformed theology, intended to introduce students to the basics of the Christian theological tradition.

For Ames, theology was one of the arts (subject to universal rules just as were logic, grammar, and physics), but unlike the other arts its doctrine and first principles arose out of revelation and not from nature and human inquiry. Ori-ented toward the formation of the will and human activity, theology was pri-marily practical, not speculative, having as its end the "art of living well."

The central governing concept in Ames' *Marrow* was the covenant of grace, which he saw as the integrating idea of the entire Bible. The covenant was the saving promise of a God whose initiative and love created a new people. It was that which the Christian experienced as in living to God; it was the goal of religious discipline, repentance, and faith; it was appropriated only by faith and not by works, but works demonstrated clearly the power of grace that was inherent in the covenant. This covenant of grace was manifested in five stages of Christian life: calling, justification, adoption, sanctification, and glorification. To some extent Ames' description of the Christian life of grace was a long commentary on Rom 8:30.

Although he followed Calvin* and other Reformed theologians in emphasiz-ing divine predestination in the Christian's life of grace, Ames did not place predestination under the general heading of the work of God as did William Perkins, Theodore Beza,* and some other Reformed theologians. In the *Marrow*, Ames placed predestination in a chapter (ch. 25) that followed those on faith, the nature of God, sin, and the person and work of Christ, and before the chapters on the stages of Christian growth in grace. For Ames, predestination had an instrumental value. It led to the Christian life, served as a divine assur-ance that Christians had been placed on their pilgrimage into grace by God, was an invitation to sinful and anxious humans to begin their pilgrimage in faith, and was an incentive to spiritual introspection.

For Ames, the covenant of grace was closely associated with the church cov-enant, which bound those predestined into a special relationship of love to one another and to God.

Bibliography

A. *Bellarminus Enervatus*, 4 vols. (n.p., 1626); *Conscience with the Power and Cases Thereof. Divided into V. Bookes* (n.p., 1639); *Opera omnia*, ed. M. Nethenus, 5 vols. (Amsterdam, 1658); *The Workes of . . . W. Ames* (London, 1643); *The Marrow of Theology*, ed. and trans. John D. Eusden (Boston, 1968); *Technometry*, trans. Lee W. Gibbs (Philadelphia, 1979).

B. DNB 1:355–57; LThK³ 1:527; ODCC 51–52; RGG 1:332; TRE 2:450–53; Douglas Horton, *William Ames* (Cambridge, Mass., 1965); idem, "Let Us Not Forget the Mighty William Ames," *Religion in Life* 29 (1960): 434–42; Keith L. Sprunger, *The Learned Doctor William Ames: Dutch Background of English and American Protestantism* (Urbana, Ill., 1972); idem, "Ames, Ramus, and the Method of Puritan Theology," HTR 59 (1966): 133–51.

Patrick W. Carey

ANDREWES, LANCELOT (1555, Barking, England–26 September, 1626, Southwark, England). *Education*: B.A., Pembroke Hall, Cambridge, 1575. *Career*: Master, Pembroke Hall, 1589–1605; Dean of Westminster, 1601–5; Bishop of Chichester, 1605–9; Bishop of Ely, 1609–19; Bishop of Winchester, 1619–26.

Andrewes was one of the main influences on the formation of a distinctively Anglican theology. He was one of the Caroline Divines who distinguished Anglicanism both from Roman Catholicism and from the theology of the Continental reformers. He was a distinguished biblical scholar and one of the translators of the Authorized (King James) Version of the Bible. He was largely responsible for the translation of the Pentateuch and the historical books. His *Tortura Torti* (London, 1609) replied to Cardinal Robert Bellarmine's* criticism of King James' apology for the Oath of Allegiance that followed the Gunpowder Plot of 1605. Andrewes was best known for his learned sermons, and for his devotional anthology from the Scriptures and the ancient liturgies, *Preces Privatae* ("Private Devotions," London, 1647). In 1605 he began to serve as a court preacher in the court of King James, and preached at court on almost all major feasts of the church year for about twenty years. Andrewes' preaching was learned and deeply rooted in his experience of faith. Theology and spirituality were inseparable for Andrewes. His life is commemorated in the Episcopal Calendar on September 26.

Bibliography

A. *Ninety-Six Sermons*, ed. W. Laud and J. Buckeridge (London, 1629); *A Pattern of Catechistical Doctrine* (London, 1641); *The Greek Devotions of Bishop Andrewes*, trans. J. H. Newman (London, 1840); *The Works of Lancelot Andrewes*, ed. J. P. Wilson and James Bliss, 11 vols. (Oxford, 1841–54); *The Preces Privatae of Lancelot Andrewes*, trans. F. E. Brightman (London, 1908); *Lancelot Andrewes: Sermons*, ed. G. M. Story (Oxford, 1967).

B. DNB 1:401–5; DTC 1:1186–87; ECatt 1:1211; LThK³ 1:635–36; NCE 1:497;

ODCC 61; RGG 1:369; TRE 2:683–87; T. S. Eliot, *For Lancelot Andrewes* (New York, 1929); Maurice F. Reidy, *Bishop Lancelot Andrewes, Jacobean Court Preacher* (Chicago, 1951); John Booty, *Three Anglican Divines on Prayer* (Cambridge, Mass., 1978); Trevor A. Owen, *Lancelot Andrewes* (Boston, 1981), Nicholas Lossky, *Lancelot Andrewes, The Preacher*, trans. Andrew Louth (Oxford, 1991).

Robert B. Slocum

ANSELM OF BEC AND CANTERBURY (1033, Aosta–21 April 1109, England). Anselm was a pious boy, but, as Eadmer, his friend and first biographer puts it: "With health of body, youth and worldly well-being smiling upon him, he began little by little to cool in the fervor of his desire for a religious life— so much so that he began to desire to go the way of the world rather than to leave the world for a monastic life. He gradually turned from study, which had formerly been his chief occupation, and began to give himself up to youthful amusements." Yet by 1059 Anselm had made his way to the Abbey of Bec, some twenty miles south of Rouen. By 1042 Bec had been enriched by the arrival of Lanfranc* (ca. 1015–89). Modern verdicts on Lanfranc's intellectual achievements vary, but he had a considerable reputation as a scholar even before he came to Bec, and he quickly became a powerful figure there. There can be little doubt that it was he who drew Anselm to Bec.

Anselm became a monk of Bec in 1060. The available evidence attests that he always did his best to abide by the *Rule* of St. Benedict. It also suggests that monastic life was the one undertaking in which he most wished to succeed. Readers of his letters will quickly get a sense of him as someone who thought himself to be a bad Christian, yet he always held that the life of a monk was the best form of life. And this was the life he wanted to live.

In 1063 Anselm succeeded Lanfranc as prior of Bec and started to produce the texts for which people now remember him most. His first serious work was the *De grammatico*, which he probably wrote between 1060 and 1063, and which he describes as "an introduction to dialectic." But this is not his most distinguished work, and by 1076 he had written something rather different: the *Monologion*, his first really important book. To begin with, he called it an "Example of Meditating about the Substance of Faith" (*Exemplum meditandi de ratione fidei*). Then he called it a "*Monoloquium* on the Substance of Faith." In the end, though, he settled on the title *Monologion* ("monologue" or "soliloquy") because, so Eadmer tells us, "in it he alone speaks and argues with himself."

Anselm's *Monologion* is a treatise on the existence and nature of God and the doctrine of the Trinity. It represents a new way of writing theology. It is a theological treatise presented by someone who wants us to see the force of what he is saying on its own terms. In many ways, it is a very modern book. Its author presupposes that his arguments and conclusions ought to be acceptable to any clear-thinking reader. The same must be said of Anselm's next book, the *Proslogion*. It was written around 1077–78, so its production coincided with a major event in Anselm's life: Anselm became abbot of Bec in 1078. But readers of the *Proslogion* will get no sense of what was happening to its author when he was working on it. The *Proslogion* is a timeless kind of work, elegantly written and reading, in parts, like poetry. Its subject matter is similar to that of the *Monologion*, but its tone is different. The *Monologion* is very much a treatise. The *Proslogion* is cast in the form of a prayer.

Anselm was abbot of Bec for fifteen years, and he did a lot to increase its fame and material standing. He also managed to produce three notable texts between the years 1080 and 1086. These are the dialogues *De veritate* ("On Truth"), *De libertate arbitrii* ("On Freedom of Choice"), and *De casu diaboli* ("On the Fall of the Devil"). The first two dialogues deal directly with the subjects cited in their titles. The third, however, is mostly about evil in general, and evil choices in particular: Where does evil come from? How does it fit into God's plan for his creation? Is it something real? Or is it a kind of failure to be? These are the main questions dealt with in *De casu diaboli*.

From 1089 Anselm had to extend his intellectual horizons beyond his meditations at Bec and the interests and needs of his students there. From this time he found himself involved in serious argument with opponents in the world at large. And, to begin with, he found himself at odds with Roscelin. Probably born around 1050 at Compiègne, Roscelin was a teacher of theology and philosophy at various French cathedral schools. He was drawn to Anselm's attention in a letter from John, a monk at Beauvais, who said that Roscelin was claiming that the divine Trinity either included three distinct things, as three angels are three things, or that the Father and the Holy Spirit became incarnate with the Son. According to the report given to Anselm, Roscelin was also claiming that this is what Lanfranc and Anselm were teaching. Since the teaching on the Trinity ascribed to Roscelin by John was unorthodox, Anselm was naturally alarmed to find himself associated with it, and said so in some of his letters. He also felt the need to state his position with care and attention to detail.

Anselm's definitive reply to Roscelin, *Epistola de incarnatione Verbi* ("Letter on the Incarnation of the Word"), took several years to complete. The final version was not ready until around 1094. And by then Anselm was facing the world outside the monastery more directly than before. For as he was worrying about Roscelin and the Trinity, he was swept away from Bec and plunged into a very different situation. In 1093 he succeeded Lanfranc as archbishop of Canterbury.

Soon after Anselm became archbishop, the English king (William II) requested a large sum of money from him to finance an expedition to Normandy. Anselm refused the request since he judged that paying it would lead to hardship for his tenants. When William returned from Normandy Anselm asked to travel to Rome to receive his pallium (the symbol of his appointment as archbishop) from Pope Urban II. But William did not recognize Urban as pope, and in a meeting of clergy and nobles a majority of bishops sided with him against Anselm.

As matters turned out, Anselm received his pallium in May 1095. And then, for a while, there was peace between king and archbishop. Yet by summer 1097 William was complaining about the quality of troops provided for him by Anselm during a military exercise in Wales. Anselm therefore decided that royal opposition to himself as archbishop was still in the air and unlikely to diminish. He repeatedly asked the king's permission to leave for Rome, and permission was finally given. Anselm reached Rome in April 1098, and he stayed away from England until after the death of William Rufus in 1100. The period was clearly a satisfying one for him, and it marked the completion of three more writings: the *Cur Deus homo* (a discussion of the fittingness of the Incarnation), a meditation on human redemption, and *On the Virgin Birth and Original Sin* (*De conceptu virginali*). Yet conflict was on the way again.

William's successor, Henry I, welcomed Anselm back to England. But it soon became clear that Anselm found Henry's policies regarding the church as unacceptable as William's were. Following what he took to be the papal position, Anselm thought the king to be claiming more rights over the church than were proper. A period of disputation followed, with Anselm leaving England yet again. But Henry and Urban's successor, Pascal II, managed to agree on a compromise between themselves. Anselm did not welcome it, but he was obliged to accept it and return to England, where he arrived for the last time by September 1106. Eadmer tells us that when Anselm came to England he "was received with great joy and honor by holy church." Eadmer also says that the king "was heartily glad that he had made his peace with Anselm." By now, however, Anselm was close to death. He showed signs of serious illness before returning to England, and he fell sick again around Easter 1107. His literary work continued, for he wrote a treatise called *De concordia* on the subject of God and human freedom. Yet he became feeble enough to need carrying on a litter to travel, and he died.

Although most of Anselm's writings are short, the range of his interests is broad. One will find him reflecting on, for example, truth, logic, rightness, freedom, eternity, and the nature of Christ. One will also find him talking about sin, goodness and badness, existence, the Eucharist, and the nature and importance of sacraments. In most of Anselm's writings, however, one idea in particular continually emerges: that people can approach God as those who seek to understand. He agrees that God is incomprehensible. He also agrees that Christian truth raises difficult intellectual questions. Yet he is also sure that God wants us to seek him using the abilities he has given us. And, for this reason, he holds that we can try to understand the things of God and to love them accordingly. In one of his letters he says: "The Christian ought to progress through faith to understanding, and not through understanding to faith. Let him rejoice if he is able to attain understanding; if he cannot, let him revere what he cannot apprehend." Yet Anselm is certain that, having believed, we can seek to understand. As he writes in the *Proslogion*: "For I do not seek to understand so that I may believe; but I believe so that I may understand." In the *Cur Deus homo* he adds: "It seems to me to be negligence, if, after we have been established in the faith, we do not make the effort to understand what we believe." Anselm's thought is that of a devout Christian believer confident that his belief is ultimately something that makes sense. This confidence produced and pervades his major treatises from the *Monologion* onwards, and it is his most distinguishing characteristic as a thinker. In his *Monologion* it leads him to the conclusion that something like the existence of God as Trinity can be demonstrated philosophically and without recourse to Christian revelation, a view echoed later by Richard of St. Victor.*

Anselm is especially famous for arguing that there is an absurdity in the denial that God exists. He is often cited as the author of the "ontological argument," traditionally understood as maintaining that God must exist since God, by definition, is supremely perfect and existence is a perfection. In fact, Anselm never used the premise that existence is a perfection as part of an argument for the existence of God. But he certainly held that people who deny the existence of God might be trapped in a contradiction.

Anselm is often reported as saying that there is some logical necessity involved in God's becoming incarnate. But his major treatment of the Incarnation (the *Cur Deus homo*) argues for the necessity of God's becoming incarnate on the basis of premises that cannot be taken as intended to establish that God must become incarnate on pain of simple logical contradiction. Anselm's discussions of the Incarnation draw on and depend upon the Old Testament and Christian texts, which he inherited and used in his attempt to understand while also believing.

Anselm's writings are also heavily indebted to the thinking of St. Augustine.* His theme of faith seeking understanding is Augustinian, though he pursues it with a sense of philosophical rigor generally lacking in Augustine. In the *De concordia* he embraces an argument of Augustine to the effect that God's knowledge is not a threat to human freedom since what God knows might be that some people act freely. Lanfranc wrote to Anselm complaining that the *Monologion* was insufficiently deferential to Augustine. But the text of that work is full of Augustinian themes and emphases. Like all his writings, Anselm's *Monologion* does not appeal directly to authorities. Their aim is to get people to think for themselves. But it is not too hard to discern the authorities on which Anselm draws, and people who read him with an eye on the history of Christian theology will quickly come to see how accurate he was in describing himself as seeking to move from faith to understanding. They will also see how, among early medieval thinkers, he is someone able to challenge his readers intellectually and to encourage them to follow some subtle forms of argument.

Bibliography

A. *Anselmi Cantuariensis Archiepiscopi opera omnia*, ed. F. S. Schmitt, 6 vols. (Rome and Edinburgh, 1938–68); *The Life of St. Anselm by Eadmer*, ed. R. W. Southern

(Oxford, 1962); *Anselm of Canterbury: The Major Works*, ed. Brian Davies and G. R. Evans (Oxford, 1998).

B.   DTC 1:1327–60; LThK³ 1:711–12; NCE 1:581–83; ODCC 73–74; TRE 2:759–78; G. R. Evans, *Anselm* (London, 1989); R. W. Southern, *Saint Anselm: A Portrait in a Landscape* (Cambridge, 1990).

Brian Davies

ANSELM OF HAVELBERG (end of 11th century–12 August 1158, Milan). Little is known of Anselm's education and early life; he was a Premonstratensian canon before his consecration as archbishop of Havelberg, 1129–55; represented Emperor Lothair III in discussions on issues dividing Greek and Latin churches at Constantinople, 1136; served Frederick I Barbarossa, 1152, negotiating a treaty with Eugene III; sent again to the Byzantine court in debate with prelates of the Byzantine church, 1154; archbishop and exarch of Ravenna, 1155–58.

Anselm defended the Canons Regular against criticism from monastic authors. In this defense, Anselm developed a theology of history based on the evolution of religious orders and their differing means of increasing the understanding of the faith throughout church history. He insisted that this growth was the result of the continuing reformation of the church by the Holy Spirit. This theology also allowed him to defend the western church against the charges of doctrinal novelty by Eastern theologians.

Bibliography

A.   *Epistola apologetica pro ordine canonicorum regularium*, PL 188, 1117–40; *Dialogues*, ed. Gaston Salet, SC 118 (Paris, 1966).

B.   LThK³ 1:712–13; NCE 1:583–84; L. F. Barmann, "Reform Ideology in the *Dialogi* of Anselm of Havelberg," CH 30 (1961): 379–95; Gottfried Wentz, *Das Bistum Havelberg* (Berlin, 1963); Walter James Edyvean, *Anselm of Havelberg and the Theology of History* (Rome, 1972); Bernard McGinn, *Visions of the End: Apocalyptic Traditions in the Middle Ages* (New York, 1979); Karl Morrison, "Anselm of Havelberg: Play and the Dilemma of Historical Progress," in *Religion, Culture, and Society in the Early Middle Ages: Studies in Honor of Richard E. Sullivan*, ed. Thomas F. X. Noble and John J. Contreni (Kalamazoo, Mich., 1987), 219–56; Carol Neel, "Philip of Harvengt and Anselm of Havelberg: The Premonstratensian Vision of Time," CH 62 (1993): 483–93.

Daniel Marcel La Corte

ANSELM OF LAON (1050, Laon?–1117, Laon). A pupil of Anselm of Canterbury,* Anselm of Laon takes his epithet from his long association with the cathedral school at Laon in northern France, where he taught together with his brother Radulphus (d. 1136) for many years. The two brothers educated several of the men who were to leave their mark on twelfth-century theology, including Peter Abelard* and Gilbert of Poitiers.* Abelard, who attended Anselm's lectures sometime around 1113, judged him to be without originality or insight, but modern scholarship has mitigated the harshness of that criticism, juxtaposing instead Anselm's "erudite" approach to theology, in which a mastery of the authoritative sources is most pronounced, with Abelard's more personal and speculative reading of Scripture. Anselm, in fact, pioneered the method of scriptural exegesis upon which Abelard built, wherein apparent contradictions among authorities are reconciled through critical analysis.

Anselm and his followers also began the work of systematizing theology, by collecting and comparing related arguments on various topics, which they published as *sententiae*. One such collection is the *Liber pancrisis*. Many of the sections within the *Pancrisis* begin with the words *quaeritur* or *quaestio*, indicating a tendency to move beyond simple commentary and to weigh evidence on either side of a theological problem. The school at Laon is thus sometimes credited with originating two of the literary genres ubiquitous in later scholastic theology: the systematic *summa* and the disputed question. Anselm and his brother also produced several biblical commentaries, which became part of the *Glossa ordinaria*.

Bibliography

A. *Liber pancrisis*, ed. Odon Lottin, in *Psychologie et morale au XII*e *et XIII*e *siècles* (Louvain, 1959), 5:32–81; idem, "Nouveaux fragments théologiques de l'école d'Anselme de Laon," RTAM 11 (1939): 305–23; 12 (1940): 49–77; 13 (1946): 202–21, 261–81; 14 (1947): 5–31; 157–85.

B. LThK³ 1:714; NCE 1:584; ODCC 74; TRE 3:1–5; Joseph de Ghellinck, *Le mouvement théologique du XII*e *siècle*, 2d ed. (Bruges, 1948), 113–48; Ermenegildo Bertola, "Le critiche di Abelardo ad Anselmo di Laon ed a Guglielmo di Champeaux," *Rivista di filosofia neo-scolastica* 52 (1960): 495–522; idem, "La 'Glossa ordinaria' biblica ed i suoi problemi," RTAM 45 (1978): 34–78; Valerie I. J. Flint, "The 'School of Laon': A Reconsideration," RTAM 43 (1976): 89–110.

M. Michèle Mulchahey

ANTONINUS OF FLORENCE (1 March 1389, Florence–2 May 1459, Florence). *Career*: joined the Dominicans, 1405; became a leader of the reform movement within the order; with the aid of Cosimo di Medici founded the convent of San Marco, Florence, 1436; prior, San Marco, 1439–44; took part in the Council of Florence, 1439–45; archbishop of Florence, 1446; renowned for his charitable work during the plague of 1448 and the earthquake of 1453; canonized by Adrian IV in 1523.

Earned the title "Antoninus the Counselor" for his work as a spiritual director. His *Confessionale*, a work on the sacrament of penance, has three distinct parts: one, in Italian, was intended to help the faithful prepare for confession, while the other two are manuals for priests administering the sacrament. His *Summa moralis*, also called *Summa theologiae*, exemplifies the practical bent of his theology. Its four volumes deal with the soul, its passions, sin, and the law; with kinds of sin; with states of life and vocations; and with the cardinal and theological virtues. His *Chronicon* is a history of the world in three volumes drawn from Scripture and ecclesiastical authors to illustrate how people ought to live. Though he was proclaimed to be among the doctors of the church in the bull of canonization, the title was never conferred.

Bibliography

A.   *Confessionale* (Florence, 1490); *Summa moralis* (Florence, 1477).

B.   DMA 1:342; DTC 1:1450–54; LThK³ 1:784; NCE 1:646–47; ODCC 80; R. Morçay, *Saint Antonin, fondateur du couvent de Saint-Marc, archevêque de Florence, 1389–1459* (Tours, 1914); J. B. Walker, *The "Chronicles" of Saint Antoninus: A Study in Historiography* (Washington, D.C., 1933); Raymond A. De Roover, *San Bernardino of Siena and Sant' Antonino of Florence: The Two Great Economic Thinkers of the Middle Ages* (Boston, 1967); John P. Donnelly, "Marriage from Renaissance to Reformation: Two Florentine Moralists," *Studies in Medieval Culture* 11 (1977): 161–71.

Roland J. Teske

APOLLINARIUS OF LAODICEA (ca. 310, Laodicea–ca. 392). *Career*: bishop of the Christian community faithful to the Nicene creed, ca. 360.

Apollinarius was a biblical exegete and prolific writer against a variety of contemporary heretics, including Eunomius and Marcellus of Ancyra.* Admired for his upright life and trinitarian orthodoxy during most of his life, Apollinarius ordained Vitalis, a student of his, to the see of Antioch ca. 376/77, although there were already two orthodox bishops struggling over it, thereby initiating a schismatic movement in the East. He and his followers were condemned and deposed in Rome ca. 378, and by Eastern synods and imperial legislation in the late 370s and 380s.

Apollinarius claimed that Christ has no human soul, the vital and intellectual functions of the Savior being provided directly by the indwelling divine Word. For Apollinarius, Christ is one incarnate divine person (or *hypostasis*), and one unique divine and human organism or nature (*physis*). The controversy aroused by his ideas sparked several decades of debate that culminated in the Chalcedonian definition of 451, which asserted against Apollinarius that Christ is one person in two natures—one fully divine, one fully human.

Bibliography

A.   *Apollinaris von Laodicea und seine Schule*, ed. Hans Lietzmann (Tübingen, 1904; repr. Hildesheim, 1970); *The Christological Controversy*, ed. Richard A. Norris (Philadelphia, 1980), 103–11.

B.   DTC 1:1505–6; EEC 1:58–59; LThK³ 1:826–28; NCE 1:667–68; TRE 3:362–71; Guillaume Voisin, *L'Apollinarisme* (Louvain, 1901); Charles E. Raven, *Apollinarianism* (New York, 1923); Richard A. Norris, *Manhood and Christ: A Study in the Christology of Theodore of Mopsuestia* (Oxford, 1963); Ekkehard Mühlenberg, *Apollinaris von Laodicea* (Göttingen, 1969).

Kelley McCarthy Spoerl

AQUINAS. *See* THOMAS AQUINAS.

ARIUS (ca. 260, Libya?–336, Constantinople). Little is known of Arius' early career. He may have studied in Antioch or Nicomedia with the teacher Lucian. He is alleged to have supported Meletius, a schismatic bishop of Alexandria, in the early part of the fourth century. Under Alexander, who became bishop of Alexandria ca. 313, Arius ministered as a presbyter in the Baucalis, a region of the city near the docks, where he became a popular preacher. Arius' views regarding the eternity and the divine status of the second person of the Trinity began to arouse controversy later in the decade. Alexander called an Egyptian synod ca. 318 (or possibly a few years later) that condemned Arius' views and excommunicated Arius himself. Thereafter, Arius sought support elsewhere in the East, and succeeded in acquiring at least two influential supporters, Eusebius of Nicomedia* and Eusebius of Caesarea.* Despite their and others' support, Arius' views were again condemned at the first ecumenical council of Nicaea in 325, after which Arius was exiled. Within a few years, however, pressure started to mount for his rehabilitation. Recalled from exile sometime earlier, Arius was reinstated at the Council of Tyre in 335, but died in Constantinople in 336 before he could return to Alexandria.

Christology was the focus of Arius' controversial teaching. Arius taught that God the Son, incarnate in Christ, is a preexistent personal entity (or *hypostasis*) created out of nothing by the will of God the Father for the purposes of creation. As such, the Son does not share the Father's divine substance, has a lesser rank and glory than the Father, and knows the Father only imperfectly. Because he is created at a contingent moment prior to the creation of the world, the Son is not coeternal with the Father. In some passages, Arius suggests that the Son is not Son by nature, but by adoption, in view of the merits he would gain in his incarnate career.

The sources for reconstructing Arius' thought are fragmentary and uncertain, most of them reported in hostile accounts. Scholars continue to debate the major influences on Arius' Christology, and whether it is shaped primarily by soteriological concerns, Neoplatonic philosophy, or other factors. In the eyes of his critics, Arius' Christology compromised the divinity of Christ, thereby endangering his status as divine revealer and savior.

Theses attributed to Arius soon became a stereotyped feature of theological debate in the fourth century, although the historical Arius seems to have been quickly forgotten. In the fourth century, Arius' teaching was responsible for the rise of trinitarian speculation, which sought to explain how Christians could assert the full divinity of Christ and the Holy Spirit and simultaneously claim to be monotheists.

Bibliography

A. *Athanasius Werke*, ed. Hans Georg Opitz (Berlin, 1934), 3:1–2.

B. DTC 1:1779–99; EEC 1:76–78; LThK³ 1:981–89; NCE 1:814–15; TRE 3:698–703; Robert C. Gregg and Dennis Groh, *Early Arianism: A View of Salvation* (Philadelphia, 1981); G. Christopher Stead, *Substance and Illusion in the Christian Fathers*

(London, 1985); Rowan Williams, *Arius: Heresy and Tradition* (London, 1987); Maurice Wiles, *Archetypal Heresy: Arianism through the Centuries* (Oxford and New York, 1996).

Kelley McCarthy Spoerl

ARMINIUS, JACOBUS (10 October 1560, Oudewater–19 October 1609, Leiden). *Education*: studied at Univ. of Leiden, 1576–82; read theology under Theodore Beza,* Geneva, 1582–85. *Career*: ordained, 1588; pastor, Amsterdam, 1588–1603; professor of theology, Univ. of Leiden, 1603–9.

Arminius was spokesman for the resistance to strict Calvinist orthodoxy in the formative years of the Dutch Reformed Church. While serving as pastor in Amsterdam, he was asked to write a refutation of the views of Coornheert, who had attacked the supralapsarian views of Beza. As a result of this theological inquiry, Arminius came to largely agree with Coornheert and to question the strict Calvinistic doctrine that held sway in the Dutch Reformed Church. This led him to preach the universality of God's grace and the possibility of a free-will response to grace by faith. During his fifteen-year pastorate in Amsterdam, he became the favorite of the merchant oligarchy, many of whom were not attracted to the strict Calvinism of other clergy.

From 1603, as newly appointed professor of theology at Leiden, Arminius was drawn into a long and bitter controversy with faculty colleague Franciscus Gomarus* (a strict Calvinist). In subsequent years, Arminius clarified his opposition to the Calvinist perspective on predestination and human freedom, believing it made God the author of sin and denied the possibility of human freedom.

In 1608, Arminius requested that the States of Holland and West Friesland appoint a national synod to consider the theological issues involved, including the Calvinists' desire to make binding on all clergy the authority of the Belgic Confession and the Heidelberg Catechism. Arminius viewed this as an attempt to canonize a high Calvinist view of predestination. In contrast, Arminius maintained that God's first absolute decree regarding salvation was not the assignment of certain individuals to eternal life and others to damnation, but the appointment of his Son, Jesus Christ, to be the savior of the human race. God has predestined to salvation all who trust in Christ, having granted sufficient prevenient grace to all humankind to enable repentance and faith. Thus, God's decree of salvation or damnation of individuals is based on his foreknowledge of their faith and perseverance, or lack thereof.

In 1609 Arminius appeared before the States General to defend his views, but became ill and died before the conference's conclusion. After his death, the leadership of the "Arminians" fell to Simon Episcopius and Janus Uytenbogaert. John van Olden Barneveldt and Hugo Grotius* were sympathetic supporters of the cause. In 1610, the Arminians sent a treatise, called the *Remonstrance*, to the States of Holland and West Friesland. This set forth their theological views and requested the appointment of a synod to settle the dispute.

Several years later, the Synod of Dort (1618–19) was called. Composed almost entirely of Calvinists, the synod passed a point-by-point refutation of the *Remonstrance*, confirmed the Belgic Confession and the Heidelberg Catechism as the standards of orthodoxy, condemned Arminianism, and banned the Remonstrants.

The Remonstrants insisted that Divine sovereignty was compatible with human freedom, and that election unto salvation was conditioned upon a free-will response of faith. They also maintained that Christ died for all, not just the elect; that God's grace could be resisted; and that perseverance unto salvation was conditioned upon continued faith and obedience. Arminian theology sought to maintain the biblical antinomy of divine sovereignty and human freedom, without an overemphasis on Divine agency (Determinism) or human free will (Pelagianism). Although agreeing with the Calvinists on the doctrine of total depravity, the Arminian view of prevenient grace, with its emphasis on the supernatural restoration of human freedom, led to a different understanding of the place of human cooperation in the process of salvation.

Outside the Netherlands, Arminianism found expression in England, where the anti-Calvinistic Laudian revival of the seventeenth century was dubbed ''Arminian'' by its opponents. The term was later adopted by John Wesley* (1703–91) to designate his synthesizing school of non-Calvinist evangelicalism. ''Arminian evangelicalism'' is perhaps the most enduring theological contribution of the Methodist movement, as reflected in the Arminianizing of the American Protestant church during the nineteenth and twentieth centuries.

Bibliography

A.   *The Works of James Arminius*, 3 vols. (Leiden, 1629; repr. London, 1991).

B.   DTC 1:1968–71; ECatt 1:1994–97; LThK³ 1:305; NCE 1:840; ODCC 107–8; OEncR 1:72–73; RGG 1:622; TRE 4:63–69; Carl Bangs, *Arminius: A Study in the Dutch Reformation* (repr. Grand Rapids, Mich., 1985); A. W. Harrison, *Arminianism* (London, 1937); J. H. Maronier, *Jacobus Arminius* (Amsterdam, 1905).

R. David Rightmire

ARNAULD, ANTOINE (5 February 1612, Paris–8 August 1694, Brussels). *Education*: B.A., Sorbonne, 1633–35. *Career*: subdiaconate, 1638; ordained priest, 1641; priest at Port-Royal, 1641–79; priest in Netherlands, 1679–94.

Arnauld is primarily known as the foremost popularizer of Jansenist principles and spirituality during the middle of the seventeenth century. He was influenced to a considerable extent by his widowed mother and his older sister Jacqueline Marie Angelique, the mother superior of the convent of Port Royal, both of whom introduced him to Abbé Saint-Cyran (Jean Duvergier de Hauranne, 1581–1643), a Jansenist spiritual director at the Port-Royal convent.

Arnauld studied Cartesian philosophy and theology at the Sorbonne with the intention of becoming a priest. While there in 1635 he wrote and defended a proto-Jansenist thesis on the doctrine of grace, six years prior to the publication of Cornelius Otto Jansen's* (1585–1638) *Augustinus* (1641).

Like Saint-Cyran and Jansen, Arnauld saw the necessity of retrieving biblical and patristic sources, which they all believed had been taken for granted and indeed been replaced by scholastic theologies. In particular they wanted to restore the thought of St. Augustine,* whom they believed had been neglected in the theology of grace. Following Michael Baius,* Arnauld emphasized the victorious and efficacious nature of grace to such an extent that he made grace humanly irresistible in the process.

In 1643, Arnauld's theology became a bone of contention in French Catholicism when he published his *De la fréquente communion*, which emphasized the necessity of scrupulously preparing right dispositions for the reception of communion. The book propagated some distinctively Jansenist principles and rigorous spiritual practices. It also brought a storm of protests from the French Jesuits who considered the book and the Jansenist principles it contained as dangerous to the faith and a manifestation of Calvinist rather than Catholic theology.

After 1643, Arnauld became a forceful supporter of Jansenist positions, asserted that those positions were not Calvinist but Augustinian, attacked Jesuit confessional principles and practices, and in the process drew the support of Blaise Pascal* and other admirers of the Port-Royal spirituality. After five propositions in the *Augustinus* were condemned in Pope Innocent X's *Cum Occasione* (1653), Arnauld led the Jansenists in subscribing to the condemned positions; but, while he accepted the general principles that were condemned, he could not accept the charge that they were to be found in the *Augustinus*, creating a famous distinction between fact and law that would serve the Jansenists for generations in their relations with Rome.

Arnauld was censured and condemned by the Sorbonne in 1656, restored to honor by King Louis XIV in 1669, but after a decade of relative theological peace between 1669 and 1679, he was forced to leave France in 1679 when the Jansenist controversy revived. He moved to the Netherlands where he continued to support Jansenist causes. The author of more than 320 works, he became a major force in diffusing Jansenist principles.

Bibliography

A.   *Oeuvres de Messire Antoine Arnauld*, 43 vols. (Lausanne, 1775–83; repr. Brussels, 1964–67).

B.   DHGE 4:447–85; DTC 1:1978–83; ECatt 1:2005–8; LThK³ 1:1016–17; NCE 1:841–42; ODCC, 108–9; RGG 1:629; Jean Laporte, *La doctrine de Port-Royal* (Paris, 1923); Steven M. Nadler, *Arnauld and the Cartesian Philosophy of Ideas* (Manchester, 1989); *Interpreting Arnauld*, ed. Elmar J. Kremer (Toronto, 1996).

Patrick W. Carey

ARNDT, JOHANN (17 December 1555, Edderitz, Germany–11 May 1621, Celle, Germany). *Education*: studied at Univ. of Helmstedt, 1576; Univ. of Wittenberg, 1577; Univ. of Strasbourg, 1578; Univ. of Basel, 1579–82. *Career*: diaconate at Ballenstedt, 1583; pastorates, Badeborn, 1584; Quedlinburg, 1585–99; Braunschweig, 1599–1609; Eisleben 1609–11; general superintendent, Celle, 1611–21.

Arndt's chief theological contribution was conveyed in his writings, particularly in his devotional treatises contained in the *Four Books of True Christianity* (1605–10). Arndt was deeply opposed to the polemical spirit that characterized the Christianity of his day. His books were of a devotional rather than a dogmatic nature. He brought an emotional, spiritual, and practical emphasis into the stricter and sometimes sterile dogmatism that dominated the newly formed Lutheran Church following the demise of its founder. Arndt's chief concern was to provide practical aid to those seeking to live the Christian life. His writings described concrete ways in which Christians could express love to God in a tangible way through acts of kindness and compassion for their fellow human beings. The immediate popularity of Arndt's works gave testimony to the fact that they met a deep-felt need. His *Four Books on True Christianity*, was reprinted over twenty times during his lifetime and before the close of the eighteenth century had been published in over 125 editions. Next to the Bible and Luther's* *Small Catechism*, no other work has been so often read and deeply revered among Lutherans everywhere. It retained this appeal throughout the entire nineteenth century. Never, before Arndt's *True Christianity*, had there been expressed within Lutheranism such a deep moral concern and strong emphasis on practical piety. In spite of the popularity of his literary efforts, Arndt was condemned by a number of the leaders of Lutheran orthodoxy for his dependence on medieval mysticism and for placing too much emphasis on sanctification. On several occasions he faced formal charges of heresy. In each instance, he defended his works on the basis of the Lutheran confessional books and was exonerated. Arndt's impact upon the founders of classical German Lutheran Pietism was immense. Both Philipp Spener* and August Francke* frequently expressed admiration for his works, and Arndt's theological tenets provided the heart and soul of Lutheran Pietism's emphatic ethical thrust.

Bibliography

A. *True Christianity*, trans. by A. W. Boehm (London, 1712; Philadelphia, 1868) and Peter Erb (New York, 1979).

B. DTC 1:1983–84; ECatt 1:2008–9; LThK³ 1:1017–18; ODCC 109; RGG 1:629; TRE 4:121–29; James B. Morris, *The Life of John Arndt* (Baltimore, Md., 1853); Wilhelm Koepp, *Johann Arndt, Eine Untersuchung über die Mystik in Luthertum* (Berlin, 1912).

Paul K. Kuenning

ATHANASIUS OF ALEXANDRIA (295/300–373). Athanasius was one of the most controversial and dynamic figures of his time. His importance lies not just—perhaps not primarily—in his controversy with the Arians and their successors, but also in his supervision of the church during a time of dramatic transition. Athanasius' career represents the pivot between the martyr church and the ascetic church. Both his ascetical writings and his ecclesiastical activity with the desert ascetics rank among his most significant and lasting achievements. Still, it is his role in the Nicene controversy that is the source of Athanasius' lasting fame. Although his actual theological influence on the resolution of this conflict has been overestimated, his career and personality became the touchstone for the Nicene cause in the East and the West. Finally, recent reevaluations of Athanasius have helpfully demonstrated his political skill and, at times, his political unscrupulousness. But these traits should not be stressed at the expense of his personal faith and depth of commitment to Nicene orthodoxy.

Many accounts of Athanasius' episcopal career survive, and its basic outline is readily apparent. He was a protégé of Alexander of Alexandria, and he seems to have accompanied his bishop to the Council of Nicaea in 325. Alexander hand-picked Athanasius to be his successor, and despite intense opposition he was elected bishop in 328 at a very young age. He inherited two problems from Alexander: the Arian controversy and the Melitian schism. The latter seems to have occupied his immediate attention, and he dealt with it in a typically heavy-handed manner. This, coupled with his refusal to readmit Arius into communion, led to his condemnation in 335 by a synod in Tyre and subsequent exile by Constantine. He returned to Alexandria after Constantine's death in 337, but was deposed again by a council led by Eusebius of Nicomedia* in 339. This time Athanasius fled to Rome, where he cultivated the support of the Roman bishop Julius and met Marcellus of Ancyra,* who also had been exiled and was in Rome to appeal for Julius' help. During this time Athanasius began to develop the fundamental features of his anti-Arian polemic, probably as a result of his association with Marcellus. Athanasius returned to Alexandria in 346, largely owing to the patronage of Constantine's son Constans. The bishop continued his ''anti-Arian'' activity and was again deposed by Constantius, who in 356 used military force to drive Athanasius from Alexandria. Athanasius fled the city and spent six years hiding among the desert monks of Egypt. In 361 he returned, and with the exception of a brief exile in 365 spent the rest of his life in possession of his see.

Athanasius wrote a great deal, most of which has survived. Some dispute exists about the exact chronology of his writing, but a rough chronology can be ascertained. Among his earliest works are *Against the Heathen* and *On the Incarnation*, neither of which contains overt reference to the Arian controversy. His important *First Oration against the Arians* was probably composed during a visit to Rome, where he appealed to Julius and met his fellow exile, Marcellus of Ancyra; two other *Orations against the Arians* survive as well. Upon his return from Rome he produced his *Apology against the Arians*, and during his third exile he wrote *Apology to Constantius*, *Apology for His Flight*, and *History of the Arians*. His great *Life of Antony* was probably written shortly after the monk's death in 356. Although much of this corpus was ostensibly written against "Arians," his later writings do reflect awareness of later theologies. Athanasius seems to have used "Arian" as a rhetorical device to label his opponents with an already condemned heresy. Starting in the early 340s Athanasius developed an appreciation of the creed of Nicaea (325) as the touchstone of orthodox trinitarian theology and by the late 350s understood the acceptance of that creed, in particular the creed's language of consubstantiality or "same in essence" (*homoousios*), as necessary for an orthodox doctrine of the Trinity.

In his early theology especially, Athanasius revealed himself to be an "Alexandrian" in the tradition of Origen.* Athanasius accepted the broad outlines of Origen's scheme, including a modified form of Origen's double creation. His Logos theology also shows Origen's influence. It is Athanasius' Christology that shows the greatest debt to Origen, and by the end of the fourth century it would be seen as a limitation in Athanasius' understanding of the Incarnation. If human nature may generally be understood as consisting of a rational component, the *logos* or mind, lower psychological functions, and the body, then the divine Word exists incarnated in Jesus as Logos (in place of a human mind or logos). Apollinarius'* version of this doctrine would later be repudiated by Nicenes such as Gregory of Nazianzus,* Gregory of Nyssa,* and Nemesius of Emesa, although Athanasius died before this controversy flared.

In both his ascetical and trinitarian theologies Athanasius gave his own creative spin to the tradition he inherited. The fact that even "pre-Fall" humans were created with bodies means that we are inherently unstable and thus ultimately die. (Athanasius is one of the very few fathers of the early church who believed that bodily death preceded sin.) After the Fall, however, death is no longer the natural event marking transition from a physical to a spiritual existence; it is the mark of our being held in bondage to another law, the mark of an existence separated from its source of life, God. Athanasius' Christology, his soteriology, and his asceticism all come together to describe the problem of our fatal separation from God and the restoration of the possibility of a restored life with God through the Incarnation. Athanasius sees the Incarnation in terms of three central concerns or areas of activity: first, the Word's act of revelation of God to humanity; second, his act of restoration of humanity's original nature; and third, his act of sacrifice in the crucifixion, freeing us from a law of sin and the paralyzing fear that the sign of that bondage, death, instilled in humanity. After Christ, humans die natural deaths, not the deaths of fear of bondage. Athanasius knew the reality of this freedom from fear and a death of bondage from the martyrs and from ascetics, like Antony, who had indeed died but had died without fear, calmly, and in control of their bodies. It is important to note, however, that Athanasius emphasized that Antony's victory is really Christ's victory, and that Christ's victory is only possible because he shares in the divine substance. Even in the desert, Athanasius' theology built on his doctrine of the Trinity.

Bibliography

A. Patrology 3:22–66.

B. DTC 1:2143–78; LThK³ 1:1126–31; NCE 1:996–99; ODCC 119–20; TRE 4:333–49; F. L. Cross, *The Study of St. Athanasius* (Oxford, 1945); T. E. Pollard, "Logos and Son in Origen, Arius and Athanasius," StPatr 2 (1957): 282–87; G. Florovsky, "The Concept of Creation in Saint Athanasius," StPatr 6 (1962): 36–57; Charles Kannengiesser, "Athanasius of Alexandria and the Foundations of Traditional Christology," ThSt 34 (1973): 103–13; E. P. Meijering, "Athanasius on the Father as the Origin of the Son," in *God Being History* (Amsterdam, 1975), 89–102; Frances Young, *From Nicaea to Chalcedon* (London, 1983); Charles Kannengiesser, "The Athanasian Decade: 1974–84," ThSt 46 (1985): 524–41; Maurice Wiles, "The Philosophy in Christianity: Arius and Athanasius," in *The Philosophy in Christianity*, ed. Godfrey Vesey (New York, 1989), 41–52; Leslie Barnard, *Studies in Athanasius' Apologia Secunda* (New York, 1992); Timothy D. Barnes, *Athanasius and Constantius* (Cambridge, Mass., 1993); Peter Widdicombe, *The Fatherhood of God from Origen to Athanasius* (Oxford, 1994).

Michel René Barnes

AUGUSTINE OF HIPPO (13 November 354, Thagaste–28 August 430, Hippo). More is known about Augustine than about anyone else in classical antiquity. His early schooling probably took place in Thagaste; he was then sent to Madaura (modern Mdaurouch) to study rhetoric and grammar. At seventeen, he went to Carthage (now Tunis) to complete his rhetorical formation. There, when he was about nineteen, he read Cicero's now-lost *Hortensius*, which introduced him to philosophy; became acquainted with the *Categories* of Aristotle; attempted to read the Bible, but was repelled by the style of the available Latin translations; and joined Manichaeism, a religion to which he belonged for nine years, and which, among other things, rejected the Old Testament, partly because it seemed to condone immorality.

After his formal education, Augustine taught in Thagaste, and then in Carthage. In 383, disillusioned with his students, he traveled to Rome to teach rhetoric. There he found that, if students were less ruly than at Carthage, they were also less willing to pay. Doubtful by now about Manichaeism, he toyed briefly with the thought of the Academics, or skeptics, who expressed doubt about everything.

In 384 he was appointed rhetor to the imperial court of Milan. There he began listening to sermons of the bishop, Ambrose,* at first for their style, and later for their content. Through them he came to realize that Scripture can be interpreted in more than a literal sense. At the same time, he began reading works in Neoplatonism, which helped him resolve some of his intellectual difficulties with Catholic Christianity. He now leaned toward the latter, but problems with chastity (which he thought of as, for him, necessary for baptism) blocked his final conversion until the famous scene in the garden described in Book 8 of his *Confessions*.

When he was ready to commit himself fully to Christianity, Augustine resigned his position and retired with some relatives and friends to a villa near Milan, where he prepared for baptism and wrote the first of his extant works. He was baptized by Ambrose on Easter of 387. Some months later he began the journey back to Africa, but had to winter in Rome after the death of his mother.

In 388 Augustine returned to Thagaste, where he formed a community of fellow Christians dedicated to serving God. For three years he was able to pursue a life of "divine leisure"; but in 391 he happened to be in Hippo Regius (today Annaba, Algeria) when Valerius, its bishop, asked his congregation for a presbyter to assist him. The assembly forcibly detained Augustine for ordination, which he accepted on conditions that he would be able to establish a community at Hippo like the one in Thagaste and that he would have time to study Scripture more intensively. Both conditions were met, and Augustine served the church of Hippo for the rest of his life, as presbyter, coadjutor bishop (395), and, from 396, as chief pastor.

Augustine's literary output is immense, and a major reason for his enduring influence on western Christian thought. Besides hundreds of sermons and letters, he has left us over ninety treatises, which fall into three main groups: commentaries on biblical books; polemical writings, such as those against Pelagianism; and various books on theological subjects. He is especially known for three works: *Confessions*, *The Trinity*, and *The City of God*.

Another reason for his influence is the range of ideas that he expounds, although these are far from systematically arranged. This fact makes it impossible to provide a succinct overview of his entire thought in brief compass. It may be said, though, that his primary focus—which never wavers—is on the relationship between the human being and God. This is where Christianity becomes all-important. Humans find fulfillment in God, and nowhere else. Like other Christian writers of the time, Augustine employs philosophical (primarily Neoplatonist) language and concepts to convey the Christian message, when non-Christian philosophy and Christianity do not conflict. So he admits that the philosopher is correct to view the attainment of Wisdom as the goal of human life; but, in a non-Christian context, this Wisdom makes no move toward humanity. The God-fearing person identifies Wisdom with God, as in Judaism; but this Wisdom is not received as a Wisdom become one of ourselves.

The Christian is, then, the true philosopher, for whom Wisdom is identified with Christ, the incarnate God, who maintains us in being with the same love that created us. Questions about the origin of the universe and about human destiny had been largely responsible for the journey that finally led Augustine to Christianity. The same questions continued to fascinate him, which is why throughout his commentaries on the opening chapters of Genesis, his purpose was to affirm the overall goodness of creation, though some have accused Augustine (even in his own lifetime) of maintaining Manichaean views on corporality, marriage, and sex.

The question of our creation raises another: what does grace add to our nature? It does not give us a new destiny for, to Augustine, humankind has always had only the one; nor does it supply new powers to attain a destiny we are otherwise incapable of reaching, because the mind is by nature attuned to God, from whom it is held back only by sin. Grace operates chiefly in the will, arousing within it a fervent love that strains toward the heavenly, unceasing vision of God; for it is clear that Augustine thinks of grace as leading ultimately to the perfecting of our instability by stabilization, of initial *formatio* by full *reformatio* in God, according to that perfect image in which we were created and which is the divine Son.

The theater wherein *reformatio* occurs is history, which is the record of God's interaction with humanity. This interaction reaches peak intensity in the Incarnation, which is central to history, in the sense that all history derives meaning from it. Hence, all history is sacred (an idea worked out chiefly in *Christian Doctrine*), a long march under Providence that stretches from humankind's initial creation to the fullness of time in which God sent the Son, and then beyond to the end time. We know this from God's revealed Scripture, which speaks to everyone because its pages speak of a universal God; God in turn reveals the universal church; and the universal church is entrusted with guarding the Scriptures, a task fulfilled within history.

The City of God further develops this theology. Christianity is no intruder into history; rather, Christianity gives history its definition, centering on the Incarnation, for which all the events that took place among all peoples of pre-Christian times were a preparation. As for the future, Augustine thinks of the church on earth in two ways: (1) as *peregrina*, "pilgrim" (Christ continuing in time and space), or *in via* ("under way"), as the present, historical, visible reality of the church-institution; (2) as *beata* ("blessed"), in a more speculative, future-oriented sense, or *in patria* ("home"), where the ultimate destiny of its members (and for some, already in actuality) is concerned. A person partakes in this twofold activity by faith, which "opens the way to understanding."

At this point there comes a radical, but not complete, break with Neoplatonism. Augustine accepts many Neoplatonist ideas: all being is in hierarchy; earthly being consists of the triad material, animate, and rational; humans in turn consist of the triad flesh, animate soul, rational soul; and the soul's triadic function is exercised in intellect, memory, and will. Humankind's true home lies at the level of the rational soul; we prepare for this true home by purifying the mind of all distractions, enabling us to contemplate the One (True, Good, Beautiful, unchangeable and beyond being itself). In Neoplatonism the human mind is illuminated, and thus oriented towards its true end, by the divine *Logos* (Reason).

With all of this Augustine agrees, to the point of incorporating it into his theology of the Trinity. Where he parts company with Neoplatonism is in identifying the divine Logos or Wisdom with the (incarnate) Word, and in his insistence on faith as the gateway to understanding: "unless you believe, you will not understand" (Is 7:9). This is because he considers the will to have primacy even over knowledge: anything not properly known cannot be properly loved, which happens when the will (not reason) is corrupted. Faith is, then, the means of cleansing the will and orienting it towards God.

For Augustine, Neoplatonism had reached the threshold of Christianity without actually crossing it. This limits its value, because human nature is fallen and needs faith to come to the truth. This does not mean reason is undervalued, because, in properly using intellect, memory, and will, human nature finds fulfillment. Reason is the receiver of that illumination by which anything is known, the human faculty that most fully demonstrates that we are made in God's image and are therefore eligible to participate in the divine nature. God, the inward "Illuminator," is the cause of whatever certainty humankind attains, because memory contains whatever reason comes to know, and reason knows whatever is drawn out of memory through illumination.

The presence of God within oneself constitutes the essential starting point for "renewing" one's knowledge of God (*recognitio*), for God could not be recollected if totally wiped from memory. Reason therefore has the priority of order, but not of time. This is so, not because reason is intrinsically incompetent, but because it remains unreliable in the person who has not yet submitted to the Illuminator. In Augustine's view, we do not begin with faith and then go to understanding; we begin in faith in order to go to understanding.

Still, one cannot know or possess God without the will. This makes a purely rationalistic approach to God completely unacceptable to Augustine: it would render any sort of personal commitment dependent on the previous acquisition of intellectual vision. Besides, one can intellectualize about God without (as Augustine well knew) actually bending one's will to God. This is because of the reality of sin: as sinners, we all have a blinded vision that cannot be cleared until the (distorted) will has made its commitment. Caught between the fact of sin and the end for which it was intended, the human will is ambivalent: all desire happiness, and in that sense all have a yearning for it, which really means for God; but not all would agree that God is what they really yearn for.

Recognitio is the casting off of blindness, a realization that God chose to become humble in history. This God humbled is Christ "the disturber," so-called because he causes upset in the ambivalent will of human beings until they are forced to seek divine healing. Faith, then, may be defined as the acknowledgement (*agnitio*) of the power of the servant Christ, the humble physician, to heal the wounds created by sin. But not even the Word incarnate could induce faith and love of God in us if the eternal Word (Logos) had not already visited our reason. Were this not so, there would be no connection between the historical and the eternal. The fact that such a connection exists permits the response between God and ourselves to take place.

Bibliography

A.   Critical editions of many of Augustine's works are printed in CSEL and CCSL. Translations of many of his works are found in NPNF and FC.

B.   DTC 1:2270–2471; LThK³ 1:1241–47; NCE 1:1041–58; ODCC 128–30; TRE 4: 646–99; Peter Brown, *Augustine of Hippo: A Biography* (Berkeley, Calif., 1967); Eugene TeSelle, *Augustine the Theologian* (New York, 1970); Terry L. Miethe, *Augustinian Bibliography, 1970–1980: With Essays on the Fundamentals of Augustinian Scholarship* (Westport, Conn., 1982); Gerald P. Bonner, *St. Augustine of Hippo: Life and Controversies*, 2d ed. (Norfolk, Va., 1986); Mary T. Clark, *Augustine* (London, 1994).

J. Kevin Coyle

AULÉN, GUSTAF (15 May 1879, Ljungby, Sweden–16 December 1977, Lund, Sweden). *Education*: Ph.D., Univ. of Uppsala, 1909. *Career*: assistant professor, Univ. of Uppsala, 1907–13; professor of systematic theology, Univ. of Lund, 1913–33; founder, *Svénsk Teologisk Kvartalskrift* (Swedish Theological Quarterly), 1925; bishop of Strängnäs, 1933–52; active retirement, 1952–77.

Aulén is the father of "Lundensian theology." He built this approach to theological investigation on the foundation laid by his Uppsala professors, Nathan Söderblom* and Einar Billing.* From them he learned a concern for Luther,* a respect for the historical-critical method, and the certainty that Christianity is unique.

The first of his books was *The Faith of the Christian Church* (1923; Philadelphia, 1948), a systematic theology in a trinitarian shape. Aulén's next book on the Christian conception of God (translated only into German) was laid out in the historical pattern now characteristic of Lund. In this schema, dogma (the church's normative interpretation of the apostolic witness) developed to high points in the patristic era (Irenaeus*) and the Reformation (Luther). Medieval scholasticism and Lutheran orthodoxy, in contrast, are low points at which the primitive and apostolic faith was radically betrayed. This evaluative periodization appears to have been his original contribution.

Christus Victor (New York, 1931), the English translation of his lectures on the Christian idea of the Atonement, uses this same periodization. In it, he argues that the second-century bishop of Lyons and the sixteenth-century reformer most faithfully expound the "classic" early teaching. This paradigmatic monograph has had wide reception as evidenced by its translation into English, German, French, Dutch, Chinese, and other languages. It initially identified "Lundensian theology."

Aulén's historical analysis avoided liberal subjectivism even as it gave scant comfort to reactionary confessionalism. He scandalized the rationalist critics by affirming that Paul and the church fathers rightly interpreted the Christ of the gospels; he offended the theological biblicists by boldly using the historical-critical method. He joined in the continental neo-orthodox criticisms of German fascism though he did so on the basis of Luther's idea of the "two kingdoms," the very doctrine Barth* rejected to criticize Hitler's ideology on Christocentric grounds.

Following his translation into the episcopate, he was active in ecumenical assemblies (Edinburgh, 1937; Amsterdam, 1948). The international ecumenical links Söderblom had forged became the bridges across which Swedish theological investigation stimulated dogmatic and exegetical thought in other countries. He spoke and acted for renewal in the Church of Sweden. He was a modern hymn composer and urged liturgical relevance.

He continued to speak to live issues of the Church in Sweden and beyond. His lectures (during his only trip to North America) on *Church, Law and Society* (New York, 1948) drew from the same wells as *Christus Victor* to anchor Christian social action in God's creative intention, not merely in the recovery provided in the divine redemption. Since his retirement, two volumes addressed contemporary issues in the Swedish Church, but in ways that apply not only in Sweden: *Eucharist and Sacrifice* (Philadelphia, 1958) and *Reformation and Catholicity* (Philadelphia, 1961). To help English readers past Swedish obscurities, he wrote an exposition of the spiritual reflections of Sweden's most famous diplomat. Nearing ninety years of age, he undertook to read and summarize for the nontechnical reader the "Jesus research" that had been published only in the previous ten years.

He was a scholar and a churchman. His lasting contribution is the judgment that Irenaeus and the church fathers serve to answer distinctively Protestant questions no less than to ground "catholic" theology. His continuing challenge to theologians of every land and confession is the insistence that Luther is an epochal expositor of the apostolic witness for the whole church.

Bibliography

A. *Die Dogmengeschichte im Lichte der Lutherforschung* (Stockholm, 1932); *Jesus in Contemporary Historical Research* (London, 1970); *Dag Hammarskjöld's White Book* (Philadelphia, 1969).

B. LThK³ 1:1251–52; ODCC 132; TRE 4:748–52; Edgar M. Carlson, *The Reinterpretation of Luther* (Philadelphia, 1948); Philip S. Watson, *Let God Be God! An Interpretation of the Theology of Martin Luther* (Philadelphia, 1948); Gustaf Wingren, "Gustaf Aulen" in *Handbook of Christian Theologians*, ed. Martin E. Marty and Dean G. Peerman, 2d ed. (Nashville, Tenn., 1984), 308–19.

David T. Priestley

B

BAADER, FRANZ XAVER VON (27 March 1765, Munich–23 May 1841, Munich). *Education*: studied medicine, Ingolstadt and Vienna, 1781–85; studied mining technology, the Erzgebirge, 1788–92; trained in British mining, 1792–96. *Career*: held increasingly responsible positions, the Bavarian mining administration, 1799–1820; ennobled, 1807; honorary professor of speculative theology, Univ. of Munich, 1826; with J. J. Görres, coeditor, *Eos*, 1826–29.

Franz von Baader was the most prominent Roman Catholic lay theologian of the German romantic-idealist generation, in dialogue with Schelling and Hegel and influencing Kierkegaard,* Soloviev* and Berdiaev.* His work was wide-ranging, from a philosophy rooted in a system of polarity held together in the ''world-soul'' (a notion that Schelling seized upon and propagated) to proto-ecumenical and social-critical essays.

The works of the Lutheran mystic, Jakob Boehme* (1585–1624), exercised a major lasting influence on Baader. In Baader's thought, the polar opposites of Romantic philosophy came to unity not via a dialectic of objects or concepts but in a dialogue of persons, grounded in the dialogue initiated by God at creation with his human creatures. Against Descartes (and Kant, Fichte, etc.), he asserted a dialogal anthropology: *Cogitor ergo cogitans sum*: I am conceived [in God's thought], therefore I am, a thinking being, addressed and known by God (hence *Gewissen*, con-science). Nor should the human subject be reduced to a solipsistic self, an assumption he regarded as the fatal flaw of modern philosophical anthropology. Other human beings are equally acknowledged by God, equally selves, rather than simply ''not (my)self.'' Theologically, this social aspect is seen to derive from Christ, the Logos who associates persons, also in his work of redemption, in the church.

Baader coined the adjective ''Christian-social.'' His 1835 work, *Über die*

Proletairs, is but one sign of the interest he had in economic problems since his critical reflections on Adam Smith's liberal economics in 1802. From 1832 to 1835 he wrote some articles anticipatory of the social Catholicism that developed later in the century. It was perhaps the papacy's alliance in the 1830s with the forces of reaction that led him to question whether the papacy was essential to the church or not. This in turn, along with the obscurity and randomness of his writings, made his thought rapidly seem to be quite dated. He has still not received the detailed scholarly study that his importance would seem to warrant.

Bibliography

A. *Franz von Baaders sämtliche Werke*, ed. F. Hoffmann, 16 vols. (Leipzig, 1851–60; repr. Aalen, 1963); for a chronological listing of his works, see 16: 51–58.

B. LThK³ 1:1327–29; BBKL 1:313–14; KThD 1:274–302; NCE 2:3; TRE 5:64–67; E. Susini, *Franz von Baader et le romantisme mystique*, 2 vols. (Paris, 1943); S. Schmitz, *Sprache, Sozietät und Geschichte bei Franz Baader* (Frankfurt/Bern, 1975); L. Procesi Xella, *Baader: Rassegna storica degli studi (1786–1977)* (Bologna, 1977); W. Lambert, *Franz von Baaders Philosophie des Gebets* (Innsbruck, 1978).

Paul Misner

BACON, ROGER (ca. 1214/1220, Somerset, England–1292, Oxford). The facts about Bacon's life are few and uncertain. He probably studied arts first at Oxford and then at Paris; began teaching arts at Paris, possibly as early as 1237, and continued to teach there until 1247; gave up his teaching position to do research on topics he considered neglected; possibly studied theology at Oxford from 1247 to 1252, where he may have come under the influence of Robert Grosseteste*; entered the Franciscans ca. 1256; was sent to the Franciscan house in Paris, where he was frustrated by strict Franciscan censorship policy in the aftermath of the controversy over Joachim of Fiore* and the Franciscan Spirituals; made contact with Cardinal Guy le Gos de Foulques (the future Clement IV) with regard to his plans for curricular reform; in 1265 or 1266 ordered by Clement IV to send him the remedies Bacon proposed for the reformation of Christian doctrine; by 1267 wrote his *Greater Work* (*Opus majus*) which he sent to Clement IV in the hope that the pope would implement his plan; followed it with his *Lesser Work* (*Opus minus*) and *Third Work* (*Opus tertium*), when the pope failed to take action; in 1277 was condemned by his Franciscan superiors for his allegedly dangerous teachings, which may have involved his views on astrology and alchemy, his sympathies for the apocalyptic ideas of Joachim of Fiore, or simply his harsh criticisms of his Franciscan brethren; imprisoned probably between 1277 and 1279, but according to some for much longer; probably lived in the Franciscan house of studies at Oxford from 1279 to 1292, the year of his death, when he wrote *The Compendium of Theological Studies*; known as *Doctor mirabilis* (the amazing teacher).

Bacon was among the first to study the newly translated works of Aristotle, and during the years prior to 1247 he commented extensively on various Aristotelian works, especially the *Physics* and the *Metaphysics*, and the *Liber de causis* (*The Book of Causes*), which was then taken to be Aristotle's; during this period he also wrote several works on logic and grammar. In his *Opus majus* Bacon presented his proposal for curricular reform; he insisted on the need for Hebrew and Greek in biblical studies, claimed that the study of mathematics was essential to all knowledge, including the study of theology, and pointed out the usefulness of philosophy to theology in the conversion of unbelievers. Bacon was an ill-tempered man who railed against his most illustrious contemporaries, both Franciscans and Dominicans, accusing Alexander of Hales,* Bonaventure,* Albert,* and Thomas* of destroying theology by commenting on the *Sentences* of Peter Lombard* rather than on the Bible. Bacon's work in logic and semiotic theory has attracted some contemporary interest. His insistence upon the value of mathematics for scientific inquiry, his emphasis upon experience, and his work in optics have made him seem a man whose vision reached far beyond that of his contemporaries. As recent studies have shown, his influence upon later medieval philosophy and theology has been important though further study is needed.

Bibliography

A. *The 'Opus Majus' of Roger Bacon*, ed. J. H. Bridges, 3 vols. (Oxford, 1897–1900; repr. Frankfurt, 1964); *Opera hactenus inedita Rogeri Baconi*, ed. Robert Steele et al., 12 vols. (Oxford, 1905–40); *Rogeri Baconis Moralis Philosophia*, ed. F. M. Delorme and E. Massa (Zurich, 1953); trans. Roger Belle Burke, 2 vols. (Philadelphia and London, 1928); *Roger Bacon's Philosophy of Nature*, ed. and trans. David C. Lindberg (Oxford, 1983); *Compendium of the Study of Theology*, ed. and trans. Thomas S. Maloney (Leiden and New York, 1988).

B.   DTC 2:8–31; LThK³ 8:1356–57; ODCC 143; Theodore Crowley, *Roger Bacon: The Problem of the Soul in His Philosophical Commentaries* (Louvain, 1950); Stewart C. Easton, *Roger Bacon and His Search for a Universal Science: A Reconsideration of the Life and Work of Roger Bacon in the Light of His Own Stated Purposes* (New York, 1952); Thomas S. Maloney, "The Extreme Realism of Roger Bacon," *Review of Metaphysics* 38 (1985): 807–37; Jeremiah Hackett and T. S. Maloney, "A Roger Bacon Bibliography (1957–1985)," *New Scholasticism* 61 (1987): 184–207; J. Hackett, "Roger Bacon," in *Dictionary of Literary Biography*, vol. 115, *Medieval Philosophers* (Detroit, Mich., 1992), 90–102; J. Hackett, "Roger Bacon on Magnanimity and Virtue," *Les philosophies morales et politiques au Moyen Age* (Ottawa, 1995), 1:367–77; Georgette Sinkler, "Roger Bacon," in *Cambridge Dictionary of Philosophy*, ed. R. Audi (Cambridge, 1995), 61–62.

Roland J. Teske

BAIUS (DE BAY), MICHAEL (1513, Meslin l'Évêque [Hennegau], Belgium–16 September 1589, Leuven). *Education*: studied philosophy, Louvain, 1533–35; theology, Louvain, 1536–41. *Career*: ordained priest, 1542; taught philosophy, Louvain 1544–50; doctor and professor of theology, Louvain, 1550–89.

Baius' main concern was to oppose Luther's* teaching on justification as alien justice imputed to the sinner, while taking a rigorously antipelagian stance. He was not willing to let Luther and Calvin* appropriate Augustine* for their views. His lectures were assiduously attended and widely noted. One must realize that the Council of Trent's decree on justification was not promulgated until 1564, after Baius and others had already developed their positions.

In 1560, the Sorbonne, followed eventually by other universities, condemned positions attributed to him in lectures. He replied with a number of publications between 1563 and 1566 and defended himself at Trent during the last session of the Council. Further condemnations followed (among others from the universities of Alcalá and Salamanca), in particular the bull *Ex omnibus afflictionibus* of Pope Pius V (Oct. 1, 1567; see DS 1901–80). A major ambiguity bedeviled later assessments: depending on the placement of a comma (the *Comma Pianum*), the propositions listed were said to be condemned (even though some of them might be open to benevolent interpretations) either (1) because of the way they were likely to be taken, or, alternatively, (2) in the very sense the author intended. Baius came to terms with the condemnations, as did his colleagues at Louvain. His main connection with the posthumous controversies that kept his name prominent was simply that he promoted study of scriptural and patristic texts as superior to scholastic approaches. Such Louvainian "positive theology" would collide with the views of Molina* and Lessius in the controversies over grace and free will, especially in the condemnations of Jansenism a half century and more after his death.

The propositions condemned by Pius V in 1567 account for the opinions about Baius that have prevailed since his time, at least until recently. Against the Aristotelian-leaning scholastic thesis of a state of pure nature, he arrived at the paradoxical position of insisting that Adam's original integrity, including the indwelling Holy Spirit, was "natural" (DS 1926). He fell into this awkwardness by adopting the perspective of his adversaries and avoiding the classic term "grace," with its emphasis on personal offer and response. He seems to have taken the Thomistic distinction of the natural order and the supernatural order as if they were two "human natures," one better than the other, and reasoned that if Adam's descendants were deprived of their ancestor's original integrity by his sin, then that integrity must have been "natural" in the first place.

Bibliography

A. *Michaelis Baii opera*, ed. G. Gerberon (Cologne, 1696).

B. LThK³ 1:1360–62; NCE 2:19–21; TRE 5:133–37; Henri de Lubac, *Augustinianism and Modern Theology* (New York, 1969); idem, "Le 'De prima hominis justitia' de M. Baius: Une relecture critique," in *L'Augustinisme à l'ancienne faculté de théologie de Louvain* (Leuven, 1994), 123–66; repr. in Alfred Vanneste, *Nature et grâce dans la théologie occidentale: Dialogue avec H. de Lubac* (Leuven, 1996), 185–228.

Paul Misner

BALTHASAR, HANS URS VON (12 August 1905, Lucern–26 June 1988, Basel). *Education*: studied German literature and philosophy at Univs. of Zurich, Vienna, Berlin, 1925–28; Ph.D., Univ. of Zurich, 1928; studied philosophy, Pullach, Germany, 1931–33; theology, Fourvière (near Lyons), France, 1933–37. *Career*: entered Society of Jesus, 1929; ordained priest, 1936; staff, *Stimmen der Zeit*, Munich, 1936; student chaplain, Univ. of Basel, 1937; editor and translator for the "European Series" of the Klosterberg collection, 1940; established the Johannes Verlag, 1947; departure from the Society of Jesus, 1950; public lectures in Germany, retreat activity, early 1950s; incardinated, Diocese of Chur, 1956; Golden Cross of Mount Athos, honorary doctorates Edinburgh, Münster, Fribourg, 1965; member International Theological Commission, 1969–88; cofounder *Communio: International Catholic Review*, with Jean Daniélou,* Henri de Lubac,* Joseph Ratzinger et al., 1972; corresponding Fellow, British Academy, 1973; associé étranger, French Academy, 1975; honorary doctorate, Catholic Univ. of America, 1980; International Paul VI prize by Pope John Paul II, 1984; symposium in Rome on "Adrienne von Speyr and her Ecclesial Mission," 1985; Wolfgang Amadeus Mozart Prize, 1987; cardinal, 1988.

Author of eighty-five separate volumes, over 500 articles and contributions to collected works, almost 100 translations, editor of sixty volumes of the works of Adrienne von Speyr and other pieces, Swiss theologian Hans Urs von Balthasar yet insisted that his most important work was cofounding, with Adrienne von Speyr, a "secular institute," the Community of Saint John (Johannesgemeinschaft).

Called by Henri de Lubac "the most cultured man of his time," von Balthasar never held an academic chair. Most renowned as a theologian, his early years were formed by lifelong interests in literature and music. He chose literature as his field of endeavor, never acquiring a doctorate in either philosophy or theology, considering himself a "Germanist" by specialization.

From an old, distinguished Lucerne family, he early experienced formative influences from leading intellectual and spiritual figures.

Jesuit philosopher Erich Przywara* schooled him in the analogy of being. Przywara and Karl Barth* had been disputing analogy, a conversation Balthasar pursued with greater fruitfulness. Balthasar's early, definitive work *Karl Barth* attempted to connect Barth and the Catholic tradition by bridging "the analogy of faith" and the "analogy of being." His friendship with Barth was cemented by a shared passion for Mozart.

From Henri de Lubac he discovered the church fathers and the sense of the catholicity and "*communio*" nature of the church. Balthasar was most interested in Irenaeus,* Origen,* Gregory of Nyssa,* and Maximus the Confessor,* all of whom he treated extensively especially in his earlier work, three of them receiving separate volumes.

In music and architecture Balthasar celebrated the baroque as a full-bodied proclamation of the Catholic spirit, the "Catholica." In literature he was particularly influenced by Goethe. He largely translated Claudel, but also others such as Peguy, Bernanos, and Calderon, whom he held was Christendom's master playwright.

Central to Balthasar's life and work was his transforming encounter with Swiss physician and mystic Adrienne von Speyr (1902–67). He insisted that their work was part of an inseparable whole, of which her contribution was the more important. His belief in a shared mission with her to found a secular institute led to his departure from the Society of Jesus which did not accept this mission, although his theology remained profoundly Ignatian.

Critical of the fortress mentality of the preconciliar church, he argued for openness to the world and for the role of the laity in making visible the glory of God that is in the world. This attitude was confirmed by the Second Vatican Council, at which, however, he was not invited to participate. After the Council, he condemned the degeneration of the longed-for openness to the world into world-accommodation. Critical of movements seeking positions of worldly influence, he urged a simple presence in the de-Christianized world: contemplation was at the core of the lay life.

His aesthetic orientation convinced him that the loss of the transcendental, beauty, had been disastrous for modern Christianity. Balthasar urged that his "theological aesthetics" was not a theological frill, but likely the one possible way to transcend the limitations of the regnant cosmological and anthropological methods. He sought to create a theological aesthetics in which beauty would once again be the entry point into the human encounter with the divine. Concerned for the "one thing needful," Balthasar maintained that one who has lost a sense of beauty will soon lose the ability to pray and to love.

The transcendentals serve as framework for his masterwork, the *Trilogy*. From 1961 to 1987, he wrote the fifteen volumes of this *magnum opus*.

The heart of his *Trilogy* is a rediscovery of the Glory of the Lord (*Herrlichkeit*) as a vision witnessed to throughout the Scriptures and one accessible to all in the descent of Christ, the form in which God has chosen to reveal Himself to the world. At the peak of the beautiful is the Cross, where the fullness of Godhead is revealed to the cosmos. The beautiful is "formosa," form (Gestalt) and splendor combining to draw the beholder beyond himself. Because God is interpersonal love, the ecstasy into which He draws His beholder is one of obedience and not merely intoxication.

The *Theodramatik* deals with the clash of freedoms in divine human intercourse, finding in drama the key analogy for God's creation of a cosmic/historical theater. Themes of mission and eschatology emerge strongly.

A three-volume *Theologik* concludes the *Trilogy*, in which beauty leads through goodness to truth. Questions of the Holy Spirit and of the two natures in Christ are treated here, where meaning in communication between God and man is explored. The whole is summarized in an *Epilog*.

Prior to the Vatican Council he found theology "languishing in the desert of neoscholasticism" and found relief in a scripturally oriented theology. In his subsequent polemical writing, he attacked those he felt were separating the "little ones" from encountering Christ in Scripture. Although he criticized much contemporary exegesis, he yet was well versed in such scholarship and made ready use of it when beneficial.

Another well-known polemic was joined with that theology represented by Karl Rahner,* particularly over the issue of the "anonymous Christian." Balthasar warned that the cross was in danger of being stripped of its meaning, that the decisive test of martyrdom could be lost to an overly intellectualized theology.

For Balthasar, the greatest historical tragedy to befall Christianity was the split between systematic and mystical theology, what he called "sitting" and "kneeling" theologies. His work attempts to bridge that gap by returning the evidence of the saints and particularly of the mystics to the theological conversation, hence his interest in theology and holiness. It is his singular contribution to have taken the claims of the mystics, not least Adrienne von Speyr, seriously, placing their vision at the foundation of his theology. He did pioneering studies in the "theology of the saints," focusing on women mystics from Hildegard* and Mechthilde to Therese of Lisieux* and Elizabeth of the Trinity.

Distinct from other traditions where mysticism is central, for Christianity obedience to the will of God (mission) makes the saint, mystic or not: "the saint is the best apology for the Christian religion." Key to his notion of spirituality is the stance of "availability" seen most clearly in Mary, "Handmaid of the Lord."

His anthropology builds on modern personalism's belated discovery of relation as constituent of the human. Relation, the I-Thou, constitutes the person, beyond the human subject: interpersonal love is the very stuff of human existence. The uniqueness of the free person—the fruit of each one's relation with the divine "Thou" in which each human "I" finds itself—is the saving hope in a world of mass man. This also informs his passionate opposition to any systematization in the things of God.

Relation as the heart of reality reflects the nature of God, who for Balthasar is emphatically interpersonal, where "otherness" is in the very Godhead. Only Christianity can hold that God is love, that Being is identified with Love. The unity in diversity of Christianity resolves the problem of the One and the Many, Being and beings—the central problem facing humanity—in a way that allows both to be. The being of God, and of man, is dialogical, characterized by the Word.

Along with personalism, he was much concerned with freedom. This inclined him to accept a modified form of Barth's doctrine of universal election.

In his theology of the sexes, he finds the antitype for human sexuality—and its spiritual expressions—in the life of the Trinity, where the Father is giver of being, and so masculine, while the Son is receptive and feminine. In Creation, Mary receives the seed-word in a preeminent way: her bridal "yes" allows the Father's will to be realized in the world. Balthasar's theology is thoroughly Marian.

His ecclesiology reflects his conviction of the spousal nature of God's relation to His People.

Overcoming both cosmology and anthropology, he insists that "love alone" is the way, that in Jesus Christ God has fully and finally revealed who He is. Unique among world religious figures who teach "ways," Christ points to His person as the way: He is the concrete universal. The higher, the more unique and irreplaceable a being is, the more capable it is of a definitive death. This reaches its summit on Calvary, the moment of God-forsakenness, when, in place of humanity, Christ experiences the full weight of sin and its separation from God. Christ experienced the full horror of hell, forsakenness by God—and thus opened the possibility of salvation for all sinners who will accept His love. Curiously, hell as definitive rejection of love first becomes possible after Christ: the God who has been abandoned by God offers solidarity with all sinners, who yet are free to reject Him.

Balthasar rejects Origen's theory of apocatastasis, insisting that hell is the abode of the devil and a real possibility for every human. However, he insists that charity demands that one consider oneself the worst of sinners and that one hope for the salvation of all. As to whether there are any humans in hell, he finds the Scripture texts finally contradictory, recalling that the church which has canonized so many has never declared any as damned.

Critically sensitive to the concerns of liberation theology, Balthasar wrote that if only one book were to survive the twentieth century, it should be Solzhenitsyn's *Gulag Archipelago*.

Bibliography

A.   *Heart of the World* (San Francisco, 1980); *The Von Balthasar Reader*, ed. Medard Kehl and Werner Löser (New York, 1982); *Prayer* (San Francisco, 1986); *Explorations in Theology*, 3 of 5 vols., San Francisco, 1989–); *Love Alone* (Dublin, 1989); Cornelia Capol, *Hans Urs von Balthasar: Bibliographie, 1925–1990* (Einsiedeln, 1990); *The Glory of the Lord*, 7 vols. (Edinburgh, 1982–91); *Theo-Drama*, 4 of 5 vols. (San Francisco, 1989–); *Theo-Logic*, 3 vols. (San Francisco, in preparation); *The Theology of Karl Barth* (San Francisco, 1992); *My Work: In Retrospect* (San Francisco, 1993); *Mysterium Paschale* (Grand Rapids, Mich., 1993); *Our Task* (San Francisco, 1994).

B.   LThK[3] 1:1375–78; NCE 18:29–30; Manfred Lochbrunner, *Analogia Caritatis: Darstellung und Deutung der Theologie Hans Urs von Balthasars* (Freiburg, 1981); John Riches, ed., *The Analogy of Beauty: the Theology of Hans Urs von Balthasar* (Edinburgh, 1986); *Hans Urs von Balthasar: His Life and Work*, ed. David Schindler (San Francisco, 1991); John O'Donnell, *Hans Urs von Balthasar* (London, 1992); Edward T. Oakes, *Pattern of Redemption* (New York, 1994); Raymond Gawronski, *Word and Silence: Hans*

Urs von Balthasar and the Spiritual Encounter between East and West (Edinburgh, 1995).

Raymond T. Gawronski

BÁÑEZ, DOMINGO (29 February 1528, Valladolid, Spain–22 October 1604, Medina del Campo). *Education*: studied arts and philosophy, Salamanca, 1542–48; theology, 1548–52. *Career*: professed as Dominican, 1547; professor, Salamanca, 1551–61, 1570–73; Avila, 1561–67; Alcalá, 1567–70; Valladolid, 1573–76; prior, Toro, 1576–77; principal chair, Salamanca, 1581–99; retirement, 1599–1604.

As a leading Thomist of the day, Báñez became involved in the two activities for which he is principally remembered, a profound association with the Carmelite mystic and reformer, St. Teresa of Avila,* and the bitter conflict between the Dominican and Jesuit schools over grace and free will.

Báñez supported and, at Avila in 1562, saved Teresa's reform even before meeting her. The two were at Avila until 1567, meeting frequently, and they remained in contact until her death in 1582. During this time he was not only her confessor and spiritual director but also her theological adviser. The Thomistic flavor of her writings is probably due to his influence.

Báñez's theology of grace and free will (''Banezianism'') was worked out in reaction to that of the Jesuit Luis de Molina,* whose *Concordia liberi arbitrii cum gratiae donis* (''The Harmony of Free Will with the Gifts of Grace'') appeared in 1588. Báñez with certain Dominican confreres responded in 1595 with their *Apologia fratrum praedicatorum* (''Apology of the Friars Preachers''). His principal response, however, was his *De vera et legitima concordia liberi arbitrii cum auxiliis gratiae* (''The True and Legitimate Harmony of Free Will with the Helps of Grace'') of 1600. In these works Báñez and colleagues presented a system based on Thomistic principles, though couched in new terminology. Their concern was to counter by positive argument what they saw as the baneful tendency of Molina's thought, namely, to compromise the divine sovereignty in the interaction of God and human beings.

Central to Báñez's thought was the notion of a supernatural *praemotio physica* (''physical pre-motion'') by which God intrinsically determines the will to a particular salutary act. Under the *praemotio*, however, the will remains free, for in all creatures a divine *concursus* (assistance) is needed for the movement from rest to action, and God only moves creatures according to their natures, and so moves free creatures freely. This scheme certainly preserves the sovereignty of God, the doctrine of predestination, and the gracious character of salutary acts. Its critics, however, maintained that it (a) compromised human freedom in that it surrendered the latter's very essence, namely, *self*-determination, and (b) denied the existence of a (purely) sufficient grace in that without the effective *praemotio* the will remains radically incapable of salutary action.

The controversy between Banezianism and Molinism was never officially resolved. Today both are of historical interest only, as the question, to which no fully satisfactory answer has ever, and arguably can ever, be given, is approached from the standpoint of the divine transcendence and the uncreated and indeed trinitarian character of grace.

Bibliography

A.   J. Quétif and J. Échard, *Scriptores Ordinis Praedicatorum*, 5 vols. (Paris, 1719–32), 2:352–53.

B.   BBKL 1:362; Catholicisme 1:1202–4; DTC 2:140–45; LThK³ 1:1384–86; NCE 2:48–50; *La Ciencia tomista* 25–28 (1922–23), 37–39 (1928–29), 47 (1933).

David Coffey

BARONIUS, CAESAR (31 October 1538, Sora in Campagna–30 June 1607, Rome). *Education*: doctoral degree in law, Rome, 1561. *Career*: ordained priest, 1564; prefect, Cong. of the Oratory, 1584; religious superior, Cong. of the Oratory, 1593–96; protonotary apostolic, 1596; cardinal, 1596; librarian of the Roman Church, 1597; papal confessor and theologian, 1597–1605; member of Cong. *de auxiliis*, 1597.

Baronius was a humanist-influenced church historian who appropriated some of the historical tools of the Renaissance and based his histories upon primary documents. His history of the church, however, served the theological and ecclesiastical needs of the Roman Church during the late sixteenth century. Educated in Rome during the late Renaissance, Baronius came under the influence of humanism and those in Rome who were interested in the religious reformation of morals and discipline in the church. In the 1550s, moreover, Baronius came under the religious and spiritual direction of Philip Neri, founder of the Congregation of the Oratory, experienced a religious conversion under Neri's direction, and remained faithful to him throughout his life.

In 1558, one year before the publication of Matthias Flacius Illyricus'* (1520–75) first volume of the so-called *Centuriae Magdeburgenses* (i.e., *Historia Ecclesiae Christi*, Basle, 1559–74), Neri ordered Baronius to give the Oratory a series of lectures on the history of the church as part of his attempt to improve the religious knowledge of Roman priests and prominent lay people. He continued this series of lectures and the research necessary to give them for the next thirty years, prior to publishing his famous history of the church, the *Annales ecclesiastici* (12 vols., 1588–1607).

The publication of the *Annales* was a direct attempt to refute Flacius' Lutheran interpretation of church history and to demonstrate the uninterrupted evolution of the church just as Christ had designed it, rebutting the *Centuries* view that somewhere between the third and the seventh centuries the church had deviated from the path that Christ had established for it. As the *Centuries* asserted that one of the main reasons for this diversion was the establishment of the papacy as the supreme authority in the church, so the *Annales* collected documents to demonstrate the unbroken connection of the papacy with the development of the church.

While researching and writing his multivolume history, Baronius also revised the Roman Martyrology, wrote biographies of St. Gregory Nazianzus* and St. Ambrose,* and published a series of commentaries on the Acts of the Apostles. These works as well as his own history of the church were based on extensive use of primary documents and manuscripts, moving away from an undocumented and hagiographical approach to church history. In the end, though, the *Annales* became a Catholic theological apologetic for the church's development in opposition to the Lutheran defense of its own theological view of church history.

Bibliography

A.   *Annales Ecclesiastici*, 12 vols. (Rome, 1588–1607); 37 vols. (Bar-le-Duc, 1864–87); *Cesare Baronio: Scritti Vari* (Sora, 1963).

B.   DHGE 6:871–82; DTC 2:426; LThK³ 2:31–32; NCE 2:105–6; ODCC 160; OEncR 1:122–23; Generoso Calenzio, *La Vita e gli Scritti del Cardinale Cesare Baronio* (Rome, 1907); Cyriac K. Pullapilly, *Caesar Baronius: Counter-Reformation Historian* (Notre Dame, Ind., 1975).

Patrick W. Carey

BARTH, KARL (10 May 1886, Basel, Switzerland–10 December 1968, Basel). *Education*: studied theology, Univ. of Bern, Switzerland, 1904–6, 1907; Univ. of Berlin, 1906–7; Univ. of Tübingen, 1907–8; Univ. of Marburg, 1908–9. *Career*: ordained, 1908; assistant pastor, Geneva, 1909–11; pastor, Safenwil, Switzerland, 1911–21; professor, Univ. of Göttingen, 1921–25; Univ. of Münster, 1925–30; Univ. of Bonn, 1930–34, Univ. of Basel, 1935–62.

Barth was the most influential Protestant theologian of the twentieth century. During his early career, by his own admission, he was "second to none" among his contemporaries in his approval of "modern" theology. His experience in the ministry, however, led him to question and eventually change his theological outlook, and exposed him to political and social issues (such as the plight of workers) that led to his involvement in socialism, and especially in the trade union movement. The outbreak of the First World War on August 1, 1914, moreover, shook Barth's theology to its foundations. To his dismay, ninety-three German intellectuals (including most of his teachers in Germany) signed and published a manifesto supporting the war policy of Kaiser Wilhelm II. In response, Barth said that the "ethical failure" of liberal Protestantism on this matter exposed the error of its whole exegetical and dogmatic position.

Barth also found liberal Protestant theology to be inadequate for his work as a pastor, especially for preaching, which must deal with both the content of the Bible and the problems of human life. He began to wonder how human beings can speak of God at all: how can the Word of God be on human lips? What had gone on for 1900 years (namely, talk about God) suddenly seemed problematic. He became convinced that Christians—even theologians—used God as the "crowning touch" to what people had begun on their own.

So Barth made an about-face. Instead of starting with human speech and thought about God, he began with God and what God speaks and thinks about humanity: "The Lord has spoken"; theology is a mere stammering repetition of what God has said. The theologian cannot learn the truth of God from historical study, or from the pious human consciousness, or philosophical speculation, but only by listening to the Word of God and expounding it. Barth developed his theology during this period by writing a commentary on the epistle to the Romans. He followed the first edition of 1919 with a substantially revised second edition in 1922. In this commentary Barth did not pursue historical-critical questions about the Bible, which he considered to be a human attempt to bring the Word of God under our control, but instead tried to understand what the book of Romans says.

Barth concluded, for example, that we must recognize God once more as God; alongside this all other duties are mere child's play. Rejecting liberal theology's focus on humanity—its belief, piety, religion, culture, emotions, or whatever—Barth said the bedrock of Scripture is the *deity* of God. God is qualitatively different from humanity: God cannot be known as other things are known, but instead breaks forth, like a flash of lightning, revealing himself as he is. Barth emphasized God's superiority and humanity's sinfulness. He said his theological ancestors were Jeremiah, Paul, Martin Luther,* John Calvin,* and Søren Kierkegaard,* all of whom reduced humanity and the universe to "nothing" in comparison with God. For Barth, his was a "theology of crisis," since the revelation of God is the crisis of the world. God, who is wholly other, advances on this world from beyond it, like a cry of alarm, shattering everything here below. In Christ, God intersects the plane of human reality vertically, from above. The divine touches this world only as a tangent touches a circle: like a mathematical point, this intersection has no historical or psychological breadth, said Barth. Revelation conceals more than it manifests, and to us God remains unknown. The finite cannot comprehend the infinite, and time cannot comprehend eternity.

How, then, can creatures speak about God? Barth's answer was the dialectical method: the truth of God must be expressed in statement and counter-statement. So, when speaking of the revelation of God in the creation, we must immediately speak of God's hiddenness in creation. When speaking of humanity as created in the image of God, we must immediately speak as well of human sin and frailty. Since all human statements about God are inadequate, we can speak no final word about God.

In sum, Barth saw himself as protesting against Friedrich Schleiermacher,* Albrecht Ritschl,* Adolf von Harnack,* and Ernst Troeltsch.* For Barth, the subject of theology is not humanity, but God alone; theology does not lead from below to above, but from above to below. Barth said he wanted to turn Schleiermacher on his head.

In 1921, Barth wrote his first dogmatics, published posthumously as *The Göttingen Dogmatics*. In 1925, he began writing a second dogmatics, called the

Christliche Dogmatik (Christian Dogmatics), which was to have extended over several volumes, although only the first volume ever appeared. In 1930 he began studying Anselm's theology, especially his method of "faith seeking understanding." After writing a book on Anselm's proof for the existence of God in 1931 (a book many take to mark as decisive a change in his thought as does the Romans commentary), Barth decided that he needed to begin his dogmatics yet again. So he abandoned the *Christliche Dogmatik* he had begun at Münster and started writing another dogmatic theology, the *Church Dogmatics* (*Kirchliche Dogmatik*). The first part-volume appeared in 1932. He continued working on this dogmatics until the end of his life. He died without finishing it.

When the Nazis, along with Adolf Hitler, came to power in Germany, Barth sided with the opposition. When all university professors were required to open their lectures with the so-called Hitler salute, Barth refused, saying he always began his lectures with a prayer and considered the "German salute" out of place in that context. Barth's opposition to the Nazis led him, in 1934, to write the first draft of the "Barmen Declaration." This declaration became the basis for the "Confessing Church" in Germany. Later he lamented not having made the "Jewish question" part of the Barmen Declaration, although he realized that at the time not even the Confessing Church would have accepted such a document.

Also in 1934, Barth had a major disagreement with Emil Brunner* on natural theology. In response to Brunner, who said the task of that generation was to find a way back to a legitimate natural theology, Barth fired off an angry response entitled *Nein*! (*No!*), arguing that there is no way to knowledge of God by way of human reason.

Barth saw his objections to liberal Protestantism, Nazism, and Brunner to be all of one piece. For him, the issue was whether, in addition to Jesus Christ, there can be other sources of revelation, such as the progress of history, the German state, the Aryan race, or the *Führer*. He rejected any attempt to set alongside the Word of God a second source of authority: no historical event or reality can transcend the Word of God.

Near the end of 1934, Barth was suspended from his teaching position for refusing to take the obligatory oath of loyalty to Hitler. In 1935, after his appeal of the suspension was denied, he accepted a special chair at the University of Basel, where he stayed until his retirement in 1962. During the Second World War, he served willingly as a soldier in the Swiss auxiliary army, protecting Switzerland, which remained neutral in the conflict.

After the war, Barth returned to Germany during the summers of 1946 and 1947, lecturing and renewing friendships. He considered returning permanently to Germany and helping with the rebuilding effort, thus effectively leaving teaching; but he finally decided to stay on in Basel, working on his *Church Dogmatics*. During the postwar period he became widely known outside Germany and Switzerland.

Barth was criticized (by Emil Brunner,* Reinhold Niebuhr,* and others) when, after the Second World War, he did not issue a call to oppose communism just as he had done in opposition to Nazism. In response, Barth argued that the church should not take sides in the Cold War, but should find a "third way" between both communism and anticommunism.

Barth wrote most of his *Church Dogmatics* during his tenure as a professor at the University of Basel. Only Volume I, Part 1 had been written before he came to teach at Basel. The first volume, which appeared in two parts, covers issues in theological prolegomena as well as the doctrines of the Trinity and the Incarnation. The second volume, again in two parts, addresses the doctrine of God; the third volume consists of four part-volumes on the doctrine of Creation. The four parts of the fourth volume consider various aspects of the doctrine of reconciliation. Already in the first volume, Barth argued that ethics should be part of dogmatics, not a separate enterprise. He carried through on that commitment by including an ethical component in each of the subsequent volumes of the *Church Dogmatics*.

Barth's lectures and other teaching paralleled the progress of his *Dogmatics* and stimulated his writing. Each section of the *Church Dogmatics* served as the text of his academic lectures before being sent off to the publisher. Later in his career, his seminars also focused on his *Dogmatics*. Thus, although he planned a fifth volume of the *Church Dogmatics* on "the doctrine of redemption," he did not reach that topic in his lectures and never wrote the volume.

After retiring from teaching in 1962, Barth took his first trip to the United States, lecturing at several locations, visiting some prisons (he had regularly preached in the Basel prison), and touring Civil War battlefields (he took great interest in the U.S. Civil War). He continued working on his *Church Dogmatics*, but made little progress, especially after his health began to decline in 1964.

Bibliography

A. *Anselm: Fides Quaerens Intellectum*, trans. Ian W. Robertson (London, 1960; repr. Pittsburgh, Pa., 1975); *Church Dogmatics*, ed. G. W. Bromiley and T. F. Torrance, 14 vols. (Edinburgh, 1956–75); *Dogmatics in Outline*, trans. G. T. Thomson (New York, 1959); *Evangelical Theology*, trans. Grover Foley (1963; repr. Grand Rapids, Mich., 1979); *The Epistle to the Romans*, trans. Edwyn C. Hoskyns (Oxford, 1933); *The Göttingen Dogmatics*, ed. Hannelotte Reiffen, trans. G. W. Bromiley, 2 vols. (Grand Rapids, Mich., 1991–); *The Humanity of God*, trans. John Newton Thomas and Thomas Weiser (Atlanta, Ga., 1960); *The Word of God and the Word of Man*, trans. Douglas Horton (1928; repr. New York, 1957).

B. LThK³ 2:35–37; NCE 2:130–31; ODCC 162–63; TRE 5:251–68; Hans Urs von Balthasar, *The Theology of Karl Barth: Exposition and Interpretation*, trans. Edward T. Oakes (San Francisco, 1992); Eberhard Busch, *Karl Barth: His Life from Letters and Autobiographical Texts*, trans. John Bowden (Philadelphia, 1976); Herbert Hartwell, *The Theology of Karl Barth: An Introduction* (London, 1964); George Hunsinger, *How to Read Karl Barth: The Shape of His Theology* (New York and Oxford, 1991); Eberhard Jüngel, *Karl Barth: A Theological Legacy*, trans. Garrett E. Paul (Philadelphia, 1986); Hans Küng, *Justification: The Doctrine of Karl Barth and a Catholic Reflection*, with a new introductory chapter by the author and the original response of Karl Barth, trans. Thomas Collins et al. (Philadelphia, 1981); Bruce McCormack, *Karl Barth's Critically Realistic Dialectical Theology* (Oxford and New York, 1995).

Ronald J. Feenstra

BASIL THE GREAT OF CAESAREA (330, Caesarea in Cappadocia [modern Kayseri, Turkey]–1 January 379). *Education*: studied at home with his father, a rhetorician, and in Athens with the most celebrated teachers of the day, among them Prohaeresios and Himerios. *Career*: taught rhetoric briefly; in 357 joined an ascetic movement with close ties with the local church community; ordained presbyter in 362 and bishop of Caesarea in Cappadocia in 370. Wrote over 300 letters to friends, officials, private people, colleagues, and church communities as far away as Italy and Gaul; preached forty homilies on the psalms and various moral topics, and nine on the six days of creation; wrote treatises on asceticism; defended the Christian faith against Eunomios (on the Trinity) and his former teacher Eustathios of Sebaste (on the Holy Spirit).

An aristocrat by birth, Basil of Caesarea combined classical learning with the Christian gospel demands to lead a humble life dedicated to the service of others. He excelled in championing the rights of the poor and all those, such as widows and orphans, who were in need of assistance. To that effect he made available to them the vast resources of his family, who owned properties in five different provinces. During a drought and famine that struck Cappadocia in 369 he offered assistance not just to Christians but also to pagans and Jews. His involvement in the ascetic (nonmonastic) movement illustrates further this desire to be of service to others rather than to attend to his own needs. His followers were supposed to be educated, a rare occurrence among contemporary and later monks. They were also expected to make available to others their private properties, rather than renounce and abandon them. Whereas for some, ascetic life was an excuse to depend on the charity of others, Basil's followers were ordered to work, either by teaching or farming and trading. If their needs were satisfied, they were to help the needy through their work.

For Basil "faith working through love" (Gal 5:6) was the quintessence of his human and Christian vision of reality. There was no room in such an outlook for compromise and fragmentation: all reality, where God, one in essence but three in person, rules supreme, is one. Hence a human being is graced from the moment of creation. His or her goal is to cooperate with that divine gift in order to develop fully the human-divine potential. "No man is an island"—Basil knew all too well that no person or community can be self-sufficient. Hence in order to solve the problems in his homeland associated with the policies of an emperor (Valens, 364–78) who sided with heresy, he constantly appealed for help to Athanasius of Alexandria in Egypt and the churches of the far West. In doing so he was misunderstood by some, like the bishop of Rome Damasus, who saw in him an ambitious provincial leader and one perhaps not altogether orthodox. The latter suspicion stemmed from Basil's persistent friendship with people such as Eustathios of Sebaste and Apollinaris of Laodicaea* whom most condemned as heretics with no hope for amendment. Basil insisted on keeping ties with similar people and tried, in the words of Athanasius, "to be everything to everybody, so as to save everybody" (cf. 1 Cor 9:22).

Basil's unprecedented discussion in the *De litteris* of the uses and profitability for Christians to read and study the classic authors fostered in Greek and non-Greek speaking readers respect for a heritage that was dismissed by many as the work of the devil. The book was hailed during the Renaissance as the most powerful manifesto for Christians to continue reading and studying the classics despite the overt opposition of many ecclesiastical authorities. (Most candidates for ordination at the time were forbidden to read non-Christian authors, particularly the poets.) In Miguel de Cervantes Saavedra's novel *Don Quijote* the protagonist, besides fighting imaginary enemies, was in the habit of perusing Basil's work.

Besides defending the Christian faith and fostering ascetic and classical ideals, Basil was also involved in the revision of liturgical and canonical texts, both of which played an important role in his pastoral activity. For Basil a bishop-*episkopos* more than a supervisor-administrator was a *proestôs*—"a leader who cares" for the body and soul of his flock. The epithet "Great" was bestowed on Basil unanimously soon after his death by Christians, pagans, and Jews alike, all of whom attended his funeral.

Bibliography

A.   CPG 2835–3005; FC 9, 13, 28, 46; LCL (4 vols; 1926–34); NPNF 2, 8; PG 29–32; *The Ascetic Works of St. Basil*, trans. W. K. Lowther Clarke (New York, 1925).

B.   DTC 2:441–59; EEC 1:114–15; LThK³ 2:67–68; NCE 2:142–46; ODCC 166–67; TRE 5:301–13; Paul J. Fedwick, *Bibliotheca Basiliana universalis* (Corpus Christianorum; Turnhout) will contain a complete bibliography of Basil: vols. 1 (the letters; 1993), 2 (the homilies; *Hexaemeron*; *De litteris*; 1996), 3 (the ascetica, and other works; 1997), and 4 (liturgy, canonical recollections, florilegia, and catenae; 1998) provide comprehensive studies of all the manuscripts, translations, and editions of works written by, or attributed to, Basil; Paul J. Fedwick, *The Church and the Charisma of Leadership in Basil of Caesarea* (Toronto, 1979); *Basil of Caesarea: Christian, Humanist, Ascetic: A Sixteen-hundredth Anniversary Symposium*, ed. idem, 2 vols. (Toronto, 1981); Frances Young, *From Nicaea to Chalcedon* (Philadelphia, 1983), 342–43; 369–73; Benoît Gain, *L'Église de Cappadoce au IVᵉ siècle d'après la correspondance de Basile de Césarée (330–379)* (Rome, 1985); Klaus Koschorke, *Spuren der alten Liebe. Studien zum Kirchenbegriff des Basilius von Caesarea* (Freiburg, Switzerland, 1991); Robert Pouchet, *Basile le Grand et son univers d'amis d'après sa correspondance. Une stratégie de communion* (Rome, 1992); John R. K. Fenwick, *The Anaphoras of St. Basil and St. James: An Investigation into their Common Origin* (Rome, 1992); Philip Rousseau, *Basil of Caesarea* (Berkeley, Calif., 1994).

Paul J. Fedwick

BAUR, FERDINAND CHRISTIAN (21 June 1792, Schmiden, Württemberg–2 December 1860, Tübingen). *Education*: studied philosophy and theology, Univ.

of Tübingen, 1809–14. *Career:* taught history and philosophy, Blaubeuren, 1817–26; professor of theology, Univ. of Tübingen, 1826–60.

Baur was one of the most important historical theologians of the nineteenth century. His intellectual journey began with the supernaturalism and orthodoxy of the older Tübingen School. Although influenced by Friedrich Schlegel and Friedrich Schleiermacher* early in his career, Baur's thought was most profoundly affected by Georg Hegel's philosophy and view of history. Baur founded the new Tübingen School which applied Hegel's conception of historical development to primitive Christianity, the New Testament canon, and Christian doctrine.

Baur saw a conflict in primitive Christianity between the Jewish Christianity of Peter and the Gentile Christianity of Paul. The Catholic Church was the synthesis that resulted from this conflict. He dated the various books of the New Testament according to how their content fit in this developmental process. Following this approach Baur believed that the only authentic Pauline epistles were Rom, 1 and 2 Cor, and Gal. He taught that the other epistles attributed to Paul, the book of Acts and most of the rest of the New Testament, were post-apostolic. He considered Mt the earliest gospel because of its Jewish flavor, followed by Lk which gives evidence of Paul's influence. He believed Mk to be later because it shows a tendency to minimize party differences. The Gospel of Jn indicates the final reconciliation of the two parties and gives evidence of second century controversies.

A pioneer in the study of the history of doctrine, Baur authored important studies of the Atonement, the Trinity, and the Incarnation. He claimed that the essence of Christianity lay in the ethical teachings of Jesus and his doctrine of the kingdom of God.

During the final decade of his life Baur turned his attention to writing the history of the Christian Church from its beginnings to the nineteenth century. The first three volumes were prepared for publication by Baur himself. The fourth and fifth volumes were edited and published from his lecture notes after his death. Baur's presupposition was that the history of the Christian Church contained nothing supernatural or miraculous from beginning to end.

The Tübingen School declined after Baur's death although his methods and some of his conclusions reappeared in the twentieth century.

Bibliography

A. *Paul the Apostle of Jesus Christ*, trans. Allan Menzies and Eduard Zeller, 2 vols. (London, 1875–76); *The Church History of the First Three Centuries*, trans. Allan Menzies, 2 vols. (London, 1878–79); *Ferdinand Christian Baur on the Writing of Church History*, trans. and ed. Peter C. Hodson (New York, 1968).

B. BBKL 1:427–28; LThK³ 2:95–97; NCE 2:173–74; ODCC 171; TRE 5:352–59; Horton Harris, *The Tübingen School: A Historical and Theological Investigation of the*

School of F. C. Baur (Grand Rapids, Mich., 1990); Peter C. Hodson, *The Formation of Historical Theology: A Study of Ferdinand Christian Baur* (New York, 1966); A. B. Bruce, *F. C. Baur and His Theory of the Origin of Christianity* (New York, 1886).

                                                                John M. Brenner

BAVINCK, HERMAN (13 December 1854, Hoogeveen, The Netherlands–29 July 1921, Amsterdam, The Netherlands). *Education*: Doctor of Theology, Univ. of Leiden, 1874–80. *Career*: minister, Christian Reformed Church, Franeker, The Netherlands, 1880–83; professor of theology, Kampen Theol. Sch., 1883–1902; professor of theology, Free Univ. of Amsterdam, 1902–21.

Though less well-known in the English-speaking theological world than his contemporary fellow neo-Calvinist Abraham Kuyper,* Herman Bavinck was the real theologian of the nineteenth-century Dutch Calvinist revival. His *magnum opus*, the four-volume *Gereformeerde Dogmatiek*, now in its fifth edition and being translated into English, remains the standard reference work for classic Dutch Reformed theology more than one hundred years after its initial publication.

Bavinck was born into a devout and orthodox Reformed family. His father was an influential minister in the secessionist Dutch Christian Reformed Church formed in 1834 in protest against state control of the national Dutch Reformed Church. Shaped by centuries-old Reformed experiential spirituality, thanks to his theological training at the liberal University of Leiden, Bavinck was also absorbed by the challenges posed by modern thought and culture to Reformed theology. In the view of one of his contemporaries, Bavinck was thus a man between two worlds, at the same time "a Secession preacher and representative of modern culture."

Bavinck, however, was not satisfied with keeping an experiential piety tending toward otherworldliness simply in tension with a world-affirming modern culture but sought to integrate the two. The theological tool he utilized was the trinitarian and profoundly Irenaean theme that *grace restores nature*. His favored and oft-repeated definition for Christianity was some version of the following: "The essence of the Christian religion consists in this, that the creation of the Father, devastated by sin, is restored in the death of the Son of God, and re-created by the Holy Spirit into a kingdom of God." In an important address on Common Grace he summarized his understanding of grace this way: "Christianity does not introduce a single substantial foreign element into the creation. It creates no new cosmos but rather makes the cosmos new. It restores what was corrupted by sin. It atones the guilty and cures what is sick; the wounded it heals."

By thus insisting that the Christian faith is the restoration and fulfillment of the truly natural, the truly human, Bavinck provided Dutch Reformed Christians with a theological rationale for a more catholic, culturally and socially engaged vision of the Christian life.

Bibliography

A.   *Our Reasonable Faith*, trans. Henry Zylstra (Grand Rapids, Mich., 1956); *The Doctrine of God*, trans. William Hendriksen (Grand Rapids, Mich., 1951); *The Last Things: Hope for this World and the Next*, ed. John Bolt, trans. John Vriend (Grand Rapids, Mich., 1996); "Common Grace," trans. Raymond Van Leeuwen, *Calvin Theological Journal* 24 (1989): 35–65.

B.   Eugene P. Heideman, *The Relation of Revelation and Reason in Emil Brunner and Herman Bavinck* (Assen, The Netherlands, 1959); H. E. Dosker, "Herman Bavinck," *The Princeton Theological Review* 20 (1922): 448–64; John Bolt, "Christ and the Law in the Ethics of Herman Bavinck," *Calvin Theological Journal* 28 (1993): 45–73.

John Bolt

BEA, AUGUSTIN (28 May 1881, Riedböhringen, Baden, Germany–16 November 1968, Rome). *Education*: attended Lender Institute of Instruction and Education (junior high school), Sasbach, Germany, 1893–97; Constance (Switzerland) High School, 1897–98; Rastatt High School, 1898–1900; studied Univ. of Freiburg, 1900–1902; entered the Society of Jesus (Jesuits), 1902; studied philosophy in German Jesuit scholasticate, Valkenburg, Holland, 1904–7; theological studies, Valkenburg, 1910–13; ordained priest, 1912; studied at the Pontifical Biblical Institute, Rome, 1913–16. *Career*: professor for Old Testament exegesis, Valkenburg, 1917–21; Provincial Superior of Upper German Jesuit Province, 1921–24; Superior of Jesuit International House of Studies, Rome, and professor at the Pontifical Biblical Institute and Gregorian Univ., 1924–30; Rector of the Biblical Institute, 1930–49; Cardinal, 1959; President, Pontifical Secretariat (later Council) for Promoting Christian Unity, 1960–68.

One of the outstanding ecumenists of the twentieth century, Bea spent much of his life teaching Sacred Scripture and serving in various administrative and diplomatic positions for the Catholic Church, especially in Rome. He was influential in the founding by the Jesuits of Sophia University, Tokyo. His ecumenical interests and skills grew out of his many contacts with Protestant biblical scholars. When he was given approval by Pope Pius XI in 1935 to participate in a congress of Protestant Old Testament scholars in Göttingen, this was considered an extraordinary concession.

Bea was confessor to Pope Pius XII from 1945 to 1958. He also served on the Pontifical Biblical Commission under Pius XII and influenced the formulation of the pope's encyclical *Divino afflante Spiritu* (1943), a document which freed Catholic scholars to engage in historical-critical studies of the Bible. He also collaborated from 1941–48 in the project to prepare a new Latin translation of the Psalms.

He was also a close confidant of Pope John XXIII and was influential even during the preparatory stage of Vatican II. Prior to the council he was created a cardinal by John XXIII, who shortly thereafter established the Secretariat for Promoting Christian Unity (SPCU) on 5 June 1960, appointing Bea as its first president. He was assisted in that function by Monsignor (later Cardinal) Jan

Willebrands, who became his successor in 1970. Bea fostered ecumenical contacts with the Archbishop of Canterbury, Arthur Michael Ramsey. He oversaw
the choice of official non-Catholic observers at the Council and sought to improve relations between Catholics and Jews. In October 1962 the secretariat was
elevated to the rank of a conciliar commission.

As curial cardinal Bea made a notable impact on the sessions of Vatican II
(1962–65) and the formulation of its documents, especially those dealing with
divine revelation, non-Christian religions, religious freedom, and the Eastern
Catholic Churches. He participated in a famous Harvard colloquium, 27–30
March 1963, at which some 150 university professors, Catholics and Protestants,
discussed the theological significance of Vatican II, which was still in session.
Bea delivered three important lectures at the Harvard symposium later published
in *Ecumenical Dialogue at Harvard*, ed. S. J. Miller and G. E. Wright (Cambridge, Mass., 1964).

Together with the general secretary of the World Council of Churches, Willem
A. Visser 't Hooft, he received the peace prize at the Frankfurt Book Fair in
1966. After Vatican II he helped in the establishment of numerous bilateral
consultations between the Catholic Church and the Orthodox and Protestant
churches. He also promoted closer contacts with the World Council of Churches
and oversaw the promulgation of ecumenical guidelines through the first part of
a *Directory on Ecumenism* (1967).

Bea's funeral liturgy was held in St. Peter's Basilica on 19 November 1968,
and he was then buried next to his parents in the village church of his hometown
Riedböhringen on 21 November. Stjepan Schmidt, S.J., a Croatian Jesuit who
served as his personal secretary from 1959 to 1968, published a richly documented biography of this extraordinary individual and edited for publication his
spiritual diary.

Bibliography

A.   *The Unity of Christians* (New York, 1963); *Unity in Freedom: Reflections on the
Human Family* (New York, 1964); *The Church and Mankind* (Chicago, 1967); *The Way
to Unity after the Council* (New York, 1967); *Peace Among Christians*, with A. Visser
't Hooft (New York, 1967); *The Word of God and Mankind* (Chicago, 1967); *Ecumenism
in Focus* (London, 1969); *Augustin Cardinal Bea: Spiritual Profile: Notes from the Cardinal's Diary*, ed. S. Schmidt (London, 1971).

B.   BBKL 1:434–37; LThK³ 2:105–6; TRE 5:390–403; E. M. Jung-Iglesias, *Augustin
Bea, Cardinal de l'unité* (Paris, 1963); Stjepan Schmidt, ed., *The Augustin Bea Prize:
United of Mankind in Freedom* (Lugano, 1971); idem. *Augustin Bea: The Cardinal of
Unity*, trans. E. M. Stewart (New York, 1992); Gundrun Griesmayr, *Die eine Kirche und
die eine Welt: Die ökumenische Vision Kardinal Augustin Beas* (Frankfurt, 1997).

                                                              Michael A. Fahey

BEDE THE VENERABLE (672/73, Jarrow, Northumbria–25 May 735, Jarrow; feast day, 25 May). Anglo-Saxon exegete, historian, theologian, and doctor
of the church. Given to the monastery of St. Peter at Wearmouth (Durham) at

age seven and entrusted to the abbot there, St. Benedict Biscop; by 685 transferred to St. Paul's in Jarrow; ordained a deacon at 19, and a priest at 30.

Bede spent his whole life in Northumbria. The author of works on grammar,
chronography, history, and exegesis, he was one of the great polymaths of the
early medieval church. His chronological works dealt mostly with the date of
Easter, which Romans and Celts in Britain computed differently. His chronography fostered the dating of events from the year of the Incarnation. Bede wrote
the life of St. Cuthbert in prose and in verse and the lives of five other English
abbots in prose. But he is best known for his *Ecclesiastical History of the
English People*, completed in 731, which earned him the title "Father of English
History." He began with Julius Caesar's invasion of Britain and ended with the
events of 731. Bede considered his sources carefully and tried to exercise critical
judgment. The work is unified and sober; Bede had a gift for memorable descriptions. Among Bede's scriptural works are fifty homilies that he preached
to monks of his abbey; they are mostly commentaries on gospel passages. In
his exegetical works Bede transmitted and explained the work of Augustine,*
Jerome,* Ambrose,* and Gregory the Great,* although he also knew Greek and
some Hebrew. Bede commented on most of the Old Testament and almost all
of the New Testament. His study of the tabernacle and sacred vessels is noteworthy. Bede's exegetical works were highly valued in the Middle Ages.

Bibliography

A. *The Complete Works of the Venerable Bede*, ed. J. A. Giles, 12 vols. (London,
1843–44); PL 90–95; recent critical editions in CCSL, 118A-123C, 126, 175; *A History
of the English Church and People*, trans. Leo Sherley-Price (Harmondsworth, 1955) and
rev.; *The Commentary on the Seven Catholic Epistles*, trans. David Hurst (Kalamazoo,
Mich., 1985); *Commentary on the Acts of the Apostles*, trans. Lawrence T. Martin (Kalamazoo, Mich., 1989); *On the Tabernacle*, trans. Arthur G. Holder (Liverpool, 1994);
Bede's Ecclesiastical History of the English People, trans. Bertram Colgrave (New York,
1995); *Bede: On the Temple*, trans. Seán Connolly (Liverpool, 1996); *On Tobit and the
Canticle of Habakkuk*, trans. Seán Connolly (Portland, Ore., 1997).

B. DHGE 7:395–402; DTC 2:523–27; TRE 5:397–402; A. Hamilton Thompson,
Bede: His Life, Times, and Writings (Oxford, 1935); Thomas Aquinas Carroll, *Venerable
Bede: His Spiritual Teachings* (Washington, D.C., 1946); P. Hunter Blair, *Bede's Eccle-
siastical History of the English Nation and Its Importance Today* (Jarrow, 1959); idem,
The World of Bede (London, 1970); G. H. Brown, *Bede the Venerable* (Boston, 1987);
J. M. Wallace-Hadrill, *Bede's Ecclesiastical History of the English People: A Historical
Commentary* (Oxford, 1988); Benedicta Ward, *The Venerable Bede* (Kalamazoo, Mich.,
1998).

                                                                Joseph T. Lienhard

BELLAMY, EDWARD (26 March 1850, Chicopee Falls, Mass.–22 May 1898,
Chicopee Falls, Mass.). *Education*: special student, Union Coll., Schenectady,
N.Y., 1867–68; law apprentice, Springfield, Mass., 1869–71; passed Massachu-
setts bar exam, 1871. *Career*: editorial writer, *Springfield Union*, 1872–77; foun-

der and editor, *Daily News* (Springfield, Mass.), 1880–84; editor, *New Nation* (Boston, Mass.), 1891–94; periodically worked as freelance journalist and fiction writer.

Bellamy grew up the son of a Baptist minister, but later abandoned traditional Christianity. Influenced by Transcendentalism and August Comte's religious humanism, Bellamy envisioned a society converted from self-centeredness to organic unity. His significance principally rests upon the popularity of his utopian novel, *Looking Backward* (Boston, 1888).

Bellamy's "religion of solidarity" stressed self-sacrifice and universal cooperation, with a complete sharing of wealth. Key to his revolution in values was the application of Christ's Golden Rule to all aspects of life. Bellamy envisioned a Great Revival that would bring an end to sectarianism and create an ideal state built upon equal and ethical treatment for all. He believed that establishing this disciplined social order would effect the Second Coming of Christ within the hearts of all. Bellamy's version of Christian socialism meshed well with more idealistic elements within the Social Gospel Movement.

Bibliography

A. *Equality* (New York, 1897); "The Religion of Solidarity," in Arthur E. Morgan, *The Philosophy of Edward Bellamy* (New York, 1945).

B. DAB 1:163–64; NYT 23 May 1898, 7; Arthur E. Morgan, *Edward Bellamy* (New York, 1944); Sylvia E. Bowman, *Edward Bellamy* (Boston, 1986).

Terrence Crowe

BELLAMY, JOSEPH (20 February 1719, Cheshire, Conn.–6 March 1790, Bethlehem, Conn.). *Education*: B.A., Yale Coll., 1735; read theology with Jonathan Edwards,* Northampton, Mass., 1735–36. *Career*: preacher, various places in Conn., 1736–39; minister, Bethlehem, Conn., 1739–90.

Bellamy was one of a number of eighteenth-century New England pastor-theologians who were called New Divinity Men because they extended and modified the theological vision of Jonathan Edwards. Bellamy became an active itinerant preacher during the Great Awakening (1740–45) in New England shortly after he was settled as pastor of Bethlehem, Connecticut. In 1750, after the initial enthusiasm of the Great Awakening had worn off, he published what was perhaps his most important work on religious experience, *True Religion Delineated* (Boston, 1750). The book was a popularization of Edwards' more sophisticated analysis of religious experience.

Like Edwards, Bellamy supported the revivals, criticized their enthusiastic promoters for their excessive emotionalism and antinomianism, and argued against the excessive rationalism of an Arminian and Enlightenment understanding of religious experience that had little room for religious affections.

Bellamy departed somewhat from the strict Dortian Calvinism and philosophical subtlety that had characterized Edwards' positions. Bellamy's God was neither the Edwardsean sovereign nor the Deist's clockmaker, but an eighteenth-century moral governor of the universe (i.e., a mixture of Edwards' sovereign God and the Enlightenment's reasonable lawgiver). Unlike Edwards, moreover, Bellamy emphasized the voluntary nature of all sin. In these and other modifications of the Edwardsean system of theology, Bellamy opened the way for further modifications in the Calvinist system during the early nineteenth century as the Reformed tradition in America appropriated more and more of the voluntary spirit of the Enlightenment.

Bellamy had a significant influence on a host of young ministers. Prior to the establishment of theological seminaries in America, he conducted a theological school in his home for the education of aspiring ministers. His apprenticeship school in Bethlehem provided a theological education for more than sixty ministers who were eventually placed in pulpits throughout Connecticut.

Bibliography

A. *The Great Evil of Sin* (Boston, 1753); *The Wisdom of God in the Permission of Sin, Vindicated* (Boston, 1769); *A Careful and Strict Examination of the External Covenant* (New Haven, Conn., 1770); *The Works of Dr. Joseph Bellamy*, 3 vols. (New York, 1811–12); 2 vols. (Boston, 1853; 1987).

B. AAP 1:404–12; DAB 2:165; DARB, 45–46; NCAB 7:78; SH 2:33–34; Mark R. Valeri, *Law and Providence in Joseph Bellamy's New England: The Origins of the New Divinity in Revolutionary America* (New York, 1994).

Patrick W. Carey

BELLARMINE, ROBERT (4 October 1542, Montepulciano, Italy–17 September 1621, Rome). *Education*: philosophical studies at the Coll. Romano, 1560–64; theological studies, Padua and Louvain, 1564–69. *Career*: Jesuit novice, Rome, 1560; ordained priest, 1570; taught theology, Louvain, 1570–76; chair in controversial theology, Coll. Romano, 1577–94; provincial superior, Neapolitan Jesuits, 1594–97; theological advisor to Pope Clement VIII, 1597; cardinal, 1599; archbishop of Capua, 1602–5; curial administrator, Rome, 1606–21.

Bellarmine was one of the principal theological apologists for Roman Catholic Christianity in the wake of the Protestant Reformation in late Renaissance Rome. His theological lectures at Louvain had immersed him in the study of Protestant theologians. This study also undergirded his lectures at Rome. Later published and known as Bellarmine's *Controversies* (*Disputationes de controveriis Christianae fidei adversus huius temporis haereticos*), their three volumes (1586, 1588, and 1593) became the most important Catholic answer to Protestant theologians in the sixteenth century. The last volume offended Sixtus V, who felt that Bellarmine's theory of indirect papal power in civil matters hurt papal authority. Although strongly influenced by the scholastic theologians, especially St. Thomas Aquinas,* Bellarmine put less stress on the philosophical foundations of theology and more on its historical development. In this he stands in contrast to most of the Spanish theologians of the second scholasticism. Bellarmine's polemic against Protestant theologians, moreover, was relatively polite compared to most Reformation era polemics.

Throughout his career Bellarmine became involved in theological disputes, several with political dimensions. Thus, he defended his fellow Jesuit Leonard Lessius, whose teaching on grace and predestination were attacked by Michael Baius* and condemned by the University of Louvain. In the controversy *de auxiliis* on nature, grace and predestination he took a more traditional stance than did his fellow Jesuit, Luis de Molina.* Bellarmine objected to the often arbitrary interventions made by Sixtus V in the preparation of the Sixto-Clementine Vulgate, the standard Catholic version of the Bible for three centuries. Clement VIII put Bellarmine in charge of its final revision. He argued against Henry of Navarre's claim to the French throne. Bellarmine also wrote several pamphlets that supported the papal Interdict (1606) against Venice. Late in life he defended papal authority and English Catholics in several tracts against James I, but the king quickly tired of the controversy and entrusted the task of refuting Bellarmine to Bishop Lancelot Andrewes.* Bellarmine also became involved in a bitter exchange with the British Catholics Thomas Preston and William Barclay over the relative authority of church and state.

Periodically throughout his life Bellarmine was involved in the theological and spiritual formation of young Jesuits and in the more general catechetical and spiritual direction of the Catholic people. He served as spiritual director and then as rector of the Collegio Romano, a theological school for the training of young Jesuits. His sermons to the young Jesuit students there were published in the 1940s. In 1597 he wrote a short catechism that eventually ran through hundreds of editions in many languages; the next year he wrote a longer version of his catechism. When Bellarmine was appointed archbishop of Capua in 1602, he quickly resigned his curial offices and took up residence at Capua, where he devoted three years to preaching, visiting parishes, helping the poor, and reforming the small archdiocese.

Bellarmine returned to Rome in 1605 for the election of a new pope. Many in the conclave regarded him as a leading candidate, but his reputation for poverty and austerity plus his personal opposition to being made pope saved him from a burden he dreaded. After the election, Paul V, the new pope, ordered him to stay in Rome and resume work at the curia. Bellarmine resigned his benefice at Capua. For the rest of his life Bellarmine served on various papal commissions that required theological training, especially in the Holy Office. His days were taken up with administration, and his writing and scholarship leveled off. In 1616 Bellarmine told Galileo that the Holy Office forbade him to teach a heliocentric universe.

In his last years Bellarmine was able to devote time to spiritual writings. His long commentary on the psalms (*In omnes Psalmos dilucida expositio*), published in 1611, was more noteworthy for piety than exegesis. Each year from 1614 to 1619 Bellarmine devoted thirty days to remaking the Spiritual Exercises of Ignatius of Loyola. During each of these retreats he wrote a devotional book:

on the ascent of the mind to God (1614), the happiness of the saints (1615), the miseries of this life (1616), Christ's seven last words on the cross (1617), the duties of a Christian prince (1618), and the art of dying well (1619). All but the fifth of these became immensely popular. Bellarmine's writings are generally marked by a clear Latin style, careful organization, and great erudition. In 1930 Pius XI canonized Bellarmine.

Bibliography

A. *Opera omnia*, 6 vols. (Naples, 1862); *Opuscula ascetica*, 3 vols. (Regensburg, 1925); *Opera oratoria postuma*, ed. Sebastian Tromp, 9 vols. (Rome, 1942–50); *A Short Catechisme* (1614, repr. Menston, 1973); *Robert Bellarmine: Spiritual Writings*, ed. J. P. Donnelly and R. J. Teske (New York and Mahwah, N.J., 1989).

B. DTC 2:560–99; LThK³ 2:189–91; NCE 2:250–51; ODCC 181; OEncR 1:139–40; Joseph La Servière, *La théologie de Bellarmin*, 2 vols. (Paris, 1909); Xavier-Marie Le Bachelet, *Bellarmin avant son Cardinalat (1542–1598)* (Paris, 1911); James Brodrick, *The Life and Work of Blessed Robert Francis Cardinal Bellarmine, S.J. (1542–1621)* 2 vols. (London, 1928); Edward A. Ryan, *The Historical Scholarship of Saint Bellarmine* (Louvain, 1936); James Brodrick, *Robert Bellarmine: Saint and Scholar* (Westminster, Md., 1961); Manfred Biersack, *Initia Bellarminiana: die Prädestinationslehre bei Robert Bellarmin S.J. bis zu seinen Löwener Vorlesungen 1570–1576* (Stuttgart, 1989); *Roberto Bellarmino: arcivescovo di Capua, teologo e pastore della riforma cattolica*, ed. Gustavo Galeota, 2 vols. (Capua, 1990); Richard Blackwell, *Galileo, Bellarmine and the Bible* (Notre Dame, Ind., 1991).

John Patrick Donnelly

BERDIAEV, NIKOLAS ALEKSANDROVICH (6 March 1874, Kiev–24 March 1948, Clamart, France). *Education*: Corps of Cadets, 1884; Univ. of Kiev, Faculty of Law, 1894. *Career*: imprisoned for Marxist activism, 1898; exiled to Vologda, 1901–2; returned to Kiev, 1903; St. Petersburg, editor, *Voprosi Zhizni* and *Novy Put'*, 1904; trip to western Europe, moved to Moscow, 1907; publication of *Vekhi*, 1909; trial by Holy Synod, escaping sentence because of Revolution, 1914; founder and director, Liberal Academy of Moral Sciences, Moscow, 1919; professor of philosophy and history, Moscow Univ., 1920–22; arrested, exiled from Russia, 1922; founder of Religious Philosophical Society, Berlin, 1922–24; founder and editor-in-chief, YMCA Press, 1924–48; founder and editor, *Put'*, 1925–40; editor, *Orient und Occident*, 1929–34; member editorial board, *Cahiers de la Nouvelle Epoque*, 1945; honorary DD, Cambridge Univ., 1947.

Philosopher of freedom, Christian personalist and existentialist, Nikolas Berdiaev was a lifelong rebel, more a prophet than a systematic philosopher. Sympathetic to Marx, he came to see the Communists as successors of the Grand Inquisitor, offering material security at the price of freedom.

Berdiaev rejected ontology: freedom, not being, was at the basis of his philosophy. He was influenced by Jacob Boehme* for whom God created Himself from an "Ungrund." Grounded in God, freedom and personhood are of the sphere of spirit, above the objectified world of nature. The creative act is the way in which truth is attained in the world. Heavily mystical, his philosophy tended to "dissolve into vision." Discursive reason was a tool of intuition, thus mysticism was foremost in knowledge of God, against metaphysics/rationalism/objectification. Human greatness was spiritual and creative: the Fall was objectification that debased and eventually destroyed the creative impulse.

Freedom was embodied in the "God-Man." Only the religion of the God/man reconciled "formal" freedom and creative freedom. Passionately committed to the absolute priority of the person, Berdiaev confronted other existentialisms: one does not create oneself in the face of the world, against death, but rather with the power of the Holy Spirit. True community was "sobornost."

Quarreling with the Orthodox Church, he yet remained a member. Eschatologically, he felt that God worked only through human freedom in renewing the world: the Second Coming would be a result of divine-human creative activity. He rejected the doctrine of eternal torment in hell. He acknowledged as intellectual masters Jacob Boehme,* Maine de Biran, Kant, Franz von Baader,* Nietzsche, Dostoevski, and V. S. Soloviev.*

Bibliography

A. *Freedom and the Spirit* (London, 1935); *Dream and Reality. An Essay in Autobiography* (London, 1950); *The Beginning and the End* (London, 1952); *The Russian Idea* (London, 1947).

B. HDOC 61; LThK³ 2:243; NCE 2:319–20; ODCC 190; TRE 5:595–98; Tamara Klepnine, *Nicolas Berdiaev, Bibliographie* (Paris, 1978); G. Seaver, *Nicholas Berdiaev* (New York, 1950); Donald A. Lowrie, *Rebellious Prophet: A Life of Nicolai Berdyaev* (New York, 1960); Juan Luis Segundo, *Berdiaeff: une réflexion chrétienne sur la personne* (Paris, 1963); Olivier Clement, *Berdiaev: un philosophe russe en France* (Paris, 1991).

Raymond T. Gawronski

BERENGARIUS OF TOURS (ca. 1010–1088). *Education*: studied at Chartres under Fulbert, ca. 1028. *Career*: canon at Tours, and teacher at the collegiate school by 1031; in the service of Geoffrey Martel, Count of Anjou, 1040–60; archdeacon at Angers cathedral, 1040–60; master of the schools, St. Martin's, from ca. 1070; retired to St. Côme, after 1080.

Applying highly refined dialectical methods to the doctrine of the Eucharist, Berengar ignited the first great eucharistic controversy in the West. He began to publish his teachings on the Eucharist by 1047, denying that the bread and wine are essentially changed into the historical body and blood of Christ. At the Roman council of 1059 Berengar was forced to sign an excessively realistic confession of Christ's presence. Berengar immediately repudiated the confession of 1059 and began an extensive debate with Lanfranc of Bec,* maintaining that after consecration there was no material or essential conversion of the bread and wine, but rather an intelligible conversion by which Christ was present in faith, insofar as the elements had become visibile signs of invisible grace.

Bibliography

A. *Rescriptum contra Lanfrannum*, ed. R. B. C. Huygens (Turnhout, 1988).
B. LThK³ 2:244–45; NCE 2:320–21; ODCC 190–91; TRE 5:598–601; A. J. Mac-Donald, *Berengar and the Reform of Sacramental Doctrine* (New York, 1930); R. W. Southern, "Lanfranc of Bec and Berengar of Tours," in *Studies in Medieval History Presented to F. M. Powicke*, ed. R. W. Hunt et al. (Oxford, 1948), 27–48; Jean de Montclos, *Lanfranc et Bérengar* (Louvain, 1971).

Ian Christopher Levy

BERNARD OF CLAIRVAUX (1090, Fontaines-lès-Dijon–20 August 1153, Clairvaux, France). *Education*: studied with canons of Châtillon; after entering Cîteaux about 1112, received a traditional monastic education based on Scripture and the Fathers. *Career*: After his year as novice and two years in profession, Bernard was elected at age twenty-five to found a new community in Champagne, at Clairvaux, which he led as abbot for thirty-eight years. Under his abbacy, Clairvaux became the motherhouse of sixty-five new foundations. Bernard's literary accomplishments paralleled his abbatial success and attest to his tireless passion for reform. Through his letters and spiritual treatises, he effected the Cistercian reform movement and also shaped religious life throughout Europe. Outside the cloister, Bernard preached organizational and individual reform to clerics and seculars alike.

Bernard published numerous treatises on the spiritual life. Between 1124 and 1125, he published his first treatise, *The Steps of Humility and Pride*, which expands on the discussion of humility in Benedict's *Rule*. During this time he also published *Four Homilies in Praise of the Blessed Virgin*. In 1125, he addressed the conflict between the Cistercians and the Cluniacs concerning the Cistercian interpretation of the *Rule*. In this work, he rebuked the Cistercians for complacency, satirized Cluniac customs, and encouraged simplicity in ecclesiastical art and architecture. Before 1136, Bernard composed *On Grace and Free Choice*, a theological treatise on the faculties of the soul and their restoration. Bernard supported the newly founded Knights Templar and wrote his *In Praise of the New Knighthood* (between 1128 and 1136) for them and all lay leaders. *On Loving God* (before 1144) is an analysis of the progress of the soul in its return to the likeness of God. Bernard wrote a treatise on the Benedictine *Rule*, *On Precept and Dispensation*, addressed to the monks of Saintes-Pères of Chartes, no later than 1144. He offered *Five Books on Consideration* (1148–53) to Pope Eugenius III, a former monk at Clairvaux, to help this pope maintain his spiritual life among the distractions of his pontificate. He wrote eighty-six sermons on the *Song of Songs*, one of his most profound and influential works. He also composed many sermons for the seasons and principal feasts of the liturgical year.

Bernard's persuasive and passionate preaching and writing brought him into contact with many lay and ecclesiastical authorities of his day. He wrote over five hundred letters between 1116 and 1153, to kings, popes, bishops, abbots, nobles of every rank, and lay people of humbler rank. His letters witness his attempts to counsel the most powerful men of his day. Bernard addressed the Council of Troyes, which established the Templars, and enthusiastically supported the election of Innocent II at Étampes. Throughout his preaching on behalf of Innocent in France, Italy, and Germany, he was instrumental in healing the papal schism. At the Council of Sens (1140), Bernard debated Abelard* and secured an episcopal condemnation against him. Bernard also preached against heresy in Languedoc (1146) and was commanded to promote the Second Crusade, which carried him throughout France and the Empire. In the winter of 1146–47, Bernard successfully preached the Crusade along the Rhine; there, he encountered the anti-Semitic activities promoted by a certain Rasul, against whom he directed a public letter denouncing the anti-Jewish sentiment (*Epistle* 363). The failure of the crusade was a point of embarrassment for Bernard; he addressed the point in a chapter of *On Consideration*. Bernard insisted that the crusade's failure was due to the moral failings of the crusaders.

Bernard's writings evidence a thorough education in Scripture, the classics, and the Fathers, which permeates his vision of the Christian life. While Bernard adapted his style to his audience, he constantly emphasized the theme that God is love and that this love alone can satisfy the longings of the human soul. Bernard's soteriology centers on the grace-full capacity for restoration of the human soul to the likeness of God.

For Bernard, restoration begins in the true conversion of the human will. Conversion, Bernard stresses, is a response by an individual to God's call. He teaches that this first stage of restoration is humility, an honest evaluation of oneself and one's relationship to the world, to others, and to God. When one begins to know oneself one realizes the natural dignity residing in the human soul. Likewise, one recognizes a lack of harmony within one's faculties and one's base desires. This discord occurs in one's will, where one suffers between powerful attractions: toward God, one's true happiness, and towards self-centered gratifications, one's ultimate ruin. Restoration begins in reordering one's will towards true happiness, God.

Bernard taught that the process of restoration follows a four-stage progression of love. Once one understands one's place in relation to God and one's fellows, one can, under grace, begin to reorder one's desires. For Bernard, people begin in a state of self-centered love and, as they grow in humility, their love turns toward others and toward God. When one begins to find happiness not in what God does for his creatures, but to enjoy God for who and what he is, this new relationship enables one to love oneself and others unselfishly, for God's sake alone. Bernard's definition and description of the special grace of contemplative union with God in love was crucial in the formation of twelfth-century, and subsequent, spirituality.

Bibliography

A. *Sancti Bernardi opera*, ed. Jean Leclercq et al., 8 vols. (Rome, 1957–77); *The Works of Bernard of Clairvaux*, 7 vols. (Kalamazoo, Mich., 1970–); *The Letters of St. Bernard of Clairvaux*, trans. Bruno Scott James (Chicago, 1953).

B. DTC 2:746–85; LThK³ 2:268–70; NCE 2:335–38; ODCC 192–93; TRE 5:644–51; Edward Cuthbert Butler, *Western Mysticism: The Teaching of SS. Augustine, Gregory and Bernard on Contemplation and the Contemplative Life, with Afterthoughts*, 2d ed. (London, 1927); Etienne Gilson, *The Mystical Theology of Saint Bernard*, trans. A. H. C. Downs (New York, 1955); Bede K. Lackner, "The Monastic Life According to St. Bernard," in *Studies in Medieval Cistercian History*, ed. J. R. Sommerfeldt (Kalamazoo, Mich., 1976), 2:49–62; Jean Leclercq, *Bernard of Clairvaux and the Cistercian Spirit*, trans. Claire Lavoie (Kalamazoo, Mich., 1976); Michael Casey, *Athirst for God: Spiritual Desire in Bernard of Clairvaux's Sermons on the Song of Songs* (Kalamazoo, Mich., 1988); John R. Sommerfeldt, *The Spiritual Teachings of Bernard of Clairvaux* (Kalamazoo, Mich., 1991).

Daniel Marcel La Corte

BERNARD SILVESTRIS. *See* BERNARD OF TOURS.

BERNARD OF TOURS, Bernard Silvestris (fl. ca. 1140/50, Tours). Almost nothing is known of Bernard's life, though he most probably wrote his main work, the *Cosmographia*, between 1143 and 1148; a letter dedicating it to Thierry of Chartres need not connect Bernard to Chartres. *Cosmographia*, or *The Universe of the World* (*De mundi universitate*) is divided into two parts: the *Megacosmos*, which describes allegorically the story of creation along the basic lines of Platonic cosmology as found in the *Timaeus*, and the *Microcosmos*, which describes the creation of human beings as the centerpiece of the universe. Though Gilson argued that Bernard was a Christian writer, McCrimmon has shown convincingly that Bernard's sources were pagan and not Christian. The commentary on the *Aeneid*, whose authenticity is at best possible, is likewise highly allegorical and presents a treatise on wisdom, the liberal arts, and moral philosophy. The *Experimentarius*, a work in geomancy at times ascribed to Bernard, is also of only doubtful authenticity.

Bibliography

A. *Commentum Bernardi Silvestris super sex libros Eneidos Virgilii* (*Commentary on Six Books of Vergil's Aeneid*), ed. W. Riedel (Greifswald, 1924); *Cosmographia*, ed. P. Dronke (Leiden, 1978); *Experimentarius*, ed. M. Brini Savorelli, in *Rivista critica della storia della filosofia* 20 (1965): 182–230.

B. LThK³ 2:276; NCE 2:343; TRE 5:642–44; Etienne Gilson, "La cosmogonie de Bernardus Silvestris," *Archives d'histoire doctrinale et littéraire du moyen âge* 3 (1928): 5–24; M. McCrimmon, "The Classical Philosophical Sources of the De Mundi Universitate of Bernard Silvestris," Ph.D. diss., Yale, 1952; J. R. O'Donnell, "The Sources and Meaning of Bernard Silvester's Commentary on the Aeneid,'' *Mediaeval Studies* 24 (1962): 233–49; Brian Stock, *Myth and Science in the Twelfth Century: A Study of Bernard Silvester* (Princeton, N.J., 1972).

Roland J. Teske

BEZA, THEODORE (24 June 1516, Vézelay, France–7 October 1605, Geneva, Switzerland). *Education*: studied with the humanist, Melchior Wolmar, Orléans, 1525–30; Bourges, 1530–35; studied law, Orléans, 1535–39. *Career*: practiced law, Paris, 1539–48; moved to Geneva, 1548; professor of Greek, Lausanne Academy, 1549–57; rector and professor of theology, Geneva Academy, 1557–99; pastor, Geneva Church, 1557–1605.

The dying John Calvin* bequeathed his Geneva reform to a contemporary of like mind and training, Theodore Beza. Beza joined Calvin in Geneva in 1548, where a decade later he became rector of the Academy and professor of theology. Through this post and that of ''Moderator of the Venerable Company of Pastors of Geneva,'' which he received after Calvin's death, Beza became one of the most influential of the Reformed leaders.

His two most important theological works were the *Confession de la foi christienne* of 1557, and his *Quaestionum et Responsionum Christianorum libellus*, written in two parts in 1570 and 1576. At the Colloquy of Montbéliard Beza defended Calvin's position on the Lord's Supper and stood firm against the Lutheran Jakob Andreae, stating that Christ's body and blood cannot be physically present in the bread and wine because Christ has ascended into heaven. Beza preferred, however, to set aside Calvin's concern and emphasized that in the sacrament the bread and wine have a new relationship with Christ's body and blood and because of this relationship, the bread and wine become instruments of grace.

Beza also taught a doctrine of supralapsarian predestination, stating clearly what Calvin had only suggested. Beza believed that God's decree of election was metaphysically prior as cause to all its consequences, such as Creation and Fall. With this theology, Beza drew together God's decree and its implementation, a tendency that he also displayed in his theology of justification and sanctification.

Politically, Beza's treatise *Du droit des Magistrats sur leurs subiets* of 1574 reversed the position of Calvin and stated that the people had a right to revolt against tyrannical rulers. His theory was that royal position came from God through the people. Therefore, when rulers no longer served the people, they could be removed.

His biblical legacy is perhaps best preserved with the important ancient New Testament manuscript that bears his name, the *Codex Bezae*. He also annotated, edited, and translated the Bible, his most notable project being his contribution to the *Geneva Bible* of 1588.

Beza stepped aside from his role as moderator in 1580 and in 1599 retired from his position at the Academy. He died peacefully in his beloved Geneva on October 7, 1605, having succeeded Calvin, but himself having no true heir in position or influence.

Bibliography

A. *Correspondance de Théodore de Bèze*, ed. Alain Dufour, 19 vols. (Geneva, 1960–86); *Theodori Beza Vezelii volumen primum Tractationum Theologicarum* (Geneva, 1582).

B. LThK³ 2:358; NCE 2:379; OEncR 1:149–51; TRE 5:765–74; Paul F. Geisendorf, *Théodore de Bèze*, 2d ed. (Geneva, 1967); Frederic Gardy, *Bibliographie des oeuvres théologiques, littéraires, historiques et juridiques de Théodore de Bèze* (Geneva, 1960); Robert M. Kingdon, *Geneva and the Consolidation of the French Protestant Movement, 1564–1572* (Madison, Wis., 1967); Jill Raitt, "Theodore Beza," in *Shapers of Religious Traditions in Germany, Switzerland and Poland, 1560–1600*, ed. Jill Raitt (New Haven, Conn., 1981), 89–104.

Troy Pflibsen

BIEL, GABRIEL (ca. 1414, Speyer–7 December 1495, Einsiedel, Schönbuch). Little is known about Biel's early life or primary education. He burst upon the academic scene when he entered the faculty of arts at the University of Heidelberg on 13 July 1432. Before he came to the university, Biel was ordained to the priesthood and served as matinal priest at the Chapel of the Ten Thousand Martyrs at Saint Peter's in Speyer. At Heidelberg, Biel received a baccalaureate degree on 21 July 1435 and a master's degree three years later, on 21 March 1438.

After three more years within the faulty of arts at Heidelberg, Biel moved to the faculty of theology at the University of Erfurt in 1451. There, he acquired an intimate knowledge of the emerging Occamist school of thought known as the *via moderna*. His association with this school of thought was not to remain one-sided; after his short stay at Erfurt, Biel enrolled, in 1453, at the University of Cologne, where he was immersed in the *via antiqua*, which emphasized the scholastic traditions of Thomas Aquinas* and Duns Scotus.* Biel did not pursue his highly prized academic career, but became concerned with local church life and for almost a decade served as cathedral preacher and vicar in Mainz. Although the exact date of his appointment and tenure are unknown, by 1462 Biel was already acknowledged by the people of Mainz as a famous preacher and well-respected pastor. While yet a preacher at the cathedral church in Mainz, Biel came into contact with the *Devotio Moderna* and the Brethren of the Common Life. During the late 1460s, Biel lived at various Brethren Houses and in 1471 established a general chapter of the Brethren Houses on the Upper Rhein. Six years later, in 1477, he joined Benedict of Marienthal to convert Saint Amandus to a Brethren House. In 1479 he was elected provost of this new house.

On 22 November 1484 Biel was appointed to the theological faculty of the newly founded University of Tübingen. Biel considered himself representative of the new theological school, the *via moderna*, among a faculty that was dominated by the *via antiqua*. He quickly surrounded himself with young, enthusiastic students and thereby secured his place for the future. Biel's popularity was evidenced by his election as rector of the university in 1485 and 1489.

After his retirement from the University of Tübingen, Biel served as provost of the new Brethren House, Saint Peter's at Einsiedel in Schönbuch. Under his leadership, the ideals of the *Devotio Moderna* were emphasized, and the Brethren's characteristics of piety and the simple life were maintained well into the sixteenth century. Biel's final years exemplified the piety he preached and taught throughout his life.

Bibliography

A. *Tractatus utilis artis grammatice regiminum* (Reutlingen, ca. 1486); *Gabriel Byel sacre theologie licentiatus* (Tübingen, 1479); *Regula* (Leipzig, ca. 1497); *Epithoma pariter et collectorium circa quattuor sententiarum libros* (Tübingen, 1501); *Sermones* (Hagenau, 1510); *Defensorium obedientie apostolice* (Hagenau, 1510); *Tractatus de potestate et utilitate monetarum* (Oppenheim, 1516), trans. R. B. Burke, *Treatise on the Power and Utility of Moneys* (Philadelphia, 1930); *Sermones de sanctis* (Basel, 1519); *Sacrosancti canonis misse expositio . . . in Epitomen contracta* (Antwerp, 1565); *Tractatus magistri Gabrielis Byell de communi vita clericorum*, Koninklijke Bibliotheek 's Gravenhage, MS 75.958; fol. 1r-21v; ed. W. M. Landeen in "Appendix: Biel's Tractate on the Common Life," *Research Studies, Washington State University* 28 (1960): 79–95.

B. DTC 2:814–25; LThK³ 2:437; NCE 2:552; ODCC 207–8; TRE 6:488–91; F. X. Linsenmann, "Gabriel Biel und die Anfänge der Universität zu Tübingen," *Theologische Quartalschrift* 47 (1865): 195–226; C. Feckes, "Gabriel Biel, der erste grosse Dogmatiker der Universität Tübingen in seiner wissenschaftlichen Bedeutung," ibid. 108 (1927): 50–76; W. M. Landeen, "Gabriel Biel and the Brethren of the Common Life," CH 20 (1951): 23–36; idem, "Gabriel Biel and the Devotio Moderna in Germany," *Research Studies, Washington State University* 27 (1959): 135–76, 214–29; 28 (1960): 21–45, 61–78; Heiko A. Oberman, *The Harvest of Medieval Theology: Gabriel Biel and Late Medieval Nominalism* (Grand Rapids, Mich., 1967).

Peter W. Breitsch

BILLING, EINAR (6 October 1871, Lund, Sweden–17 December 1939, Västerås). *Education*: Univ. of Uppsala, 1900. *Career*: professor of theology, Univ. of Uppsala, 1900–20; bishop of Västerås, 1920–39.

Billing was, with Nathan Söderblom,* the author of the twentieth-century renewal of Swedish theology. Although he is recognized as the more original of the two Uppsala professors, Anglophones have only one brief essay in which to hear his voice; all the rest of our knowledge of him depends on the secondhand testimony of interpreters of Swedish theological development.

His academic focus was in Old Testament studies. Like Söderblom, he was unthreatened by critical methods, using them to expound traditional doctrine in a rapidly changing context.

Lundensian theology, as represented in Gustaf Aulén,* Ragnar Bring, Anders Nygren,* Per Erik Persson, and Gustaf Wingren,* preserves four elements highlighted in Billing's work: (1) the doctrine of the Atonement as God's free act is central to the Faith; (2) the church is the arena where God acts in the sacraments; (3) the Bible and Luther* are the theologian's two great sources; (4) Luther is the biblical interpreter for the whole church (Wingren, 124).

As a bishop in the Church of Sweden, he used his analytical skills in administration and in addressing and moderating issues within the COS and within the ecumenical movement. He was engaged in the preparations for full intercommunion of the COS with the Church of England, though the theological terms in which he articulated the grounds were not exactly those advanced by the Anglicans.

Bibliography

A. *Luthers lära om staten* [Luther's Teaching on the State] (Uppsala, 1900); *De etiska tankarne i urkristendomen* [The Ethical Thought of Early Christianity] (Stockholm, 1907, 1936); *Luthers storhet* [Luther's Greatness] (Uppsala, 1917); *Försoningen* [The Atonement] (Stockholm, 1908, 1921); *Our Calling* (Philadelphia, 1964).

B. TRE 6:645–48; Conrad Bergendoff, "The Ethical Thought of Einar Billing," in *The Scope of Grace*, ed. Philip Hefner (Philadelphia, 1964); Gustaf Wingren, *An Exodus Theology: Einar Billing and the Development of Modern Swedish Theology* (Philadelphia, 1969).

David T. Priestley

BILLOT, LOUIS (12 January 1846, Sierck, Moselle, France–18 December 1931, Galorro by Ariccia, Italy). *Education*: undergraduate studies, Coll. Saint-Clément in Metz, Coll. de la Sauve, and Coll. de Tivoli, Bordeaux, 1861–65; ecclesiastical studies, the major sem., Blois, 1865–69. *Career*: ordained priest, 1869; entered Jesuits, 1869; lectured on Sacred Scripture, Laval, 1871–75; preached in Paris, 1875–78, and Laval, 1878–79; taught dogmatic theology, the Catholic Univ. of Angers, 1879–82, and Jesuit scholasticate on the Island of Jersey, 1882–85; chair of dogmatic theology, Gregorian Univ., Rome, 1885–1911; consultor to the Holy Office of the Inquisition, 1910–31; cardinal-deacon 1911–27; resigned the cardinalate, 1927; retirement, 1927–31.

History remembers Billot on several counts. First, he was a brilliant teacher-scholar, prolific author of Latin manuals, and avid proponent of neo-Thomism after the program launched by Leo XIII's encyclical *Aeterni Patris* (24 August 1879). Billot was arguably the best of the Roman-school scholars assembled by Leo. However, his teaching suffered the ahistorical, ascientific, and excessively intramural defects of the neo-Thomist system—virtually guaranteed by its commitment to Latin: its philosophy was theologically biased; and its theology, too content with a verbal dialectic based on a priori definitions, repeated formulae instead of thinking them out afresh and thus abused the argument from authority. Lacking biblical and patristic foundations, Billot's theology soon became obsolete.

Second, Billot was an equally avid opponent of the so-called "modernists" who opposed Billot's brand of neo-Thomism as an inadequate vehicle for authentic Christian teaching in the modern world.

But third, Billot's name appears most often in historical studies because of his ideological resistance to the papal campaign against Action Française. When Pius XI forbade Catholic membership in that and similar organizations and levied severe penalties, Billot, on the counsel of his superiors, resigned from the college of cardinals and retired to the Jesuit novitiate at Galloro, a subdivision of Ariccia, and vowed to live out his days in absolute silence. He broke that vow only once, with a letter of 2 March 1928 to the editor of the Jesuit journal *Études*, repudiating the argument of Action Française that his example could be taken as legitimating its resistance and urging members to "end by submitting themselves to the common Father of the faithful."

Bibliography

A. *De Verbo Incarnato* (Rome, 1892); *De Ecclesiae sacramentis*, 2 vols. (Rome, 1894–95); *De peccato originali* (Rome, 1912); *De Deo uno* and *De Deo trino* (Rome, 1895); *De Ecclesia Christi*, 2 vols. (Rome 1898, 1910); *De virtutibus infusis* (Rome, 1901); *Quaestiones de novissimis* (Rome, 1902); *De inspiratione Sacrae Scripturae* (Rome, 1903); *De sacra traditione* (Rome, 1904); *De gratia Christi* (Rome, 1912).

B. Catholicisme 2:61–62; DTC 1:144–46; LThK³ 2:459; NCE 2:557–58; Henri Le Floch, *Le Cardinal Billot* (Paris, 1947); Jules Lebreton, "S. É. Le Cardinal Billot," *Études* 129 (1911): 514–25; *Tables générales* 1:444–46; Edgar Hocedez, *Histoire de théologie au XIXᵉ siècle*, vol. 3 (Brussels, 1952).

David G. Schultenover

BILLUART, CHARLES-RENE (18 January 1685, Revin, Belgium–20 January 1757, Revin). *Education*: studied philosophy and theology, Revin, 1702–8; theology, Liége, 1708–10. *Career*: entered Order of Preachers, Revin, 1701; taught philosophy, Douai and Revin, 1710–11; theology, Revin, 1711–15; prefect of studies and professor, Dominican Coll. of St. Thomas, Douai, 1715–21; prior, Revin, 1721; provincial, 1728, 1741, 1752.

Billuart was much admired as a religious administrator and as a preacher and controversialist but is most important for his theological and historical scholarship. His major work was his *Summa Sancti Thomae Hodiernis Academiarum Moribus accommodata*, a version of the *Summa* adapted to contemporary school use (19 vols. octavo, Liége, 1746–51). This work, which was requested by his Dominican chapter, presented the ideas of Thomas* following largely Aquinas' order, and as far as possible the same words as the *Summa* itself. In addition, the work undertook to inform the reader on historical questions relevant to the theological points being made by Thomas. For his historical material Billuart seems to have relied especially on Natalis Alexander's ecclesiastical history. Billuart's work was greatly admired for its order and clarity and the large amount of informative material incorporated into it. It was widely used in his own time and throughout most of the nineteenth century, going through thirteen editions. Billuart also prepared an abridged edition entitled *Summa Summae S. Thomae, sive Compendium Theologiae*, which also saw a number of editions, being published anew as late as 1903. Billuart also wrote numerous polemical essays on current issues, some involving the controversy surrounding the bull *Unigenitus* and some in which he endeavored to clarify Thomistic doctrines.

Bibliography

A. *Summa S. Thomae hodiernis academiarum moribus accommodata*, 19 vols. (Liége, 1746–51); *Summa Summae S. Thomae, sive Compendium Theologiae*, 6 vols. (Liége, 1754).

B. DHGE 8:1485–86; DTC 2:1 890–92; LThK³ 2:459–60; NCE 2:558; F. Deodato Labye, O.P., "Vita R. P. C. R. Billuart," at beginning of most editions of Billuart's *Summa S. Thomae*; L. Flynn, *Billuart and his Summa Sancti Thomae* (London, Ontario, 1938).

Richard F. Costigan

BLISS, WILLIAM DWIGHT PORTER (20 August 1856, Constantinople, Turkey–8 October 1926, New York, N.Y.). *Education*: B.A., Amherst Coll., 1878; B.D., Hartford Theol. Sem., 1882. *Career*: pastor, Congregational churches in Denver, Colo., and South Natick, Mass., 1882–85; rector, Lee, Mass., 1885–87; rector, Grace Episcopal Church, Boston, 1887–90; editor, *The Dawn*, 1889–96; rector, Church of the Carpenter, Boston, 1890–94; itinerant lecturer, Christian Social Union, 1894–98; editor, *The American Fabian*, 1895–96; rector, Church of Our Saviour, San Gabriel, Calif., 1898–1902; rector, Amityville, N.Y., 1902–6; special investigator, U. S. Bureau of Labor, 1907–9; rector, West Orange, N.J., 1910–14; student, pastor, and YMCA worker, Switzerland, 1914–21; rector, St. Martha's Episcopal, New York, 1921–25.

Bliss was a leading Episcopal Christian Socialist and a major Christian Socialist writer. He was also the founder of the Church of the Carpenter, a parish effort to carry out the principles of Christian Socialism. Raised a Congregationalist and ordained a pastor in that tradition, he joined the Episcopal Church in 1886 and was ordained. Bliss founded several organizations to promote social reform. In 1887 he worked with William Reed Huntington* in organizing the Church Association for the Advancement of the Interests of Labor, and in 1889 he helped organize the Christian Socialist Society.

Bibliography

A. *The Encyclopedia of Social Reform* (New York, 1897); *A Handbook of Socialism* (New York, 1895).

B. DAB 2:377–78; NCAB 20:91–92; NYT 9 October 1926, 17; SH 2:204; Christopher L. Webber, "William Dwight Porter Bliss (1856–1926): Priest and Socialist,"

Historical Magazine of the Protestant Episcopal Church 28 (March 1959): 9–39; Bernard Kent Markwell, ''William Dwight Porter Bliss: American Christian Socialist,'' in *The Anglican Left: Radical Social Reformers in the Church of England and the Protestant Episcopal Church, 1846–1954* (Brooklyn, N.Y., 1991).

Donald S. Armentrout

BLONDEL, MAURICE (2 November 1861, Dijon, France–4 June 1949, Aix, France). *Education*: École Normale Supérieure, 1881–85; defended dissertation, *L'action*, Sorbonne, 1893. *Career*: taught philosophy, Univ. of Lille, 1895–96; Univ. Aix-en-Provence, 1896–1927; retired, 1927–49.

Blondel was a French philosopher who was remarkable for his time in that he was a committed Catholic who received his philosophical training in the secular and generally antireligious French academy—fully immersed in the current of modern philosophy rather than in the scholastic tradition. Although he insisted on the strictly philosophical nature of his work, he rejected the idea of a ''separated philosophy,'' separated from the question of religion and of a supernatural destiny. In *L'action* (1893), Blondel analyzed human action and discerned a structure that leads to an unavoidable choice for or against God. Human action inevitably calls for an infinite, for what is radically supernatural. Philosophy uncovers a natural necessity for a supernatural religion, a need that philosophy itself is unable to fill.

As he explained in his Letter of 1896 ''On the Exigencies of Contemporary Thought in the Area of Apologetics and on the Method of Philosophy in the Study of the Religious Problem'' (*Letter on Apologetics*), Blondel was opposed to conceiving of the natural and supernatural as two parallel realities with no intrinsic relation—a widespread tendency in the Catholic neoscholastic apologetics of his time. While Blondel's basic approach to the relationship between natural and supernatural was later adopted and further developed by theologians such as De Lubac,* Rahner,* and Balthasar,* it was attacked during Blondel's day by philosophers as well as neoscholastic theologians. Philosophers charged Blondel with having compromised the autonomy of philosophy. At the same time, several Catholic theologians accused him both of confusing the natural and the supernatural and of various errors such as subjectivism attributable to his immersion in modern philosophy.

After the spate of early works, Blondel published occasionally but rather devoted himself to the preparation of his magnum opus, a trilogy on Thought, Being, and Action, whose large volumes appeared in rapid succession in the 1930s. In the trilogy Blondel was finally able to develop the full philosophical system of which the early *L'action* (1893) represented only a part, completing the early, basically phenomenological analysis of action with a metaphysical investigation of thought, being, and action.

Bibliography

A. *L'Action* (Paris, 1893); *Action*, trans. Oliva Blanchette (Notre Dame, Ind., 1984); *The Letter on Apologetics and History and Dogma*, trans. Alexander Dru and Illtyd

Trethowan (Grand Rapids, Mich., 1995); *La Pensée*, 2 vols. (Paris, 1934); *L'Etre et les êtres* (Paris, 1935); *L'Action*, 2 vols. (Paris, 1936–37); *La philosophie et l'esprit chrétien*, 2 vols. (Paris, 1944, 1946); *Les exigences philosophiques du christianisme* (Paris, 1950).

B.   LThK³ 2:528–29; NCE 2:617–18; ODCC 215–16; Henri Bouillard, *Blondel and Christianity*, trans. James M. Somerville (Washington, D.C., 1969); Henry Duméry, *La philosophie de l'action: Essai sur l'intellectualisme blondélien* (Paris, 1948); *Blondel et la religion: Essai critique sur la "lettre" de 1896* (Paris, 1954); James M. Somerville, *Total Commitment: Blondel's L'Action* (Washington, D.C., 1968).

James LeGrys

BODENSTEIN, JACOB. *See* KARLSTADT, ANDREAS.

BOEHME, JACOB (? 1575, Alt-Seidenberg, near Görlitz in Silesia, Germany– November 1624, Görlitz, Germany). *Career*: farmer and shoemaker, 1583–92; burger and mystic writer, 1593–1612; linen merchant, mystic and author, 1612– 24.

Boehme, who has been called "philosophus Teutonicus," is a difficult writer to characterize. He was a mystic and a religious philosopher more than a theologian, but he did appropriate much of the Christian biblical tradition and the Lutheran tradition in which he was raised into his mystical writings, which represent a mixture of Neoplatonism, astrology, alchemy, the Jewish Kabbalah, and Paraclesian philosophy.

Living in the midst of religious wars—particularly between Lutherans, Calvinists, Crypto-Calvinists, Spiritualists, Schwenckfeldians, and Catholics—he was particularly conscious of the need to restore some unity to the shattered peace of Christendom. From his first published work, *Aurora*, to his posthumously published *The Way to Christ*, he attempted to uncover a fundamental unifying religious philosophy of life that could transcend the doctrinal conflicts of the period in which he lived. He sought in particular to explain Christian doctrinal perspectives on the Trinity, grace, and sacraments in terms that he believed transcended the confines of confessional particularism.

For Boehme, God was the primal abyss containing the possibilities and even the necessity of both good and evil. The problem of theodicy was for him a key issue that was a recurring motif in his works. The indwelling divine spirit, present in all beings, revitalized the human will and illuminated the human understanding, making the human will free through the divine immanence.

In his last major work, *Mysterium Magnum*, which recapitulated much of his earlier work, he demonstrated the correspondences of his nature philosophy and Scripture. That work also illustrated that for him the world was a sacramental mystery, revealing and simultaneously hiding the real presence of the eternal Word. This sacramental vision of the world, moreover, was broad enough to encompass various Christian and non-Christian beliefs and practices. Grace and salvation are extended to non-Christians as well as Christians.

His thought influenced some within Germany during his lifetime, even though his published as well as unpublished works were condemned as heretical by his own Lutheran pastors and by the Lutheran town council of Görlitz. Most of his writings, though, were published after his death and they had a strong influence upon German and English idealists and romantics.

Bibliography

A. *Jakob Bohmes Schriften* (Leipzig, 1938); *The Works of Jacob Behmen, the Teutonic Theosopher* (London, 1764–81; New York, 1976); *The Way to Christ* (New York, 1976); *Personal Christianity: The Doctrines of Jacob Boehme* (New York, 1891, 1957–58, 1977).

B. HERE 2:778–84; LThK³ 2:550–51; ODCC 218–19; OEncR 1:186–87; TRE 6: 748–54; H. Vetterling, *The Illuminate of Gorlitz: or, Jakob Bohme's Life and Philosophy: A Comparative Study* (Leipzig, 1923); H. Grunsky, *Jacob Boehme* (Stuttgart, 1956); J. J. Stoudt, *Sunrise to Eternity: A Study in Jacob Boehme's Life and Thought* (Philadelphia, 1957); H. Tesch, *Jakob Böhme* (Munich, 1976); A. Weeks, *Boehme: An Intellectual Biography of the Seventeenth-Century Philosopher and Mystic* (Albany, N.Y., 1991).

Patrick W. Carey

BOETHIUS, ANICIUS MANLIUS SERVERINUS (480–524). Boethius was born into a Roman senatorial family; held the office of senator; was taught catechesis by John the Deacon; was found guilty of treason by Theodoric, Ostrogoth king of Italy, because he had supported a friend who criticized the king in a letter to Emperor Justinian; was imprisoned, tortured and clubbed to death in 524. While in prison, he wrote the classic *De consolatione philosophiae*; among his other writings are five *Opuscula sacra* dealing with the Trinity, substances, and Chalcedonian Christology; his philosophical thought was influenced by the Neoplatonists. *De consolatione philosophiae* greatly influenced medieval and Renaissance thought. Its themes—the folly of dependence on Fortune, the struggle between good and evil, God as the final aim of all humanity, the meaning of eternity—are presented clearly and logically in a dialogue with personified Philosophy. In spirit and method, the *Opuscula sacra* look forward to scholastic theological method—particularly Tractate Four, *De fide catholica*, which discusses permissible application of reason to belief. Boethius' trinitarian theology concentrates on the relation of equals and identicals among the three persons.

Bibliography

A. CPL 878–95; *The Consolation of Philosophy*, trans. Richard Green (Indianapolis, Ind., 1978); *The Theological Tractates and the Consolation of Philosophy*, trans. Hugh F. Stewart et al., LCL (Cambridge, Mass., 1990).

B. DTC 2:918–22; LThK³ 2:547–48; NCE 2:631–33; ODCC 219; TRE 7:18–28; Gilbert of Poitiers, *The Commentaries on Boethius*, ed. Nikolaus Häring (Toronto, 1966); Thierry of Chartres, *The Commentaries on Boethius*, ed. idem (Toronto, 1971); Henry

Chadwick, *Boethius: the Consolations of Music, Logic, Theology and Philosophy* (Oxford, 1981); Margaret Gibson, *Boethius: His Life, Thought and Influence* (Oxford, 1981).

Thomas S. Ferguson

BONAVENTURE (ca. 1217, Bagnoregio, near Orvieto–15 July 1274, Lyons). *Education*: Franciscan Friary, Bagnoregio; master of arts, bachelor of scripture, licentiate and doctorate in theology, Univ. of Paris, 1235–53. *Career*: entered the Franciscan order in Paris, probably in 1243; taught as regent master at the school of the Friars at Paris, 1253–57; minister general of the Franciscan order, 1257–74; named cardinal bishop of Albano, 1273; took an active part in the Second Council of Lyons, 1274; canonized a saint by Sixtus IV, 1482, and declared a doctor of the church by Sixtus V, 1588, with the title Seraphic Doctor.

In an age that produced the comprehensive complexity of both the Gothic cathedral and the scholasticism of the universities, Bonaventure developed one of the most comprehensive and complex syntheses of the Middle Ages. He drew from the vision of the patristic era but suffused it with new elements inspired by Francis of Assisi. He took his theological anthropology and epistemology directly from Augustine,* but not his trinitarian theology. Through a complex transmission of texts, he produced a trinitarian theology that is strikingly similar to that of the Greek Fathers. In his theology of history, he was influenced by Joachim of Fiore,* but modified the Joachimite emphases on the Holy Spirit with his own Christocentricity. Although he assimilated into his vision significant elements from Aristotle, he did not make Aristotle's metaphysics integral to his system.

Bonaventure's theological method differs from that of Thomas Aquinas.* In a technical sense it was formulated by Anselm of Canterbury,* developed by Richard of St. Victor,* and in the thirteenth century flowed into the early Franciscan school. It is called "seeking necessary reasons" (*rationes necessariae*) for revealed mysteries; once a mystery, such as the Trinity, has been revealed, it is possible to search for its intrinsic reason (*ratio*), which is found in the realm of the good rather than of being. Bonaventure's primary use of this method consisted in his applying to the Trinity the principle of the self-diffusiveness of the good.

Perhaps his major contribution to theology is his explicit formulation of the strong metaphysical structure that undergirds his theological synthesis. This metaphysics is the flowering of centuries of Christian Neoplatonism, which he summarized as follows: "This is our whole metaphysics: emanation, exemplarity, consummation, to be illumined by spiritual rays and to be led back to the Highest Reality." Bonaventure grounds this metaphysics in the inner life of the Trinity, as is illustrated in the very context of his statement, quoted above from the first of the *Collations on the Six Days*, which deals with Christ as the metaphysical center in his eternal generation from the Father. This he develops in an original way, basing his metaphysics of emanation, exemplarity, and consummation on the Father as the fountain fullness of fecundity in the Trinity.

From all eternity the Father's boundless fecundity flows within the Trinity in the generation of the Son and the spiration of the Holy Spirit. This eternal intra-trinitarian fecundity overflows in creation and Christocentricity. Bonaventure, however, explicitly denies that creation is necessary, for the divine fecundity is fully actualized within the Trinity. But if God freely decides to create the finite world in space and time, then this creative act would flow from the primordial fecundity within the Trinity. Out of his intra-trinitarian fecundity, then, emerges the theophanic, or God-manifesting, structure that pervades Bonaventure's theology of the created world. All created reality manifests in multiple ways the richness and fecundity of the inner life of God. This is the quintessential theme of his theology and it is here that he gives a metaphysical and epistemological basis for the vision that is poetically expressed in Francis of Assisi's *Canticle of Brother Sun.*

Bonaventure identified different ways in which the Trinity is manifested in creation. All creatures are vestiges of the Trinity, reflecting the divine power, wisdom, and goodness. Power ultimately reflects the Father's power to generate the Son, who is the Image, Word, and Wisdom of the Father. The goodness of creatures reflects the goodness of the Spirit, who is the love between the Father and the Son and the gift through whom all good gifts are given. "Image" is the term used for the way rational creatures reflect the Trinity in the depths of their interiority, in the soul's faculties of memory, understanding, and will. The Father is reflected in our memory, the Son in our understanding, and the Holy Spirit in our will and affectivity. A higher level of reflection of the Trinity is found in the likeness, a term which is used of our faculties reformed by grace. Bonaventure's theophanic universe is perhaps most comprehensively expressed in his treatment of the three books: the book of creation, the book of Scripture, and the Book of Life (Christ). In his *Disputed Questions on the Mystery of the Trinity*, he explores how the divinity is manifested in the book of creation: in vestiges and in souls as images. However, because of the sinfulness of the human situation, we find it difficult to read this book. So God has given us another book, the book of Scripture, which guides us to penetrate the meaning of the book of creation. Finally, God provides a third book, namely, the Book of Life, that is Christ himself, the Image of the Father, who becomes incarnate in order to manifest the meaning of the other two books. By reading these books in harmony, we can perceive more fully the multileveled divine manifestation in the finite world.

Closely connected with his metaphysics of the theophanic universe is his epistemology of illumination. Derived from Augustine, this epistemology is the counterpart on the level of human consciousness to the metaphysical structure of his system. God is present in the human mind, illuminating our faculties of memory, understanding, and will to perceive the divine eternity, truth, and goodness. In the light of this illuminating presence, we can have certitude of God's existence. This means that the existence of God is a truth that cannot be intrinsically doubted, although our minds may be clouded over and not grasp this truth reflexively. In his *Disputed Questions on the Mystery of the Trinity*, Bonaventure gives in brief fashion twenty-nine versions of proofs for God's existence, ten directly on illumination, ten proceeding from the contingency of created being, and nine versions of the ontological argument. However, he presents all of these as truths that cannot be doubted and refers to them as "exercises" rather than formal proofs.

We can also have certitude about objects in the finite world, even though these objects and our minds themselves are changeable. This certitude is grounded in the metaphysics of the eternal ideas in the divine mind. From all eternity the Father generates the Son as his perfect Image and Word, and within the Son are generated the eternal ideas of all he can create in the finite world. In the fourth of the *Disputed Questions on the Knowledge of Christ*, Bonaventure claims that our minds can be illumined by the eternal ideas in the divine mind as regulative and motivating sources of certitude. This comes about by a process he calls "contuition." We have direct perception of sense objects and simultaneously an awareness of the ground of certitude in the divine mind.

Bonaventure's theophanic universe reaches its climax in the incarnate Christ. It is in the coincidence of opposites of the divine and the human that the fountain-fullness of fecundity in the inner life of the Trinity achieves its counterpart in creation. And it is here that the divine fullness was united with emptiness in the suffering of the incarnate Christ. In 1259, some two and a half years after he was elected Minister General, Bonaventure wrote in the prologue of his *Soul's Journey into God* that he visited La Verna in Tuscany, the site of Francis' vision of the six-winged Seraph in the form of Christ crucified, after which he received the stigmata. Bonaventure tells how he perceived a symbolic meaning in the vision, that the six wings symbolized the six stages of the soul's journey into God. He also saw that there was "no other path but through the burning love of the Crucified." From that time on, the suffering, death, and resurrection of Christ take on new meaning in Bonaventure's spiritual writing and his theology. And it is Francis who exemplifies these mysteries.

In the *Soul's Journey into God*, Bonaventure makes a major contribution to the history of western Christian mysticism by charting a path, with Francis as his guide, first through the reflections of God in creation and ultimately into apophatic darkness which, at the same time, is inflamed with the fire of love. Bonaventure developed these themes of crucified love through poverty and humility in his *Life of St. Francis* (*Legenda maior*), which he was officially commissioned to write by the general chapter of the Franciscan order. In terms of its dissemination in the medieval period and its effect on spirituality and culture at large, this is the most influential life of St. Francis ever written. Bonaventure developed these themes in a different way in *The Tree of Life*, the first major set of meditations on the life of Christ. Emerging out of monastic centers in the twelfth century, this form of prayer contained a new use of the imagination in visualizing a scene in the life of Christ and then responding affectively as an actor in the drama. Bonaventure's meditations gave a major impetus to the developing devotion to the humanity and passion of Christ in the Middle Ages, which flowed into the *Exercises* of Ignatius of Loyola* in the sixteenth century and into modern times.

The focus on Christocentricity, which had been evolving in Bonaventure's writings since his studies at the University of Paris, reached a climax in his final work: the twenty-three lectures or *Collations on the Six Days* that he delivered in the spring of 1273. These lectures express his final synthesis and show the impact of Francis on his deepening understanding of poverty and humility, and his integration of the opposites of fullness and emptiness. They bring to a climax the themes of the theophanic universe and the poverty and humility of the suffering Christ. The first lecture, entitled ''Christ the Center of All the Sciences,'' sets the framework for the unfolding of the whole. Christ is the metaphysical center in his eternal generation from the Father, the physical center in his incarnation, the mathematical center in his crucifixion, the logical center in his resurrection, the ethical center in his ascension, the juridical center in his final judgment, and the theological center in his drawing all things back to the Father. In this context, Bonaventure deals with the mysteries of the life of Christ on a cosmic level and not on the level of imagining the scenes from the gospels as he did in his meditations on the life of Christ. Through the perspective of Christ the center, Bonaventure reaffirms his metaphysics of the theophanic universe and draws his thought into a comprehensive vision that produces one of the major theologies of history in the Middle Ages.

Bibliography

A.   *S. Bonaventurae opera omnia*, 10 vols. (Quaracchi, 1882–1902); *Works of Saint Bonaventure*, 6 vols. (St. Bonaventure, N.Y., 1955–96); *The Works of Bonaventure*, 5 vols. (Paterson, N.J., 1960–70); *Bonaventure: The Soul's Journey into God, The Tree of Life, The Life of St. Francis* (New York, 1978).

B.   DTC 2:962–86; LThK³ 2:570–72; NCE 2:658–64; ODCC 222–23; TRE 7:48–55; Jacques Guy Bougerol, *Introduction to the Works of Bonaventure* (Paterson, N.J., 1964); Étienne Gilson, *The Philosophy of St. Bonaventure* (Paterson, N.J., 1965); Joseph Ratzinger, *The Theology of History in St. Bonaventure* (Chicago, 1971); *S. Bonaventura 1274–1974*, 5 vols. (Grottaferrata, 1972–74); John Quinn, *The Historical Constitution of St. Bonaventure's Philosophy* (Toronto, 1973); Ewert Cousins, *Bonaventure and the Coincidence of Opposites* (Chicago, 1978); Zachary Hayes, *The Hidden Center* (St. Bonaventure, N.Y., 1992).

Ewert Cousins

BONHOEFFER, DIETRICH (4 February 1906, Breslau, Silesia, Germany [Poland in 1998]–9 April 1945, Flössenberg Concentration Camp, Bavaria, Germany). *Education*: studied at Univ. of Tübingen, 1923–24; Ph.D., Alexander von Humboldt Univ., Berlin, 1924–27; habilitation, 1929–30; post-graduate study, Union Theol. Sem., New York City, 1930. *Career*: ordained Lutheran minister, 1931; lecturer in systematic theology, Alexander von Humboldt Univ., Berlin, 1931–36; pastor, German expatriate congregation, London, 1933–35; director, Preachers' Sem. of the Confessing Church, Finkenwalde and Zingst, Pommerania, 1935–37; German Armed Forces Counterintelligence, 1940–43; arrest, 1944; execution, 1945.

Bonhoeffer is known primarily for his Christian witness against the Nazi regime in Germany. In February of 1932, following Adolf Hitler's election as Chancellor, Bonhoeffer gave a radio broadcast on "The Leader and the Younger Generation," in which he was critical of the *Führerprinzip* ("leader principle") of a Nazi Party determined to turn Germany into a totalitarian state. That spring semester he gave a series of lectures on Christology and published essays on the Christian Church in relation both to the Jews and to the question of excluding them from civil and ecclesiastical service. The Christ of the three ecumenical Creeds and the Lutheran Confessions was, for Bonhoeffer, the focal point of all reality, divine and human. This Christ is historic, sharing in and sanctifying historic time (in the sense of Martin Kähler and not in the sense of the "historical Jesus" of Ritschl* and Schweitzer*). The rootedness of Jesus and his whole identity as a member of the historic covenant people of God, the Jews, is integral to the reality of the Incarnation of God in Christ. Bonhoeffer opposed attempts by "German-Christian" theologians and popular publicists in sympathy with the Aryan supremacist notions of National Socialism to Aryanize the Son of Mary and to excise the Jewish element from Christian faith and practice.

On 5 April 1943 Bonhoeffer was arrested by the *Gestapo* without warrant and remanded to a regular army (*Wehrmacht*) prison in Berlin-Tegel. A warrant for his arrest was later drawn up on a charge of "subversion of the Armed Forces" in connection with his participation in attempts to smuggle Jews and Christians of Jewish heritage across the Swiss border. During his time in Tegel, Bonhoeffer continued work on what he considered to be his most important book, the "Ethics" (a book he had started to write in 1940 during his sojourn at the Benedictine Monastery in Ettal, Bavaria). In "Ethics" he developed the theme of responsibility before God within the real structures of the world, both as created and sustained by God and as corrupted by sin. Bonhoeffer contrasted the "man of conscience" (who was primarily interested in maintaining his own moral innocence, even under a truly criminal state and who therefore could not be relied upon to behave in a responsible manner, though it meant risking his own reputation) with the "responsible man" who was willing to risk not only the charge of treason but even death in order to be responsible to God in upholding the right and taking responsibility for the oppressed. The "Man for others" (Christ—a phrase Bonhoeffer borrowed from Barth*) was the living, dynamic reality to which life in the historic moment was to be conformed in obedience and love to God.

Sometime after 17 January 1945 Bonhoeffer was transferred to the *Gestapo* and *SS* (Schutzstaffel, or elite guard corps) prison in Berlin's Prinz Albrecht Strasse, thence to Buchenwald Concentration Camp, 7 February 1945 and from there to three successive sites in Bavaria: Regensburg, Schönberg, and finally to Flössenberg Concentration camp for summary court martial and execution by hanging.

Bonhoeffer was an articulate witness of Christian faith radically engaged in responsible action on behalf of the oppressed, a silent witness of the "other Germany" (of the German political and military resistance to a criminal regime), and an enduring theological voice who transposed the ensemble of classical Protestant theology into a contemporary mode. The twin themes in his ecclesiology of the servant church "without privileges" and the church as the living congregation of Christ, which seeks and forms community with others, continued to be a driving force behind the ecumenical movement within his own Lutheran communion and world Christianity. Interest in Bonhoeffer cut very much across all denominational lines and was itself a factor for Christian unity and theological dialogue. As the Roman Catholic lay theologian, William Kuhns, put it, Dietrich Bonhoeffer was a "bridge theologian," one who made it possible for Orthodox, Catholics, and Protestants to enter his world and that of one another under the sign of a faith in solidarity with the suffering Christ.

Bibliography

A. *Gesammelte Schriften*, ed. Eberhard Bethge, 6 vols. (Munich, 1958–74); *Life Together*, trans. John Doberstein (San Francisco, 1954); *Act and Being*, trans. Bernard Noble (San Francisco, 1962); *The Cost of Discipleship*, trans. Reginald Fuller, rev. Irmgard Booth (New York, 1963); *The Communion of Saints*, trans. Ronald Gregor Smith et al. (San Francisco, 1963); *Ethics*, trans. Neville Horton Smith (New York, 1965); *No Rusty Swords: Letters, Lectures and Notes, 1928–1936*, trans. Edwin H. Robertson and John Bowden (San Francisco, 1965); *The Way to Freedom: Letters, Lectures and Notes, 1935–1939*, trans. Edwin H. Robertson and John Bowden (San Francisco, 1966); *Letters and Papers from Prison*, enlarged ed., trans. Reginald Fuller et al. (New York, 1972); *True Patriotism: Letters, Lectures and Notes, 1939–1945*, trans. Edwin Robertson and John Bowden (San Francisco, 1973); *Christ the Center*, rev. trans. Edwin Robertson (San Francisco, 1978); *Dietrich Bonhoeffer: Werke*, ed. Eberhard Bethge et al., 16 vols. (Munich, 1986–); *Dietrich Bonhoeffer's Works*, ed. and trans. Wayne W. Floyd, Jr., et al., 16 vols. (Minneapolis, Minn., 1996–); *A Testament to Freedom. The Essential Writings of Dietrich Bonhoeffer*, ed. Geffrey B. Kelly and F. Burton Nelson (San Francisco, 1990).

B. LThK^3 2:574; ODCC 223; TRE 7:55–66; Clifford J. Green and Wayne W. Floyd, Jr., *Bonhoeffer Bibliography. Primary and Secondary Sources in English* (Philadelphia, 1986–); Eberhard Bethge, *Dietrich Bonhoeffer: Man of Vision—Man of Courage*, ed. Edwin Robertson, trans. Eric Mosbacher et al. (New York, 1970); William Kuhns, *In Pursuit of Dietrich Bonhoeffer* (Garden City, N.Y., 1969); Ernst Feil, *The Theology of Dietrich Bonhoeffer*, trans. Martin Rumscheidt (Philadelphia, 1985); A. J. Klassen, ed., *A Bonhoeffer Legacy: Essays in Understanding* (Grand Rapids, Mich., 1981); Geffrey B. Kelly, *Liberating Faith. Bonhoeffer's Message for Today* (Minneapolis, Minn., 1984); Edwin Robertson, *The Shame and the Sacrifice: The Life and Martyrdom of Dietrich Bonhoeffer* (New York, 1988); Charles Marsh, *Reclaiming Dietrich Bonhoeffer: The Promise of His Theology* (New York, 1994); Joachim Fest, *Plotting Hitler's Death: The Story of the German Resistance*, trans. Bruce Little (New York, 1996).

Guy C. Carter

BOOTH, WILLIAM (10 April 1829, Nottingham, England–20 August 1912, Hadley-Wood). *Education*: tutored in theology within the Methodist New Connexion. *Career*: ministry as a circuit preacher, 1852–61; evangelistic work, 1861–65; founder, the Christian Mission, 1865; general, Salvation Army, 1878–1912.

From 1842 until 1851 Booth worked as a pawn-broker's assistant, where he developed a compassion for the disadvantaged of Victorian society. As a minister, he became increasingly dissatisfied with the limitations the Methodist New Connexion placed upon his calling to preach the gospel to the poor. In 1855, he married Catherine Mumford (1829–1890), who shared his aspirations and who became a famous preacher and advocate of female ministry. Upon his departure from the New Connexion, Booth adopted Finneyan revivalistic tactics and employed them in reaching the lowest strata of society. These tactics included taking the message of salvation to the people; attracting them by a variety of novel means; immediately pressing his hearers for a decision; and employing every convert in the task of evangelism. Adapting measures to meet the needs of the total person, Booth creatively synthesized his evangelistic efforts with relevant social action.

Booth had eleven articles of faith of the Salvation Army established by deed poll in 1878. With these articles, he sought to convey the essentials of Christian faith and practice in a pragmatic and utilitarian spirit. The movement's doctrines of salvation and sanctification, when clothed in the dramatic and sensational garb of militaristic worldwide conquest and spiritual warfare, impressed the gospel on the impoverished masses by means of vivid imagery. Booth's *Orders and Regulations of the Salvation Army* (1878), provided organizational structure and rules of governance for his organization. By 1879 the Army had eighty-one mission stations and 127 full time evangelists. In 1880 the movement spread to the United States, and to Australia the following year.

Booth lived to establish Army work in fifty-eight countries and colonies, traveled over 5 million miles, preached nearly 60,000 sermons, and was received in audience by kings, emperors, and presidents around the world. Of his many publications, *In Darkest England and the Way Out* (1890) was the most notable, providing the framework for the Army's subsequent social ministry. In 1912 he was succeeded as General of the Salvation Army by his son, William Bramwell Booth (1856–1929).

Bibliography

A.   *Salvation Soldiery* (London, 1889); *In Darkest England and the Way Out* (London, 1890).

B.   DHGE 9:1166–67; DNB, 1912–21, 50–52; LThK³ 2:590–91; NCE 2:702; ODCC 226; Harold Begbie, *The Life of General William Booth, the Founder of the Salvation Army*, 2 vols. (New York, 1920); St. John Ervine, *God's Soldier: General William Booth*, 2 vols. (New York, 1935).

R. David Rightmire

BOSSUET, JACQUES-BENIGNE (27 September, 1627, Dijon–12 April 1704, Paris). *Education*: Jesuit Coll. des Godrans, Dijon, 1635–42; Coll. de Navarre,

Paris, 1642–48; Doctor of Divinity, Paris, 1652. *Career*: ordained priest, 1652; archdeacon of Metz, 1654–59; preacher in Paris, 1659–70; bishop of Condom, 1670–81; tutor to the Dauphin, 1670–81; member of the French Academy, 1671; bishop of Meaux, 1681–1704.

Bossuet was renowned above all as an orator, but was also author of a number of significant books, participant in religious controversies such as Jansenism and Quietism, personal adviser to King Louis XIV, and leading defender of the ecclesiology of Gallicanism. Bossuet's books embody great learning and contain many judicious insights into theological and historical questions. His *Discourse on Universal History* (1681), a pioneering work in the theology of history written for the instruction of the Dauphin (and the king), presents the great lessons taught by human history: the providence of God, the superiority of the Christian (especially the Catholic) faith, and the need of everyone, including rulers, to learn from the rise and fall of great kingdoms.

Bossuet's hope that recovery of unity with the Protestants could somehow be achieved showed itself in several works. His *Exposition de la doctrine catholique sur les matières de controverse* (1671) attempted to clear up misunderstandings of Catholic doctrine in a clear, non-polemical way. His *Histoire des Variations des Eglises protestantes* (1688), working from the maxim, "perpetuity [in one faith] is a mark of truth, variation is a mark of error," and recounting the ceaseless variations of Protestant doctrines, showed his hope that Protestant readers could be induced to rethink their attachment to the Reformed Church.

This kind of thinking showed itself also in Bossuet's ecclesiology, in which he was a major proponent of Gallican positions. He thought that the Roman doctrine of absolute papal monarchy was a latter-day variation from the church's historic faith in a more collegial form of authority. He was the principal redactor of the Declaration of the Gallican Clergy (Gallican Articles) of 1682, and wrote a massive *Defensio* of the articles (published only posthumously) in which, with great historical erudition, he undertook to disprove papal claims of supremacy over an ecumenical council and papal infallibility in defining doctrine.

Not involved in a major way in the Jansenist controversy, Bossuet admired the piety and strict morals of leading Jansenists, but thought that the five propositions condemned, rightly he felt, by Innocent X in 1653 definitely permeated the work of Jansenius.* In the controversy over Quietism Bossuet's lack of sympathy for mysticism led him unfortunately to use his great prestige to cooperate in unjust judgments on Fénelon* and on Madame Guyon.*

Bibliography

A.   *Oeuvres completes*, ed. F. Lachat, 31 vols. (Paris, 1862–66); *Oeuvres oratoires*, ed. J. Lebarq, 7 vols. (Paris, 1922–27); *Discourse on Universal History*, ed. Orest Ranum (Chicago, 1976); *Histoire des variations des Eglises protestantes*, 4 vols. (Versailles, 1817); *Politics Drawn from the Very Words of Scripture* (New York, 1990).

B.   DSAM 1:1874–83; DTC 2:1049–89; LThK³ 2:612–13; NCE 2:717–18; ODCC

228; TRE 7:88–93; E. K. Sanders, *Jacques-Benigne Bossuet: A Study* (New York, 1922); A. G. Martimort, *Le gallicanisme de Bossuet* (Paris, 1953); T. Goyet, *L'Humanisme de Bossuet* (Paris, 1965); J. LeBrun, *La spiritualité de Bossuet* (Paris, 1972).

Richard F. Costigan

BOUQUILLON, THOMAS JOSEPH (16 May 1840, Warnêton, Belgium–5 November 1902, Brussels, Belgium). *Education*: liberal arts, St. Louis at Menin, Belgium, 1854–60; philosophy, petite sém., Roulers, Belgium, 1862; theology, Sem. of Bruges, Belgium, 1862; S.T.D., Gregorian Univ., Rome, 1867. *Career*: ordained priest, 1865; professor of moral theology, Sem. of Bruges, 1867–77; Catholic Univ. of Lille, 1877–85; entered Benedictine Abbey, Maredsous, Belgium, 1885–89; professor of moral theology, Catholic Univ. of America, 1889–1902.

Bouquillon was a Catholic moral theologian who was significantly influenced by the Roman scholastic and Thomistic revival in philosophy and theology. Like his Roman professors Johann Baptist Franzelin* (1816–86) and Anthony Ballerini (1805–81), he understood moral theology as a science of the Christian means to salvation, not just the science of ethical activity. He was, moreover, a progressive scholastic in the sense that he was sympathetic with the scientific spirit of the late nineteenth century. While teaching in the United States in particular he called upon moral theologians to establish a dialogue between Thomas Aquinas'* moral principles and the new developments in the empirical social sciences (especially sociology and economics). His advocacy of the use of the social sciences had a profound effect upon moral theology, especially in fostering the development of a twentieth-century social Catholicism that focused upon issues of social and economic justice in American society. His teachings significantly influenced his students, two of whom, John A. Ryan* (1865–1945) and William J. Kerby (1870–1936), became intellectual and social leaders within early twentieth century American Catholicism.

Bouquillon believed he was particularly well suited to American life. As a Belgian Catholic, he grew up in a nation where the Catholic clergy had supported the political movements to establish a free nation and where Catholics had experienced and valued the benefits of religious freedom. In the United States he was considered a member of the liberal wing of the faculty at the Catholic University and sided with Americanizing bishops and priests. He became most widely known in the United States during his involvement in an American Catholic debate on the state's role in education. In 1891, Bouquillon supported Archbishop John Ireland's argument for the state's right and duty to provide for public education, a position that was hotly contested in American Catholic circles. Bouquillon argued on the moral grounds that the state had the duty to provide for the "temporal common welfare" and that the diffusion of knowledge was among the most necessary means for that end. The state, therefore, had a duty to provide education where parents and churches were incapable of doing so. The battle over the state's right to educate would continue

here and there within American Catholicism for another fifty years before Bouquillon's position gained universal acceptance.

Bibliography

A. *Institutiones theologiae moralis fundamentalis* (Bruges, 1873; rev. ed. 1890;
1903); *Tractatus de virtutibus theologicis* (Bruges, 1878; 1890); *Tractatus de virtute
religionis* (Bruges, 1880); *Education: To Whom Does It Belong?* (Baltimore, Md., 1891);
"Theology in Universities," *Catholic University Bulletin* 1 (January, 1895): 25–34;
"Moral Theology at the End of the Nineteenth Century," *Catholic University Bulletin*
5 (April, 1899): 244–68.

B. DAB 2:481–82; DTC 2:1093–94; NCE 2:731; H. Rommel, *Thomas Bouquillon
. . . Notice biobibliographique* (Bruges, 1903); Laurent Janssens, "Maitre Thomas Bou-
quillon," *Revue Bénédictine* 20 (1903): 2–6; C. J. Nuesse, "Thomas Joseph Bouquillon
(1840–1902), Moral Theologian and Precursor of the Social Sciences in the Catholic
University of America," *Catholic Historical Review* 72 (1986): 601–19; idem, "Before
Rerum Novarum: A Moral Theologian's View of Catholic Social Movements in 1891,"
Social Thought 17 (1991): 5–17.

Patrick W. Carey

BOUYER, LOUIS JEAN (17 February 1913, Paris–). *Education*: studied at
State Univ. of Strasbourg, 1932–36; State Univ. at Paris, 1940–42; S.T.D., Institut Catholique, Paris, 1946. *Career*: after membership in various Protestant
congregations in Paris, became a Lutheran pastor; professor, Institut Catholique,
1946; ordained Catholic priest and became member of French Oratory, 1947;
taught at the Univ. of Notre Dame, summer sessions after 1951.

The productive and creative Bouyer must be numbered among that distinguished group of European theologians whose scholarship made possible the
firm grounding of the theological and liturgical renewals of Vatican II. Bouyer
had been raised a Protestant and had studied with the Calvinist Auguste Lecerf
and with the Lutheran biblical scholar Oscar Cullmann.* Before he became a
Catholic priest, moreover, he was influenced by Sergei Boulgakoff, a Russian
Orthodox scholar.

Bouyer's Protestant background left him with an unshakable conviction of
the primacy of the Bible, which for him was *the* Christian text, especially as
the Bible is proclaimed in the liturgy. For Bouyer all renewal begins with the
Bible. One can read about his move from Protestantism to Catholicism in his
The Spirit and Forms of Protestantism (ET 1958). A central idea that gave
direction to all Bouyer's thought was the necessity of returning to the sources,
the great French theological principle of *ressourcement*. From the beginning
Bouyer maintained a corporate sense of Christianity and of the liturgy. He opposed all individualistic piety; in fact, in 1943 he published a work in the famous
Unam Sanctam series on the Body of Christ in the theology of Athanasius of
Alexandria.* This emphasis on the Body of Christ gave a distinctively ecclesial
foundation to all of Bouyer's theology. His interests and publications have been
cast widely: the Bible, liturgy, ecumenism, ritual, history of spirituality, system-

atic theology, mariology, monasticism, and biography. Bouyer even wrote pseudonymously three novels. Many of his books have been translated into English, some of which have remained standard, much consulted studies. At first Bouyer espoused the ideals of the Second Vatican Council, but he subsequently became less amenable to and more cautious about some of the Council's results. Bouyer was never one to disguise his convictions, although in the 1940s he advised caution and restraint about liturgical changes that could come as too much too soon. He favored careful, pastoral groundwork in the revision of the liturgy.

For some time those interested in the revival of studies in Christian spirituality had at hand only the collaborative effort *The History of Christian Spirituality*, in which Bouyer took a major role. (Original French editions were published in 1960, 1961, 1965, and 1966). Louis Bouyer's scholarship and strongly held liturgical positions became well known and influential not only in Europe but also in North America especially through books like *Liturgical Piety* (1954), *Christian Initiation* (1958), and *Eucharist* (1968). Many, though not all, of Bouyer's ideas on the liturgy became prime elements in the liturgical renewal initiated by Vatican II.

Bibliography

A.   *Le métier du théologien. Entretiens avec Georges Daix* (Paris, 1979); Karin Heller, *Ton Créateur est Ton Époux, Ton Rédempteur; Contribution à la Théologie de l'Alliance à Partir des Écrits du R. P. Louis Bouyer, de 'Oratoire'*. Thesis ad Doctoratum in Theologia (Paris, 1996), 431–46; Martin Klöckener, "Bio-bibliographisches Repertorium der Liturgiewissenschaft," in *Archiv für Liturgiewissenschaft* 35–36 (1993–94): 285–357; "Letter to Father Duployé," *Communio* 16 (Summer 1989): 283–91; *Orbis Liturgicus*, ed. Anthony Ward and Cuthbert Johnson (Rome, 1995), 577.
B.   LThK[3] 2:620; Erasmo Leiva-Merikakis, "Louis Bouyer the Theologian," *Communio* 16 (Summer 1989): 257–76, to which is added (pp. 277–82) a bibliography of books from 1938 to 1988; Grant Sperry-White, "Louis Bouyer, Theologian, Historian, Mystagogue," in Robert L. Tuzik, *How Firm a Foundation: Leaders of the Liturgical Movement* (Chicago, 1990), 96–104.

Keith J. Egan

BRADWARDINE, THOMAS (ca. 1290–26 August 1349, Avignon). Bradwardine was a contemporary of Robert Holcot, and like Holcot both a student and a lecturer at Merton College in Oxford. Among his interests at Merton were theology and mathematics. In an early treatise, *De proportionibus velocitatum in motibus* (1328), Bradwardine asserted that an arithmetic increase in velocity corresponds with a geometric increase in the original ratio of force to resistance. Although his assertion was incorrect, it remained the dominant view in European theories of mechanics for over a century.

While still at Merton College, Bradwardine came under the strong influence of Pelagian orthodoxy, and began to struggle with the matters of grace and free will. He concluded that God's grace precedes human free will and began writing his chief treatise against the Pelagians while still at Merton College. In 1335,

Bradwardine left Merton College and joined the bishop of Durham, Richard de Bury. It was here that Bradwardine encountered one of the richest libraries in medieval England as well as a very stimulating and learned group of theologians, including the future archbishop of Armagh, Richard FitzRalph, and Bradwardine's old friend and theological opponent, Robert Holcot.

In 1337, Bradwardine was appointed chancellor of Saint Paul's Cathedral, London, where he completed his major work, *The Case of God Against Pelagius*. In this work, Bradwardine emphasized the prevenience of God's grace. Reviving the study of Augustine,* he wrote that God's eternal predestination selected those elect who would receive God's prevenient grace and thus be freed from the bondage to sin. This gift of God's grace was not offered on the grounds of some foreseen human effort but simply on the basis of God's own election. For Bradwardine, the offer of this grace implied an acceptance on the part of the believer, but that acceptance was directly aided by God's grace and was not possible without it. Therefore, every act of the individual was preceded by, and related to, God's special act of grace.

This led to the major criticism of Bradwardine's work—God's determinism. Using the image of the "potter and the pot" (Rom 9:21), Bradwardine insisted that human beings were dependent upon God for determining all of their actions. This interpretation left little or no room for human rebellion against God. Bradwardine's reliance on Augustine, and his emphasis on grace, influenced the Reformation theologians in the next century.

Bradwardine continued to serve in the church as royal chaplain and subsequently as confessor to King Edward III. In 1349, he was consecrated archbishop of Canterbury in Avignon, but died thirty-eight days later from the Black Death.

Bibliography

A. *De causa Dei contra Pelagium et de virtute causarum ad suos Mertonenses, libri tres*, ed. H. Savile (London, 1618).

B. DMA 2:357–59; DTC 15:765–73; LThK² 10:137–38; NCE 14:116; ODCC 231; Justus F. Laun, "Thomas von Bradwardin: Der Schüler Augustins und Lehrer Wiclifs," ZKG 47 (1928): 333–56; idem, "Die Praedestination bei Wiclif und Bradwardin," in *Imago Dei: Festschrift für G. Krüger*, ed. H. Bornkamm (Giessen, 1932), 63–84; Gordon Leff, *Bradwardine and the Pelagians* (Cambridge, 1957); Heiko Oberman, *Archbishop Thomas Bradwardine, A Fourteenth-Century Augustinian: A Study of His Theology in its Historical Context* (Utrecht, 1957); idem, "Thomas Bradwardine: Un précurseur de Luther?" RHPhR 40 (1960): 146–51.

Peter W. Breitsch

BRENZ, JOHANNES (1499, Weil der Stadt, Germany–10 September, 1570, Stuttgart, Germany). *Education*: studied at Univ. of Heidelberg, 1518–19. *Career*: lecturer on Scriptures, Heidelberg, 1519–22; town preacher, priest, Lutheran Reformer, Schwäbisch Hall, 1522–48; advisor, Dukes of Württemberg, 1548–70.

Brenz heard Martin Luther* at the Heidelberg Disputation of 1518 and became an advocate of the new evangelical theology. He had a role in developing the constitutions of the Lutheran Reformation in several German jurisdictions. He helped launch the Lutheran attack upon Zwingli's* symbolic interpretation of the Lord's Supper and upheld the Lutheran concept of the real bodily presence of Christ in the Lord's Supper. Brenz's two Christological treatises utilized the doctrine of the communication of attributes to state that the two natures of Christ participate in each other's reality. He affirmed that God the Son really shared in the death on the cross and the baby in the manger truly was the creator of the world. Brenz emphasized this realistic notion of the hypostatic union, against Zwingli's and Melanchthon's* verbal interpretation of the communication of attributes. He also attempted to distinguish his doctrine from Monophysitism. Lutheran orthodoxy rejected his Christology as paradoxical. However, Brenz sensed that Christ's divine participation in human suffering and human participation in divine exaltation is salvific. Similar approaches have resurfaced in nineteenth-century "kenotic" theology and twentieth-century considerations of the suffering of God.

Bibliography

A. *Operum Reverendi et Clarissimi Theologi, D. Ioannis Brentii, Praepositi Stutgardiani*, 8 vols. (Tübingen, 1576–90); *Frühschriften*, ed. Martin Brecht et al., 2 vols. (Tübingen, 1970–74); *Die christologischen Schriften*, vol. 1, ed. Theodor Mahlmann (Tübingen, 1981).

B. LThK³ 2:675–76; NCE 2:786; ODCC 235; OEncR 1:214–15; TRE 7:170–81; Martin Brecht, *Die frühe Theologie des Johannes Brenz* (Stuttgart, 1971); Eric Gritsch and Robert W. Jenson, *Lutheranism* (Philadelphia, 1976); Hans Christian Brandy, *Die späte Christologie des Johannes Brenz* (Tübingen, 1991).

Melvin G. Vance

BRIGGS, CHARLES AUGUSTUS (15 January 1841, New York City–8 June 1913, New York City). *Education*: Univ. of Virginia, 1858–61; The Union Theol. Sem., New York City (hereafter, UTS), 1861–63; Univ. of Berlin, 1866–69. *Career*: Presbyterian pastor, Roselle, N.J., 1870–74; professor of Hebrew and Cognate Languages, UTS, 1874–91; coeditor (for UTS), *The Presbyterian Review*, 1880–89; Edward Robinson professor of biblical theology, UTS, 1891–1904; tried for heresy in church courts of the Presbyterian Church, 1892–93; suspended from the Presbyterian ministry, 1893; ordained Episcopal priest, 1899; professor of theological encyclopedia and symbolics, UTS, 1904–13.

Briggs was the foremost Protestant biblical scholar in late-nineteenth-century America as well as one of the earliest (and most controversial) voices in the American ecumenical movement in the early twentieth century. He is best known, however, for his "heresy trial" of 1892–93. Brigg's inaugural address, "The Authority of Holy Scripture," delivered at UTS on the evening of January 20, 1891, and the ensuing series of "heresy trials" that it unleashed between

1892 and 1893 have been termed "the most notorious event in nineteenth-century American church history." Many historians of American religion rank the "Briggs Case" (as the address and trials are collectively designated), along with the Salem Witchcraft Trials of 1691 and the "Monkey Trial" in Dayton, Tennessee, in 1925, as the most important religious trials in American history.

Converted as an undergraduate to "heart religion," Briggs remained committed throughout his turbulent life to the evangelical values that emerged from that experience. Briggs' ministerial education in New York under Edward Robinson and Henry Boynton Smith, and his further study at the University of Berlin with Isaac Dorner, however, helped Briggs to recognize the intellectual threat posed by historical criticism—especially as that criticism was applied to the Bible in "higher criticism"—to American evangelical culture.

As a teacher and scholar at UTS for close to forty years, Briggs devoted his entire personal and professional career to reconciling the seemingly irreconcilable claims of evangelicalism and historical criticism in a succession of much-heralded and often controversial scholarly works: his work as seminary librarian as well as his manuscript research tracing the Puritan roots of his own denomination led to the publication of *American Presbyterianism* and close to thirty articles on American religious history. His reputation as the foremost biblical scholar in late-nineteenth-century America was founded on a succession of important and ground-breaking works like *Biblical Study* and *General Introduction to the Study of Holy Scripture* as well as on standard biblical reference works like the *International Critical Commentary* and the magisterial *Hebrew and English Lexicon of the Old Testament* (still used today).

Invited in 1891 to inaugurate a new chair named in memory of one of his teachers at Union (Robinson), Briggs delivered what is perhaps the most famous inaugural address in American religious history. Briggs' address, which advocated the use of the historical-critical method among mainline American Protestants in understanding the Bible, marked the arrival of biblical criticism as a neuralgic issue among American Protestants and helped to define the fault line between emerging camps of theological modernists and Fundamentalists. The address immediately set off a firestorm of criticism, leading directly to heresy charges against Briggs in the Presbytery of New York and in the General Assemby of the Presbyterian Church. Along with the "Henry Ward Beecher Case," the Briggs Case was nineteenth-century America's most publicized ecclesiastical event. After a series of bitter and closely fought courtroom trials, Briggs was suspended from the ministry, entered the Episcopal Church, and spent the remaining twenty years of his life working for church union.

Bibliography

A. *American Presbyterianism: Its Origin and Early History* (New York, 1885); *The Authority of Holy Scripture: An Inaugural Address* (New York, 1891); *Biblical Study: Its Principles, Methods, and History* (New York, 1883); *Church Unity: Studies of Its Most Important Problems* (New York, 1909); *General Introduction to the Study of Holy*

Scripture (New York, 1899); *Whither? A Theological Question for the Times* (New York, 1889); with Francis Brown and S. R. Driver, *A Hebrew and English Lexicon of the Old Testament, with an Appendix Containing the Biblical Aramaic* (Boston, 1906); with S. R. Driver and A. Plummer, *International Critical Commentary on the Holy Scriptures of the Old and New Testaments* (New York, 1895ff.).

B. . DAB 3:40–41; NCAB 7:318–19; NCE 2:802; NYT 9 June 1913, 1; SH 2:270–71; Richard L. Christensen, *The Ecumenical Orthodoxy of Charles Augustus Briggs* (Lewiston, N.Y., 1995); Mark S. Massa, *Charles Augustus Briggs and the Crisis of Historical Criticism* (Minneapolis, Minn., 1990); Max Rogers, "Charles A. Briggs: Conservative Heretic," Ph.D. diss., Columbia Univ., 1964; George Shriver, *American Religious Heretics* (Nashville, Tenn., 1966).

Mark S. Massa

BROWN, WILLIAM ADAMS (29 December 1865, New York City–15 December 1943, New York City). *Education*: B.A., Yale, 1886; M.A., Yale, 1888; Union Theol. Sem. New York City (hereafter, UTS), 1887–90; Univ. of Berlin, 1890–92; Ph.D., Yale, 1901. *Career*: ordained Presbyterian minister, 1893; lecturer, UTS, 1893–98; professor of systematic theology, UTS, 1898–1930; research professor in Applied Christianity, UTS, 1930–36; executive Secretary of the General War-Time Commission of the Churches (of the Federal Council of Churches of Christ), 1917; first chairman of the Department of Research and Education, Federal Council of Churches, 1924; president, Religious Education Association, 1928–31; retirement, 1936–43.

Brown was a modernist Presbyterian theologian and teacher, leader in the American ecumenical movement in the first three decades of the twentieth century, moving spirit behind the formation of the Federal Council of Churches of Christ in America (now the National Council of Churches), and one of the chief architects of the World Council of Churches. Studying under Charles Briggs* at UTS and Adolf Harnack* in Berlin, Brown absorbed the ideal of church unity from both, and spent his ministerial and professorial careers advancing the cause of social reform and ecumenism, which were linked in his thought. From his Berlin studies Brown likewise developed a lifelong loyalty to Albrecht Ritschl's* belief that the "essence of Christianity" lay in experience and not in dogma, and that the experience of God's redemptive power is "as positive a fact as any of those which enter into the catalogue of the positivist philospher." Indeed, he asserted that more evidence existed for the reality of God as savior than could be adduced for many of the conclusions of physics or biology.

A lifelong organizer and leader in reform crusades, Brown was one of a group of UTS alumni who founded Union Settlement House (N.Y.C.), worked in the 1904 anti-Tammany Hall campaign led by the Reverend Charles Parkhurst, assisted Charles Stelzle in founding the Labor Temple (N.Y.C.), and was a member of the "Committee of Fourteen" investigating commercialized vice in New York City.

Brown regarded church unity as both a spiritual necessity and a precondition for effective pastoral outreach, especially in the urban ministry of bringing ethnic, racial, and class groups together for the cause of social reform. He was a leader in the American delegation to the ''Universal Christian Conference on Life and Work,'' held in Stockholm in 1925 and was responsible for planning the ''World Conference on Faith and Order'' at Lausanne in 1927. He brought both of these groups together in Britain in 1937, a union which culminated in the organization of the World Council of Churches in 1938.

Bibliography

A.   *Christian Theology in Outline* (New York, 1906); *The Essence of Christianity: A Study in the History of Definition* (New York, 1902); *Is Christianity Practicable?* (New York, 1916); *A Teacher and His Times: A Story of Two Worlds* (New York, 1940).

B.   DAB 3:110–11; DARB 71–72; NCE 2:825; NYT 16 December 1943, 27; *The Church Through Half a Century: Essays in Honor of William Adams Brown*, ed. Samuel McCrea Cavert and Henry Van Dusen (New York, 1936).

Mark S. Massa

BROWNSON, ORESTES AUGUSTUS (16 September 1803, Stockbridge, Vt.–17 April 1876, Detroit, Mich.). *Education*: studied at Balston Academy, Balston Spa, N.Y., 1818–19; read theology with Samuel Loveland, Reading, Vt., 1825–26. *Career*: school teacher, Detroit, Mich.; Elbridge, N.Y., 1824–25; ordained Universalist Minister, Jaffrey, N.H., 1826; Universalist preacher, Hartland, Vt., Lichtfield, Ithaca, Geneva, Auburn, N.Y., 1826–30; editor, *Gospel Advocate and Impartial Investigator*, 1829; corresponding editor, *The Free Enquirer*, 1829–30; editor, *Genesee Republican and Herald of Reform*, 1830; unaffiliated minister, Ithaca, 1831; founding editor, *The Philanthropist*, 1831–32; Unitarian minister, Walpole, N.H., 1832–34; Canton, Mass., 1834–36; editor, *The Boston Reformer*, 1836–38; organizer and minister, the Society for Christian Union and Progress, Boston, 1836–38; founding editor, *Boston Quarterly Review*, 1838–42; staff, *United States Magazine and Democratic Review*, 1842–44; founding editor, *Brownson's Quarterly Review*, 1844–64, 1873–75; independent journalist and author, 1844–76.

Brownson was primarily a self-taught religious thinker who before his conversion to Catholicism in 1844 had embraced a variety of religious positions that reflected some of the plasticity of religious culture in the United States during the early nineteenth century. He identified himself first with the Presbyterian tradition and then he moved to Universalism to social radicalism to Unitarianism and to Transcendentalism. The ambit of his early theological orientations was fixed by the discussions taking place in the Reformed tradition in America. Throughout this religious and intellectual journey he sought to reconcile two doctrines he found intermittently attractive: the sovereignty and benevolent fatherhood of God and the freedom of the human person. During his twenties, influenced by the Universalist and rationalist-Deist traditions, he emphasized human freedom and free scientific inquiry into the Christian tradition.

By his early thirties he began to appropriate a romantic reaction to the excessive rationalism of his early years and began to emphasize the transcendental spirit of Christian individualism, associating himself with the Unitarianism of William Ellery Channing.* By his early forties, under the influence of the French St. Simonian Pierre Leroux, he moved away from the Universalist and Unitarian liberal Christian tradition and the Romantic individualism of Transcendentalism toward an emphasis upon ecclesial communion and tradition, emphasizing, like a number of other conservative religious reformers during the 1840s, the necessity of the church in the process of salvation, sanctification, and reform. This change in his theological perspective led him into the Catholic Church in 1844.

From 1844 until his death in 1876, Brownson became the foremost American Catholic lay theologian and philosopher, developing in dialectical fashion a concept of "life by communion" that he appropriated in 1842 from Pierre Leroux and that he modified in the 1850s under the influence of the Italian ontologist Vincenzo Gioberti* (1801–52). For Brownson, God's creative act established a dialectical harmonious communion between God and the human subject. That divine creative act was manifested most perfectly and most definitively in the Incarnation of the Word. The continuing presence of the Incarnate Word was made manifest in the church. The church thus became the medium through which God's creative act and the Incarnation bound a community of believers organically and transcendentally to God, Christ, each other, and history. Thus, the church was for him an historical organism that continually sought to appropriate and to express in outward tradition the inner tradition of God's creative and Incarnate Word.

In a variety of ways and with obvious as well as subtle changes, Brownson applied his doctrine of the dialectical harmony of the divine and the human to his understanding of the individual, the church, society, literature, democratic government and politics, and the emerging industrial and economic order. In the period before the Civil War he focused upon the necessity of the church for salvation and for societal peace and harmony. In the period after the war he, like Pope Pius IX, concentrated his intellectual guns upon what he perceived to be a rising secularism in science, politics, education, and religion. Although he criticized the direction of American society after the war, he emphasized the necessity of preserving in dialectical harmony and tension the American spirit of freedom and the Catholic sense of authority and community.

Bibliography

A. *The Works of Orestes A. Brownson*, ed. Henry F. Brownson, 20 vols. (Detroit, Mich., 1882–87); *Boston Quarterly Review*, 1838–42; *Brownson's Quarterly Review*, 1843–65, 1873–75; *Selected Writings: Orestes A. Brownson*, ed. Patrick W. Carey (New York, 1991); *Orestes A. Brownson: A Bibliography, 1826–1876*, comp. Patrick W. Carey (Milwaukee, Wis., 1997).

B. DAB 3:178–79; DARB, 72–74; NCAB 7:197; NCE 2:827–29; NYT 18 April 1876, 7; SH 2:281; Henry F. Brownson, *Life of Orestes Brownson*, 3 vols. (Detroit,

Mich., 1898–1900); Arthur M. Schlesinger, Jr., *Orestes A. Brownson: A Pilgrim's Progress* (Boston, 1939); Theodore Maynard, *Orestes Brownson: Yankee, Radical Catholic* (New York, 1943); Americo D. Lapati, *Orestes A. Brownson* (New York, 1965); Thomas R. Ryan, *Orestes A. Brownson: A Definitive Biography* (Huntington, Ind., 1976).

Patrick W. Carey

BRUNNER, H. EMIL (23 December 1889, Winterthur, Switzerland–6 April 1966, Zurich). *Education*: Univs. of Zurich and Berlin, 1908–10; Ph.D., Univ. of Zurich, 1912. *Career*: English teacher, Leeds, England; vicar with Herman Kütter, Neumünster, Zurich; pastor, Obstalden, Glarus, 1916–24; professor of systematic and practical theology, Univ. of Zurich, 1924–55; guest professor, Princeton Sem., N.J., 1938–39; visiting professor of Christianity and Ethics, International Christian Univ., Tokyo, 1953–55.

Brunner was one of the most influential theologians in the world during the mid-twentieth century. Although overshadowed in many ways by his Swiss compatriot, Karl Barth,* from approximately 1930 to 1960 he was the most widely read theologian in the English-speaking world. Already in the 1920s Brunner was invited to give lectures at theological schools in the Netherlands and in the United States, and in the 1930s in England, Scotland, Hungary, and Scandinavia. Several of his key works—*The Mediator* (Philadelphia, 1934), *The Divine Imperative* (Philadelphia, 1937), and *Man in Revolt* (Philadelphia, 1939)—were standard texts in many Protestant seminaries in Great Britain, North America, and Asia.

This popularity and influence were due not only to his scholarship and his role as one of the leaders in the movement variously known as dialectical theology or neo-orthodoxy but also to the accessibility and lucidity of his theological writings. In his theology he also relates a thoroughgoing Christocentrism to contemporary social and political situations.

Early influences in Brunner's development were his Swiss nationality and the Reformed tradition, particularly as mediated by the Swiss reformer, Ulrich Zwingli.* He was also indebted to Luther* and Calvin,* but his view of the church and sacraments is closer to that of Zwingli.

A third early influence was that of the Religious Socialist Movement whose founders were two German Lutheran pastors, the Blumhardts, father and son. They were concerned about social and political reforms, but unlike their liberal contemporaries, they were Christologically oriented and gave more place to the work of the Holy Spirit in their vision of the Kingdom of God.

Later influences in the shaping of Brunner's theology were the phenomenology of Husserl, the I-Thou philosophy of Ferdinand Ebner and Martin Buber, and above all the Christian existentialism of Søren Kierkegaard.*

This new approach to theology was worked out for the first time in Brunner's seminal study originally given as lectures in Upsala, Sweden in 1936: ''Wahrheit als Begegnung,'' first published in English as *The Divine Human Encounter* in 1943 and later entitled more accurately in an expanded edition in 1964 as *Truth as Encounter*. Here Brunner developed what he regarded as "the Christian concept of truth, truth as encounter, revelation conceived as God's self-communication."

This central motif in Brunner's theology is simple insofar as it points to a meeting or experience of another person, but it is complex in that "encounter" is Brunner's way of relating revelation and faith, the Truth (Jesus Christ) and truth, Word as event and Word as doctrine. As he explains in *Truth as Encounter*,

To know God in trustful obedience is not only to *know* the truth, but through God's self-communication to *be* in it, in the truth that as love is at the same time fellowship. The truth about man is founded in the divine humanity of Christ, which we apprehend in faith in Christ, the Word of God. This is truth as encounter. . . . Here *truth happens*, here we *are* in the truth, which is not in us but comes to us, which makes us free by restoring to us our true being, our being in the Thou, and our being for the Thou. In this truth as encounter, in which we understand our personal being as being in the love of the Creator and Redeemer . . . to have and to be are one.

Brunner believed that this personalistic, existential notion of truth as encounter was a fruitful—and biblical—alternative to the liberalism and subjectivism of Schleiermacher* and the intellectualistic objectivism found in traditional Roman Catholicism and orthodox Protestantism. Against the former he posited the once-for-all (*einmalige*) character of revelation as a historical event centering in Jesus Christ. Against the latter he pointed out that revelation is not primarily a doctrine but an act. To use another of his favorite phrases, revelation is a "personal correspondence" between God and humanity. "God does not reveal this and that—he reveals Himself by communicating Himself" (*Christianity and Civilization* I).

Despite his insistence on the personal character of revelation and its correlate, faith, Brunner did not deny the importance of doctrine. In a chapter in *Truth as Encounter* titled "Doctrine As Token and Framework, Indissolubly Connected with the Reality It Represents" he explains:

God, to be sure, does not deliver to us a course of lectures in dogmatic theology or submit a confession of faith to us, but he *instructs* us authentically about himself. . . . Consequently, we can never abstract the abstract framework from the personal Presence contained in it, although certainly we must differentiate them.

Brunner's theological contributions extend also to the fields of epistemology, anthropology, Christology, personal and social ethics, eschatology and eristics (Brunner's preferred approach to apologetics), as well as helpful treatments of the standard topics in theology.

Brunner was no armchair theologian; in an intriguing variety of ways he lived out his apologetic, pastoral, and missionary concerns. He was active in local church life, preaching once a month in his home church, the Fraumünster; he also supported a variety of church renewal movements: the Oxford Movement, the YMCA, the nonchurch movement in Japan (*Mukyōkai*), and the lay academy movement in Switzerland.

His crowning achievement in this regard was his appointment in 1953 as the first visiting professor of Christianity and ethics at the recently organized International Christian University in Tokyo. The two-year stay in Japan was exciting and fruitful, although it took its toll on his health.

Brunner's theology, like that of many of his distinguished contemporaries, is now in eclipse. Most of his works are out of print, and the present generation of theological students hardly recognizes his name. He is best known today for his famous dispute with Karl Barth concerning a "point of contact" (*Anknüpfungspunkt*) for the gospel in the consciousness of "natural man" and the nature of the theological task. This division began in 1929 and came to a climax in 1934 when Brunner published a monograph, *Nature and Grace: Discussion with Karl Barth*, to which Barth responded with a sharp rebuttal entitled *Nein!* (*No!*).

Brunner's influence continued indirectly through his former students and their impact on a later generation. His influence is seen more directly in the late-twentieth-century theologies of evangelical theologians such as Donald Bloesch and Paul Jewett.

Bibliography

A. *Dogmatics*, 3 vols. (Philadelphia, 1950–60).

B. NCE 16:42–43; ODCC 144; TRE 7:236–42; *The Theology of Emil Brunner*, ed. Charles W. Kegley, (New York, 1962); J. Edward Humphrey, *Emil Brunner* (Peabody, Mass., 1976); Hans Heinrich Brunner, *Mein Vater und sein Ältester* (Zurich, 1986); *Emil Brunner in der Erinnerung seiner Schüler* (Zurich, 1989).

I. John Hesselink

BUCER, MARTIN (11 November 1491, Schlettstadt in Alsace–28 February 1551, Cambridge, England). *Education*: instructed as a Dominican friar in Schlettstadt, 1507–17; sent to Heidelberg in 1517 to acquire his doctorate. *Career*: ordained priest, 1521; pastor, Landstuhl, 1521–23; excommunicated, 1523; pastor in Strasbourg, 1524–48; head of clergy, Strasbourg, 1531–48; regius professor of theology, Cambridge, 1549–51.

Bucer was a German Reformed theologian and church leader known for his work in the city of Strasbourg. While studying in Heidelberg as a Dominican he became attracted to humanism and to the theology of Luther,* whom he heard at the disputation there in 1518. He obtained release from his vows and became a secular priest in 1521, married, and was excommunicated in 1523 for trying to initiate reforms in Alsace. He emigrated to Strasbourg, and by the early 1540s was established as a major Protestant leader.

A theological moderate, Bucer tried to reconcile Protestant factions, especially on the issue of the Eucharist. He accepted a real, though not local, presence in the sacrament, even if he was closer to Zwingli* than to Luther, something the latter was quick to recognize. Bucer agreed with Melanchthon* on the Cassel Formula (1534), which decreed that Christ's body and the sacramental bread were one, and accepted the Wittenberg Concord (1536), which produced an agreement among the imperial cities of southern Germany on the nature of the real presence. He was willing to recognize different points of emphasis among Protestants but believed that all were agreed on substantive issues. His attempts at ecclesiastical reconciliation also extended beyond the Protestant camps, as he often tried—unsuccessfully—to bring together Catholics and Protestants.

An emphasis on sanctification is noticeable in Bucer's theology from his earliest works as he stressed the gift of Christian love, which enabled believers to live according to God's plan through the aid of the Holy Spirit. He also wrote several works on pastoral theology and throughout his career was occupied with social and political issues. He was very active as an ecclesiastical and political adviser, not only in southern Germany but also in France and England.

Bibliography

A.   *Martini Buceri Scripta Anglicana fere omnia*, ed. C. Hubert (Basel, 1577); *Correspondance de Martin Bucer*, ed. Jean Rott, 2 vols. (Leiden, 1979–); *Martin Bucer's Deutsche Schriften*, ed. Robert Stupperich, 10 vols. (Gütersloh, 1960–); *Martini Buceri Opera Latina*, ed. François Wendel et al., 5 vols. (Paris and Leiden, 1954–).

B.   DNB 7:172–77; LThK³ 2:739; ODCC 246–47; OEncR 1:221–24; TRE 7:258–70; Constantin Hopf, *Martin Bucer and the English Reformation* (Oxford, 1946); Jean Rott, *Investigationes Historicae*, ed. M. de Kroon and M. Leinhard, 2 vols. (Strasbourg, 1986); W. P. Stephens, *The Holy Spirit in the Theology of Martin Bucer* (Cambridge, 1970); Martin Greschat, *Martin Bucer. Ein Reformator und seine Zeit* (Munich, 1990).

Anthony D. DiStefano

BUGENHAGEN, JOHANNES (24 June 1485, Pomerania–20 April 1558, Wittenberg, Germany). *Education*: classics, Univ. of Greifswald, 1502–10; studied at Univ. of Wittenberg, 1521; doctorate in theology, Univ. of Wittenberg, 1533. *Career*: ordained priest, 1509; lecturer on Bible, monastery sch., Belbuck, Germany, 1517–20; pastor, Wittenberg, 1523–57; professor of theology, Univ. of Wittenberg, 1535–58.

Bugenhagen is perhaps best known as Martin Luther's* pastor and confessor, but his own ecclesiastical and biblical efforts also played a key role in the Protestant Reformation. He was a key translator for the Wittenberg reformation. Literally, he became a member of the editorial board for Luther's German Bible and in 1524 translated its New Testament into Low German. Figuratively, he was the translator of Luther's theological insights into the practice of congregational life. Because of his knowledge of the language, he frequently assisted in the ecclesiastical reforms of the territories to the north, writing church orders and ordaining superintendents to replace the deposed Catholic bishops. Though specific to each context, each of the church orders addressed three areas: (1) liturgical reforms, (2) the revitalization of education, and (3) the establishment of a relief system for the poor. His organizational genius was the balance he found between maintaining the autonomy of each congregation and providing for their supervision.

Highly regarded in Bugenhagen's own day but soon forgotten were his treatises and his commentaries. He was the first of the Wittenberg group to respond to Zwingli's* symbolic understanding of the Lord's Supper. In 1525 he wrote an open letter to the city of Hamburg, *Of the Christian Life and Proper Good Works*, which became a key summary of the Wittenberg Theology. In 1524 he published his most popular biblical work, *Harmony of the Accounts of the Passion and Resurrection*. Throughout his career he wrote biblical commentaries, including works on Psalms, Paul's letters and Matthew.

Bibliography

A. *Die evangelischen Kirchenordnungen des XVI. Jahrhunderts*, ed. Emil Sehling, 15 vols. (Tübingen, 1902–80), see vols. 4–7; *Dr. Johannes Bugenhagens Briefwechsel*, ed. Otto Vogt (Stettin, 1888–99).

B. NCE 2:860–61; ODCC 248; OEncR 1:226–27; TRE 7:354–63; *Bibliotheca Bugenhagiana*, ed. Georg Geisenhof (Leipzig, 1908); Karl A. T. Vogt, *Johannes Bugenhagen Pomeranus* (Elberfeld, 1867); Ernst Wolf, "Johannes Bugenhagen, Gemeinde und Amt," in *Peregrinatio* (Munich, 1954).

Troy Pflibsen

BULLINGER, HEINRICH (18 July 1504, Bremgarten–17 September 1574, Zurich). *Education*: B.A., M.A., Univ. of Cologne, 1520, 1522. *Career*: head teacher, Cistercian monastery, Kappel, 1523; pastor, Bremgarten, 1529–31; chief pastor, Zurich, 1531–74.

Bullinger is known chiefly as Zwingli's* successor as the leader of the Reformed Church in Zurich. While a student at Cologne he became interested in the theological controversies surrounding Luther and began a study of patristic theology, Luther's* early treatises, Melanchthon's* *Loci Communes*, and the New Testament. By 1522 he was committed to the Reformation.

In 1523 Bullinger became head teacher at the monastery at Kappel. There he wrote commentaries on most of the books of the New Testament and helped further the reform of the monastery. In 1525 the Mass was abolished there, and the next year the Reformed Eucharist was celebrated. Bullinger replaced his father as pastor at Bremgarten in 1529, and in late 1531 was appointed as Zwingli's successor as chief pastor in Zurich. Here he spent the rest of his life preaching, writing, caring for refugees, and trying to solidify and extend the reforms introduced by Zwingli.

Among Bullinger's writings his *Decades*, a collection of his sermons, provides the best summary of his theology. He wrote a history of the Swiss Reformation up to 1532, tracts against Lutherans and Anabaptists, and numerous theological treatises. He also collaborated with John Calvin* on the *Consensus Tigurinus* (1549), which helped to settle dogmatic disputes in Switzerland, and in 1566 published the Second Helvetic Confession, which was widely accepted throughout Protestant Europe and is one of the most comprehensive Reformed creeds. Bullinger's voluminous correspondence, along with his writings, helped to extend his influence in Europe.

The most distinctive part of Bullinger's theology is his teaching on the covenant, which is found in many of his works. He taught that God established one covenant with his people, and it remained the same throughout both testaments and into contemporary times. It was conditional in that God required his people to have faith in him and to love their neighbors. This view of the covenant established for Bullinger the unity of the chosen people in all ages, as well as the unity of the two testaments.

Bibliography

A.   *Werke* (Zurich, 1972–92); *Heinrich Bullingers Diarium der Jahre 1504–1574* (Basel, 1904); *Heinrich Bullinger Werke*, Pt. 1, *Bibliographie*. vol. 1, *Beschreibendes Verzeichnis der gedruckten Werke von Heinrich Bullinger*, ed. Joachim Staedtke (Zurich, 1972); *Heinrich Bullinger Werke*, Pt. 2, *Briefwechsel*, 5 vols. (Zurich, 1973–).
B.   DHGE 10:1210–11; LThK³ 2:778–79; NCE 2:883; ODCC 249–50; OEncR 1: 227–30; TRE 7:375–87; J. Wayne Baker, *Heinrich Bullinger and the Covenant: The Other Reformed Tradition* (Athens, Ohio, 1980); Fritz Blanke and Immanuel Leuschner, *Heinrich Bullinger: Vater der reformierten Kirche* (Zurich, 1990); Walter Hollweg, *Heinrich Bullingers Hausbook: Eine Untersuchung über die Anfänge der reformierten Predigtliteratur* (Neukirchen-Vluyn, 1956); Carl Pestalozzi, *Heinrich Bullinger* (Elberfeld, 1858); Joachim Staedtke, *Die Theologie des jungen Bullinger* (Zurich, 1962).

Anthony D. DiStefano

BULTMANN, RUDOLF (20 August 1884, Wiefelstede, Oldenburg–30 July 1976, Marburg). *Education*: studied at Tübingen, 1903–4; Berlin, 1905; and Marburg, 1906, where he received his Diploma, 1907, and Dr.Theol., 1910. *Career*: Privatdozent, Marburg, 1912–16; professor, Breslau, 1916–20; Giessen, 1920–21; Marburg, 1921–51; retirement 1951–76.

German New Testament exegete who combined historical, theological, and philosophical concerns to articulate a position that played a central role in Protestant, and increasingly in Catholic, theological debates in the twentieth century. Son and grandson of Lutheran pastors and missionaries, a Lutheran pastor himself, he was the heir of the liberal theological tradition represented by his teachers J. Weiss, A. von Harnack,* W. Herrmann,* and H. Gunkel.

With M. Dibelius and K. L. Schmidt, his early work sought to apply to the synoptic gospels the methods of *Formgeschichte*, which had been developed primarily by Gunkel in the study of the Old Testament and first identified as important for understanding the New Testament by Weiss. Bultmann argued in *Die Geschichte der synoptischen Tradition* (1921) that the gospel narratives we now possess are best seen as collections of individual literary units strung together like beads on a string. These units, which can be identified by their characteristic forms, were initially the product of the oral traditions of the earliest

Christian communities who created and shaped the Jesus material to serve their devotional and apologetic needs. In the process, as he later claimed, the historical person of Jesus was thoroughly "mythologized" (i.e., interpreted according to the mythological worldview of antiquity). As a consequence, although we can infer much about the early Christian communities from the gospel traditions, "we can now know almost nothing concerning the life and personality of Jesus" (*Jesus*, 1926).

That historical skepticism was for Bultmann, however, not the end but the beginning of the matter. It cleared the ground for what he took to be the true theological issue concerning knowledge of Jesus Christ: not what historical science can recover concerning the man who lived long ago, but what the Evangelical proclamation about that individual means for us today. The theological task is therefore not that of history but of interpretation (i.e. of enabling those who live here and now to hear the word of God addressed to humanity in Jesus Christ there and then). The problem, he believed, is that the mythology of the New Testament stands in the way of such a hearing. "It is impossible to use electric light and the wireless and to avail ourselves of modern medical and surgical discoveries," he wrote in his seminal essay, *Neues Testament und Mythologie* (1941), "and at the same time to believe in the New Testament world of demons and spirits." Thus, in order to make the New Testament comprehensible to modern, scientifically minded individuals, he proposed a hermeneutical program of "demythologizing" the New Testament, in which what he took to be its kerygmatic substance—the new human self-understanding arising out of God's decisive activity in Jesus Christ—is separated from its ancient mythological form and interpreted according to that form of contemporary discourse that he believed best represents the substance of New Testament proclamation: the existentialist philosophy of the early M. Heidegger of *Sein und Zeit*.

Bultmann's thought represents at its core, therefore, a struggle with the modern questions of faith and history. He understood his work as a positive appropriation and critical advance on the liberal theological tradition in which he was schooled. The hermeneutical program he proposed was, he claimed, implicit in the nature of myth itself and already emergent in the New Testament, above all in the Johannine and Pauline literature. Moreover, in his response to the modern question of knowledge of Christ, he believed himself to be faithful to the Evangelical doctrine of *justificatio fidei* in offering a modern understanding of the burden of Pauline, Augustinian, and Lutheran theology.

Bibliography

A. *History of the Synoptic Tradition*, rev. ed., trans. J. Marsh (New York, 1963); *Jesus and the Word*, trans. L. P. Smith and E. H. Lantero (New York, 1958); *Theology of the New Testament*, trans. K. Grobel (New York, 1951 and 1958); "New Testament and Mythology," in: *Kerygma and Myth*, ed. H. W. Bartsch, trans. R. H. Fuller (New York, 1961); *History and Eschatology: The Presence of Eternity* (New York, 1957).

B. LThK³ 2:768–69; ODCC 209–10; TRE 7: 387–96; Norman Perrin, *The Promise of Bultmann* (Philadelphia, 1979); Walter Schmithals, *An Introduction to the Theology of Rudolf Bultmann*, trans. J. Bowden (Minneapolis, Minn., 1968); John Painter, *Theology as Hermeneutics: Rudolf Bultmann's Interpretation of the History of Jesus* (Sheffield, England, 1987); Klaus Hollmann, *Existenz und Glaube; Entwicklung und Ergebnisse der Bultmann-Diskussion in der katholischen Theologie* (Paderborn, 1972); Eberhard Jüngel, *Glauben und Verstehen: zum Theologiebegriff Rudolf Bultmanns* (Heidelberg, 1985).

D. Lyle Dabney

BUSHNELL, HORACE (14 April 1802, Bantam, Conn.–17 February 1876, Hartford, Conn.). *Education*: B.A., Yale Coll., 1827; studied at Yale Law Sch., 1829–31; B.D., Yale Sem., 1833. *Career*: school teacher and journalist, Conn. and N.Y., 1827–29; tutor, Yale Coll., 1829–31; minister, North Congregational Church, Hartford, Conn., 1833–59; travel and writing, 1859–76.

A Congregationalist minister from Hartford, Connecticut, Bushnell was perhaps the most innovative American Protestant theologian of the nineteenth century. As a theologian, Bushnell, like Friedrich Schleiermacher* and F. D. Maurice,* inspired a paradigmatic shift in nineteenth-century theology. As the "father" of American Protestant liberalism, he nurtured later liberals and Social Gospel advocates like Theodore Munger,* Washington Gladden,* and Walter Rauschenbusch.* Progressing beyond dogmatic scholasticism, he claimed that all doctrinal/theological disputes resulted from an improper understanding of language. For him language was symbolic, and therefore particular dogmatic construals were but fragments of a larger "comprehensive" theological truth. Theological language, if it is indeed "biblical," should not consist of rigid literal or "scientific" definitions and metaphysical speculation but embrace the "comprehesiveness" of paradox and polarity. Hence, unlike traditional orthodoxy, Bushnell's method fostered a theology "from below" and a Christocentric perspective. Logically arguing from the human to the divine, he claimed the divine mystery of the trinitarian God can only be understood through its symbolic (human) manifestation in the life and death of Jesus; it is Jesus, as the Christ, who discloses the Father, Son, and Spirit. Likewise, Christ's suffering, in the Atonement, reveals the loving, not punishing, nature of God's eternal character. Divine-human reconciliation can only occur when both God and humanity, moved by love, experience both grief (suffering) and joy of forgiveness/reconciliation. Although Bushnell's later works were significantly more "scientific" than his earlier ones, he wrote no "comprehensive" systematic theology. Yet, saying this, he consistently applied his method to these later works as well as to other theological topics he addressed such as biblical interpretation, human sinfulness, sacraments, ecclesiology, and eschatology.

One of the greatest preachers of his era, he was a much-sought-after orator on public occasions of social and political importance. His admiration for American society was matched by his penetrating criticism. Against all forms of individualism—economic, political, and religious—he often argued how "rights language" and "social contracts" were undermining American institutions; he was a communitarian and an institutionalist, but no separatist. Indeed, as a democratic realist, he argued that Christians must fight cultural and political battles for the good of society. Moreover, he was used to battles. His early writings were so controversial that Congregationalist conservatives from different parts of New England between 1849 and 1854 repeatedly attempted to bring him to trial for heresy. Congregational polity prevented this because the local Association and the congregation both, in the end, supported Bushnell. Nonetheless, this Congregational trial of 1849, the greatest heresy crisis in Connecticut's history, proved to be a catalyst for Congregationalism's later shift toward liberalism.

Despite his scholarly interests, he was a restless and creative spirit who enjoyed amateur engineering and inventing, city planning, mountaineering, sailing, and exploring. As "The First Citizen of Hartford," he labored excessively to establish the first large urban park in America ("Bushnell Park" in Hartford), and devoted much of his energy to other civic projects in education, public works, and the arts.

Bibliography

A. *Christian Nurture* (Boston, 1847; rev. 1860, and many subsequent eds.); *God in Christ* (Hartford, Conn., 1849); *Christ in Theology* (Hartford, Conn., 1851); *Nature and the Supernatural* (New York, 1858); *The Vicarious Sacrifice* (New York, 1866); *Forgiveness and Law* (New York, 1874).

B. DAB 3:350–54; DARB 89–90; NCAB 8:303; NCE 2:910; NYT 18 February 1876, 4; SH 2:318–19; Theodore T. Munger, *Horace Bushnell: Preacher and Theologian* (Boston, 1899); Barbara M. Cross, *Horace Bushnell: Minister to a Changing America* (Chicago, 1958); William A. Johnson, *Nature and the Supernatural in the Theology of Horace Bushnell* (Lund, 1963); David L. Smith, *Symbolism and Growth: The Religious Thought of Horace Bushnell* (Chico, Calif., 1981); James O. Duke, *Horace Bushnell on the Vitality of Biblical Language* (Chico, Calif., 1984); Robert L. Edwards, *Of Singular Genus of Singular Grace: A Biography of Horace Bushnell* (Cleveland, Ohio, 1992); David W. Haddorff, *Dependence and Freedom: The Moral Thought of Horace Bushnell* (Lanham, Md., 1994).

David Haddorff

BUTLER, JOSEPH (18 May 1692, Wantage, England–16 June 1752, Bath, England). *Education*: studied at the Latin Sch., Wantage, at an academy in Gloucester and then Tewkesbury, and at Oriel Coll., Oxford; B.A., Cambridge, 1718. *Career*: preacher at the Rolls Chapel, London, 1719–26; prebendary, Salisbury, 1721–38; rector, Haughton-le-Skerne; rector, Stanhope, 1726–40; prebendary, Rochester, 1733–40; chaplain to the lord chancellor, 1733–36; clerk of the closet to Caroline, queen consort of George II, 1736–37; bishop of Bristol, 1738–50; bishop of Durham, 1750–52.

Butler was raised a Presbyterian, but before entering Oriel College, conformed to the Church of England, and was ordained deacon and priest in 1718. In 1736 Butler wrote *The Analogy of Religion, Natural and Revealed, to the Constitution and Course of Nature*, on which rests his reputation and fame. It was the last of his few major publications. In the Advertisement, or what we might call the preface, to the *Analogy*, Butler stated what has become two famous sentences: "It is come, I know not how, to be taken for granted, by many persons, that Christianity is not so much as a subject of inquiry; but that it is, now at length, discovered to be fictitious. And accordingly they treat it, as if, in the present age, this were an agreed point among all the people of discernment; and nothing remained, but to set it up as a principal of mirth and ridicule, as it were by way of reprisals, for its having so long interrupted the pleasures of the world." Butler argued that there is strong evidence for the truth of Christianity, and that no reasonable person can be convinced to the contrary.

In this volume, Butler challenged the supernatural rationalists, the more conservative Deists, who believed in a God who was the moral governor of the universe but not in the particular claims of Christian revelation, such as the virgin birth, the resurrection, and the miracles of Jesus. Many of these Deists were opposed to the historical forms of Christianity and insisted upon the absolute authority of individual thought free from all external authority. They wanted to find a religion that all persons could subscribe to—a "natural religion," a religion that was in harmony with scientific thought. For them, true religion lies in its universality, and supernatural revelation is superfluous.

Butler began his argument against the Deists by admitting that absolute proof for the facts of revealed religion cannot be given. Scripture does have ambiguities and contradictions, but so does nature. Nature, on which the Deists based their natural religion, is no more reliable than Scripture, but Scripture is as reliable as nature. Natural religion and revealed religion are both baffling and mysterious. But from humanity's experience of the world people can draw conclusions for the reasonableness and probability of a higher order, an eternal realm. For finite human beings, "probability is the very guide of life."

Butler roots his argument in one of the major thinkers of the early church. "Hence, namely from analogical reasoning, Origen* has with singular sagacity observed, that, 'he who believes the Scriptures to have proceeded from him who is the Author of nature, may well expect to find the same sort of difficulty in it, as are found in the constitution of nature.' " For years this volume served as the most complete and best answer to the Deist objections to revealed religion. Butler was also a practical ethicist and argued that ethics is the practice of common virtues, compassion, and benevolence.

Butler was not optimistic about the Methodist movement or the future of the Church of England. In 1739 he said to John Wesley,* "Sir, the pretending to extraordinary revelation and gifts of the Holy Ghost is a horrid thing, a very horrid thing." In 1747 it is reported that he refused to be Archbishop of Canterbury, claiming that it was "too late for him to try to support a falling church."

Bibliography

A. *The Works of Bishop Butler*, ed. W. E. Gladstone, 2 vols. (Oxford, 1896); *The Works of Bishop Butler*, ed. Samuel Halifax (New York, 1844).

B. Catholicisme 2:336; DNB 8:67–72; LThK³ 2:859–60; NCE 2:916; ODCC 256–57; TRE 7:496–97; R. W. Church, *Pascal and Other Sermons* (London, 1910); Ernest C. Mossner, *Bishop Butler and the Age of Reason* (New York, 1936); W. J. Norton, Jr., *Bishop Butler, Moralist and Divine* (New Brunswick, N.J., 1940); P. Allan Carlsson, *Butler's Ethics* (London, 1964); *Joseph Butler's Moral and Religious Thought: Tercentenary Essays*, ed. Christopher Cunliffe (New York, 1992).

Donald S. Armentrout

C

CAJETAN, THOMAS DE VIO (20 February 1469, Gaeta, Italy–10 August 1534, Rome). *Education*: studied at Naples, Bologna, and Padua, 1484–93. *Career*: joined Dominicans, 1484; professor of theology, Padua, 1493–97; Pavia, 1497–99; Milan, 1499–1501; Rome, 1501–8; Dominican Procurator General, 1501–8; Master General of the Dominicans, 1508–18; cardinal, 1517; papal legate to Germany, 1518–19; bishop of Gaeta, 1519–23; papal legate to Hungary, 1523; study and writing, Rome, 1523–34.

Cajetan was probably the greatest Catholic theologian of the early sixteenth century and was a major force in the Thomistic revival of the era. Given his administrative duties for the Dominicans and the papacy, Cajetan's output of 150 published works is striking. His career as a scholar breaks neatly into philosophical, theological, and exegetical phases. Up to 1498 he devoted himself to philosophy and wrote commentaries on Porphyry and Aristotle, among other works. In his commentaries on Aristotle, Cajetan defended the Thomistic understanding of the soul and its immortality against Paduan Averroism. His later (1510) commentary on Aristotle's *De Anima*, however, admitted that Aristotle probably taught the soul's mortality; for Cajetan belief in the soul's immortality comes from revelation and not from reason. He clung to this view when voting on the immortality question at the Fifth Lateran Council in 1513. In philosophy Cajetan saw himself as a disciple of Aquinas,* but some modern Thomists often judge that he neglected the richness of Aquinas' metaphysics of existence and was influenced by Scotism.

From 1507 to 1524 he produced works of systematic theology and polemics against Protestants. His great work was his commentary (1507–1520) on Thomas' *Summa theologiae*; it became standard and was printed by papal command with the 1570 and 1888–1906 editions of the *Summa*. In 1511 he wrote a tract defending the papal cause against the Schismatic Council of Pisa.

Cajetan devoted his last decade to studying Scripture and writing nine biblical commentaries. These were based on the Greek and Hebrew texts and contain many criticisms of the Latin Vulgate. Cajetan appropriated humanist critical methods, which led him to anticipate many modern positions, especially regarding the authorship of various New Testament books—much to the annoyance of more conservative Catholic scholars of his age. His main goal was to refute Protestantism.

Bibliography

A. *Opera omnia quotquot in sacrae Scripturae expositionem reperiuntur*, 5 vols. (Alcalá, 1639); *Scripta philosophica: Commentaria in De anima Aristotelis*, ed. J. Coquelle (Rome, 1938–39); *Commentary on Being and Essence*, ed. L. H. Kendzierski and F. C. Wade (Milwaukee, Wis., 1964); *Cajetan Responds: A Reader in Reformation Controversy*, ed. Jared Wicks (Washington, D.C., 1978); *Cajetan et Luther en 1518*, ed. Charles Morerod, 2 vols. (Fribourg, 1994).

B. LThK³ 2:884–85; NCE 2:1053–55; ODCC 263; OEncR 1:233–34; TRE 7:538–46; *Revue thomiste* 17 (1934–35); Joseph F. Groner, *Kardinal Cajetan, eine Gestalt aus der Reformationzeit* (Freiburg/Louvain, 1951); G. Hennig, *Cajetan und Luther* (Stuttgart, 1966); Dennis Doherty, *The Sexual Doctrine of Cardinal Cajetan* (Regensburg, 1966); Marvin O'Connell, "Cardinal Cajetan: Intellectual and Activist," *New Scholasticism* 50 (1976): 310–22; Barbara Hallensleben, *Communicatio, Anthropologie und Gnadenlehre bei Thomas de Vio Cajetan* (Münster, 1985).

John Patrick Donnelly

CALVIN, JOHN (10 July 1509, Noyon, Picardy, France–27 May 1564, Geneva). *Education*: studied Latin grammar and the arts, Univ. of Paris, 1523–27/28 (or 1520–25); studied civil law, Univ. of Orléans, 1528–29 (or 1525–29); licentiate in law, Univ. of Bourges, 1529–31, or 1532; studied Greek and Hebrew, Univ. of Paris, 1531–32; and studied or taught at the Univ. of Orléans, 1532–33. *Career*: Protestant refugee and author, Basel, 1534–36; minister, Geneva, 1536–38, Strasbourg, 1538–41, and Geneva, 1541–64; founder of the Genevan Academy, 1559.

Calvin ranks second in influence only to Martin Luther* among sixteenth-century Protestant reformers. He wrote polemical works and catechisms as well as commentaries on most of the books of the Bible. His *Institutes of the Christian Religion*—which follows the broad outlines of the Apostles' Creed and is shaped by biblical and patristic thought—is the cornerstone of Reformed theology.

In the opening line of every edition of the *Institutes*, Calvin says, "Nearly the whole of sacred doctrine consists in these two parts: knowledge of God and of ourselves." For Calvin, self-knowledge leads us to be displeased with ourselves and thereby arouses us to seek God, while knowledge of God is required for a clear awareness of ourselves, and especially of our own folly and corruption.

Rejecting as pointless all speculation about a God with whom we have nothing to do, Calvin says that genuine knowledge of God involves not only knowing that there is a God but also revering and loving God—which Calvin calls "piety." True piety results from recognizing that we owe everything to God, are nourished by his fatherly care, and should seek nothing beyond him.

Calvin recognizes several means by which we gain knowledge of God. All humans have, by natural instinct, an awareness of divinity (*sensus divinitatis*). God has implanted in all people a "seed of religion," a natural awareness "that there is a God and that he is their Maker" (*Inst.*, 1.3.1). God has also "engraved unmistakable marks of his glory" upon the universe so that no one can plead the excuse of ignorance. God displays his glory, moreover, outside the ordinary course of nature, providentially administering human society: declaring clemency to the godly, showing severity to the wicked, protecting the innocent, and caring for the poor in their desperate straits.

Nevertheless, all people degenerate from the natural knowledge of God, not apprehending God as he reveals himself, but presumptuously fashioning a deity of their own imagining, thereby worshiping a figment rather than the true God. Although God represents himself in the mirror of his works with great clarity, we grow dull toward such clear testimonies and "forsake the one true God for prodigious trifles" (*Inst.*, 1.5.11). Our minds are like labyrinths of confusion, or like springs pouring forth gods we have invented for ourselves. Even philosophers adore a shameful diversity of gods. So if we were taught only by nature, we would end up worshiping an unknown god. Consequently, we need the witness of God himself, "illumined by the inner revelation of God through faith" (*Inst.*, 1.5–13,14). In a well-known passage, Calvin says, "Just as old or bleary-eyed men and those with weak vision" can scarcely see until they put on spectacles, "so Scripture, gathering up the otherwise confused knowledge of God in our minds, having dispersed our dullness, clearly shows us the true God" (*Inst.*, 1.6.1). God uses not only mute teachers, such as nature and providence, but also "opens his own most hallowed lips" (*Inst.*, 1.6. 1). Thus, although it is fitting to contemplate God's works, as spectators in a "most glorious theater," it is also fitting to listen to God's Word in Scripture, since our feeble human minds cannot grasp God without being aided by his sacred Word (*Inst.*, 1.6.2,4).

Calvin recognizes, however, that the Scriptures must be confirmed as the living words of God. Piety requires certainty and assurance that can be found neither in the consent of the church nor in arguments, but only in the testimony of the Holy Spirit. The same Spirit who spoke through the authors of Scripture must work in our hearts to persuade us that these authors faithfully proclaimed what God spoke to them. Once we have embraced Scripture, arguments that were not sufficient by themselves become useful aids: Calvin cites Scripture's ability to move us, its sublime thoughts, its antiquity, miracles that confirmed the teaching of Moses and others, the fulfillment of its prophecies, and the consent of the church as secondary aids to our feebleness. Still, Scripture can lead to "a saving knowledge of God only when its certainty is founded upon the inward persuasion of the Holy Spirit," and not upon mere external arguments (*Inst.*, 1.8.13).

In response to religious fanatics or enthusiasts who abandon Scripture and claim a new revelation from the Spirit, Calvin argues that God has forged a mutual bond between Word and Spirit: the Spirit, as the author of Scripture, attests the Word of God in Scripture and the Word leads us to recognize the true Spirit of God. Calvin also sees a connection between the revelation of God in creation and in Scripture: the knowledge of God set forth in Scripture has the same goal as the knowledge imprinted in creatures, inviting us "first to fear God, then to trust in him" (*Inst.*, 1.10.1–2). So the Spirit leads us to the Word, which—like nature—is a *mirror* in which faith may contemplate the invisible God (*Inst.*, 3.2.6).

Rejecting any notion of faith as simple agreement with the gospel history or with the teachings of the church, Calvin insists that faith is "a firm and certain knowledge of God's benevolence toward us, founded upon the truth of the freely given promise in Christ, both revealed to our minds and sealed upon our hearts through the Holy Spirit" (*Inst.*, 3.2.7). Knowledge of the unseen God does not involve comprehension, as with objects of sense perception, but rather consists in assurance. Because unbelief is so deeply rooted in our hearts that we can only with hard struggle persuade ourselves that God is faithful, the assurance of faith depends on our feeling the sweetness of God's goodness toward us and experiencing it in ourselves. Then, when believers are shaken by temptations and doubts, they will "either rise up out of the very gulf of temptations, or stand fast upon their watch," confident of God's mercy to them (*Inst.*, 3.2.21, 37).

Calvin affirms that God created the world good and by his own free will. Like Augustine,* he rejects speculation about why God created the world when he did. Instead of focusing on the duration or sequence of the events of creation, he focuses on the spiritual value of observing that God created, out of nothing, an abundance and variety of creatures, each with its own nature and assigned functions; that God formed humanity as "the most excellent example of his works"; and that God has provided for the preservation of the entire creation (*Inst.*, 1.14.20).

Proper self-knowledge, says Calvin, involves knowing both that human beings as created had the moral knowledge and strength of will to choose between good and evil and that, as a consequence of the Fall, Adam's descendants lack the ability to carry out their duty. Still, we are not held liable for the transgression of another; the contagion imparted by Adam resides in us. Calvin's view of original sin reflects Augustine's teaching on the matter.

In his doctrine of providence, Calvin insists that we see God's power as much in the continuing state of the universe as in its creation. God does not merely generally superintend everything or even direct a few particular acts, but regulates individual events so that they all proceed from his plan and "nothing takes place by chance"—not even when a branch falls and kills a passing traveler (*Inst.*, 1.16.4–6). Unlike the Stoic dogma of fate, says Calvin, the doctrine of providence sees God as the ruler of all things who "in accordance with his wisdom'' has from eternity decreed what he was going to do and now carries it out (*Inst.*, 1.16.8).

If God wills everything that occurs, does he also will evil? Although Augustine and others (including much of the Reformed tradition) answer this question by distinguishing between God's active and permissive will, Calvin rejects the idea that God merely permits certain events, "as if God sat in a watchtower awaiting chance events, and his judgments thus depended upon human will" (*Inst.*, 1.16.8, 1.18.1). In response to the charge that God would then have two contrary wills—a revealed will that forbids sin and a secret will that decrees evil actions—Calvin says that God's will is one and simple in him but appears manifold to us because we cannot grasp how God both wills and does not will something to take place.

Calvin's affirmation of God's goodness in relation to evil events hinges on Augustine's insight that God is not limited to doing only what humans may do, or only what humans consider acceptable for God to do. Conceding that his doctrine of providence might seem harsh, Calvin defends it by saying that it is biblical and that it allows believers to have gratitude for favorable outcomes, patience in adversity, and freedom from worry about the future because they know that all things are ruled by their heavenly father.

Like Martin Luther, Calvin says that the doctrine of justification by faith is pivotal for true religion. Those who are justified have in heaven a gracious father, not a judge. God justifies by freely embracing sinners who are utterly void of good works and conveying such a sense of divine goodness that sinners will despair of works and rely wholly on God's mercy. The faith through which sinners are justified is a divine gift through which they receive God's mercy, not a work that qualifies them for salvation. Without the doctrine of justification by faith, says Calvin, we diminish God's glory by trusting in works rather than God's grace for salvation and we also generate spiritual anxiety by lacking assurance of salvation. Only unmerited righteousness conferred as a gift of God can quiet consciences before God.

In his doctrine of predestination, Calvin identifies the twin dangers of either probing without restraint matters that God wills to remain hidden or avoiding what Scripture says. Based on biblical passages such as Paul's discussion of election in Rom 9–11, Calvin argues that predestination is God's eternal decree regarding each individual, foreordaining eternal life for some and eternal damnation for others. This divine decree is not based on God's foreknowledge of the holiness of the elect or the sinfulness of the reprobate but only in God's inscrutable will. God's sovereign election of some and reprobation of others reveals his glory, says Calvin, by showing his justice as well as by impressing upon the elect God's infinite mercy to them. In contrast to Calvin, many Reformed theologians hold that reprobation does not mirror election, since God actively chooses the elect, but leaves the reprobate in the ruin they incur by their sins.

Calvin argues that God has given each individual—not just the clergy—a calling or vocation "as a sort of sentry post" to prevent heedless wandering about throughout life. Each person, says Calvin, will fulfill his or her calling willingly, bearing its weariness and anxieties, if it is seen as a duty to God. "No task," says Calvin, "will be so sordid and base, provided you obey your calling in it, that it will not shine and be reckoned very precious in God's sight" (*Inst.*, 3.10.6).

Bibliography

A. *Ioannis Calvini opera quae supersunt omnia*, ed. J. W. Baum, A. E. Cunitz, and E. Reuss, 59 vols. (Brunswick and Berlin, 1863–1900); *Calvin's Commentaries*, trans. Calvin Translation Society, 22 vols. (Grand Rapids, Mich., 1979); *Calvin's Old Testament Commentaries*, The Rutherford House Trans. ed. D. F. Wright, 26 vols. (Grand Rapids, Mich., and Carlisle, Pa., 1993–); *Concerning the Eternal Predestination of God*, trans. J. K. S. Reid (Cambridge, 1962); *Institutes of the Christian Religion*, 1536 ed., trans. Ford Lewis Battles, rev. ed. (Grand Rapids, Mich., 1986); *Institutes of the Christian Religion*, LCC, ed. John T. McNeill, trans. Ford Lewis Battles, 2 vols. (Philadelphia, 1960); *Selected Works of John Calvin: Tracts and Letters*, ed. Henry Beveridge and Jules Bonnet, 7 vols. (Grand Rapids, Mich., 1983).

B. DTC 2:1377–98; ECatt 3:402–17; LThK³ 2:895–900; NCE 2:1087–90; ODCC 266–68; TRE 7:568–92; Edward A. Dowey, Jr., *The Knowledge of God in Calvin's Theology*, expanded ed. (Grand Rapids, Mich., 1994); Alexandre Ganoczy, *The Young Calvin*, trans. David Foxgrover and Wade Provo (Philadelphia, 1987); W. Fred Graham, *The Constructive Revolutionary: John Calvin and His Socio-Economic Impact* (Richmond, Va., 1971); Wulfert de Greef, *The Writings of John Calvin: An Introductory Guide*, trans. Lyle D. Bierma (Grand Rapids, Mich., 1994); John T. McNeill, *The History and Character of Calvinism* (Oxford, 1954); Richard A. Muller, *The Unaccommodated Calvin* (New York, 1999); T. H. L. Parker, *Calvin: An Introduction to His Thought* (Louisville, Ky., 1995); T. H. L. Parker, *John Calvin: A Biography* (Philadelphia, 1975); Susan Schreiner, *The Theater of His Glory: Nature and the Natural Order in the Thought of John Calvin* (Durham, N.C., 1991); David C. Steinmetz, *Calvin in Context* (New York and Oxford, 1995); François Wendel, *Calvin: Origins and Development of His Religious Thought*, trans. Philip Mairet (New York, 1963).

Ronald J. Feenstra

CAMPBELL, ALEXANDER (12 September 1788, Ballymena, Ireland–4 March 1866, Bethany, W.Va.). *Education*: studied at Glasgow Univ., Glasgow, Scotland, 1808–9. *Career*: minister, Brush Run, Pa., 1812–40; editor, *Christian Baptist*, 1823–30; *Millennial Harbinger*, 1830–64; founder and president, Bethany Coll., 1840–66; president, American Christian Missionary Society, 1849–66.

Campbell was a leading force behind the "Restoration Movement," an early nineteenth century impulse ostensibly dedicated to Christian unity. Blaming the divisions of Christendom on "creeds of human contrivance" and "the kingdom of the clergy," Campbell argued for a program based exclusively on New Testament authority. His efforts were primarily ecclesiastical and not political, but he believed that his principles could deliver the millennium on the fertile soil of the new republic. He argued for the perspicuity of Scripture, using purely objective biblical studies to seek the essential outlines of primitive Christianity. On the weekend of New Year's Day, 1831–32, Campbell's "Disciples" began a tenuous (but lasting) union with the "Christian" movement of Barton W. Stone. He remains, however, the primary founder of the Churches of Christ, Christian Churches, and Disciples of Christ.

Campbell's religious heritage began in the Seceder Presbyterian Church in Ireland, but this affiliation ended prior to his departure from Glasgow. His primary influences must begin with his father, Thomas, through whom he encountered John Locke. During his year in Glasgow, he discovered various independent Christian movements and was surely influenced by the Scottish Common Sense philosophy of Thomas Reid. These influences preceded his arrival in the United States on 29 September 1809.

Campbell's restoration movement rested on substantial theological premises. Repulsed by Deism, Campbell rejected the (Lockean) belief that unaided human reasoning can use empirical data to arrive at the idea of God. The witness of Scripture is primary to spiritual ideas, and reason plays a subsequent, supporting role. Moreover, the Spirit convicts human souls only through the mediation of Scripture. In his landmark "Sermon on the Law" (September 1816), Campbell rejected the Old Testament as a guide to the Restoration program. The Old Testament contains true revelation, but Campbell believed that its regulations were limited to the Jewish nation and have been supplanted by the full revelation of the New Testament. Campbell granted considerable latitude to various theological opinions but took his stand on visible church practices, believing the latter could be easily restored to their New Testament purity. Campbell's primitivist program was initially aimed at the reformation of "Protestant popery," but in his last thirty years he became less iconoclastic and more sympathetic to Protestant establishments.

Bibliography

A.   *The Christian Baptist*, 7 vols. in 1 (abridged ed., Cincinnati, Ohio, 1835; repr. Joplin, Mo., 1983); *The Millennial Harbinger*, 35 vols. (repr. Joplin, Mo., 1987); *The Christian System* (1835; repr. Joplin, Mo., 1989).

B.   DAB 3:446–48; DARB, 97–98; NCAB 4:161; NCE 2:1111–12; NYT 11 March 1866, 5; ODCC 273; SH 2:370–72; Eugene Boring, "The Formation of a Tradition: Alexander Campbell and the New Testament," *The Disciples Theological Digest* 2 (1987): 5–62; Everett Ferguson, "Alexander Campbell's 'Sermon on the Law,' " *Restoration Quarterly* 29 (1987): 71–85; Leroy Garrett, *The Stone–Campbell Movement* (Joplin, Mo., 1994); Robert Richardson, *Memoirs of Alexander Campbell*, 2 vols. (Philadelphia, 1868–70); Frederick R. West, *Alexander Campbell and Natural Religion* (New Haven, Conn., 1948); Richard Hughes, *Reviving the Ancient Faith: A History of the Churches of Christ* (Grand Rapids, Mich., 1996).

Keith Huey

CANO, MELCHIOR (6 January, 1509, Tarancón, Spain–30 September, 1560, Toledo, Spain). *Education*: theology, Univ. of Salamanca under Francis de Victoria, 1527–31; read theology, St. Gregory's Coll., Valladolid, Spain, 1532. *Career*: entered Dominicans, Salamanca, 1523; master of students and second chair in theology, St. Gregory's, 1534–42; professor of theology, Alcalá, Spain, 1543; professor of theology, Salamanca, 1546–52; theological adviser, Council of Trent, 1551–52; rector, St. Gregory's Coll., 1554–57; provincial of Dominicans, 1557–60.

Cano has been called the father of theological method in the post-Reformation Catholic tradition. His most important work, *De locis theologicis* (published posthumously in Salamanca, 1563), was frequently republished throughout Europe during the sixteenth and seventeenth centuries and had a significant and long-lasting impact on post-Tridentine Catholic theology (particularly upon the theological manual tradition, which lasted well into the twentieth century). Cano's treatise systematically outlined the various sources (authorities) of theological argumentation. After distinguishing between arguments based on authority from those based on reason, Cano enumerated ten *loci*, or sources, of theology: Scripture, tradition, general church councils, the Roman Church, the Fathers, the schoolmen, natural reason, the philosophers, the doctors of civil law, and history.

Cano's attempt to establish a Catholic method of theology must be seen within the general context of the Protestant Reformation. To some extent Cano's *De locis* was a counter to Philipp Melanchthon's* *Loci Communes* (1521), which presented an outline of the chief Christian doctrines whose foundations he located in the Bible as the only rule of faith. Using the same term and attempting to establish a broad Catholic grounding for the sources of theological argumentation, Cano wrote his *De locis* as a treatise on the fundamental principles or sources of theological science (understood in an Aristotlean sense) that emphasized the multiple sources for understanding Christian doctrine.

De locis, moreover, reflected the tensions inherent in two sixteenth-century intellectual traditions that Cano inherited in his attempt to articulate a method for doing theology: Renaissance humanism (Salamanca had become a center of humanism and theological renovation since the end of the fifteenth century) with its emphasis upon the retrieval of sources, and Thomistic scholasticism with its emphasis upon deductive reasoning and its view of theology as an Aristotelian science that drew its arguments and proofs chiefly from authority. To some extent, Cano's work became a tentative, though not very adequate, synthesis of the scholastic and the humanist methodical approaches to theology, and those two approaches to theological method would in many of Cano's Catholic theological successors battle for dominance in the modern Catholic theological world.

Bibliography

A. *De locis theologicis* (Salamanca, 1563, and many subsequent ed.); *Opera* (Cologne, 1605).

B. DTC 2:1537–40; ECatt 3:533–34; LThK³ 2:924–25; NCE 3:28–29; ODCC, 276;

OEncR 1:255; RGG 1:1609; A. Lang, *Die Loci Theologici des Melchior Cano und die Methode des dogmatischen Beweises* (Munich, 1925); E. Marcotte, *La nature de la théologie d' après Melchior Cano* (Ottawa, 1949); T. Tshibangu, "Melchior Cano et la théologie positive," in *Collectanea Moralia in Honorem Eximii Domini Arthur Janssen* (Louvain, 1964): 300–339; J. Belda Plans, *Los lugares teológicos de Melchor cano en los comentários a la Suma* (Pamplona, 1982); J. Tapia, *Iglesia y teología en Melchor Cano* (Rome, 1989); B. Körner, *Melchior Cano De locis theologicis: Ein Beitrag zur theologischen Erkenntnislehre* (Graz, 1994).

Patrick W. Carey

CAPREOLUS, JOHN (ca. 1380, Rodez, France–6 April 1444, Rodez). Entered the Dominicans; studied and earned degrees at Paris; taught at Paris, 1408–11, later at Toulouse, where he commented on the *Sentences*, and then at Rodez; upheld the theology of St. Thomas Aquinas* against various adversaries such as Henry of Ghent,* Scotus,* Aureoli, Durandus,* and Ockham*; wrote his only known work, *The Defenses of the Theology of Thomas Aquinas*, between 1408 and 1433. Composed in the form of a commentary on the *Sentences*, the four volumes of the *Defensiones* represent a profound explanation and defense of the teachings of Aquinas and were the first to emphasize Thomas' *Summa Theologiae* instead of his *Commentary on the Sentences*. As the first interpreter of St. Thomas whose actual aim was to present the teachings of the master, and because of his fidelity to Aquinas' thought, Capreolus was later known as "the soul of St. Thomas" and as "the prince of Thomists," though he interpreted Aquinas' real distinction between essence and existence in creatures in the sense of one that holds between two distinct beings.

Bibliography

A. *Defensiones theologiae divi Thomae Aquinatis*, 7 vols. (Tours, 1900–1908; repr. Frankfurt, 1967).

B. DTC 2:1694; LThK³ 5:888; NCE 3:91–92; ODCC 285; T. M. Pèques, "Capréolus 'Thomistarum Princeps.' À propos de la nouvelle édition des ses oeuvres," *Revue Thomiste* 7 (1899): 63–81; Karl Forster, *Die Verteidigung der Lehre des heiligen Thomas von der Gottesschau durch Johannes Capreolus* (Munich, 1955); Martin Grabmann, "Johannes Capreolus O.P. der 'Princeps Thomistarum' (d. 1444), und seine Stellung in der Geschichte der Thomistenschule," *Mittelalterliches Geistesleben* (Munich, 1956), 3:370–410; Johannes Hegyi, *Die Bedeutung des Seins bei den klassischen Kommentatoren des heiligen Thomas von Aquin: Capreolus, Silvester von Ferrara, Cajetan* (Pullach, 1959); James Reichman, "St. Thomas, Capreolus, Cajetan, and the Created Person," *New Scholasticism* 33 (1959): 1–31; Norman J. Wells, "Capreolus on Essence and Existence," *Modern Schoolman* 39 (1960): 1–24.

Roland J. Teske

CARLSTADT, ANDREAS. *See* KARLSTADT, ANDREAS.

CARNELL, EDWARD JOHN (28 June 1919, Antigo, Wis.–14 April 1967, Oakland, Calif.). *Education*: B.A. Wheaton Coll., Wheaton, Ill., 1937–41; Th.B. and Th.M. Westminster Theol. Sem., Philadelphia, Pa., 1941–44; Th.D. Harvard Div. Sch., Cambridge, Mass., 1944–48; Ph.D., philosophy, Boston Univ., Boston, Mass., 1944–49. *Career*: pastor, Baptist Church, Marblehead, Mass., 1945–47; teacher, Gordon Coll. and Div. Sch., Mass., 1945–48; teacher and president, Fuller Theol. Sem., Pasadena, Calif., 1948–67.

Carnell was a seminal thinker and chief apologist for "new evangelicalism." This movement—initiated by Harold Ockenga, Carl F. H. Henry, and others—sought to move conservative evangelicals from the cultic orthodoxy that dominated Protestant fundamentalism by the 1940s. Carnell was a product of this fundamentalism, yet a person made more complex by exposure to vastly more liberal thought patterns at Harvard and Boston University. He recognized that the stigma of his youth was a closed-minded view of truth, a propositional approach that damaged the intellectual standards of those involved and that promoted an attitude of exclusion. Carnell experienced lifelong internal conflicts over issues related to his eclectic theological background and struggled to maintain allegiance both to an inerrant view of Scripture and to selected contemporary views, especially an existential approach to Christianity. During his highly controversial presidency at Fuller Theological Seminary (1955–59) in particular, Carnell came under criticism from fundamentalists who found his views heterodox. He intemperately described these opponents as needing pity more than scorn.

In his desire to integrate diverse theological tendencies, Carnell asserted the viability of an inerrant reading of Scripture to answer present human needs. He attempted to reconcile the validity of conservative evangelical claims for the Bible with modern claims to the validity of natural knowledge, even using elements of Paul Tillich's* method of correlation to further his argument. But Carnell refused to accept the more extreme forms of dialectical theology. He did not embrace the existential "leap of faith" as valid, instead calling it irrational and extreme. Carnell proposed a balanced approach to revelation, depending upon the normative truths of Scripture. This approach ironically led him back into propositionalism.

For Carnell, God might not be fully known propositionally but traditional language still remained the only reliable way to approach the truth concerning relations between human beings and divinity. In his most creative and mature apologetic, *Christian Commitment* (1957), Carnell went further. He posited the superiority of a "knowledge of acquaintance" over a "knowledge by inference," a distinction that opened new evangelicals to move towards a more direct affective knowledge of God and gave grounds for a dialogue with other Christians on the full impact of the biblical revelation.

Carnell's lifelong struggle took its toll and he suffered from severe insomnia as well as recurrent clinical depression. In April 1967 he died of an overdose of barbituates while attending an ecumenical conference in Oakland, California.

Bibliography

A. *The Burden of Søren Kierkegaard* (Grand Rapids, Mich., 1956); *The Case for Orthodox Theology* (Philadelphia, 1959); *Christian Commitment* (New York, 1957); *An Introduction to Christian Apologetics* (Grand Rapids, Mich., 1948); *The Theology of Reinhold Niebuhr* (Grand Rapids, Mich., 1950); *The Kingdom of Love and the Pride of Life* (Grand Rapids, Mich., 1960).

B. *Who Was Who* 4:155; Rudolph Nelson, *The Making and Unmaking of an Evangelical Mind: The Case of Edward John Carnell* (New York, 1987); John A. Sims, *Edward John Carnell: Defender of the Faith* (Washington, D.C., 1979); Ronald H. Nash, *The New Evangelicalism* (Grand Rapids, Mich., 1963).

Terrence Crowe

CASEL, ODO (27 September 1886, Koblenz-Lützel, Germany–28 March 1948, Herstelle-Weser). *Education*: gymnasium, Andernach, 1899–1905; sem. studies, Maria Laach, 1905–9; S.T.D., San Anselmo, Rome, 1913; Ph.D., philosophy, Bonn, 1919. *Career*: entered Order of St. Benedict, Maria Laach, 1905; ordained priest, 1911; editor, *Jahrbuch für Liturgiewissenschaft*, 1921–41; chaplain, Benedictine convent, Herstelle, 1922–48.

Casel is widely recognized as the most influential liturgical theologian of the twentieth century. Early in his career he formulated a theology of Christian liturgy as the ritually enacted presence of the Pauline "Mystery" on external analogy with ancient Mediterranean mystery religions. He went on to explain, develop, and defend his theory in many of his 308 writings, which were frequently published in the *Jahrbuch für Liturgiewissenschaft*.

"The Mystery," according to Casel, is Jesus Christ himself in the saving events of his life, death, and resurrection, made present again in history in the life of the church, especially in its sacred liturgy. Just as through transubstantiation at the Eucharist Christ's body and blood become "substantially" present, without any of their "accidental" properties, in the forms of bread and wine, so also in the liturgy and in other Christian faith practices is the unitary reality of Christ's once-and-for-all saving *transitus* through death to eternal life, without any of its historical limitations, made objectively present and effective in the lives of the faithful. Christian sacraments, therefore, are the redemptive historical work itself of Christ, but in its sacramental mode of being.

Although Pius XII in "Mediator Dei" (1947) and the scholarly community in general rejected as too objectivistic Casel's explanation for *how* Christ's saving events are present and active in the church, his teachings *that* they are present served to awaken the twentieth-century church to a new self-awareness, resulting in much of the theology both of "Mediator Dei" itself and of Vatican II. In addition, Casel anticipated as early as 1922 (*Das Gedächtnis des Herrn in der altchristlichen Liturgie*) the importance given by later theologians to the role of eucharistic memorial (*anamnesis*) in making the church present to Christ in his saving events.

Recent studies reveal that, for Casel, the study of liturgy is fundamentally not a science of rubrics or even historical investigation of church practice. It is rather theology itself since God, revealed as love in Jesus Christ, continues to be known only in and through committed relationship and not as an objective super-reality discoverable by disinterested intellectual analysis. Consequently, theology in all its branches must be judged finally in light of how it helps the church find and respond to God better in its sacred liturgy and, through the liturgy, in all of Christian life. In other words, true theology is ultimately doxology.

Bibliography

A.   "Mysteriengegenwart," *Jahrbuch für Liturgiewissenschaft* 8 (1929): 10–224; *The Mystery of Christian Worship* (London, 1962); "Glaube, Gnosis und Mysterium," *Jahrbuch für Liturgiewissenschaft* 15 (1941): 155–306.

B.   LThK³ 2:966–67; NCE 3:176–77; ODCC 294; TRE 7:643–47; *La Maison-Dieu* 14 (1948): 5–66; *Vom christlichen Mysterium*, ed. A. Mayer et al. (Düsseldorf, 1951), with complete bibliography; André Gozier, *Dom Casel* (Paris, 1968); Burkhard Neunheuser, "Odo Casel in Retrospect and Prospect," *Worship* 50 (1976): 489–504; Angelus A. Häussling, "Odo Casel— Noch von Aktualität?" *Archiv für Liturgiewissenschaft* 28 (1986): 357–87; Maria-Judith Hertha Krake, *Der Herr ist der Geist: Studien zur Theologie Odo Casels* (St. Ottilien, 1986).

John D. Laurance

CASSIAN, JOHN. *See* JOHN CASSIAN.

CATHERINE OF SIENA (1347, Siena–1380, Rome). Caterina di Giacomo di Benincasa (St. Catherine of Siena) is one of the three women doctors of the Roman Catholic Church. One of twenty-five children born to Jacopo Benincasa and his wife Lapa (a fairly prosperous couple), she vowed herself to virginity as a young girl and at the age of sixteen joined a female penitential group (the *Mantellate*) associated with the Order of Preachers founded by St. Dominic Guzman (1170–1221). She subsequently spent some three years living in seclusion at home, and then worked among the poor and sick of Siena. She acquired a number of influential friends and contacts, traveled widely in Italy, and acted as an ambassador between the papacy and the city-state of Florence. She also encouraged a crusade to the Holy Land and influenced the move of the papacy from Avignon (which she visited) to Rome. She was severely ascetical, and her contemporary biographer, Raymond of Capua (ca. 1330–99), associates her with the occurrence of miracles and attributes to her "visions" and a "spirit of prophecy." She was canonized in 1461. Today, she is probably best known for her spiritual writings (mostly dictated, though she did learn to write), chiefly the *Dialogue of Divine Providence* (presented as a set of interchanges between Catherine and God the Father), and a collection of over 300 letters (Catherine was one of the great correspondents of her age). All of her writings employ her own Sienese dialect, not Latin.

Catherine's writings, especially her letters, suggest that she was a formidably independent individual with a strongly practical nature. They also offer a consistently presented theological vision that is at once simple (in that it can be stated fairly quickly) and orthodox (in that it brings together the essentials of Christian doctrine). Being Trinity and Creator, Catherine repeatedly insists, God is entirely and changelessly happy apart from creatures, who owe all that makes up their existence entirely to God, and who add nothing to the divine perfection. And yet, so Catherine also repeatedly insists, God became a human being, which indicates the degree of God's love for the human race. From the theological point of view, the notable feature of Catherine's writings is not their originality but the way in which she constantly dwells on these notions while combining an exalted doctrine of God as the ineffable and immutable source of existence (a doctrine that is very like that associated with writers such as St. Augustine* and St. Thomas Aquinas*) with a resolutely Christocentric vision of the work and meaning of divinity, a vision that leads Catherine to a triumphant exultation in human beings as things of incomparable worth and value.

At one level, so Catherine frequently maintains, creatures are nothing at all, for their being is wholly derived and they are, in many ways, imperfect. Yet, so she adds, creatures derive from the eternal plan of God and are, so to speak, found in God from eternity. In the light of the Incarnation, the conclusion Catherine draws from this teaching is that the human creature is an eternal object of trinitarian love and that this conviction is the final meaning of the teaching that God is Love. In Catherine's theology, this teaching is also a call to self-knowledge (a major topic in her writings) as something revealing both human imperfection and human dignity. For Catherine, this teaching is also a call to the exercise of charity, by which the life of the Trinity is imaged or reflected (as it was incarnate in Christ), and to a life lived in love for God as that from which one derives and as that to which one is called to return. The chief threat to the living of such a life is, so Catherine thinks, sin, which she thinks to be a kind of unreality (as, for example, do Augustine and Aquinas). She also thinks of it as something that derives from ignorance. One of her favorite names for God is "Truth," and, on her account, wickedness is essentially a form of stupidity. It comes from failing to recognize what God is and what people are as creatures and as objects of God's love.

Bibliography

A. *Epistolario di Santa Caterina da Siena*, ed. Eugenio Dupre-Theseider (Rome, 1940); *Il Dialogo della Divina Provvidenza ovvero Libro della Divina Dottrina*, ed. Giuliana Cavallini (Rome, 1968); *The Dialogue*, ed. Suzanne Noffke (New York and London, 1980); *I, Catherine: Selected Writings of St. Catherine of Siena*, trans. Kenelm Foster and Mary John Ronayne (London, 1980); *The Letters of Catherine of Siena*, ed. Suzanne Noffke (Binghamton, N.Y., 1988).

B.   LThK[3] 5:1333–34; NCE 3:258–60; ODCC 304–5; TRE 18:34–36; Raymond of

Capua, *The Life of Catherine of Siena*, trans. Conleth Kearns (Wilmington, Del. and Dublin, 1980); Giuliana Cavallini, *Catherine of Siena* (London, 1998).

Brian Davies

CHANNING, WILLIAM ELLERY (7 April 1780, Newport, R.I.–2 October 1842, Bennington, Vt.). *Education*: Harvard Coll., 1794–98; private theological studies, Cambridge, Mass., 1801–2. *Career*: tutor, private family, Richmond, Va., 1798–1800; pastor, Federal Street Congregational Church, Boston, 1803–42.

Channing was the foremost representative of American Unitarianism in the early nineteenth century. During his early years he had been exposed to the consistent Calvinism of his Newport, R.I., pastor Samuel Hopkins.* His Harvard education, however, had convinced him that the liberal Arminian opposition to Calvinism was well founded and consistent with the progressive and enlightened age of reason in which he lived. By 1815, Channing had emerged as the foremost defender of Unitarianism and in 1819 he published a famous sermon, *Unitarian Christianity*, that defined American Unitarianism. That famous sermon was a theological declaration of independence from what he and others considered the irrationalism and logical immorality of basic Calvinist positions.

As a disciple of the Age of Reason, Channing asserted that all of Christian revelation was to be received, interpreted, and judged according to the God-given gift of human reason. Such a view of reason's role in revelation governed most of Channing's theological perspectives.

On the basis of this view of supernatural revelation, Channing rejected the traditional (Nicene) trinitarian notion of God, the Calvinist doctrines of an inherited original sin and human inability, the belief in Christ's divine nature and equality with the Father, limited Atonement, the notion of a predestining divine election, and divine perseverance of the saints. This rejection of trinitarian and Christological doctrines and of the five points of Dortian theology was part of a focused movement of liberation from New England Puritan theological traditions that had a significant influence upon a number of congregations in Massachusetts.

On the positive side of the theological ledger, Channing emphasized the absolute unity and the Fatherhood of God, the communion of all human beings, the exemplary leadership of Jesus who showed human beings how to realize the potential power of the divine image within the human soul, the salvation from sin and evil through character formation and moral development (brought about by education and attention to the divine dwelling within), and the gradual progress and moral perfectibility of human beings in the march of history.

Channing's optimistic views of human nature and destiny did not deny the potential human beings had for evil, but the source of human evil was in free choice, not in some inherited nature that was inevitably incapable of doing good or choosing the path toward salvation.

Channing's emphasis upon human consciousness of the divine within and his focus upon human likeness (or kindred nature) to the divine prepared the way for a transition from the rationalism of the Enlightenment in American theology to the more romantic strains that would be taken up among American Transcendentalists like Ralph Waldo Emerson.*

Bibliography

A. *The Works of William E. Channing, D.D.*, 8th ed., 6 vols. (Boston, 1848, and many subsequent editions); *Unitarian Christianity and other Essays*, ed. with intro. I. H. Bartlett (Indianapolis, Ind., 1957); *Discourses on War*, intro. E. D. Mead (New York, 1972); *Slavery and Emancipation*, 3d ed. rev. (1836; New York, 1968); *The Works of William E. Channing*, 2 vols. (New York, 1970); *William Ellery Channing: Selected Writings*, ed. D. Robinson (New York, 1985).

B. AAP 8:360–84; DAB 4:4–7; DARB 107–9; NCAB 5:458–59; NCE 3:449; ODCC 318; SH 3:3–4; D. P. Edgell, *William Ellery Channing: An Intellectual Portrait* (Boston, 1955); A. W. Brown, *Always Young for Liberty: A Biography of William Ellery Channing* (Syracuse, N.Y., 1956); Madeline H. Rice, *Federal Street Pastor: The Life of William Ellery Channing* (New York, 1961); A. W. Brown, *William Ellery Channing* (New York, 1962); J. Mendelsohn, *Channing the Reluctant Radical: A Biography* (Boston, 1971); A. Delbanco, *William Ellery Channing: An Essay on the Liberal Spirit in America* (Cambridge, Mass., 1981).

Patrick W. Carey

CHANNING, WILLIAM HENRY (25 May 1810, Boston, Mass.–23 December 1884, London). *Education*: A.B., Harvard Coll., 1829; graduated from Harvard Div. Sch., 1833. *Career*: preacher, Boston area and Meadville, Pa., 1833–34; Unitarian minister-at-large, New York City, 1836–37; Unitarian minister, Cincinnati, Ohio, 1837–41; editor, *Western Messenger,* 1839–41; Unitarian minister, New York City, 1843–45; founder, Religious Union of Associationists, 1847–50; minister, Rochester, N.Y., 1850–52; Unitarian minister, Liverpool, England, 1854–61; Washington, D.C., 1861–63; chaplain, U.S. House, 1863–64; preacher, England, 1866–84.

This nephew of William Ellery Channing* was an aristocrat by birth and a radical by disposition. He saw himself as a vessel to bring in a "holy and hopeful" transfiguration of humanity. Believing self-absorption the root of all evil, he desired to become the conscience of Transcendentalism and to transform the excessive individuality of the movement through political and social activism.

Upon graduating from Harvard, Channing embarked on a host of enterprises. After an unsuccessful stint as minister-at-large to New York City's poor, he became a Unitarian pastor in Cincinnati and editor of *The Western Messenger*, an influential Transcendentalist journal. He underwent a faith crisis there that was based in his disillusionment with organized religion and the intractable class differences. Channing returned East in the early 1840s, emphasizing the need for independent ministries and "associationism," a utopian socialism based in the ideas of Charles Fourier. Channing closely identified with the Brook Farm Commune and moved it towards Fourierism. After the 1846 collapse of this experiment, Channing largely distanced himself from Transcendentalism. He was active in the social reform issues of his day and, following the Civil War, came to rest as an expatriate preacher in England.

Bibliography

A. *Memoirs of William Ellery Channing*, 3 vols. (Boston and London, 1848).

B. DAB 4:9–10; NYT 24 December 1884, 1; O. B. Frothingham, *Memoir of William Henry Channing* (Boston, 1886); David Robinson, ''The Political Odyssey of William Henry Channing,'' *American Quarterly* 34 (1982): 165.

Terrence Crowe

CHATEAUBRIAND, RENE-FRANÇOIS DE (4 September 1768, St. Malo, France–4 July 1848, Paris). *Education*: studied at schools in Rennes and Dinan, Brittany, 1781–86. *Career*: lieutenant in regiments of Navarre at Cambrai, 1786–91; émigré in United States, 1791; emigre in England, 1793–1800; travels to Greece, Jerusalem, Africa, Spain, 1806–7; active in French politics, largely on the royalist or conservative side—foreign minister, 1822–24; diplomatic posts in Rome, 1802–4, 1828–29, Berlin, 1821, and London, 1822; writer, 1830–48.

Chateaubriand had enormous influence in the growth of the Romantic movement in literature, aesthetics, and religion. He wrote a continuous stream of books on literary, political and historical subjects, many of them with a religious dimension. His novel, *Atala* (1801) extolled the unspoiled life of the natives in America, with a devout missionary showing the added benefits of Christianity. His major work, *Le Genie du Christianisme* (1802), gives a glowing and comprehensive portrayal of the merits and beauties of Catholic Christianity. His *Memoires d'Outre-Tombe* (1848–50) distilled a lifetime of thoughts and comment.

Chateaubriand's personal belief in the Christian religion is shown on a grand scale in *The Genius of Christianity*, written with the explicitly apologetic intent of refuting the harsh and scornful criticism of the Voltaireans and all rationalists. Noting that a professedly theological work would probably not be read, he adopted a way to show that the Christian (meaning really Catholic) religion, of all religions, ''is the most humane, the most favorable to liberty and to the arts and sciences,'' and that ''nothing is more divine than its morality, nothing more lovely and sublime than its tenets, its doctrine, and its worship.'' To this end he summoned all the ''charms of the imagination'' and appealed to ''all the interests of the heart.'' Since humans are always drawn to mysteries, finding nothing more beautiful and pleasing, he showed that the church's dogmas, starting with the Trinity, are steeped in mystery and really appeal to the heart and to sentiment. Similarly, the doctrine of redemption ''contains the wonders of man and the inexplicable history of his destination and his heart.'' All the church's teachings on faith and morals are treated in this same way.

At great length and with enormous erudition, Chateaubriand told how the creativity of Christianity was shown in poetry, the fine arts, and literature, and then also in the church's liturgy and sacraments. Glowing accounts of the religious orders, the missionaries, and the hierarchy filled out this portrayal. Though he did not develop an ecclesiological theme, a brief section on popes—"to the Holy See Europe owes her civilization, part of her best laws, and almost all her arts and sciences"—gave an early impetus to the Ultramontane movement that was soon to burgeon in France.

Bibliography

A.   *Oeuvres completes*, 14 vols. (Paris, 1864–73); *The Genius of Christianity*, trans. Charles White (Baltimore, 1856; New York, 1976); *Memoires d'Outre-Tombe*, ed. M. Levaillant, 4 vols. (Paris, 1948).

B.   LThK³ 2:1030–32; NCE 519–21, ODCC 325–26; TRE 7:710–12; V. Giraud, *Le Christianisme de Chateaubriand*, 2 vols. (Paris, 1928); P. Moreau, *La conversion de Chateaubriand* (Paris, 1933); Ghislain de Diesbach, *Chateaubriand* (Paris, 1995).

Richard F. Costigan

CHEMNITZ, MARTIN (7 November 1522, Treuenbreitzen [Brandenburg], Germany–8 April 1586, Braunschweig). *Education*: studied at Univs. of Magdeburg, 1539–42; Frankfurt an der Oder, 1543–45; Wittenberg, 1545–47; M.A., Königsberg, 1547. *Career*: ducal librarian, Königsberg, 1547–53; ordained Lutheran minister, 1553; pastor, St. Aegidi, and assistant to Superintendent Joachim Mörlin, Braunschweig, 1554–67; founder and rector, Univ. of Helmstedt, 1576; superintendent, 1567–86.

Chemnitz was a theologian and churchman who contributed significantly to the establishment of the Lutheran reformation. He helped to reorganize the Lutheran Church in Prussia, Braunschweig, and Wolfenbüttel after the churches there had been influenced by Andreas Osiander.* He also contributed to the development of a Lutheran confessional stance in the late sixteenth century. Although sympathetic to Melanchthon* in his early years, he moved away from that influence in his later years, reasserting some of Luther's* positions. "*Si Martinus non fuisset*" runs the popular saying, "*Martinus vix stetisset*": "If there had been no Martin [Chemnitz], Martin [Luther] would not have survived." He developed a theological system that, unlike the confessional writings of Melanchthon, incorporated Luther's 1536 Smalcald Articles. He thus became the leader of a party inclined to take a position between the Philippists (partisans of Melanchthon) and their opponents, the Gnesio ["genuine"] Lutherans. The real author of the 1577 Formula of Concord, which united the Lutheran churches, he influenced its Christology by his *De duabus naturis in Christo* (1570) and its sacramental teaching by his *Repetitio sanae doctrinae de vera praesentia corporis et sanguinis in coena* (1561). His dogmatics *Loci theologici* (1591–92), edited by successor Polykarp Leyser, was widely accepted as authoritative.

Chemnitz was also important for his Lutheran examination of the doctrines of the Council of Trent. In his extensive *Examen Concilii Tridentini* (1566–73), in which he argued that the Lutheran churches represented the oldest Christian tradition, he delivered the authoritative Lutheran critique of the decrees of the Council of Trent.

Bibliography

A.   *The Two Natures in Christ*, trans. J. A. O. Preus (St. Louis, Mo., 1971); *Loci Theologici*, trans. J. A. O. Preus, 2 vols. (St. Louis, Mo., 1989); *Examination of the Council of Trent*, trans. Fred Kramer, 4 vols. (St. Louis, Mo., 1971–86).

B.   LThK³ 2:1034; ODCC 326–27; OEncR 1:309–10; TRE 7:714–21; Theodore R. Jungkuntz, "Martin Chemnitz: The Confessor?" in *Formulators of the Formula of Concord: Four Architects of Lutheran Unity* (St. Louis, Mo., 1977), 46–68; Fred Kramer, "Martin Chemnitz, 1522–1586," in *Shapers of Religious Traditions in Germany, Switzerland, and Poland, 1560–1600*, ed. Jill Raitt (New Haven, Conn., 1981), 39–51; W. A. Jünke, ed., *Der zweite Martin der Lutherischen Kirche: Festschrift zum 400. Todestag von Martin Chemnitz* (Braunschweig, 1986).

Oliver K. Olson

CHENU, MARIE-DOMINIQUE (baptismal name MARCEL-LÉON) (7 January 1895, Soisy-sur-Seine, France–11 February 1990, Paris). *Education*: entered Order of Preachers (the Dominicans), 1913; studied philosophy and theology, Rome, 1914–20; doctorate under R. Garrigou-Lagrange, Angelicum, Rome, 1920. *Career*: professor, Dominican House of Studies, Le Saulchoir (then in Kain-les-Tournai, Belgium), 1920–32; regent of studies, relocated Le Saulchoir, Etoilles, near Paris, and editor of *Revue des sciences philosophiques et théologiques* and *Bulletin thomiste*, 1932–42; teaching and pastoral work, Paris, 1942–53; assigned to Rouen, 1953–63; further pastoral activities at the Dominican Convent Saint-Jacques, Paris, 1963–90.

Chenu is now widely recognized as an important twentieth-century medievalist and interpreter of the theology of Thomas Aquinas.* He was a major figure in the renewal of Thomistic studies through his historical, contextual writings. In 1930 he founded, together with Etienne Gilson, the Institute for Medieval Studies in Canada. While teaching at the Dominican *studium generale* (Le Saulchoir), he produced for private circulation a booklet entitled *Une école de théologie: Le Saulchoir* (1937) which was subsequently delated to Rome because of alleged subjectivism and relativism. In 1942 the work was placed on the *Index of Forbidden Books*. He was deprived of his title as Master of Theology, removed from Le Saulchoir, and sent to Paris. There he taught at the Sorbonne and the Institut Catholique, and became a theological and pastoral adviser to Cardinal Suhard for several innovative pastoral attempts at evangelization among the disadvantaged, known as the Mission de France, 1941, and the Mission de Paris, 1942. He also encouraged and advised a number of Dominican worker-priests who had assumed a new apostolate among de-Christianized workers, an experiment viewed with suspicion by the Vatican and eventually suppressed. Because of ongoing uneasiness about how his ministries were perceived by officialdom, his Dominican superiors moved him away from Paris and relocated him to Rouen (1954–63).

Perhaps because of these antecedents, he was not officially invited as a *peritus* to Vatican II, although he stayed in Rome during the council as a private adviser to the bishop of Antsirabe, Madagascar (a former student) and was active behind the scenes. His theological perspective is reflected in parts of *Gaudium et spes* (e.g., on the unity of Creation and Redemption, and on the salvific significance of work). His religious vision, especially his Christian anthropology and soteriology, can also be perceived in sections of the Pastoral Constitution on the Church in the Modern World and the Decree on the Laity. At the age of 95, he died while living at the Convent Saint Jacques, Paris.

Bibliography

A.   *La théologie comme science au XIIIe siècle* (Paris, orig. ed., 1927, rev. ed. 1957); *Une Ecole de théologie: Le Saulchoir* (Le Saulchoir, 1937); *Les études de philosophie médiévale* (Paris, 1939); *La Parole de Dieu, I: La Foi dans l'intelligence; II: L'Evangile dans la vie* (Paris, 1964); *Toward Understanding Saint Thomas*, trans. A. M. Landry and D. Hughes (Chicago, 1964); *La théologie au douzième siècle* (Paris, 1957) [ET (partial): *Nature, Man, and Society in the Twelfth Century* (Chicago, 1983)]; *Saint Thomas d'Aquin et la théologie* (Paris, 1959); see also his pastoral writings, esp. *Spiritualité du travail* (Liège, 1941); *The Theology of Work*, trans. Lilian Soiron (Chicago, 1966).
B.   LThK³ 2:1034; NCE 18:85–86; André Duval, "Bibliographie du P. Marie-Dominique Chenu (1921–1965)," *Mélanges offerts à M.-D. Chenu* (Paris, 1967), 9–29; O. de la Brosse, *Le Père Chenu: La Liberté dans la foi* (Paris, 1969); François Leprieur, *Quand Rome condemne: Dominicains et prêtres-ouvriers* (Paris, 1989); *L'Hommage différé au Père Chenu*, ed. Claude Geffré et al. (Paris, 1990).

Michael A. Fahey

CHILLINGWORTH, WILLIAM (12 October 1602, Oxford, England–30 January 1644, Chichester). *Education*: B.A., Trinity Coll., Oxford Univ., 1620; fellow, Trinity Coll., 1628; Jesuit Coll., Douai, 1630. *Career*: prebendary, Chester, 1635–39; proctor, Salisbury chapter, 1640; chaplain, Royalist army, 1640–44; imprisonment, Chichester, 1644.

Chillingworth was an Anglican theologian best known as an apologist for Protestant Christianity in general and its Anglican form in particular. After graduating from Trinity College, Oxford, he publicly debated the Jesuit John Fisher (1569–1641) on a series of theological issues. The controversy led to Chillingworth's conversion to Catholicism. In 1630 he went to Douai to join the Catholic community there. One year later, however, he returned to England and in 1634 rejoined his Anglican communion where he became a forceful spokesman for Protestantism.

Chillingworth's most important apologetical work was the *Religion of Protestants a Safe Way to Salvation* (1638) in which he argued that Protestantism provided all the necessary and essential means to salvation, a position he took in opposition to Catholic arguments to the contrary. He asserted, moreover, that the "Bible only is the religion of Protestants," denied that any church had the gift of infallibility, and defended a Christian's right to use reason and free inquiry in doctrinal matters.

Bibliography

A. *The Religion of Protestants, A Safe Way to Salvation* (London, 1638); *The Works of William Chillingworth* (London, 1719; and many subsequent editions).

B. DNB 10:252–57; ODCC 329–30; TRE 7:745–47; J. D. Hyman, *William Chillingworth and the Theory of Toleration* (Cambridge, Mass., 1931); J. Waller, "William Chillingworth," Ph.D. thesis, Cambridge, 1952; R. R. Orr, *Reason and Authority: The Thought of William Chillingworth* (Oxford, 1967).

Patrick W. Carey

CHRYSOSTOM. *See* JOHN CHRYSOSTOM.

CLARKE, WILLIAM NEWTON (2 December 1841, Cazenovia, N.Y.–14 January 1912, Deland, Fla.). *Education*: graduated from Oneida (Cazenovia) Sem., 1858; B.A., Madison (now Colgate) Univ., 1858–61; Hamilton (Colgate) Theol. Sem., 1861–63. *Career*: pastor, First Baptist Church, Keene, N.H., 1863–69; First Baptist Church, Newton Center, Mass., 1869–80; Olivet Baptist Church, Montreal, Quebec, Canada, 1880–83; First Baptist Church, Hamilton, N.Y., 1887–90; professor, New Testament at the Baptist Theol. Sch., Toronto, Ontario, Canada, 1883–87; J. J. Joslin Professor of Christian Theology, Colgate Theol. Sem., Hamilton, N.Y., 1890–1908; lecturer in ethics, Colgate Theol. Sem., 1908–12.

Clarke was a Baptist theologian and pastor, major figure in the American Protestant "New Theology" movement at the end of the nineteenth century, mission theorist, and author of America's first work of systematic theology from a liberal perspective.

As a theology professor in a "liberalized" Protestant seminary (Colgate), Clarke found himself unable to use any of the standard evangelical textbooks of theology and was forced to produce an "outline" that gradually evolved into a published compendium of the American Protestant liberal faith. Clarke's epoch-making work, *An Outline of Christian Theology* (1898), adumbrated in systematic form the emerging "modernist" Protestant theology that followed Schleiermacher* in positing religious sentiment/experience as the starting point for the theological task, and not the "irreducible facts" of the Bible, as previous mainline Protestant systematizers had argued. Rejecting older views of biblical inspiration and the "proof texting" use of Scripture revered by many evangelicals, Clarke argued that the "religious feeling" was the source of all particular faiths and norms, so that other religions differ from Christianity not as the false differs from the true, but rather as the "less complete differs from the more complete form.'' Clarke's *Outline* became the standard (and most quoted) work of systematic theology studied by several generations of Protestant seminarians in ''progressive'' divinity schools, many of whom—like Harry Emerson Fosdick*—made this theology of ''Christocentric liberalism'' well known and widely accepted in the pews through their preaching.

In 1900, Clarke published a chastened theological evaluation of the American missionary enterprise (*A Study of Christian Missions*), delineating in the process a severe ''crisis in missions'' that helped to initiate a radical rethinking of Protestant foreign missions in the first two decades of the twentieth century. Rejecting traditional motives for ''saving the lost'' and criticizing Western nations for the often-imperialistic motives masked in their support of non-Western missions, Clarke called for a more culturally sensitive missionary enterprise, preaching a simpler and more ''scientific'' faith marked as much by service as by preaching.

Bibliography

A.   *An Outline of Christian Theology* (New York, 1898); *The Ideal of Jesus* (New York, 1911); *Sixty Years with the Bible: A Record of Experience* (New York, 1912); *A Study of Christian Missions* (New York, 1900).

B.   DAB 4:164; DARB 117–18; NCAB 22:264–65; NCE 3:918; NYT 16 January 1912, 13; SH 3:128; Emily S. Clarke, *William Newton Clarke: A Biography* (New York, 1916); Bernard H. Cochran, *William Newton Clarke, Exponent of the ''New Theology''* (Durham, N.C., 1962); Claude L. Howe, *The Theology of William Newton Clarke* (New York, 1980).

Mark S. Massa

CLEMENT OF ALEXANDRIA (ca. 150, Athens?–ca. 215, Palestine?). Little is known of Clement's life. He seems to have converted to Christianity in adulthood and studied with teachers from different parts of the Roman Empire in search of deeper knowledge about the faith. Clement eventually settled in Alexandria, where he became a student of Pantaenus. Clement himself taught in the city as a Christian philosopher, giving instruction to a general audience on intellectual, cultural, and ethical matters from a Christian perspective. In 202/3, probably because of a local persecution, Clement left Alexandria, possibly for Palestine.

Clement wrote three major works and several minor works. His first major work is the *Protreptikos*, or *Exhortation to the Greeks*, an apologetic work that encourages its non-Christian readers to reject paganism and embrace Christianity as the true philosophy. The *Paidagogos* or *Tutor* is addressed to those who have already converted to Christianity. Its first book presents Christ as the true teacher; the following two discuss how Christians should live out their faith in their daily lives, treating such ordinary concerns as food, drink, household management, recreation, bathing, marriage, and family life. The *Stromateis* or *Miscellanies* consider the relationship between Christian faith and Greek philosophy and refute the false religious and moral principles of Gnosticism. In addition to these major works, Clement composed the *Excerpts from Theodotus*, planned to refute statements from a Valentinian Gnostic, and wrote a homily entitled *Who Is the Rich Man Being Saved?* Other works survive in fragmentary form, and several lost works are attributed to Clement.

The Alexandria of Clement's day provided an intellectual atmosphere rich in Graeco-Roman, Jewish, Egyptian, and Christian influences, many of which are reflected in Clement's thought. In a competitive marketplace of ideas, Clement argued for the compelling truth of Christianity. For Clement, Christ is the Logos, the reason that generates and directs the universe and that was definitively revealed in Jesus of Nazareth. Other philosophies and religions have been able to discern this reason, which is why their insights can help Christians understand their faith. Clement's thought thus represents an approach to Christianity that is open to the surrounding culture and even to certain aspects of heterodoxy within the church, as when he tries to present the orthodox, observant Christian as the true Gnostic. In addition, probably in response to the wealthy, well-connected individuals who came to him for guidance, Clement argued that Christianity was compatible with the possession of property and with marriage, a stance that set him apart from the ascetic tendencies in other quarters of the church of his day.

Bibliography

A.   SC 2, 23, 30, 38, 70, 108, 158, 278, 279; ANF 2; *Alexandrian Christianity*, trans. John E. L. Oulton and Henry Chadwick (London, 1954).

B.   DTC 3:137–99; EEC 1:179–80; LThK³ 6:126–27; NCE 3:943–44; ODCC 364–65; TRE 8:101–13; Eric F. Osborn, *The Philosophy of Clement of Alexandria* (Cambridge, 1957); André Méhat, *Étude sur les 'Stromates' de Clément d'Alexandrie* (Paris, 1966); S. R. C. Lilla, *Clement of Alexandria* (Oxford, 1971); A. van den Hoek, *Clement of Alexandria and His Use of Philo in the Stromateis* (New York, 1988).

Kelley McCarthy Spoerl

CLEMENT OF ROME (end of the first century). Tradition makes Clement the third successor of St. Peter in Rome: he is otherwise unknown. A letter addressed (probably in A.D. 96) by the church in Rome to the church in Corinth became known as the *First Letter of Clement*; it is included among the works of the Apostolic Fathers. Another early work, sometimes called the *Second Letter of Clement*, is the oldest extant Christian homily; its author is unknown. Later tradition attributed two *Letters to Virgins* to Clement, and a novel about the apostles in two versions, called the *Clementine Homilies* and the *Recognitions*.

The occasion of *First Clement* was disorder at Corinth: some younger members of the community had removed the presbyters or elders from office. In response, the church at Rome urged the Corinthian Christians to restore the presbyters to their place and to observe good order. About one-fourth of the letter comprises quotations from the Old Testament, which the author uses as the source for examples of virtue. The letter attests to the government of the church by "bishops and deacons," who may collectively be called "elders." It is also the oldest witness to the persecution of Nero and the martyrdom of Peter and Paul in Rome and suggests that Paul traveled to Spain. The author knew 1 Cor well. *First Clement* was highly revered in antiquity and was sometimes included in the canon of the New Testament.

Bibliography

A.   A. Lindermann and H. Paulsen, *Die Apostolischen Väter* (Tübingen, 1992); R. M. Grant and H. H. Graham, *First and Second Clement* (New York, 1965).
B.   DTC 3:48–54; EEC 1:181; LThK³ 2:1227–28; NCE 3:926–28; ODCC 360–61; TRE 8:113–20; D. A. Hagner, *The Use of the Old and New Testaments in Clement of Rome* (Leiden, 1973); B. Bowe, *A Church in Crisis: Ecclesiology and Paraenesis in Clement of Rome* (Philadelphia, 1988).

Joseph T. Lienhard

COLERIDGE, SAMUEL TAYLOR (21 October 1772, Ottery St. Mary, Devonshire–25 July 1834, Highgate). *Education*: attended Jesus Coll., Cambridge, 1791–93, 1794; toured Germany with the Wordsworths and studied Kant, 1798–99. *Career*: enlisted in 15ᵗʰ Light Dragoons, 1793; met Southey at Oxford and planned American pantisocracy which later failed, 1794; author and traveler, 1794–1815; author in residence at Highgate under the care of surgeon James Gillman, 1816–34.

Though he built his earliest reputation through poetic endeavors with writers including Wordsworth and Southey, Coleridge's impact on nineteenth century religious thought, especially through the theological and philosophical prose of his mature years, is significant not only in Britain, where his writings were widely read and subsequently influenced several groups including the so-called Broad Church Movement of F. D. Maurice* and Newman's* Oxford Movement, but also in America where both the Transcendentalism of Emerson* and Alcott as well as the Protestant liberalism of Bushnell* owe Coleridge a great debt. Coleridge's religious affections evolved throughout his life from Unitarianism early on to orthodox Anglicanism in his later years. His religious thought has been linked to numerous philosophers, especially the German idealists, including Kant, Schelling, Fichte, and Schlegel.

All of Coleridge's later theology emanates from a single foundation, his distinction between the two ways of knowing: Reason and Understanding. Reason is the intuitive source of fixed and absolute truths: it is "the Revelation of an immortal soul." Understanding, however, relies on sensory perception and reflection; in *The Friend* (1809), Coleridge calls this "the faculty of thinking and forming *judgements* on the notices furnished by the Sense, according to certain rules existing in itself." In *Aids to Reflection*, Coleridge explored this distinction further and argued that Christianity's purpose, through Redemption, is to emancipate the human soul from its slavery to Understanding. In all, Coleridge's theology promotes a religious paradigm vastly different from that of eighteenth-century rationalism; in *Aids* he maintained that "Christianity is not a Theory, or a Speculation, but a *Life*. Not a *Philosophy* of Life, but a Life and a living Process."

Bibliography

A. *The Collected Works of Samuel Taylor Coleridge*, Bollingen Series LXXV, gen. ed. Kathleen Coburn, 16 vols. (London and Princeton, N.J., 1969–); *The Collected Letters of Samuel Taylor Coleridge*, ed. E. L. Griggs, 6 vols. (Oxford, 1956–71); *The Notebooks of Samuel Taylor Coleridge*, Bollingen Series L, ed. Kathleen Coburn, 4 vols. (New York, 1957–).

B. BBKL 1:1089–93; DNB 4:758–73; HERE 3:710–13; NCE 3:988–90; ODCC 374–5; TRE 8:149–54; James Dykes Campbell, *Samuel Taylor Coleridge: A Narrative of the Events of His Life* (London, 1894); J. Robert Barth, *Coleridge and Christian Doctrine* (Cambridge, 1969; repr. New York, 1987); Charles Richard Sanders, *Coleridge and the Broad Church Movement*, Duke University Series (New York, 1972); Robert C. Wendling, *Coleridge's Progress to Christianity: Experience and Authority in Religious Faith* (Lewisburg, Va., 1995).

Jeffrey W. Barbeau

CONGAR, YVES MARIE-JOSEPH (13 May 1904, Sedan in the French Ardennes–22 June 1995, Paris). *Education*: studied at Parisian sem. "of the Carmelites," 1921; attended Thomistic courses of Jacques Maritain at the "Univ. Sem.," 1921; studied at the Dominican study-house of Le Saulchoir (Kain-la-Tombe, Belgium), 1925–30. *Career*: entered Dominican novitiate, Amiens, France, 1925; ordained priest, 1930; professor of theology and apologetics, Le Saulchoir, in Belgium, 1931–37, in Etoilles (southeast of Paris), 1937–54; medical orderly in World War II, 1938–40; prisoner of war, Colditz, 1940–45; writer, École Biblique, Jerusalem, 1954; Rome, 1955; ministerial work, Cambridge, England, 1955; author, Strasbourg, 1956–58; member, preparatory theological commission for Vatican II, 1959–63; *peritus* (theological expert), Vatican II, 1963–65; author, Paris, 1968–95; cardinal, 1994.

Congar is generally regarded as the greatest Catholic ecclesiologist of the twentieth century. He was influenced in his early education by the neo-Thomists, but his contacts with Etienne Gilson (1884–1979) and especially Marie-Dominique Chenu,* the director of his thesis on the unity of the church in the thought of Johann Adam Möhler,* gradually removed him from the neo-Thomist influence and moved him toward an appreciation of the historical method. During his early teaching career, moreover, he studied the Catholic Modernists and particularly Maurice Blondel,* which reinforced his interest in the historical method and the philosophical "turn to the subject."

In 1936 Congar established the series of ecclesiological studies, *Unam Sanctam*. Its first volume was Congar's *Chrétiens désunis; Principes d'un œcuménisme catholique* (Paris, 1937). In Congar's words, the series aimed to restore and make available a certain number of themes and profoundly traditional ecclesiological values that had been more or less forgotten or hidden by other less profound themes of less value within the Tradition. It proposed to restore as much as possible the totality of the catholic heritage by using the resources in approaching contemporary problems of the church. It would reexamine the sources, but in order to nourish a living thought.

In the years prior to the Second Vatican Council Congar's historical approach to theology came under suspicion in the neo-Thomist Roman circles of theology. While imprisoned at Colditz during World War II he learned of Rome's condemnation of Chenu's "A School of Theology, Le Saulchoir" for what was called semi-Modernism. The Vatican feared that the emphasis of the Saulchoir theologians on historical context would turn theology into cultural anthropology divorced from its divine subject matter, revelation.

In 1954 the superior general of the Dominican order, Emmanuel Suárez, under threats from the Vatican that the Order of Preachers in France would be dissolved, removed the French Dominicans' major superiors, the head of their publishing house, Cerf, and forbade Congar, Chenu, and others to teach. The Dominicans also had to withdraw all their priests from the priest-worker movement. Congar retreated to the École Biblique in Jerusalem where he was prohibited from accepting the chair of the Hautes-Etudes which was offered to him. While there he wrote *Le Mystère du Temple ou l'économie de la présence de Dieu à sa créature de la Genèse à l'Apocalypse* (Paris, 1958 [*The Mystery of the Temple*]), a study of the biblical sources of the Christian community. Publication and translation of his works were made difficult, and he had to appear in Rome several times for examinations. After his time in Jerusalem, Congar spent four months in Rome, then went to Cambridge, England, to do ministerial work, where he was forbidden contact with Protestants, and from there went to Strasbourg where he was more or less left alone.

Suspicion of Congar's theology was officially lifted in 1959 when Pope John XXIII appointed him to the preparatory theological commission for Vatican II. During the council as a *peritus* (theological expert) he assisted in the drafting of many of the major documents: the *Dogmatic Constitution on Divine Revelation*, the *Dogmatic Constitution on the Church*, nos. 9, 13, 16, 17, the *Pastoral Constitution on the Church in the Modern World*, the *Decree on the Church's Missionary Activity*, chapter 1, the *Decree on Ecumenism*, the *Decree on the Life and Ministry of Priests*, and the *Declaration on Religious Freedom*. Pope Paul VI named him to the newly-founded Pontifical International Theological Commission, which was to bring a broader expertise and vision to the work of the Roman Congregation for the Doctrine of the Faith. Pope John Paul II invited him to attend the extraordinary synod of 1985, although he was forced to decline the invitation for reasons of ill health. Pope John Paul II named Congar a cardinal in the church in 1994. Congar happily accepted even though he had written that the papal creation of the college of cardinals in the eleventh century had all but destroyed episcopal collegiality in the Roman Church.

Congar's primary theological interests were fundamental theology, ecclesiology, and ecumenism, although all his work is fundamentally reducible to some form of ecclesiology. His theological productivity was massive: more than 1,600 books, articles, and translations. The four great books which comprise the core of his life's work are *Chrétiens désunis, Vraie et fausse réforme dans l'Eglise* (Paris, 1950, 2d ed. 1968 [*True and False Reform in the Church*]), *Jalons pour une théologie du laïcat de l'Eglise* (Paris, 1953 [*Lay People in the Church*]), and *La Tradition et les traditions* (Paris, 1960, 1963 [*Tradition and Traditions*]). It is appropriate that his last major work after the council, the three-volume *Je crois en l'Esprit Saint* (Paris, 1979–80 [*I Believe in the Holy Spirit*]), was on the Holy Spirit, the source of unity and the soul of a living and dynamic tradition. A neurological disease from which Congar suffered since the mid-1930s curtailed his physical activities after 1968 and made scholarly research nearly impossible after 9 October 1984, when his health made it necessary to move from Saint Jacques, the Dominican house that held the library of Le Saulchoir, to the hospital of the Invalides in Paris for permanent hospital care.

As an ecclesiologist Congar was interested in church reform through a "return to the sources," and his interest in historical texts permeates all his work. Initially in the 1930s, planning a lecture course on the church, he attempted to develop an ecclesiology based on the categories of the Thomistic philosophy of society; however, he abandoned this effort as a false start. Much more fruitful were his efforts, undertaken years later, to think in an organically unified way about the unity of the church. His aim was to reform the juridical and authoritarian ecclesiology of the baroque period by returning to the concept of the church as mystery in its trinitarian foundations. The structures of the church are entirely relative to the mystery they serve. Consequently authority in the church is not primarily a juridical power, but a service of charity. Congar worked for an eschatological vision of the church as the people of God, Body of Christ, and temple of the Holy Spirit, images consonant with the sacramental and communal character of the church. His ecclesiology is both Christocentric and pneumatological.

His work on the laity accentuated their identity as priestly, kingly, and prophetic members of the people of God, a theme that he contributed to the Second Vatican Council. For Congar, the entire people of God is priestly and there is no sacrament of the priesthood except baptism. There is a sacrament of order; some are ordained to the ministerial priesthood as followers of the apostles and ministers instituted by them to serve the priesthood of the faithful.

Congar's major contribution to fundamental theology lies in his work on tradition (*La Tradition et les traditions*). Originally published in two volumes, the first is a historical essay on tradition from the Old Testament to 1950. The second volume is a theological essay that examines tradition as transmission, as history and development, the church as subject of tradition, the relationship between Scripture and tradition with regard to revelation, the principal monuments or witnesses to tradition, and the questions of tradition in contemporary Protestant thought. He views tradition, not as the "purely mechanical transmission of an inert deposit,'' but dynamically as the organic life, always fresh and living, of the church as it continually reflects on revelation. Other contributions to fundamental theology include his concept of faith as the act by which a person hands himself over to God and his theology of revelation as being the act of God's self-revelation rather than primarily a propositional truth.

From the time of his ordination, Congar had an interest in the ecumenical movement, an interest that originated from his meditations on the seventeenth chapter of St. John. A series of his sermons at Sacré-Cür in Paris in January 1936 mark a beginning for Catholic involvement in the ecumenical movement, which until then was a Protestant movement. A pioneering ecumenist, Congar wrote the first theology of ecumenism from a Roman Catholic perspective, *Chrétiens désunis*. In the late 1930s his principal ecumenical interests were in Anglicanism and Orthodoxy. Later his primary interests would be in the Lutherans and the Orthodox. He preached the Week of Christian Unity every year from 1936 to 1964. A strong impetus for the ecumenical movement was the rejection of the old rationalistic apologetic methodology in favor of a more historical understanding of the Reformation that placed Luther* in his own historical context as reformer and representative of late medieval spirituality. Another breakthrough came with the realization that ecumenical unity did not mean a surrender of the separated traditions and loss of ecclesial identity, but mutual understanding within ecclesiological diversity.

Congar's *Vrai et fausse Réforme dans l'Eglise*, unfortunately never translated into English and initially withdrawn from circulation upon orders by the Vatican even though it had been submitted to sixteen censors before publication, contains a historical and positive portrait of Luther as well as a program of renewal for Roman Catholicism. Congar was a member of the Catholic Conference for Ecumenical Questions under the leadership of Johannes Willebrands. He participated in the early drafts of the World Council of Churches' Toronto statement and frequently reflected on Faith and Order papers. In 1965 he became a member of the official Catholic-Lutheran commission of dialogue. His final ecumenical book was *Diversités et communion* (Paris, 1982). The Franciscans of the Atonement awarded Congar for his work in ecumenism in November 1984.

In his obituary for Congar, Richard J. Beauchesne summarized Congar's theological contribution:

In part, it is about ecumenism as an authentic mark of the church, along with holiness, unity, catholicity and apostolicity. It is about the primacy of tradition (the Trinitarian ''handing over'' of God's life to the church) over traditions (found in the church, but not contained formally in scriptures) such as the Roman primacy. It is about the primacy of worship as life over worship as ritual; the primacy of universal priesthood over the ordained priesthood; the primacy of church as community over church structures. It is about Congar's most fundamental creed: ''I believe the holy church is conditioned by the absolute: I believe in the Holy Spirit.''

Bibliography

A. *Dialogue between Christians: Catholic Contributions to Ecumenism* (Paris, 1964; Westminster, Md., 1966); *L'ecclésiologie du haut moyen âge* (Paris, 1968); *L'Église de saint Augustin à l'époque moderne* (Paris, 1970).

B. LThK³ 2:1295–96; NCE 18:104–5; NYT 24 June 1995; ODCC 397–98; Jean-Pierre Jossua, *Yves Congar: Theology in the Service of God's People* (Chicago, 1968), 213–72 for list of Congar's works; T. I. MacDonald, *The Ecclesiology of Yves Congar: Foundational Themes* (Lanham, Md., 1984); *Fifty Years of Catholic Theology: Conversations with Yves Congar*, ed. Bernard Lauret (Philadelphia, 1988); Aidan Nicols, *Yves Congar* (Wilton, Conn., 1989); Thomas O'Meara, "Ecumenist of Our Times: Yves Congar," *Midstream* 27 (1988): 67–76.

Susan Wood

CONTARINI, GASPARO (16 October 1483, Venice–24 August 1542, Bologna). *Education*: studied classical literature, philosophy, science and theology, Univ. of Padua, 1501–9. *Career*: Venetian ambassador to Charles V (1521–25) and Clement VII (1528–30), 1521–30; cardinal, 1535; chairman, Vatican Reform Commission, 1536; bishop of Belluno, 1536–41; papal legate to Regensburg Colloquy, 1541; papal legate to Bologna, 1541–42.

Contarini was a skilled diplomat and a strong upholder of the institutional church and the papacy, but as a theologian he lacked depth and originality. Most of his theological writings, which included a catechism, a treatise on the sacraments, and a defense of double justification, were published posthumously and heavily censored in his *Opera* (Paris, 1571).

Paul III appointed him first cardinal in 1535, then chair of the committee that drew up reform proposals (the *Consilium de emendanda ecclesia*) in 1537. He befriended Ignatius of Loyola* and the first Jesuits and urged reform in his diocese of Belluno. Paul III sent Contarini as legate to the colloquy of Regensburg, which Charles V convened in 1541 to seek reunion between Catholics and Protestants. The Colloquy managed an uneasy compromise on several questions—notably justification—but broke down over the sacraments. Both Luther* and Paul III later repudiated double justification—a position defended by Contarini and many Italian *spirituali*. Leadership among the cardinals slipped away to Gian Pietro Carafa who favored repression over compromise. Contarini's last year was spent as legate at Bologna, a major post but far from Rome.

Bibliography

A. *Opera* (Paris, 1571); *Gegenreformatorische Schriften (1530c.–1542)*, ed. Friedrich Hünermann (Münster, 1923).

B. DHGE 13:771–84; LThK³ 2:1305–6; NCE 4:257–58; ODCC 408–9; OEncR 1: 419–20; TRE 8:202–6; Peter Matheson, *Cardinal Contarini at Regensburg* (Oxford, 1972); Gigiola Fragnito, *Gasparo Contarini: un magistro veneziano al servizio della christianità* (Florence, 1988); Elisabeth Gleason, *Gasparo Contarini: Venice, Rome and Reform* (Berkeley, Calif., 1993).

John Patrick Donnelly

COTTON, JOHN (4 December 1584, Derby, England–23 December 1652, Boston, Mass.). *Education*: B.A., M.A., Trinity Coll., Cambridge Univ., 1603, 1606; B.D., Emmanuel Coll., Cambridge Univ., 1613. *Career*: fellow and occasional dean, Emmanuel Coll., 1607–12; rector, St. Botolph's Anglican Church, Boston, England, 1612–33; minister, First Church, Boston, Mass., 1633–52.

An author of nearly fifty books and hundreds of sermons, John Cotton was initially viewed as a moderate noncomformist in an era of religious extremism. Cotton showed early brilliance and entered Cambridge University at thirteen. In 1602, his education took a Calvinistic turn and he was converted through impassioned preaching of the pulpiteer William Perkins. Having thrown off any pretense to spiritual self-sufficiency, Cotton became a resident of Puritan-centered Emmanuel College. The young religious scholar was famed for his preaching ability and moved increasingly in the direction of nonconformity. He also displayed a gift for innate caution in his years as head lecturer, dean, catechist, and tutor at Emmanuel.

In 1612, Cotton went forth to test noncomformist principles as rector of St. Botolph's Church, Boston, Lincolnshire. Over the next twenty years, he gained a reputation as a brilliant intellectual with moderate Puritanical tendencies. The mild-mannered minister became vexed with instances of coercion and corruption in the Anglican Church, preached against abuses, and modified Saint Botolph's liturgical practices. With the accession of William Laud* to Archbishop of Canterbury in 1633, Cotton was forced to answer for his views and chose exile to the Massachusetts Bay Colony.

Cotton's arrival in New England was anticipated with prayers and fasting and he was revered as the foremost noncomformist minister to arrive from England. As chief teacher and pastor of First Church, Boston, he became embroiled in two major controversies. The first was the advent of Antinomianism when his disciple, Anne Hutchinson, began to promote direct inner experience as superior to traditional signs of election. After initially shielding her, Cotton realized the danger of separating the covenants of grace and works and joined in the banishment of Hutchinson from the colony. A second issue concerned Roger Williams'* assertion that the magistrate could not enforce church precepts. Cotton engaged in a polemical exchange with Williams over the issue of the authority of secular power to ensure religious obedience.

Cotton was instrumental in drafting the Cambridge Platform of 1648. This document organized the churches of the commonwealth on a mixed presbyterial and congregational basis. The description of the emerging New England Way had an oligarchic tone, imposing serious controls on what initially had been a highly democratic system. The Cambridge Platform marked Cotton's retreat from his previous moderating position to a more legalistic and authoritarian stance.

Bibliography

A. *The Way of Life* (London, 1641); *The Way of the Churches of Christ in New England* (London, 1645); *The Bloudy Tenent, Washed and Made White in the Bloude of the Lambe* (London, 1647); *A Treatise of the Covenant of Grace* (London, 1659).

B. AAP 1:25–30; DAB 4:460–62; NCAB 7:27–28; NCE 4:368; SH 3:278; Larzer Ziff, *The Career of John Cotton: Puritanism and the American Experience* (Princeton, N.J., 1962); Everett H. Emerson, *John Cotton* (New York, 1965).

Terrence Crowe

CRANMER, THOMAS (2 July 1489, Aslacton, Nottinghamshire, England–21 March 1556, Oxford). *Education*: B.A., M.A., B.D., Jesus Coll., Cambridge, 1512, 1515, 1521. *Career*: public examiner in theology, Cambridge, and reader in divinity, Jesus Coll., 1526–29; ambassador, emperor's court, Charles V, Ratisbon, Germany, 1532; archbishop of Canterbury, 1533–53.

Cranmer was the first Protestant archbishop of Canterbury, the primary writer of the 1549 *Book of Common Prayer*, and the major figure driving the Reformation in England. It was he who suggested that King Henry VIII should take his divorce issue away from the lawyers and give it to the divines at the universities. Before long Cranmer was summoned to Henry's court, and in 1530 was attached to the embassy at Rome and given the responsibility of presenting Henry's position to the continental universities and to the pope. Later he was named ambassador to the court of Charles V and used this position to promote theological and political union between England and Germany. While in Germany, Cranmer married Margaret, the niece of Andreas Osiander,* a Lutheran theologian. Since Cranmer was a priest, this violated the canons of the Roman Church and showed his growing independence from the Mother Church.

While Cranmer was in Germany, the archbishop of Canterbury, William Warham, died, and after much dilatory action on the part of Pope Clement VII, Cranmer was consecrated archbishop of Canterbury on 30 March 1533. One of his first official acts came on 23 May 1533, when he formally ruled that Henry's marriage to Katherine of Aragon was null and void.

When Henry VIII died in 1547, he was succeeded by his son, Edward VI, who was greatly influenced by Protestant advisers, and Cranmer was free to do more reformation work. In 1547 the first *Book of Homilies* was issued, and it was edited by Cranmer and Nicholas Ridley. On 21 January 1549, the Act of Uniformity made the *Book of Common Prayer*, in English, the required liturgical usage. This was primarily Cranmer's work and showed him as the master of English prose. In 1552 a second *Book of Common Prayer* was made the uniform usage and the ''Forty-two Articles'' were drawn up by Cranmer and others.

Mary, a devoted Roman Catholic, became queen in 1553, and the Protestant Cranmer was in trouble. On 13 November 1553, he was removed as archbishop and was imprisoned. Under pressure, he signed six recantations, but on a "foul and rainy" March morning he renounced his recantations and thrust the hand that had signed them first into the fire that consumed his body.

Bibliography

A. *The Remains of Thomas Cranmer*, ed. Henry Jenkyns, 4 vols. (Oxford, 1833); *Cranmer's Works*, ed. John E. Cox, 2 vols. (Cambridge, 1844–46).

B. DNB 5:19–31; LThK³ 2:1337–38; NCE 3:413–14; ODCC 428; OEncR 1:448–50; TRE 8:226–29; A. F. Pollard, *Thomas Cranmer and the English Reformation* (London, 1904); G. W. Bromiley, *Thomas Cranmer: Archbishop and Martyr* (London, 1955); idem, *Thomas Cranmer: Theologian* (New York, 1956); Jasper Ridley, *Thomas Cranmer* (Oxford, 1962).

Donald S. Armentrout

CULLMANN, OSCAR (25 February 1902, Strasbourg–). *Education*: diploma in classical philology, 1920, and theology, 1924, Strasbourg; Dr. theol., Strasbourg, 1930. *Career*: teacher of Greek and German at Ecole des Batignolles, Paris, 1925–26; director of the Thomasstift, 1926–27; instructor in Greek, Strasbourg, 1927–30; professor of New Testament and early church history, Strasbourg, 1930–38; Basel, 1938–; director of the Collegium Alumnorum, Basel, 1942–; professor, Ećole des Hautes-Etudes, Paris, 1949–; Faculté Libre de Théologie Protestante, Paris, 1953; professor, Sorbonne, Paris, 1954–.

Cullmann is a German/French Lutheran New Testament exegete and historian of the early church who has made significant contributions to the discipline of New Testament theology and has had a profound impact upon the ecumenical movement in the twentieth century. Introduced by his teachers at Strasbourg to the nineteenth-century *Leben-Jesu* research and to the early work in *Formgeschichte*, Cullmann became convinced that the latter scientific discipline now made it possible to escape the captivity to the philosophical presuppositions that had been imposed upon our understanding of the New Testament by ancient as well as modern interpreters and to objectively recover the original convictions and motives that had shaped earliest Christianity's witness to Christ. He took as his research agenda, therefore, the task of identifying the central message of the New Testament and demonstrating how that had been developed and deformed in subsequent church history. In *Christus und die Zeit* (1946), he argued that, if we set aside our pre-understanding and listen to the text, we come to the realization that the central and unique character of the New Testament encompasses both the form and the substance of its proclamation. The form or framework of the New Testament is, he claimed, an original conception of linear time, which, in contrast to the cyclical notion of Hellenism, views the whole of time as a purposeful history defined by *Heilsgeschichte*, that series of redemptive acts of God beginning with creation and ending with consummation, to which the Bible witnesses. The essence or substance of the New Testament was the declaration that what Judaism expected only at the end of time, the redemptive appearance of God's Messiah, had already occurred in the middle of time in the person of Jesus of Nazareth. On this reading, therefore, contrary to both Greek and Jewish understandings, the New Testament proclaims that God's purposes for all of history have been realized in Jesus Christ, the decisive moment at the midpoint of all history. We now live in that period of eschatological tension between that midpoint and the end in which the Christian community proclaims the "already" of God's redemption of creation in Christ and lives in expectation of the "not yet" of his final appearance and the consummation of all things. The church thus plays, according to Cullmann, a crucial role in *Heilsgeschichte* in that it participates in God's final redemptive activity leading up to the end. He subsequently traced these conceptions back not just to early Christianity but in principle to Jesus himself in *Die Christologie des Neuen Testaments* (1957). And in *Heil als Geschichte* (1964), he extended his debates with Bultmann* over demythologization with the consistent eschatology of Werner and the realized eschatology of Dodd, as well as with Barth* over the concept of eternity.

The importance accorded to the church—and to the exegesis of Scripture to discover the church's true voice—in Cullmann's theology, as well as his personal gifts for forging scholarly friendships across confessional lines, contributed to his long involvement in the ecumenical movement. As early as his first year in Paris he studied with Catholic theologians, among whom were Loisy,* and his years at Strasbourg saw him involved in New Testament exegesis with the likes of Bouyer* and Congar.* During these Paris years, too, he began to gain a hearing from members of the Roman hierarchy. Among his many publications on ecumenical themes, his 1952 *Petrus-Jünger, Apostel, Märtyrer* was perhaps the most striking application of his research agenda to the question of the rise of, and relations between, the western churches. At Basel he hailed the founding of the World Council of Churches in 1948 as a signal event in *Heilsgeschichte* and became involved in consultations with Orthodox theologians. He was an official observer at Vatican II and wrote extensively on the theological issues that animated it. He has well earned the sobriquet that has often been applied to him: a father of modern ecumenism.

Bibliography

A. *Christ and Time: The Primitive Christian Conception of Time and History*, trans. F. V. Filson, rev. ed. (Philadelphia, 1964); *Salvation in History*, trans. S. G. Sowers (New York, 1967); *The Christology of the New Testament*, trans. S. C. Guthrie and C. A. M. Hall, rev. ed. (Philadelphia, 1963); *Peter: Disciple, Apostle, Martyr. A Historical and Theological Study*, trans. F. V. Filson., 2d rev. and exp. ed. (Philadelphia, 1962); *Catholiques et protestants; un projet de solidarité chrétienne* (Neuchatel, 1958); *Einheit in Christus* (Zurich, 1962); *Vrai et faux oecumenisme. Oecumenisme après le Concile* (Neuchatel, 1971); *Unity through Diversity: Its Foundation, and a Contribution to the Discussion Concerning the Possibilities of its Actualization*, trans. M. E. Boring (Philadelphia, 1988).

B. ODCC 365; S. G. Guthrie, Jr., "Oscar Cullmann," *A Handbook of Christian Theologians*, ed., M. E. Marty and D. G. Peerman (Cleveland, Ohio, and New York,

1965), 338–54; Otto Karrer, *Peter and the Church: An Examination of Cullmann's Thesis*, trans. R. Walls (New York, 1963); Liugi Bini, *L'intervento di Oscar Cullmann nella discussione Bultmanniana*, (Rome, 1961); Karl-Heinz Schlaudraff, *"Heil als Geschichte"?: die Frage nach dem heilsgeschichtlichen Denken, dargestellt anhand der Konzeption Oscar Cullmanns* (Tübingen, 1988).

D. Lyle Dabney

CYPRIAN OF CARTHAGE (ca. 200–14 September 258, Carthage). Cyprian's life may be reconstructed from a careful reading of his treatises and letters. Other information is provided by Jerome's* *On Illustrious Men*, Pontius' *Life of Cyprian* and the *Proconsular Acts of Cyprian*. Born into a wealthy pagan family, Cyprian was an expert rhetorician. Under the influence of Caecilian, he converted to Christianity and distributed his wealth to the poor. In 248 he was ordained a priest and in 249 was elected bishop of Carthage by popular acclamation. He fled during the Decian persecution, which broke out in 250, but continued to direct his church from exile. He returned to Carthage in 251 after the persecution had ended. As bishop he faced two major problems—the lapsed and the controversy on rebaptism.

His two most famous and important works are *On the Lapsed* and *On the Unity of the Church*. *On the Lapsed* not only gives insight into life within the Christian community during the time of persecution but also addresses the very serious problem of dealing with those Christians who apostatized during persecution. Flight was considered a legitimate way of dealing with persecution, since Jesus himself had fled to Egypt when pursued by Herod. However, sacrificing to idols was absolutely forbidden. Even securing forged certificates of sacrifice without actually performing the act of sacrifice was considered wrong. These Christians would have to submit to formal ecclesiastical penance. Cyprian is especially critical of Christians who presented themselves to the magistrate when the edict was issued and offered pagan sacrifice without being forced to, yet he is understanding of those who succumbed under torture. The Council of Carthage in 251 used Cyprian's treatise as the basis for the formulation of a policy on how to deal with the lapsed.

Cyprian also wrote *On the Unity of the Church* (251), the first treatise on the church. Upon the death of Pope Fabian, Cornelius, rather than the distinguished Novatian,* was elected bishop of Rome. Displeased with the situation, Novatian had himself consecrated by three Italian bishops and set himself up as the first antipope. Novatian insisted that sacraments, specifically baptism, administered outside the church were not valid. Cyprian agreed with this assessment since it reflected a rather firmly entrenched African custom, found earlier in the writings of Tertullian* and later among the Donatists. According to Cyprian there is no salvation outside the church. He used the image of Noah's ark: only those in the ark, in the church, are saved. Heretics baptized outside the church would have to be rebaptized; the Roman practice was to receive them with the imposition of hands. Nevertheless, Cyprian supported Cornelius as the legitimately elected bishop of Rome against Novatian. Cyprian also supported Cornelius' successor, Lucius, but ran into conflict with Rome's next bishop, Stephen, who tried to impose the Roman practice upon the African church. *On the Unity of the Church* is also important because its fourth chapter is preserved in two versions. A longer version stresses the primacy of Peter. When W. Hartel edited Cyprian's works in 1868, he treated the longer version as interpolated. J. Chapman was the first to suggest the longer version was a revision introduced into the text by Cyprian himself. Today the prevailing opinion gives chronological priority to the longer version, stressing the primacy of Peter, which Cyprian revised when he came into conflict with Pope Stephen over the rebaptism controversy. The conflict ended abruptly when Stephen was martyred in 257 and Cyprian, the following year.

Cyprian wrote other treatises and letters. *To Donatus* is a personal description of his conversion and baptism. *To Demetrianus* is apologetic. *On the Dress of Virgins*, *On the Lord's Prayer*, *On the Good of Patience* and *On Jealousy and Envy* deal with moral issues. *Testimonies, To Quirinus* has three parts: an apology against the Jews, a compendium of Christology and a summary of the moral duties of Christians. *On Mortality* consoles Christians for the plague that struck in 252. *On Works and Almsgiving* urges good works and liberal almsgiving. *To Fortunatus* is an exhortation to martyrdom. Having suffered martyrdom during the persecution of Valerian and having articulated a specifically African ecclesiology, Cyprian was championed in the next century by the Donatists as their guiding light and inspiration.

Bibliography

A.   ACW 25, 43, 44, 46, 48; ANF 5; CCSL 3–3A; CPL 38–67; CSEL 3; FC 36, 51; PL 4.

B.   DTC 3:2450–70; EEC 1:211–12; LThK³ 2:1364–66; NCE 4:564–66; ODCC 441; TRE 8:246–54; John Chapman, "Les interpolations dans le traité de S. Cyprien sur l'unité de l'église," *Revue Bénédictine* 19 (1902): 246–54, 357–73; 20 (1903): 26–51; Peter Hinchliff, *Cyprian of Carthage and the Unity of the Christian Church* (London, 1974); Michael M. Sage, *Cyprian* (Cambridge, Mass., 1975); Charles Saumagne, *Saint Cyprien, évêque de Carthage et "pape" d'Afrique, 248–258* (Paris, 1975); Charles A. Bobertz, "Cyprian of Carthage as Patron: A Social Historical Study of the Role of Bishop in the Ancient Christian Community of North Africa," diss. Yale, 1988; J. Patout Burns, "On Rebaptism: Social Organization in the Third Century Church," JECS 1 (1993): 367–403; since 1986 the *Revue des Etudes Augustiniennes* publishes an annual *Chronica Tertullianea et Cyprianea*.

Kenneth B. Steinhauser

CYRIL OF ALEXANDRIA (ca. 378–444, Alexandria). A brilliant theologian who came to be called the "seal of the Fathers," Cyril succeeded his uncle Theophilus as patriarch of Alexandria in 412. He is best known for his leading role at the Council of Ephesus (431), which condemned Nestorius* and Christological dualism and proclaimed the Virgin Mary as *Theotokos* ("God-

Bearer''). During the early years of his episcopacy Cyril took strong measures against the Novatianists, Arians, Adoptionists, Sabellians, Manichees, and varying forms of Egyptian folk religion. Cyril also battled theologically and civically against the strong, vigorous Jewish community in Alexandria. Before the Council of Ephesus and the Nestorian controversy, Cyril's theological works consisted primarily of commentaries on the Scriptures. During this time he penned numerous commentaries on the Old Testament and a massive commentary on the Gospel of John.

In 429 Nestorius, patriarch of Constantinople, objected to the title *Theotokos* for the Virgin Mary on the grounds that Mary was the mother of the humanity of Christ. Nestorius circulated a series of sermons that argued that Mary should be called *Christotokos*, thereby avoiding any implication that the eternal Logos was mutable and passible. These notions could not but offend Cyril whose thought and piety were firmly focused upon the eternal Son of God who became man and entered into fallen humanity with all its infirmities (except for sin) in order to transform it. To deny that Mary was the Mother of the Son of God made man struck at the very heart of salvation. Cyril initially responded to Nestorius' views in a letter to Egyptian monks where he argued that to refuse to confess the Virgin Mary as *Theotokos* was to refuse the confession of the full divinity of Christ laid down at Nicaea. Nestorius and Cyril exchanged letters on the matter. In what came to be known as his *Second Letter* to Nestorius, Cyril accused Nestorius of dividing the Lord Jesus Christ into two sons. In the meantime, a Roman synod on 11 August 430 condemned the teachings of Nestorius. Pope Celestine made Cyril the executor of the decrees of the synod, which insisted that if Nestorius did not recant and make a profession of faith that conformed to the faith of Rome and Alexandria he would be deposed and excommunicated. After convoking an Egyptian synod that repeated the Roman condemnation, Cyril sent a letter to Nestorius (Cyril's *Third Letter*) informing him of the condemnation of his doctrines and requiring him to consent to twelve anathemas, which upheld the single subjectivity of Christ in very strong language. The twelve anathemas, one of which insisted that God died in the flesh, led some Antiochene theologians to accuse Cyril of Apollinarianism.

The Emperor Theodosius called for an ecumenical council to open on 7 June 431 in order to resolve the dispute. After waiting several weeks for the Syrian bishops to arrive, Cyril began the council under his own presidency without them. The council formally condemned the doctrines of Nestorius, deposed him, and upheld the orthodoxy of the title *Theotokos*. Upon their arrival the Syrians at Ephesus held a counter-council that pronounced Cyril deposed and excommunicated. Theodosius initially recognized the deposition of Cyril, but quickly reversed himself. In 433 Cyril and John of Antioch reached an agreement known as the Formula of Reunion, which mentioned both the Alexandrian insistence upon the oneness of Christ and the Antiochene emphasis on the two natures of Christ. Nevertheless, the same Christological issues surfaced again, especially after Cyril's death in 444.

Cyril's soteriological concerns governed his Christology. Salvation for Cyril was essentially the ontological re-creation of the human race by the Son of God, who took on the human condition in order to raise it to a new, transformed state. This salvation was communicated chiefly in the Eucharist, whereby the faithful receive the life-giving body and blood of the Word made flesh and are joined to his body. Cyril insisted that this divinization of humankind required an understanding of the Incarnation whereby the Son of God did not come to dwell in a man but really became man. According to Cyril, if the Word of God is not the subject of the Incarnation then it is not God who saves humanity, and salvation then comes to nothing. Far from being an Apollinarian, Cyril emphasized that the kenosis or self-emptying of the Son of God into the flesh involved the assumption not of a mindless body but a complete human life with all its fragile and limiting conditions. The ontological re-creation of human nature demanded nothing less than this. On the other hand, the humanity of Christ, for Cyril, was not an independently acting agent or person. Rather, the Logos alone was the bearer of all human actions in Christ. Thus Cyril argued that humanity and divinity in Christ should be understood not as an association but as a union (*henosis*) of two realities. He sometimes expressed this with the formula "union according to hypostasis," which signified that the Logos truly united himself with a human reality and made it his own. It followed, for Cyril, that if the Son of God is the subject of the Incarnation then it is necessary to say that the Son of God was born, suffered, and died. This language of cross-referencing or communication of idioms was a short way of expressing the doctrine of the Incarnation whereby God becomes man so that human beings might become like God.

Cyril sometimes used the formula "one enfleshed nature of the Word" to express his thought. He mistakenly believed that the phrase came from Athanasius, when in fact it was Apollinarian in origin. Cyril intended the formula to connote that the Son of God is the personal subject of the Incarnation and now stands truly enfleshed. The Alexandrian archbishop often used the term "nature" (*physis*) to signify a concrete individual subject rather than the defining qualities of a thing. This, of course, inevitably caused misunderstandings about his thought. Cyril took great pains to explain that he did not understand the Christological union as a mixture of divine and human realities. He repeatedly stressed that the distinctiveness and completeness of the divine and human realities remained fully intact and alive after the union. Cyril also later acknowledged that one could speak of two natures abiding in Christ as long it was also admitted that the natures were united and not separated in the one Christ.

Cyril's theology exercised an enormous influence on the conciliar decrees of the fourth and fifth centuries. At Chalcedon (451) his Christology was of primary importance if not the primary authority, while at Constantinople II (553) his thought was the clear norm, as his twelve chapters were accepted as an orthodox expression of faith.

Bibliography

A. ACO, *Concilium universale Ephesinum*, ed. Eduard Schwartz (Berlin and Leipzig, 1927–30), 1:1–5; John A. McGuckin, *St. Cyril of Alexandria: The Christological Controversy; Its History, Theology, and Texts* (New York, 1994).

B. DTC 2:2476–2527; EEC 1:214–15; LThK³ 2:1368–70; NCE 4:571–76; ODCC 443–44; TRE 8:254–60; Robert Wilken, *Judaism and the Early Christian Mind: A Study of Cyril of Alexandria's Exegesis and Theology* (New Haven, Conn., 1970); Lawrence J. Welch, *Christology and Eucharist in the Early Thought of Cyril of Alexandria* (San Franscisco, 1994).

Lawrence J. Welch

CYRIL OF JERUSALEM (ca. 315, Jerusalem or Palestinian Caesarea–Jerusalem, March, 387). Cyril was ordained bishop ca. 348, allegedly with the support of Acacius of Caesarea, an important figure in the fourth-century "Arian" movement. Cyril's episcopacy was disrupted by three exiles. He was first deposed at a council in Jerusalem in 357 and reinstated by the council of Seleucia in 359. His second exile was decreed at the council of Constantinople in 360 and was ended in 362 after Julian the Apostate became emperor. Cyril was exiled a third time ca. 367 by the pro-Arian emperor Valens and only returned to his see upon the latter's death in 378. Cyril participated in the councils of Constantinople in 381 and 382.

Cyril's most important literary work is a series of twenty-four catechetical lectures delivered ca. 350. The first nineteen talks were addressed to catechumens preparing for baptism at the Easter vigil. After the introductory lecture, or *procatechesis*, these talks discuss the origin and nature of faith as well as the proper means of preparing for baptism and offer a detailed doctrinal exposition of the creed of Jerusalem. The last five catecheses, called the *Mystagogical Catecheses*, were delivered during Easter week to those Christians who had just been baptized and explain the three sacraments that comprised the initiation they had just undergone: baptism, confirmation, and the Eucharist. Scholars have questioned the attribution of the *Mystagogical Catecheses* to Cyril, claiming that they may have been composed instead by his episcopal successor, John. In any case, these lectures offer scholars invaluable information about the catechumenate and the liturgy in this important part of the Christian world in the fourth century.

Despite his early association with Acacius of Caesarea, Cyril's theology was largely orthodox by the standards of his time. Against the Arians, Cyril believed in the Son's full divinity and eternity, as well as in the Holy Spirit's divinity and personal distinction from the Father and Son. Against the claims of his contemporary Marcellus of Ancyra,* who denied the enduring character of the personal distinctions in the Trinity, Cyril argued for the eternal reality of these distinctions in the Godhead. Cyril did not officially endorse the doctrine of the Trinity's consubstantiality, first affirmed at the Council of Nicaea in 325, until late in his career, probably because of its nonscriptural provenance and the support it might give to Marcellus' views. Nevertheless, with his clear repudiation of both Arianism and Marcellus' "neo-Sabellianism," Cyril's thought is representative of the conservative eastern tradition in trinitarian theology stemming from Eusebius of Caesarea,* which by the end of the fourth century was absorbed by Nicene orthodoxy.

Bibliography

A. PG 33; NPNF 7; *St. Cyril of Jerusalem's Lectures on the Christian Sacraments*, ed. F. L. Cross (Crestwood, N.Y., 1951); *Catéchèses Mystagogiques*, SC 126 (Paris, 1966).

B. DTC 3:2527–77; EEC 1:215; LThK³ 2:1370; NCE 4:576–78; ODCC 442–43; Antoine Paulin, *Saint Cyrille de Jérusalem, catéchète* (Paris, 1959); Ignace Bertin, "Cyrille de Jérusalem, Eusèbe d'Émèse et la théologie semi-arienne," RSPhTh 52 (1968): 38–75; Robert C. Gregg, "Cyril of Jerusalem and the Arians," in *Arianism: Historical and Theological Reassessments* (Cambridge, Mass., 1985), 85–105.

Kelley McCarthy Spoerl

D

D'AILLY, PIERRE (ca. 1350/51, Compiègne–9 August 1420, Avignon). *Education*: M.A., Master of Theology, Univ. of Paris, 1368, 1381. *Career*: taught arts and theology at Paris; rector, Coll. de Navarre, 1384–89; chaplain to Charles VI of France, 1389; chancellor, Univ. of Paris, 1389–95; bishop of Le Puy, 1395, Noyon, 1396, and Cambrai, 1397–1411; cardinal, 1411; leader, Council of Constance, 1414–18; papal legate to Avignon, 1418–20.

D'Ailly wrote more than 170 works on theology, philosophy, Scripture, piety, reform, ecclesiology, and apocalypticism. He also wrote *Imago mundi*, an astrological and geographical treatise that greatly influenced Christopher Columbus. A leading church statesman of his troubled era, d'Ailly was a moderate who played a prominent role in resolving the Great Schism and reforming diocesan pastoral care. His theological principles are found primarily in his commentary on Peter Lombard's* *Sentences* (ca. 1375). His thinking relied on divine law contained in Scripture and on natural law, and reflected Ockham's* nominalism. He did not believe that every tenet of faith could be fully comprehended intellectually; certain doctrines, like the essence of the Trinity, must ultimately be taken on faith. He saw the power of God as both absolute (*potentia absoluta*) and ordained (*potentia ordinata*). God is not bound by created laws and can take any action that does not contradict itself; however, God may choose to act within certain parameters that he establishes, unless he chooses to transcend them.

D'Ailly's major contribution was in ecclesiology. Slowly embracing conciliarism and assigning a large mediating role to cardinals, he balanced extremes between papalists, who assigned full authority to the pope, and constitutionalists, who were especially active during the schism, contending that a general council governed the church. Drawing on canon law, Aristotle, and Paul, d'Ailly depicted the church as a mixed polity: monarchy (papacy), aristocracy (cardinals), populace (general council). For d'Ailly, Christ, not a council, gave full juridical authority to Peter in Jn 21:17 ("Feed my sheep") and his papal successors to serve the church, which was, therefore, a hierarchy led by the divine institution of the papacy. Only in extraordinary circumstances—the schism, heresy, notorious crimes—could the council determine if the pope was doing his duty.

Bibliography

A. *Quaestiones Magistri Petri de Aylliaco cardinalis cameracensis super primum, tertium et quartum libros Sententiarum* (Paris, 1499); conciliar works in *Jean Gerson. Opera omnia*, ed. Louis Ellies Dupin (Antwerp, 1706), 1:641–93; 2:925–60; *Imago mundi*, ed. Edmond Buron, 3 vols. (Paris, 1930), trans. E. F. Keeber (Wilmington, Del., 1948); *Tractatus de materia concilii generalis*, in *The Political Thought of Pierre d'Ailly. The Voluntarist Tradition*, ed. Francis Oakley (New Haven, Conn., 1964), 252–342; trans. idem in "The 'Propositiones utiles' of Pierre d'Ailly: An Epitome of Conciliar Theory," CH 29 (1960): 398–403; *Tractatus et sermones* (Strasbourg, 1490, repr. Frankfurt, 1971).

B. DHGE 1:1154–65; DTC 1:642–54; LThK² 8:329–30; NCE 11:208; ODCC 446–47; TRE 26:278–81; Louis Salembier, *Le Cardinal Pierre d'Ailly* (Tourcoing, 1932), with a complete list of d'Ailly's works; F. Oakley, *The Political Thought of Pierre d'Ailly: The Voluntarist Tradition* (New Haven, Conn., 1964); Louis B. Pascoe, "Theological Dimensions of Pierre d'Ailly's Teaching on the Papal Plenitude of Power," AHC 11 (1979): 357–66; Bernard Guenée, *Between Church and State: The Lives of Four French Prelates in the Late Middle Ages*, trans. Arthur Goldhammer (Chicago, 1991), 102–258; Laura Ackerman Smoller, *History, Prophecy, and the Stars: The Christian Astrology of Pierre d'Ailly, 1350–1420* (Princeton, N.J., 1994).

Christopher M. Bellitto

DANIÉLOU, JEAN (14 May 1905, Neuilly-sur-Seine–20 May 1974, Paris). *Education*: degree in letters, the Sorbonne, 1927; studied philosophy, Jersey, England, 1931–34; studied theology, Lyon-Fourvière, 1934–36; Ph.D., the Sorbonne, 1943; Ph.D., Institut Catholique, 1944. *Career*: entered the Society of Jesus, 1929; ordained priest, 1938; appointed to the Chair of Christian Origins, Institut Catholique, Paris, 1944–69; coeditor with de Lubac, *Sources Chrétiennes*, 1944; member, editorial board of *Études*, 1943; editor, *Bulletin d'histoire des origines chrétiennes*, 1946–71; founder with Mère Marie de l'Assomption of the "Circle of St. John the Baptist," a group of young people who attempted to deepen their knowledge and understanding of non-Christian religions; *peritus* (theological expert), Second Vatican Council, 1962–65, where he was a consultant for the *Pastoral Constitution on the Church in the Modern World*; ordained bishop, 1969; named cardinal, 1969; succeeded cardinal Eugène Tisserant in the Académie Française, 1972.

Daniélou was associated with a theological movement in France known as the "New Theology." The movement was mostly identified with the Jesuit faculty of Fourvière, who were particularly interested in the retrieval of Scripture and patristic literature as theological sources. Henri de Lubac,* a member of the Fourvière faculty, along with Hans Urs von Balthasar,* initiated Daniélou into the New Theology and especially into his lifelong study of the Fathers. Daniélou sketched the general orientation of this New Theology in an article, "Les orientations présentes de la pensée religieuse" (*Études*, 1946), where he noted the distance that had developed between theology and the pressing concerns of the day, a progressive rupture between exegesis and systematic theology with each discipline developing according to its own method, and a consequent progressive aridity within systematic theology. The new orientation, aimed at a reunification of theology, included a return to Scripture, a return to the Fathers, and a liturgical revival. The controversy surrounding the New Theology tended to set the proponents of scholasticism against those wishing to return to patristic sources. The theologians associated with Fourvière were known for their adoption of the typological and allegorical interpretation of Scripture. Daniélou's contributions to this renewal include *Sacramentum futuri: études sur les origines de la typologie biblique* (1950) and *Bible et liturgie* (1958). The "New Theology" movement encountered resistance during the 1940s from neoscholastic theologians who thought the new movement suffered from a tendency to modernism. The new movement was also criticized in Pope Pius XII's encyclical *Humani Generis* (1950).

Daniélou was noted as an intellectual, a theologian, a preacher, a spiritual director, and a polemicist. His primary area of expertise was patristics. He was known especially for his study of the mysticism of St. Gregory of Nyssa* (*Platonisme et théologie mystique*, 1953). His translation of Gregory's *Life of Moses* was the first volume of the series *Sources chrétiennes*, which made critical patristic and medieval texts accessible to a larger public. He was also noted for his books on Philo of Alexandria, Origen,* Judeo-Christian theology, and the pre-Nicene Fathers. He identified *Le Signe du Temple* (*The Presence of God*, 1958) as programmatic for his entire career. However, other writings emerged from his varied activities. Work issuing from his chaplaincy included *Dieu et Nous* (*God and Us*, 1957) and *Approaches du Christ* (*Christ and Us*, 1961). His interest in the non-Christian world and the dialogue between faith and culture found expression in *Le mystère du salut des nations* (*The Salvation of the Nations*, 1949) and *Le mystère de l'Advent* (*Advent*, 1950). Perhaps most polemical was *L'oraison: problème politique* (*Prayer as a Political Problem*, 1967), a book not accepted by the majority of his former friends in the New Theology movement.

He further distanced himself from the more progressive element in the church when he promoted a letter of loyalty to Pope Paul VI, signed by 100,000 French, in the controversy over *Humanae Vitae* and the "Credo of Paul VI." Yet he detested sectarianism. As G. Vallquist noted, Daniélou's dialectical approach defended the theological renewal after World War II against an authoritarian Thomism, and a quarter of a century later he defended Thomism against a theology disdainful of traditional scholasticism. He detested what he called the intellectual poverty of the post–Vatican II progressives and protested against what he saw as the secularism of the church after the council.

His later years found him engaged in conferences, pamphleteering, and television interviews as a critic of those whom he thought distorted both the gospel and the Council, but he never abandoned his theological work. His mature work includes the three-volume study *A History of Early Christian Doctrine before the Council of Nicea* (1973) as well as the spiritual works *La Trinité et le mystère de l'existence* (*God's Life in Us*, 1969) and *La Resurrection* (1969).

His death in 1974 at the apartment of a prostitute occasioned a certain notoriety, but a statement issued on 22 April 1975 (subsequently published in *Communio*) by the Reverend André Costes, S.J., provincial of France, and Professor Henri-Irénée Marrou, member of the Institute of Human and Moral Sciences and president of the Society of Friends of Cardinal Daniélou, provided a detailed sequence of events and circumstances prior to Daniélou's death that enabled them to assert that the allegations that Daniélou had led a double life were groundless. One of his eulogists was his long-time friend, Henri de Lubac.

Bibliography

A.   *Et qui est mon prochain?/ Memoires* (Paris, 1974); "Bibliographie des travaux du Cardinal J. Daniélou sur le Judéo-Christianisme," RechScRel 60 (1972): 11–18; Charles Kannengiesser, "Bibliographie patristique du J. Daniélou," in *Epektasis: mélanges patristiques offerts au Cardinal Jean Daniélou*, ed. Jacques Fontaine and Charles Kannengiesser (Paris, 1972).

B.   LThK³ 3:16–17; NCE 17:173–75; *Daniélou, Jean 1905–1974* (Paris, 1975); Henri de Lubac, "On the Death of Cardinal Danielou," *Communio* 2 (1975): 93–95; André Costes and H. I. Marrou, "Death of Cardinal Danielou," *Communio* (1975): 317–18; Françoise Jacquin, *Histoire du cercle Saint Jean-Baptiste: L'enseignment du Père Danielou* (Paris, 1987); Geoffrey Wainwright, "Bible et liturgie: Danielou's Work Revisited," *Studia Liturgica* 22 (1992): 154–62.

Susan Wood

DE BAY, MICHAEL *See* BAIUS, MICHAEL.

DE LA TAILLE. *See* LA TAILLE, MAURICE DE.

DE LUBAC. *See* LUBAC, HENRI DE.

DE MAISTRE. *See* MAISTRE, JOSEPH DE.

DENCK, HANS (ca. 1500, Heybach, Upper Bavaria–November 1527, Basel, Switzerland). *Education*: Univ. of Ingolstadt, 1517–20. *Career*: language teacher, Regensburg; proofreader, Basel 1522–23; teacher, Nuremberg 1523–25; dissenter and writer, locations include, Schwyz prison, St. Gall, Basel, Augsburg, Strasbourg, and Worms, 1525–28.

Denck entered the Reformation as a follower of the more moderate Oecolampadius.* Denck rejected the doctrine of eucharistic grace conveyed through Christ's presence and espoused revelation through an "inner Word," which is in all persons and to which Scripture is an imperfect witness. He opposed both infant baptism and predestination on the grounds that humans must covenant with God in baptism and must choose self-renunciation to become righteous. For him God's goodness ruled out the possibility of hell, making it possible for all humans to be converted eventually. He emphasized the imitation of Christ's human obedience and became a pacifist. Denck probably saw Christ's divinity as a matter of Christ's unique unity with the "inner Word." Denck finally turned to the idea of a private religion and renounced Anabaptism as producing continual divisions. When he died he was in the process of seeking reconciliation with Oecolampadius.

Bibliography

A. *Selected Writing of Hans Denck*, trans. and ed. E. J. Furcha (Pittsburgh, Pa., 1976); *The Spiritual Legacy of Hans Denck*, ed. Clarence Bauman (Leiden, 1991).

B. LThK³ 3:93; OEncR 1:469–70; TRE 8:488–90; Werner O. Packull, *Mysticism and the Early South German-Austrian Anabaptist Movement 1525–1531* (Scottsdale, Pa., 1976); George H. Williams, *The Radical Reformation*, 3d ed. (Kirksville, Mo., 1992).

Melvin G. Vance

DENIS THE CARTHUSIAN. *See* DIONYSIUS THE CARTHUSIAN.

DENZINGER, HEINRICH JOSEPH (10 October 1819, Liège–19 June 1883, Würzburg). *Education*: studies in Würzburg Sem., 1838–41; German Coll., Rome, 1841–45. *Career*: ordained, 1844; professor, New Testament, and professor, dogmatic theology, Univ. of Würzburg, 1848–83.

The work for which Denzinger became famous is his collection of sources and rulings that serve as authorities in Roman Catholic theology. Entitled *Enchiridion Symbolorum*, it is referred to simply as "Denzinger." Since its first appearance in 1854, it has been revised by several successive editors, who have improved it substantially, and it is still in use in its 36th and 37th editions. It was an indispensable vademecum for all students of Catholic theology between the First and the Second Vatican Councils. It continues to meet a real need, though theological argumentation built exclusively upon it has been derided as "Denzinger theology."

Denzinger was one of the theologians in Catholic Germany of his time who were trained in Rome and inclined more to scholastic perspectives than their peers of a more speculative or historical bent. The University of Würzburg was their first stronghold among the German universities and was a base for the more decidedly Ultramontane wing of German Catholic theology in the second half of the nineteenth century.

Bibliography

A. *Enchiridion symbolorum et definitionum, quae in rebus fidei et morum a conciliis oecumenicis et summis pontificibus emanarunt* (Würzburg, 1854, and many subsequent eds.); *Vier Bücher von der religiösen Erkenntnis,* 2 vols. (Würzburg, 1856–57); *Ritus Orientalium, Coptorum, Syrorum et Armenorum in administrandis sacramentis,* 2 vols. (Würzburg, 1863–64).

B.   DTC 4:450–51; LThK³ 3:99; NCE 4:777; M. Weitlauff, ''Zur Entstehung des 'Denzinger','' *Historisches Jahrbuch der Görres-Gesellschaft* 96 (1978): 312–71; P. Walter, *Die Frage nach der Glaubensbegründung aus innerer Erfahrung auf dem I. Vatikanum* (Mainz, 1980); *History of the Church,* ed. H. Jedin (New York, 1981), 8: 237–47.

Paul Misner

DE SALES. *See* FRANCIS DE SALES.

DIDYMUS OF ALEXANDRIA. *See* DIDYMUS THE BLIND.

DIDYMUS THE BLIND (313–398). Athanasius* himself appointed Didymus the Blind head of the catechetical school of Alexandria, a position in which Origen* rose to prominence. Beyond this fact, very little is known about Didymus' life. Jerome,* Rufinus, and Palladius each claim to have studied with him, and all three held him in high respect. Rufinus especially was influenced by the Alexandrian: he spent eight years in Alexandria learning from Didymus, and he used Didymus' commentary on Origen's *On First Principles* in his own translation of that work. Jerome acknowledges the influence of Didymus' exegesis, while Palladius was attracted to the teacher's asceticism and purity of life. According to Jerome, Rufinus, and Palladius, Didymus was blinded early in his life, perhaps by age four. In his writings, however, he displays a wide range of classical and Christian learning. He seems to have developed an outstanding facility for memorization. The paucity of information about Didymus' career is surprising given the turbulence in Alexandria during the mid-fourth century; though his writings exhibit explicit pro-Nicene sympathies, he seems to have stayed free of ecclesiastical controversy. His reputation was tarnished after his death, however, by his association with Origen, and he was condemned as an Origenist both by Jerome (much to Rufinus' chagrin) and by a council in 553.

Didymus reportedly wrote a large number of works, primarily scriptural commentaries and doctrinal works. These writings were widely circulated during the fourth century, especially in the West. Indeed, until recently his treatise *On the Holy Spirit* was known only in Jerome's Latin translation. Besides Jerome and Rufinus, Didymus' writings also influenced Ambrose of Milan,* and perhaps even Augustine.* Our knowledge of Didymus' writings was expanded during the Second World War by the discovery of papyri in Tura that contained several of his commentaries. Most scholars accept Didymus as the author of a Greek *De trinitate,* though a strong dissenting opinion has emerged. Less certain are attempts to link Didymus with books IV and V of Basil of Caesarea's* *Contra Eunomium.* Didymus is among the first Greek theologians to explore the role of the Holy Spirit. He affirms that the Father, Son, and Holy Spirit share the same substance, resulting in a unity of will and operation. Didymus contrasts the nature of the Trinity, which is good, wise, and holy in itself, with human, created nature, which receives these qualities through participation in the divine. As an exegete and theologian he depends heavily on Origen, especially in his skillful use of allegorical exegesis. He develops Origen's theology in some important ways, however, including a sophisticated account of Christ's two natures and a more robust description of the Spirit's role as the source of divine sanctification. As a theologian Didymus is thus important as one of the last great Alexandrian theologians of the patristic era and for the way in which he adapted his local tradition to pro-Nicene theology, foreshadowing the accomplishments of Cyril of Alexandria.*

Bibliography

A.   Patrology 3:85–100; CPG 2:2544–72.
B.   DTC 4:748–55; LThK³ 3:212–13; NCE 4:861; ODCC 480; TRE 8:741–46; Wolfgang A. Bienert, *Allegoria und Anagoge bei Didymos dem Blinden von Alexandria* (Berlin, 1972); Alasdair Heron, "The Holy Spirit in Origen and Didymus the Blind: A Shift in Perspective from the Third to the Fourth Century," *Kerygma und Logos*, ed. Adolf Ritter, (Göttingen, 1979), 298–310; Walter M. Hayes, "Didymus the Blind Is the Author of Adversus Eunornium I-V," StPatr 17 (1982): 1108–14.

Michel René Barnes

DIONYSIUS AREOPAGITA (Pseudo–). A slim body of works purporting to the writings of St. Paul's convert at the Areopagus in Athens (see Acts 17) first appeared in the Christian East around A.D. 500. After some debate, "Dionysius" was accepted as a genuinely apostolic witness and his works accorded a corresponding authority in both the Greek- and Syriac-speaking East and, particularly from the twelfth century on, in the Latin West. Modern scholarship begins properly with two essays, published simultaneously in 1895 by J. Stiglmayr and H. Koch, that demonstrated Dionysius' debts to the pagan Neoplatonist philosopher Proclus Diadochus (d. 486). Recent attempts to identify the mysterious Dionysius with a known personality from the late fifth century, however, have been notably unsuccessful. Proposals range from pagan disciples of Proclus, to non-Chalcedonian (i.e., "Monophysite") Christians, to orthodox defenders of Chalcedon.

The variety of identities proposed reveals the degree to which the interpretation of the Dionysian writings remains a matter of debate and conjecture. Those writings include four treatises: *Celestial Hierarchy, Ecclesiastical Hierarchy, Divine Names,* and *Mystical Theology.* The latter works are accompanied by ten "Epistles" of varying length, arranged in a hierarchical sequence. The first four letters are addressed to monks, the fifth and sixth to a deacon and priest, the seventh and ninth to Bishop Timothy (intended doubtless to be taken as the addressee of the Pastoral Epistles), and the tenth to John the Evangelist in exile at Patmos. The eighth letter, addressed to a monk, breaks the ascending sequence, but this device is deliberate since the monk in question has flouted divinely willed order in the church by presuming to exercise the functions belonging to ordained clergy.

Dionysius' concern for law and order is clear to all his interpreters. He appears to have been the inventer of the word "hierarchy," and he roots his understanding of ecclesiastical order in the eternal structures of the angelic world. The three orders of angels, each including a sequence of three ranks, hand down the gifts of divine purity, illumination, and perfection. The names of the nine ranks, and the number nine itself, had precedents in Christian tradition. What was original to the Dionysian scheme was their arrangement into three triads, each with higher, middle, and lower ranks. The source of this structure is clearly the Neoplatonism of Proclus and Iamblichus but, unlike the pagan philosophers, Dionysius accords his intermediates no causal function. His angels are not demiurges but revealers and communicators of grace.

This triadic system is then applied to the church which, as the image of heaven, reflects the angelic universe on the plane of material existence. As with the angels, the church finds the ground of its being in the Second Person of the Trinity. The triad of sacraments that mediate Christ's presence comprises Baptism, the Eucharist, and the consecration of the oil, *myron*, used to confirm the newly baptized and consecrate the altar. Mediating the sacraments to the laity is the ancient triad of sacred ministers: bishops, priests, and deacons. The laity are also divided into three ranks: those being perfected, the monks; those illumined, the baptized generally; and those being purified, among whom Dionysius included catechumens, penitents, and the possessed.

In the *Divine Names*, Dionysius turns to the knowledge of God and draws again both on prior Christian tradition and on late Neoplatonism. Notable especially throughout this work and the *Mystical Theology*, though never absent in his other works, is his emphasis on God's intrinsic unknowability or transcendence. Negation, *apophasis*, is thus the method Dionysius prefers in approaching the divine mystery. Here his thought is in harmony with a theme common in late antique theology both to pagan and to Christian thinkers. Likewise, both the long Platonic tradition of commentary on the *Parmenides* and the data of biblical revelation contribute to Dionysius' explanation of the names positively ascribed to God. After reviewing the mystery of Trinity in *Divine Names* 2, and doing so in a way quite in accord with Christian orthodoxy, Dionysius turns to the other names of God, including goodness, beauty, love (*eros*), being, and wisdom. Here he is both indebted to his master, Proclus, and departs significantly from him. The treatment of *eros* as the divine force that creates, sustains, and wills all things to return to the Maker could only have been written by a Christian. At two other points Dionysius takes explicit exception to Proclus' intermediate causes. The divine names, he insists twice, do not denote subsistent entities, but point instead to God's own powers or activities in creating and sustaining the cosmos.

Mystical Theology is finally both more and less than the intellectual exercise of abstraction, a sort of metaphysical trampoline, as some modern critics have described it. It is more, insofar as this brief treatise, which deals with the ascent to divinity via negation, presupposes the preceding treatises on the hierarchies and the names. It is less, because it requires the succeeding epistles (in particular 3 and 4 on the mystery of Christ) for its proper comprehension. The presence toward which Dionysius urges his readers in this little work is the same as the one revealed at the altar of the church's liturgy (see *EH*, esp. chap. 4) and to the sanctified ascetic at prayer (see *Ep.* 3). In this union and harmony of the liturgical and the mystical, the institutional and the personal, one finds the core of the Dionysian message as well as the key to its subsequent reading by later thinkers in the Christian East. Among the latter, one should note especially John of Scythopolis, Dionysius' first commentator (ca. 550), Maximus the Confessor,* John of Damascus,* Symeon the New Theologian,* and Gregory Palamas.*

Bibliography

A.   PG 3; *Corpus Dionysiacum* 1, ed. Beate Regina Suchla (Berlin and New York, 1990); idem, 2, ed. Günter Heil and A. M. Ritter (Berlin and New York, 1991); *Pseudo-Dionysius: The Complete Works*, trans. Colm Liubhéid (New York, 1987).

B.   DTC 4:429–36; EEC 1:238–40; LThK³ 3:242–43; NCE 11:943–44; ODCC 484–85; TRE 8:772–80; Josef Stiglmayr, "Der neuplatoniker Proklos als Vorlage des sog. Dionysius Areopagita in der Lehre vom Übel," *Historisches Jahrbuch* 16 (1895): 253–73, 721–48; Hugo Koch, *Pseudo-Dionysius Areopagita in seinen Beziehungen zum Neuplatonismus und Mysterienwesen* (Mainz, 1900); Réné Roques, *L'Univers dionysien* (Paris, 1954); E. Corsini, *Il tratto DE DIVINIBUS NOMINIBUS dello Pseudo Dionigi e i commenti Neoplatonici al Parmenide* (Turin, 1962); Roland Hathaway, *Hierarchy and the Definition of Order in the Letters of Pseudo-Dionysius* (The Hague, 1969); Bernhard Brons, *Gott und die Seienden. Untersuchungen zum Verhältnis von neuplatonischer Metaphysik und christlicher Tradition bei Dionysius Areopagita* (Göttingen, 1976); Paul Rorem, *Biblical and Liturgical Symbols within the Pseudo-Dionysian Synthesis* (Toronto, 1984); Andrew Louth, *Denys the Areopagite* (Wilton, Conn., 1989); Alexander Golitzin, *Et Introibo ad Altare Dei: The Mystagogy of Dionysius Areopagita, with Special Reference to Its Predecessors in the Eastern Christian Tradition* (Thessalonica, 1994).

Alexander Golitzin

DIONYSIUS (DENIS) THE CARTHUSIAN (1402, Ryckel, Belgium–12 March 1471, Roermond, Holland). *Education*: began studies in 1415 at the school of the Brethren of the Common Life in Zwolle where he came under the influence of the *devotio moderna*; M.A., Univ. of Cologne. *Career*: entered the Carthusians at Roermond where he spent the greatest part of his life in prayer and scholarly writing; procurator, 1432–34; assisted Nicholas of Cusa* in his reform visitation of Carthusian foundations, 1451, 1452; placed in charge of the monastery at Bois-le-Duc, 1465–69; returned to Roermond, 1469.

Denis' writings fill forty-three volumes in quarto—about 25,000 pages—twice the amount written by Augustine of Hippo.* The edition of his *Opera Omnia* includes 174 works. Among these there are, first of all, fourteen volumes of commentary on Scripture. Secondly, there are works in dogmatic theology and philosophy. These include larger works, such as his *Commentary on the Sentences* of Peter Lombard,* which is his principal theological work; a work on the nature of the true and sovereign God; a theological consideration of creatures in relation to God; a compendium of philosophy; a compendium of theology; commentaries on the works of Pseudo-Dionysius*; and a commentary on Boethius'* *Consolation of Philosophy*. There are also smaller theological works written more from the perspective of Christian spirituality—for example, works on the four last things, on the praises of God, and on the loveliness of the world and the beauty of God. The latter work, entitled *De venustate mundi et pulchritudine Dei* is regarded as the most important work on aesthetic philosophy written in the Middle Ages. Denis' influential work *On Contemplation* describes contemplation as a negative knowledge of God by which the soul, set aflame with love for God, arrives at ecstatic union with God by reason of special gifts. Finally, there are works aimed at the reformation of the church and society, as well as a series of sermons on both the temporal and the sanctoral cycles. Denis' spiritual writings enjoyed a wide popularity and were read and quoted by such later saints as Ignatius Loyola,* Francis de Sales,* and Alphonsus Liguori.*

Bibliography

A. *Doctoris ecstatici D. Dionysii Cartusiani Opera Omnia*, 43 vols. (Montreuil, Tournai, Parkminster, 1886–1935); *Dionysii Cartusiensis Opera selecta*, CCCM 121–121A (Turnhout, 1991).

B. DTC 4:436–48; NCE 4:764–65; ODCC 486; TRE 9:4–6; Martin Beer, *Dionysius' des Kartäusers Lehre vom desiderium naturale des Menschen nach der Gottesschau* (Munich, 1963); Johannes Möllerfeld, "Die Schönheit des Menschen nach Dionys dem Karthäuser," in *Dr. L. Reypens-Album*, ed. A. Ampe (Antwerp, 1964), 229–40; Norbert Maginot, *Der Actus humanus moralis unter dem Einfluss des Heiligen Geistes nach Dionysius Carthusianus* (Munich, 1968); Raymond Macken, *Denys the Carthusian: Commentator on Boethius' "De consolatione Philosophiae"* (Salzburg, 1984); Hans-Günter Gruber, *Christliches Eheverständnis im 15. Jahrhundert. Eine moralgeschichtliche Untersuchung zur Ehelehre Dionysius' des Kartäusers* (Regensburg, 1989); Kent Emery, "Denys the Carthusian and the Doxography of Scholastic Theology," in *Ad Litteram*, ed. M. Jordan and K. Emery (Notre Dame, Ind., 1992), 327–59; idem, "Denys the Carthusian and the Invention of Preaching Materials," *Viator* 25 (1994): 377–409.

Roland J. Teske

DIX, GREGORY, born George (4 October 1901, Woolwich, England–12 May 1952, Nashdom Abbey). *Education*: Westminster Sch., 1915–20; Merton Coll.,

Oxford, 1920–23; Wells Theol. Coll., 1923–24; M.A., B.D., and D.D., Oxford, 1927, 1949. *Career*: lecturer in modern history, Keble Coll., Oxford, 1924–26; ordained priest, 1925; entered Anglican Benedictines, Pershore, 1926; lecturer, St. Augustine's Coll., Gold Coast, Ghana, 1926–29; monk, Nashdom Abbey, 1929–52.

Dix was the most influential Anglican liturgical scholar of the twentieth century primarily because of his major work, *The Shape of the Liturgy* (London, 1945). In it Dix argued that all classic eucharistic liturgies possess a four-fold structure. Whereas Jesus at the Last Supper (1) took, (2) blessed, (3) broke, and (4) gave the bread, and after supper (5) took, (6) blessed, and (7) gave the wine; the church early on conflated those seven actions into four: (1) taking bread and wine—offertory, (2) saying the blessing—eucharistic prayer, (3) breaking the bread—fraction rite, (4) giving the consecrated bread and wine—communion. Dix saw the offertory as an essential part of the Eucharist because it effectively symbolized that it was the self-offering of all in the church that is transformed in the bread and wine by being taken up fully into Christ's own self-offering through the blessing of the eucharistic prayer. Accordingly, for Dix it is not the "words of consecration" nor even the eucharistic prayer alone that consecrated, but the rite as a whole. Although rightly emphasizing the Jewish origins of Christian liturgy, Dix offered no solid proof in following W. O. E. Oesterley's thesis that the Last Supper was a *chaburah* meal. On the other hand, his espoused theory that the eucharistic prayer developed from the Jewish *berakah* has become accepted fact and the stimulus for great strides in recent liturgical theology.

Dix's 1937 critical edition of Hippolytus'* *Apostolic Tradition* made this liturgical treasure available for the first time in a reliable way, giving direction and impetus to the many liturgical revisions and new eucharistic prayers that followed in the Western church. Although this work securely established Dix's reputation as a scholar, he was criticized in his use of sources and for occasionally making corrections based on personal theological presuppositions.

Confirmation was an early concern of Dix. He argued that Christian initiation comprised baptism, confirmation, and eucharist in a way that confirmation was essential to initiation. Water baptism acted to remove sin and to unite one to Christ in his death-resurrection as a precondition for receiving the saving Pentecostal baptism of the Spirit in confirmation. Blessed with a brilliant and intuitive mind, Dix sometimes posed theories on little evidence. Some theories, however, withstood the test of time, revolutionizing theology and church practice.

Bibliography

A. *The Question of Anglican Orders* (London, 1944); *The Theology of Confirmation in Relation to Baptism* (London, 1946).

B. DNB [1951–60], 301–2; LThK³ 3:276–77; NCE 4:933; ODCC 493; Kenneth W. Stevenson, *Gregory Dix—Twenty-Five Years On* (Bramcote Notts, 1977); Bryan D.

Spinks, "Mis-Shapen. Gregory Dix and the Four-Action Shape of the Liturgy," *Lutheran Quarterly* 4 (1990): 161–77; Pierre-Marie Gy, O.P., "Re-Visiting Dom Gregory Dix After Fifty Years," *Worship* 70 (1996): 2–15.

John D. Laurance

DÖLLINGER, JOHANNES JOSEPH IGNAZ VON (28 February 1799, Bamberg–10 January 1890, Munich). *Education*: theological studies, Univ. of Würzburg, 1817–20, and sem. in Bamberg, 1820–22; doctorate, Univ. of Landshut, 1826. *Career*: taught church history and canon law, Aschaffenburg, 1823–26; professor of church history, Univ. of Munich, 1826–90, except for 1847–49 when he was suspended for speaking out about the Bavarian king's involvement with a certain Lola Montez. Much engaged in the Catholic revival after the Napoleonic era, he contributed often to the journals *Eos* (starting in 1829) and *Historisch-Politische Blätter* (1838).

Döllinger's historical writings had an apologetic tendency, aimed mostly against Protestantism until 1848. In the second half of the century he gradually became more critical of the papacy, in the measure in which he came to see it as inimical to church unity in its own methods and aims.

He looked with a certain measure of disdain upon the neoscholastic revival in the form in which it was being brought back to Germany by some clerics who studied in Rome. In 1863, he organized a conference of Catholic scholars in Munich and expounded his views on the issue to them. Rome took this as an attack on the control it was exercising more and more in theological matters. Pope Pius IX sent a letter of 21 December 1863 to the archbishop of Munich ("Munich Brief," *Tuas libenter*, DS 2875), asserting such control and forbidding unauthorized congresses such as the Munich conference. The following year came the Syllabus of Errors (DS 2901–2980), which alienated Döllinger still more.

The movement to define papal infallibility without regard for historical difficulties brought his relationship to the Ultramontane ascendancy in Catholicism to the breaking point. In the run-up to the First Vatican Council he marshaled all his objections to a possible definition in a series of anonymous newspaper articles that set off a furious controversy (notably with M. Scheeben* and J. Hergenröther). During the council, with the help of Lord Acton, he published the *Römische Briefe vom Concil* by "Quirinus." Unable to accept the (relatively moderate and interpretable) definition when it came, Döllinger, excommunicated, did not actually join the Old Catholic Church—"*je suis isolé*," he wrote—but many of those who looked to him did. His ecumenical orientation only became more pronounced in the years after Vatican I.

Bibliography

A. *Die Lehre von der Eucharistie in den drei ersten Jahrhunderten* (Mainz, 1826); *Lehrbuch der Kirchengeschichte*, 2 vols. (Regensburg, 1836–38); *Die Reformation*, 3 vols. (Regensburg, 1846–48); *Die Freiheit der Kirche* (address for the Catholic Association, Regensburg, 3 October 1849); *Hippolytus und Callistus oder die römische Kirche in der ersten Hälfte des 3. Jahrhunderts* (Regensburg, 1853); *Christentum und Kirche in der Zeit der Grundlegung* (Regensburg, 1860); *Kirche und Kirchen, Papsttum und Kirchenstaat* (Munich, 1861); "Die Vergangenheit und Gegenwart der katholischen Theologie" (1863), repr. in J. Finsterhölzl, *Ignaz von Döllinger* (Graz, 1969), 227–63; *Die Papstfabeln des Mittelalters* (Munich, 1863); Janus, *Der Papst und das Konzil* (Leipzig, 1869); *Über die Wiedervereinigung der christlichen Kirchen* (1872; Nördlingen, 1888); *Geschichte der Moralstreitigkeiten in der römisch-katholischen Kirche* (Nördlingen, 1889); *Briefe und Erklärungen von I. von Döllinger über die Vaticanischen Decrete 1869–1887* (Munich, 1890; repr. 1968); Ignaz von Döllinger—Lord Acton, *Briefwechsel 1850–1890*, ed. V. Conzemius, 4 vols. (Munich, 1963–81).

B.   DHGE 14:553–63; KThD 3:9–43; LThK³ 3:306–7; NCE 4:959–60; ODCC 496; TRE 9:20–26; J. Friedrich, *Ignaz von Döllinger*, 3 vols. (Munich 1899–1901); P. Neuner, *Döllinger als Theologe der Ökumene* (Paderborn, 1979); W. Klausnitzer, *Päpstliche Unfehlbarkeit bei Newman und Döllinger* (Innsbruck, 1980); R. Boudens, ed., *Alfred Plummer. Conversations with Dr. Döllinger 1870–1890* (Leuven, 1985); *Geschichtlichkeit und Glaube*, ed. G. Denzler and E. L. Grasmück (Munich, 1990); K. Schatz, *Vaticanum I* (Paderborn, 1992–94); J. P. Boyle, *Church Teaching Authority* (Notre Dame, Ind., 1995).

Paul Misner

DOSITHEUS OF JERUSALEM (30 May 1641, Jerusalem–7 February 1707, Jerusalem). *Education*: studied in a monastery, Jerusalem. *Career*: archdeacon of Jerusalem, 1661; Metropolitan of Caesarea, 1666.

Dositheus spent the greater part of his active life in Romanian Moldavia where, at a distance from the Turkish authorities in Istanbul and under the patronage of the autonomous local princes, he was free to set up the first printing press in the Ottoman Empire in the city of Jassy. This press printed the Synod of Jassy's earlier (1642) condemnation of the *Confession* of the "Calvinist Patriarch," Cyril Lucaris.* Dositheus, presiding over and directing the Synod of Bethlehem in 1672, would also improve upon Jassy's statement by toning down the heavily latinate language that the earlier council had used, refuting Lucaris in point by point detail, and by likewise correcting the *Confession* of Metropolitan Peter Mogila* of Kiev, who had been the earliest (1640) to respond to Lucaris. The *Confession of the Orthodox Faith*, which came out of the Synod of Bethlehem, remains Dositheus' best known work, a genuine landmark of Orthodox theology.

His other works included a multivolume *History of the Jerusalem Patriarchate*, and the invaluable editing and publication of later Byzantine theological works in the *Tome of Joy* (*Tomos Kharas*). The latter rescued from oblivion the acts of the pro-Photian council of 879 A.D., a council that Dositheus reckoned as the eighth ecumenical (together with many Orthodox today). The *Tomos* also made works by Gregory Palamas* available for the first time in print, together with other theologians from the last century of Byzantium, usually writing in a polemical vein against Latin Christianity. It is arguable that Dositheus was the most important Orthodox Church leader of the seventeenth century. He was certainly a strikingly able one in a grim era.

Bibliography

A. *Acts and Decrees of the Synod of Jerusalem* (London, 1899; repr. New York, 1969); *Historia peri ton in ierosolumois patriarcheusanton* (Bucharest, 1715); *Dositheou, Patriarchou Hierosolymon: Tomos Charas* (repr. Thessalonike, 1985); *Dositheou, Patriarchou Hierosolymon: Theologikon* (repr. Thessalonike, 1987).

B. DTC 4:1788–1800; HDOC 109–10; LThK³ 3:350; ODCC 503; Aurelio Palmieri, *Dositeo patriarca greco di Girusalemme* (Florence, 1909); Kurt Robert Armin Georgi, *Die Confessio Dosithei* (Jerusalem 1672). *Geschichte, Inhalt und Bedeutung*, Ph.D. diss., Marburg, 1940; I. V. Dura, *Dositheos Hierosolymon kai he prosphora autou eis tas Roumanikas choras kai ten ekklesian auton* (Athens, 1977).

Alexander Golitzin

DREY, JOHANN SEBASTIAN VON (17 October 1777, Killingen, Germany–19 February 1853, Tübingen). *Education*: gymnasium, Ellwangen; studied theology, Augsburg, 1797–99; attended sem., Pfaffenhausen, 1899–1901. *Career*: ordained, 1801; assistant pastor, Röhlingen, 1801–6; taught physics, mathematics, and philosophy, Catholic Lyzeum, Rottweil, 1806–12; professor of theological encyclopedia, apologetics, dogmatics, and history of dogma, Catholic Univ., Ellwangen, 1812–17; Univ. of Tübingen, 1817–46; cofounder of *Theologische Quartalshcrift*, 1819.

Drey's first publication, "Revision of the Present State of Theology" (1812), championed the revision of theology through the realignment of its deepest mystical and dialectical impulses and accomplishments, which have been threatened in one way or another in medieval, reformation, and modern theologies. His four-part essay, "On the Spirit and Essence of Catholicism," published in the inaugural year of the *Theologische Quartalschrift* (1819), defended Catholicism as a "living tradition," the continuation of original apostolic Christianity and the productive mediation of the inner subjectivity of faith and its objective historical basis. Religion is an affair of the heart, engendering thought and action; and the church is an organic institution that communicates its essential Christological and sacramental identity according to the spirit and the needs of times, places, and peoples. His first book, *Brief Introduction to the Study of Theology with Reference to the Scientific Standpoint and the Catholic System* (1819), offered an impressive statement of the nature of Catholic theology in the context of the modern university and reflected his critical engagement with Enlightenment, Romantic, and Idealist ideas, and especially the work of Friedrich Schelling and Friedrich Schleiermacher.* His view of theology builds on an anthropological explanation of religion, a historical approach to revelation, and a vision of Christianity governed by the idea of the kingdom of God. Theology has three parts: historical, scientific, and practical. Exegesis and historical theology construct an organic interpretation of the data that should serve as the necessary propadeutic for the entire theological enterprise. The scientific nature of theology entails fundamental theology, which includes apologetics and polemics, and dogmatic theology, which deduces the system of doctrines and the church from the idea of the kingdom of God. Theology, like law and medicine, is a positive science, because it aims at the education of clergy, who will serve and adminster in their communities.

After publishing several essays on revelation, Drey produced his major three-volume work, *Die Apologetik als wissenschaftliche Nachweisung der Göttlichkeit des Christentums in seiner Erscheinung* (1838–47). His apologetics offers a philosophy of revelation that provides a scientific defense of the divine origins of the content of Christianity in terms of its revelatory and saving character. The first volume treats the basic characteristics of religion as immediately present to the human subject and mediated through creation and history. The second volume provides a descriptive analysis of nature-based religions and historical religions (Eastern and Western) in comparison with the positive and historical character of Christianity that culminates in a defense of the fullness of revelation in Jesus Christ. The third volume seeks to demonstrate the divinely revealed nature of the Catholic Church—its hierarchical structure, priesthood, and constitution.

Drey's literary remains include lecture notes on dogmatics that execute his early plan: the various dogmatic loci are deduced from the drama of the kingdom of God.

Bibliography

A. *Kurze Einleitung in das Studium der Theologie, mit Rücksicht auf den wissenschaftlichen Standpunkt und das katholische System* (Tübingen, 1819; repr. Frankfurt am Main, 1966; ed., Franz Schupp, Darmstadt, 1971); *Brief Introduction to the Study of Theology with Reference to the Scientific Standpoint and the Catholic System*, trans. Michael Himes (Notre Dame, Ind., 1994); *Die Apologetik als wissenschaftliche Nachweisung der Göttlichkeit des Christentums in seiner Erscheinung*, 3 vols. (Mainz, 1838, 1843; 1847; repr. first ed. Frankfurt am Main, 1967); *Geist des Christentums und des Katholizismus. Ausgewählte Schriften katholischer Theologie im Zeitalter des deutschen Idealismus und der Romantik*, ed. Josef Rupert Geiselmann (Mainz, 1940).

B. DTC 4:1825–28; LThK³ 3:373–74; NCE 4:1060–61; Wayne Fehr, *The Birth of the Catholic Tübingen School: The Dogmatics of Johann Sebastian Drey* (Chico, Calif., 1981); Abraham Kustermann, *Die Apologetik Johann Sebastian Dreys (1777–1853)* (Tübingen, 1988); Bradford E. Hinze, *Narrating History, Developing Doctrine: Friedrich Schleiermacher and Johann Sebastian Drey* (Atlanta, Ga., 1993); *Revision der Theologie—Reform der Kirche. Die Bedeutung des Tübinger Theologen Johann Sebastian Drey in Geschichte und Gegenwart*, ed. Abraham Kustermann (Würtzberg, 1994).

Bradford Hinze

DROZDOV, FILARET [PHILARET] [Vasilij Michajovi Drozdov] (26 December 1782, or 6 January 1783, Kolomna–19 November or 1 December 1867, Moscow). *Career*: professor, Petersburg Spiritual Academy, 1810–17; rector, 1812–17; archbishop of Tver, 1817–20; archbishop of Moscow, 1821–26; metropolitan, 1826–67.

Philaret was known as the foremost Russian preacher of his day and for other accomplishments as well. In 1823 he wrote and published the catechism that still plays an important role in Russian Orthodox catechetics today. Philaret was renowned for his work on the Russian Bible translation project. In the early stages of the project (1816–1825), before he had become metropolitan, he set forth guidelines for translation that were to be used throughout the second half of the nineteenth century. Translation was to be based on the Masoretic Hebrew text, then from the Greek, when the latter was the original language, giving both preference over Church Slavic.

Philaret directed that the spirit of the text must be painstakingly observed, so that conversation should be rendered in a colloquial style, narration in a narrative style, and so forth. He ranked translational priorities as accuracy, clarity, and finally literary purity. He also gave stylistic directions, such as that Holy Scripture derives its majesty from the power, not the glitter, of its words. In 1856 Philaret personally urged the Holy Synod to undertake the translation that would provide the Orthodox people with the means to read Holy Scripture for instruction in the home and with the easiest possible comprehension. His proposal was accepted by the Synod, and under his watchful eye the Gospel Book was published in 1860, the complete New Testament in 1862, fascicles of the Old Testament in 1868, and the complete edition in 1875.

Philaret wrote no formal theology other than his catechism. It was in his correspondence and particularly in his sermons that his absorption of the patristic and liturgical wealth of the church made itself felt. It was also this sense of the Tradition that directed and sustained his herculean administrative labors. In the reform and improvement of the Russian Church's schools, seminaries, and academies (i.e., institutions of advanced theological education) and in their revival of patristic and biblical scholarship, in the encouragement of the church's reviving monasticism, missionary work, and ecumenical contacts, and in resistance to the continually overbearing character of the tsars' appointed representatives to the Russian Holy Synod, the Ober Procurators, Metropolitan Philaret led the way for over two generations. He stood thus at the very center of an extraordinarily lively and too seldom appreciated era in the history of both Russian Orthodoxy and of the Orthodox Church worldwide.

Bibliography

A.   *Prostranyi kristianskii katikhizis provoslavnyia katolicheskiia vostochnyia tserkvi*, ed. V. Siialski and A. Kreshman (Berlin, 1845), ET: Archbishop Fan Noli, *Eastern Orthodox Catechism* (Boston, 1954); *Filareta Mitropolita Moskovskogo, Socheneniia: Slova i Rechi*, ed. A. I. Mamontov (Moscow, 1873–85); *Perepiska Filareta, Mitropolita Moskovskogo*, ed. S. A. Nechaevym (St. Petersburg, 1895); P. Hauptmann and G. Stricker, eds., *Die Orthodoxe Kirche in Rußland. Dokumente ihre Geschichte (860–1980)* (Göttingen, 1988), 471–538.

B.   HDOC 280–83; G. Florovsky, *The Ways of Russian Theology*, vol. I, trans. R. L. Nichols (Belmont, Mass., 1979), 201–20; Kallistos Ware, ''Metropolitan Philaret of Moscow, 1782–1867,'' *Eastern Churches Review* 2 (1968): 24–28; P. Kovalevsky, ''Le Métropolite Philaret (Drozdov) de Moscou, 1782–1867,'' *Irénikon* 40 (1967): 593–95;

M. S. Ivanov, "Academy's Theology (a Historical Survey): for the 300th Anniversary of the Moscow Theological Academy," *Journal of the Moscow Patriarchate* 1 (1986): 65–75; Ioann, Metropolit Sanktpeterburga, *Zhizn'i deiatol'nost' Filareta Mitropolita Moskovskogo* (Tula, Russia, 1994).

Alexander Golitzin

DUBOSE, WILLIAM PORCHER (11 April, 1836, Winnsboro, S.C.–18 August, 1918, Sewanee, Tenn.). *Education*: The Citadel, 1855; M.A., Univ. of Virginia, 1859; Theol. Sem. of the Protestant Episcopal Church, Camden, S.C., 1859–61. *Career*: ordained priest, 1865; pastor in Winnsboro and Abbeville, S.C., 1866–71; chaplain, Univ. of the South, Sewanee, Tenn., 1871–83; professor in the Coll. and Sch. of Theol., Univ. of the South, 1871–1908; dean, Sch. of Theol., 1894–1908.

DuBose is widely recognized as the most significant and original theologian in the history of the Episcopal Church. He published seven books of theological significance. His first book, *The Soteriology of the New Testament* (New York, 1892), presents his systematic approach to theology. DuBose emphasized soteriology and Christology, especially in terms of the role of human participation in the life/death/resurrection experience of Christ, as the basis for the process of salvation. DuBose also considered the role of the Holy Spirit relative to salvation and the life of the church. DuBose applied his theological system to the history of the early church in *The Ecumenical Councils* (New York, 1896), and to the study of the New Testament. His theology was deeply rooted in the lessons of his experience, which he discussed in his autobiographical *Turning Points in My Life* (New York, 1912). In this book he recalled his own experiences of conversion, loss, and discovery. DuBose was ecumenical in outlook and a frequent contributor to the ecumenical journal *The Constructive Quarterly*. He encouraged the working out of extremes through open discussion. He believed in the continuity of church tradition, but he also believed that the truth must be rediscovered in each time and situation. DuBose has been described as a "liberal catholic." He is commemorated in the Episcopal calendar of the church year on August 18.

Bibliography

A.   *The Gospel in the Gospels* (New York, 1906); *The Gospel According to Saint Paul* (New York, 1907); *High Priesthood and Sacrifice* (New York, 1908); *The Reason of Life* (New York, 1911); *Unity in the Faith*, ed. W. Norman Pittenger (Greenwich, Conn., 1957); *A DuBose Reader*, ed. Donald S. Armentrout (Sewanee, Tenn., 1984); *William Porcher DuBose, Selected Writings*, ed. Jon Alexander, O.P. (Mahwah, N.J., 1988).

B.   DAB 5:472–73; DARB 152–53; NCAB 18:43; NYT 22 August 1918; SH 4:16; Ralph E. Luker, *A Southern Tradition in Theology and Social Criticism, 1830–1930: James W. Miles, William P. Dubose and Edgard G. Murphy* (New York, 1984); John Macquarrie, "William Porcher DuBose and Modern Thought," *Saint Luke's Journal of Theology* 31 (1987): 15–24; Robert B. Slocum, "The Lessons of Experience and the

Theology of William Porcher DuBose," *Anglican Theological Review* (1997): 341–68; Robert B. Slocum, "Life, Movement and Being: William Porcher DuBose's Christology, Soteriology, and Ecclesiology," Ph.D. diss., Marquette Univ., 1997.

Robert B. Slocum

DUCHESNE, LOUIS-MARIE-OLIVIER (13 September 1843, Saint-Servan, France–21 April 1922, Rome). *Education*: studied at the Coll. de Saint-Servan, the minor sem. of Saint-Méen, and at the Coll. Saint-Charles at Saint-Brieuc, 1850s; higher studies at the major sem. of Saint-Brieuc, 1860–64; Gregorian Univ., Rome, 1863–65; Saint-Brieuc, 1865–67; École des Carmes and the École pratique des hautes études, Paris, 1871–73. *Career*: ordained priest, 1867; taught mathematics, physics, and rhetoric, École Saint-Charles in Saint-Brieuc, 1867–71; appointed to the École archéologique française, Rome, 1874–76; chair of church history, Institut Catholique, Paris 1877–85; founder, *Bulletin critique de littérature, d'histoire, et de théologie*, 1880; chair, École pratique des hautes études, 1885–95; director, École archéologique française de Rome, 1895–1922; prothonotary apostolic, 1900; member, French Academy, 1910.

Historical judgment on Louis Duchesne is divided. He applied the methods of his mentor, the distinguished Christian archaeologist Giovanni Battista De Rossi, to church history and influenced in that direction gifted students in Paris such as Alfred Firmin Loisy,* whose inferences from historical research to doctrine cost him papal condemnation as a "modernist."

No one discounts Duchesne's great contribution to historical method and to ancient and early church studies. The rub comes elsewhere. He had not at first realized the impact that historical studies could have on doctrine. Having encouraged Loisy to apply scientific methods to Scripture, Loisy in turn encouraged Duchesne to explore for himself their impact on the traditional reading of the gospels, especially on Christology. Duchesne replied on 18 August 1881 that his preliminary investigations indicated the need for a new apologetic, and he encouraged Loisy to "not be afraid of going ahead." Duchesne himself, however, soon recognized that the church's theologians and magisterium, who had no appreciation of historical methods, would be hostile to their doctrinal implications. He concluded, as Loisy said of him, that "a scientific evolution on the terrain of the Bible in the Roman Church is a moral impossibility." He then withdrew to safer ground and advised Loisy, Houtin, and Hébert to do the same.

This choice separated Duchesne from the "modernists" and earned him conflicting evaluations. Although he himself occasionally ran into trouble (students forbidden to attend his lectures, a work placed on the *Index*), he avoided the stigma of modernism, because, as Houtin observed, he did not allow himself to philosophize upon his conclusions and propose a new apologetic. He would not allow himself to consider the possibility of the evolution of dogma, even though scientific historical studies pointed to that conclusion.

Duchesne was ambivalent about his own position. On 18 January 1900, he wrote to Hébert: "It may be that, in spite of all appearances, the old ecclesiastical edifice is going one day to tumble down. . . . If it happens so, no one will blame us for having supported the old establishment as long as possible."

Bibliography

A. *Les origines du culte chrétien* (Paris, 1889); *Fastes épiscopaux de l'ancienne Gaule*, 3 vols. (Paris, 1894–1915); *Histoire ancienne de l'Église chrétienne*, 3 vols. (Paris, 1906–10), ET, *Early History of the Church*, 3 vols. (London, 1905–24), vol. 4, *L'Église au VIe siècle* (Paris, 1924, posth.); *Liber pontificalis*, ed. with commentary, 2 vols. (Paris, 1886–92; 2d ed., Cyril Vogel, 1955–57); *Scripta minora: études de topographie romaine et de géographie ecclésiastique*, with comprehensive bibliography by Jean Charles Picard (Rome, 1973).

B. DHGE 14:965–84; DTC 4:1844–45; LThK[3] 3:395–96; NCE 4:1088; ODCC 511–12; Henri Marrou et al., *Monseigneur Duchesne et son temps: Actes du colloque organisé par L'École Française de Rome* (Rome, 1975); Brigitte Waché, *Monseigneur Louis Duchesne (1843–1922)* (Rome, 1992).

David G. Schultenover

DUNS SCOTUS, JOHN (ca. 1266, Duns, a village of southern Scotland–8 November 1308, Cologne). *Education*: early studies at the Franciscan convent in Northampton; theological studies at Oxford around 1288 and finished them under William of Ware, regent Master from 1291 to 1293. In the fall of 1302 he moved to Paris and began a new set of lectures on Lombard's* *Sentences*, the *Reportationes Parisienses* (or *Parisian Reports*), working there under Gonsalvus of Spain. Exiled to England by Philip the Fair in 1303 for siding with Boniface VIII in their dispute, he returned to Paris in the autumn of 1304 to finish the *Reportationes Parisienses* and was promoted to Master of Theology in 1305. Scotus was given the scholastic title *Subtle Doctor*, a well-deserved honor for a man who developed highly detailed and nuanced positions in attempting to settle the academic conflicts between Thomas Aquinas,* Henry of Ghent,* and Godfrey of Fontaines, and their followers. *Career*: ordained priest, 1291; Scotus left a large and complicated collection of philosophical and theological works. His philosophical works are presumably earlier and date, except for later revisions, from the years before he began his theological studies. These include his *Questions on Porphyry's Isagoge*, *Questions on the Categories of Aristotle*, his two works on Aristotle's *Perihermenias*, and his *Questions on the Sophistical Refutations*. His important *Questions on the Metaphysics* seems to follow immediately after these logical works in time, but books 7–9 of the nine authentic books show some very late revisions. Scotus' other philosophical works are even more problematic, since the texts of the *Questions on Aristotle's "De anima"* and the *Theoremata* show signs of corrections and further explanations deriving from Scotus' followers, such as the early Antonius Andreas (d. 1320) in the case of the *De anima*, or the later Maurice de Portu (d. 1513) in regard to the *Theoremata*. Scotus' theological efforts, which are his strongest contributions, began in Oxford, probably around 1288. His *Lectura* is the earliest of his commentaries on Lombard's *Sentences*, but by 1300, and certainly during the school year 1301–2, he was revising it. We also know that in 1300 he participated in the disputation of his fellow Franciscan, Philip Bridlington. Finally, we know of a first collection of *Collationes* (oral disputations or conferences) that must also be connected with Oxford. When Scotus moved to Paris in 1302, his *Reportationes Parisienses*, particularly in Book 1, show a more mature response than the *Ordinatio* to the teachings of Henry of Ghent and Godfrey of Fontaines. The collection of *Quodlibet* questions, dating from Paris in the academic year 1306–7, must likewise be taken as representing Scotus' most mature thought. His second *Collationes*, whose authenticity, like that of the first, is verified by William of Alnwick, derives from Paris. Finally, although the *De primo principio*, which provides a full treatment of the transcendentals as well as formal proofs for the existence and infinity of God, is without doubt the work of Scotus, half of its text comes verbatim from the *Ordinatio*, and it thus has the character of a compilation. In sum, the works of Scotus, especially his theological works, are very complicated texts: he revised his original manuscripts over time, providing numerous additions and annotations; and his secretaries and students filled in many places that were incomplete. Scotus left Paris in the fall of 1307 to become lector at the Franciscan house of studies in Cologne, where he died in 1308. While long honored within the Franciscan order, he was declared a blessed of the universal church only in 1993.

In his portrayal of the nature of theological study, Scotus principally examined the positions of Henry of Ghent and Godfrey of Fontaines. Henry claimed for theologians a special light that provides enough evidence or understanding to warrant declaring theology a science of the realities of the Christian faith. Godfrey reduces theology principally to a study of the Scriptures, claiming that we can have little evidence for the truths that in the present life remain truths of faith. While denying any special light and without reducing theology principally to a study of the Scriptures, Scotus attempted to reconcile the two positions, arguing that believers can have some science or knowledge of the objects of Christian faith, since theologians develop arguments, especially metaphysical ones, that support Christian truths, and they, while remaining believers, thus go beyond the knowledge of the simple believer. For Scotus, the study of theology demands the development of both intellectual and practical habits. To attain his end of loving God as he should, man needs a distinct knowledge of the nature of this goal and the necessary and sufficient means to attain it. Such knowledge can only be attained through the understanding of the Scriptures entrusted to the church. The growing character of such understanding is especially noticeable in the various creeds. When new heresies arose, for example, it was necessary to declare explicitly the truth involved. Such a truth was already a matter of faith; it was, however, not declared explicitly before the new credal statement.

In his effort to guarantee some knowledge of the realities proclaimed in the Scriptures, Scotus went beyond Henry's peculiar doctrine of analogy and defended man's ability to have a univocal concept common to God and creatures that prescinds from their proper modes of "infinite" and "finite." In fact, Scotus argued, some common univocal concept is presupposed by our analogous, proper concepts of God, and even contended that his position was both accepted and implied within the tradition of natural theology. Our proper concept of God is thus composite, made up of a common univocal concept that expresses the quiddity of God (as well as of creatures) and a distinguishing concept that expresses the qualitative difference that is proper to the divine reality. The concept of being common to God and creatures is not like a genus that is in potency to its differences, which are outside it; the modes "infinite" and "finite" are intrinsic grades of perfection. In a way, they resemble the various intensities or shades of a color, like whiteness. Whiteness is a common and imperfect concept compared to a concept like "whiteness of a certain intensity," and yet nothing outside of whiteness is added to a concept expressing the grade of intensity. A common concept and a proper concept of God, however, in order to be real concepts, do not require a common reality distinct from the proper reality of God and of creatures. The proper concept is a perfect concept and the common concept is an imperfect concept, but of the same reality.

The mode "infinite" not only gives an essential attribute of God; it provides his most distinctive perfection. No other concept compares to it: neither another divine perfection nor an attribute linked to created things. That the latter falls short is evident when one considers the superiority of the inner life of God. Yet, in a totally different way, one might say that "infinite" likewise falls short: not because it is not God's most distinctive perfection, but because of the weakness of our minds in the present earthly state. "Infinite" does not provide us with as much definite knowledge as less distinctive concepts. We can more definitely conceive of the infinite being of God by considering it according to his more proper perfections, such as simplicity or immutability. Between God's essence and his proper perfections Scotus introduces his famous formal distinction, since he found the distinction of reason admitted by Thomas Aquinas and, to a lesser degree, by Henry of Ghent incapable of protecting the formal and objective character of the essential attributes of God. While admitting a real identity of the divine essence and its attributes, Scotus champions a formal nonidentity or distinction among them, since the formal and objective concept of each perfection is not identical with the formal and objective concept of the divine essence or the other divine attributes.

The divine intellect and divine will also are formally distinct from the divine essence. Scotus portrays God's ideas or knowledge of possible created realities not just as objective aspects of the divine essence as imitable in different ways. Rather, he portrays them as objective concepts formed by the infinite intellect, each of which has intelligible being distinct from other possible realities. The divine will creates all things freely, and although their radical contingency is underscored, the created order is chosen from among many wise orders of possible reality and produced not capriciously, but in a most reasonable manner. The actually chosen order is secure: by God's power the three boys in the fiery furnace in Daniel were not burned; but on its own part, as a creature of God, fire always burns.

Scotus speaks of all the possible orders of reality as the objects of God's absolute power and of the actually chosen order as the object of his ordained power. It is evident that the distinction does not imply any competing actual powers in God, but allows Scotus to speak of the contingency of the actually created order, including grace. In other words, the actually created order can be viewed in two different ways: as one of many possible wise orders and as the actually chosen order. Scotus' portrait of man's justification stresses that God could have chosen by his absolute power to grant man eternal life by any wise means, but that his ordained order is that this attainment of eternal life with God could only be merited if man performed morally good acts in a state of habitual grace. Habitual grace can thus be viewed as among the possible wise means for eternal life, and is thus not absolutely necessary; and it can be viewed also as necessary because of God's chosen plan for salvation. A man in the state of grace thus does not merit by his morally good acts eternal life according to an absolute demand of justice, since both grace and morally good acts are contingent realities that only are accepted because God wisely chooses to accept them as worthy of eternal life. In themselves, they are not worthy of such a recompense.

Scotus, strongly stressing God's free choice and the essential contingency of creation, occasioned frequent challenges to many of his theological and philosophical positions both in his own time and later. This helps, at least in part, to explain his continually developing positions in the *Lectura*, the *Ordinatio*, and the *Reportationes Parisienses*, and the constant efforts at clarification and justification by such early disciples as Anfredus Gonteri, Antonius Andreas, Francis of Mayronnes, Henry of Harclay, Hugh of Newcastle, John of Bassolis, Peter of Aquila, Robert Cowton, and William of Alnwich.

Bibliography

A.   *Opera omnia. Editio nova iuxta editionem Waddingi XII tomos continentem a patribus Franciscanis de observantia accurante recognita*, 26 vols. (Paris, 1891–95; this collection also contains some spurious works); *Opera omnia studio et cura Commissionis Scotisticae ad fidem codicum edita* (the critical edition of Scotus' works); vols. 1–7, *Ordinatio*; vols. 16–19, *Lectura* (Rome, 1950–); *Opera philosophica*, vols. 3–4, *Quaestiones super libros Metaphysicorum Aristotelis* (the first two of the five volumes of Scotus' philosophical treatises for which the Franciscan Institute at St. Bonaventure University has accepted editorial responsibility; St. Bonaventure, N.Y., 1998–); A. B. Wolter, trans., "Duns Scotus on the Necessity of Revealed Knowledge," *Franciscan Studies* 11 (1951): 231–71; *A Scholastic Miscellany: Anselm to Ockham*, ed. E. Fairweather (London, 1956), 428–39 (*Ordinatio* question concerning God's existence as self-evident); *Philosophical Writings*, trans. A. B. Wolter (Indianapolis, Ind., 1962); *A Treatise on God as First Principle*, ed. A. B. Wolter, 2d ed. (Chicago, 1966); *Medieval Philosophy: From St. Augustine to Nicholas of Cusa*, ed. J. F. Wippel and A. B. Wolter (New York, 1969): 402–19 (*Lectura* version of Scotus' proof for the existence of God); *God and Creatures:*

The Quodlibetal Questions, trans. F. Alluntis and A. B. Wolter (Princeton, N.J., 1975); A. B. Wolter and M. M. Adams, "Duns Scotus' Parisian Proofs for the Existence of God," *Franciscan Studies* 42 (1982): 248–321; *Duns Scotus on the Will and Morality*, ed. and trans. A. B. Wolter (Washington, D. C., 1986); *Contingency and Freedom: Lectura I, 39*, trans. A. Vos (Dordrecht, 1994); *Five Texts on the Medieval Problem of Universals: Porphyry, Boethius, Abelard, Duns Scotus, Ockham*, trans. P. V. Spade (Indianapolis, Ind., 1994), 57–113; *Duns Scotus, Metaphysician*, ed. and trans. A. B. Wolter and W. A. Frank (West Lafayette, Ind., 1995).

B. *Bibliographia de vita, operibus et doctrina Ioannis Duns Scoti, Saec. XIX-XX*, ed. O. Schaefer (Rome, 1955); O. Schaefer, "Resenha abreviada da bibliographia escotista mais recente (1954–66)," *Revistas Portuguesa de Filosofia* 23 (1967): 338–63; D. Cress, "Toward a Bibliography on Duns Scotus on the Existence of God," *Franciscan Studies* 35 (1975) 45–65; *John Duns Scotus, 1265–1965*, ed. J. K. Ryan and B. Bonansea, Studies in Philosophy and the History of Philosophy, 3 (Washington, D.C., 1965); *Philosophy of John Duns Scotus in Commemoration of the 700th Anniversary of his Birth*, Monist 49 (1965); *De doctrina Ioannis Duns Scoti*, 4 vols. (Rome, 1968); *Deus et homo ad mentem I. Duns Scoti* (Rome, 1972); *Regnum hominis et regnum Dei*, ed. C. Bérubé, 2 vols. (Rome, 1978); *Homo et mundus*, ed. C. Bérubé (Rome 1981); A. B. Wolter, *The Philosophical Theology of John Duns Scotus*, ed. M. M. Adams (Ithaca, N.Y., 1990); *Duns Scotus*, ed. A. B. Wolter, *American Catholic Philosophical Quarterly* 67 (1993); *Via Scoti: Methodologica ad mentem Joannis Duns Scoti*, ed. L. Sileo, 2 vols. (Rome, 1995); *John Duns Scotus: Metaphysics and Ethics*, ed. L. Honnefelder, M. Dreyer, and R. Wood (Leiden, 1996); O. Boulnois, *Duns Scot: La rigueur de la charité* (Paris, 1998). For a list of books and articles on various subject matters, see S. D. Dumont, "Henry of Ghent and Duns Scotus," in *Medieval Philosophy*, ed. J. Marenbon, 327–28, Routledge History of Philosophy, 3 (London and New York, 1998).

Stephen F. Brown

DURANDUS OF ST. POURÇAIN (ca. 1270, Saint Pourçain, France–1334, Meaux, France). Entered the Dominican order at 19; studied theology in Paris by 1303; opposed in his first commentary on the *Sentences* in 1307–8 various positions of Thomas Aquinas,* whose teachings had been made mandatory for the Dominicans since 1296; revised his commentary between 1310 and 1313 without satisfying his order; began teaching as a master in theology in 1312, but was soon called to Avignon to lecture at the papal court; in 1317 appointed bishop of Limoux, then of Le Puy, and finally of Meaux.

Durandus denied the real distinction between essence and existence in creatures as well as a real distinction between the agent and possible intellects. He held that theology could not be a true science, that God causes free actions only insofar as he creates and conserves free will, and that the sacraments are only occasions, not true instrumental causes, of grace; he also taught that it is probable that marriage is not a sacrament and that Christ could by God's absolute power be present in the Eucharist along with the substance of bread and wine.

Bibliography

A. *In Petri Lombardi sententias theologicas commentariorum libri IIII* (*Commentary on the Sentences of Peter Lombard*) (Venice, 1571; repr. Ridgewood, N.J., 1964); *Quolibeta Avenionensia tria* (*Three Avignon Quodlibets*), ed. P. T. Stella (Zurich, 1965).

B.   DTC 4:1964–66; LThK³ 3:411–12; NCE 4:1114–16; ODCC 517; TRE 9:240–42; Josef Koch, *Durandus de S. Porciano O.P.: Forschungen zum Streit um Thomas von Aquin zu Beginn des 14. Jahrhunderts* (Münster, 1927); Mark G. Henninger, ''Durand of Saint Pourçain,'' in *Individuation in Scholasticism: The Later Middle Ages and the Counter-Reformation, 1150–1650*, ed. Jorge J. E. Gracia (Albany, N.Y., 1994), 319–32.

Roland J. Teske

E

ECK, JOHANN (13 November 1486, Egg, Swabia, Germany–10 February 1543, Ingolstadt, Bavaria, Germany). *Education*: studied at Univ. of Heidelberg, 1498; further studies at Tübingen, Cologne, and Freiburg im Breisgau, 1499–1510. *Career*: ordained priest, 1508; professor of theology and pastor, Ingolstadt, 1510–41; papal nuncio to Germany, 1519.

Eck's early theology reflected antischolastic tendencies and humanist influence but his later work was largely controversialist and directed to specific theological questions under debate rather than to systematic theology. He was a combative anti-Protestant theologian who debated Andreas Carlstadt* and Martin Luther* at Leipzig (1519) and Oecolampadius* (for Zwingli*) at Baden (1526). He was also instrumental in securing and circulating the papal bull *Exsurge Domine* (1520) against Luther. He opposed, moreover, Lutherans at Augsburg (1530) and reunion efforts by Catholic and Protestant irenicists at Regensburg (1540).

In 1537, futhermore, he translated the Vulgate into German dialect for Catholic use. In the midst of his debates with the Protestant reformers he insisted that Scripture must be interpreted by ecclesial authority and that general councils cannot err in doctrinal matters because they are guided by the Holy Spirit. In debates he presented his positions with extensive proofs from Scripture, the Fathers, and declarations of councils. His *Enchiridion locorum communium* (1525) was a valuable source for the debated issues of his time. On the basis of Scripture and tradition, moreover, Eck supported Petrine primacy, seven sacraments, the sacrifice of the Mass, and the need for both faith and works in the process of salvation.

Although Eck agreed with the Lutherans on the cause of sin, God's judgment, and to some extent on free will, he was inflexibly obedient to what he understood as orthodox Catholic teachings. His pugnacious, though talented, style of debate, however, served at times to needlessly polarize positions while they were still in an embryonic state, widening the breach between Reformers and the Roman Catholics rather than attempting to mend it. At the same time, the pastoral side of this complex man shone forth in his thirty years of faithful ministry to his parishioners at Ingolstadt and his respect for the beauty of liturgy.

Bibliography

A. *Enchiridion of Commonplaces against Luther and Other Enemies of the Church*, trans. F. L. Battles (1525–43; Münster, 1979; Grand Rapids, Mich., 1978); *De sacrificio missae, libri tres* (1526), ed. Erwin Iserloh et al., Corpus Catholicorum, 36 (Münster, 1982).

B. DTC 4:2056–57; LThK³ 441–43; NCE 5:37; OEncR 2:17–19; TRE 9:249–58; Erwin Iserloh, *Die Eucharistie in der Darstellung des Johannes Eck* (Münster, 1950); idem, *Johannes Eck (1486–1543)* (Münster, 1988); Max Ziegelbauer, *Johannes Eck, Mann der Kirche im Zeitalter der Glaubensspaltung* (St. Ottilien, 1987).

Joan Skocir

ECKHART, MEISTER, Johannes Eckhart (ca. 1260, Hochheim, Thuringia–1327/8, Avignon). *Education*: studied arts at Paris and theology at Cologne, after 1275. *Career*: entered the Dominican order, Erfurt, ca. 1275; commented on the *Sentences* at Paris, 1293–94; prior of the Dominican house at Erfurt; master of theology in Paris and lectured there, 1302–3; provincial of the Dominican province of Saxony, 1303–11; returned to Paris for his second regency in theology; professor of theology, Strasbourg, 1313–23; preacher and spiritual director to contemplative nuns in the Rhine valley while prior in Strasbourg; professor of theology in Cologne where, under a Franciscan bishop hostile to the Dominicans, he was charged with heresy, 1320; published a work in his own defense (*Rechtfertigungsschrift*) and asked to be transferred to the papal court in Avignon; died before John XXII condemned, in March of 1329, twenty-eight propositions drawn from several lists of over 100 propositions taken from his writings.

In Eckhart's philosophy the neoplatonic metaphysics of the One reemerges with vigor so that God is the One, pure of all being. He takes the words of Ex 3:14 as expressing God's wish to remain unknown as the cause of all being beyond being. Yet, he also says that, because God is one, he has being—so much so that in comparison to him creatures are pure nothingness. He maintained that there is in the soul a divine element, a spark of the divine Intellect—something uncreated and uncreatable.

Eckhart is recognized as the greatest of the German mystics. Though his thought embodies elements from Greek, Neoplatonic, Arabic, and scholastic sources, it arises out of his personal mystical experience. His mature works describe four stages of the soul's union with God: dissimilarity, similarity, identity, and breakthrough. The first stage emphasizes the nothingness of creatures in comparison with the being of God. In the second stage the soul finds itself to be the image of God with a resemblance to God. The third stage of identity does not involve a substantial oneness but rather a oneness of God's operation and man's becoming. The fourth stage moves beyond identity with God to a breakthough beyond God to the point that the soul is the Father and engenders the Son. Eckhart's language can easily be misunderstood, as is shown by the accusations of heresy brought against him in his lifetime, though his teaching can be understood as completely orthodox. In his philosophical and theological insights Eckhart was forced to coin many new abstract terms and thus contributed greatly to the development of the German language.

Bibliography

A. *Eine lateinische Rechtfertigungsschrift des Meister Eckhart*, ed. Augustinus Daniels (Münster, 1923); *Die lateinischen Werke* (Stuttgart, 1956—); *Die deutschen Werke*, ed. Josef Quint (Stuttgart, 1958–); *Meister Eckhart: The Essential Sermons, Commentaries, Treatises, and Defense*, trans. Edmund Colledge and Bernard McGinn (New York, 1981); *Meister Eckhart: Teacher and Preacher*, ed. Bernard McGinn (New York, 1986); *Le commentaire de l'Evangile selon Jean: Le Prologue*, trans. Alain de Libera et al. (Paris, 1989).

B. DTC 4:2057–81; LThK³ 2:443–46; NCE 5:38–40; ODCC 527; TRE 9:259–64; James M. Clark, *Meister Eckhart: An Introduction to his Life and Works* (London, 1957); Reiner Schürmann, *Meister Eckhart, Mystic and Philosopher* (Bloomington, Ind., 1978); Frank Tobin, *Meister Eckhart: Thought and Language* (Philadelphia, 1986).

Roland J. Teske

EDDY, MARY BAKER (16 July 1821, Bow, N.H.–3 December 1910, Brookline, Mass.). *Education*: private tutoring, 1830–34; studied at Sanbornton Academy, N.H., 1842; studied with Phineas P. Quimby, Portland, Maine, 1862, 1864. *Career*: itinerant teaching in Mass., 1866–75; minister, Christian Science Association, Lynn, Mass., 1876–81; founder, *Christian Science Monitor*, 1908; minister, Church of Christ (Scientist), Boston, 1881–1910.

Eddy, founder of the Church of Christ, Scientist, was not a systematic theologian but an evangelist for the divine self-healing power inherent in human beings. Influenced to some extent by the mesmerism of Phineas Quimby, she searched the Scriptures and the human soul to discover a "science" of health. For her, human beings were created perfectly in the image of God, and thus they could discover in themselves and in the spiritual world around them a freedom from the materialism of sin, sickness, and death.

In 1875 Eddy published her *Science and Health*, a text that has become the bible for Christian Scientists and others who hope to discover in reading it the healing power that it points to.

Bibliography

A. *Science and Health, with Key to the Scriptures* (Boston, 1875, and over 200 subsequent and revised editions); *Miscellaneous Writings* (Boston, 1896); *Christian Healing and the People's Idea of God* (Boston, 1909).

B.   DAB 6:7–15; DARB 139–41; NAW 1:551–61; NCAB 3:80–81; NYT 5 December 1910, 1; SH 4:73; Georgine Milmine and Willa Cather, *The Life of Mary Baker Eddy and the History of Christian Science* (New York, 1909); Robert Peel, *Mary Baker Eddy: The Years of Discovery* (New York, 1966); Robert D. Thomas, *With Bleeding Footsteps: Mary Baker Eddy's Path to Religious Leadership* (New York, 1994).

Patrick W. Carey

EDWARDS, JONATHAN (5 October 1703, East Windsor, Conn.–22 March 1758, Princeton, N.J.). *Education*: B.A., Yale Coll., 1720; postgraduate study of theology, Yale Coll., 1721–22. *Career*: pastor, Presbyterian Church, New York City, 1722–23; tutor, Yale Coll., 1724–26; pastor, Congregational Church, Northampton, Mass., 1726–50; pastor, Stockbridge, Mass., 1751–58; president, Coll. of New Jersey, 1758.

Edwards was the most important and creative American theologian of the colonial era and one of the more significant theologians within eighteenth-century Christianity. He was an American Puritan of Congregationalist polity whose doctrinal positions were in strict conformity with the Synod of Dort. He was also a thinker conversant with the thought of the world in which he lived, familiar with thinkers as diverse as the French Catholic Oratorian ontologist Nicholas Malebranche, the British empiricist John Locke, the British natural philosopher and mathematician Isaac Newton, the Scottish Common Sense philosopher Francis Hutcheson, and British evangelists John Wesley* and George Whitefield.*

Edwards' theology was an attempt to make intelligible in the eighteenth century the Reformed and Dortian doctrinal positions that were coming under severe criticism from various sides. His theology emerged from within the theological and pastoral context of the American Puritan tradition whose covenant theology and emphasis upon an evangelical conversion experience continued on in Edwards' thought. William Ames,* William Perkins, and a host of other Puritan Reformed theologians provided the theological justification for the Puritan experience and Edwards worked within that seventeenth-century context, but his eighteenth-century world was changing rapidly in the American colonies, and he was aware of the challenges that were coming to the Puritan tradition, not only in the form of an emerging Arminianism in the Boston area but also in the form of the new philosophical orientation emerging from the Scottish and British Enlightenment. His theology tried to meet these challenges head on in order to preserve and pass on with more acceptable conceptual tools than he had inherited from the seventeenth century the substance of the Christian faith.

One of the defining moments in the history of Edwards' theological development was certainly the so-called Great Awakening of the early 1740s. From North Carolina to Maine during those years a major revival of religious life helped to change the face of religion and indeed of theology in the American colonies. In the midst of this major revival of religious life, in which he played a major role as an evangelical pastor and theological defender, he published a major work on religious experience that has had a continuing influence on subsequent thinkers in the American religious tradition.

A Treatise Concerning Religious Affections (1746) was Edwards' attempt to defend religious revivals and appeals to religious affections against the Arminian (Edwards' loosely defined designation for almost anyone who disagreed with the Dortian system of theology) opponents of the revival. The *Treatise*, however, was also critical of those within the Awakening whose enthusiasm for the revival produced an anti-intellectual form of spiritualism that tended to degrade true religion. In the end, the *Treatise* was an attempt to define clearly the nature and biblical signs of an authentic religious experience.

The *Treatise* answered a central question in the Puritan tradition: how shall the presence of the divine spirit be discerned? He defined the nature of religious affections as "vigorous and sensible" exercises of the will or inclination, then he demonstrated how ambiguous the signs of religious affections could be, and finally he outlined twelve distinguishing signs of truly gracious affections (that is, affections that had their origin in grace and not in the movement of purely human passions or desires) culminating with love as the twelfth and most perfect sign of gracious affections. All these signs were not infallibile indicators of the presence of saving grace in a person's life, but were certain guides that helped a person discern the presence of the Spirit within.

With the help of Lockean and Calvinist psychology Edwards developed an understanding of religious affections that demonstrated great pastoral experience with the religious life of the converted and with the dangers and ambiguities inherent in trying to discern and claim the presence of God within the human soul. The work was an introspective religious masterpiece that brought to an intellectual climax the Puritan search to distinguish true and false claims of religious experience.

Religious Affections dealt with a local problem, the Great Awakening, but it contained a theological vision that had more universal significance in the emerging Enlightenment mentality because it reinforced a theocentric view of human life that the Age of Reason was gradually overturning. Two other major Edwardsean works, *Freedom of the Will* (1754) and the *Doctrine of Original Sin* (1758), more directly addressed an emerging Enlightenment anthropocentrism than did *Religious Affections*.

Although he lived on the frontier of the Colony of Massachusetts, Edwards was conversant with the direction of thought during the Age of Reason and he foresaw how the anthropocentric starting point of much of modern Enlightenment thought would undermine the Christian and Reformed view of the absolute sovereignty and glory of God, a theology of justifying and saving grace, and a sense of the divine control and direction of human history. *Freedom of the Will* and the *Doctrine of Original Sin* attacked what Edwards perceived to be the linchpin doctrines of the new movements in eighteenth-century thought: that is, the idea of a self-determining free (or autonomous) will (or a liberty of indifference) and the idea that human beings were perfectible with their own innate powers.

Edwards agreed with John Locke that human beings were free to do, but they were not free to will—in the sense that the will was not an autonomous, uncaused cause that provided grounds for a self-determining human agent. The will was not only organically connected to the intellect and human affections, it was also ultimately connected to the total human condition of the sons and daughters of Adam and to the Creator God who was the source of its existence and power. The will was not a self-determining agent, but a power possessed by a human who was under the influence of either saving grace or human corruption. Edwards saw the increasing emergence (within Arminianism and within the new Age of Reason) of an autonomous voluntarism as an essential assault upon the Christian idea of divine sovereignty and total human dependence, but it was also an assault upon his understanding of the inherent interrelatedness of all created things in the divine mind. A self-determining liberty was a fundamental threat to the sense and glory of the divine that was at the heart of all human activity and Christian life.

Edwards' *Doctrine of Original Sin* was a defense of the Calvinist doctrine of total depravity and an attack upon the British Congregationalist John Taylor's (1694–1761) *Scripture Doctrine of Original Sin* (1740), which was influential in undermining the Calvinist doctrine in England, Scotland, and America. Again, Edwards saw that the traditional Calvinist doctrine of original sin was part of a total vision of the Christian life, the need for redemption in Christ, and a view of the interrelatedness of the human community. The Enlightenment movement to undermine that doctrine had implications for the entire Christian vision. Edwards argued, against Taylor and a number of others who had attacked the doctrine, that original sin was empirically evident, clearly revealed in the Bible, and intelligible in light of a divinely given principle of identity between Adam and the entire human race.

In another major work, *The Nature of True Virtue* (originally written in 1755, but published posthumously in 1765), Edwards provided a Christian and Reformed alternative to an emerging Enlightenment-influenced moral philosophy that attempted to develop a moral system independent of Christian revelation. The Scottish philosopher Francis Hutcheson had since the early eighteenth century been developing the idea that all human beings had an inherent autonomous ''moral sense.'' Hutcheson based his new philosophy of the moral sense upon aesthetics, linking the ideas of beauty and virtue. Humans had an inherent moral sense of the harmony and beauty in the universe, and this sense motivated human beings to act in accord with that harmony and beauty. The moral sense was a purely natural sense that ultimately looked to benevolence as the primary motivating factor in all human activity.

Edwards saw the new movement toward an exclusively natural view of morality as another manifestation of a modern spirit that undermined a Christian and Reformed view of morality as a gracious movement of humans to praise and glorify God. Morality for him was not a self-determining movement toward human perfectibility, but a sense of the glory, beauty, and goodness (benevolence) of God. The true moral sense or true virtue, then, consisted in a benevolence to Being in general (i.e., that consent, propensity, and union of heart to Being in general that is immediately exercised in a general good will). True virtue was an openness to, a gratitude for, and a fundamental consent to being in general. Such an understanding of virtue led to holiness (i.e., union with God) and the glorification of God, not to human perfectibility. Morality, then, is for Edwards essentially a religious phenomenon, an essential expression of God's love in human beings. Morality, too, flows not from an autonomous human power, but from a sense of the heart that originates in God's love and saving grace. What Edwards accomplished in this essay on disinterested love was a metaphysical, theocentric understanding of morality that almost all his immediate successors missed.

Edwards' theology certainly took into account the new philosophical and scientific movements of his day and borrowed the conceptual framework of the new systems of thought, but he filled the new philosophies with a content that reinforced the Christian and Reformed vision of reality. What was new and creative in Edwards' theology was his language and conceptual framework that preserved while it transformed the Reformed doctrinal tradition that he inherited. In this sense he was a modern evangelical theologian for whom reason and philosophy were not alien nor autonomous; under grace and divine sovereignty they served the Christian tradition and the glory of God.

Bibliography

A. *The Works of President Edwards*, ed. S. E. Dwight, 10 vols. (New York, 1829–30); *Works of Jonathan Edwards*, ed. Perry Miller et al., 15 vols. to date (New Haven, Conn., 1957–); *The Printed Writings of Jonathan Edwards, 1703–58: A Bibliography* (Princeton, N.J., 1940).

B. AAP 1:329–35; DAB 6:30–37; DARB 160–62; NCAB 5:464–65; NCE 5:183–84; SH 4, 80–81; Perry Miller, *Jonathan Edwards* (Boston, 1949, 1959, 1981); D. J. Elwood, *The Philosophical Theology of Jonathan Edwards* (New York, 1960); Conrad Cherry, *Theology of Jonathan Edwards: A Reappraisal* (Garden City, N.Y., 1966); Norman Fiering, *Jonathan Edwards' Moral Thought and Its British Context* (Chapel Hill, N.C., 1981); Robert Jenson, *America's Theologian* (New York, 1988); *Jonathan Edwards and the American Experience*, ed. Nathan O. Hatch and Harry S. Stout (New York, 1988); Nancy Manspeaker, *Jonathan Edwards: Bibliographical Synopses* (Lewiston, N.Y., 1981); M. X. Lesser, *Jonathan Edwards: A Reference Guide* (Boston, 1981); idem, *Jonathan Edwards: An Annotated Bibliography, 1979–1993* (Westport, Conn., 1994); John E. Smith, *Jonathan Edwards: Puritan, Preacher, Philosopher* (Notre Dame, Ind., 1992); Arni Morimato, *Jonathan Edwards and the Catholic Vision of Salvation* (University Park, Pa., 1995).

Patrick W. Carey

EDWARDS, JONATHAN, JR. (26 May 1745, Northampton, Mass.–1 August 1801, Schenectady, N.Y.). *Education*: B. A., Coll. of New Jersey, 1765; read theology with Joseph Bellamy,* Bethlehem, Conn., 1765–66. *Career*: tutor, Coll. of New Jersey, 1767–69; pastor, New Haven, Conn., 1769–95; pastor, Colebrook, Conn., 1796–99; president, Union Coll., Schenectady, N.Y., 1799–1801.

Jonathan Edwards Jr. was one of the so-called New Divinity men who preserved the theological tradition of his famous father and transformed it in light of the needs of an emerging democratic culture in late-eighteenth-century America. Although both of his parents died when he was thirteen, Jonathan Jr. was educated in his father's theology by Joseph Bellamy (1719–90), one of his father's notable disciples.

The New Divinity Movement of which Edwards Jr. was a part was a highly metaphysical system of theology that was consistent with Dortian doctrine. But it was also conversant with an emerging democratic culture that emphasized benevolence and freedom. Like other New Divinity Men he maintained a governmental, rather than a satisfaction, theory of the Atonement, in an attempt to emphasize the goodness as well as the power of God. Such a theory asserted that the work of Christ in the Atonement demonstrated how the natural world was regulated by moral government, by conformity to moral law. It demonstrated both the power and benevolence of God, and Edwards Jr. used it, among other things, to meet the arguments of the Deists and Universalists head on by demonstrating the metaphysical and logical consistency of a divine predestination and a limited atonement.

Beginning in 1791, Edwards opposed the slave trade and thus became one of the first New England theologians (another was the New Divinity pastor Samuel Hopkins* of Providence, R.I.) to do so.

Bibliography

A. *The Works of Jonathan Edwards . . . Late President of Union College*, ed. T. Edwards, 2 vols. (Andover, Mass., 1842; New York, 1987); *The Salvation of All Men Strictly Examined* (New Haven, Conn., 1790).

B. AAP 1:653–60; DAB 6:37–38; NCAB 7:169–70; SH 4:82–83; R. L. Ferm, *Jonathan Edwards the Younger, 1745–1801: A Colonial Pastor* (Grand Rapids, Mich., 1976).

Patrick W. Carey

EMERSON, RALPH WALDO (25 May 1803, Boston, Mass.–7 April 1882, Concord, Mass.). *Education*: B.A., Harvard Coll., 1821; studied theology, Harvard Div. Sch., 1825–26. *Career*: instructor in private school, Boston, 1821–25; minister, Second Congregational Church, Boston, 1829–32; travel and study in Europe, 1832–33; writer and lecturer, Concord, Mass., 1833–82.

Emerson was not a systematic theologian, but he was important for American theology as a representative of the romantic mood especially from the mid-1830s to the mid-1840s. He was educated within the liberal and Unitarian theological ambiance of Harvard College and Divinity School, but shortly after being ordained as a minister, he found himself increasingly uncomfortable preaching an historical Christianity and celebrating the Eucharist, which he saw as an empty symbol and useless activity. The experience of the ministry made him disaffected with Christianity. In 1832, therefore, he resigned his ministry and took up a career as a writer, lecturer, and poet.

By the early 1830s he was becoming dissatisfied with the cold rationalism that was a part of his liberal and Unitarian theological education and background. Influenced to some extent by Samuel T. Coleridge* and German idealism, he quickly moved away from historical and incarnational Christianity and into an idealist or purely spiritualized understanding of human nature and religion.

In 1836, he published his first major work, *Nature*, which was a clear articulation of his romantic idealism. Through *Nature* Emerson became the outstanding spokesperson for the transcendental movement in the country, emphasizing in particular the spiritual dimension that was inherent in all nature and in all human existence.

Nature was followed in 1838 with Emerson's explicit declaration of independence from historical Christianity in his so-called "Divinity School Address" at Harvard University. He argued there for an emancipation from historic forms of Christianity and for a sensitivity to the spirit dwelling within the human soul. Christ for him was a symbol of the highest human achievement of consciousness of the divine within human reach.

Although he continued to present an idealist version of human spirituality after 1838, he had completely abandoned the Christian theological tradition in his poetry, writings, and lectures. He was not hostile to historical Christianity, he simply abandoned it as an outmoded form of the human spirit—even though he continued in Concord to attend church services.

Bibliography

A.   *The Complete Works of Ralph Waldo Emerson*, ed. E. W. Emerson, 12 vols. (New York and London, 1903–4); *Letters of Ralph Waldo Emerson*, ed. Ralph L. Rusk, 6 vols. (New York, 1939); *Journals and Miscellaneous Notebooks of Ralph Waldo Emerson*, ed. W. Gilman et al., 16 vols. (Cambridge, Mass., 1960–82); *Bibliography of Ralph Waldo Emerson*, ed. G. W. Cooke (New York, 1908; repr. 1968).

B.   DAB 6:132–41; DARB 169–70; NCAB 3:416–18; NCE 5:302–3; NYT 28 April 1882, 1; J. McAleer, *Ralph Waldo Emerson: Days of Encounter* (Boston, 1984); S. Paul, *Emerson's Angle of Vision* (Cambridge, Mass., 1952); R. L. Rusk, *The Life of Ralph Waldo Emerson* (New York, 1947; London, 1957); S. E. Wicher, *Freedom and Fate* (Philadelphia, 1953); David Robinson, *Apostle of Culture* (Philadelphia, 1982); Evelyn Barish, *Emerson and the Roots of Prophecy* (Princeton, N.J., 1989).

Patrick W. Carey

EMMONS, NATHANIEL (1 May 1745, East Haddam, Conn.–23 September 1840, Franklin, Mass.). *Education*: B.A., Yale Coll., 1767; read theology with Nathan Strong, Coventry, Conn., and John Smalley, Berlin, Conn., 1767–69.

Career: unattached supply preacher, 1769–73; minister, Franklin, Mass., 1773–1827; retirement, 1827–40.

Emmons was a New Divinity pastor-theologian who followed to some extent the Hopkinsianism (after Samuel Hopkins*) that had characterized much of Connecticut and Massachusetts theology after the 1750s. He was a consistent Calvinist who, like other New Divinity Men, supported and promoted the experimental religion of the revivals.

Emmons fostered the New Divinity theology in New England during the late eighteenth and early nineteenth century primarily through the ministerial school he conducted at his home. Like many other New Divinity pastor-educators, he used Hopkins' *System of Doctrines* (1793), a systematic presentation of the New Divinity theology that Emmons believed confirmed the main doctrines of Calvinism with a greater degree of consistency and perfection than any other system of theology.

Like Hopkins, he emphasized the absolute sovereignty and causality of God and tried to reconcile that divine sovereignty and human freedom. He emphasized sovereignty to such an extent that he made God the efficient cause and immediate agent of sin. But, he also maintained that God created the human person as a free (and therefore responsible) moral agent. For him, though, freedom was not to be understood in the Arminian sense of self-determination. Such an autonomous concept of human freedom he believed denied divine causality and sovereignty. Freedom was applicable to human activity not to human powers (i.e., humans were free regardless of what power produced the activity). Emmons tried to escape from the charge that his system made God the author of sin by saying that sin was one thing and the taking place of sin was quite another. For him the same act could be simultaneously the product of divine energy and wholly the act of the creature. In this way he thought he had reconciled sovereignty and free agency. The distinction he drew, however, was an assertion rather than a demonstration of the compatibility of freedom and divine sovereignty.

Bibliography

A. *The Works of Nathaniel Emmons*, ed. Jacob Ide, 6 vols. (Boston, 1842–45).

B. AAP 1:693–706; DAB 6:150–51; DARB 150–51; NCAB 5:141; NCE 5:308; SH 4:121; Edwards A. Park, *Memoir of Nathaniel Emmons* (Boston, 1861); Henry B. Smith, "The Theological System of Emmons," in *Faith and Philosophy* (New York, 1877; 1987), 215–63.

Patrick W. Carey

EPHREM THE SYRIAN (ca. 306, Nisibis, Syria–373, Edessa [Urhay], Syria). *Education:* studied Christian doctrine during the tenure of bishop Jacob of Nisibis (d. 338) who had attended the Council of Nicaea. *Career:* deacon and teacher of the local church under Jacob and three successors: Babu (338–46), Vologeses (346–49) and Abraham (361–63); traditional founder of the theological School of Nisibis; "son of the covenant" (i.e., a member of the church living a life of virginity and asceticism in imitation of Christ); rhetor and poet in the Syriac tradition and composer of numerous hymn-cycles, exegesis in poetry and prose, and doctrinal expositions. After the death of emperor Julian in 363 and the secession of Nisibis to the Persian Sassanids, Ephrem went with many local Christians to Edessa, inside the Roman Empire; there he served bishop Barses until Barses was moved (371) to Harran; Ephrem wrote polemical works, hymns, and sermons until his death.

Ephrem the Syrian was a genius at the composition of liturgical poetry in the service of the church. Along with Aphrahat (fl. 340s) he is the first known writer of the Great Church in Syria, and his fame spread to Greek- and Latin-speaking regions, contributing to the production of spurious works ascribed to him. He was renowned as an *ihidaya*, a single person serving God and assisting as "herdsman" the "shepherd" of the Nisibene flock.

His writings can be divided into two major types: the *memra* (metrical homily) and the *madrasha* (hymn). In addition he wrote prose works, mostly scriptural exegesis. Among the *memre* are the *Sermons on Believing*, *Sermons on Nicomedia*, and *Sermons on Holy Week*. The *madrashe* include the *Nisibene Hymns*, *Hymns against Julian*, *Hymns against Heresy*, *Hymns on Believing*, *Hymns on the Nativity*, *Hymns on Fasting*, and *Hymns on the Unleavened Bread, Holy Thursday, and the Crucifixion*. Prose works include the *Commentary on Genesis*, *Commentary on Exodus*, *Commentary on the Diatessaron*, and *Prose Refutations of Mani, Marcion, and Bar Daisan*.

Ephrem's works represent a well-developed Christian culture that owed much to its Jewish matrix. Few written records of the prior tradition survive, and connections with Greek philosophy are scant. Rather, targum, midrash and the later *piyyutim* are closer to Ephrem's understanding, even though doctrinally he was a Nicene theologian emphasizing the orthodox teaching of the Trinity and the divine salvation manifested in Christ. Marian themes are prominent in his work, as is the cosmic drama of salvation reflected in the personified forces of Death, Hell and Satan, and in the heroic labors of holy people, both biblical and contemporary. Ephrem saw in both nature and Scripture an infinite, interlinked number of *raze* (a Syriac word, from the Persian, meaning "symbol" or "mystery") which coinhered with the biblical narrative understood historically. His exegesis and his theology were contemplative, and perhaps most closely resemble that of the earlier Greek-speaking authors Irenaeus* of Lyons and Melito of Sardis.

Bibliography

A. *Prose Refutations*, ed. and trans. C. W. Mitchell, E. A. Bevan, and F. C. Burkitt, 2 vols. (London, 1912–21); *In Genesim et in Exodum commentarii*, ed. Raymond Tonneau, CSCO 152–53 (Louvain, 1955); *Commentarius in Evangelium Concordans*, ed. L. Leloir (Dublin, 1960) and *Folios additionels*, ed. idem (Louvain, 1990); *Syriac Hymns and Homilies*, ed. and trans. Edmund Beck, CSCO (Louvain, 1955–79).

B. DTC 5:188–93; LThK³ 3:708–10; NCE 5:463–64; ODCC 551; TRE 9:755–62; Robert Murray, *Symbols of Church and Kingdom: A Study in Early Syriac Tradition* (Cambridge, 1975); Sebastian Brock, *The Harp of the Spirit*, 2d ed. (London, 1983); T. B. Mansour, *La pensée symbolique de S. Ephrem le Syrien* (Kaslik, 1988); Kathleen McVey, *Ephrem the Syrian: Hymns* (New York, 1989); Sebastian Brock, *The Luminous Eye: The Spiritual World Vision of St. Ephrem* (Kalamazoo, Mich., 1992); Sidney H. Griffith, *'Faith Adoring the Mystery': Reading the Bible with St. Ephraem the Syrian* (Milwaukee, Wis., 1997).

Robin Darling Young

ERASMUS, DESIDERIUS (27 or 28 October 1467?, Rotterdam, the Netherlands–11 July 1536, Basel, Switzerland). *Education*: studied at Deventer and 's-Hertogenbosch, 1484–87; studied theology, Coll. de Montaigue, Univ. of Paris, 1495. *Career*: joined Augustinian Canons, 1487; ordained priest, 1492; writer and translator, France, Netherlands, England, Venice, Basel, Louvain, Freiburg, 1495–1536.

Erasmus was the foremost humanist of his generation. For him theology was primarily a practical affair of learning to know and follow Christ. In 1499 Lord Mountjoy invited Erasmus to visit England, where he met leading humanists such as John Colet and Thomas More. They taught him how the humanist critical study of the Scriptures and church fathers flavored by a dash of Neoplatonism could provide learned piety as an alternative to the dry late scholasticism, which Erasmus despised. Erasmus applied himself in England to mastering Greek as the necessary tool for understanding the New Testament and the Greek Fathers.

In 1500 Erasmus returned to the Continent and spent four years wandering from university to university. In 1503 he published his *Enchiridion Militis Christiani*, the best summary of his developing *philosophia Christi*. His philosophy of Christ owed a considerable debt to the *devotio moderna*, most notably in its rejection of scholasticism and speculative theology and its stress on inward piety. Erasmus also rejected much of popular piety, especially outward practices such as pilgrimages, relics, and devotion to the saints. He downplayed the sacraments and the institutional church but did not reject them. He did not share the anti-intellectualism of the *devotio moderna*; rather he felt linguistic, historical, and literary skill were essential to the renewal of Christianity. Thus, when in 1505 he published Lorenzo Valla's annotations on the New Testament, his preface stressed philology's contribution to a proper understanding of Scripture. After being awarded a doctorate by the University of Turin in 1506 Erasmus worked for two years at Venice with the great printer Aldus Manutius; during these years he prepared and published a greatly expanded version of his *Adages*.

From 1508 to 1514 Erasmus was back in England, mainly at Cambridge. It was in 1508 as a guest of Thomas More that he wrote his most famous work, the *Praise of Folly*, which held up for ridicule scholastic theologians, greedy churchmen, and superstitious friars and peasants. After his English sojourn Erasmus spent several years in Brabant, mainly teaching at Louvain; in these years he wrote two works intended for young Charles V, the *Institutio principis Christiani* and the *Querela pacis* and began his detailed paraphrases of the New Testament. Erasmus' battle cry against his scholastic opponents was *ad fontes*: the renewal of Christianity depended mainly upon a return to the Scriptures and Fathers of the early church. Erasmus devoted most of his last twenty years to editing these sources—this work proved his greatest contribution to theology. In 1516 he rushed out the first printed edition of the Greek New Testament together with his own Latin translation, notes, and several introductions. The work was widely praised and damned but ran through more than two hundred editions. Working with several assistants he then began an immense project of publishing the works of the Latin and Greek Fathers. First came his beloved St. Jerome*—four volumes in 1516—then Cyprian* in 1520, Pseudo-Arnobius in 1522, Hilary* in 1523, Irenaeus* in 1526, Ambrose* in 1527, Augustine* in 1528, John Chysostom* in 1530, Basil* in 1532, and Origen* in 1536. Erasmus also insisted that many writings of classical Greek and Latin authors supported Christian morality; accordingly he also continued to edit and publish these works. In 1521 Erasmus settled down for the next thirteen years at Basel where he had the humanist publisher John Froben as a friend. The majority of Erasmus' torrent of publications henceforward came from Froben's press.

In 1517 Erasmus was Europe's leading religious and literary figure. Suddenly Martin Luther* eclipsed him. Erasmus and Luther shared so many of the same enemies and attitudes toward popular Catholicism that some conservatives claimed that ''Erasmus laid the egg that Luther hatched.'' Both Catholics and Lutherans tried to enlist Erasmus and his pen. For several years Erasmus tried to steer a middle course, urging mutual forbearance, but in 1524 he attacked Luther with his *De Libero Arbitrio*. Luther replied in his *De Servo Arbitrio* with devastating effect, dismissing Erasmus as a feeble skeptic. Erasmus tried to answer with his lengthy *Hyperaspistes* (1526–27).

In 1527 the death of Froben and the triumph of Zwinglian reformers made life in Basel increasingly distasteful to Erasmus. He moved to Catholic Freiburg in 1529 where he remained for six years. In 1535 he returned to Basel to publish his *Ecclesiastes*, a manual on preaching. His death continued the ambiguities of his life: he left no money for masses and did not receive the last sacraments.

Bibliography

A.   *Opera omnia*, 11 vols. (Leiden, 1703–6; repr. Hildesheim, 1961–62); *Opera omnia*, 21 vols. to date (Amsterdam, 1969–); *Opus epistolarum Desiderii Erasmi Roterodami*, ed. Percy S. Allen, 12 vols. (Oxford, 1906–58); *The Collected Works of Erasmus*, 86 vols. to date (Toronto, 1974–).

B.   DTC 5:388–97; LThK³ 3:735–37; NCE 5:508–11; ODCC 556–57; OEncR 2:55–59; TRE 10:1–18; Margaret Mann Phillips, *Erasmus and the Northern Renaissance* (London, 1981); Roland Bainton, *Erasmus of Christendom* (New York, 1969); Marjorie O'Rourke Boyle, *Erasmus on Language and Method in Theology* (Toronto, 1977); James

McConica, *Erasmus* (Oxford, 1991); Cornelis Augustijn, *Erasmus: His Life, World, and Influence* (Toronto, 1991); E.-E. Halkin, *Erasmus: A Critical Biography* (Oxford, 1993); Hilmar Pabel, ed., *Erasmus' Vision of the Church* (Kirksville, Mo., 1995).

John Patrick Donnelly

ERIGENA, JOHN SCOTUS (ca. 810, Ireland–d. after 870). Educator, translator, and theologian, Erigena was at the palace school of Charles the Bald by 847, teaching grammar and dialectics. In 851 Hincmar of Rheims,* involved in the controversy with Gottschalk* over predestination since 849, consulted Erigena, who offered his *De divina praedestinatione liber*. Though it argued against the double predestination taught by Gottschalk, its difficulty and its idiosyncratic defense of single predestination gained it little favor, and it was condemned by councils at Valencia (855) and Langres (859). Later (860–62), commissioned by Charles, Erigena undertook what became his most influential work, translations of the works of Pseudo-Dionysius* (superceding the earlier and inferior translation of Hilduin, Abbot of St.-Denis). Erigena also wrote a commentary on the Dionysiac literature (*Expositiones super ierarchiam caelestem sancti Dionysii*, 865–70). His translations from the Greek continued with the *Ambigua* of Maximus the Confessor* and *De opificio hominis* (otherwise known as *De imagine*) of Gregory of Nyssa* (862–63), and, later, the *Quaestiones ad Thalassium* of Maximus (864–66). A reported translation of Epiphanius's *Ancoratus* has not survived. Erigena's work as a teacher of the liberal arts is reflected in his *Annotations* to Martianus Capella (859–60). Homilies on the Prologue to John's Gospel and an (incomplete) commentary on John's Gospel were written towards the end of his life, and letters and poems also survive.

Erigena's most original work by far, however, is his *De divisione naturae* or *Periphyseon* (864–66) in five books. This work displays an enormous erudition drawn from a great variety of sources, both Latin and Greek, including especially Dionysius, Augustine,* Gregory of Nyssa, and Maximus the Confessor, but also Ambrose,* Basil of Caesarea,* Boethius,* Chrysostom,* Gregory of Nazianzus,* Gregory the Great,* Hilary,* Isidore,* Jerome,* Origen,* and many classical sources as well. Erigena attempts a harmonization of Eastern and Western writers, attempting to read, for example, Augustine through a spiritual cosmology and eschatology drawn from Gregory of Nyssa and Dionysius. The results are not as stilted as one might expect. Erigena is a sophisticated and subtle interpreter, who easily amplifies the Platonic overtones in Augustine's doctrines. He has a keen sense for the genuine ambiguities in Augustinian thought (as, for example, the precise status of the original bodies of Adam and Eve, and of the spiritual bodies of the eschaton).

Erigena divides all ''natures'' into four categories: (1) nature that creates, itself uncreated; (2) nature that creates, itself created; (3) nature that is created and does not create; and (4) nature that does not create, itself uncreated. The first is God as First Principle and ''superessential'' cause, beyond all categorization and predication. Even the category of relation can only be predicated metaphorically, and the same is true of "love" as a designation of God. Thus Erigena teaches an apophaticism more absolute than even Dionysius'. Nature that creates, itself created, is the set of primordial causes that reside in the Word. They are eternal, but their eternity is created. They are the "paradigms" that eternally mediate the intentions of the uncreated Word into creation proper—that is, nature that is created and does not create. A double universe of intelligible and sensible realities, these are the "effects" of the causes that are themselves always present together with the effects. They are the "work" of God, but also are in a way God Himself, God created by Himself.

The Fall of man, his turning towards the material in place of the spiritual, resulted in the fall of the rest of creation, which as a result descends or "flows down" as far as the bodily and sensible, though even as such sensible creation is good, an expression of the Word in the face of sin. Man's nature becomes as it were divided against itself, mind and body, thought becoming dependent upon sensation, and bodily nature itself divided into two sexes. The ascent of Man in return to God is not possible without Christ, the Word who became fully human, descending to the realm of multiplicity because of His mercy, and as such recalling all things to Himself as God.

The fourth category of nature, nature that is not created and does not create, is once again God as cause, only in this case as end, final cause, the point of return, God as final good, truly lovable, the object of our desire, for which we yearn, having been taught by God's mercy in the Incarnation and the subsequent economy of symbol, Scripture, and sacrament, and to which we return in ascent. Our return is our divinization, *theosis*, an absorption in or union with God, which is nevertheless by grace and which does not entail a change of substance on either part, though again Erigena can sometimes speak about this and other issues regarding the relation between Creator and creation in language strong enough to have prompted condemnations on the grounds of pantheism (Council of Paris, 1210; Honorius III, 1225; *Index of Forbidden Books*, 1681).

Bibliography

A.   PL 122; *Epistolae*, ed. E. Dümmler, MGH *Epistolae* 6; *Iohannis Scoti Annotationes in Marcianum*, ed. Cora E. Lutz (New York, 1939); *Carmina*, ed. M. W. Herren, Scriptores Latini Hiberniae 12 (Dublin, 1993); *Commentarius in Evangelium Johannis*, ed. É. Jeauneau, SC 180 (1972); *De divina praedestinatione liber*, ed. G. Madec, CCCM 50 (1978); *Le "De Imagine" de Grégoire de Nysse* [Erigena's translation], ed. M. Cappuyns, RTAM 32 (1965): 205–62; *Homilia in prologum Sancti Evangelii Secundum Johannem*, ed. É. Jeauneau SC 151 (1969); *Expositiones in Ierarchiam Coelestem*, ed. J. Barbet, CCCM 31 (1975); *Maximi Confessoris Ambigua ad Iohannem juxta . . . Eriugenae . . . interpretationem*, ed. É. Jeauneau, CCSG 18 (1988); *Maximi Confessoris Quaestiones ad Thalassium*, ed. C. Laga and C. Steel, CCSG 7, 22 (1980, 1990); *Periphyseon libri V (De divisione naturae)*, I-III, ed. I. P. Sheldon-Williams; IV, ed. É. Jeauneau, Scriptores Latini Hiberniae 7, 9, 11, 13 (1968–96); Guy-H. Allard, *Johannis Scoti Eriugenae Periphyseon: Indices Generales* (Montreal, 1983).
B.   BBKL 3:563–67; LThK³ 5:966–68; NCE 7:1072–74; ODCC 558–59; TRE 17:

156–72; É. Jeauneau, in SC 151.171–98; 180.88–90 [bibliographies]; J. J. O'Meara, *Eriugena* (1969); Mary Brennan, "A Bibliography of Publications in the Field of Eriugenian Studies 1800–1975," *Studi Medievali* 3d ser. 18 (1977): 401–77; idem, *A Guide to Eriugenian Studies . . . 1930–87* (1985); idem, "Materials for the Biography of J. Scottus Eriugena," *Studi Medievali* 3d ser. 27 (1986) 412–60; Werner Beierwaltes, *Eriugena. Grundzüge seines Denkens* (Frankfurt am Main, 1994, with bibliography).

John C. Cavadini

EUSEBIUS OF CAESAREA (ca. 260, Palestine–ca. 339, Caesarea, Palestine). *Education*: studied under Pamphilus, a disciple of Origen.* *Career*: bishop of Caesarea in Palestine, ca. 313, and was an early supporter of Arius.* After being condemned for this at an Antiochene synod in 324, he vindicated himself at the Council of Nicaea in 325 by subscribing to the Creed with some qualifications.

Eusebius was a prolific writer in many genres. His *Ecclesiastical History* preserves many original documents pertinent to early Christianity. His biblical exegesis (on the Psalms and Isaiah) sought to balance allegorical and literal or historical interpretations of Scripture. His apologies (*Preparation for the Gospel* and *Demonstration of the Gospel*) sought to prove the truth of Christianity by showing the fulfillment of prophecy and Scripture in Christian history. As a political theorist (*In Praise of Constantine* and *Life of Constantine*), Eusebius described the Roman emperor as the image and representative of Christ on earth. As a dogmatic theologian (in *Against Marcellus* and *Ecclesiastical Theology*), Eusebius taught a preexistent Trinity of three persons or *hypostaseis*. The Son is begotten by the Father, but is subordinate to him and not eternal. The Holy Spirit is the first and most exalted creature of the Son. Eusebius' Christology anticipates that of Apollinarius of Laodicea*: becoming incarnate, the Son takes on human flesh, but not a human soul.

Bibliography

A. *Eusebius Werke*, GCS 7, 9, 11, 14, 20, 23, 43, 47; NPNF 2, 1.

B. DHGE 15:1437–60; LThK³ 1007–9; NCE 5:633–36; ODCC 574; TRE 10:537–43; H. Berkhof, *Die Theologie des Eusebius von Caesarea* (Amsterdam, 1939); D. S. Wallace-Hadrill, *Eusebius of Caesarea* (Westminster, Md., 1961); T. D. Barnes, *Constantine and Eusebius* (Cambridge, Mass., 1981).

Kelley McCarthy Spoerl

EUSEBIUS OF NICOMEDIA (d. ca. 342). Eusebius of Nicomedia, a disciple of Lucian of Antioch, became the most important Christian leader in the period between the Council of Nicaea (325) and his death. Eusebius received Arius* after his expulsion from Alexandria and supported the presbyter by launching a letter-writing campaign against Alexander of Alexandria. He attended the Council of Nicaea and seems to have assented, reluctantly, to its creed and its condemnation of Arius. Immediately after the council, however, he communicated with some of Arius' supporters, an act that resulted both in his exile and an angry letter from the emperor to the church at Nicomedia. Due in part to his familiarity with Constantine's sister, however, Eusebius was restored to his see in 328 and sometime in 337 became bishop of Constantinople. Upon his reinstatement to Nicomedia, Eusebius began to campaign actively against Marcellus of Ancyra* and Athanasius of Alexandria,* presiding over synods that deposed both of these, as well as Eustathius of Antioch. Eusebius enjoyed a close relationship with and great influence over Constantine; it was he who baptized the dying emperor. The ecclesiastical historians, with Athanasius, portray Eusebius as an ambitious, power-hungry scoundrel, but he was a gifted leader who was willing to put ideology over personal security. Eusebius may also have encouraged missionary efforts outside the Roman Empire.

Almost nothing survives of Eusebius' writing except a brief letter that he wrote to Paulinus of Tyre (c. 320) and a few fragments quoted by his opponents. Although little survives from his postexilic period, enough exists to provide a coherent picture of his early trinitarian theology, favorable to Arius. Eusebius worries that Alexander's theology results either in two gods, the one God being divided into two, or, worst of all, in God's experiencing change. To counter this Eusebius asserts that there is one "Unbegotten" (*agennêtos*) who produced another of a different substance and power. In Eusebius' opinion, to say that the Son is "from God" does not mean that the Son shares God's substance, since all things are "from God" without sharing in his substance. God creates all things by his will without communicating his substance. Especially noteworthy is Eusebius' exegesis of Prv 8:22, a text that was crucial in subsequent trinitarian debates. This text, for Eusebius, shows that the Son was "created and founded," thus proving that the Son is not an "emanation" from the Father; he could not both "emanate" and be created. Unlike Arius, or at least the Arius who was anathematized by Nicaea, Eusebius does not claim that the Son was created "out of nothing," and he may have been responsible for changing Arius' position on this doctrine. Instead he decries the possibility of knowing "the mode of his beginning." Despite this difference, Eusebius' early theology must be judged "Arian." Like Arius, Eusebius emphasizes God's inability to communicate his essence and the reduction of the Son's divinity that this incomparability implies.

Bibliography

A. *Theodoret, Jerome, Gennadius, Rufinus: Historical Writings*, trans. Blomfield Jackson, NPNF 2, 3 (New York, 1892); Hans Georg Optiz, ed., *Athanasius Werke* 3, 1. *Urkunden zur Geschichte des arianischen Streites* (Berlin, 1934), 318–28; L. Parmentier and F. Scheidweiler, *Theodoret Kirchengeschichte* (Berlin, 1954).

B. DTC 5:1539–51; LThK³ 3:1007–9; NCE 5:633–36; ODCC 574; TRE 10:537–42; Pierre Nautin, "Note critique sur la lettre d'Eusèbe de Nicomédie à Paulin de Tyr," VC 17 (1963): 24–27; G. C. Stead, " ' Eusebius' and the Council of Nicea," JTS 24 (1963): 85–100; Colm Luibhéid, "The Arianism of Eusebius of Nicomedia," *Irish Theological Quarterly* 43 (1976): 3–23; Rowan Williams, *Arius: Heresy and Tradition* (London,

1987); R. P. C. Hanson, *The Search for the Christian Doctrine of God* (Edinburgh, 1988); Timothy D. Barnes, *Athanasius and Constantine* (Cambridge, Mass., 1993).

Michel René Barnes

EVAGRIUS OF PONTUS (Ibora, Pontus [Asia Minor], 345–Kellia [near Alexandria] Egypt, 399). *Education*: rhetoric and philosophy in Pontus; theology under Gregory of Nazianzus,* in Cappadocia and Constantinople; monastic teaching, theology in Jerusalem under Melania and Rufinus and in Egypt under Macarius the Great, Macarius the Egyptian, et al. *Career*: ordained lector perhaps by Basil of Caesarea*; deacon by Gregory of Nazianzus, 379; assisted Gregory in Constantinople, 379–81, wrote letter *De Fide*; fled to Jerusalem and vested as monk by Melania before 383; to Nitria, site of monastic settlements, 383; to Kellia where he participated in study-circles, composed numerous treatises, advised visitors, corresponded with like-minded monks and nuns, and copied manuscripts to support himself, 385–99.

Evagrius of Pontus was, after Antony of Egypt, the chief theorist of intellectualist monasticism and Christian spirituality in the patristic period. Trained by two of the Cappadocians, he was attached early to the Nicene party and promoted its theology. However, he wrote no doctrinal treatises or formal scriptural commentaries; rather, almost all his works were directed toward those attempting to live the full ascetic life as solitaries or as members of monastic communities. Unlike Antony, he wrote in the form of *apophthegmata*, short sayings meant to stimulate thought in their hearer; he was the first to set down on paper the *apophthegm*, perhaps following the oral interview of the monks and their disciples, and his example was followed by the better-known *Sayings (Apophthegmata) of the Desert Fathers*.

The learned monasticism of lower Egypt emphasized biblical exegesis and a theology of the contemplative life. Therefore, Evagrius composed *scholia* and collections of sayings that helped monks to understand how their craft of spiritual exercises, or *praktike*, followed the teachings of Christ revealed in the Bible. He outlined monastic *paideia* in this same context in the more programmatic, three-volume *Praktike, Gnostikos*, and *Kephalaia Gnostika*. Evagrius also wrote treatises to monks and nuns on the evil *logismoi* or the thoughts obsessively occurring to those attempting to pray, on scriptural texts for use against demonic temptation, and on prayer. A large corpus of letters survives.

The Alexandrian theologians Clement* and Origen,* as interpreted for monastic endeavors, form the basis for Evagrius' thought. But Evagrius did not begin with an "Origenistic," quasi-philosophical system of thought with which to promote a solipsistic contemplation of the Godhead. Rather, he began with a diagnosis of human ills and suggested a carefully-sequenced program of curing the fragmented human self by defeating the passions and the *logismoi* by means of *askesis* and the imitation of Christ. Once *apatheia* (purity of heart) is achieved, the monk may love and know the natural world and God and come to a *gnosis* of the Trinity. His writings were condemned as Origenist in 553 under Justinian, and most were lost in Greek, though preserved in Syriac and Armenian. He influenced Latin, Benedictine monasticism through Cassian,* Syrian through Philoxenos, and Greek through Diadochos, Palladius, John Climacus, and Maximus the Confessor.*

Bibliography

A.   *Evagriana syriaca*, ed. J. Muyldermans (Louvain, 1952); *Les six Centuries des "Kephalaia gnostica,"* ed. Antoine Guillaumont, PO 28, 1 (Turnhout, 1958); Evagrius Ponticus, *The Praktikos: Chapters on Prayer*, trans. John E. Bamberger (Spencer, Mass., 1970); *Traité pratique ou Le moine*, ed. Antoine Guillaumont and Claire Guillaumont, SC 170–71 (Paris, 1971); *Le Gnostique*, ed. with comm. by Antoine Guillaumont and Claire Guillaumont, SC 356 (Paris, 1989); Gabriel Bunge, *Evagrios Pontikos. Über die acht Gedanken* (Würzburg, 1992); J. Driscoll, *The Mind's Long Journey to the Holy Trinity: The* Ad Monachos *of Evagrius Ponticus* (Collegeville, Minn., 1993); *Scholies à l'Ecclesiaste*, ed. Paul Gehin, SC 397 (Paris, 1993).

B.   DTC 5:1611–12; LThK³ 3:1027–28; NCE 5:644–45; ODCC 578; TRE 10:565–70; Irénée Hausherr, *Les leçons d'un contemplatif* (Paris, 1960); A. Guillaumont, *Les "Kephalaia Gnostica" d'Evagre le Pontique et l'histoire de l'origénisme chez les Grecs et chez les Syriens* (Paris, 1962); M. Parmentier, "Evagrius of Pontus and the 'Letter to Melania,' " *Bijdragen* 46 (1985): 2–38.

Robin Darling Young

F

FAUSTUS OF RIEZ (ca. 405–ca. 490). Bishop of Riez (Reii) in Southern Gaul. Probably a Briton by birth and a Gaul by upbringing, Faustus as a young man became a monk of the influential island monastery of Lérins (present-day Île St. Honorat) in southern Gaul, rising to be abbot ca. 433. Translated to the see of Riez ca. 457 as successor to Maximus, he became perhaps the most revered Gallic preacher and theologian of the late fifth century.

His extant works consist of a long treatise *De gratia*, a shorter treatise *De spiritu sancto*, eleven letters (the longest of which, *Ep.* 3, seems to have circulated as a pamphlet), and several sermons. The collected sermons of "Eusebius Gallicanus" (CCSL 101–101B), once attributed to Faustus, are now thought to be the product of a sixth-century redaction, though they undoubtedly contain some material from him. Faustus' reputation in the history of Christian thought is due primarily to two doctrinal positions: his assertion of the corporeality of the soul, as set forth in *Ep.* 3 (rebutted in the tractate *De statu animae* of Claudianus Mamertus) and his treatise on grace, which has been taken by many to be a classic statement of the "semi-Pelagian" position. Written ca. 474 against a presbyter, Lucidus, who had adopted a rigid predestinarian position in describing the operation of divine grace, Faustus' *De gratia* probably reflected the consensus of the bishops of Provence as expressed in synods convened against Lucidus. Gennadius of Marseilles refers to the treatise in very favorable terms in his *Liber de viris inlustribus* 86 (ca. 490), but is considered doctrinally suspect in the so-called *Decretum Gelasianum* (late fifth/early sixth century).

Faustus clearly regarded the "Pelagian" assertion of free will and the predestinarian logic of Augustine's* later anti-Pelagian works as a theological Scylla and Charybdis. Between the two extremes, Faustus, in a manner reminiscent of John Cassian,* stressed the general availability of the means of salvation and the perduring, though enfeebled, human endowments of intellect and will, while stressing the need for the grace of Christ to bring about authentic freedom. He attempted to produce a balanced scriptural account of the rapport between divine grace and the human free will, grafting many aspects of Augustine's thought into that account without explicitly attaching Augustine's name to the seeming excesses of predestinarianism.

Bibliography

A. *Fausti Reiensis praeter sermones pseudo-Eusebianos opera*, ed. August Engelbrecht, CSEL 21.

B. DTC 5:2101–5; LThK³ 3:1199–1200; NCE 5:861; ODCC 601; TRE 11:63–67; Gustave Weigel, *Faustus of Riez: An Historical Introduction* (Philadelphia, 1938); Carlo Tibiletti, "Libero arbitrio e grazia in Fausto di Riez," *Augustinianum* 19 (1979): 259–85; Ralph W. Mathisen, *Ecclesiastical Factionalism and Religious Controversy in Fifth-Century Gaul* (Washington, D.C., 1989); Marianne Djuth, "Faustus of Riez: Initium Bonae Voluntatis," *Augustinian Studies* 21 (1990): 35–53; Thomas A. Smith, *De Gratia: Faustus of Riez's Treatise on Grace and Its Place in the History of Theology* (Notre Dame, Ind., 1990); Rebecca Weaver, *Divine Grace and Human Agency: A Study of the Semi-Pelagian Controversy* (Macon, Ga., 1996).

Thomas A. Smith

FEBRONIUS, JUSTUS. *See* HONTHEIM, JOHANN.

FÉNELON, FRANÇOIS DE SALIGNAC DE LA MOTHE (6 August 1651, Gascony–7 January 1715, Cambrai). *Education*: studied at the Jesuit coll. in Cahors, 1663–65; the Univ. of Plessis, 1666–73; Sem. of St. Sulpice, ca. 1663–75. *Career*: ordained, 1675; served in parish of St. Sulpice, 1675–78; superior of the New Catholics convent, a community for Protestant converts, in Paris, 1678–89; missionary to the Huguenots in Saintogne, 1686–88; preceptor of the Duke of Burgundy, the grandson of Louis XIV and heir to the throne, 1689–97; elected to the French academy, 1693; archbishop of Cambrai, 1695–1715.

Fénelon was a French ecclesiastic, educator, and author who adopted semi-Quietist perspectives through the influence of Madame Guyon,* whom he met in 1688. Although Fénelon rejected many of Madame Guyon's more extreme spiritual views, he expressed agreement with much of her teaching on contemplative prayer and the inner spiritual life. He believed that his own spiritual doctrine was simply a reexpression of the teaching of earlier orthodox mystics. For Fénelon, the ascent towards mystical union and Christian perfection consists of suppressing one's own self-dependence, direct action, and reasoning, and waiting upon God in passive contemplation. Ultimately, through contemplation, the individual's love of God becomes pure and "disinterested," with no concern for gaining merit or benefits such as salvation. Compared to Quietists such as Madame Guyon and Miguel de Molinos, though, Fénelon gave greater emphasis to active aspects of the spiritual life, stressing that the active practice of each virtue was a necessary dimension of the authentic life of faith.

Fénelon's career took a significant turn in the events surrounding the Church's Conference of Issy (1695). When Madame Guyon's writings were being evaluated at the conference, Fénelon, despite pressure from leadership, refused to denounce her work in terms that implied a condemnation of her person or motives. With these conditions, Fénelon signed the Thirty-Four Articles of the Conference of Issy, which condemned her teaching and that of Quietism. Fénelon later wrote *The Maxims of the Saints* as a response to, and clarification of, the Thirty-Four Articles, with the intent of distinguishing true and false mysticism. For his resistance during the conference, though, he was banished from his position as tutor at the royal court and remained under the close scrutiny of the church and king for the rest of his life. In 1699, Pope Innocent XII condemned twenty-three propositions from *The Maxims of the Saints* but allowed Fénelon to continue in his office as archbishop of Cambrai, where he served with significant influence until his death.

Bibliography

A. *The Maxims of the Saints Explained Concerning the Interiour Life* (London, 1698); *Oeuvres de Fénelon*, 22 vols. (Versailles, 1820–24); *Christian Perfection*, trans. Mildred Whitney Stillman and Charles F. Whiston (New York, 1947); *Fénelon Letters*, ed. and trans. John McEwen (London, 1964).

B. DTC 5:2137–69; LThK³ 3:1231; NCE 5:882–84; ODCC 605; TRE 11:81–82; Charles Butler, *The Life of Fénelon, Archbishop of Cambray* (New York, 1811); Paul Janet, *Fénelon, His Life and Works*, trans. and ed. Victor Leuliette (London, 1914); Elie Carcassonne, *Fénelon: l' homme et l' oeuvre* (Paris, 1946); Marguerite Haillant, *Fenelon et la predication* (Paris, 1969); Henk Hillenaar, *Fénelon et les Jesuits* (Paris, 1967); James Herbert Davis, *Fénelon* (Boston, 1979); Aimé Richardt, *Fénelon* (Ozoir-la-Ferriere, 1993).

Clyde Glass

FENTON, JOSEPH CLIFFORD (16 January 1906, Springfield, Mass.–7 July 1969, Chicopee Falls, Mass.). *Education*: A.B., Holy Cross Coll., Worcester, Mass., 1926; J.C.B., S.T.L., Grand Sem./Univ. of Montreal, 1930; S.T.D., Institutum Angelicum, Rome, 1931. *Career*: ordained priest, 1930; curate, Easthampton, Mass., 1931–33, Leicester, Mass., 1933–34; professor of philosophy, St. Ambrose Coll., Davenport, Iowa, 1934–35; professor of special dogmatic theology, St. Bernard's Sem., Rochester, N.Y., 1935–38; professor of dogmatic theology, Catholic Univ. of America, Washington, D.C., 1938–64; editor, *American Ecclesiastical Review*, 1944–64; charter member, Catholic Theological Society of America, 1946; ordinary member, Pontifical Roman Theological Academy, 1956–69; member, Preparatory Pontifical Theological Commission, Second Vatican Council, 1960–62; *peritus*, Second Vatican Council, 1962–65; pastor, Chicopee, Mass., 1964–69.

Educated under the renowned Reginald Garrigou-Lagrange* (1877–1964), Fenton became one of the leading American Catholic theological proponents of the antimodernist, neoscholastic theology that had been prevalent in the Roman schools since the First Vatican Council (1869–70). As a theological educator and editor, Fenton had a profound conservative influence on the theological education of the American Catholic clergy in the period prior to the Second Vatican Council (1962–65).

Like many Roman theologians in the period after the modernist crisis of 1908, Fenton believed that the scholastic method of theology and even its terminology were constants that could not and would not experience any substantial change without threatening the authenticity of the word of God. Throughout his career he appealed to the authority of Vatican I, the papal encyclical tradition, and other ecclesiastical pronouncements as the source of his theological argumentation. For him the appeal to these authorities was the surest way to ward off the dangers of a twentieth-century modernism that he believed was as threatening to divine revelation as were Gnosticism, Montanism, and Arianism in the early church.

In the late 1940s and throughout the 1950s he upheld the thesis-hypothesis tradition on church and state issues. He developed this position in continuity with the Roman scholastic theologians and in opposition to his fellow American Catholic theologian John Courtney Murray,* who supported religious liberty. Fenton considered Murray's innovative approach to religious freedom a manifestation of modernism, an excessive willingness to accommodate the church's traditions to the modern zeitgeist.

At the Second Vatican Council, Fenton generally supported the theological positions of Cardinal Alfredo Ottaviani (1890–1979) and the conservative Roman scholastic theological tradition. He was extremely disappointed with the new theological spirit behind many of the conciliar decrees and with the ecclesiastical changes the council promoted. In 1964, after he either resigned or was asked to resign his professorship at the Catholic University of America, he was appointed a pastor in Chicopee, Massachusetts. He spent the remaining years of his life attacking from the pulpit the liberal reforms within the American church.

Bibliography

A. *The Concept of Sacred Theology* (Milwaukee, Wis., 1941); *The Concept of the Diocesan Priesthood* (Milwaukee, Wis., 1951); *We Stand with Christ: An Essay in Catholic Apologetics* (Milwaukee, 1942); coeditor, *Studies in Praise of our Blessed Mother* (Washington, D.C., 1952); *The Catholic Church and Salvation* (Westminster, Md., 1958).

B. *National Catholic Reporter*, 16 July 1969, 5; *Catholic Authors*, ed. Matthew Hoehn, vol. 2 (Newark, N.J., 1948), 243–44; *Contemporary Authors*, ed. Barbara Harte and Caroline Riley, 1st rev., vols. 5–8 (Detroit, Mich., 1969), 369–70.

Patrick W. Carey

FILARET. *See* DROZDOV, FILARET [PHILARET].

FINNEY, CHARLES GRANDISON (29 August 1792, Warren, Conn.–16 August 1875, Oberlin, Ohio). *Education*: studied law, Adams, N.Y., 1818–21; read theology with Presbyterian minister George Gale, 1822–23. *Career:* converted in 1821; licensed to preach, 1823; ordained a Presbyterian minister, 1824; revivalist in upstate N.Y., 1824–29; pastor, Second Presbyterian Church, New York City, 1832–36; pastor, Broadway Tabernacle, New York City, 1836–37; professor of theology, Oberlin Coll., 1835–75; pastor, First Congregationalist Church, Oberlin, Ohio, 1835–72; president, Oberlin Coll., 1851–66.

Finney was perhaps the most widely known of the American Protestant revivalists of the mid-nineteenth century. Although Finney was educated by a Presbyterian pastor whose theological sympathies were with traditional Calvinism, Finney himself, from the very beginning of his training for the ministry, found the Calvinist doctrine of original sin and Atonement unreasonable, unbiblical, and from the viewpoint of preaching the gospel in a democratic culture, impractical and ineffective. Theologically his emphasis on the inherent freedom of the Christian placed him more in the Arminian than the Calvinist camp of the Reformed tradition.

Like eighteenth-century American evangelical Protestants, Finney focused upon the necessity of conversion, but he stressed, as never before, the importance of revivalistic means to bring sinners to an experience of grace and conversion. In upstate New York, where he earned a reputation as an effective evangelical preacher, he first constructed a series of protracted revival meetings and developed what was called the ''anxious bench'' as a means of bringing individuals to an awareness of their sinfulness and providing them with an occasion for conversion. Although he repeatedly spoke of the power of divine grace in the conversion process, he so emphasized human effort that many considered his theology Pelagian or at least semi-Pelagian.

As a revivalist in upstate New York, a pastor in New York City, and as a professor at Oberlin College in Ohio, Finney emphasized the necessity of bringing sinners to conversion. But, after the 1830s, he increasingly stressed the possibilities of complete sanctification. Developing the traditional Calvinist doctrine of sanctification along Methodist lines, he began to talk of ''entire sanctification,'' a Christian perfectionism that flowed from his earlier emphasis upon conversion but developed into an emphasis upon Christian lives of holiness. His position, however, was more Calvinist than Methodist on the issue of holiness and perfectionism.

Bibliography

A. *Lectures on Revivals of Religion* (New York, 1835; 1960); *Sermons on Various Subjects* (New York, 1835); *Sermons on Important Subjects* (New York, 1836); *Lectures on Systematic Theology,* 2 vols. (Oberlin, Ohio, 1846–47; London, 1851); *View of Sanctification* (Oberlin, Ohio, 1840; Minneapolis, Minn., 1986); *Lectures to Professing Christians* (New York, 1837; Oberlin, Ohio, 1880); *The Memoirs of Charles G. Finney,* ed. Garth M. Rosell and Richard A. G. Dupuis (Grand Rapids, Mich., 1989).

B. DAB 6:394–96; DARB 181–82; NCAB 2:462–64; NCE 5:928; NYT 17 August 1875, 4; SH 4:316–17; David L. Weddle, *The Law as Gospel: Revival and Reform in the Theology of Charles G. Finney* (Metuchen, N.J., 1985); Keith J. Hardman, *Charles Grandison Finney, 1792–1875: Revivalist and Reformer* (Syracuse, N.Y., 1987; Grand Rapids, Mich., 1990); C. E. Hambrick-Stowe, *Charles G. Finney and the Spirit of American Evangelicalism* (Grand Rapids, Mich., 1996).

Patrick W. Carey

FLACIUS, MATTHIAS (3 March 1520, Labin, Istria [near Trieste]–11 March 1575, Frankfurt am Main, Germany). *Education*: studied at San Marco Sch., Venice, 1536–39; Univs. of Basel and Tübingen, 1540–41; Univ. of Wittenberg, 1541–44. *Career*: chair of Hebrew, Wittenberg, 1544–49; Magdeburg, 1549–57; Univ. of Jena, 1557–61; Regensburg, 1562–66; Strasbourg, 1567–73; Frankfurt, 1574–75.

Influenced by both Luther's* and Melanchthon's* lectures at the University of Wittenberg, Flacius became a major force in the settlement of the Lutheran Reformation and is widely regarded as the father of modern church history.

In 1547, Emperor Charles V conquered Lutheran forces and imposed a religious law, the "Augsburg Interim," a first step in reversing the Reformation and remaking the Empire into a Hapsburg monarchy. From the presses of Magdeburg, "Our God's Chancery," Flacius and associates carried on a resistance campaign. They influenced the 1552 Princes' Revolt, which defeated Charles' hopes and laid the military basis for the Peace of Augsburg in 1555, giving Lutherans legal rights. The controversies between the followers of Philipp Melanchthon (Philippists), and Flacius' Lutheran party (Gnesio-Lutherans, Flacians) provoked by the Interim were resolved in the (official Lutheran) Formula of Concord of 1577. Whereas Flacius' advocacy of Luther prevailed in the Formula, his opposition to "Samaritanism" (Erastianism, state rule over the church) was ignored.

He combined fiery agitation with a (Venetian) passion for rescuing and publishing manuscripts. Convinced that "collation is the mother of truth," he assembled a 1557 *Catalog of Testimonies of the Truth* and organized the massive *Magdeburg Centuries*, the first comprehensive church history since Eusebius'* in the fourth century, both documented collections meant to furnish polemical resources and to demonstrate the catholicity of the Reformation. His use of primary sources transformed the discipline. Opposing him, Robert Bellarmine* and others had to abandon the artificial "lives of saints" tradition and employ his method.

At Jena, as church official and professor at the new "true University of Wittenberg," his struggle for the freedom of the church from the state (censorship, excommunications) led to his dismissal from the university. Early absolutist princes, led by Elector August of Saxony against an independent church, were able to cite a "Flacian heresy": that sin is man's substance. Anticipating existentialism, Flacius meant that man *is* his relationship to God. Confronting any residual Pelagianism, he made his provocative point using traditional Aristotelian language. Although, as Karl Barth* notes in the *Church Dogmatics*, he did not depart from Luther, the statement struck other theologians as unusual (*inusitata*).

Finding refuge in Regensburg, he failed to found a university, and at the 1563 *Landtag* at Ingolstadt he failed to influence Bavaria to accept the Augsburg Confession. At the same time, he worked on a *Clavis Scripturae Sacrae*, which combined a biblical dictionary (based on the insight that biblical Greek words were informed by Hebrew content) with a collation of ancient and Reformation commentators, and other material on biblical interpretation, earning him recognition (Dilthey, Gadamer) as Father of Hermeneutics. Exiled again, during the 1565/66 "Miracle Year" that began the Dutch Revolt, he wrote a confession and liturgical order for the short-lived "Martinist" Church at Antwerp, which was eliminated in 1566 in the "Council of Blood" of the Spanish Duke of Alba. "Hunted down like a boar" by Elector August, he found refuge in Strasbourg, and, finally, at Frankfurt am Main, where the Lutheran Church refused him a Christian funeral.

Bibliography

A. *Triglot Concordia: The Symbolical Books of the Ev. Lutheran Church*, ed. Gerhard Friedrich Bente (St. Louis, Mo., 1921).

B. DHGE 17:311–16; LThK³ 3:1312–13; NCE 5:954; ODCC 616; OEncR 2:110–11; TRE 11:206–14; Oliver K. Olson, "Matthias Flacius," in Jill Raitt, *Shapers of Religious Traditions in Germany, Switzerland and Poland* (New Haven, Conn., 1981), 1–17.

Oliver K. Olson

FLOROVSKY, GEORGES V. (28 August 1893, Odessa, Russia–11 August 1979, Princeton, N.J.). *Education*: B.A., M.A. in philosophy and science, Univ. of Odessa, Russia, 1911–16; Phil. Mag, Univ. of Prague, 1923. *Career*: lecturer in philosophy, Univ. of Odessa, 1919–20; taught philosophy of law in the Russian Faculty of Law, Univ. of Prague, 1922–26; professor of patristics and systematic theology, St. Sergius Orthodox Theol. Institute, Paris, 1926–48; ordained priest, 1932; professor of divinity, St. Vladimir's Orthodox Theol. Sem., 1948–55, dean, 1950–55; associate professor of Orthodox Church history and dogma, Holy Cross Greek Orthodox Theol. Sch., Brookline, Mass., 1955–59, 1963–65; professor of Eastern church history, Harvard Div. Sch., 1956–64; professor emeritus, Harvard, 1964–79; visiting professor of religion and Slavic studies, Princeton Univ., 1964–72.

With one notable exception, Florovsky's *oeuvre* consists of occasional essays rather than extended studies or attempts at system-building. His style is laconic, as Nicholas Berdiaev* observed of his writing: "His reviews are articles, his articles—monographs, and his monographs—multi-volume tomes." The four volumes of his *Collected Works* dedicated to the church fathers and ancient ascetic writers represent in fact the collected and translated notes from his lectures on patristics taken down by his students in the 1930s. The one large work that he consciously authored as a single study is his *The Ways of Russian Theology*, a vast examination of the Russian theologico-intellectual tradition from the fourteenth through the early twentieth centuries. Yet this work, too, served as a vehicle for the two themes that characterize Florovsky's thought, and that may be summed up in the two phrases he coined: "pseudomorphosis," and "neo-patristic synthesis."

Florovsky's thesis, for which *Ways* served as his most extended discussion, was simple: the formal, theological thought of the Orthodox East should return to the "mind of the Fathers." By this return, however, he did not have in mind the simple reiteration of early Christian formulae, but rather the reacquisition, in harmony with Orthodoxy's never-abandoned liturgical and ascetico-spiritual traditions, of that intellectual component of patristic literature which he understood as embodying the eternally, indeed, divinely based perspectives of the biblical revelation. He saw this reacquistion as necessary because of the deformation—hence "pseudomorphosis"—of Orthodoxy's school theology after the fall of the Byzantine Empire and, particularly, in the seventeenth and eighteenth centuries when, since they were without their own schools in Muscovy and the Ottoman East, authorities in the Orthodox Church felt obliged to borrow the theological manuals of Roman Catholic and Protestant divines. The result, as Florovsky put it, was a "theology on stilts," no longer in living contact with the liturgical and ascetical sources, which continued to feed both popular piety and monastic spirituality. *The Ways of Russian Theology* was his most sustained protest against this development which, not without some ferocity and injustice, he presented as five centuries of theological amnesia and spiritual "dreaminess." The one, unique figure in the whole work whom he treats with unreserved respect and admiration is the remarkable Metropolitan Philaret Drozdov* of Moscow.

While *Ways* must be read against the background of debates among Russian exiles over the causes of the Revolution and also as a counter to the Sophiology of the man who was otherwise Florovsky's friend and patron, Fr. Sergei Bulgakov, still, exactly the same thrust lies behind all Florovsky's other works: the intellectual and spiritual-ascetic patrimony of "Christian Hellenism" received through the church fathers comprises the true perennial philosophy. At Florovsky's hands, this credo served to illumine and explain the works of Christian antiquity. Even though now over sixty years old, his lecture notes and occasional essays on patristic scholarship may still be consulted with great profit. His vast reading and inerring instinct for the pulse of an issue or theological problem have informed three generations of scholars, both within and outside the Orthodox Church, and will surely continue to illumine readers yet to come. His energetic advocacy of the ecumenical movement and unflagging interest in the problematics of the Western Christian tradition were also of a piece with his lifelong emphasis on the Fathers. Florovsky was never an obscurantist, never a narrow apologist of some "oriental" Christianity. He rather saw the Orthodox Church as inextricably bound up with the dynamics of Western European civilization, as both informed by it—in ways both good and ill—and as offering to it the recovery of essential elements in a common past. His commitment to this shared biblical and patristic tradition, coupled with his conviction that it offered ways out of the impasses of modernity, governed his scholarly and churchly life to his death, just as it moves and inspires his many students to this day.

Bibliography

A. *Collected Works*, 14 vols. to date (Belmont, Mass., 1974–), especially *Ways of Russian Theology*, vols. 6 and 7 of the *Collected Works*; *Human and Divine Wisdom* (1922); *The Death on the Cross* (1930); *The Eastern Tradition in Christianity* (1949); complete bibliography in *The Heritage of the Early Church: Essays in Honor of Rev. G. V. Florovsky*, ed. D. Nieman and M. Shatkin, in *Orientalia Christiana Periodica* 195 (Rome, 1973).

B. HDOC 131–32; LThK[3] 3:1332; NCE 18:168; ODCC 620; E. L. Mascall and Rowan Williams, "George Florovsky (1893–1979)," *Sobornost* 2 (1980): 69–72; Anatoliy Vdernikov, "Archpriest Professor George Florovsky (1893–1979) in memoriam," *Journal of the Moscow Patriarchate* 2 (1980): 54–57; Iioann Sviridov, "Certain Aspects of the Theology of Archpriest George Florovsky (for the 10th anniversary of his demise)," *Journal of the Moscow Patriarchate* 4 (1989): 67–74; Andrew Blaine, ed., *Georges Florovsky: Russian Intellectual and Orthodox Churchman* (New York, 1993).

Alexander Golitzin

FOSDICK, HARRY EMERSON (24 May 1878, Buffalo, N.Y.–5 October 1969, Bronxville, N.Y.). *Education*: B.A., Colgate Univ., Hamilton, N.Y., 1900; Colgate Theol. Sem., 1900–1901; M. Div., Union Theol. Sem., New York City, 1903; M.A., Political Science, Columbia Univ., 1908. *Career*: pastor, First Baptist Church, Montclair, N.J., 1903–15; First Presbyterian Church, New York City, 1915–25; Park Avenue Church, New York City, 1925–26; Riverside Church, New York City, 1926–46; professor, Union Theol. Sem., 1908–46; radio preacher, "National Vespers," 1927–46; retirement, 1946–69.

Fosdick—a nationally-known anti-Fundamentalist, preacher, devotional writer, and author of over forty books—grew up in a religiously tolerant atmosphere. After academic success at Colgate University, the sensitive overachiever experienced severe reactive depression. This period colored all of Fosdick's later ministry, and he was acutely aware of the human psyche and its entire dependence upon God. By 1911, Fosdick had taken a public stand against sectarianism, refusing to identify authentic religion with denominational forms.

In 1915, the Baptist minister took a post at First Presbyterian Church, New York, a move symbolizing Fosdick's growing commitment to the organic union of evangelical churches. In 1922, he preached his controversial sermon "Shall the Fundamentalists Win?" In it, he charged Fundamentalists with intolerance because they imposed antiquated doctrines and forced openminded elements out of the church. The ensuing controversy took Fosdick's liberal reputation worldwide, as fundamentalists labeled him "modernism's Moses," a chief heretic and iconoclast to Protestant evangelicalism.

After his forced resignation from his First Presbyterian pastorate in 1925, John D. Rockefeller, Jr., invited Fosdick to become pastor for the new interdenominational Riverside Church. A key vehicle in Fosdick's increasing influence was his radio ministry, "National Vespers." From both pulpit and microphone, Fosdick preached a gospel of comprehensive evangelical liberalism. The leitmotiv for his views was the need to relate Christianity to a scientific age. He stressed the reconciliation of science and religion and promoted an immanentist view of God, involving experiential divine/human continuity. Fosdick was an unabashed popularizer and his assertion that preaching was counseling on a group scale was criticized by both fundamentalists and neo-orthodox thinkers such as Reinhold Niebuhr.*

Fosdick became identified with many causes. He was an ardent pacifist and internationalist after World War I as well as a promoter of social justice. Though always of progressive faith, he became disillusioned with the overoptimism of many liberals and also conflicted with secular humanists such as Joseph Wood Krutch and Walter Lippmann over their simplistic representations of Christianity.

Bibliography

A.   *On Being a Real Person* (London, 1943); *The Modern Use of the Bible* (New York, 1921); *Christianity and Progress* (New York, 1922); *The Living of These Days: An Autobiography* (New York, 1956).

B.   DARB 184–85; NCAB, E 266–67; NYT 6 October 1969, 1; ODCC 626; Robert Moats Miller, *Harry Emerson Fosdick: Preacher, Pastor, Prophet* (New York, 1985); William R. Hutchison, "The Great War and the Logic of Modernism" and "The Odd Couple: Fundamentalism and Humanism in the Twenties," in *The Modernist Impulse in American Protestantism* (Durham, N.C., 1992).

Terrence Crowe

FOX, GEORGE (July 1624, Drayton, England–January 1691, London, England). *Career*: itinerant Quaker preacher and author, 1648–91; trip to American Colonies, 1671–72; trip to Holland and Germany, 1677.

Fox was the founder of the Quakers (i.e., the Religious Society of Friends) and was not a systematic theologian. Coming to his late teens and early twenties during the English Civil War, Fox came to the conclusion that the inner voice of the spirit was supreme over external standards such as creeds, churches, rituals, ministries, and even the Bible. From that basic position he never wavered during the remainder of his life. Without any formal education he believed he was as capable as any learned Oxford don of interpreting the Bible for himself. By 1646, Fox was convinced that a person's private encounter with God was the final test of all authentic faith and thus he began, under trying circumstances and numerous imprisonments, to preach his new gospel of the inner light and gained numerous converts to his movement during the remainder of his life. His emphasis upon the movements of the inner spirit, moreover, led him to insist upon religious liberty in the state.

Bibliography

A. *A Journal, or Historical Account of the Life ... of ... George Fox* (London, 1694; and various subsequent editions); *The Works of George Fox*, 8 vols. (Philadelphia, 1831); *George Fox's "Book of Miracles,"* ed. Henry J. Cadbury (Cambridge, 1948); *Narrative Papers of George Fox*, ed. Henry J. Cadbury (Richmond, Ind., 1972); "The Power of the Lord is Over All," *The Pastoral Letters of George Fox*, ed. T. Canby Jones (Richmond, Ind., 1989).

B. DARB, 166–67; DNB 7:557–61; NCAB 7:10; NCE 5:1047–48; SH 4:348–49; Rufus M. Jones, *George Fox: Seeker and Friend* (London, 1933); Vernon Noble, *The Man in Leather Breeches: The Life and Times of George Fox* (New York, 1953); H. Larry Ingle, *First Among Friends: George Fox and the Creation of Quakerism* (New York, 1994).

Patrick W. Carey

FRANCISCUS ZABARELLA. *See* ZABARELLA, FRANCISCUS.

FRANCIS DE SALES (21 August 1567, Château de Sales, Thorens, Savoy– 28 December 1622, Lyons, France). *Education*: studied humanities and philosophy, Jesuit Coll. of Clermont, Paris, 1582–88; studied law and theology, Univ. of Padua, 1588–91. *Career*: ordained priest, 1593; provost of exiled Genevan canons, Annecy, 1593–99; missionary to the Chablais, 1594–98; trip to Rome, 1598–99; coadjutor bishop-elect of Geneva-Annecy, 1599–1602; bishop of Geneva-Annecy, 1602–22; cofounder with Madame de Chantel, Visitation of Holy Mary, 1610; canonized saint, 1665; doctor of the church, 1877.

Francis de Sales was a religious reformer in Savoy and a theologian of Christian spirituality. Educated under the guidance of the Jesuit humanist tradition, he became during his years in the Catholic diocese of Geneva, which had been exiled to Annecy, Savoy, a spiritual guide to lay and religious within his diocese. He wrote numerous letters of spiritual guidance and eventually collected them into two books—*The Introduction to a Devout Life* (1608, rev. 1609) and *A Treatise on the Love of God* (1616)—which became classics of the Western Christian spiritual tradition.

The *Introduction* was intended to provide spiritual guidance for those who were leading "an ordinary life to all outward appearances." It reflected the Erasmian humanism that focused upon finding the love of God and Christ in daily activities. The *Treatise* was intended for those living in an advanced state of Christian perfection; it focused on charity as the form of all virtues.

In all of his pastoral as well as published work, Francis tried to counter what he considered the pessimistic theology of Calvinism, with its emphasis upon human sinfulness and predestination, and emphasized in Molinistic fashion the freedom of the human will and the natural desire and yearning for God that was harmonized with divine grace. His Christian optimism was based upon his understanding of the doctrines of creation and redemption.

Bibliography

A.   *Oeuvres*, 27 vols. (Annecy, 1892–1932, 1964); *Francis de Sales, Jane de Chantal: Letters of Spiritual Direction*, trans. Peronne Marie Thibert, intro. Wendy M. Wright and Joseph F. Power (New York, 1988); *Finding God Wherever You Are: Selected Spiritual Writings*, ed. Joseph F. Power (New Rochelle, N.Y., 1993).

B.   DHGE 8:753–60; DSAM 5:1057–97; LThK³ 4:52–54; NCE 6:34–36; ODCC 633–34; André Ravier, *Francis de Sales: Sage and Saint* (San Francisco, 1988); Michael de la Bedoyere, *François de Sales* (New York, 1960); E. J. Lajeunie, *Saint François de Sales: L'Homme, la pensée, l'action*, 2 vols. (Paris, 1966); William C. Marceau, *Optimism in the Works of St. Francis de Sales* (Lewiston, N.Y., 1989); Hélène Bordes and Jacques Henniquin, ed., *L'Unidivers Salésien: Saint François de Sales hier et aujourd'hui. Actes de colloque international de Metz* (Paris, 1994).

Patrick W. Carey

FRANCIS XAVIER (7 April 1506, Castle Xavier, Spain–3 December 1552, Sancian, China). *Education*: studied philosophy, Univ. of Paris, 1525–31; studied theology, Paris, 1533–37. *Career*: with Ignatius of Loyola* a cofounder of the Jesuits, 1540; secretary to Ignatius Loyola, Rome, 1540–42; papal nuncio to India and Jesuit superior, 1542–45, 1548–49; missionary, Goa and in southern India, and in Indonesia, 1545–47; Japan, 1549–52; China, 1552; canonized, 1622; named patron of the foreign missions, 1927.

Xavier was not really a theologian, but he had to face the challenge of adapting the Catholic faith to rich and ancient Asian civilizations. His letters reveal how he both wrestled with this problem and directed the work of his Jesuit subordinates with a strong hand. The publication of selected letters stimulated missionary zeal among Counter-Reformation Catholics, and he laid the groundwork for later Jesuit missionary work in Asia.

Bibliography

A.   *The Letters of Saint Francis Xavier, 1506–1552* (St. Louis, Mo., 1992).

B.   DSAM 5:1099–1107; ECatt 5:1616–20; LThK³ 4:55–56; NCE 14:1059–60; ODCC 634; OEncR 4:305; James Brodrick, *St. Francis Xavier, 1506–1552* (New York, 1952); Georg Schurhammer, *Francis Xavier: His Life, His Times*, 4 vols. (Rome, 1973–82).

John Patrick Donnelly

FRANCK, SEBASTIAN (1499, Donauworth, Bavaria–October 1542, Basel, Switzerland). *Education*: Univ. of Ingolstadt, 1515–17, studies for the priesthood, Heidelberg, Germany. *Career*: reforming priest, Augsburg, Germany 1524–28; private citizen, writer, translator, printer, Nuremberg, Strasbourg, Ulm, Basel, 1528–42.

Though he had been a Lutheran pastor, Sebastian Franck rejected Luther's* doctrine of "salvation by faith alone" as ineffective for moral renewal. As part of his renunciation of politically established religion, Franck extended Erasmus'* criticism of the immorality of rulers. Franck also rejected armed resistance to political authorities. Regarding attempts to gather the church as sinfully presumptuous he wrote a world history to demonstrate that the external church is of the devil. He regarded those condemned as heretics as often being the truly enlightened members of their generation. Asserting that righteousness comes from God's internal work, he rejected Catholicism for reliance on the performance of sacraments, Protestantism for reliance on true doctrine, and Anabaptism for trust in church discipline and the righteousness of suffering. He regarded the literal sense of the Scripture as false and the spiritually mature as outgrowing their need for Scripture. He affirmed that instruction about Christ's inner presence will bring ethical renewal and that unevangelized "heathens" who obey their "inner Word" will be saved.

Bibliography

A. *Spiritualist and Anabaptist Writers*, ed. G. H. Williams (Philadelphia, 1957); *Two Hundred Eighty Paradoxes or Wondrous Sayings*, trans. E. J. Furcha (Lewiston, N.Y.: 1986).

B. LThK³ 4:15; ODCC 636; TRE 11:307–12; Steven Ozment, *Mysticism and Dissent* (New Haven, Conn., 1973); George H. Williams, *The Radical Reformation*, 3d ed. (Kirksville, Mo., 1992).

Melvin G. Vance

FRANCKE, AUGUST HERMANN (22 March 1663, Lübeck, Germany–8 June 1727, Halle, Germany). *Education*: studied at Univs. of Erfurt, Kiel, Hamburg and Leipzig, 1679–85. *Career*: teacher of Greek, Hebrew and Scripture, Leipzig Univ., 1685–89; Lutheran pastor, Erfurt, 1690–91; professor of theology, Halle Univ., and pastor, Glaucha, 1691–1727; founder and administrator, Orphan Home and Schools, 1695–1727.

Under the leadership of Francke the movement later known as classical Lutheran Pietism attained the apex of its growth and influence. Francke, in large measure, adopted the theological stance of his mentor, Philipp Spener,* and translated into reality many of the reforms Spener had advocated. Francke excelled in the study of languages and was primarily a biblical theologian who initiated the first exegetical journal. His chief concern was to relate the teachings of the Bible in a practical way to the daily life of the Christian believer. While maintaining his credence in the confessions of Lutheranism and their cardinal doctrine of salvation by faith alone, Francke insisted that faith and good works are inseparably connected. His concept of piety contained a deep concern to serve humanity and improve the conditions of this life. It was this latter aspect that became the driving force and lasting impact of his career.

As a direct result of this theological perspective, Francke developed and implemented a practical program of social ministry aimed to aid the poorest and most needy members of society. In 1695 he started a school for the poor children of his parish. Other institutions were quickly added. By 1697 these included a grammar school and orphanage, a teacher training school and a high school. As a pioneering effort in social ministry and teaching methods, Francke's Orphan Home and Schools achieved worldwide renown and became a model for similar endeavors. Under Francke's leadership Pietism exercised a growing ascendency within the entire Lutheran Church of Germany and Scandinavia. From Halle, pastors and teachers traveled as missionaries to nearly every part of the world. Included among them was Henry Melchoir Mühlenberg, the acknowledged 'patriarch' of the Lutheran Church in North America. The life and work of August Francke contributed greatly to the dominant influence of Pietism on Lutheranism during the eighteenth and nineteenth centuries.

Bibliography

A. *Memoirs* (Philadelphia, 1830); *Nicodemus, or, A Treatise Against the Fear of Man* (London, 1709); *Pietas Hallensis, a Demonstration of the Foot-Steps of a Divine Being in the World* (London 1705); *August Hermann Francke's Werke in Auswahl* (Berlin, 1969).

B. LThK³ 4:2–3; ODCC 636; TRE 11:312–20; Henry E. F. Guerike, *The Life of Augustus Hermann Francke*, trans. Samuel Jackson (London, 1837); F. Ernest Stoeffler, *The Rise of Evangelical Pietism* (Leiden, 1965); Erich Beyreuther, *August Hermann Francke* (Marburg, 1969); Gary R. Sattler, *God's Glory, Neighbor's Good* (Chicago, 1982).

Paul K. Kuenning

FRANZELIN, JOHANN BAPTIST (15 April 1816, Aldein, diocese of Trent, South Tirol, Austria–11 February 1886, Rome). *Education*: philosophical studies, Galicia at Tarnapol, Poland, 1835–42; theological studies under several prominent teachers, Carlo Passaglia,* Clemens Schrader, and Giovanni Perrone,* Rome, 1845–48; theological studies, Ugbrook in Devonshire, England, 1848, and Leuven (Louvain), 1849. *Career*: entered the Jesuit novitiate, Graz, 1834; taught in the gymnasium, Lemberg (Lvov), Poland, 1842–45; ordained priest, 1849; taught Hebrew and exegesis, Vals, 1849–50; taught Semitic languages, Roman Coll., 1850–57; chair of dogmatic theology, Gregorian Univ., 1857–86; consultor for Propaganda and the Holy Office, 1857–86; member of a preparatory commission for Vatican I, 1868–69; pope's theologian, Vatican I, 1869–70; cardinal, 1876.

Franzelin's theological expertise and his reflections on tradition as a source of Christian revelation earned him an appointment as papal theologian at the First Council of the Vatican. Although preliminary drafts of matters to be debated at the council were considerably revised, his work helped develop an emerging new branch of Roman Catholic theology (viz., ecclesiology). This new tract or treatise moved the consideration of the Christian Church from a polemic and apologetic treatise to a proper dogmatic treatise. Although numbered among the neo-scholastic theologians, his mastery of scriptural exegesis and positive theology anticipated a later renewal in dogmatic theology. His examination of the works of Macarius Bulgakov on Eastern Christianity, moreover, displayed a pioneering ecumenical interest.

Bibliography

A. *Tractatus de Deo Trino secundum Personas* (Rome, 1869); *Tractatus de Verbo Incarnato* (Rome, 1870); *Tractatus de Divina Traditione et Scriptura* (Rome, 1870); *Theses de Ecclesia Christi* (Rome, 1907).

B. DTC 6:765–67; LThK³ 4:29; NCE 6:80–81; ODCC 636–37; Sommervogel, 3: 950–51; Hurter, 5:1507–8; Leo Scheffczyk, "Johann Baptist Franzelin (1816–1886)," in *Katholische Theologen Deutschlands im 19. Jarhundert*, ed. Heinrich Fries and Georg Schwaiger (Munich, 1975), 2:345–66; T. Howland Sanks, *Authority in the Church: A Study in Changing Paradigms* (Missoula, Mont., 1974); Peter Walter, *Johann Baptist Franzelin (1816–1886), Jesuit, Theologe, Kardinal: Ein Lebensbild* (Bosen, 1987).

William J. Kelly

FULGENTIUS OF RUSPE (467, Telept, North Africa–527, Ruspe, North Africa). *Education*: received classical training in Greek authors (and later, Latin authors), concentrating on rhetoric. *Career*: entered the monastery at Ruspe at an early age and quickly attained the rank of abbot; briefly fled Vandal occupation, intending to go to Egypt and live in the Thebaid, but, being warned of monophysitism among the monks, turned back after traveling as far as Rome; consecrated bishop, 507; exiled twice to Sardinia with other Catholic bishops by Arian Vandal rulers; acted as the bishops' secretary; recalled to Carthage, 515–17, by the Vandal king Thrasamund to discuss treatment of Catholic clergy and to debate theology; after Thrasamund's death, returned to Ruspe until his death.

Fulgentius was the foremost North African theologian of his day. His extant theological works date from 515–27; important treatises include *Ad Monimum*, *Dicta regis Trasamundi et contra ea responsiones*, and the letters *De veritate praedestinationis et gratiae* and *De remissione* (other letters treat virginity and marriage). An alphabetic hymn that teaches Christian theology also survives. His works exhibit a wholehearted reception of Augustinian thought, especially in the areas of predestination and grace. He teaches that the human soul, because of the body's perpetual revolt against it, is inclined towards evil and cannot save itself. The disorder of the senses that causes the struggle is the essence of original sin, passed down to humanity through procreation. The only help for human souls comes from grace procured by Christ in his incarnation, death, and resurrection. This grace is gratuitous, distributed by God according to his will. Fulgentius supports, but with less precision than Augustine,* the view that God predestines people not to evil or sin, but to salvation, according to his will.

Fulgentius' polemical works include the debate with Thrasamund, attacks on Arian theologians and semi-Pelagians, and sermons and epistles defending Chalcedonian Christology. The pastoral side of Fulgentius' identity as monk-bishop appears in his letter to Euthymius, who sent "from the heart" questions on the remission of sins.

Despite his training in rhetoric, Fulgentius' mature treatises show little, if any, classical rhetorical style. They are works of a mature and dedicated theologian, carefully crafted in order to make theological and polemical points, but they rarely rise to the level of greatness. His sermons exhibit the rhetorical technique of *sermo humilis*, used by preachers in order to reach an audience whose first language was Berber (Punic) rather than Latin. Discussion of the theory that these works were preceded by the livelier fancies of a youthful Fulgentius (the Mythographer) continues. In addition to his reliance on Augustine, Fulgentius' theological sources include Ambrose* and Hilary.* He takes care to promote Chalcedonian orthodoxy concerning the two natures in Christ. Fulgentius' writings frequently appeared in Carolingian *florilegia* and influenced theological thought in the Middle Ages.

Bibliography

A. CCSL 91–91A; CPL 814–46; *The Life of Fulgentius, On the Forgiveness of Sin, To Monimus, Selected Letters*, trans. Robert Eno, FC 95 (Washington, D.C., 1997).

B. DTC 6:1968–72; LThK³ 4:220–21; NCE 6:220; ODCC 646; TRE 10:723–27; Ferrandus, Deacon of Carthage, *Vita s. Fulgentii*, trans. and ed. G. Lapeyre (Paris, 1929); Hans Diesner, *Fulgentius von Ruspe als Theologe und Kirchenpolitiker* (Stuttgart, 1966); Susan Stevens, "The Circle of Bishop Fulgentius," *Traditio* 38 (1982): 327–41.

Thomas S. Ferguson

G

GABRIEL BIEL. *See* BIEL, GABRIEL.

GARRIGOU-LAGRANGE, REGINALD (21 February 1877, Auch, France–15 February 1964, Rome). *Education*: studied medicine, Univ. of Bordeaux, 1890s; studied philosophy and theology, Dominican House of Studies, Flavigny, France, 1898–1904; philosophical study, Paris, Switzerland, Austria, and Germany, 1904–5. *Career*: entered the Dominican novitiate, Amiens, 1897; ordained priest, 1902; professor of philosophy and theology, Le Saulchoir, the Dominican House of Studies, Kain, Belgium, 1905–9; professor of apologetics and dogmatic theology, Angelicum (Pontifical Univ. of St. Thomas), Rome, 1909–59; chair of spiritual theology, Angelicum, 1917–60; retirement, 1960–64.

Garrigou-Lagrange was one of the most important Thomist theologians in the first half of this century. A prolific author (28 books and over 600 articles), he also influenced a wider circle of priests, religious, and educated laity through his lectures and spiritual direction. The esteem in which he was held by powerful Roman Congregations (among them, the Holy Office, the Congregation for Religious, and the Congregation for Seminaries and Universities) enabled him more than once to influence indirectly the teaching of theology in his own order and in the church as a whole. Following St. Thomas,* as understood by his great Dominican commentators, Garrigou-Lagrange created a coherent speculative system in which philosophy, apologetics, and dogmatic and spiritual theology were linked to one another in his own Thomistic synthesis.

As a student at Flavigny, Garrigou-Lagrange had learned his Thomism from Ambroise Gardeil, a great pioneer of the French Thomist revival. When he began to teach, during the Modernist crisis, Dominican Thomists had taken a firm stand against idealism and Bergsonian process philosophy. Consequently, his first major work (1909) was directed against Emile Le Roy, whose Bergsonianism was thought to compromise the abiding validity of the church's dogmatic statements. Its epistemology was built upon the Thomistic notion of being acquired through abstractive intuition. Contrary to the claims of the idealists, that notion, which grounded the principles of identity, sufficient reason, causality, and finality, brought the mind into immediate contact with reality. It also grounded the Aristotelian metaphysics of act and potency which, in his second major work, *God, His Existence and His Nature*, Garrigou-Lagrange employed to defend St. Thomas' proofs for God's existence and justify the mind's natural knowledge of God's attributes through the analogy of being.

Like Gardeil, Garrigou-Lagrange preferred the nineteenth century "extrinsic" apologetics of signs and miracles to the more recent "intrinsic" apologetics of Maurice Blondel* based upon the exigencies of the human will. In the Dominican tradition the act of faith was a strictly supernatural act that unaided human reason could not make. Apologetics, therefore, could do no more than show the credibility of revelation; its arguments, proposed as they were by Christian believers, belonged to theology. Although they made revelation accessible to unbelievers, they preserved its supernatural character and defended the truths of faith against the attempts of natural reason to pass judgment on them.

In his speculative theology Garrigou-Lagrange followed St. Thomas faithfully and, in twelve major Latin works, made his way through all the parts of the *Summa Theologiae*. Nearly all the major topics were covered in them: the Trinity, the Incarnation, Redemption, predestination, grace, the virtues, the gifts of the Holy Spirit, and eschatology. A summary of Garrigou-Lagrange's theology can be found in his more popular work, *Reality: A Synthesis of Thomistic Thought*. Grace, in his view, was one of the most significant topics in speculative theology, and in his treatment of it, he followed the Dominican tradition of Bañez,* as he made clear in his French work, *La Prédestination des saints et la grâce*. In his spiritual theology, to which he devoted a number of popular works, he again was faithful to the Dominican tradition. Asceticism could be distinguished from mysticism but never separated from it, since all Christians, not just the elite, were destined through their grace of baptism to infused contemplative prayer and, unless impeded, as many were, they could reach it with the help of the infused virtues and the gifts of the Holy Spirit. Garrigou-Lagrange's great strength was his gift for speculative synthesis. He could locate the major principles of a system, explain them, relate them to each other, and draw conclusions from them with coherent clarity. That power enabled him to close the gap between spirituality and theology and link the mystical wisdom of St. John of the Cross* to the speculative wisdom of St. Thomas. He had little interest in historical research, however, and often failed to distinguish between St. Thomas' own thought and the Thomism of his Dominican commentators. Exegesis and biblical theology held little interest for him, and he could be intolerant toward other theologians, including Thomists, who disagreed with him. His influence declined after Vatican II, and the work of younger French Dominicans, like M.-D. Chenu* and Yves Congar,* moved the theology of his order in a different direction.

Bibliography

A. *Le Sens commun, la Philosophie de l'être et les Formules dogmatiques* (Paris, 1909); *God, His Existence and His Nature: A Thomistic Solution of Certain Agnostic Antinomies* (St. Louis, Mo., 1934); *The Three Ways of the Spiritual Life* (London, 1938); *Predestination* (St. Louis, Mo., 1939); *Reality: A Synthesis of Thomistic Thought* (St. Louis, Mo., 1950); *The Last Writings of Reginald Garrigou-Lagrange* (New York, 1969); for a complete bibliography see *Angelicim* 42 (1965): 200–72.

B.   Catholicisme 4:1764; LThK³ 4:295; NCE 6:293–94; B. Lavaud, ''Le P. Garrigou-Lagrange. In Memoriam,'' *Revue Thomiste* 64 (1964): 181–92; idem, ''Le Père Garrigou-Lagrange. Maître spirituel. Témoignage d'un disiciple et ami,'' *Vie Spirituelle* 111 (1964): 237–54; Georges van Riet, *L'Epistémologie thomiste* (Louvain, 1946), 338–49; Helen James John, S.N.D, *The Thomist Spectrum* (New York, 1966); Gerald A. McCool, *The Neo-Thomists* (Milwaukee, Wis., 1994); the first issue of *Revue Thomiste* 64 (1964) is devoted to an overview of Garrigou-Lagrange's work.

Gerald A. McCool

GEERT DE GROOTE. *See* GROOTE, GEERT DE.

GERDIL, [HYACINTHE] GIACINTO SIGISMONDO (20 June 1718, Samoëns, Savoy, Italy–12 August 1802, Rome). *Education*: theological studies, Bologna, 1734–37. *Career*: joined Barnabites, Annecy, 1733; professor of philosophy, Macerata, 1737–48; professor of moral philosophy, Casal, 1748–54; professor of philosophy and moral theology, Turin, 1754; tutor to Charles Emmanuel IV, 1764; cardinal in petto, 1773; residence in Rome, 1776; cardinal, 1777; bishop of Biddon, consultor of the Holy Office, corrector of the oriental books, and prefect of Propaganda, 1777–98; residence in Abbey Della Chiusa, 1798–1800; residence in Rome, 1800–2.

A theologian of wide learning, Gerdil wrote on philosophy, education, canon law, history, and the physical and natural sciences as well as theology. His most important works were written in defense of a spiritual philosophy against what he perceived to be the materialism of John Locke's empiricism, a supernatural religion against the naturalism of Deism, and on the spiritual supremacy of the papacy against Febronianism and the Synod of Pistoia. His most important contribution was in the area of the knowledge of God, where he supported to some extent the ontologism of Malebranche.

Bibliography

A. *Opere edite ed inedite*, 20 vols. (Rome, 1806–21); *Opere edite et inedite . . . nuova collectione*, 7 vols. (Naples, 1853–56); *L'Immortalité de l'âme démontrée contre Locke et défense du P. Malebranche contre ce philosophe*, 2 vols. (Turin, 1747–48); *Brief Exposition of the Origin, Progress, and Marks of the True Religion*, trans. Edmond William O'Mahony (London, 1869).

B.   DTC 6:1299–1300; ECatt 6:96–99; LThK³ 4:1198; G. Piantoni, *Vita del Card. G. S. Gerdil ed analisi delle sue opere* (Rome, 1831); Angelo Gnemmi, *L'apologia razionale religiosa fondamento parmenideo e affermazione di Dio nel contributo di G.S. Gerdil* (Padua, 1971); Massimo Lapponi, *Giacinto Sigismondo Gerdil e la filosophia christiana dell' età moderna* (Rome, 1990).

Patrick W. Carey

GERHARD, JOHANN (17 October 1582, Quedlinburg, Upper Saxony–17 August 1637, Jena). *Education*: studied philosophy and medicine, Univ. of Wittenberg, 1599–1601; studied theology, Wittenberg, Jena, 1601–3; M. A., Univ. of Marburg, 1604; doctorate in theology, Univ. of Jena, 1615. *Career*: professor of theology, Univ. of Jena, 1606–15; general superintendent of Lutheran Church, Coburg, 1606–15; professor of theology, Univ. of Jena, 1616–37.

Gerhard was the chief representative of Lutheran orthodoxy, a "classical theologian" ranking with Thomas Aquinas* (Robert Scharlemann), and the "third man of the Reformation," after Luther* and Chemnitz*" (Jacques Bossuet, chaplain to Louis XIV). The influence of the pietist Johann Arndt,* who was a pastor in Quedlinburg and who assisted Gerhard at the age of fifteen in overcoming an acute neurosis, is apparent in Gerhard's youthful work, *Meditationes sacrae* (1606), in which he quotes Augustine,* Anselm,* Bernard,* and Thomas à Kempis. It was translated into nine languages, including English. Influenced by Cornelius Martini of Helmstedt and Francis Suárez,* he was the first professor in Jena to lecture on metaphysics.

He participated in the convocations sponsored by the Dresden court chaplain Mathias Hoe von Hoenegg, which claimed doctrinal leadership for the Lutheran Church. He took part in rejection of the theology and philosophy of the University of Helmstedt, the *Decisio Saxonia*, which settled the Christological controversy between the theologians from Tübingen and Giessen on *kenosis* ("emptying," Phil, 2:7), and the answer in 1628 and 1630 to the Jesuits, who charged that the Evangelical church had violated the provisions of the 1555 Augsburg Peace by departing from the Augsburg Confession.

His main exegetical work is the *Harmonia Evangelistarum* (1626–27); his ethical teaching is found in his *Schola Pietatis* (1622–23). His chief polemical work is his *Confessio Catholica* (two books in four sections, 1633–37), which, after Chemnitz' *Examen Concilii Tridentini*, is the most important apologia for Lutheran theology. His *Patrologia* (1653) may be the source of the term "patrology." His most important dogmatic work was the nine volumes of the *Loci theologici* (1610–22), the most comprehensive dogmatics of Lutheran high orthodoxy, in which he makes use of neo-Aristotelianism which, under the influence of Melanchthon* and late Spanish scholastics, had spread to Lutheran universities. His system is presented in six divisions: Death, Resurrection, Judgment, the End of the World, and Eternal Salvation or Condemnation. His interest in practical application is shown by a discussion, *De usu*, in every section.

Bibliography

A. *Loci theologici*, ed. I. F. Cotta, 20 vols. (Tübingen, 1762–89); *The Doctrine of Man in Classical Lutheran Theology*, ed. Herman A. Preus and Edmund Smits (Minneapolis, Minn., 1962).

B. LThK³ 4:512–13; NCE 6:382–83; ODCC 666–67; TRE 12:448–53; *Encyclopedia of the Lutheran Church* 2:905–6; Robert D. Preus, *The Theology of Post-Reformation Lutheranism*, 2 vols. (St. Louis, Mo., and London, 1970/72); Robert P. Scharlemann, *Thomas Aquinas and John Gerhard* (New Haven, Conn., and London, 1964); Heinrich Schmid, *The Dogmatics of the Evangelical-Lutheran Church*, trans. Charles A. Hay and Henry E. Jacobs (St. Louis, Mo., 1875).

Oliver K. Olson

GERSON, JEAN (14 December 1363, Gerson-lès-Barbey, France–12 July 1429, Lyons). *Education*: Master of Arts, Master of Theology, Univ. of Paris, 1381, 1394. *Career*: preacher and writer on pastoral and reform topics; chancellor, Univ. of Paris, 1395–1429, although absent after 1415; leader, Council of Constance, 1415–18; pastoral service, Lyons, 1419–29.

A leading late medieval theologian and church statesman, Gerson embodied the diverse intellectual and spiritual movements of an era marked by an upsurge in spiritual devotion and the institutional chaos of the Great Schism. Key to Gerson's theology is his conception of the church as a mystical body and an institutional hierarchy modeled after trinitarian angelic archetypes. The church, guided by the Holy Spirit, especially during a general council such as Constance, led her members in a process of purgation, illumination, and perfection that produced her constant reformation and led to charity, unity, and peace. The theologian's task is to interpret law to maintain hierarchical order, and the bishop's practical role is to revive the church by overseeing doctrinal and moral reform.

Gerson's emphases on restoring hierarchical order and the Holy Spirit's role coincided in his support of a conciliar solution to the schism. At Constance, he delivered his famous sermon *Ambulate dum lucem habetis* (23 March 1415, on Jn 12:35), later adapted in the conciliar decree *Haec sancta* (6 April 1415), which provided the theological grounds for continuing the council when Pope John XXIII (d. 1419), who had called the council, fled. The general council, Gerson argued, was led by the Holy Spirit and not one particular pope. Representing the church, the council validated itself by the grace of the Holy Spirit. With others, he then led the council in uniting the church under one pope.

Gerson was not only concerned with power politics; he was also a pastoral theologian. As Parisian chancellor, he criticized the sophistic, impractical excesses of late medieval scholasticism. Gerson reoriented scholastic education toward pastoral goals by emphasizing personal penitence, the study of Scripture, and training in pastoral care and preaching. His efforts as chancellor, his vernacular sermons, his directions for pastors at work in parishes, and his own pastoral service demonstrate that, although he envisioned reform as starting with the head of the church and trickling down through the hierarchy to her members, Gerson was neither a church statesman who allowed himself to be entirely consumed by high-level matters nor an academic theologian interested more in theory than praxis.

Bibliography

A.   *Jean Gerson. Opera omnia,* ed. Louis Ellies Dupin, 5 vols. (Antwerp, 1706); *De mystica theologia,* ed. André Combes (Lugano, 1958); *Oeuvres complètes,* ed. Palémon Glorieux, 10 vols. (Paris, 1960–73); *Selections from A Deo exivit, Contra curiositatem, and De mystica theologia speculativa,* trans. Steven E. Ozment (Leiden, 1969).

B.   DTC 6:1314–30; LThK³ 5:909–10; NCE 6:449–50; ODCC 669–70; TRE 12:532–38; Louis B. Pascoe, *Jean Gerson: Principles of Church Reform* (Leiden, 1973); D. Catherine Brown, *Pastor and Laity in the Theology of Jean Gerson* (New York, 1987); Mark Stephen Burrows, *Jean Gerson and De Consolatione Theologiae (1418): The Consolation of a Biblical and Reforming Theology for a Disordered Age* (Tübingen, 1991).

Christopher M. Bellitto

GILBERT OF LA PORRÉE (ca. 1075, Poitiers–1154, Poitiers). *Education*: studied at the cathedral schools of Poitiers and at Chartres. *Career*: chancellor of the cathedral at Chartres several times; taught at Paris, 1141; bishop of Poitiers, 1142; denounced by two of his deacons to Pope Eugenius III for his teachings on the Trinity. The pope ordered an inquiry, and at the Council of Rheims in 1148, Gilbert's views were examined. Bernard of Clairvaux* drew up a profession of faith in reply to the errors of which Gilbert was accused. Chief among these were that he said that the divine essence is not God and rejected the statement that God is the divinity, along with the implications of such statements for the Incarnation. Problems with Gilbert's language about the Trinity arose from his application of rules of speculative grammar to theology so that he was understood to maintain that divinity or divine essence is not God, but a quality or form by which God is. Gilbert accepted the profession of faith devised by Bernard, was acquitted of all charges, returned to his diocese, and even pardoned the deacons who accused him.

Bibliography

A.   *The Commentaries on Boethius,* ed. Nikolaus M. Häring (Toronto, 1966).

B.   DTC 6:1348–58; LThK³ 4:648–49; NCE 6:478–79; ODCC 675; TRE 13:266–68; Nikolaus M. Häring, "The Case of Gilbert de la Porrée, Bishop of Poitiers, 1142–1154," *Mediaeval Studies* 13 (1951): 1–40; idem, "A Treatise on the Trinity by Gilbert of Poitiers," ibid. 39 (1972): 14–50; Lauge Olaf Nielsen, *Theology and Philosophy in the Twelfth Century: A Study of Gilbert Porreta's Thinking and the Theological Expositions of the Doctrine of the Incarnation during the Period, 1130–1180* (Leiden, 1982); Theresa Gross-Diaz, *The Psalms Commentary of Gilbert of Poitiers: From Lectio Divina to the Lecture Room* (Leiden, 1996).

Roland J. Teske

GILBERT OF POITIERS. *See* GILBERT OF LA PORRÉE.

GILES OF ROME, Aegidius Romanus (ca. 1243, Rome–23 December 1316, Avignon). *Education*: studied under Thomas Aquinas,* Paris, 1269–72. *Career*: entered the Augustinian Hermits in Rome ca. 1257; refused to retract his position on the unicity of the substantial form in each being after its inclusion among the 219 propositions condemned by the bishop of Paris in 1277; exiled from Paris, lived for a year at Bayeux, and then traveled to Rome; reinstated at Paris, 1285; prior general of his order, 1292; defended Boniface VIII who was accused of wrongly acquiring the papacy, 1294; bishop of Bourges, 1295; sided with Boniface against Philip IV on privileges of the clergy; over a territorial dispute in 1305 pressed for the excommunication of the bishop of Bordeaux who was soon elected Pope Clement V; removed from his see and confined to quarters in Bourges until 1310 when he regained his freedom by helping Clement against the Templars; attended the Council of Vienne; known as *Doctor fundatissimus* (the most solid teacher); adopted as the official teacher of his order in 1287.

Giles wrote his most popular work, *The Rule of Princes*, ca. 1285 for his pupil, the future King Philip the Fair. His *Ecclesiastical Power*, which emphasized the supremacy of spiritual over temporal power, strongly influenced Boniface VIII's famous bull, *Unam Sanctam*. In his teaching Giles followed St. Thomas in holding a real distinction in creatures between being and essence, but conceived it as a distinction between two things (*res a re*). He disagreed with Aquinas in maintaining the primacy of the will over the intellect.

Bibliography

A.   *Super libros De anima, De materia caeli, De intellectu possibili, De gradibus formarum* (Venice, 1500; repr. Frankfurt, 1982); *Commentaria in octo libros Physicorum Aristotelis* (Venice, 1502; repr. Frankfurt, 1968); *De esse et essentia, De mensura angelorum, De cognitione angelorum* (Venice, 1503; repr. Frankfurt, 1968); *De regimine principum* (Rome, 1607; repr. Aalen, 1967); *Defensorium seu correctorium librorum S. Thomae Aquinatis* (Cologne, 1624; repr. Frankfurt, 1968); *De ecclesiastica potestate*, ed. Richard Scholz (Weimar, 1929; repr. Aalen, 1961); trans. A. Monahan (Lewiston, N.Y., 1990) and R. W. Dyson (Dover, N.H., 1986); *Theoremata de esse et essentia*, ed. E. Hocedez (Louvain, 1930), trans. M. V. Murray (Milwaukee, Wis., 1952); *Errores philosophorum*, ed. J. Koch; trans. J. Reidl (Milwaukee, Wis., 1944); *De renunciatione papae*, ed. J. Eastman (Lewiston, N.Y., 1992).

B.   DTC 6:1358–65; NCE 6:484–85; ODCC 676–77; Peter W. Nash, ''Giles of Rome: A Pupil but Not a Disciple of Thomas Aquinas,'' in *Readings in Ancient and Medieval Philosophy*, ed. J. Collins (Westminster, Md., 1960), 251–57; Palémon Glorieux, ''Les premiers écrits de Gilles de Rome,'' RTAM 41 (1974): 204–8; Thomas A. Losoncy, ''Giles of Rome,'' in *Dictionary of Literary Biography*, vol. 115, *Medieval Philosophers* (Detroit, Mich., 1992), 214–21.

Roland J. Teske

GIOBERTI, VINCENZO (5 April 1801, Turin, Italy–26 October 1852, Paris, France). *Education*: after studies with the Oratorians, he obtained his doctorate in theology at Turin in 1823. *Career*: ordained priest, 1825; professor of theology, Turin Univ., 1825–31; chaplain to the court of Charles Albert of Sardinia-Piedmont, 1831–33; arrested on suspicion of republican views, imprisoned for four months and banished, 1833; private tutor and engaged in philosophical, theological, and political studies, Brussels, 1834–47; returned in triumph to Turin, 1847; elected deputy for Turin and president of the chamber, appointed prime minister of the Piedmontese government, 1848–49; resigned his post, February 1849; undertook an unsuccessful mission to Paris as ambassador-plenipotentiary for his government, 1849; resigned as ambassador and remained in Paris in self-imposed exile until his death.

Gioberti was a devout Catholic and convinced upholder of Italian unity. His political writings and practical influence carried considerable weight during the Italian *Risorgimento,* although his early republican ideas changed in favor of constitutional monarchy. He advocated a federation of Italian states headed by the pope. His endeavors to bring about a rapprochement between nascent political Italy and the papacy collapsed after the assassination in Rome of Pellegrino Rossi, Pius IX's prime minister, in 1848, while his refusal to countenance military action alienated him from his own colleagues. His final ideas, published shortly before his death, moved closer to complete acceptance of democracy.

Gioberti's philosophy and theology, more enduring than his political views, were in many ways molded by his reaction to Kant, whose subjectivism he rejected. Gioberti's own ontological views revolve around: (1) the concept of being, the given, self-evident, intuited object of human intelligence; (2) reflection, which appropriates the object in thought; and (3) language, the instrument of reflection. The initial intuition of the idea of being *(Ente)* depends upon God, "the Idea, from whom as creative force proceeds the cognitive and operating power of the [human] spirit." Such a description of human intelligence led to well-founded accusations of ontologism and pantheism, although Gioberti's primary intent was undoubtedly to safeguard the objectivity of thought. While "being does not act as external and limited cause, but as infinite, eternal cause producing our activity," "immanent thought makes its own splendor shine on the mediate cognition through which we raise ourselves to it." For Gioberti, divine activity does not harm but initiates human activity, which then, by way of reflection and the God-given gift of the word, articulates the vague cognition present in the primal intuition. Revelation and civil society both have their actualization through this union between God and the human intelligence.

The suspicions aroused by Gioberti's political, philosophical, and theological theories, and his virulent attacks on the Jesuits, provoked the inclusion of all his works in the *Index of Forbidden Books.*

Bibliography

A. *Opere Edite e Inedite,* ed. Giuseppe Mazzari (Naples, 1856–63, and many subsequent editions); see especially *Del Primato morale e civile degli Italiani, Filosofia della rivelazione* and *Protologia.*

B.   ECatt 6:414–22; LThK³ 4:654; NCE 6:492; ODCC 678; L. Stefanini, *Gioberti* (Milan, 1947); G. Saitta, *Il pensiero di Gioberti* (Florence, 1927).

Denis Cleary

GLADDEN, SOLOMON WASHINGTON (11 February 1836, Pottsgrove, Pa.–2 July 1918, Columbus, Ohio). *Education*: B.A. Williams Coll., 1859. *Career*: minister in Brooklyn, N.Y., 1860–61, Morrisonia, N.Y., 1861–66, North Adams, Mass., 1866–71; editorial staff, *Independent*, 1871–75; minister, Springfield, Mass., 1875–82, Columbus, Ohio, 1882–1914; retirement, 1914–18.

Gladden was a pioneer of the Christian social movement, the Social Gospel. Pastoral charges served as the grounds for his pragmatic theological analysis of American social questions (1870–1918).

Gladden deliberated on social systemic dilemmas in light of the advances in the New Theology. The writings of Horace Bushnell* and Frederick W. Robertson intellectually inspired his ardent application of the insights from liberal biblical criticism and the new sciences to daily congregational life. In *Applied Christianity* (New York, 1886), the most substantive of his thirty-eight books, Gladden revealed himself more the experimentalist than the theoretician. He assessed issues like labor-management relations, taxation, and political corruption in light of cooperative Christian principles. The inclusion of racial and religious analyses in his social judgments set his proposals apart from other religious reformers. Gladden earned the enmity of the Nativists and the industrial monopolists alike because he called for Christian life to move from the private sphere into the public realm.

He won the appellation "the Father of the Social Gospel," because his groundbreaking thought and action stressed that redemption was more than an individual regenerative experience. According to Gladden, societies and social systems were also in need of gracious transformation. Ecumenical relationships between Protestant, Catholic, and Jew as well as cooperation between the races and classes were some of the signs of God's redemptive grace at work in the world.

Gladden's abiding legacy to the history of social Christianity resides in his pastoral ministry. Whether the text was *Plain Thoughts on the Art of Living* (New York, 1868) or *Burning Questions in Modern Theological Issues* (New York, 1890), the prolific theologian affirmed that at its center Christianity is a community of faith reflecting on its life in the human city in light of God's Word. Critical Christian deliberation on daily life must lead to the practice of agapic service in order to realize social justice. Gladden is an historic figure in the reconception of American Protestantism from an old Calvinism resistant to modern life to a new social Christianity, a friend both to modernity and its citizenry.

Bibliography

A.   The Washington Gladden Collection (Ohio Historical Society, Columbus); *Being a Christian* (New York, 1871); *The Church and Modern Life* (New York, 1908).

B.   DAB 7:325–27; DARB 204–5; NCAB 10: 256; *The Congregationalist* 11 July 1918; NYT 3 July 1918, 13; SH 4:492–93; Jacob H. Dorn, *Washington Gladden, Prophet of the Social Gospel* (Columbus, Ohio, 1966); Richard D. Knudten, *The Systematic Thought of Washington Gladden* (New York, 1968).

Dominic P. Scibilia

GOGARTEN, FRIEDRICH (13 January 1887, Dortmund–16 October 1967, Göttingen). *Education*: studied at Berlin, Jena, Heidelberg, 1908–12. *Career*: Lutheran vicariate in Stolberg in the Rhineland; assistant pastor in Bremen; pastor in Stelzendorf in Thuringia, 1917–25; and at Dorndorf on the Saale, 1925–31; assistant professor of theology, Univ. of Breslau, 1931–35; professor of systematic theology, Univ. of Göttingen, 1935–55; retired, 1955–67.

Gogarten was a "crisis" or "dialectical" theologian. Influenced by the theological personalism of Eberhard Griesbach and Martin Buber and by the renaissance in Luther* studies, led by Karl Holl, Erich Seeberg, and others, he developed a theological position that posited the sociality of God as the central category of biblical theology; the corollary category was the sociality of humanity created in God's image and redeemed through Christ.

Gogarten found the perfect theological resource for this theology of crisis in the Lutheran theological dialectic between "Law" (divine judgment of humanity *coram Deo*) and "Gospel" (divine forgiveness of believers *propter Christum*). The "dialectic" between God and world and between divinity and humanity in Christ form the tension within which life is to be discovered anew.

The Lutheran doctrine of the divine basis of civil authority (the doctrine of the "Two Realms" or "Two Kingdoms") was used by Gogarten to the fullest in his political thought. An authoritative form of government that vigorously carries out the divine mandate to govern and to limit chaos and sin for the sake of life (a form of government such as Germany had under the deposed Hohenzollern Emperors) was to be preferred to the weak confusion he perceived in the Weimar Republic, not simply as a matter of hurt German national pride but as a matter of faith.

Gogarten's emphasis upon the essential sociality and this-worldly character of the Incarnation of God in Christ and the church made him an early proponent of secularity and the "world come of age," a phrase that Gogarten himself would never abandon and that was brought into popular coinage by Dietrich Bonhoeffer.* The secular world come of age had to hear the message of the Bible through the miracle narrative, which makes up much of the sacred text. The central content of that message is the personalist I-Thou reality of humanity standing in judgment and redemption before God. The ethical corollary of that reality of faith is freedom and responsibility from which the believer may not honestly escape through an obscurantist retreat into religion understood as magical thinking.

Bibliography

A. *Die Schuld der Kirche gegen die Welt* (Jena, 1928); *Einheit von Evangelium und Volkstum?* (Hamburg, 1933); *Gericht oder Skepsis: eine Streitschrift gegen Karl Barth* (Jena, 1937); *Der Zerfall des Humanismus und die Gottesfrage vom rechten Ansatz des theologischen Denkens* (Stuttgart, 1937); *Demythologizing and History*, trans. N. H. Smith (New York, 1955); *Der Mensch zwischen Gott und Welt* (Heidelberg, 1952); *The Reality of Faith. The Problem of Subjectivism in Theology* (Philadelphia, 1959); *Christ the Crisis*, trans. R. A. Wilson (Richmond, Va., 1970); *Despair and Hope for Our Time*, trans. Thomas Wieser (Philadelphia, 1970); *Luthers Theologie* (Tübingen, 1967).

B. LThK³ 4:819; NCE 16:195–96; ODCC 689; TRE 13:563–67; Larry E. Shiner, *The Secularization of History. An Introduction to the Theology of Friedrich Gogarten* (Nashville, Tenn., 1966); Eckhard Lessing, *Das Problem der Gesellschaft in der Theologie Karl Barths und Friedrich Gogartens* (Gütersloh, 1972); Alexander Schwan, *Geschichtstheologische Konstitution und Destruktion der Politik: Friedrich Gogarten und Rudolf Bultmann* (Berlin, 1976).

Guy C. Carter

GOMARUS, FRANCISCUS (30 January 1563, Bruges–11 January 1641, Groningen). *Education*: studied at Strasbourg with humanist Johann Sturm, 1574–77; at Neustadt with Ursinus, Zanchius, and Tossanus, 1578–81; at Oxford, Cambridge, 1582–83; doctorate in theology, Univ. of Heidelberg, 1593. *Career*: pastor, Frankfurt, 1587; professor of theology, Leiden, 1594–1611; minister, Reformed congregation at Middelburg, 1611–14; taught at the Heugenot seminary in Saumur, France, 1614–18; professor of theology, Groningen, 1618–41.

Gomarus was a leading representative of predestinarian Calvinist theology in the Netherlands and an ardent opponent of Arminianism. Deeply influenced by the theology of Theodore Beza,* Gomarus' theological system centered on supralapsarian predestination, as evidenced in his treatise *De divinae praedestinationis hominum objecto* (1650). Known for his Contra-Remonstrant views, he was chosen as a delegate to the Synod of Dort (1618–19). At Dort he was among the principal opponents of Arminianism and helped secure the condemnation of the Remonstrants. Polemical in nature, Gomarus was an uncompromising defender of strict Calvinism.

Bibliography

A. *Opera theologica omnia*, 3 vols. (Amsterdam, 1644).

B. LThK³ 4:831; NCE 6:604; ODCC 689–90; OEncR 2:181–82; G. P. Van Itterzon, *Franciscus Gomarus* (The Hague, 1929); Douglas Nobbs, *Theocracy and Toleration: A Study of Disputes in Dutch Calvinism from 1600 to 1650* (Cambridge, 1938); Carl Bangs, *Arminius: A Study in the Dutch Reformation* (repr. Grand Rapids, Mich., 1985).

R. David Rightmire

GORE, CHARLES (22 January 1853, Wimbledon, London, England–17 January 1932, Kensington, London, England). *Education*: first class in classical moderation and in *literae humaniores*, Balliol Coll., Oxford, 1872, 1875. *Career*: fellow, Trinity Coll., Oxford, 1875–80; ordained priest, 1878; vice principal, Cuddesdon Theol. Coll., 1880–84; principal, Pusey House, 1884–93; founder, Community of the Resurrection, Oxford, 1892; vicar, Radley, Berks, 1893–94; canon of Westminster, 1894–1902; bishop of Worcester, 1902–5; bishop of Birmingham, 1905–11; bishop of Oxford, 1911–19.

Gore was the foremost proponent of Anglican liberal catholicism, which sought to express catholic tradition in light of contemporary knowledge. Gore firmly upheld the catholicity of the church in terms of the succession of bishops and sacramental ministry, the creeds, and the canon of Scripture. He understood catholicism as the establishment of a "visible society" that is to be "the one divinely constituted home of the great salvation." Gore's liberal catholicism also welcomed the contribution of knowledge and insights from a variety of sources, including natural science and biblical criticism. He emphasized the importance of moral decisiveness in the Christian life. Gore believed liberal catholicism to be embodied in the Anglican appeal to Scripture, tradition, and reason as sources of church authority. He edited *Lux Mundi* (1889), a collection of essays by a group of Oxford Anglican teachers who sought "to put the Catholic faith into its right relation to modern intellectual and moral problems." Gore's essay "The Holy Spirit and Inspiration" in *Lux Mundi* included a statement that acknowledged Jesus' human limitation of knowledge. This statement led to considerable controversy, and represented Gore's break with the dogmatic conservatism of the older Tractarians. The doctrine of Christ's kenosis, or self-emptying under conditions of human nature, was subsequently developed by Gore and others and became prominent in Anglican theology. Gore's 1891 Bampton Lectures, *The Incarnation of the Son of God*, was one of the most important Anglican works of the time on the Incarnation. His teaching on the Incarnation reflected both patristic dogma and contemporary interest in the historical life of Christ.

Bibliography

A. *The Church and the Ministry* (New York, 1889); *Dissertations on Subjects Connected with the Incarnation* (New York, 1895); *The Creed of the Christian* (London, 1895); *The Body of Christ* (New York, 1901); *The Basis of Anglican Fellowship* (London, 1914); *Belief in God* (New York, 1921); *Christian Moral Principles* (London, 1921); *Belief in Christ* (New York, 1922); *The Holy Spirit and the Church* (New York, 1924); *The Anglo-Catholic Movement To-day* (London, 1925).

B. DNB [1931–40] 349–53; LThK³ 4:839; NCE 6:631–32; ODCC 691; TRE 13: 586–88; Paul Avis, *Gore: Construction and Conflict* (Worthing, 1988); James Carpenter, *Gore, A Study in Liberal Catholic Thought* (London, 1960); Gordon Crosse, *Charles Gore, A Biographical Sketch* (London, 1932); Albert Mansbridge, *Edward Stuart Talbot and Charles Gore* (London, 1935); G. L. Prestige, *The Life of Charles Gore, A Great*

Englishman (London, 1935); Arthur Michael Ramsey, *An Era in Anglican Theology, From Gore to Temple* (New York, 1960).

Robert B. Slocum

GOTTSCHALK OF ORBAIS (ca. 803–ca. 869), monk, theologian, poet. Oblated by his father Count Berno to the abbey of Fulda, Gottschalk later sought release from the monastic life, but Rabanus Maurus,* his abbot, successfully opposed him. He moved to Orbais and was made a priest, though his ordination was irregular. His subsequent study of Augustine issued in a theology of double predestination—of the elect to glory and of the reprobate to Hell (but not to sin), compromising the universality of God's salvific will and of redemption in Christ. Rabanus Maurus, then archbishop of Mainz, had him condemned at the Synod of Mainz (848), and the metropolitan, Hincmar of Rheims,* convened a synod at Quiercy-sur-Oise ratifying the condemnation. Gottschalk was flogged, stripped of orders, and imprisoned for life in the monastery of Hautvillers. Hincmar wrote a rebuttal of Gottschalk's views, eliciting replies from Gottschalk (his *Confessio prolixior*), but also Jonas of Orléans, Servatus Lupus, Ratramnus,* Florus of Lyons, and others objecting to Hincmar's imprecision. The controversy was settled at the council of Touzy (860), but left the issue itself still awaiting the more precise theological categories of a later century. Gottschalk appealed for rehabilitation, but Nicholas VI died before hearing the case (867), and Gottschalk himself died, disturbed and refusing even clothing from Hincmar, two years later. Gottschalk also had opposed Radbertus* on the Eucharist, and Hincmar's replacing the phrase *trina deitas* with *summa deitas* in a common Vespers hymn. Gottschalk was also a poet, probably the best of the whole Carolingian Renaissance.

Bibliography

A. MGH *Poetae Latini* 1.623–24; 3.707–738; 4.934–36; 6.86–106; *Oeuvres théologiques et grammaticales de Godescalc d'Orbais*, ed. Cyrille Lambot (Louvain, 1945); idem, "Lettre inédite de Godescalc d'Orbais," *Revue bénédictine* 68 (1958): 41–51.

B. BBKL 2:275–76; DTC 12:2901–35; LThK³ 4:955–57; NCE 6:648; ODCC 696; TRE 14:108–10; Klaus Vielhaber, *Gottschalk der Sachse* (Bonn, 1956); Jean Jolivet, *Godescalc d'Orbais et la Trinité* (Paris, 1958); O. Stegmüller, "Martin von Tours oder Gottschalk von Orbais?" *Revue bénédictine* 76 (1966): 177–230; Jean Devisse, *Hincmar, Archevêque de Reims, 845–882*, 1:115–279 (Geneva, 1975); David Ganz, *Corbie in the Carolingian Renaissance* (Sigmaringen, 1990); Marie-Luise Weber, *Die Gedichte des Gottschalk von Orbais* (New York, 1992); John Marenbon, "Carolingian Thought," in *Carolingian Culture: Emulation and Innovation*, ed. Rosamond McKitterick, 171–92 (New York, 1994).

John C. Cavadini

GREBEL, CONRAD (1498, Zurich, Switzerland–1526, Maienfeld, Oberland). *Education*: studied at Basel, Vienna, Paris, 1514–20. *Career*: resided in Zurich,

1520–23; broke with Zwingli,* 1523; preacher and founder, Swiss Brethren, 1523–26.

Grebel became converted to the Protestant reform under the influence of Ulrich Zwingli, whose protégé he became. Dissatisfied with what they considered the slow pace of reforms in Zurich and especially with a council edict that mandated baptism for all infants by the age of eight weeks, Grebel, Felix Manz, George Blaurock, and others met to pray for guidance on January 2, 1525. They signaled their break with the Zurich church and their call for religious liberty by rebaptizing each other and leaving Zurich to evangelize their beliefs, founding what came to be known as the Swiss Brethren or (among detractors) Anabaptism.

While Grebel held to separatist discipleship, he also provided a modifying effect on the more radical Anabaptists of southern Germany. As a biblicist, he taught the necessity of fulfilling the law of Christ in exact adherence to the New Testament, which does not mention infant baptism or explain how Christ is present in the Lord's Supper. Opposed to hymnology and ecclesial ritual, Grebel also taught nonviolence, especially among Christians, and the sacredness of every place.

Bibliography

A.   *The Life and Letters of Conrad Grebel*, ed. Harold S. Bender et al. (Goshen, Ind., 1950).

B.   LThK³ 4:995; NCE 6:717; OEncR 2:191–93; *Mennonite Encyclopedia* 2:566–75; John L. Ruth, *Conrad Grebel, Son of Zurich* (Scottdale, Pa., 1975); George H. Williams, *The Radical Reformation* (Philadelphia, 1962).

Joan Skocir

GREGORY I, THE GREAT (ca. 550, Rome–604, Rome). *Career*: became a civil servant; in 574, sold his patrimony in Sicily, founded seven monasteries there, and turned his father's house into a monastery dedicated to St. Andrew; never attained the rank of abbot, but was content to remain a monk; while at St. Andrew's, wrote sermons on 1 Kings and Song of Songs; deacon, Rome, 579; papal emissary to Constantinople, where he lived for six years, 579–85; while there he began the *Moralia in Job*, a work of dogmatic, ascetical, and mystical theology, which he revised and completed in 595; pope, 590–604; concluded a peace with the Lombards, 592–93; during his papacy, composed sermons on Ezekiel, and the *Dialogues*, as well as letters.

Because the exarch at Ravenna was inactive, Gregory acted in the secular as well as sacred sphere during his papacy. His ability to manage the affairs of both Italy and the church has its roots in the concept of *consideratio*, self-knowledge and reflection, which balances the contemplative and the active, the temporal and the spiritual. Gregory provided an intellectual framework in which to integrate all aspects of life with Christian teachings. The *Rule for Bishops* contains practical and theoretical aspects of episcopal responsibility, using as a model the angelic hierarchy. *Consideratio* requires that clerics exhibit a sense of balance. Gregory saw the role of the preacher as an essential guide to the spiritual life, which unfolds the mysteries of Scripture and directs the faithful on an inward journey of self-discovery to the inner recesses of the heart.

The *Dialogues* treat the soul, the nature of death, resurrection, and the life to come through observance of the lives and deaths of holy men. Sainthood for Gregory does not stem only from miraculous events, but from a daily living out of the virtues of Christian life, charity, observance, and discipline.

Gregory undertook to revise and fix the text of the liturgy. He seems to have written a portion of a sacramentary to which later liturgists contributed. An important innovation was his placement of the Lord's Prayer in its present position, caused by his conviction that Christ's own words, rather than the composition of a liturgist, ought to be prayed over Christ's Body and Blood. Gregory was interested in the revival and reform of church music but probably did not compose the chant modes given the title "Gregorian."

Bibliography

A. CPL 1708–21; CCSL 140–44; PL 77; SC 251; *Dialogues, Book II*, trans. Odo Zimmerman (Westport, Conn., 1980).

B. DTC 6:1776–81; LThK³ 4:1010–13; NCE 6:766–70; ODCC 706–7; TRE 14:135–45; Dag Norberg, *In registrum Gregori Magni studia critica*, 2 vols. (Uppsala, 1937–39); H. Ashworth, "Did St. Gregory the Great Compose a Sacramentary?" StPatr 2 (1953): 3–16; Gillian Evans, *The Thought of Gregory the Great* (New York, 1986); Carole Straw, *Gregory the Great: Perfection in Imperfection* (Berkeley, Calif., 1988).

Thomas S. Ferguson

GREGORY OF NAZIANZUS (330, Nazianzus–390, Arianzus). *Education*: wealth supported primary education in Nazianzus, later rhetorical study in Cappadocian Caesarea, and with the rhetorician Thespesius in Palestinian Caesarea—which held Origen's library expanded by Eusebius and Pamphilus. In Alexandria Gregory may have met Athanasius* and Didymus the Blind.* For ten years he studied with the rhetoricians Himerius and Prohaeresius (a Christian) in Athens. There he resumed his friendship with Basil* and probably met Julian, who became the apostate emperor. Gregory so excelled in rhetoric that he evidently was invited to teach in Athens but left the city in the hope of founding a monastic retreat with Basil. *Career*: Gregory never sought the episcopacy. He resisted becoming a priest but finally accepted his father's call to be an auxiliary bishop of Nazianzus. After his parents' death he entered the monastery of St. Thecla in Seleucia. Basil appointed him bishop of Sasima, a dusty outpost town, but Gregory furiously refused to serve; he smelled ecclesiastical politics. A persuasive female cousin drew him to a struggling Orthodox congregation in Constantinople. Although there less than three years, the capital occasioned twenty-two of his forty-four extant orations. He was chosen the second president of the 381 Council of Constantinople, yet resigned in disgust when Alexandrian and Macedonian bishops insisted that canon law stood against his being bishop there after serving at Sasima. He retired to Arianzus, edited his works, and wrote poetry.

Along with Basil the Great and John Chrysostom,* Gregory Nazianzus is one of the three hierarchs of Eastern Orthodoxy. Only he and the apostle John are called "the Theologian" in that tradition. Gregory was born into a Christian Cappadocian family of means and died on the family estate at Arianzus. Gregory's corpus is extensive: the orations, over two hundred and forty letters, and three hundred poems including a long autobiography, the most self-reflective in antiquity (surpassed only partially by Augustine's* *Confessions*). The *Theological Orations* are classics. He so mastered rhetoric that Byzantine commentators on ancient Greek manuals of the subject often replaced illustrations from Demosthenes with ones from Gregory.

His theological projects were communal. He shared theological treatises, letters, and lists of biblical words with Basil, Gregory of Nyssa,* and others. Although Gregory of Nyssa probably first developed Cappadocian technical trinitarian terminology, Gregory of Nazianus helped make the conceptions palatable. He found the non-Nicenes, Eunomius and his community, trapped in materialistic logic and mean-spirited. They preferred precise terms supported by syllogisms, which treated biblical language about Christ's divinity as homonyms. Their Constantinopolitan leaders were often bright but immature logicians rather than mature contemplative poets who knew that God's nature was ultimately incomprehensible and thus inexpressible. Nazianzen worked within Nicene definitions, including *homoousios*, but he warned that his opponents did not confess Father, Son, and Spirit in scriptural terms. For him doctrine developed beyond Holy Writ; only in his time had the sense of the Holy Spirit as God become plain, yet he balked at anything less than inclusive use of the Bible. His citation of over seven hundred fifty passages in the *Theological Orations* backed his claim that he and his supporters made more sense of more Scripture than did his opponents. He spelled out clear grammatical rules of exegesis but used allegory because he saw all Scripture as intending the confession of his worshipping community.

Gregory introduced *perichoresis*, "interpenetration," to depict the union of human and divine natures in Jesus Christ and used a threefold predication to deal with Scripture: the Son before incarnation, the Son incarnate, and the man Jesus. He fought Sabellians and Arians, and handily dealt with Apollinarians by insisting that a Christ without human mind and soul would not heal the most sinful elements: "What is not assumed is not saved." He avoided the suggestion of totally separate natures or a minimized divinity.

For him salvation needed many metaphors: death in our place, cleansing blood, ransom—but Satan deserved no payment. He emphasized *theôsis*, "deification," more than any other theologian: Christ became human that we might become divine. The Eucharist is mysterious but depends on presence and majestic power. Baptism is threefold immersion in the name of Father, Son, and Spirit because each is divine and enables humans to become divine.

God's grace secures salvation, but the image of God in humans was not destroyed. It was badly distorted. Thus God does not coerce; God cajoles. An understanding of rhetorical persuasion enhances preaching. Human will is free enough to make each person responsive and responsible. Grace is everything, but contemplation, discipline, and virtue are never nothing.

God is not a male, thus both men and women exist in God's image. Eve sinned, but so did Adam. Christ died for both. The truth of the faith has been taught and sustained by honored women—for example, his mother Nonna, his sister Gorgonia, and others. Marriage and childbirth are good; without them there would be no people to pursue celibacy. Marriage is a partnership of fellow servants, not a relationship of master and slave. In the end, however, celibacy is preferable.

Ecclesiastical structure must be watched. Leaders should be tested people, not new converts. Only the contemplative can pursue theology; it is not for everyone, every topic, every audience, or every occasion. Too many mediocre bishops lack classical education and Christian virtue.

Gregory's invectives against Julian and his occasionally vitriolic rejection of Judaism make him appear to deny truth in other religions. He knew that pagans worshiped many gods whose tales were considered immoral even by their believers who allegorized them; Jews rejected Jesus yet lived morally. Nazianzen honored Plato and Aristotle when they talked about God with certain metaphors. He applauded the meditative practices of some pagans who disciplined their bodies and sought truth for their souls. His father had lived a virtuous life as a Hypsistarian and thus was well prepared to take the name of Jesus.

The Theologian remains a remarkable guide. His quirky, overly sensitive personality gave him fits, but many of his theological proposals still fit.

Bibliography

A.   PG 35–38; SC 208, 247, 250, 270, 284, 309, 318, 358, 384; GCS 53; C. G. Browne and J. E. Swallow, NPNF 2, 7, 185–498; E. R. Hardy, LCC 3 (1954): 113–232; FC 22, 75; J. McGuckin, *Gregory Nazianzen: Selected Poems* (Oxford, 1986); L. Wickham and F. Williams in Norris (see below).

B.   DTC 6:1839–44; LThK³ 4:1004–6; NCE 6:791–94; ODCC 711–12; TRE 14:164–73; Donald F. Winslow, *The Dynamics of Salvation: A Study in Gregory of Nazianzus* (Cambridge, Mass., 1979); Anna-Stina Ellverson, *The Dual Nature of Man: A Study in the Theological Anthropology of Gregory of Nazianzus* (Uppsala, 1981); Frederick W. Norris, *Faith Gives Fullness to Reasoning: The Five Theological Orations of Gregory Nazianzen* (New York, 1990); Peter L. Gilbert, "Person and Nature in the Theological Poems of St. Gregory of Nazianzus," Ph.D., diss. Catholic University of America, 1994; Jean Bernardi, *Saint Grégoire de Nazianze. Le théologien et son temps (330–390)* (Paris, 1995).

Frederick W. Norris

GREGORY OF NYSSA (ca. 335, Cappadocia—ca. 395). Together with his older brother Basil of Caesarea* and Gregory of Nazianzus,* Gregory of Nyssa was one of the three celebrated Cappadocian Fathers whose collective contribution to early Christian theology, particularly in the resolution of the trinitarian controversies, was profound. They struggled against the so-called "neo-Arianism" which, during the second half of the fourth century, raised the philosophical and theological stakes of the trinitarian debates. Gregory of Nyssa was perhaps the least adept at episcopal ministry but the most theologically prolific of the three Cappadocians. He carefully negotiated the language of one essence (*ousia*) and three persons (*hypostaseis*) of God, and constructed an entire mystical theology and theological anthropology grounded in the first principle of God's (the Trinity's) essential infinity and incomprehensibility.

Gregory of Nyssa was born into a Christian family and was profoundly influenced in his youth by his oldest sibling, Macrina, a respected ascetic theologian, and by his older brother Basil, whom Gregory credits as his tutor. Unlike the other two Cappadocian Fathers, Gregory did not study in one of the great philosophical or rhetorical centers of his time. He received ordination as a lector in the church and appeared to be headed toward the priesthood but instead married and assumed a position as a teacher of rhetoric—a controversial action at a time when Christianity was struggling to surmount the vestiges of pagan culture. Gregory of Nazianzus reproached Gregory for loving the "name of rhetor" more than the "name of Christian," for repudiating the divine mysteries, and for needing, as it were, to be resurrected from the dead (Gregory Nazianzus, *Ep.* 11). His secular career was short-lived, however. In 372 Basil, as the metropolitan bishop of Cappadocia, recruited his younger brother to serve as bishop in Nyssa, a modest but strategic outpost in the battle against Arianism and a place that Gregory himself described as a virtual wilderness (*Ep.* 9). Gregory was a poor administrator even by Basil's account. In 376 Arians maneuvered to depose Gregory from his see, but he regained it in 378. In this early period of his episcopacy, Gregory's interests in asceticism and spiritual theology intensified, and he produced several significant works, including his treatises *On Virginity* and *On the Dead*, homilies on the Lord's Prayer, the Beatitudes, and Ecclesiastes, and a commentary *On the Inscriptions of the Psalms*.

Gregory's career took another dramatic turn after Basil's death (379), when he assumed a more forceful role in opposing Arianism during the period from the synod of Antioch in 379 to the councils of Constantinople in 381, 382, and 383. He was a strong presence in all of those anti-Arian assemblies, and the emperor Theodosius I singled him out as a champion of the Orthodox faith. In the 380s Gregory produced his treatise *Against Eunomius*, the most important work of Orthodox trinitarian theology in the fourth century. To this same period belong his *Hexaemeron* (a commentary on the six days of creation), his *Life of Macrina* honoring his sister, his speculative anthropological treatises *On the Soul and Resurrection* and *On the Creation of Humanity*, his *Great Catechetical Oration* (for Christian catechists) and substantial Christological works against Apollinarianism. His last significant trinitarian work, *To Ablabius: That There Are Not Three Gods*, and two mature works of spiritual theology, the *Commen-*

tary on the Song of Songs and the *Life of Moses*, stem from the period of his retirement in the early 390s.

Within his fourth-century context, Gregory was a constructive critic of Platonism and Origenism and a steadfast opponent of Eunomian (neo-) Arianism. Already in his early writings such as *On Virginity*, Gregory was developing his views on cosmology, anthropology, and the economy of salvation. He holds up the virgin life (which he himself, unlike Basil and Gregory of Nazianzus, had not embraced) as the model "philosophical life" for Christians because its ascetic disciplines are the primary means to reverse the residual effects of the Fall—namely, irrationality, sexuality, deviant bodily passions, and mortality.

Gregory sets out a more theoretical frame for his theological anthropology in his treatises *On the Soul and Resurrection* and *On the Creation of Humanity*, where he categorically repudiates Platonic concepts of preexistence and Origenist speculation about dual acts of creation (spiritual and corporeal). He in turn develops his own constructive theology of human ensoulment and embodiment, built on a sophisticated exegesis of the narratives of creation and the Fall in Gn 1–3. God, he asserts, created human souls and bodies in an ideal coexistence (Gn 1:26); nonetheless, the "concrete" reality of the Fall (which he explains as a fault of Adam's ignorance and accompanying ill choice) devastated the original communion of human nature with God. Structurally, then, human nature remains a microcosm of the intelligible and spiritual realms of God's one created order and enjoys an exalted mediatorial position in that order. The soul is essentially the image of God, the body derivatively so (an "image of the image"). Existentially, however, by the addition after the Fall of the remedial "garments of skins" (Gn 3:21)—the constraints on bodily existence that God intends for an ultimately redemptive purpose—the ascetic life of human beings is a kind of microcosm of salvation history. The soul's internal struggles to purify the body and to bring about harmony among the higher and lower faculties of human nature reflect, in miniature form, the process of moral restoration operative in the macrocosm of creaturely nature. It is a process already perfected, however, through the grace of Jesus Christ, who by his incarnation, death, and resurrection, has integrated the fallen and ruptured elements of creaturely nature and effected a new creation.

The originality of Gregory's contribution to Christian anthropology stands out in his treatment of three interrelated themes: mutability, freedom, and passion. Opposing the Platonic tendency to equate mutability with degenerativeness (and thus immutability with perfection), Gregory redefines human mutability in Christian terms as the perpetual openness of creaturely nature to its Creator. Created beings, *qua* creatures, retain a tendency to drift toward aimless movement and moral degeneration; but built into their nature as intellectual beings made in the image of God is a freedom always to transcend their limitations, to choose the Good, and to persist in constant change for the better ("from one degree of glory to another," 2 Cor 3:13). Human free will (*prohairesis*), informed by reason and acting in steady cooperation with divine grace, can thus enter a mode of continued moral and spiritual progress—the perpetual "striving" or *epektasis* to which Gregory sees Paul alluding in Phil 3:13. Good choices, however, are only one aspect of it. The will must also redirect and transmute the errant passions, turning anger, for example, into courage, cowardice into caution, fear into obedience, hatred into an aversion to vice, love into burning passion for God, and so on. All the potencies or faculties of human nature must be rallied in the pursuit of divine virtues and communion with God.

Basic to this doctrine of human transformation and perpetual spiritual progress is Gregory's interpretation of the "image of God." Unlike Origen, who distinguished in Gn 1:26–27 between the "image" of God as a rational endowment and the "likeness" of God as an eschatological goal to which souls are directed by divine pedagogy, Gregory envisioned the image and the likeness as essentially the same reality, a principle of final causality within the original human constitution, signaling the predisposition to virtue, the potency of godlikeness, and the dynamic character of creaturely nature. The human vocation, then, is perpetual assimilation to God, "deification," a restoration to "original" perfection.

At the peak of his career, Gregory confronted the neo-Arian theologian Eunomius in his long treatise *Against Eunomius*, the summa of his trinitarian doctrine (composed 380–83). Eunomius basically challenged the Cappadocians to explain how the one "ingenerate" (also "uncreated," "uncaused") God could share that status with another, the Son. Philosophical first principles dictated that the pure simplicity of divine being admitted of no distinction or compositeness. Any "generation" or "begetting" on the part of God had to mean a willed action extrinsic to God's essence (*ousia*). The "begotten" Son could therefore only be a creature, the metaphysical inferior of his "Father." Gregory, in response, could accept the premise of the uncreated simplicity of the Godhead, but as an exponent and interpreter of the Nicene faith he begins, *a priori*, with the eternally irreducible interrelation between Father and Son (and Holy Spirit) in sharing that uncreated essence. The "generation" of the Son is an ineffable reality that does not admit of a greater or lesser share in the Father's divinity. The same can be said of the "procession" of the Holy Spirit from the Father "through the Son"; no diminution is implied by that relation.

Gregory's central contribution to trinitarian doctrine is the articulation of the formula "one [divine] essence (*ousia*) in three persons (*hypostaseis*)," which was affirmed by the Council of Constantinople of 381, and which reinterpreted the Nicene principle of the consubstantiality (*homoousia*) of Father, Son, and Holy Spirit in terms of a unity of the equality of the divine persons rather than a sheer numerical unity. Clearly that reinterpretation risked being targeted as "tritheism," but for Gregory the risk was worth it (cf. *To Ablabius: That There Are Not Three Gods*). Granted the paradox of confessing the oneness and threeness of God as logically simultaneous, the formula moved Christian theology beyond the impasse of an overly abstract philosophical monotheism that to a great degree had bogged down earlier debates over the meaning of the divine *homoousia*. Gregory for his part vigorously defends the absolute mystery of the divine essence, spurning Eunomius' claims to have captured the essence of God through the concept of "ingeneracy"; thus Gregory insists that all "apophatic" and "cataphatic" (or theologically "negative" and "affirmative") language about God, even biblical language, serves merely to provide boundaries for speaking about God, not to identify positively what God is. The principle of divine "infinity" proved to be especially useful to Gregory in signaling God's absolute and mysterious transcendence.

This principle in turn provides a crucial link between Gregory's *theologia* proper and his theological anthropology and spirituality. The eternal progress (*epektasis*) of human beings toward assimilation to God, as is summarily portrayed in one of Gregory's last works, the *Life of Moses*, genuinely has no terminus; it extends even beyond death because creatures can never ultimately be "stretched" to the point of reaching the infinite and ineffable God. For the ontological "gap," or *diastêma*, between the Uncreated, whose own being knows no *diastêma*, and creation, which is inherently diastemic, constitutes at once the metaphysical and epistemic delimitation of created nature and the "frontier," as it were, across which creatures must forever strain toward God. Precisely in that perpetual striving, however, lies the creature's sabbatical rest: a sublime paradox.

The chasm between the Uncreated and the created is for Gregory truly bridged only through Jesus Christ himself. Although in his anti-Apollinarian writings Gregory stresses a careful distinction of divine and human natures for polemical purposes, he strongly affirms, overall, the Incarnation as an intimate "mingling" of the divine Logos with the full human nature (soul and body) of Jesus. Here he echoes a soteriological principle, going back to Irenaeus* and Athanasius,* and carried over to the Cappadocians by Gregory of Nazianzus: "what is not assumed [by the incarnate Son] is not healed; what is united is saved." Conversely, Nyssa asserts the full divinization of Christ's humanity on behalf of all humankind, even claiming that the peculiar properties (*idiômata*) of Christ's earthly nature were preempted by the divine attributes of the Son. While some of these Christological nuances are unsatisfactory by later (fifth-century) accounts of the "communication of attributes" in Christ, they nevertheless serve Gregory's own grand vision of the instrumentality of the Incarnation in the economy of the human redemption and deification.

Bibliography

A.   PG 44–46; *Gregorii Nysseni Opera*, ed. W. Jaeger et al., 9 vols. (Leiden, 1952–); SC 1 bis, 6, 119, 178, 363; *Select Writings and Letters of Gregory, Bishop of Nyssa*, trans. W. Moore and H. Austin Wilson, NPNF 2, 5 (repr. Grand Rapids, Mich., 1954); *The Lord's Prayer; The Beatitudes*, trans. H. Graef, ACW 18 (Westminster, Md., 1954); *From Glory to Glory: Texts from Gregory of Nyssa's Mystical Writings*, ed. and trans. H. Musurillo (New York, 1961); *Ascetical Works*, trans. V. Callahan, FC 58 (Washington, D.C., 1967); *The Life of Moses*, trans. A. Malherbe and E. Ferguson, CWS (New

York, 1978); *Commentary on the Song of Songs*, trans. C. McCambley (Brookline, Mass., 1987); *Homilies on Ecclesiastes*, trans. S. Hall (New York, 1993); *Treatise on the Inscriptions of the Psalms*, trans. R. Heine (New York, 1995).

B.   DTC 6:1847–52; LThK³ 4:1007–8; NCE 6:794–96; ODCC 712; TRE 14:173–81; J. Daniélou, *Platonisme et théologie mystique* (Paris, 1944; rev. ed., 1954); G. Ladner, "The Philosophical Anthropology of St. Gregory of Nyssa," *Dumbarton Oaks Papers* 12 (1958): 59–94; D. Balás, *"Metousia Theou": Man's Participation in God's Perfections according to Saint Gregory of Nyssa* (Rome, 1966); W. Jaeger, *Gregor von Nyssas Lehre vom Heiligen Geist* (Leiden, 1966); E. Mühlenberg, *Die Unendlichkeit Gottes bei Gregor von Nyssa* (Göttingen, 1966); J. Daniélou, *L'être et le temps chez Grégoire de Nysse* (Leiden, 1970); *Écriture et culture philosophique dans la pensée de Grégoire de Nysse*, ed. M. Harl (Leiden, 1971); R. Hübner, *Die Einheit des Leibes Christi bei Gregor von Nyssa* (Leiden, 1974); R. Heine, *Perfection in the Virtuous Life: A Study in the Relationship between Edification and Polemical Theology in Gregory of Nyssa's "De Vita Moysis"* (Cambridge, Mass., 1975); M. Canévet, *Grégoire de Nysse et l'herméneutique biblique* (Paris, 1983); R. P. C. Hanson, *The Search for the Christian Doctrine of God: The Arian Controversy 318–381* (Edinburgh, 1988); V. Harrison, *Grace and Human Freedom According to St. Gregory of Nyssa* (Lewiston, N.Y., 1992); J. Pelikan, *Christianity and Classical Culture: The Metamorphosis of Natural Theology in the Christian Encounter with Hellenism* (New Haven, Conn., 1993); M. Barnes, "The Polemical Context and Content of Gregory of Nyssa's Moral Psychology," *Medieval Philosophy and Theology* 4 (1994): 1–24; H. Urs von Balthasar, *Presence and Thought: An Essay on the Religious Philosophy of Gregory of Nyssa*, trans. M. Sebanc (San Francisco, 1995).

Paul M. Blowers

GREGORY PALAMAS. *See* PALAMAS, GREGORY.

GREGORY OF RIMINI (ca. 1290, Rimini, near Venice–November, 1358, Vienna). During his academic career Gregory came under the influence of the nominalist philosophy of William of Occam.* With the intervention of Pope Clement VI (1342–52), Gregory finally obtained his degree from the University of Paris and received teaching positions at Bologna and Padua. In 1357, he was elected superior general of the Augustinian monastic order.

Scholars debate whether or not Gregory of Rimini should be considered a nominalist, a moderate nominalist, a modern teacher, or some synthesis of all. Gregory was not completely subsumed by the Occamist school, since he was able to synthesize a theology of divine grace, based on Augustine's,* with his nominalist training. Gregory openly defended the Augustinian doctrine of double predestination and passionately opposed the rising Pelagian tendencies of his day. Gregory allowed for proofs of the existence of God and a rational demonstration of the spirituality of the soul. He assigned more importance to personal experience than the traditional nominalist school did. Under Augustinian influence, he claimed that the intellect knows the individual objects of experience by an intuitive process before it can fashion any abstract ideas. He further maintained that the immediate object of knowledge and science was not the object that exists outside the mind, but rather the total meaning of logical propositions.

On the question of human salvation and spiritual blessing, Gregory taught what he believed to be an Augustinian doctrine, which emphasized the inability of each person to lead a moral life by free will alone without divine grace. Following Augustine, he held to the principle of predestination based upon God's gracious election of the just and their eternal reward in God's kingdom. Gregory also insisted that it was impossible for any human being to initiate the process of salvation by making the moral choice to live according to God's will. Christians cannot aspire to see God without the help of God.

One of Gregory's less favorable teachings was related to the Black Death and concerned infant baptism. Gregory believed that all children should be baptized at an early age because those children who were dying without baptism would suffer eternal punishment. This teaching earned him the nickname "infant torturer."

Gregory's principal teachings are assembled in his major work, in which he cited the twelfth-century scholastic theologian Peter Lombard.* The widespread influence of Gregory's teachings on much of late medieval Europe is evidenced by the similar teaching emanating from the sixteenth-century Augustinian faculty at the University of Wittenberg, Germany, the monastic order and school of the Protestant reformer, Martin Luther.*

Bibliography

A. *Super Primum et Secundum Sententiarum* (Saint Bonaventure, N.Y., 1955 [repr. of the Venice edition of 1522]).

B. DTC 6:1852–54; LThK³ 4:1025; NCE 6:797; ODCC 713; TRE 14:181–84; Martin Schuler, *Prädestination, Sünde und Freiheit bei Gregor von Rimini* (Stuttgart, 1934); Gordon Leff, *Gregory of Rimini: Tradition and Innovation in Fourteenth Century Thought* (Manchester, 1961).

Peter W. Breitsch

GROOTE, GEERT DE (16 October 1340, Deventer–20 August 1383, Deventer). *Education*: studied for the priesthood in Paris; M. A., ca. 1358; studied canon law. *Career*: in 1374 underwent a conversion, gave up his considerable wealth, and lived for two years as a guest at the Carthusian monastery of Monnikhuizen; left the monastery, determined to live a religious life outside the cloister; made his large home a haven for poor women, who became the first Sisters of the Common Life; began in 1379 to preach as a deacon in the diocese of Utrecht for the reform of the faith and morals of the clergy and the laity; banned from preaching in 1383 after strongly denouncing the incontinence of the clergy in the presence of the bishop and his clergy; died of the plague soon afterwards. His writings include some eighty letters and ten treatises. Groote is recognized as the founder of the New Devotion with its emphasis on life in Christ, on the reading of Scripture, on progress in moral holiness, and on development in interiority. In 1386 some of his disciples founded Windesheim, which became the center of the spiritual revival known as the *Devotio moderna*, and they themselves became the Brethren of the Common Life.

Bibliography

A. *Devotio Moderna: Basic Writings*, trans. with intro. John Van Engen (New York, 1988).

B. NCE 6:809; ODCC 716; TRE 14:274–77; Ernest F. Jacob, "Gerard Groote and the Beginnings of the New Devotion in the Low Countries," JEH 3 (1952): 40–57; T. P. van Zijl, *Gerard Groote: Ascetic and Reformer, 1340–1384* (Washington, D.C., 1963); Otto Gründler, "Devotio Moderna atque Antiqua: The Modern Devotion and Carthusian Spirituality," in *The Spirituality of Western Christendom*, ed. E. Rozanne Elder (Kalamazoo, Mich., 1984), 2:176–93; Mark S. Burrows, "Devotio Moderna: Reforming Piety in the Later Middles Ages," in *Spiritual Traditions for the Contemporary Church*, ed. R. Maas (Nashville, Tenn., 1990), 133–42.

Roland J. Teske

GROSSETESTE, ROBERT (ca. 1170, Suffolk–9 October 1253, Buckden). *Education*: studied at Oxford and probably Paris; M.A. between 1186 and 1191; D.Th. by ca. 1220. *Career*: member of Oxford faculty of theology by early 1220s; taught at Oxford Franciscan house of studies, 1224–35; bishop of Lincoln, 1235–53.

Grosseteste was one of the leading lights of his era. He wrote theological treatises, biblical commentaries, and philosophical tracts, as well as works of natural science and mathematics. He also provided translations of significant Greek texts. His interest in the Greek language increased about the time he was made bishop of Lincoln in 1235, and he translated from Greek into Latin several patristic works, including those of Pseudo-Dionysius,* as well as Aristotle's *Nicomachean Ethics*.

Very much in the Augustinian tradition, Grosseteste set forth a light-metaphysic that was more indebted to Platonism than to Aristotelianism. Drawing on Arabic studies of optics, he propounded a philosophy of nature in which God acts upon the world through light, fusing this theory with an epistemology that centered on divine illumination. Insofar as anything is true it is conformed to the eternal Word, since all truth manifests itself in the light of the highest truth, which is God. Yet, for Grosseteste, such contemplation of the highest truth, the eternal exemplars, was only possible for those who were pure in heart.

Biblical commentators in the thirteenth-century schools became increasingly interested in doctrinal questions; Grosseteste's commentaries were more reminiscent of earlier medieval exegesis with its more pastoral and spiritual emphasis. Though appreciative of philosophical methods, he upheld the absolute authority of the Bible over the pagan philosophers and admonished the masters of Oxford to afford the Bible the principal place in the curriculum.

A most conscientious bishop, who publicly denounced clerical corruption,

Grosseteste refused to grant a prebend in Lincoln to Pope Innocent IV's nephew, disobeying a papal request on the grounds that an unjust papal mandate by its very nature had no true apostolic authority. He enjoyed an excellent reputation in the English church well after his death.

Bibliography

A. *Roberti Grosseteste episcopi quondam Lincolniensis Epistolae,* ed. Henry R. Luard (London, 1861); *Die philosophischen Werke des Robert Grosseteste, Bischofs von Lincoln,* ed. Ludwig Baur (Münster, 1912); *Commentarius in VII libros physicorum Aristotelis,* ed. Pietro Rossi (Florence, 1981); *Hexaëmeron,* ed. Richard C. Dales and Servus Gieben (Oxford, 1982); *Opera Roberti Grosseteste Lincolniensis,* ed. James McEvoy, Richard C. Dales, Philipp W. Rosemann (Turnhout, 1995–).

B. DTC 6:1885–87; LThK² 8:1339; NCE 12:530–32; ODCC 717–18; TRE 14:271–74; Alistair C. Crombie, *Robert Grosseteste and the Origins of Experimental Science, 1100–1700* (Oxford, 1953); *Robert Grosseteste, Scholar and Bishop: Essays in Commemoration of the Seventh Centenary of His Death,* ed. Daniel Callus (Oxford, 1955); James McEvoy, *The Philosophy of Robert Grosseteste* (Oxford, 1982); R. W. Southern, *Robert Grosseteste: The Growth of an English Mind in Medieval Europe,* 2d ed. (New York, 1992).

Ian Christopher Levy

GROTIUS, HUGO, born Huigh De Groot (10 April 1583, Delft, Netherlands– 28 August 1645, Rostock, Germany). *Education*: studied at Leiden Univ., 1594– 98; doctorate in law, Orleans, 1598. *Career*: practiced law, The Hague, 1599– 1607, appointed official historiographer of province of Holland, 1601; advocate-fiscal (public prosecutor) of Holland, 1607–14; pensionary (chief magistrate) of Rotterdam, 1614–18; after involvement in the Dutch Calvinist-Arminian controversy arrested for treason and sentenced for life, 1618; imprisoned at Loevestein castle, 1619–21; escaped prison and fled to Paris, 1621; lived meagerly on royal pension in Paris while pursuing scholarly interests, 1621–31; returned to Netherlands, 1631, but exiled again in Hamburg, 1632–34; Swedish ambassador to French court in Paris, 1635–45.

Grotius is best known for his famous *De Jure Belli ac Pacis* (*On the Law of War and Peace,* 1625), the first systematic treatise on international law, which argued that relations between nations should be regulated by laws, the law of nature and the law of nations. Although his career was in legal and diplomatic fields, Grotius was intensely interested in theological matters, as witnessed by the four tomes of his collected theological works. His legal thought shaped his theological ideas. While Grotius closely sympathized with and politically defended the Arminians in the Arminian controversy, he was not strictly Arminian, but a Christian humanist scholar in the tradition of Erasmus.* His ideal was early Christian antiquity, seen as a time of peace and unity.

His most popular theological work was *De Veritate Religionis Christianae* (1627), an apology to convince non-Christians of the truth of Christianity based largely on extra-biblical arguments. In *Defensio Fidei Catholicae de Satisfac-*

tione Christi adversus Faustum Socinum (1617) Grotius argued that the Arminian view of Christ's Atonement was not the Socinian position, which rejected the traditional Reformation view of Christ's death as vicarious satisfaction for sin. Yet Grotius diverged from the traditional view by stating that God relaxes the penalty of his law and Christ rendered satisfaction, not as a full equivalent for the penalty of sin, but as a nominal equivalent that God is pleased to accept. Grotius' *De Imperio Summarum Potestatum circa Sacra* (1647) contended that the state should have authority over religious matters; the church may arrange only its own internal affairs.

His extensive *Annotationes* on the Old and New Testaments (1641–50) belong to the Christian humanist tradition of philological annotation, not the commentary tradition. Grotius' humanistic exegesis sought the meaning of the text in its original context rather than seeking proof for a doctrinal system. Grotius intensely desired peace among Christians and advocated church union, first among Protestant churches, later also with Roman Catholics. Hence in *De Antichristo* (1640) he denied the pope was the Antichrist.

Bibliography

A.   *Opera Omnia Theologica*, 4 vols. (Amsterdam, 1679; facsimile, Stuttgart, 1972); a new series, *Opera Theologica*, is being published with English translations.
B.   LThK³ 4:1066; NCE 6:812–13; ODCC 718–19; OEncR 2:197–98; TRE 14:277–80; A. Haentjens, *Hugo De Groot als Godsdienstig Denker* (Amsterdam, 1946); *The World of Hugo Grotius (1583–1645)*, ed. R. Feenstra (Amsterdam, 1984); *Hugo Grotius Theologian*, ed. Henk Nellen and Edwin Rabbie (Leiden, 1994).

Donald Sinnema

GUARDINI, ROMANO (17 February 1885, Verona, Italy–1 October 1968, Munich, Germany). *Education*: studied chemistry and economics, Univ. of Tübingen, Munich, and Berlin, 1903–5; studied theology, Freiburg, Tübingen, and Mainz, 1905–10; Ph.D. in theology, Univ. of Freiburg, 1915; Habilitation, Univ. of Bonn, 1922. *Career*: ordained priest, 1910; parish priest, 1910–12 and 1915–20; professor of "Philosophy of Religion and the Catholic Worldview," Univ. of Berlin, 1923–39; professor of "Philosophy of Religion and the Christian Worldview," Univ. of Tübingen, 1945–47, Univ. of Munich, 1948–63; professor emeritus, 1963–68.

Guardini was one of the most creative Catholic minds in the first half of the twentieth century. He played a major role in the liturgical and theological renewal that led to the Second Vatican Council. By the end of his life, he had written approximately seventy books and 100 articles. In the early 1900s, as a university student, Guardini came to the insight that human life and also human thought involve an interplay of polarities (*Gegensätze*) that possesses an underlying unity. Given this view, he was attracted to the Neoplatonism of St. Bonaventure,* the German Idealism of the later Schelling, and also the phenomenology of Max Scheler.

Guided by his theory of the coincidence of opposites, Guardini undertook analyses of the Christian life and its beliefs and also of world literature and contemporary culture. These studies cluster around a few recurring topics. On prayer and worship, he described how the Christian life requires both private prayer and liturgy (e.g., the Mass) and also how worship involves a congregation's participation in words (e.g., common prayers and songs) and actions (e.g., standing, sitting, and walking in procession). In his ecclesiological writings, he shed light on the church's communal, prophetic, and sacramental dimensions. In his Christology, while reaffirming the church's teachings (e.g., the doctrine of the Council of Chalcedon), he emphasized the contemporaneity of Jesus Christ, who encounters the Christian community in the Eucharist. Using biblical and ecclesial images of Jesus Christ, he sought to show that the Christian faith primarily involves a commitment to a mysterious, personal reality (i.e., Jesus Christ alive in the Holy Spirit), and only secondarily does it entail the adoption of specific ideas or formulas. In his literary analyses of works by Dante, Dostoyevsky, and Rilke, Guardini illumined their implicit religious themes and compared these ideas to the wisdom (springing from divine revelation) available within the Judeo-Christian tradition. Writing on contemporary life, Guardini called attention to the dignity and complexity of being a person as well as to the possibilities for and threats to self-realization within modern society. In his elucidation of these topics, Guardini helped lead the way out of the "ghetto" or self-enclosed Catholicism of the nineteenth century to the Second Vatican Council's "church in the modern world." While teaching at the University of Berlin, Guardini emerged as a national leader within the Catholic youth movement, especially at Burg Rothenfels am Main (near Würzburg). Here, he experimented with liturgical innovations that Catholics now take for granted (e.g., scripture readings not in Latin but in the vernacular, dialogue homilies, and communal responses to the priest's prayers during Mass).

In 1939 the Third Reich forced Guardini to resign from his professorship because he refused to support Nazism. From 1943 into 1945 he lived in the village of Mooshausen. In 1945 Guardini declined an invitation to succeed Martin Heidegger at the University of Freiburg, choosing instead to teach at Tübingen (1945–47) and then Munich (1948–63). In 1952 he argued that Germans had a moral and financial responsibility to assist the Jewish people. From 1949 until 1963 Guardini preached on Sundays at St. Ludwig's Church in Munich to overflowing congregations. After his retirement, Guardini's academic position at the University of Munich was assumed by Karl Rahner.*

During the 1920s church officials were suspicious of Guardini's new ideas, liturgical reforms, and creative activities with youth. However, after the war, they saw him in a new light. In 1952 Pope Pius XII appointed Guardini a papal monsignor, and in 1965 Pope Paul VI invited Guardini to become a cardinal, but the ailing theologian declined. Among the numerous awards that Guardini received were the Peace Prize of the German Book Association (1952), an honorary doctorate in philosophy from the University of Freiburg (1954), the Peace Award of the Order "Pour le Merite" (1958), and the Erasmus Prize (1962).

Bibliography

A. *The Spirit of the Liturgy, and The Church and the Catholic* (Freiburg, 1918, and Mainz, 1922; New York, 1935); *Der Gegensatz* (Mainz, 1925); *The Conversion of St. Augustine* (Leipzig, 1935; Westminster, Md., 1960); *The Lord* (Würzburg, 1937; Chicago, 1954); *The World and the Person* (Würzburg, 1939; Chicago, 1965); *Meditations Before Mass* (Dusseldorf, 1939; Westminster, Md., 1955); *The Death of Socrates* (Berlin, 1943; New York, 1948); *Freedom, Grace and Destiny* (Munich, 1948; New York, 1961); *The End of the Modern World* (Mainz, 1950; New York, 1956); *Power and Responsibility* (Mainz, 1951; Chicago, 1961); *Rilke's Duino Elegies* (Munich, 1953; Chicago, 1961); *The Virtues* (Würzburg, 1963; Chicago, 1967); *Berichte über mein Leben* (Düsseldorf, 1984).

B. LThK³ 4:1087–88; NCE 16:198–99; TRE 14:294–97; Kurt Hoffman, "Portrait of Father Guardini," *The Commonweal* 60 (September 17, 1954): 575–77; Joseph B. Gremillion, "Interview with Romano Guardini," *America* 100 (November 15, 1958): 194–95; Jakob Laubach, "Romano Guardini," in *Theologians of Our Time*, ed. Leonhard Reinisch, trans. C. Henkey (Munich, 1960; Notre Dame, Ind., 1964), 109–26; Hanna Barbara Gerl, *Romano Guardini* (Mainz, 1985); Regina Kuehn, "Romano Guardini: Teacher of Teachers," in *How Firm a Foundation*, ed. Robert Tuzik (Chicago, 1990), 36–49; Alfons Knoll, *Glaube und Kultur bei Romano Guardini* (Paderborn, 1993); *Romano Guardini*, ed. Robert Krieg (Chicago, 1995); Robert A. Krieg, *Romano Guardini: A Precursor of Vatican II* (Notre Dame, Ind., 1997).

Robert A. Krieg

GUÉRANGER, PROSPER LOUIS PASCAL (4 April 1805, Sablé-sur-Sarthe–13 January 1875, Solesmes). *Education*: Coll. Royal, Angers, 1818–22; Sém. diocésain, Le Mans, 1822–26. *Career*: ordained priest, 1827; secretary to bishop of Le Mans, 1826–29; entered the Order of St. Benedict, Rome, 1837; Abbot, Solesmes Abbey, 1837–75.

Dom Guéranger's efforts to renew the church through informed popular participation in its sacred liturgy (his "liturgical movement") led eventually to Vatican II and the modern understanding of all in the church as the body of Christ.

Besides Scripture and the Fathers, works by Châteaubriand,* de Maistre,* de Lamennais,* Gerbet, and Möhler* shaped Guéranger's theological vision. For Guéranger, the church was the continuation on earth of Christ's Incarnation. It is, therefore, through the liturgy that the individual is most powerfully brought, body and soul, into the church's communal life in Christ. The ancient and doctrinally authoritative Roman liturgy, celebrated worldwide, is best suited to overcome the subjective rationalism and alienating individualism of the industrial, post-Enlightenment world. Guéranger refounded Solesmes in the hope that once again monastic liturgical communities would transform Western society.

Mistaken identification of Guéranger with Romantic medievalism and his oftentimes polemical tone have obscured the major role he played in forging the faith-practice and self-understanding of the Catholic Church.

Bibliography

A. *Institutions liturgiques*, 4 vols. (Paris, 1840–85); *L'Année liturgique*, 9 vols. (Paris, 1841–66).

B. LThK³ 4:1091–92; NCE 6:831–32; ODCC 720–21; Cuthbert Johnson, *Prosper Guéranger (1805–1875): A Liturgical Theologian* (Rome, 1984); R. W. Franklin, *Nineteenth-Century Churches: The History of a New Catholicism in Württemberg, England, and France* (New York and London, 1987).

John D. Laurance

GÜNTHER, ANTON (17 November 1783, Lindenau [now Czech Republic]– 24 February 1863, Vienna). *Education*: studied in Prague with the philosopher Bernard Bolzano, 1809; legal and theological studies, 1809–20. *Career*: ordained priest, 1821; scholar in Vienna, 1824–63.

Though Günther's speculative efforts cannot be said to be successful, he was nevertheless the most significant philosophical thinker in the German Catholic nineteenth century. He had quite a following in Austria, including two leading cardinals. Because of reservations he expressed about the neoscholastic revival, his writings were delated to Rome and censured in a papal brief of 1857, *Eximiam Tuam* (see DS 2828–31).

Taking seriously the subjective starting point of knowledge in self-consciousness, like the German Idealist philosophers, he nevertheless constructed a system wherein the dualisms of finite reality and God, of self and nature, and of state and society were not denied in an ultimate monism. By neoscholastics he was regarded as ''semi-rationalist'' (DS 2914); his doctrine of creation was targeted at Vatican I as inadequate (DS 3025).

The Güntherian or Viennese ''school'' eventually fell victim to a general recession of speculative or idealist thought and to the advances scored by Ultramontanism and neoscholasticism in Catholic milieus, though it has had its admirers (A. Dempf, E. K. Winter) in the twentieth century as well.

Bibliography

A. *Vorschule zur spekulativen Theologie*, 2 vols. (Vienna, 1828–29); *Gesammelte Schriften*, 9 vols. (Vienna, 1882; repr. Frankfurt, 1968); *Späte Schriften*, ed. J. Reikerstorfe (Vienna, 1978).

B. BBKL 2:384–86; ChP 1:266–84; DHGE 22:668–69; KThD 1:348–75; LThK³ 4: 1105–7; NCE 6:865; ODCC 722–23; J. Pritz, *Glauben und Wissen bei A. Günther* (Vienna, 1963); B. Osswald, *Anton Günther* (Paderborn, 1990).

Paul Misner

GUYON, MADAME JEANNE (18 April 1648, Montargis, France–9 June 1717, Blois, France). *Education*: Madame Guyon had no formal education beyond the sporadic training she received at Benedictine, Ursuline, and Dominican convents while in her youth. *Career*: writer and itinerant teacher throughout France, 1681–88; imprisoned for her Quietist doctrine, 1688; writer and itinerant teacher, primarily in Paris, Versailles, and St. Cyr, 1688–95; imprisoned for heretical teaching, 1695–1702; released from prison and retired to Blois, 1702.

Born Jeanne Marie Bouvier de la Mothe, Madame Guyon was a French Quietist and author. As a youth she sought a religious vocation but was constrained by her mother to marry Jacques Guyon in 1664. Her marriage to Guyon, who was an invalid and twenty-two years her senior, was a difficult one, which prompted her towards increasing introspection and mystical perspectives. Following her husband's death in 1676, Madame Guyon became enchanted with the Quietist teaching of Miguel de Molinos. A Barnabite friar, François Lacombe, subsequently served as her spiritual director and encouraged her in applying Molinos' highly apophatic teaching. During an extended journey through France (1681–88), with Lacombe often accompanying her, she gained converts to her extreme mystical outlooks. She presented her teaching in *A Short and Easy Method of Prayer*, stressing that the loftiest attainment of the human soul is to contemplate God with entire passivity of the intellect, will, and emotions. The resultant rest in the presence of God would lead to indifference even regarding eternal salvation.

In the life of her followers, her doctrines consequently led to disdain for spiritual exercises and a disregard for the sacraments of the church. She was arrested for suspected heresy in 1688 but was released through the intercession of Madame de Maintenon. Madame Guyon's popularity continued to grow as she was welcomed into the company of the Royal Court and found a sympathetic heart in François Fénelon,* who dialogued with her through a series of spiritual letters and adopted many of her views. Bishop Bossuet* of Meaux, though, expressed concern over her doctrine in 1694. Madame Guyon's request to clear her name resulted in the evaluation of her teaching at the Conference of Issy (1695). Despite Fénelon's efforts to defend her, her teaching was condemned. She was again arrested and imprisoned in Vincennes and later at the Bastille. She was released in 1702 and lived the rest of her life in Blois.

Bibliography

A. *Oeuvres de Madame de La Mothe-Guion*, ed. Jean Philippe Dutoit, 39 vols. (Paris, 1767–68, 1790–91); *A Short and Easy Method of Prayer*, trans. Thomas Digby Brooke (Baltimore, Md., 1812); *The Life and Religious Experience of the Celebrated Lady Guion*, trans. William Cowper (New York, 1820); *Spiritual Torrents*, trans. A. W. Marston (Philadelphia, 1883).

B. DTC 6:1997–2006; LThK[3] 4:1122; NCE 6:869–71; ODCC 725; Thomas C. Upham, *Life, Religious Opinions and Experience of Madame de La Mothe Guyon* (London, 1851); Michael De La Bedoyere, *The Archbishop and the Lady: the Story of Fénelon and Madame Guyon* (New York, 1956).

Clyde Glass

H

HALL, FRANCIS JOSEPH (24 December 1857, Ashtabula, Ohio–12 March, 1932, Baldwinsville, N.Y.). *Education*: A.B., Racine Coll., 1882; A.M., Racine Coll., 1885. *Career*: instructor, Western Theol. Sem., 1886–1905; professor of dogmatic theology, Western Theol. Sem., 1905–13; General Theol. Sem., 1913–28.

Hall wrote a comprehensive treatise on theology in his ten-volume *Dogmatic Theology* (1907–22). This "Anglican *Summa Theologica*" is a systematic exposition of traditional catholic doctrine. It is based in patristic and scholastic sources. It also draws on the Caroline Divines and other Anglican sources as well as Lutheran and Calvinist sources. He also wrote the three-volume *Theological Outlines* (1892–95). Hall, an Episcopal priest, was a strong supporter of church unity and a member of the World Conference Commission. He was termed the "most notable of Anglo-Catholic theologians."

Bibliography

A.   *Theological Outlines*, 3 vols. (Milwaukee, Wis., 1892–95); *Dogmatic Theology*, 10 vols. (London, 1907–22).

B.   *Who Was Who in America, 1897–1942*, 505.

Robert B. Slocum

HARNACK, ADOLF VON (7 May 1851, Dorpat, Livonia–11 June 1930, Heidelberg, Germany). *Education*: gymnasium, Erlangen and Dorpat; Univ. at Dorpat, 1869; Univ. at Leipzig, 1872; dissertation on early Gnosticism, 1873. *Career*: privatdozent, Leipzig, 1874; professor, Leipzig, 1876; professor, Giessen, 1879; Marburg, 1886; and Berlin, 1888; cofounder and editor, *Theologische Literaturzeitung*, 1876; member, Prussian Academy of Sciences, 1890;

director general, Royal Library in Berlin, 1906; president, Kaiser Wilhelm Gesellschaft, 1911; professor emeritus, Berlin, 1921–30.

Son of a pious Lutheran theologian of strict theological orthodoxy, Harnack was the foremost church historian and historian of dogma in his generation; indeed, given his ongoing influence, arguably in the whole of the modern era. In addition, he was an accomplished organizer and manager of research projects and institutions whose work was far broader than theology or even the humanities, as well as an editor of some of the most important monograph series and journals of his age. He was a representative of the Protestant liberal theology of the nineteenth century and, thus informed, his work embodied the ideals of modern critical historiography. As such, his account of the history of the early church and the development of dogma was at variance at many points with the received ecclesiastical tradition. As a result, although deeply committed to Christianity, he was the object of profound suspicion and active opposition by church authorities. Despite the fact that he was decisively shaping the field of ecclesiastical and theological history through his voluminous writings as well as his production of numerous doctoral students, the Prussian church refused to allow him to serve as an academic examiner for prospective pastors—even for his own students. Moreover, they denied him throughout his lifetime any official role in the church and its councils. This stood in stark contrast to the extraordinary honors he received from both the contemporary academic community and German state. The former counted him as the highest exemplar of the modern critical scholar and demonstrated that by electing him to positions of great honor and responsibility. The latter, in the person of Kaiser Wilhelm II, conferred upon him the dignity of hereditary nobility—hence the 'von' in his name—and in the form of the Weimar Republic offered him the post of German ambassador to Washington, D.C.

As an historian, Harnack eschewed the writing of biography due to the ambiguities of personal motive and concentrated instead on telling the story of institutions: states, societies, groups, and corporations with their established practices, laws, codes and rules. True to his theological and philosophical convictions, he wrote that story as the history of ideas. He saw his role as historian not simply as a reporter of bygone events, but as that of a kind of judge of history's abiding truth. Having established reliable sources and carefully described their contents, therefore, he sought to tell the story of the past in the present in the service of the future by demonstrating what it was in those institutions, in his judgment, that preserved and furthered human life by liberating individuals ''from the 'service to that which passes away,' from enslavement to mere nature, and from servitude to one's own empirical self.'' In other words, he conceived of the historian as midwife to humanity's progressive self-realization through a critical process of transcending the merely finite and the physical.

As an historian of dogma, he took as his task the critical differentiation of the essential message of Christianity from the historical development of church theology so that the former could serve as liberator of life from the deadly tyranny of the latter. Thus, he quite consciously understood himself to be following in the footsteps of such earlier historical theologians as J. S. Semler* of the eighteenth century German Enlightenment as well as the modern nineteenth century figures F. C. Baur* and Albrecht Ritschl.* This agenda is seen most clearly in what were perhaps his two most influential publications: his *Grundriss der Dogmengeschichte* and *Das Wesen des Christentums*. In his *Grundriss*, he seeks to demonstrate, on the one hand, that the message of Jesus of Nazareth in the first century had little or nothing in common with the rise of the hierarchical and sacramental institution of the church and its official theology in succeeding centuries and, on the other hand, that only as it is liberated from its imprisonment in ecclesiastical dogma can that message become liberating for humanity once again. Thus, drawing on the interpretation of Luther* that had arisen in the Aufklärung, he called for the continuation of what the Reformation had only begun: the freeing of Christianity from all—and that includes ecclesiastical and theological—authoritarianism. It was to the question of what was essential to the message of Jesus that Harnack then turned in *Wesen*, a publication that began as a series of popular public lectures. There, he reviews the teachings of Jesus, their effect upon the early church, and the subsequent forms taken by Christianity in the course of its history and attempts to clarify thereby the unchanging character of the gospel taught and embodied in Jesus in the ever changing reembodiments of that gospel in the various stages of the history of Christianity. Thus he sought to substitute an historical conception of the nature of Christianity for the traditional dogmatic definition.

Bibliography

A.   *History of Dogma*, trans. from the 3d German ed., N. Buchanan, 7 vols. bound as 4 (Gloucester, Mass., 1976); *Militia Christi: The Christian Religion and the Military in the First Three Centuries*, trans. D. M. Gracie (Philadelphia, 1981); *Marcion: The Gospel of the Alien God*, trans. J. E. Steely and L. D. Bierma (Durham, N.C., 1990); *What is Christianity?* trans. T. B. Saunders (New York, 1957).

B.   BBKL 2:554–68; LThK[3] 4:1196–97; NCE 6:929–30; ODCC 736–37; TRE 14: 450–58; G. Wayne Glick, *The Reality of Christianity. A Study of Adolf von Harnack as Historian and Theologian* (New York, 1967); Wilhelm Pauck, *Harnack and Troeltsch: Two Historical Theologians* (New York, 1968); Thomas Hubner, *Adolf von Harnacks Vorlesungen über das Wesen des Christentums unter Besonderer Berücksichtigung der Methodenfragen als Sachgemässiger Zugang zu Ihrer Christologie und Wirkungsgeschichte* (Frankfurt a.M, 1994).

D. Lyle Dabney

HECKER, ISAAC THOMAS (18 December 1819, New York City–22 December 1888, New York City). *Education*: Redemptorist formation in St. Trond and Wittem, Belgium and London, 1845–49. *Career*: ordained priest, London, 1849; Redemptorist mission band, England, 1850–51; U.S., 1851–57; founder, the Paulists, New York, 1858; Paulist superior general, 1858–88; founding editor, *The Catholic World*, 1865–88; founder, Catholic Publication Society, 1866; procurator and theologian at Vatican Council I, Rome, 1870; public lectures throughout U.S., 1859–71.

One of the first American Catholics to bring the relationship between Catholicism and American culture to reflective awareness, Hecker successfully cast European Catholic Romanticism in the diverse idiom of American Calvinism. From New England theology, and especially Orestes Brownson,* he learned both the language and critique of Calvinist orthodoxy. He found a religious home in European Catholic Romanticism with its sense of the church as the historical extension of the Incarnation. God's activity in the soul preoccupied his early thought (1842–58). The church as answering the soul's questions and aspirations was his chief apologetic theme. With the founding of the Paulists in 1858, Hecker entered his most active and optimistic period (1858–70). By means of the moderate traditionalism of Brownson's providential theory of history, he made a genuine theological affirmation of American institutions as providentially compatible with Catholic faith. Giving a Catholic accent to the millennialist idiom of his evangelical contemporaries, he looked for signs of America's impending conversion to Catholicism foreshadowed in his own conversion. To hasten this "future triumph" of the church, he developed a spirituality of active involvement in the world. His emphasis on America's conversion to Catholicism included a cultural transformation that made his embrace of America not entirely uncritical.

Between 1870 and 1888, events forced Hecker to deal with the inner tensions arising from his views of God's work in the soul and in history. The pain of conflict and invalidism deepened both his interior life and his American messianism. He retained to the end his sense of a converted America's providential role with respect to the universal church.

As an American Catholic experimental alternative to the neoscholastic theological norm of his day, Hecker was without peer. He is the progenitor of the Catholic "Americanist" (implying no want of orthodoxy) tradition. In their emphasis, sometimes insufficiently critical, on the providential fit between Catholicism and American culture, figures such as John Ireland, John Keane, John A. Ryan,* and John Courtney Murray* are Hecker's theological successors.

Bibliography

A. *The Diary*, ed. John Farina (New York, 1988); *The Brownson–Hecker Correspondence*, ed. Joseph F. Gower and Richard M. Leliaert (Notre Dame, Ind., 1979); *Questions of the Soul* (New York, 1855); *Aspirations of Nature* (New York, 1857); *The Church and the Age* (New York, 1887).

B.   DAB 8:495; NCAB 9:166–67; NCE 6:982–83; SH 5:196; Walter Elliott, *The Life of Father Hecker* (New York, 1891); *Hecker Studies*, ed. John Farina (New York, 1983); Vincent Holden, *The Yankee Paul, Isaac Thomas Hecker* (Milwaukee, Wis., 1958); David O'Brien, *Isaac Hecker, An American Catholic* (New York, 1992); William Portier, *Isaac Hecker and the First Vatican Council* (Lewiston, N.Y., 1985); idem, "Providential Nation: An Historical-Theological Study of Isaac Hecker's 'Americanism,' " Ph.D. diss., Toronto, 1980.

William L. Portier

HEILER, FRIEDRICH (30 January 1892, Munich–27 April 1967, Munich). *Education*: theology and philology, Univ. of Munich, 1911–18. *Career*: professor of history of religions, Marburg, 1920–60, with interruption during the Nazi period.

Heiler's 1918 dissertation, a vast study in comparative religion on *Prayer*, reached a fifth edition in 1923, an indication of what an impact it made. A Catholic and admirer of Catholic ''Modernists'' like Friedrich von Hügel* and George Tyrrell,* he felt out of place in the Catholicism of the antimodernist purges and at home in the Swedish Lutheranism of another of his spiritual models, Nathan Söderblom,* who received him into Lutheran communion in 1919. In Marburg, however, he found German Protestantism too anti- or at least un-Catholic and took up a position ''between the confessions,'' espousing an ''evangelical catholicity.'' Even though the ecumenical movement actually developed along lines of interconfessional dialogue in which he (again) could find no place, his writings and efforts would have an indirect effect toward the breakthrough of the Second Vatican Council, which he welcomed.

Bibliography

A. *Inter confessiones*, ed. A. M. Heiler (Marburg, 1972), 154–95; *Prayer: A Study in the History and Psychology of Religion*, trans. S. McComb (Oxford, 1932); *Der Katholizismus: Seine Idee und seine Erscheinung* (Munich, 1923); *Die Religionen der Menschheit* (Stuttgart, 1959).

B. BBKL 2:660–61; LThK³ 4:1266; NCE 16:203–4; *F. von Hügel, N. Söderblom, F. Heiler: Briefwechsel 1909–1931*, ed. Paul Misner (Paderborn, 1981); P. McKenzie, *The Christians: Their Practices and Beliefs* (London, 1988); A. J. van der Bent, *Historical Dictionary of Ecumenical Christianity* (Metuchen, N.J., 1994); O. Weiss, *Der Modernismus in Deutschland* (Regensburg, 1995); H. Hartog, *Evangelische Katholizität* (Mainz, 1995).

Paul Misner

HENRY OF GHENT (ca. 1217, Ghent–29 June 1293, Tournai). *Education*: first studied at the cathedral school at Tournai; master of theology, Univ. of Paris, 1275. *Career*: canon, Tournai, 1267; master of theology, Univ. of Paris, 1276–92; archdeacon of Bruges, 1276; actively supported the condemnation of 219 propositions by the bishop of Paris, Étienne Tempier, on 7 March 1277; archdeacon of Tournai, 1278; thereafter commuted between Tournai and Paris; known as the Solemn Teacher (*Doctor solemnis*) and to some contemporaries as the Master of Digression (*Magister digressivus*).

A member of the secular clergy, Henry strongly supported the Augustinian opposition to the perceived or real excesses of Aristotelianism in the arts faculty at Paris. His two major works are his *Summa of Theology*, which contains his ordinary lectures and remains incomplete, and his *Quodlibetal Questions*, which are probably the best representatives of the genre still extant. During Advent and Lent each year a master held a public disputation during which he could deal with any (*quodlibetalis*) question he chose. Henry himself edited his fifteen quodlibetal disputations, which were held from 1277 to 1291 or 1292. The critical edition of Henry's works, in progress at Louvain, has heightened contemporary interest in his thought, and scholars have come to see that he held a more balanced view than had been supposed previously. For example, though he holds that the will is a higher power than the intellect and stresses its active character so that it is not moved even by God, he is hardly the radical voluntarist that he has been taken to be. Henry denied a real distinction between being and essence in creatures and between the soul and its powers, in each case maintaining instead an intentional distinction, which seems to be somewhere in between a real and a merely mental distinction. He held the unicity of substantial form in all but human beings and taught a highly spiritual view of the human person that is in many respects closer to Plato and Avicenna than to Aristotle and Aquinas.* His argument for the existence of God also follows along the lines of Avicenna's metaphysics.

Bibliography

A. *Summa quaestionum ordinariarum* (*Summa of Theology*) (Paris, 1518; repr. St. Bonaventure, N.Y., 1953); *Quodlibeta* (*Quodlibetal Questions*) (Venice, 1613); *Opera omnia*, ed. Raymond Macken et al. (Louvain, 1979–); *Quodlibetal Questions on Free Will*, trans. Roland J. Teske (Milwaukee, Wis., 1993).

B. DSAM 7:197–210; LThK³ 4:1386–87; NCE 6:1035–37; ODCC 754–55; J. Gomez-Caffarena, *Ser participado y ser subsistente en la metafísica de Enrique de Gante* (Rome, 1958); Anton C. Pegis, "Toward a New Way to God: Henry of Ghent," *Mediaeval Studies* 30 (1968): 226–47; 31 (1969): 93–116; 33 (1971): 158–79; Steven P. Marrone, *Truth and Scientific Knowledge in the Thought of Henry of Ghent* (Cambridge, Mass., 1985); B. B. Price, "Henry of Ghent," in *Dictionary of Literary Biography*, vol. 115, *Medieval Philosophers* (Detroit, Mich., 1992), 236–40; Raymond Macken, *Bibliographie d'Henri de Gand* (Louvain, 1994); idem, *Essays on Henry of Ghent* (Louvain, 1994); *Henry of Ghent: Proceedings of the International Colloquium on the Occasion of the 700th Anniversary of His Death (1293)*, ed. W. Vanhamel (Louvain, 1996).

Roland J. Teske

HENRY (HEINRICH) HEIMBUCHE OF LANGENSTEIN, *Doctor conscientosus* (1325, Langenstein in Hesse–11 February 1397, Vienna). *Education*: studied in Paris from 1358 on; *Magister artium*, 1363; *Doctor theologiae*, 1375. *Career*: ordained priest, between 1358 and 1367; professor of theology, Paris, 1376–84; vice chancellor, Paris, 1371–81; professor, Vienna, 1384; rector, 1393–94.

For twenty-five years, Henry led the life of a student and professor at Paris. But in the Western Schism, which began in 1378, Henry supported the Roman pope, Urban VI, against the Frenchman, Clement VII; for this reason he left

Paris for Germany in 1382. In 1384 he was called to Vienna, where he reorganized the university, which had been founded in 1365. His interests included natural science, philosophy, theology, and politics. Among his theological writings are a commentary on the *Sentences*, biblical commentaries, sermons, and short treatises. He also composed ascetical and spiritual works for priests, particularly on the Mass, the Eucharist, and confession. Early in his life Henry was a nominalist, in the school of William of Occam,* and a conciliarist and a mystic; later in his life he moved toward mitigated Thomism.

Bibliography

A. Lang (see below) has an index of his published works.

B. DMA 6:166–67; DSAM 7:215–19; DTC 8:2574–76; LThK³ 4:1390–91; NCE 6: 1037–38; TRE 15:11–13; Justin Lang, *Die Christologie bei Heinrich von Langenstein. Eine dogmengeschichtliche Untersuchung* (Freiburg i. Br., 1966).

Joseph T. Lienhard

HERMAS (second century). Hermas, a freedman formerly owned by Rhoda (whom he mentions) was the brother of Pius, bishop of Rome. Ca. 150 he composed an apocalypse entitled the *Shepherd*, after one of the figures who mediate revelations to Hermas. The work was divided into five Visions, twelve Mandates, and ten Similitudes. The main theme of the *Shepherd* is repentance. The first repentance took place in baptism. Hermas is the first Christian author to deal with the problem of second penance, or repentance for, and forgiveness of, serious sins committed after baptism. He establishes the pattern that the church was to follow for centuries: one act of public penance and reconciliation (but only one) was permitted after baptism. In Visions 1–4 the revealer is the church, at first an old woman, who then grows younger. In Visions 5–10 the Shepherd is the revealer. The twelve Mandates and Similitudes 1–5 form a teaching on Christian virtues. Similitudes 6–9 deal with penance. In the last Similitude the Son of God appears as an angel and repeats the exhortation to penance, especially for the rich. Hermas never mentions Jesus Christ, or the Word, but only the Son of God, who is also the highest angel. As holy spirit the Son dwells in flesh; this human nature is God's adopted son. The *Shepherd* found a temporary place in the canon of the New Testament: Irenaeus,* Tertullian* (before his Montanist period), Clement of Alexandria,* and Origen* all considered it canonical.

Bibliography

A. GCS 48 (1967); *The Shepherd of Hermas*, trans. G. Snyder (Camden, N.J., 1968).

B. DSAM 7:316–34; DTC 6:2268–88; LThK³ 4:1448–49; NCE 6:1074; ODCC 760; TRE 15:100–108; L. W. Barnard, "The Shepherd of Hermas in Recent Study," *Heythrop*

Journal 9 (1968) 29–36; C. Osiek, *Rich and Poor in the Shepherd of Hermas: An Exegetical-Social Investigation* (Washington, D.C., 1983).

Joseph T. Lienhard

HERMES, GEORG (22 April 1775, Dreierwald, Westphalia–26 May 1831, Bonn). *Education*: philosophical and theological studies, Univ. of Münster, 1792–98. *Career*: teacher, gymnasium, Münster, 1797–1807; ordained priest, 1799; professor of dogmatic theology, Münster, 1807–19; professor of theology, Univ. of Bonn, 1820–31.

Hermes was a post-Kantian theologian who tried to demonstrate the rational validity of the act of faith in Christian revelation and the possibility of a scientific theology. As a student he had read Immanuel Kant and Johann Gottlieb Fichte and had experienced a period of religious doubt. His later theology reflects the continuing influence of Kant and his own early encounter with religious doubt.

Hermes accepted the Kantian distinction between speculative and practical reason, even though he enlarged to some extent the powers of speculative reason. Using this distinction, Hermes tried to develop grounds for the rational validity of the act of faith, placing the act of faith within practical reason. The act of faith could be established on sound rational grounds by exercising Hermes' method of universal doubt—a rigorous methodology by which whatever could be doubted must be doubted until the mind could no longer withhold consent, thereby producing apodictic certitude. Practical reason alone could provide this certitude about the act of faith, a faith the mind was obliged to make in order to meet the moral demands of the categorical imperative. In this way he believed he had demonstrated both the rationality and the freedom of the act of faith.

Once Hermes had demonstrated that historical revelation could be rationally "accepted as true" he moved on to demonstrate the possibility of a scientific theology, holding that no proposition of revelation could be accepted as true on the basis of revelation that had contradicted the rational demands of reason.

Hermes had a large Catholic following in some of the German universities prior to and immediately following the Vatican condemnation of his so-called "rationalist" or semirationalist positions (in *Dum acerbissimus*, 1835, DS, 2738–40) four years after his death. Catholic critics saw his understanding of the act of faith as at least semirationalist because he made faith depend on a preliminary rational assent. According to his critics, his understanding of the act of faith was not based upon the supernatural authority of the revealing God, an act in traditional Catholic theology that transcended the limits of natural knowledge and the philosophical order. Hermes had not denied the supernatural order of revelation, but he was preoccupied with the rational preconditions of the act of accepting it.

Bibliography

A. *Untersuchung über die innere Wahrheit des Christentums* (Münster, 1805); *Studirplan der Theologie* (Münster, 1819); *Einleitung in die christkatholische theologie: Philosophische Einleitung* (Münster, 1819); *Positive Einleitung* (Bonn, 1829); *Christkatholische Dogmatik*, 3 vols. (Bonn, 1834–35).

B. DTC 6:2288–303; HERE 6:624; LThK³ 5:10–12; NCE 6:1075–76; ODCC 761; TRE 15:156–58; Roger Aubert, *Le problème de l'acte de foi* (Louvain, 1950), 108–11; H. H. Schwedt, *Das römische Urteil über Georg Hermes (1775–1831): Ein Beitrag zur Geschichte der Inquisition im 19. Jahrhundert* (Rome, 1980); Gerald A. McCool, *Catholic Theology in the Nineteenth Century* (New York, 1977), 59–67; Thomas Fliethmann, *Vernunftig Glauben: Die Theorie der Theologie bei Georg Hermes* (Wurzburg, 1997).

Patrick W. Carey

HERRMANN, WILHELM (6 December 1846, Melkow [Altmark]–2 January 1922, Marburg). *Education*: gymnasium, Stendal; Univ. at Halle, 1866; Lic. theol., 1875; Habilitation, 1875. *Career*: gymnasium, 1870; professor, Halle, 1875; professor, Marburg, 1879; professor Emeritus, 1917.

Son and nephew of Protestant pastors of strongly pietist persuasion, Herrmann was an important German theologian of the Wilhelmina era and a teacher who had a profound impact on the next generation of theologians. As a young man at the University of Halle he sat under such teachers as Julius Müller and F. A. G. Tholuck. He lived, in fact, for some two years in the home of the latter and there came to know the *Erweckungsbewegung* in its finest flower. At Halle he became a thorough Kantian, and in Tholuck's home met and became an ardent admirer of the theology of Albrecht Ritschl.* Herrmann's central question was that of Kant concerning the independence and justification of religious knowledge. He sought to identify the essence and ground of religion over and against science and ethics, as is indicated by the title of his first major book, *Die Religion im Verhältnis zum Welterkennen und zur Sittlichkeit* (1879). The goal of religion, he taught, following Ritschl, was to govern the relation of humanity to the world. And religion's chief expression is faith. His theology, therefore, was directed against both Protestant orthodoxy and Enlightenment rationalism, spurning the metaphysical flights of the one and the naturalism of the other. Instead, he, like the whole tradition of nineteenth-century Protestant liberal theology, beginning with Schleiermacher,* sought to return to the figure of Jesus of Nazareth and the power of his religious personality in order to identify the specifically religious human impulse. It was this Christological concentration above all that he passed on to his students at Marburg and that was critically appropriated and reinterpreted by theologians of the next generation as diverse as Karl Barth,* Rudolf Bultmann,* and Ernst Fuchs.

Bibliography

A. *The Communion of the Christian with God; Described on the Basis of Luther's Statements*, trans. R. T. Voelkel (Philadelphia, 1971); *Ethik*, 6th ed. (Tübingen, 1921);

Schriften zur Grundlegung der Theologie, ed. P. Fischer-Appelt (Munich, 1966–67); *Dogmatik. Vorlesungsdiktate*, ed. M. Rade (Munich, 1925).

B. BBKL 2: 771–73; EKL 5: 249; LThK³ 3:25; ODCC 762–63; RGG 3:275–77; TRE 15:165–72; Robert T. Voelkel, *The Shape of the Theological Task* (Philadelphia, 1968); Peter Fischer-Appelt, *Metaphysik im Horizont der Theologie Wilhelm Herrmanns* (Munich, 1965); Hermann Timm, *Theorie und Praxis in der Theologie Albrecht Ritschls und Wilhelm Herrmanns* (Gütersloh, 1967); James M. Robinson, *Das Problem des Heiligen Geistes bei Wilhelm Herrmann* (Marburg, 1952).

D. Lyle Dabney

HERVÉ OF NEDELLEC, Hervaeus Natalis (ca. 1250/69, Brittany–1323, Narbonne). Entered the Dominican order, 1276; present in Paris at Saint Jacques in 1303; supported Philip the Fair against Boniface VIII; master of theology, 1307; provincial of France, 1309; master general of the order, 1318; headed a commission to examine the works of Durandus of Saint Pourçain, found ninety-one objectionable propositions; opposed various teachings of James of Metz, Peter Aureoli, and Henry of Ghent*; wrote a defense of the teachings of Thomas Aquinas,* though he himself rejected the distinction between existence and essence in creatures; successfully worked for the canonization of Thomas Aquinas, but died at Narbonne on his way to the ceremony.

Bibliography

A. *Quatuor quodlibeta* (*Four Quodlibetal Questions*) (Venice, 1486; repr. Ridgewood, N.J., 1966); *Quaestiones disputatae* (*Disputed Questions*) (Venice, 1513); *Tractatus de secundis intentionibus* (*Treatise on Second Intentions*) (Venice, 1513); *In quatuor libros sententiarum commentaria* (*Commentary on the Sentences*) with *De potestate papae* (*The Power of the Pope*) (Paris, 1647; repr. Farnborough, 1966); *De cognitione primi principii* (*Knowledge of the First Principle*), ed. Josef Santeler in *Der kausale Gottesbeweis bei Herveus Natalis nach dem ungedruckten Traktat* (Innsbruck, 1930); *De iurisdictione* (*On Ecclesial Authority*), ed. Ludwig Hödl (Munich, 1959).

B. DTC 6:2315; LThK³ 5:47–48; Cyril O. Vollert, *The Doctrine of Hervaeus Natalis on Primitive Justice and Original Sin, as Developed in the Controversy on Original Sin during the Early Decades of the Fourteenth Century* (Rome, 1947); E. Allan, "Hervaeus Natalis: An Early Thomist on the Notion of Being," *Mediaeval Studies* 22 (1960): 1–14; Kenneth Plotnik, *Hervaeus Natalis O.P. and the Controversies over the Real Presence and Transubstantiation* (Munich, 1970).

Roland J. Teske

HEWIT, AUGUSTINE FRANCIS (27 November 1820, Fairfield, Conn.–3 July 1897, New York City). *Education*: B.A., Amherst Coll., 1839; studied for ministry, Hartford Congregationalist Sem., 1840–41; read theology with Episcopal bishop William Rollinson Whittingham, Baltimore, 1842–43; read theology with Father Patrick Lynch, Charleston, S.C., 1846. *Career*: ordained deacon, Episcopal Church, 1843; taught, Edenton, N.C., 1845; ordained Catholic priest, 1846; pastor, Charleston, 1846–49; entered Cong. of the Most Holy Redeemer

(Redemptorist); Redemptorist missionary, east coast of United States, 1851–59; member of Paulists, 1860–97; associate editor, *Catholic World*, 1865–86; editor, *Catholic World*, 1886–97; superior, Paulists, 1886–97.

After converting to Catholicism, Hewit became a Redemptorist and Paulist missionary who gave numerous parish missions along the eastern coast of the United States. He was also an editor of a Catholic periodical that tried to lift the intellectual discussion within American Catholicism. As a Catholic theologian he was at first drawn to ontologism, as is evident in his publications, particularly in his *Problems of the Age*. Gradually, however, as the papal condemnations of ontologism and traditionalism became more vigorous and more pronounced, he retreated from his ontologism and gradually supported the revival of scholasticism. Through the *Catholic World* he became a major apologist of Catholicism in America during the second half of the nineteenth century. Conservative in theology, he was progressive in his view that the Catholic Church must adapt itself to American institutions and methods of evangelization.

Bibliography

A. *A Few Thoughts Concerning the Theories of High-Churchmen and Tractarians* (Charleston, S.C., 1846); "How I Became a Catholic," *Catholic World* 46 (October 1887): 32–43; *Sermons of the Rev. Francis A. Baker, Priest of the Congregation of St. Paul. With a Memoir of his Life by Rev. A. F. Hewit* (New York, 1865, and subsequent editions); *Problems of the Age; with Studies in St. Augustine on Kindred Topics* (New York, 1868); *The King's Highway, or, The Catholic Church the Way of Salvation as Revealed in the Holy Scriptures* (New York, 1874); articles in *Catholic World*, 1865 to 1897.

B. DAB 8:604; DACB, 256–57; DARB 240–41; NCE 6:1092–93; "Editorial," *Catholic World* 65 (August 1897): 706–7; Joseph Flynn, "The Early Years of Augustine F. Hewit, C.S.P., 1820–1846," M.A. Thesis, Catholic Univ. of America, 1945; Joseph McSorley, *Father Hecker and His Friends* (New York, 1972).

Patrick W. Carey

HILARY OF POITIERS, Hilarius (ca. 300–ca. 367). Apart from Tertullian* and Augustine,* Hilary was the most original theologian of the early Latin church. He converted to Christianity later in life. His episcopate began ca. 350, just as proponents of anti-Nicenism, supported by Constantius II, began to dominate religious politics in the West.

Hilary's *Commentary on Matthew* shows almost no sign of the trinitarian controversy that would later dominate his career; the thought-world of Tertullian, Novatian* and Cyprian* is central to his exegesis in this work. In 356 Hilary was arraigned before a local council in Béziers where (he later says) false charges were brought against him and he was summarily banished to Asia Minor. It was just prior to Béziers that Hilary declared he first heard the Nicene Creed recited, although he must have known something of "Arian" ideology before this time. During his four-year exile, Hilary gained much insight into the dynamics of those theological tensions that divided East and West. He wrote

On the Synods for his episcopal brethren in the West to establish rapprochement between Eastern and Western notions of orthodoxy. *Homoiousios*, he states, can be faithfully interpreted so as to be compatible with *homoousios*, whereas the use of the Nicene watchword must be carefully monitored to prevent modalist applications, which were the ongoing cause of eastern suspicions of Western theology.

Hilary attended the eastern council of Seleucia in 359 and was in Constantinople the following year seeking an audience with the emperor in order to block the official ratification of the homoian creed promulgated at Ariminum, but to no avail. Some time during the first half of 360, he returned without imperial permission to Poitiers and in a manifesto written that same year scornfully attacked the emperor as an enemy of the true faith and a persecutor of Christians worse than Nero or Decius.

Now back in the West, Hilary published other scriptural commentaries and at least three polemical works: a dossier of credal and epistulary documents, now in fragmentary form, which implicated two leading homoian bishops, Valens and Ursacius, in doctrinal duplicity and heretical intentions; a document accusing Auxentius, the homoian bishop of Milan (355–74), of Arianism; and a composition in twelve books, the so-called *De trinitate*, or as Jerome* described it, *Adversus Arrianos libri*. In this last work, most of which was written in the East, Hilary argues that the Son shares the same divine substance as the Father and is thus ontologically equal to the Father in all the divine attributes. The Son is distinct from the Father only by his relationship of origin as the always-begotten Son of the unbegotten Father. In order to refute the "Arian" argument that the passion of the incarnate Son was proof of his inferior divinity, Hilary asserted that Christ's body, while feeling the impact of suffering, felt no pain because his soul was of divine origin and was therefore unaffected by the consciousness of suffering. As in *De synodis*, Hilary charts a middle course between subordinationism and modalism perceived as the extremes on either side of his position.

Bibliography

A.   Patrology 4, 33–60 and CPL 427–64.

B.   DSAM 6:2388–462; DTC 6:2388–2462; LThK³ 5:100–102; NCE 6:1114–16; ODCC 769–70; TRE 15:315–22; C. F. Borchardt, *Hilary of Poitiers' Role in the Arian Struggle* (The Hague, 1966); Jean Doignon, *Hilaire de Poitiers avant l'exil* (Paris, 1971); Paul Burns, *The Christology in Hilary of Poitiers' Commentary on Matthew* (Oxford, 1977); H. C. Brennecke, *Hilarius von Poitiers und die Bischofsopposition gegen Konstantius II.* (Berlin and New York, 1984); D. H. Williams, "A Reassessment of the Early Career and Exile of Hilary of Poitiers," JEH 42 (1991): 212–17; idem, "The Anti-Arian Campaigns of Hilary of Poitiers and the 'Liber Contra Auxentium'," CH 61 (1992): 7–22; P. Burns, "Hilary of Poitiers' Road to Béziers: Politics or Religion?"

JECS 2 (1994): 273–89; P. Smulders, *Hilary of Poitiers' Preface to His 'Opus Histo-ricum'* (Leiden, 1995).

Daniel H. Williams

HILDEGARD OF BINGEN (1098–17 September 1179, Rupertsberg). *Education*: at St. Disibod, by Jutta of Spanheim, 1106–36. *Career*: donated to St. Disibod by parents, 1106; elected abbess, 1136; suffered a life-threatening illness in which she received the visionary impetus to write, 1141; left St. Disibod to found a new community, 1147; installed as abbess of St. Rupert, 1151.

The tenth of ten children, Hildegard was given by her parents in tithe to God. She was educated by the aristocratic anchoress, Jutta of Spanheim, and accompanied her into the women's community at St. Disibod. At age 42, she began to dictate her visions to a monk of the adjacent monastery, reporting that they began in her childhood, but that she had at first been afraid to report them. The culminating experience, following severe illness, was the vision of a blazing light, which poured itself into her entire being, warming her from within. After that, she found that she was free to speak of her visions, and able to understand and interpret Sacred Scripture, especially the psalter, the gospels, and the creation narratives. Although a highly original thinker for her time, her themes may be compared with those of her contemporaries Rupert of Deutz* and Honorius Augustodunensis, as well as the cosmological speculations of the school of Chartres. At the center of her visionary world stands *homo microcosmos*, the human being as crown of creation and locus of the cosmic conflict between good and evil. Man and woman alike share in the glory and responsibility, as each contributes to restoration of the image of God and the achievement of justice in God's creation.

Frail but strong-willed, Hildegard published *Scivias* (1141–51) after shrewdly securing the patronage of both Bernard of Clairvaux* and Pope Eugenius III. Convinced it was God's will that she found a new community for her nuns, she used her illness to persuade Abbot Kuno to grant her permission to move to Rupertsberg. On her four preaching tours of the Rhineland, she exhorted clergy to adhere to the Gregorian reform, rebuked the emperor for falling away from the papacy, and even took Bernard of Clairvaux to task for his support of the excessively militaristic enterprise of the Second Crusade. She and her community defied their bishop and were placed under interdict for burying in their cemetery an excommunicated nobleman, but her demands for justice secured restoration of the convent's rights just months before she died.

Bibliography

A. PL 197; *Hildegard von Bingen: Lieder*, ed. Pudentiana Barth (Salzburg, 1965); *Welt und Mensch: Das Buch 'De operatione Dei,'* ed. Heinrich Schipperges (Salzburg, 1965); *Illuminations of Hildegard of Bingen*, ed. and intro. Matthew Fox (Santa Fe, N.M., 1985); *Hildegard of Bingen's Scivias*, ed. and intro. idem (Santa Fe, N.M., 1986); *Hil-*

degard of Bingen's Book of Divine Works, With Letters and Songs, ed. and intro. idem (Santa Fe, N.M., 1987); *Vita sanctae Hildegardis*, ed. Monica Klaes, CCCM 126 (Turnhout, 1993).

B.   DSAM 7:505–21; DTC 6:2468–80; LThK³ 5:105–6; NCE 6:1117; ODCC 770–71; TRE 15:322–26; Barbara Newman, *Sister of Wisdom: St. Hildegard's Theology of the Feminine* (Berkeley, Calif., 1987); Sabina Flanagan, *Hildegard of Bingen, 1098–1179: A Visionary Life* (New York, 1989); Rosel Termolen, *Hildegard von Bingen: Biographie* (Augsburg, 1990); Heinrich Schipperges, *Hildegard von Bingen* (Frankfurt, 1995).

Wanda Zemler-Cizewski

HINCMAR OF RHEIMS (ca. 806–882). Born into the Frankish nobility; educated at St.-Denis, near Paris; in 822 went to the court of Louis the Pious, and later served Charles the Bald; elected archbishop of Rheims, 845.

Seventy of Hincmar's treatises are extant; his best work involved canonical questions. He took part in the theological controversy with Gottschalk* over predestination. Gottschalk held a strong doctrine of double predestination, denying God's universal salvific will and compromising human free choice. Hincmar wrote *To the Simple* in 849/50 against Gottschalk, stressing single predestination, human free choice, and God's universal salvific will. Hincmar had Gottschalk condemned in 849. Ratramnus of Corbie* sided with Gottschalk and championed God's rights. The Synod of Quiercy (853) decided in favor of Hincmar, but the Synod of Valencia (855) opposed him. At Hincmar's request, John Scotus Erigena* wrote *On Divine Predestination*. In 859/60 Hincmar wrote *On the Predestination of God and Free Choice*, arguing that, if God predestines the wicked to hell, He must be the author of sin. A reconciliation was effected at the synod of Tuzey in 860. Another dispute arose when Hincmar changed the words *trina deitas* (threefold Deity) in the hymn at vespers for Mary to *summa deitas* (highest Deity), because he suspected the former of tritheism. Gottschalk and Ratramnus objected to the change, and ca. 865 Hincmar wrote *On the Onefold and not Threefold Deity* in response. In the controversy on the Eucharist Hincmar favored Paschasius Radbertus's* realism.

Bibliography

A.   PL 125–26.

B.   DTC 6:2482–86; DHGE 24:595–98; TRE 15:355–60; Jean Devisse, *Hincmar, archevêque de Reims, 845–882*, 3 vols. (Geneva, 1975–76); George H. Tavard, *Trina deitas: The Controversy between Hincmar and Gottschalk* (Milwaukee, Wis., 1996).

Joseph T. Lienhard

HIPPOLYTUS OF ROME (ca. 170–ca. 235, Sardinia). Under Victor of Rome (ca. 189–98) he was made a presbyter there. In 212 Origen* heard him preach at Rome. Hippolytus accused Callistus of Rome (217–22) of Sabellianism and of laxity toward sinners who sought reconciliation and formed a schismatic community. In the persecution under Maximinus Thrax, Pontian (Callistus' second successor after Urban) and Hippolytus were both condemned to the mines on Sardinia. Hippolytus was reconciled with the Roman bishops before he died. His and Pontian's bodies were brought back to Rome. They are commemorated together as saints on August 13.

Hippolytus, the last western theologian to compose in Greek, was a prolific writer. His *Refutation of All Heresies* attempted to show that heresy arises from contaminating Christian teaching with Greek ideas and practices (Books 1–4). Books 5–9 portray the heresies, including thirty-three Gnostic systems. The *Chronicle*, from the creation to A.D. 234, is anti-millennial in intent. Around A.D. 200 Hippolytus wrote a book *On the Antichrist* and ca. 204, a commentary on Daniel in four books; the latter is the oldest extant Christian commentary on any biblical book. A *Commentary on the Song of Songs* and a treatise on Jacob's blessing (Gn 49) are also extant. In recent years, the *Apostolic Tradition* has been reconstructed and edited from ancient translations and adaptations. In it, Hippolytus describes church life at Rome, and especially the liturgy, in great detail. The work contains the oldest extant eucharistic prayer (adapted as Canon II in the Roman Sacramentary); ordination prayers for bishops, priests, and deacons; a detailed account of the rite of baptism, including the oldest extant version of the creed; and many other blessings and regulations.

Bibliography

A. GCS 1, 26, and 36; Commentary on Daniel in SC 17; *La tradition apostolique de s. Hippolyte*, ed. B. Botte (Münster, 1963).

B. DSAM 7:531–71; DTC 6:2487–2511; LThK³ 5:147–49; NCE 6:1139–41; ODCC 773–74; TRE 15:381–87; A. d'Alès, *La théologie de s. Hippolyte*, 2d ed. (Paris, 1929).

Joseph T. Lienhard

HOBART, JOHN HENRY (14 September 1775, Philadelphia, Pa.–12 September 1830, Auburn, N.Y.). *Education*: B.A., Coll. of New Jersey, Princeton, 1793; studied theology under bishop William White of Pennsylvania. *Career*: parish ministry, 1798–1830, including rector, Trinity Church, New York City, 1816–30; assistant bishop of New York, 1811–16; bishop of New York, 1816–30.

Hobart was a leader in the revival of the Episcopal Church during the first decades after the American Revolution. He was also the leader of the early High Church party in the Episcopal Church. In 1806 he organized the Protestant Episcopal Theological Society for the advancement in theological knowledge and practical piety of future clergy in the Episcopal Church. Hobart was one of the founders of the General Theological Seminary in New York City in 1819, and he exerted a strong influence over General Seminary in its early years. He described his position in terms of "Evangelical Truth and Apostolic Order." He was one of the first in the Episcopal Church to produce theological and devotional manuals for the laity, which were called "tracts." In 1810 he founded the Protestant Episcopal Tract Society. He visited John Henry Newman* at

Oxford in 1824, and may well have influenced the development of the Tractarian Movement in England.

Bibliography

A. *A Companion for the Altar* (New York, 1804); *A Companion for the Festivals and Fasts* (New York, 1805); *The Origin, the General Character, and the Present Situation of the Protestant Episcopal Church, in the United States of America* (Philadelphia, 1814); *The Corruptions of the Church of Rome Contrasted with Certain Protestant Errors* (New York, 1818); *The Churchman: The Principles of the Churchman Stated and Explained in Distinction from the Corruptions of the Church of Rome and from the Errors of Certain Protestant Sects* (New York, 1819); *The High Churchman Vindicated* (New York, 1826); *The Church Catechism Enlarged, Explained and Proved from Scripture* (New York, 1827); *The Posthumous Works of the late Rt. Rev. John Henry Hobart*, ed. William Berrian, 3 vols. (New York, 1833).

B. AAP 5:440–53; DAB 9:93–94; NCAB 1:514–15; NCE 7:42; SH 5:302; William Berrian, "*Memoir* of Hobart," in vol. 1 of *The Posthumous Works of the late Rt. Rev. John Henry Hobart*; John McVickar, *The Early Life and Professional Years of Bishop Hobart* (Oxford, 1838).

Robert B. Slocum

HODGE, CHARLES (27 December 1797, Philadelphia, Pa.–19 June 1878, Princeton, N.J.). *Education*: studied at the Coll. of New Jersey, 1815; Princeton Sem., Princeton, N.J., 1816–19; Univs. of Paris, Halle, and Berlin, 1826–28. *Career*: missionary, Pa. and N.J., 1819–20; ordained minister, New Brunswick, N.J., 1821; instructor, oriental languages of Scripture, Princeton Sem., 1820–22; professor, oriental and biblical literature, 1822–40; editor, *Biblical Repertory and Princeton Review*, 1824–71; professor, exegetical and didactic theology, 1840–54; professor, exegetical, didactic and polemic theology, 1854–78.

Hodge was the foremost expositor of the Princeton Theology throughout most of the nineteenth century as well as the leading spokesperson for confessional Calvinism in nineteenth-century America. In an age characterized by the decline and fall of Calvinism as the dominant force in the American church, Hodge championed the Federal Theology of the *Westminster Confession of Faith* and was unwavering in his defense of "the old doctrines of Calvinism" against challenges from the New Haven Theology of Nathaniel W. Taylor,* the evangelical revivalism of Charles Finney,* and the Mercersburg Theology of John Nevin* and Philip Schaff.* In a letter to the Scottish theologian William Cunningham, Hodge summarized the objective that governed his exegetical and theological labors throughout his academic career. "I have had but one object in my professional career and as a writer, and that is to state and to vindicate the doctrines of the Reformed Church. I have never advanced a new idea, and have never aimed to improve on the doctrines of our fathers. Having become satisfied that the system of doctrines taught in the symbols of the Reformed

Churches is taught in the Bible, I have endeavored to sustain it, and am willing to believe even where I cannot understand.''

While modern historiography recognizes that Hodge was one of the greatest Reformed theologians of the nineteenth century, many interpreters nonetheless insist that both his defense of the Reformed faith and his unyielding adherence to the authority of Scripture were based upon an accommodation of theology to philosophical commitments that are diametrically opposed to the anthropological and epistemological assumptions of the Reformed tradition. Hodge's sustained polemic against higher criticism and doctrinal revisionism of any sort fell prey to an implicit rationalism, they contend, because it was based upon an endorsement of Scottish Common Sense Realism rather than on faithfulness to the Reformed tradition. Although Hodge's employment of induction and his insistence that theology is a science in which the theologian must organize the facts of Scripture into a comprehensive system might give credence to the notion that Hodge overintellectualized the faith, recent scholarship suggests that the charge of rationalism cannot be sustained. Not only did Hodge recognize that the operation of the intellect involves the ''whole soul''—mind, will, and emotions—rather than the rational faculty alone, but he also endorsed the classic Reformed distinction between a merely speculative and a spiritual understanding of the gospel. Indeed, he recognized that holiness is necessary to the perception of ''the truth and glory of the things of God,'' and as a consequence he insisted that piety—the fruit of the spiritual perception of revealed truth—''is the life of the minister.''

When Hodge's alleged rationalism is interpreted within a context that recognizes that the soul is a single unit that acts in all of its functions (i.e., its thinking, its feeling, and its willing) as a single substance, it becomes clear that his ''intellectualism'' was compatible with the assumptions of the Reformed tradition simply because it originated in a context that acknowledged that subjective and experiential concerns play a critical role in religious epistemology. As such, Hodge's employment of induction must not blind interpreters to the fact that he stood in the mainstream of the historic Reformed tradition, and that he did so by repudiating doctrinal innovations that set ''the rights of human nature'' over and against ''the divine supremacy and sovereignty in the salvation of men.''

Bibliography

A. *A Commentary on the Epistle to the Romans* (Philadelphia, 1835); *The Way of Life* (Philadelphia, 1841); *Essays and Reviews* (New York, 1857); *Systematic Theology*, 3 vols. (New York, 1872–73); *What is Darwinism?* (New York, 1874).

B. DAB 9:98–99; NCAB 10:245; NCE 7:44; SH 5:305–6; Archibald Alexander Hodge, *The Life of Charles Hodge* (New York, 1880); Andrew Hoffecker, *Piety and the Princeton Theologians* (Phillipsburg, N.J., 1981); Mark A. Noll, *The Princeton Theology, 1812–1921* (Grand Rapids, Mich., 1983); David F. Wells, ''Charles Hodge,'' in *Re-*

formed Theology in America, ed. David F. Wells (Grand Rapids, Mich., 1985); David
B. Calhoun, *Princeton Seminary*, 2 vols. (Edinburgh, 1994–96).

Paul Helseth

HONTHEIM, JOHANN NIKOLAUS VON [FEBRONIUS] (27 January
1701, Trier, Germany–2 September 1790, Monquintin, Luxembourg). *Education*: theology and law at the Univ. of Louvain; doctor of law, Collegium Germanicum, Rome, 1724. *Career*: ordained priest, 1728; diocesan official, Trier,
1728–32; professor of Roman Law, Univ. of Trier, 1732–38; director of the
sem., Trier, 1738–48; auxiliary bishop of Trier, 1748–90.

   Hontheim, a learned and cultured prelate, wrote several historical works, including a history of Trier, but is important mainly for his controversial book
written under the pseudonym of Justinus Febronius, *De statu presenti Ecclesiae
et legitima potestate Romani Pontificis* (1763). In the interests of ecumenism
and a desire to recover the pre-monarchical structure of the early church, he
proposed a basically democratic theory of church authority. Christ conferred the
power of the keys on the whole community of faith, and the pope and bishops
derive their authority from it. Since all the apostles were equal, Peter and his
successor have a primacy of honor and not of jurisdiction. The pope is subject
to the judgment of the whole episcopate and of an ecumenical council. The state
power also is entitled to intervene if need be to curb excesses of papal power.
The book aroused a storm of controversy. Pope Clement XIII promptly (1764)
condemned it and many authors wrote refutations of it. Von Hontheim offered
a partial retraction in 1779, but the book continued to be very widely read well
into the nineteenth century.

Bibliography

   A. *De statu presenti Ecclesiae et legitima potestate Romani Pontificis liber singularis
ad reuniendos dissidentes in religione compositus* (Bouillon and Frankfurt, 1763).
   B. DHGE 24:1066–69; DTC 5:2115–24; ODCC 603, 788–89; V. Pitzer, *Justinus
Febronius* (Göttingen, 1976); R. Duchon, "De Bossuet à Febronius," RHE 65 (1970):
372–422.

Richard F. Costigan

HOOKER, RICHARD (c. 1554, Heavitree, Devonshire, England–2 November
1600, Bishopbourne, England). *Education*: B.A., M.A., Corpus Christi Coll.,
Oxford, 1574, 1577. *Career:* ordained priest, 1582; fellow, Corpus Christi Coll.,
1577–84; reader in Hebrew, Oxford, 1579–84; rector, Drayton Beauchamp,
1584–85; Master of the Temple, London, 1585–91; rector, Boscombe, Wiltshire,
1591–95; rector, Bishopsbourne, Kent, 1595–1600.

   Hooker was the leading apologist of the Elizabethan Settlement and the
greatest articulator and defender of Anglicanism. He became nationally famous
by his reaction to the Reader at the Temple, Walter Travers, a vigorous Calvinist
Puritan, who claimed that church government should follow the pattern of John

Calvin's* Geneva. Hooker insisted that the church was under no obligation to imitate the church government of the apostolic period, much less of sixteenth-century Geneva. The issue between them was the role of Scripture in determining church polity. Travers claimed that Scripture teaches presbyterianism, and Hooker insisted that Scripture was not intended to give a pattern for church government but rather that Scripture presupposed the operation of natural law and positive human laws. Thomas Fuller said, "the pulpit spake pure Canterbury in the morning and Geneva in the afternoon until Travers was silenced." It was out of this conflict that Hooker's *magnum opus*, his monumental *Of the Lawes of Ecclesiastical Polity*, was born. Only five of the books appeared in Hooker's lifetime; I-IV in 1594 and V in 1597. Books VI-VIII appeared much later and seem to have been tampered with. The *Lawes* is the primary literary defense of the established Church of England against Puritan criticisms, and provides the philosophical basis for the Elizabethan Settlement. The Puritans insisted that all religious doctrines and institutions must be derived from the Bible and that the Scriptures are the exclusive guide for the Christian. Hooker argued that reason and tradition are also authoritative for the Christian and that church polity was much more an issue of reason and tradition than of Scripture. The Puritans taught that one may do only that which is prescribed in Scripture, and Hooker taught that one may do anything not prohibited by Scripture.

Book V is a commentary on the 1559 *Book of Common Prayer*. Here Hooker defended the written prayers of the Prayer Book and developed his opposition to the Puritan use of extemporaneous prayers. He also defended the sacramental usage of the Church of England and insisted that Christ is present in the Eucharist but rejected both consubstantiation and transubstantiation. He was somewhat indifferent to issues of substance and change in the Eucharist and taught that the real transubstantiation of the sacrament is a change in the recipients, "an alteration from death to life." Something happens not in the sacrament itself, but in the soul of the believer. "The real presence of Christ's most blessed body and blood is not therefore to be sought in the sacrament, but in the worthy receiver of the sacrament."

Hooker taught that the primary sources of authority for the Christian are Scripture, reason, and tradition, in that order. Scripture teaches what is necessary for salvation but leaves a number of things free to be ordered at the discretion of the church, using reason and tradition. The episcopal form of church government is not precisely prescribed in Scripture, but episcopacy is the best form of church government and is justified in practice by history—that is, it is the most reasonable form of church government. Reason must be used in interpreting Scripture. In fact, reason is the faculty by which people receive revelation. Both reason and revelation guide the life of a Christian; reason guides polity and revelation guides doctrine. His primary thesis is that no period in church history can reproduce the apostolic church; to try to do so "is neither possible, nor certain, nor absolutely convenient."

Bibliography

A. *The Folger Library Edition of the Works of Richard Hooker*, ed. W. Speed Hill, 5 vols. (Cambridge, Mass., 1977–90).

B. DNB 27:289–95; LThK³ 5:272–73; ODCC 789; OEncR 2:251–54; TRE 15:581–83; Lionel S. Thornton, *Richard Hooker: A Study of His Theology* (London, 1924); John S. Marshall, *Hooker and the Anglican Tradition* (London, 1963); W. Speed Hill, ed., *Studies in Richard-Hooker: Essays Preliminary to an Edition of His Works* (London, 1972).

Donald S. Armentrout

HOOKER, THOMAS (July, 1586, Marfield, Leicestershire–July 7, 1647, Hartford, Conn.). *Education*: B.A., M.A., Emmanuel Coll., Univ. of Cambridge, 1608, 1611. *Career*: professor, Emmanuel Coll., 1611–18; pastor, Esher in Surrey, 1618–25; Chelmsford, Essex, 1625–29; fled to Netherlands, 1631; pastor, Newton, Cambridge, Mass., 1633–38; founder and pastor, Hartford, Conn., 1638–47.

Hooker's pastoral writings emphasize the individual's sinfulness, "the terrour of the Lord upon the conscience," so that the believer "may come to a parley of peace, and be content to take up the profession of the truth." Avoiding "mystical cloudy discourses" and trying to kindle "spiritual heat in the heart," his ideal of "heart religion," conveyed the possibility and comfort of assurance of the humble and contrite soul's implantation into Jesus Christ.

Hooker's *A Survey of the Summe of Church Discipline* (1648) is the most complete presentation of the ecclesiology of the Congregational "New England Way." Although he was interested primarily in the spiritual workings of the individual soul in the stages of redemption (contrition, humiliation, vocation, justification, adoption, sanctification, and glorification), he exercised great political influence in New England. Hooker's congregationalism was transposed into an incipient democratic political concept in the *Fundamental Orders of Connecticut* (1639), often regarded as the first democratic constitution in America. He taught "that the choice of public magistrates belongs unto the people by God's own allowance" "because the foundation of authority is laid, firstly, in the free consent of the people" (Sermon of 31 May 1638). However, he denied an absolute sovereignty of the people ("The privilege of election, which belongs to the people, must not be exercised according to their humours, but according to the blessed will and law of God").

Bibliography

A. *Thomas Hooker: Writings in England and Holland, 1626–1633*, ed. George H. Williams, Norman Pettit, Winfried Herget, and Sargent Bush, Jr. (Cambridge, Mass., 1975), with complete bibliography of Hooker's writings; *The Application of Redemption* (London, 1657; repr. New York, 1972); *A Survey of the Summe of Church Discipline* (London, 1648; repr. New York, 1972).

B. AAP 1:30–37; DAB 9:199–200; DARB 251–52; NCAB 6:279–80; NCE 7:132;

SH 5:361; Sargent Bush, Jr., *The Writings of Thomas Hooker. Spiritual Adventure in Two Worlds* (Madison, Wis., 1980); Frank Shuffelton, *Thomas Hooker. 1586–1647* (Princeton, N.J., 1977), with bibliographical essay.

William J. Hoye

HOPKINS, SAMUEL (17 September 1721, Waterbury, Conn.–20 December 1803, Newport, R.I.). *Education*: B.A. Yale Coll., 1741; read theology with Jonathan Edwards,* Northampton, Mass., 1741–42. *Career*: minister, Housatonic (now Great Barrington), Mass., 1743–69; minister, First Congregational Church, Newport, R.I., 1770–1803.

Hopkins was perhaps the most creative and systematic representative of the New Divinity movement in American theology. The New Divinity School of Theology created a theological defense of religious revivals and experimental religion, argued against the inroads of a generalized Arminianism that had legitimized human effort and the operation of free will in the conversion process, and modified some of the strict Calvinism of the Edwardsean tradition.

Hopkinsianism, as Hopkins' system of theology came to be called, was innovative as well as in continuity with elements of Edwards' Calvinism. Like Edwards, Hopkins' defense of the experimental religion of the Great Awakening stressed God's absolute sovereignty, human spiritual inability, and the instantaneous nature of rebirth. Like Edwards, moreover, Hopkins had a hyper-Calvinist view of human nature. Hopkins' view of sin, however, helped to identify the peculiarity of Hopkinsianism. For Hopkins, God was so sovereign that he not only permitted sin, but willed it.

Unlike Edwards and like many in the late eighteenth century, Hopkins embraced God as a benevolent moral governor. His emphasis upon benevolence was also reflected in his view of true virtue, an interest he shared with Edwards. For Hopkins, though, true virtue consisted in a radical disinterested benevolence toward Being in general, requiring from the individual a complete self-denial, even to the point of being willing to be damned for the glory of God and the good of the universe.

Hopkins' emphasis on disinterested benevolence gave evangelical Calvinism an ethic that stressed corporate obligation, personal restraint, and communal harmony and simplicity—positions that countered the egocentric patterns of acquisition, self-determination, and self-assurance that were developing in the late eighteenth century. The activist and social thrust of that ethic, however, merged compatibly with the late-eighteenth-century public-spirited and antiluxury dimensions of republican political thought. When combined with an optimistic post-millennial eschatology, Hopkins' disinterested benevolence became a call for Christians to engage in moral and social reforms in society. Hopkins himself carried out the logic of his own position by arguing against the slave trade and the enslavement of Africans in the United States, thus becoming one of the first Calvinist New England ministers to speak out publicly against slavery.

In 1793 Hopkins published his *System of Doctrines*, which summarized the

New Divinity Theology. The book became a primary text for training ministers from the 1790s to the early part of the nineteenth century in New England.

Bibliography

A. *Sin . . . an Advantage to the Universe* (Boston, 1759); *The True State and Character of the Unregenerate* (New Haven, Conn., 1769); *An Inquiry into the Nature of True Holiness* (Newport, R.I., 1773); *A Dialogue Concerning the Slavery of the Africans* (Norwich, Conn., 1776); *A Treatise on the Millennium* (Boston, 1793; New York, 1972); *System of Doctrines Contained in Divine Revelation, Explained and Defended*, 2 vols. (Boston, 1793).

B. AAP 1:428–35; DAB 9:217–18; DARB, 217–18; NCAB 7:154–55; SH 5:363–64; J. A. Conforti, *Samuel Hopkins and the New Divinity Movement: Calvinism, the Congregational Ministry, and Reform in New England between the Great Awakenings* (Grand Rapids, Mich., 1981).

Patrick W. Carey

HUBMAIER, BALTHASAR (1480/85 Frieburg, Bavaria–10 March 1528, Vienna). *Education*: studied at Latin School in Augsburg; B.A. Univ. of Freiburg im Breisgau, 1503–4; Doctor of Theology, Univ. of Ingolstadt, 1512. *Career*: school teacher, Schaffhausen, 1507; professor of theology, Univ. of Freidberg, 1509–12; professor of theology, Univ. of Ingolstadt, 1512–16; vicar, Church of Our Dear Lady, 1512–16; cathedral preacher, Regensburg, 1516–20; preacher, Waldshut on the Rhine, 1521–22; preacher, reformer and revolutionary, Waldshut 1523–25; reformer and author, Nikolsburg, Moravia, 1526–28.

Hubmaier was the most competent theologian of early Anabaptism. Trained in the school of nominalism by John Eck,* he was won over to the Reformation by reading Erasmus* and Luther* and was heavily influenced by Zwingli's* reformation in Zurich. He moved in a more "radical" Anabaptist direction when he came into contact with Conrad Grebel* and Wilhelm Reublin.

Rebaptized in Waldshut by Reublin in 1525, Hubmaier attempted to convince his fellow reformers that believer's baptism should be an essential element of the general reformation. Hubmaier based his theology of baptism on the scholastic distinction between God's absolute and ordained will. God ordained a covenant because he desired the salvation of all. If an individual fulfilled the terms of the covenant, God was obligated to grant salvation. Human depravity had eliminated the ability to choose for the good (God). Under the terms of the covenant, when the Word was preached the Holy Spirit enabled the individual to choose the good. If the individual freely consented to the movement of the Holy Spirit (baptism of the Holy Spirit), the covenant was sealed by a public water baptism. Because an infant was unable to freely consent, infant baptism was understood as ineffective.

Although Hubmaier's theology of baptism was determinative for Anabaptist theology, his equally important political theology was ignored. Unlike most Anabaptists, Hubmaier believed Christians to be uniquely qualified to rule. This was graphically illustrated by his leadership in the Waldshut peasant uprising (1525). Following failure in Waldshut he moved to Nikolsburg, Moravia, where he attempted a territorial reformation along Anabaptist lines. He was arrested and under torture appeared to have recanted his views on baptism, but before he was burned (not for theological heresy, but political insurrection) he reasserted them in a letter to King Ferdinand of Austria.

Bibliography

A.   *Quellen zur Geschichte der Täufer*, in *Balthasar Hubmaier Schriften*, vol. 9, ed. Gunnar Westen and Torsten Bergsten (Gutersloh, 1962); *Balthasar Hubmaier: Theologian of Anabaptism*, in *Classics of the Radical Reformation*, 5, ed. and trans. H. Pipkin and John H. Yoder (Scottdale, Pa., 1989).

B.   LThK³ 5:296–97; ODCC 798; OEncR 2:260–63; TRE 15:611–13; Johann Loserth, *Doctor Balthasar Hubmaier und die Anfänge der Wiedertaufe in Mähren* (Bruenn 1893); Rollin S. Armour, *Anabaptist Baptism: A Representative Study* (Scottdale, Pa., 1966); Henry C. Vedder, *Balthasar Hubmaier: The Leader of the Anabaptists* (New York, 1905, 1971); Torsten Bergsten, *Balthasar Hubmaier: Anabaptist Theologian and Martyr* (Valley Forge, Pa. 1978); Christof Windshorst, "Balthasar Hubmaier: Professor, Preacher, Politician," in *Profiles of Radical Reformers*, ed. Hans-Jurgen Goertz (Scottdale, Pa., 1982), 144–57.

Matthew Brandt

HÜGEL, BARON FRIEDRICH VON (5 May 1852, Florence, Italy–27 January 1925, London). *Career*: supported by family inheritance; informally recognized as the "lay bishop" of the Roman Catholic modernism movement, 1890–1910; founder, London Society for the Study of Religion, 1905; letter writer and author, 1890–1925.

Von Hügel was indifferent about religion until the age of eighteen when, following his father's death and a severe attack of typhus that impaired his health and hearing, he experienced a prolonged moral and spiritual crisis from which he emerged a deeply committed Catholic with the help of the Dutch Dominican Raymond Hocking and the French secular priest Henri Huvelin. The latter profoundly influenced the baron, encouraging him to a vocation of scholarship but warning him away from neoscholasticism and advising that only an exceptionally deep and lively interior life—prayer as a permanent condition rather than as discrete acts—could secure him against the corrosive influence of negative criticism of Scripture and tradition and let him bear peacefully the great sorrow he would experience in the church.

Von Hügel embraced this counsel and cultivated an intense spiritual and religious life that became, both theoretically and practically, his most passionate interest and indeed the integrating factor of his personality. Although he gave himself to numerous theological interests—biblical, historical, philosophical— the religious and mystical life became the subject of his most protracted, scholarly inquiry.

The baron awakened to his vocational interests just when Western Europe was undergoing a profound revolution of thought—the fruit largely of the Enlightenment and the consequent French Revolution—to which Roman Catholic authorities reacted with alarm. His own spiritual life securely anchored, he was himself able to entertain all manner of novel ideas without the slightest danger to his faith. But church authorities, worried about the influence of religiously hostile ideas on the average Catholic, attempted often with little pastoral sensitivity to rein in scholars. Von Hügel was a personal friend of most of them. He both encouraged them in their ideas and exhorted them to remain acceptably orthodox. Not very successful in this latter effort, he nevertheless remained faithful to his friends to the end.

Von Hügel's mystical theology evolved from his long-in-writing *The Mystical Element of Religion* (influenced by Kantian epistemology), through *Eternal Life* (influenced by Bergson's notions of time's relation to eternity), to his posthumously published *The Reality of God* (influenced by "Critical Realism," his eventual philosophy of choice). Thus, he increasingly distanced himself from excessive Kantian immanentism that led some modernists to deny the objective reality of God postulated by the act of "adoration," which for von Hügel was the essence of religion. He saw the Christian vocation as essentially incarnational, requiring a lifelong struggle to integrate and balance three principal elements of religion: the institutional, intellectual, and mystical. These three elements, interacting in different ways at different periods of one's life, when held in tension, necessarily cause friction but keep one firmly grounded and engaged in the real world. This friction and world-engagement lead to purification and authentic holiness.

Bibliography

A. *The Mystical Element of Religion* (London, 1908); *Eternal Life* (Edinburgh, 1912); *Essays and Addresses on the Philosophy of Religion*, 2 vols. (London, 1921, 1926); *Selected Letters 1896–1924* (London, 1928); *The Reality of God, and Religion and Agnosticism* (London, 1931).

B. DNB [1922–30], 874–76; LThK³ 5:300–301; NCE 7:187–88; ODCC 1707–8; TRE 15:614–18; Michael De la Bedoyère, *The Life of Baron von Hügel* (London, 1951); Maurice Nédoncelle, *Baron Friedrich von Hügel* (London, 1937); Lawrence F. Barmann, *Baron Friedrich Von Hügel and the Modernist Crisis in England* (Cambridge, 1972); Peter Neuner, *Religiöse Erfahrung und geschichtliche Offenbarung: Friedrich von Hügels Grundlegung der Theologie* (Munich, 1977); James J. Kelly, *Baron Friedrich von Hügel's Philosophy of Religion* (Louvain, 1983).

David G. Schultenover

HUGH OF ST.-CHER (ca. 1195, St.-Cher [near Vienne]–1263). *Education*: master of canon law and bachelor in theology, Univ. of Paris, 1220s. *Career*: entered the Dominican order, 1225; provincial prior of the Dominican province of France, 1227–29; regent master of theology, Paris, 1230–36; prior of the convent of St.-Jacques, Paris, 1233–36; provincial, 1236–44; cardinal, 1244; papal legate to Germany, 1252, where he approved the local celebration of the feast of Corpus Christi, an important step towards the universal acceptance of the feast. He also served on the papal commissions convened to hear testimony in the controversies surrounding the writings of Joachim of Fiore* and William of St.-Amour.

A prominent early Dominican theologian and biblical scholar, Hugh of St.-Cher was also his order's first cardinal. As a theologian Hugh is known for developing the doctrine of the treasury of merits and for his writings on the hypostatic union. Hugh of St.-Cher's main contribution was not as an innovative thinker, however, but as the leader of a team of friars at St.-Jacques who produced three landmark aids to study. The first was a set of *Postillae in totam Bibliam*, a continuous commentary on all the books of the Bible that brought together the advances in biblical scholarship made since the compilation of the *Glossa ordinaria* in the mid-twelfth century. The second is a series of *Correctoria*, lists of alternate readings for the Bible, which aimed to improve the version of the Vulgate currently in use at the university of Paris. Thirdly, Hugh and his team produced the first alphabetized concordance to the Bible, which became a tool widely used by medieval preachers and exegetes alike.

Bibliography

A.   Hugh's works are largely unedited; for a list of manuscripts and partial editions see Thomas Kaeppeli, *Scriptores Ordinis Praedicatorum Medii Aevi* 2 (1975): 269–81.

B.   DTC 7:221–39; LThK³ 5:310–11; NCE 7:193–94; John Fisher, "Hugh of St. Cher and the Development of Mediaeval Theology," *Speculum* 31 (1956): 57–69; Walter H. Principe, *The Theology of the Hypostatic Union in the Early Thirteenth Century*, vol. 3, *Hugh of Saint-Cher's Theology of the Hypostatic Union* (Toronto, 1970); Richard H. Rouse and Mary A. Rouse, "The Verbal Concordance to the Scriptures," *Archivum Fratrum Praedicatorum* 44 (1974): 5–30; Robert E. Lerner, "Poverty, Preaching, and Eschatology in the Revelation Commentaries of 'Hugh of St.-Cher'," in *The Bible in the Medieval World: Essays in Memory of Beryl Smalley*, ed. K. Walsh and D. Wood (New York, 1985), 157–89.

M. Michèle Mulchahey

HUGH OF ST. VICTOR (end of 11th century–1141). Little is known of Hugh's early life; one tradition points to Saxon origins, another to Flemish; received his education with the Canons Regular of St. Augustine at Hammersleven, Saxony, and joined the community; joined St. Victor in Paris, ca. 1115; leading master at the abbey and remained so until his death.

Philosophically, Hugh's thoughts on the value of human reason as forming a natural connection to the knowledge of God's existence and attributes inform his theological works. In logic and abstractive knowledge, he was influenced by Aristotle and Boethius.* He tended towards a middle position on the discussions between the universalists and the realists. The value of reading and study, including the *trivium* and the *quadrivium*, affirmed the value of contemporary educational practice.

Hugh's exegesis concentrated on interpreting the literal meaning. Even though this focus may have signaled a return to an interpretation as old as the church itself rather than something new, attention to the letter brought fresh discourse into the field of biblical exegesis. In the end, however, Hugh's own commentaries resembled those of his contemporaries.

Theological influences on Hugh include Anselm of Canterbury,* Anselm of Laon,* William of Champeaux, Pseudo-Dionysius,* and even Abelard.* (Hugh did not take part in the condemnation of Abelard's works at Sens in 1140.) Hugh's historical theology begins with the Fall, culminates with Christ, and ends with the consummation of all creation. Original sin is a corruption that one takes on at birth, resulting in intellectual ignorance and fleshly concupiscence. Hugh's trinitarian theology is correct, if sketchy, and some slight errors concerning the human and divine knowledge in Christ occur. His sacramental theology excelled in the definition of the sacraments and emphasized the role of absolution in the sacrament of penance and the reception of divine grace in matrimony. His legacy to scholasticism includes the definition of faith as "a certainty about things absent, above opinion and below science."

Hugh's spiritual writings, although stylistically indirect, nonetheless contributed to the tradition of mystical thought for which the Abbey of St. Victor became famous.

Hugh of St. Victor remains important among medieval theologians, influencing Richard of St. Victor* and Peter Lombard,* among others. His synthesis of scholastic method and Christian orthodoxy allowed for the flourishing of scholasticism throughout his era and beyond.

Bibliography

A.   PL 175–177; *Didascalicon*, trans. Jerome Taylor (New York, 1961).

B.   DTC 7:240–308; LThK³ 5:311–12; NCE 7:194–95; ODCC 800–801; TRE 15: 629–36; Jerome Taylor, *The Origin and Early Life of Hugh of St. Victor: An Evaluation of the Tradition* (Notre Dame, Ind., 1957); R. Baron, *Études sur Hugues de Saint-Victor* (Paris, 1963); Jerome Taylor, *The Didascalicon of Hugh of St. Victor: A Medieval Guide to the Arts* (New York, 1968); Joachim Ehlers, *Hugo von St. Viktor. Studien zum Geschichtsdenken und zur Geschichtsschreibung des 12. Jahrhunderts* (Wiesbaden, 1973).

Thomas S. Ferguson

HUMBERT OF ROMANS (ca. 1200, Romans–14 July 1277, Valence). A native of France; entered the Dominican order in Paris in 1224, already a *Magister artium*; lector in theology in the Dominican *studium* at Lyons, from 1226; prior there, 1236–39; prior of the Roman province, 1240–ca. 1242; provincial of France, 1244; superior general of the Dominican order, 1254–63. Humbert might have been elected pope in the conclave of 1241 or 1243 but outside pressure intervened. His *Opus tripartitum*, which Gregory X commissioned for the Second Council of Lyons, offered a plan for the reform of the church, a defense of the crusades, and a way of healing the schism with the Greeks. He gave the constitutions of the Order of Preachers (Dominicans) their final form

(1259) and did the same for the liturgical books of the order. He wrote on the religious life and on preaching. His work *De praedicatione crucis* was a *summa* of crusade preaching. A collection of his sermons is also extant.

Bibliography

A.   *Opera de vita regulari*, ed. J.-J. Berthier, 2 vols. (Turin, 1956); *Treatise on the Formation of Preachers*, in *Early Dominicans: Selected Writings*, ed. Simon Tugwell (New York, 1982).

B.   DSAM 7:1108–16; LThK³ 5:330–31; NCE 7:231; ODCC 802; Karl Michel, *Das Opus tripartitum des Humbertus de Romanis, O.P. Ein Beitrag zur Geschichte der Kreuzzugsidee und der kirchlichen Unionsbewegungen*, 2d ed. (Graz, 1926); Edward T. Brett, *Humbert of Romans: His Life and Views of Thirteenth Century Society* (Toronto, 1984).

Joseph T. Lienhard

HUNTINGTON, WILLIAM REED (20 September, 1838, Lowell, Mass.–26 July, 1909, Nahant, Mass.). *Education*: A.B., Harvard, 1859; read theology with Rev. Frederic Dan Huntington, 1860–62. *Career*: parish ministry, All Saints Church, Worcester, Mass., 1862–83; Grace Church, New York City, 1883–1909; member, House of Deputies of the General Convention of the Episcopal Church, 1871–1907.

Huntington, an Episcopal priest, articulated a fourfold basis for Christian unity in his book, *The Church-Idea* (New York, 1870). He presented the Anglican basis for an ecumenical "Church of the Reconciliation" in America. This proposal emphasized the acceptance of the Holy Scriptures as the Word of God; the Nicene Creed as the rule of faith; Baptism and Eucharist as the two sacraments ordained by Christ; and the episcopate as the keystone of governmental unity in the church. Huntington's "foursquare" basis for church unity became known as the "Quadrilateral." It was through his influence that the House of Bishops adopted the Quadrilateral at the General Convention of the Episcopal Church meeting in Chicago in 1886. Although the Quadrilateral was not enacted by the House of Deputies at the 1886 General Convention, it was passed in a modified form by the Lambeth Conference of 1888. The Chicago-Lambeth Quadrilateral is the primary Anglican ecumenical statement and point of reference for Christian reunion.

Huntington was also a significant liturgical scholar. He urged greater liturgical flexibility to make the worship of the Episcopal Church more widely accessible. At the 1874 General Convention Huntington called for a complete revision of the Prayer Book. Huntington's *Materia Ritualis* (Worcester, Mass., 1882) came to serve as the working paper of the joint committee on revision of the Prayer Book prior to the General Convention of 1883. He had a leading role in the proposal of *The Book Annexed to the Report of the Joint-Committee* (1883), a substantial revision of the Episcopal Prayer Book. Although *The Book Annexed* was not accepted, this Prayer Book revision process ultimately resulted in the 1892 *Book of Common Prayer*. Huntington was influential in the canonical authorization of the order of deaconesses in the Episcopal Church in 1899. He was known as the "First Presbyter of the Church" in his later years. His life is commemorated in the Episcopal Church calendar of the church year on July 27.

Bibliography

A. *The Book Annexed: Its Critics and Its Prospects* (New York, 1886); *The Peace of the Church* (New York, 1891); *A Short History of the Book of Common Prayer* (New York, 1893); *A National Church* (New York, 1898).
    B. DAB 9:420–21; DARB 260–61; NCAB 38:131–32; NYT 27 July 1909, 7; SH 5: 412–13; John Wallace Suter, *Life and Letters of William Reed Huntington* (New York, 1925).

Robert B. Slocum

HUS, JAN (1373, Husinec–6 July 1415, Constance). *Education*: B.A., M.A., three baccalaureates in theology, Univ. of Prague, 1393, 1396, 1404–8. *Career*: ordained priest, 1400; dean of arts faculty, 1401–2; preacher of Bethlehem chapel, 1402; university rector, 1409–10.

When Hus arrived at the University of Prague in 1390 a struggle for control raged between the Czech masters and the Germans who had dominated the university since its foundation in 1348. This academic battle was coupled with calls for church reform by the Czechs who emphasized lay piety and the need for frequent communion. By the end of the fourteenth century the writings of the English theologian John Wyclif* were known in Prague and well received by many Czech scholars, who found solid theological support for their reforms in his writings on the nature of the true church and rightful dominion. In 1403, forty-five articles drawn from Wyclif's writings were condemned, and in 1410 Wycliffite tracts were ordered burned.

By 1407, in the wake of his violent sermons against clerical abuses, Hus was forbidden to preach. He had attacked the sale of indulgences and argued that tithes should not be obligatory, that secular lords might deprive delinquent priests of their temporalities, and that nobody is rightfully a civil lord or bishop while in mortal sin. At the heart of his calls for reform stood his doctrine of the church, which he articulated in his *De ecclesia* (*On the Church*), written in 1413. Here he proposed an ecclesiology very similar to Wyclif's, by which the church is defined as the totality of the predestined whose sole head is Christ. While many may be in the church, they are not of the church if they are not among the predestined. If the pope was among the predestined he is still only head of the Roman Church, and if he is not among the predestined his power is by definition illegitimate. Recognizing the practical limitations of such a theory, however, Hus did not advocate the dissolution of the established church order.

Excommunicated and in exile by 1413, Hus continued to write a great deal, composing many works in the Czech language, including his *On Simony*. Summoned to the Council of Constance, he was charged with thirty Wycliffite errors, some of which he did not hold (he did not deny transubstantiation, as Wyclif had done). Hus never received the fair hearing he was promised and was swiftly condemned. Refusing to recant, he was pronounced a heretic and burned at the stake on 6 July 1415.

Bibliography

A. *Opera Omnia*, ed. Fr. Rysanek et al. (Prague, 1959–); *Tractatus de ecclesia*, ed. S. Harrison Thomson (Boulder, Colo., 1956); trans. D. S. Schaff (New York, 1915); *The Letters of John Hus*, ed. Matthew Spinka (Manchester, 1972).

B. DTC 7:333–46; LThK³ 5:340–41; NCE 7:271–72; ODCC 806–7; TRE 15:710–21; Matthew Spinka, *John Hus' Concept of the Church* (Princeton, N.J., 1966); idem, *John Hus: A Biography* (Princeton, N.J., 1968); Paul de Vooght, *L'hérésie de Jean Hus*, 2 vols. (Louvain, 1975).

Ian Christopher Levy

HUTTER, JACOB (also Huter) (1500?, Moos, Tyrol–25 February 1536, Innsbruck, Austria). *Career*: hatter by trade; Anabaptist evangelist, 1529–36.

Hutter was a promoter of the Anabaptists. In his early twenties he may have participated in the Tyrolian Peasants' Revolt (1523–25) but converted to nonviolent Anabaptism after the revolt. Upon the martyrdom of the Anabaptist founder George Blaurock in 1529, Hutter became leader and organizer of Tyrol Anabaptists, later known as the Hutterite Brotherhood. Persecutions in the Tyrol forced Hutter and many of his followers to flee to the more tolerant Moravia, where he brought unity to disagreeing Anabaptist groups and laid the foundations for economic stability by emphasizing strict adherence to early Christian communal practices. In 1536, during the severe persecutions of Anabaptists mandated by King Ferdinand of Austria, Hutter was burnt at the stake and his wife was drowned.

Hutter was not an original thinker but an evangelist and organizer who during the movement's origins promoted Anabaptist principles and stabilized Moravian Anabaptist communes by insisting upon a disciplined Christian life and strict observance of the Christian principles of love and peace.

Bibliography

A. *Brotherly Faithfulness: Epistles from a Time of Persecution* (Rifton, N.Y., 1979); *The Chronicle of the Hutterian Brethren*, ed. and trans. Hutterian Brethren, vol. 1 (Rifton, N.Y., 1987).

B. LThK³ 5:346–47; OEncR 2:282–84; TRE 15:752–56; J. W. Bennett, *Hutterian Brethren* (Stanford, Calif., 1967); Victor Peters, *All Things Common: The Hutterian Way of Life* (Minneapolis, Minn., 1965).

Joan Skocir

I

IGNATIUS OF ANTIOCH (d. ca. 117). Ignatius of Antioch is known substantially through the seven letters he wrote to Christian communities while he was a prisoner en route to Rome. Ignatius' influence and his reputation depend upon these letters and the authority that accrued to these letters (and Ignatius' person) because of his martyrdom in Rome (probably during the reign of Trajan, A.D. 98–117). Beyond the minimum biographical facts provided implicitly in the letters we know nothing about Ignatius' life. He was evidently fairly well educated, a bishop in Antioch before his arrest by the Roman authorities, and a man deeply engaged in combatting problems he observed among Christian communities. And, finally, he understood his coming violent death as an act integral to his faith. Despite the paucity of our knowledge of the man, Ignatius' letters provide an excellent sense of the person who wrote them, of his devotion to Christ even to death, and of the theology that Ignatius identified with the true church of Christ.

The center of Ignatius' theology is the reality of Christ's divinity and humanity. Ignatius is particularly concerned to combat the belief that Jesus was not truly human (Docetism), a fact that has led some scholars to conclude that Ignatius' opponents represented a Christianity still very much tied to Jewish categories (i.e., ''Jewish Christianity''). For Ignatius, divine and human, spirit and matter, living and dying (because we are dying and only God is really living) come together in Jesus. Ignatius' attachment to this doctrine of the Incarnation serves the positive function of being the basis for his doctrines of the Eucharist, the church, martyrdom, and salvation. Likewise, in Ignatius' theology, the doctrine of the Incarnation has the critical function of supporting his rejection of Docetism, which he sees as robbing Christianity of its grasp of who and what Christ was, as well as robbing it of the promise of the salvation that Christ offered. The Eucharist, in particular, receives much attention in Ignatius' letters, for as the Incarnation is where divinity and humanity meet, so the Eucharist is the continuation of this meeting. The Eucharist is a kind of an enlargement of the meeting of divinity and humanity, an opening up of this meeting in such a way that believers can participate in that meeting and, by participating, be delivered from death. This is why the Eucharist is, in Ignatius' words, the "medicine of immortality." Martyrdom is related to the Incarnation in a similar way. The Incarnation—which for Ignatius includes the inevitable fact of death (if God really became human)—is a death for the sake of bringing together life and death so that death can be absorbed into life. Martyrdom is also a death so that death can be absorbed into life and, moreover, a special imitation of Christ's own death.

Ignatius' theology has received particular attention for its emphasis on the office of the bishop. Each local church was, according to Ignatius, centered on and built upon its bishop. It is the bishop who celebrates the Eucharist, forgives sins, and represents Christ to the local community of Christians; and it is the bishop, together with all other bishops in the world, who represents what Ignatius calls "the mind of God." Obviously Ignatius is an early and authoritative representative of the episcopal structure of the church that would soon come to predominate, but scholars have not determined clearly how Ignatius' own bishop-centered ecclesiology relates to the general rise of an episcopal-centered church structure.

Bibliography

A. Patrology 1, 74–75.

B. DSAM 7:1250–66; DTC 7:685–713; LThK³ 5:407–9; NCE 7:353–54; ODCC 817–18; TRE 16:40–45; Frederick A. Schilling, *The Mysticism of Ignatius of Antioch* (Philadelphia, 1932); Cyril Charles Richardson, *The Christianity of Ignatius of Antioch* (New York, 1953); Henning Paulsen, *Studien zur Theologie des Ignatius von Antiochien* (Göttingen, 1978); Peter Meinhold, *Studien zu Ignatius von Antiochien* (Wiesbaden, 1979); William R. Schoedel, *Ignatius of Antioch* (Philadelphia, 1980); Christine Trevett, *A Study in Ignatius of Antioch in Syria and Asia* (Lewiston, N.Y., 1992); Allen Brent, "The Ignatian Epistles and the Threefold Ecclesiastical Order," *Journal of Religious History* 17 (1992): 18–32.

Michel René Barnes

IGNATIUS OF LOYOLA (1491, Azpeitia, Spain–31 July 1556, Rome). *Education*: studied Latin, Barcelona, 1524–26; studied Univs. of Alcalá, Salamanca, 1526–27; studied Univ. of Paris, 1528–35; Mass., Univ. of Paris, 1535; read theology, Venice, 1535. *Career*: founder, Society of Jesus (Jesuits), 1536; superior general of Jesuits, 1536–56.

Loyola was neither a skilled writer nor a profound theologian but he had a remarkable gift in dealing with people, understanding the workings of grace and the human need for spiritual growth, and organizing the Jesuits. The Jesuits had a unique impact on the world of the Catholic Reformation as preachers, teachers, writers, and missionaries. Their spirituality grew out of Loyola's *Spiritual Exercises*, first published in 1548; the book evolved from Loyola's religious experiences in 1522 and from the notes he produced on the basis of those early experiences. The *Exercises* (more than 5,000 editions) teach several methods of systematic prayer and recast Loyola's own mystical experiences in a lower key. The full *Exercises* were to last thirty days and were given by an experienced director to persons making major decisions about their lives. Loyola's other major work was the Jesuit *Constitutions*, which are much longer and more detailed than the previous rules for religious orders. Loyola carried on a voluminous correspondence in his last fifteen years and dictated a short autobiography covering his years up to his arrival at Paris.

Bibliography

A. *Ignatius of Loyola: Spiritual Exercises and Selected Works*, ed. George Ganss (New York, 1991).
B. DSAM 7:1266–1318; LThK³ 5:410–11; NCE 7:354–56; ODCC 818–19; OEncR 2:307–10; TRE 16:45–54; Philip Caraman, *Ignatius Loyola: A Biography of the Founder of the Jesuits* (San Francisco, 1990); William Meissner, *The Psychology of a Saint: Ignatius of Loyola* (New Haven, Conn., 1992); John O'Malley, *The First Jesuits* (Cambridge, Mass., 1993); Jose I. Tellechea Idígoras, *Ignatius of Loyola: The Pilgrim Saint* (Chicago, 1994).

John Patrick Donnelly

ILLYRICUS. *See* FLACIUS, MATTHIAS.

IRENAEUS (fl. ca. 180/90). Pastor, very likely styled "bishop," of the Christian congregations at Lyons and Vienne in Roman Gaul. It was there, in the decade after 180, that he took upon himself, partly no doubt for pastoral reasons, the responsibility of exposing and refuting Christian gnosticism in the tradition of Valentinus and Ptolemy. Following the lead of Justin Martyr,* he regarded these teachers and their disciples as heretics—that is, as sectarian corrupters of Christian truth—and indeed as the paradigmatic heretics, whose rebuttal, he thought, would in principle dispose of all the rest of their ilk. If one ignores Justin, whose work "against all the . . . heresies" (*First Apology* 26, 8) is lost, Irenaeus was the first of the Christian heresiologists; but he was much more than a collector of deviations. His polemic against Christian gnostics (and against Marcion,* whom he appears to have reckoned in that category) compelled him to develop a constructive reading of Christian teaching and tradition that, though not in all respects original, became widely known and influential.

Of Irenaeus' life little is known. He was born in Asia Minor, most likely in Smyrna, where, as he himself relates, he saw the great Polycarp when he was a youth. The date of his birth cannot be fixed but might well have fallen in the decade between 130 and 140. Equally unknown is the time of his coming to

Lyons (which, being a center of government, trade, and transport, had a significant population of immigrants from the East); but it seems likely that it was preceded by a stay at Rome. What is certain is that he was a prominent member of the Christian congregation in Lyons when, in 177 or a bit later, a severe persecution broke out (see Eusebius, HE 5, 1). According to Eusebius,* Irenaeus was dispatched at this time on a mission to Bishop Eleutherus of Rome and on his return became head of the community (HE 5, 4, 1; 5, 5, 8), his predecessor having died in the course of the persecution. He is last heard of around 190, addressing letters to various bishops, in particular to Victor of Rome, on the issues of the Quartodeciman controversy (HE 5, 24, 11 and 18) and is generally thought to have died in the course of the next decade. He may for all anyone knows have been martyred, but Gregory of Tours' report to that effect is not a reason for supposing so.

In addition to missives on the Quartodeciman controversy, Eusebius names three "letters" of Irenaeus "against those at Rome who were counterfeiting the sound ordinance of the church," and provides brief excerpts from two of them (HE 5, 20, 1). He also knows a writing "against the Greeks," entitled *On Knowledge* [*epistêmê*]; some discourses (or possibly dialogues) that refer to Hebrews and the *Wisdom of Solomon*; a work titled *Demonstration of the Apostolic Preaching* (HE 5, 26) and another titled *Exposure and Rebuttal of the "Knowledge"* [*gnôsis*] *Falsely so Named* (HE 5, 7, 1), which he also refers to as a treatise "against the heresies." Of all these works, only the last two can be read today. The treatise (in five books) *Against Heresies*—for the tradition has preferred Eusebius' short title to Irenaeus' long one—has been preserved in a complete Latin translation, with significant fragments of the original Greek as well as of Armenian and Syriac versions. The *Demonstration of the Apostolic Preaching* was for many centuries lost but was rediscovered towards the end of the nineteenth century in a complete Armenian translation. Unlike *Against Heresies*, which is lengthy, full of detours, and explicitly polemical in purpose, the *Demonstration* is a relatively brief and carefully designed work that seeks to show, for purposes of catechesis, how the basic content of baptismal instruction is attested in the Jewish Scriptures. It is not itself a work of catechesis, however, and the exposition reflects the author's concern for problems of heresy.

In *Against Heresies* Irenaeus makes it clear that in his judgment he has one advantage over previous opponents of Christian Gnosticism (from whom nevertheless he derives a great deal not only of his information about his heretics but also of his attitude towards them): namely, that he has read some of their treasured writings and therefore has a solid knowledge of their "hypothesis." By this term he meant essentially the plot structure of a set of myths that spoke of the procession of reality from the ultimate God, the "error" or "passion" to which this procession gave rise as being departed from its origin, and the restoration of all things to a state of peace and order. The laying out of this "hypothesis" in some of its different forms, and of the scriptural exegeses that were used to support it, is the principal business of Book 1. Irenaeus also makes it clear, however, that he agrees with Justin in tracing all heresy back to the figure of Simon Magus. This belief supports his notion that at base, in spite of its variety and inconsistencies, heresy is a single phenomenon. In fact, however, his (or Justin's) genealogy of heresy is as unnecessary for his argument as it is improbable; for his conviction about the unity of heresy reposes in the end on his observation of two or three fundamental points on which his opponents seem to him to agree and which at the same time differ basically from Christian faith as he, and others like him, understand it.

The first of these, and the one to which Irenaeus returns again and again, is Valentinian postulation of a "God above God": that is, of an ultimate Deity and a spiritual cosmos that alike transcend the Creator-God of Gn 1–3, who is demoted to the rank of a malign, or in some cases a merely ignorant artisan. This reduplication of deities and creations, which Irenaeus interpreted as deliberate blasphemy against the Creator, is closely connected with the second focus of disagreement: the Valentinian or Gnostic view that true humanity is "spirit" and not "body," that indeed the "self" of the Gnostic is simply a displaced spark of the spiritual overworld and that "body" is accordingly either a burden or an irrelevance from the point of view of human salvation. As far as Irenaeus was concerned, this view contradicted not only the widely accepted truth that a human self is a compound of soul and body, but more importantly the promise that the body would enjoy salvation (resurrection) through the gift of God's Spirit in baptism. Finally, Irenaeus thought that this set of beliefs, all of which were made explicit in the Gnostic "hypothesis," entailed a reduplication, even a quadruplication, of Christ-figures, each of whom seemed to represent a separate being, and none of whom could be said to have taken "flesh" in the usual sense of that term or to have undergone the sort of suffering Jesus had called upon his disciples to endure when it became necessary to "martyr."

Above and beyond such material points of difference, Irenaeus protested his opponents' exegesis not only of the Jewish Scriptures but also of the four gospels and the letters of Paul. These were writings that both sides in the controversy recognized as authoritative (with the notable exception of Marcion, whose special devotion to Paul required him to dispense with any gospel save a form of that attributed to Luke). In Irenaeus' view, the Scriptures had nothing whatever to say about events in an alleged spiritual realm prior to the divine act recorded at Gn 1:1; and, therefore, the attempts of gnostic teachers to harmonize the Scriptures with their "hypothesis" by ingenious allegorical exegeses of obscure passages were, he judged, necessarily fruitless. Irenaeus did not of course object to allegorical or typological exegesis as such and indeed practiced it himself. He did however believe that the Scriptures were simply silent about the subject matter of the greater part of the Gnostic "hypothesis" (which explains why he himself was reduced, in Book 2, to a form of refutation that excluded allusion to the Scriptures); and he was also certain that when his opponents misread the Scripture with regard to subject matters that it did address it was because their thinking continued to be governed by their false "hypothesis.'' He himself upheld ''the 'hypothesis' of the truth,'' also called ''the rule of faith'' or ''the rule of truth,'' as a summary guide to the Scriptures' teaching. By this he meant the plot of the myth of creation and redemption implicit in the churches' basic catechesis, which was given to converts as an explication of the threefold confession of faith (in God, God's Word, and God's Spirit) to be made at their baptism. Needless to say, he also maintained that this same ''hypothesis'' could be gathered by a normally intelligent reader from the clear and explicit materials in the Scriptures (though he conceded that the Scriptures were not available to folk who did not understand Greek).

The primary issue for Irenaeus was, of course, that of the status of the Creator-God of Gn 1, who for him was no inferior ''artisan'' but the one and only God. The establishment of this principle of ''one God the Father, from whom are all things'' (1 Cor 8:6) was the burden not only of *Against Heresies* 2, whose aim was to portray the Valentinian overworld and its ''God beyond God'' as a foolish fiction, but also of Book 4 and a significant portion of Book 3, which are governed by the positive aim of showing that the Creator, ever acting with, in, and through Son and Spirit, is the God both of the Law and Prophets and of the Christian dispensation. Appropriating a theme developed in the tradition of Hellenistic Judaism, Irenaeus envisages God as the one who ''contains all things'' but is contained by none, and thus as the transcendent ground of everything, who is nonetheless intimately present to all creatures as the context of their being. In accord with this picture, Irenaeus insists that matter itself, far from being the waste product of the process by which the spiritual world came to be, is a direct creation of God—a presupposition, this, of his belief that body as well as soul can ultimately participate in salvation.

To understand how the biblical history of humanity with God constitutes a unity and does not, as both Marcion and the Valentinians taught, fall into two or more contrary parts, Irenaeus made use of the term *oikonomia* (cf. Eph 1:10), meaning roughly the policy or plan that governs God's ''household management'' of the created order. He often used the word in the plural, recognizing that God's ''ways'' with humanity varied according to the circumstances and needs of the creature; but in the succession of these ''economies'' he saw the working out of an overall scheme whose aim it was to raise a creature of flesh and blood to fellowship with, and so participation in, the divine life. God had this aim in mind when Adam was created on the model, ''after the image,'' of the Christ who was to be the incarnate Word. The incarnation of the Word, then, was the fulfillment of God's promises and disciplines under the Mosaic covenant, and through it the Spirit came to dwell with humanity and to elevate it to new life in God. Irenaeus thus envisaged Adam and Eve, the original humans, as immature and saw the history of humanity's dealings with God as the continuation of that first creation, to be fulfilled not only or chiefly in a thousand-year reign of Christ on earth, but in a continuing growth in God's eternity.

Bibliography

A.   The most recent critical edition of *Against Heresies* (with French translation) is that of A. Rousseau, L. Doutreleau et al., *Irénée de Lyon: Contre les hérésies*, SC, 10 vols. (Paris, 1969–82); the edition of R. Massuet (Paris, 1710) is reprinted in PG 7. Also valuable is that of W. W. Harvey (Oxford, 1859); ET John Keble (London, 1872); and A. Roberts and W. H. Rambaut, ANF 1; Book 1 trans. D. J. Unger, ACW 55 (New York, 1992); *The Demonstration of the Apostolic Preaching*, ed. and trans. into German K. Mekerttschian and E. Minassiantz, TU 31, 1 (Leipzig, 1907); trans. into English, J. A. Robinson (London, 1920); and with annotations by J. P. Smith, ACW 16 (Westminster, Md. 1952).

B.   DSAM 7:1923–69; DTC 7:2394–2533; EEC 1:413–16; NCE 7:631–32; ODCC 846–47; TRE 16:258–68; J. Lawson, *The Biblical Theology of Saint Irenaeus* (London, 1948); G. Wingren, *Man and the Incarnation: A Study in the Biblical Theology of Irenaeus*, trans. R. MacKenzie (Edinburgh, 1959); A. Benoit, *Saint Irénée. Introduction à l'étude de sa théologie* (Paris, 1960); P. Bacq, *De l'ancienne à la nouvelle alliance selon saint Irénée* (Paris, 1978); Y. de Andia, *Homo vivens. Incorruptibilité et divinisation de l'homme selon Irénée de Lyon* (Paris, 1986); A. Orbe, *Espiritualidad de San Ireneo* (Rome, 1989); D. Minns, *Irenaeus* (London, 1994); Robert M. Grant, *Irenaeus of Lyons* (London, 1997).

Richard A. Norris

ISIDORE OF SEVILLE (ca. 560–April, 636). *Education*: born to a Roman family, probably in Cartagena; received an ecclesiastical education. *Career*: bishop of Seville, ca. 600, succeeding his brother, Leander; presided at the Second Council of Seville, 619; probably presided at the Fourth Council of Toledo, 633.

Isidore's works include: *Differentiae*, which analyzes word meanings; *De natura rerum*, on physics, written for the Visigoth King Sisebutus (612–20); *Liber numerorum*, on the numbers that appear in Scripture; *Sententiae*, concerning doctrine and morals, the first book of sentences; and *Etymologiarum libri XX*, the work for which he is best remembered.

In the *Etymologiae*, a link between the culture of Late Antiquity and that of the Middle Ages, Isidore treats grammar, rhetoric, all areas of mathematics, law, chronology, human anatomy and physiology, cosmography, geography, military science, architecture, and natural science. The theological books (6–8) deal with the duties of clerics, God, order, the rule of faith, the church, and the different Christian sects.

Isidore's guiding compositional principle in the *Etymologiae* is his attitude towards word origins, and its dictionary method developed as much because of his philosophy of education as for its convenience. Isidore trusted that well-defined and well-analyzed words would naturally take their place in the whole scheme of learning and understanding.

Bibliography

A.   CPL 1186–1229; PL 82–83; *Etimologías*, trans. José Reta (Madrid, 1982).

B.   DSAM 7:2104–16; DTC 8:98–111; LThK³ 5:618–20; NCE 7:674–76; ODCC

851–52; TRE 16:310–15; Ernest Brehaut, *An Encyclopedist of the Dark Ages: Isidore of Seville* (New York, 1912); Pierre Cazier, *Isidore de Séville et la naissance de l'Espagne catholique* (Paris, 1994).

Thomas S. Ferguson

J

JAMES OF VITERBO (ca. 1255, Viterbo–1308, Naples). *Education*: studied philosophy and theology, Paris; received his bachelor's degree, 1288, and became a master, 1293. *Career*: entered the Order of Hermits of St. Augustine, ca. 1270; succeeded Giles of Rome and was regent master in 1293–1300; bishop of Benevento, 1302–3; archbishop of Naples, 1303–8.

James was known for being inventive and speculative; he composed a large number of *Quodlibeta* discussions (e.g., 32 *De praedicamentis in divinis*, 50 *De spiritu sancto*). Directed by the general chapter in 1295 to the study of Scripture, he produced commentaries on Matthew, Luke, and Paul, but these have not survived. In 1300 he was placed in charge of the *studium generale* founded in Naples. In the controversies in March to September of 1302 James composed, and dedicated to Boniface VIII, the earliest known treatise on the church, *De regimine christiano*. James was a strong defender of the rights of the papacy, asserting that papal power was also kingly power, but in this he kept his argumentation on the theological level in the conflict between Boniface VIII and Philip IV. In general his work is more a series of assertions than a strictly argued tract. James spent his last years reconstructing Naples' cathedral. He was beatified in 1914. In the past his theological writings drew more attention than his ideas on church and state, but shifting currents of interest have drawn more attention to these latter, and he is seen as a strong proponent of papal rights.

Bibliography

A. *James of Viterbo: On Christian Government*, ed. R. W. Dyson (Woodbridge, N.Y., 1995).

B. DTC 8:305–9; LThK³ 5:732; NCE 7:813; John F. Whippel, "The Relationship between Essence and Existence in Late-13th Century Thought: Giles of Rome, Henry of

Ghent, Godfrey of Fontaines and James of Viterbo,'' in *Philosophies of Existence Ancient and Medieval*, ed. P. Morewedge (New York, 1982), 131–64.

Thomas E. Morrissey

JAN HUS. *See* HUS, JAN.

JANSENIUS (JANSEN), CORNELIUS (28 October 1585, Leerdam, Holland– 6 May 1638, Ypres, Belgium). *Education*: philosophical and theological studies, Louvain, 1602–9; Univ. of Paris, 1609–11; doctorate in theology, Univ. of Paris, 1617. *Career*: head of a school (''college''), Bayonne, France, 1611–14; ordained priest, 1614; rector, new college of St. Pulcheria for Dutch students, 1617–24; professor of theology and Scripture, Louvain, 1618–35; rector, Univ. of Louvain, 1635–36; bishop of Ypres (Ieper), 1636–38.

Jansen was a Louvainian scholar whose posthumously published *Augustinus* (1640) precipitated the long-lasting Jansenist controversy and movement. The original issue was divine grace and human freedom, how they were to be reconciled in the Augustinian tradition. The Council of Trent insisted both that God's grace was absolutely necessary at every step along the way to faith and conversion and that the human response to grace was a voluntary one, for ''one can also reject'' grace. Concurrently a theory on the harmony of grace and free will was developed in the form of Molinism (see Luis de Molina*). It had been discussed in the papal court from 1597 to 1607, in the ad hoc *Congregatio de Auxiliis*—without result, except for an admonition not to publish further on the subject until the papal decision was made known. The decision not having come, this admonition was widely ignored. Another ruling about not indulging in charges of heresy over the question was better observed.

Jansen determined to study the question. He took altogether seriously the injunction of Pope Clement VIII to regard the writings of St. Augustine of Hippo,* the *doctor gratiae*, as *the* authentic guide to a Catholic solution. This papal enthusiasm for St. Augustine was unfortunate in that it did not fully reflect the previous Catholic theological tradition, which was anxious to put Augustine into a broader context. Popes had always avoided canonizing the more extreme Augustinian positions. Jansen nevertheless proceeded to retrieve everything that Augustine had written on the grace question and put it into systematic order, on the assumption that Augustine's views, once they were more fully and exactly comprehended, would prevail. He wound up, like the older Augustine, asserting human freedom and responsibility while championing the supremacy and necessity of God's all-conquering grace to the point of rendering human beings practically powerless to resist grace; nor would this grace be available always or to everyone, even newborns.

His book finished, he caught the plague and died, leaving instructions on its publication. Had he lived longer, he might have been reminded about Sixtus V's injunction not to call one's Catholic adversaries heretics (which Jansen did by drawing parallels). An unscrupulous campaign against the dead bishop's book ensued. Several paraphrases (see DS 2001–2006) were eventually derived from the *Augustinus*, out of context, and condemned as offensive and heretical in the 1653 constitution, *Cum occasione*, of Innocent X. The followers of Molina in the Society of Jesus had snatched a late victory out of their near-defeat in the *De Auxiliis* hearings.

Jansen's *Augustinus* can now be viewed as an impressive early work of "positive" or historical theology, retrieving with unprecedented exactitude and fullness the thought of Saint Augustine on the need for grace and the utter insufficiency of human beings, without grace, to find favor with God. Other historians of doctrine, such as Denis Pétau* (Petavius, S.J., 1583–1653), were able to correct Jansen's—and Augustine's—one-sidedness. Instead of allowing research to correct research, however, historical issues were thought amenable to canonical decisions, vitiating the controversy and prolonging its negative effects.

Bibliography

A. *Augustinus*, 3 vols. (Louvain 1640; repr. in one vol., Frankfurt, 1964); *Pentateuchus seu Commentarius in quinque libros Moysis* (Louvain, 1639); *Tetrateuchus seu Commentarius in quattuor Evangelia* (Louvain, 1639); *Analecta in Proverbia* (Louvain, 1644); *Correspondance de Jansénius*, ed. Jean Orcibal (Louvain, 1947).

B. LThK³ 5:744–45; NCE 7:818–19; *Nationaal Biografisch Woordenboek* 9:393–417; TRE 16:502–9; Jacques Gres-Gayer, "Jansénisme," *Dictionnaire historique de la papauté* (Paris, 1994), 921–24; J. van Bavel and M. Schrama, eds., *Jansénius et le Jansénisme dans les Pays Bas: Mélanges Lucien Ceyssens* (Leuven, 1982); *L'Image de C. Jansénius*, ed. E. J. M. van Eijl (Leuven, 1987); J. Orcibal, *Jansénius d'Ypres (1585–1638)* (Paris, 1989); L. Dupré, "Jansenius, an Intellectual Biography," JR 73 (1993): 75–82; A. Vanneste, "Pour une relecture critique de l'*Augustinus* de Jansénius," *Augustiniana* 44 (1994): 115–36, repr. in *Nature et grâce dans la théologie occidentale: Dialogue avec H. de Lubac*, A. Vanneste (Leuven, 1996), 229–50.

Paul Misner

JAN VAN RUYSBROECK. *See* RUYSBROECK, JAN VAN.

JEAN BRIÈVECUISSE, JEAN COURTECUISSE. *See* JOHN OF BREVICOXA.

JEAN GERSON. *See* GERSON, JEAN.

JEROME, Eusebius Hieronymus (ca. 347–419). Prolific writer, translator, traveler, and controversialist, Jerome was trained in Rome, where he was also baptized. By the middle of the fourth century, tales of the great desert ascetics reached the West with the result that Jerome, like many in the educated and aristocratic circles, embraced ascetic aims. After a short stay in Antioch, Jerome dwelt in the desert region of Chalcis from ca. 375 to 377, a time that he came to loathe on account of the severities of a solitary existence, although he later idealized the experience in his *Life of Malchus*. For the rest of his life Jerome's writings advocated a Christian spirituality founded upon withdrawal from the world, scriptural study, and placing sacred devotion before familial ties.

Jerome returned to Rome and there, having become secretary to the bishop Damasus, actively promoted the ascetic lifestyle already current among noble women such as Paula and Eustochium. A scandal erupted when Paula's daughter, Blesilla, died as a result of extreme fasting encouraged by an unapologetic Jerome. Shortly thereafter Jerome retired from the city never to return and, along with Paula, founded monastic communities for men and women in Bethlehem. By this time Jerome was defending the superiority of communal asceticism as more suitable than the eremetic life for developing the Christian virtues. Besides his copious correspondence, Jerome's major literary contributions lay in the following areas.

Biblical versions. Jerome is perhaps best known for his translation of the Bible into Latin, known as the Vulgate. In fact, however, he began by correcting New and Old Testament books of the Old Latin in accordance with the Septuagint and the Greek New Testament. Only after moving to Bethlehem and becoming familiar with the writings of Origen* did he discover the serious shortcomings of the Septuagint when compared with the Hebrew. He began translating the Old Testament anew from Hebrew into Latin, completing the task by 404/5. The new translation caused much consternation among Christian communities, including Augustine's,* long accustomed to the translation of the Septuagint. Of the New Testament, Jerome seems to have retranslated only the gospels; the rest of the New Testament was done by a later hand.

Translation of Commentaries. From the time of his first journey to Antioch, Jerome became acquainted with the Greek exegetical tradition, especially that of Origen. He translated many of Origen's commentaries and homilies on biblical texts. Despite Jerome's later rejection of Origenist theology, the bulk of his translations were adapted from Origen's commentaries and theological syntheses. He also translated Didymus of Alexandria's *On the Holy Spirit*. Jerome himself wrote commentaries on several books of the Old Testament, some epistles of Paul, the gospel of Mt, and the Apocalypse.

Historical. Jerome translated Eusebius'* *Chronicle*, which he freely emended, and added a continuation of the text up to the year 378. He also used material from Eusebius' *Ecclesiastical History*, while taking the form from Suetonius' registry of famous Roman rhetors and grammarians, to write an ecclesiastical version of *On Illustrious Men*.

Polemical. Against the monk Helvidius, Jerome defended the perpetual virginity of Mary; this book was the first Latin treatise devoted to Mariology. Against Jovinian, Jerome defended the superior merit of ascetic living, though he failed to convince other detractors that his views denigrated the holiness of marriage. He attacked Vigilantius for the latter's opposition to the excesses of martyr cults. Jerome published a tract against Lucifer of Cagliari, set in dialogue form, which accepted the necessity of a strong anti-Arian position while advocating communion for penitent bishops who signed the creed of Ariminum (359). Using the same format, Jerome wrote three books *Against the Pelagians* and three books against his former companion and scholarly contemporary, Rufinus.

Monastic. Based upon the model of the famous *Life of Antony*, Jerome wrote three *Lives*, almost certainly fictional; of Paul, Antony's more saintly predecessor; Hilarion, a disciple of Antony; and Malchus. In each of these accounts, the holiness and power (*virtus*) of the famous Antony is rivalled. Late in life Jerome fulfilled a request by translating the *Rule of Pachomius*.

Bibliography

A.   CPL, 580–621; Patrology 4, 212–46.

B.   DSAM 8:901–18; DTC 8:894–983; LThK³ 5:91–93; NCE 7:872–74; ODCC 867–68; TRE 15:304–15; F. Cavallera, *Saint Jérôme: Sa vie et son oeuvre*, 2 vols. (Paris, 1922); J. N. D. Kelly, *Jerome: His Life, Writings and Controversies* (London, 1975); Ch. Piétri, *Roma Christiana*, 2 vols. (Rome, 1976); *Jérôme entre l'Occident et l'Orient: XVIᵉ centenaire du départ de saint Jérôme de Rome et de son installation à Bethléem*, ed. Y.-M. Duval (Paris, 1988); Stefan Rebenich, *Hieronymus und sein Kreis: Prosopographische und sozialgeschichtliche Untersuchungen* (Stuttgart, 1992); Adam Kamesar, *Jerome, Greek Scholarship, and the Hebrew Bible* (New York, 1993); S. D. Driver, "The Development of Jerome's Views on the Ascetic Life," RTAM 62 (1995): 44–70; Catherine Tkacz, " 'Labor tam Utilis': The Creation of the Vulgate," VC 50 (1996): 42–72.

Daniel H. Williams

JEWEL, JOHN (24 May 1522, Buden in the parish of Berimber, Devonshire, England–23 September 1571, Monkton Farleigh, Wiltshire). *Education*: studied at Merton Coll., Oxford, 1535–39; B.A., M.A., Corpus Christi Coll., Oxford, 1540, 1545. *Career*: fellow, Corpus Christi Coll., 1542–53; vicar, Sunningwell, 1551–53; teacher on the continent, 1555–59; bishop, Salisbury, 1560–71.

Jewel was a reform bishop of Salisbury and a noted defender of the Elizabethan Settlement in England against the Roman Catholic Church. He defended the Reformation settlement of 1559 against the criticisms of the Roman Catholic Church just as Richard Hooker* later defended it against the Puritans. Jewel was greatly influenced by Peter Martyr* (Pietro Martire Vermigli), the Protestant reformer from Italy, who came to Oxford in 1547 as Regius professor of divinity. On the accession of Queen Mary in 1553, Jewel lost his fellowship and was forced to flee from England. He was a Marian exile at Frankfurt in March 1555 but joined Martyr at Strasbourg soon thereafter and then the next year followed him to Zurich. When Mary died in 1558, Jewel returned to England and on 21 January 1560 he was consecrated bishop of Salisbury, where he served until his death.

Jewel was chosen to lead the literary offensive against the Roman Catholics who met at the Council of Trent, 1545–63, to define their position against the Protestants. The Roman Catholic critics saw in Protestantism the multiplication of sects and gross immorality, which resulted from the Protestants' lawlessness and irreligion because of their doctrine of justification by faith and their repudiation of the doctrine of papal authority. Protestants and members of the Church of England were seen as immoral, heretical, divisive, and schismatic. Jewel was commissioned to answer these accusations, and in 1562 he published in Latin his *Apologia pro Ecclesia Anglicana*, which was the first systematic statement of the Church of England against the Church of Rome. It was translated into English as *An Apology of the Church of England.*

The *Apology* had a twofold purpose: (1) to present the truth and refute the rumors about the Church of England and (2) to show the errors of the papacy, which prevented the English from joining the Council of Trent. He defended the Church of England as the true church and insisted that the English Reformation was the restoration of the true church in England after the Roman medieval abuses. He denounced transubstantiation, purgatory, the celibacy of clergy, and the worship of saints and images as "trifles, follies, and baubles." Using Scripture and the first four ecumenical councils, Jewel defended the two sacraments of baptism and Eucharist, communion in both kinds, and the threefold orders of bishops, presbyters, and deacons. He insisted that the practices of the Church of England were older and thus better than later Roman innovations.

Bibliography

A.   *The Works of John Jewel*, ed. John Ayre, 4 vols. (Cambridge, 1845–1550); *An Apology of the Church of England*, ed. John E. Booty (Ithaca, N.Y., 1963).

B.   DNB 10:815–19; LThK[3] 5:848–49; NCE 7:971–72; ODCC 875–76; OEncR 2: 338–39; John E. Booty, *John Jewel as Apologist of the Church of England* (London, 1963).

Donald S. Armentrout

JIMÉNEZ DE CISNEROS. *See* XIMÉNES DE CISNEROS, FRANCISCO.

JOACHIM OF FIORE (ca. 1135, Celico–30 March 1202, Petrafitta). *Career:* son of a notary of the Sicilian court; junior chancery official; pilgrimage to Holy Land, 1167, after which he dedicated his life to God; lived as a hermit on Mt. Etna, then as a wandering preacher in Calabria; ordained priest; entered Benedictine abbey at Corazzo in 1171, of which he became prior, then abbot ca. 1176–77; campaigned to have abbey incorporated into Cistercian order; multiple visions at Abbey of Casamari in 1183–84, which revealed to him the fullness and harmony (*concordia*) of the Scriptures and the mystery of the Trinity; worked on three of his major works during these years *(Psalterium decem chordarum, Liber concordie Novi ac Veteris Testamenti,* and *Expositio in Apocalypsim)*; met with Pope Lucius III (1184); left Corazzo with papal permission in 1186; founded monastery of San Giovanni in Fiore and the order of "Florensians" in 1188; met with Richard Lion-Heart at Messina, 1191; met with Emperor Henry VI in Palermo in 1194, who became a generous patron of Joachim's monastery; wrote a fourth long work, the *Tractatus super Quatuor*

Evangelia (never completed); retreated to San Martino di Giove in 1201, shortly before his death the following year.

Monastic founder and theoretician, visionary, prophet, consultant to popes and emperors, and Christian millenarian, Joachim is probably best known for his highly inventive and abidingly influential theology of history, a theology based on intensive study of the Scriptures. Convinced that the inner mystery of God's existence as a Trinity of Persons was linked with the structure of history, Joachim saw salvation history unfolding in terms of three successive, overlapping "ages" (*status*), each primarily under the aegis of one of the persons of the Trinity. Each *status* is also characterized by a particular way of life, or *ordo*.

The *status* of the Father, which is coterminous with Old Testament history, began with Adam and ended with the coming of Christ. Its characteristic way of life was that of the married (*ordo coniugatorum*). Since the three *status* are overlapping, those of the Son and the Holy Spirit have their beginnings (*germinationes*) in the previous *status*. The status of the Son, begun with King Josiah, began to bear fruit in Christ and would end, Joachim speculated, around the end of the twelfth century. Its characteristic way of life was that of clerics (*ordo clericorum*). The *status* of the Holy Spirit had its beginning with St. Benedict, would come to fruition in the last days, and would last until the end of the world. Its characteristic way of life was that of monks (*ordo monachorum*). In the coming third *status*, a sort of monastic utopia, the faithful would enjoy a spiritual understanding of both scriptural Testaments and a joyful contemplative understanding of divine things in an age of peace that would endure until the final persecution of Gog.

This intricate theology of history is based on an equally complex hermeneutical theory. For Joachim, one of the major objectives of scriptural exegesis was to demonstrate the numerous literal parallels or concordances (*concordiae*) between Old and New Testament history. These *concordiae* not only shed light on the past but could also reveal the future. The gifted exegete could see in both Testaments (above all in the Apocalypse) sets of concordances, which enabled him not merely to understand the first two *status* more fully but to predict the structure and meaning of the dawning third *status* of history.

In 1215 the Fourth Lateran Council condemned Joachim's trinitarian doctrine. Later in the thirteenth century, his theology of history was used in a variety of ways, some of which were condemned as heretical. The Franciscan Gerard of Borgo San Donnino identified Joachim's three major works as the Eternal Gospel destined to supersede the Bible in the coming third *status*, for which a papal commission condemned him. Thomas Aquinas* attacked his threefold theology of history and denounced him as uninstructed in the subtle dogmas of faith. On the other hand, Dante immortalized him in the *Divina Commedia* as one "endowed with the prophetic spirit." Some have seen him as a Marx before Marx whose Christian utopianism anticipated elements of revolutionary communism. Others have even argued, quite unconvincingly, that Hitler's millennial expectations were based on Joachite speculation. Both Yeats and Jung appropriated his ideas. Whatever one's opinion of those ideas, and however those ideas have been garbled by enthusiasts, there is no doubt that Joachim ranks, along with Augustine,* as an original and influential theologian of Christian history.

Bibliography

A. *Expositio in Apocalypsim* (Venice, 1527); *Psalterium decem chordarum* (Frankfurt, 1527); *Tractatus super quatuor Evangelia,* ed. E. Buonaiuti (Rome, 1930); *Il libro delle figure,* ed. L. Tondelli et al. (Turin, 1953); *Liber de Concordia Novi ac Veteris Testamenti,* ed. E. R. Daniel (Philadelphia, 1983).

B. DSAM 8:1179–1201; DTC 8:1426–58; LThK³ 5:853–54; NCE 7:990–91; ODCC 878; TRE 17:84–88; M. Bloomfield, "Joachim of Flora: A Critical Survey of His Canon, Sources, Biography and Influence," *Traditio* 13 (1957): 249–311; M. Reeves, *The Influence of Prophecy in the Later Middle Ages* (Notre Dame, Ind., 1969); H. Grundmann, *Ausgewählte Aufsätze* (Stuttgart, 1977); B. McGinn, *The Calabrian Abbot* (New York, 1985).

Kevin Madigan

JOHN OF BREVICOXA, or Jean Courtecuisse or Brièvecuisse, *Doctor sublimis* (ca. 1350, Alaines, Normandy–4 March 1423, Geneva). French theologian and statesman; from 1367 on, studied and taught at Paris, where he received degrees in arts and theology; dean of the theological faculty there, 1416–21; elected bishop of Paris, 1420; bishop of Geneva, 1422–23.

John worked for the healing of the Western Schism, and favored the resignation of both popes; later, he urged withdrawing obedience from Benedict XIII. Benedict threatened Frenchmen disloyal to him with excommunication. John delivered a violent speech, which contained thirteen accusations against Benedict; it was burned in Paris in 1408. He took part in conferences at Pisa and Rome. In 1420, he was elected bishop of Paris, but Henry V of England, who controlled Paris, prevented him from entering the city. Pope Martin V transferred him to Geneva in 1422. Most of his large literary output remains in manuscript form. John was a conciliarist and held that a general council could teach infallibly, while the pope could err in matters of faith and, in case of heresy, could be deposed by a council.

Bibliography

A. Works in manuscript in the Bibliothèque Nationale in Paris. *Tractatus de fide et ecclesia, de Romano pontifice et concilio generali,* printed in *Opera Gersonii,* ed. L.-E. Dupin (Paris, 1706).

B. DSAM 8:404–6; DTC 3:1984–85; LThK³ 5:894; A. Coville, "Recherches sur Jean Courtecuisse et ses oeuvres oratoires," *Bibliothèque de l'école de Chartres* 65 (1904): 469–529.

Joseph T. Lienhard

JOHN CAPREOLUS. *See* CAPREOLUS, JOHN.

JOHN CASSIAN (ca. 365–ca. 433). A native of the Balkans (probably the Roman province of Scythia Minor), the young Cassian, with his friend Germanus, sojourned in Egypt, learning from the desert fathers the ways of cenobitic monasticism. Around 399, events surrounding the Origenist controversy drove him from Egypt to Constantinople, where he was ordained a deacon by John Chrysostom.* After some years in Rome, he came to Marseilles, where, ca. 415, he founded two monasteries.

Cassian, who depends upon Origen* and Evagrius* Ponticus, represents an important bridge between East and West. Two major works, the *De institutis coenobiorum* and the *Conlationes*, treat the theory and practice of the monastic life. These represent his real contribution to Christian literature: introducing the legacy of Egyptian monasticism to Gallic monks. His work *On the Incarnation of the Lord against Nestorius* is undistinguished.

The *Institutes* and the *Conferences* teach the pursuit of Christian perfection through a life of obedience, continence, contemplation, and prayer, with continual meditation on Scripture. Cassian's thirteenth *Conference* was perhaps a veiled attack on Augustine's* predestinationism, since it stresses the complementarity of the divine will and human effort.

Bibliography

A. *Conlationes*: CSEL 13; SC 42, 54, 64; *De institutis coenobiorum*: CSEL 17; SC 109; *De incarnatione*: CSEL 17.

B. DSAM 2:214–53; DTC 2:1823–29; LThK³ 5:888–90; NCE 3:181–83; ODCC 295; TRE 7:650–57; Philip Rousseau, "Cassian, Contemplation, and the Coenobitic Life," JEH 26 (1975): 113–26; Adalbert de Vogüé, "Pour comprendre Cassien: Un survoi des Conférences," *Collectanea Cisterciensia* 39 (1977): 250–72; Columba Stewart, *Cassian the Monk* (Oxford, 1997).

Thomas A. Smith

JOHN CHRYSOSTOM (ca. 340/50, Antioch–14 September 407, Comanna in Pontus). *Education*: studied philosophy and rhetoric under Andragathius and Libanius, Antioch; studied at monastic school of Diodore, ca. 367; hermit in mountains outside of Antioch, ca. 371–77. *Career*: ordained lector, Antioch, 371; ordained deacon, 381; ordained priest, 386–98; patriarch of Constantinople, 398–404; exiled to Cucusus in Armenia, 404–7.

Chrysostom is generally regarded as the most prominent preacher of the early church. (His appellation *Chrysostomus*, "golden-mouth," was given by a later generation). The corpus of his sermons, homiletical commentaries, treatises, and letters is considerable. Chrysostom has frequently been regarded as more a moralist than a theologian, but this view overlooks the considerable theological content in his work. Though not a source of original, speculative theology, Chrysostom does evaluate, and elaborate on, the major theological issues of his day, particularly the themes raised in the later Arian controversy.

Chrysostom was influenced by the high classical culture and worldliness of

Antioch. His early intellectual development included his tutelage under the great rhetorician, Libanius, who reportedly said on his deathbed that John would have been his successor if the Christians had not stolen him. John was baptized in 368 and, instead of pursuing a secular vocation, came under the care and instruction of Meletius, bishop of Antioch. In 372 John removed himself from the city to live for three years in a semi-isolated state in the hills outside Antioch. Ascetic excesses forced him back and permanently affected his health. He became lector, then deacon, then priest in the church of Antioch and witnessed the ongoing theological tensions with the neo-Arians (Anomoeans) that occupied the attention of Bishop Meletius and his successor, Flavian. He was also influenced at this time by his teacher Diodore of Tarsus, who favored historical exegesis.

Having already begun his literary activity during his days as a deacon (*On the Priesthood* and other treatises on the lives of monks and clerics), John preached one of his earliest series of sermons against Anomoean theology (*On the Incomprehensible Nature of God*), and another against Christians who were following Jewish ceremonial practices (*Against the Jews*) while still a priest. Over the next twelve years, as his fame as homilist grew, John's literary output was at its greatest. In 398 Chrysostom was compelled to become bishop of Constantinople. But his rustic temperament was ill suited for the role, resulting eventually in exile where he died.

His major exegetical series are works on Gn, Mt, Jn, and six New Testament letters, many of them transcribed sermons, but some perhaps exegetical commentaries in homiletical form, all of which take a historical-exegetical approach.

John's theological interests included the distinctiveness of Christian (vs. pagan) belief, the relationship of Christianity to Judaism, the way of salvation, and pastoral calling. But by far the most frequent theological issue that John addressed was the person of Christ: the relationship of Father to Son, the particularities of the incarnate life of the Son, and the relationship of the human and divine natures.

Past studies have most often portrayed Chrysostom as a classic representative of the so-called Antiochene Christology. Although Chrysostom's exegetical method is essentially the same as that of other theologians from Antioch, his underlying theological perspective on Christ is closer to the mainstream emphasis on one divine subject in the incarnate Christ. The divinity of Christ is Chrysostom's central doctrinal concern, as evidenced in his exegetical treatment of texts used by the various parties of the trinitarian controversy and in his polemical homilies against the Anomoeans. On the question of the humanity of Christ, Chrysostom takes account of the genuineness of the flesh and its attendant needs and vulnerabilities but does not stress the importance of the existence and functions of a human soul in Christ. He understands the relationship of the two natures as a union and conjunction, but not a confusion. When he distinguishes the humanity of Christ from his divinity, he is identifying not a distinct human nature as much as the incarnate nature of Christ—both human and divine—that exists after the union. Chrysostom frequently uses the concept of condescension, *sygkatabasis*, to explain how the divine Logos demonstrates human attributes in the Incarnation (*oikonomia*).

Bibliography

A.   NPNF 1, 9–14; PG 47–64.

B.   DSAM 8:331–55; DTC 8:660–90; LThK³ 5:889–92; NCE 7:1041–44; ODCC 342–43; TRE 17:118–27; Chrysostomus Baur, *John Chrysostom and His Time*, 2 vols. (Westminster, Md. 1959–60); R. Wilken, *John Chrysostom and the Jews* (Berkeley, Calif., 1983); R. Krupp, *Shepherding the Flock of God: The Pastoral Theology of John Chrysostom* (New York, 1991); J. N. D. Kelly, *Golden Mouth* (Ithaca, N.Y., 1995); M. Lawrenz, *The Christology of John Chrysostom* (Lewiston, N.Y., 1996).

Mel Lawrenz

JOHN OF THE CROSS (1542, Fontiveros, Spain–14 December 1591, Úbeda, Spain). *Education*: studied at the Jesuit Coll., Medina del Campo, Spain, 1559–63; studied arts and theology, Univ. of Salamanca, 1564–68. *Career*: entered Carmelites, Medina del Campo, 1563; ordained priest, 1567; entered first Discalced monastery for men, Duruelo, 1568; rector, Carmelite Coll. at the Univ. of Alcalá de Henares, 1572; vicar and confessor, Teresa of Avila's* monastery of the Incarnation, 1572; abducted and imprisoned, Carmelite friary at Toledo, 1577; escaped, August of 1578; administrative positions in the Carmelites, 1578–91; beatified, 1675; canonized, 1726; declared a doctor of the church, 1926; feast, 14 December.

Juan de Yepes, known as Juan de San Matiá as a Carmelite, then as Juan de la Cruz, had as his principal ministry spiritual guidance for Carmelite nuns and friars, laity, and clergy. His writings resulted from this ministry. His poems, especially the three major poems, "The Spiritual Canticle," "The Dark Night," and "The Living Flame of Love," report John's mystical experience. Commentaries (*The Ascent of Mount Carmel, The Dark Night, The Spiritual Canticle, and The Living Flame of Love*) were written for directees. John's *Sayings of Light and Love* recall, in form, the Sayings of the Desert. John's prologues offer help in reading his commentaries. John's letters (only thirty-three survive) reveal his compassionate nature.

John of the Cross is perhaps best known for his description of the dark night, the pain and suffering that accompany the purification/liberation of the senses and spirit as one passes from the practice of meditation to the gift of contemplation. Yet, John's writings celebrate equally the fire of love that brings one to divine union. *The Living Flame of Love*, a commentary on John's deepest experience of God, contains a theology of the Holy Spirit as the principal guide on the journey to union with God in love.

Neoscholasticism neglected John's poetry, much of which is laced with the imagery of the Song of Songs, and it tended to see John's doctrine in overly categorical terms, missing the biblical character of his teaching.

Bibliography

A.   *The Collected Works of Saint John of the Cross*, rev. ed. trans. Kieran Kavanaugh and Otilio Rodriguez (Washington, D.C., 1991).

B.   DSAM 8:407–47; LThK³ 5:927–29; NCE 7:1045–47; ODCC 890–91; OEncR 2: 351–52; TRE 17:134–40; *God Speaks in the Night; The Life, Times, and Teaching of St. John of the Cross*, trans. Kieran Kavanaugh (Washington, D.C., 1991).

Keith J. Egan

JOHN OF DAMASCUS (ca. 675–ca. 749). *Career*: Born of a family prominent in the civil service of the Damascus caliphate, John followed the family tradition until he entered monastic life around the year 700. He was never ordained to the priesthood, but remained a simple monk at the monastery of Mar Sabba in Palestine. John made major contributions to the church as a theologian, as a defender, especially of icons during the iconoclastic controversy, and finally as a hymnologist. As a theologian, John summarized the theological thought of the preceding six centuries in *Fount of Wisdom*, especially Book Three, "The Exact Exposition of the Orthodox Faith." This remains a work of penetrating brevity and concision. His *Treatises in Defense of the Holy Icons* during the iconoclastic controversy led directly to their vindication at the seventh ecumenical council at Nicaea in 787, two generations after his death. He was also one of the early church's greatest hymnologists. Taking up the poetic form of the canon, perhaps from Andrew of Crete and certainly together with his contemporary and fellow Mar Sabbaite Cosmas of Maiouma, John's compositions permanently influenced the Byzantine liturgy (e.g. the texts of the Paschal matins and of the funeral service).

Other important works credited to John of Damascus include funeral and paschal canons, and several homilies on the church's great solemnities, especially the *Homily on the Transfiguration*. All are of value as much for historical as for theological reasons, as is his compendious summary of Christian heresies. Another important work, *Sacra Parallela*, preserved only in fragments, collects scriptural and patristic sources on the ethical and ascetical life. His work was translated into Latin and influenced such Western theologians as Thomas Aquinas.*

These are the details, and there is regrettably little more. John has suffered neglect at scholarly hands because of the periodization favored by an earlier era of scholars. His position in the older schema as "last" of the Eastern "Fathers" finds him thus usually occupying the place of a relatively unoriginal—if highly intelligent—compiler of the prior tradition and thus also as a stepping stone to the newly creative age of medieval scholasticism. Yet, although there is some truth to this earlier classification, it must be recalled that John faced several new challenges, Islam and the imperial iconoclasm of Byzantium most notable among them. He was also active in an era and a place, the still largely Christian Palestine of early Ummayyad rule, that carried on a strikingly lively and, due to the isolation imposed by Muslim conquest, largely isolated intellectual and spiritual tradition. His own name is traditionally attached to the translation and propagation, in Christianized form, of the life of the Buddha (the story of Saints Barlaam and Joasaph), while his monastery, Mar Sabba, was in his lifetime and for at least a century afterwards the locus of a striking confluence of Christian traditions in the near East, Greek and Syriac. Its most striking achievement was the translation into Greek, during the early ninth century, of the corpus of the great Nestorian mystic, Isaac of Nineveh, but incorporating the writings of other East Syrian spiritual writers as well. John's own work, for example the "Homily on the Transfiguration," was a part of this ascetico-spiritual current, which would later reemerge so prominently in such writers as Symeon the New Theologian* (d. 1022) and Gregory Palamas.* His creative efforts for the justification of the sacred images involved the adaptation of ancient Christian treatments of scriptural exegesis to ecclesiastical art, together with an extensive grasp of both ancient philosophy and the theology of the Christological controversies. His polemical confrontation with Islam was among the earliest such efforts and later quite influential. Both icons and Islam are again on the scholarly agenda, as the bibliography below indicates, but the setting of this activity, John's Palestine, has only just begun to receive the attention that is its due.

Bibliography

A.   CPG 8040–70; *Exposition of the Orthodox Faith*, NPNF 2, 9, 1–101; *St. John Damascene: Barlaam and Joasaph*, intro. D. M. Lang (London and Cambridge, Mass., 1967); "Homily on the Transfiguration of Our Lord Jesus Christ," GOTR 32 (1987): 1–29; *Ecrits sur l'Islam*, ed. and trans. Raymond Le Coz, SC 383 (Paris, 1992); "Homily on the Withered Fig Tree and the Parable of the Vineyard," *Epiphany* 13 (1993): 25–29.

B.   DSAM 5:476–86, 8:452–66; DTC 8:693–751; LThK³ 5:894–95; NCE 7:1047–49; ODCC 891–92; TRE 17:127–32; Daniel J. Sahas, *John of Damascus on Islam: The "Heresy of the Ishmaelites"* (Leiden, 1972); Thomas Noble, "John Damascene and the History of the Iconoclastic Controversy," *Religion, Culture and Society in the Early Middle Ages*, ed. T. Noble and J. Contreni (Kalamazoo, Mich., 1987), 95–116; D. J. Sahas, "*Hule* and *Physis* in John of Damascus' *Oration in Defense of the Icons*," StPatr 23 (1989): 66–73; George Dragas, "St. John Damascene's Teaching about the Holy Icons," *Icons, Windows on Eternity*, ed. G. Limouris (Geneva, 1990), 53–72; Nikos Matsoukas, ed., "He orthodoxe theologia tes eikonos kai to Christologikon dogma," in *L'icône dans la théologie et l'art*, ed. D. Papandreou (Geneva, 1990), 105–12; Daniel Sahas, "The Arab Character of the Christian Disputation with Islam: The Case of John of Damascus (ca. 655–ca. 749)," *Religionsgespräche im Mittelalter*, ed. B. Lewis (Wiesbaden, 1992), 185–205; John A. McGuckin, "The Theology of Images and the Legitimation of Power in Eighth Century Byzantium," SVTQ 37 (1993): 39–58; Michael Torre, "St. John Damascene and St. Thomas Aquinas on the Eternal Procession of the Holy Spirit," ibid. 38 (1994): 303–27.

Alexander Golitzin

JOHN DUNS SCOTUS. *See* DUNS SCOTUS, JOHN.

JOHN (QUIDORT) OF PARIS (?, Paris–22 September 1308, Bordeaux). John entered the Dominican order as a young man; as bachelor of theology commented on the *Sentences* but got into difficulty because of his teachings, and so his further studies were postponed, 1284–86; he received the licentiate only in 1304.

John became noted for his strong defense of the doctrines of Aquinas* as early as 1284, when he responded to William de la Mare's *Correctorium*; from his teachings in 1284–86 a number of propositions were extracted and reported to the master general of the Dominicans, but John defended himself successfully in 1287. He soon gained fame as a preacher at Paris from his *Tractatus de unitate formarum* and his best-known work, *De potestate regia et papali*, in 1302. He signed the appeal to a council against Boniface VIII on 26 June 1303 but his most controversial teaching for that time was in 1304 in a *Determinatio* on how the Real Body of Christ existed in the Eucharist. John admitted transsubstantiation but also claimed that this doctrine was not defined by the church and hence was not the only possible explanation; his account, known later as consubstantiation, attracted attention among the Reformers of the sixteenth century. In his own day John's teaching was reviewed by a body of four bishops and other theologians and canonists. John was placed under an edict of silence and suspended from teaching or preaching. He appealed this judgment and went to Bordeaux to see Pope Clement V in person but died before any decision was made.

While a strong Thomist, John was an original thinker who did not simply repeat Aquinas' views. His most notable contribution is today seen in the areas of political philosophy and ecclesiology. His tract at the time of the dispute between Boniface VIII and Philip IV was one among many produced on the French side but by far the most able and comprehensive. It lent itself to a variety of interpretations, and so quite varied schools would claim John for their cause. The 1970s saw two modern translations of the work into English, by John Watt in 1971 and by Arthur P. Monahan in 1974.

Bibliography

B.   DTC 8:840–41; LThK³ 5:955; NCE 7:1064; Francis Oakely, "Natural Law, the Corpus Mysticum and Consent in Conciliar Thought from John of Paris to Matthias Ugonis," *Speculum* 56 (1981): 786–810; Paul Saenger, "John of Paris, Principal Author of the *Quaestio de Potestate Papae* (*Rex Pacificus*)," ibid. 41–55.

Thomas E. Morrissey

JOHN PECKHAM. *See* PECKHAM, JOHN.

JOHN DE POUILLY, De Polliaco (late 13th century–after 1321). John was a professor of theology at Paris around 1300 and a major figure in controversies of that era. He had studied with Godfrey of Fontaines, was a member of the commission that condemned the mystical writings of Marguerite Porrette and, convinced of the validity of the Templar confessions made under torture, took the view that those who later recanted their confessions were to be treated as lapsed heretics and so turned over to the secular arm.

John took a strong stand on the side of the secular masters in their disputes with the mendicant orders at Paris. He objected to what he saw as extraordinary powers granted to the mendicants for hearing confessions. Pouilly saw this power as reaching excess in the bull of Pope Benedict XII (*Inter cunctas* in February, 1304), which seemed to eviscerate the exclusive right of pastors to absolve their parishioners as expressed at Lateran IV (*Omnis utriusque sexus*). The Council of Vienne restricted these privileges but the mendicants took no heed of its prescription, and so Pouilly denounced their actions and beliefs. He was himself denounced to John XXII for his excesses in language and cited to appear at Avignon. His chief accuser, Peter de Palu, O.P., drew up a list of thirty errors. The major point at issue was Pouilly's proposition that the jurisdiction of pastors was of divine origin and held immediately from Christ, and so it could not be restricted or diminished; thus, *Inter cunctas* was null, since it tried to give a dispensation contrary to natural and divine law.

The disputed theses were reduced to three and condemned by John XXII in July 1321 in *Vas electionis*, which did not, however, deal with the issue whether the local pastorate was of divine institution, but rather condemned the manner in which Pouilly and others tried to restrain the jurisdictional powers of the mendicants granted to them by the papacy. John de Pouilly is seen today as part of the disputes in later medieval political thought over jurisdiction and sovereignty in the ecclesiastical and civil order. He was a Thomist (although opposed to the Dominicans) and while criticizing papal policy and actions submitted his ideas to the judgment of the pope whom he saw as by divine law the head of the hierarchy, the teacher and judge of the entire church. John accepted the censure of his ideas and lived quietly until his death at an unknown date. He left large numbers of *Quodlibeta* and *Quaestiones* on a variety of topics, often very metaphysical, which remain only in manuscript form. Some of his ideas point in the direction of nominalism and, as a Thomist, he criticized the Scotist position on the Immaculate Conception.

Bibliography

B.   DTC 8:797–99; LThK³ 5:958–59; J. G. Sikes, "John de Pouilli and Peter de la Palu," *English Historical Review* 49 (1934): 219–40.

Thomas E. Morrissey

JOHN OF RAGUSA, John Stojkovic (ca. 1390/95, Ragusa–1443, Lausanne). John studied at Paris after entering the Dominican order at Ragusa and received his doctorate in 1420. He was an envoy of the university to the Council of Pavia in 1423, where he was also a papal preacher, but protested the dissolution of the council. In 1431 Ragusa gave the inaugural sermon to open the Council of Basel. His years at Basel were his most significant, and he left an account of the early activities of the council. In 1433 he was one of the theologians named to negotiate with the Hussites, and debated John Rokyano on reception of communion under both species. In 1435 and 1437 he was ambassador of Basel to Constantinople and was instrumental in getting the emperor and the patriarch to send delegations to Basel. He joined the conciliarist group at Basel, and was made a bishop in 1438 and a cardinal priest by Felix V.

His importance is seen in his treatise on the church (*De ecclesia*), which was precipitated by his experiences, rather than being a purely theoretical tract. He wrote from the perspective of one who had actively worked for unity with both Hussites and Greeks, one who at the same time was pressing for reform of the Church of Rome while defending it from attacks from these two groups. In response to the Hussite writings Ragusa tried to bring together a theology of grace and the concept of the church. He rejected as impossible any construction of a concept of the church grounded in the mystery of predestination. For Ragusa the church was founded by the action of God giving grace; the offices in the church were visible signs of this grace and the church was to be a sign of salvation in and to the world. Thus Ragusa bound together the inner and outer aspects of grace and all were called to membership in this faith community. Ragusa developed his tract on the church from the key words of the Nicene Creed, *unam sanctam*, and from the text of Mt 16:18, where the rock was both Christ and faith. His ideas followed the tradition of Augustine* in his writings on the ''marks'' of the church. Ragusa's theology is representative of late medieval thinking and in fact was quite close to that of John de Torquemada, who is often seen as his opponent.

Bibliography

A. *Tractatus de ecclesia*, ed. F. Šanjek (Zagreb, 1983).

B. LThK³ 5:960; ODCC 896–97; Werner Krämer, *Konsens und Rezeption. Verfassungsprinzipien der Kirche im Basler Konziliarismus* (Münster, 1980).

Thomas E. Morrissey

JOHN OF ST. THOMAS, John Poinsot (9 July 1589, Lisbon, Portugal–17 July 1644, Fraga, Aragon). *Education*: studied at Louvain, 1606–9. *Career*: entered the Dominicans, Madrid, 1612; taught philosophy and theology, Coll. of St. Thomas, Alcalá, 1613–30; chair of theology, Univ. of Alcalá, 1630–43; royal confessor to Philip IV, Madrid, 1643–44.

John of St. Thomas was among the last giants of the Second Scholasticism, which marked the golden age of the Spanish universities, 1540–1640. His prolific writings in philosophy and theology were marked by clarity, erudition, and comprehensiveness more than originality. In philosophy he followed Aristotle, in theology Aquinas.* His commentaries on Aristotle, mainly in logic, natural philosophy, and rational psychology, followed the interpretations of Aquinas, as their title suggests, *Cursus philosophicus thomisticus* (Madrid, 1637). John's masterwork, *Cursus theologicus thomisticus* in eight volumes (Lyons, 1663), closely followed the *Summa Theologiae* of Aquinas: its first three volumes parallel the *Pars prima*, the fourth and fifth parallel the *Prima secundae*, the sixth the *Secunda secundae*, and the last two the *Pars tertia*. John edited the first four volumes; after his death his student Diego Ramirez prepared the text from his notes. John's main scholastic opponents were Duns Scotus* and the Jesuits Gabriel Vásquez, Francisco Suárez,* and Luis de Molina.*

Among his lesser works were a popular exposition of Christian doctrine in Spanish, a work on the art of dying, and a manual on making confession, which was prepared for Philip IV.

Bibliography

A.   *Cursus philosophicus thomisticus*, 3 vols. (Turin, 1930); *Cursus theologici*, 3 vols. (Solesmes/Paris, 1931); *The Material Logic of John of St. Thomas: Basic Treatises*, trans. Yves Simon et al. (Chicago, 1955); *Tractatus de signis: The Semiotic of John Poinsot*, ed. John Deely (Berkeley, Calif., 1985); *The Gifts of the Holy Spirit*, trans. Dominic Hughes (New York, 1951).

B.   DSAM 8:710–14; DTC 8:830–38; LThK³ 5:973; NCE 7:1070–71; ODCC 897; B. Lavaud, "Jean de Saint Thomas," *La vie spirituelle* 14 (1926): 384–415; Edward J. Furton, *A Medieval Semiotic: Reference and Representation in John of St. Thomas' Theory of Signs* (New York, 1995); John N. Deely, *New Beginnings: Early Modern Philosophy and Postmodern Thought* (Toronto, 1994).

John Patrick Donnelly

JOHN OF SALISBURY (1115, Wiltshire–25 October 1180, Chartres). *Education*: studied with Peter Abelard,* Alberic, Robert of Melun,* 1136, and William of Conches, 1137–40. *Career*: secretary and representative to the papal curia for archbishops Theobald and Thomas Becket, 1154–74; exiled to France, 1163–70; witnessed Becket's assassination, later compiled his letters; became bishop of Chartres, 1176; participated in Third Lateran Council, 1179.

John's greatest works are the *Policraticus* and the *Metalogicon* (1159). The *Policraticus* provides a foundation for western concepts of liberty and the legitimate use of power, based on classical authors and patristic writers. John insists that responsible leaders should rule in accordance with divine rather than human law, whereas tyranny disregards law. The *Metalogicon* satirizes the effects of the increasing overspecialization of administrators and clerks in royal, papal, and university service. The second half of the work defends the trivium (rhetoric, grammar, dialectic) and discusses the writings of Porphyry and Aristotle. John is among the first medieval scholars with a command of Aristotle's logical treatises (*Organon*).

Bibliography

A.   *Memoirs of the Papal Court*, trans. Marjorie Chibnail (London, 1956); *The Letters of John of Salisbury*, ed. W. J. Millor and H. E. Butler, rev. C. N. L. Brooke, 2 vols. (Oxford, 1979); *John of Salisbury's Entheticus maior and minor*, ed. Jan van Laarhoven (Leiden, 1987); *Policraticus: Of the Frivolities of Courtiers and the Footprints of Phi-*

losophers, ed. and trans. Cary J. Nederman (Cambridge, 1990); *Metalogicon*, ed. J. B. Hall, CCCM 98 (Turnhout, 1991); *Policraticus: I-IV*, ed. K. S. B. Keats-Rohan, CCCM 118 (Turnhout, 1993).

B.   DNB 10:876–83; DTC 8:808–16; LThK³ 5:964–65; NCE 7:1071–72; ODCC 897–98; TRE 17:153–55; C. C. Webb, *John of Salisbury* (New York, 1932); Walter Ullmann, *The Church and the Law in the Earlier Middle Ages: Selected Essays* (London, 1975), 383–92; *The World of John of Salisbury*, ed. Michael Wilks (Oxford, 1984); Frank Barlow, "John of Salisbury and his Brothers," JEH 46 (1995): 95–109.

Daniel Marcel La Corte

JOHN STOJKOVIC. *See* JOHN OF RAGUSA.

JOHN WYCLIF. *See* WYCLIF, JOHN.

JOURNET, CHARLES (26 January 1891, Vernier, near Geneva–15 April 1975, Fribourg). *Education*: Classical studies in Geneva and Mariahilf Coll., Schwyz, and St. Michael's Coll., Fribourg, and the diocesan sem., Fribourg; ordained priest, 1917. *Career*: professor, Fribourg sem., 1924–70; founded with F. Charrière the theological journal *Nova et vetera*, 1926, and served as its editor until his death in 1975; cardinal, 1965.

Swiss theologian Journet is notable for having written the only formal comprehensive systematic treatise on the church in the twentieth century, the three-volume *L'Eglise du Verbe incarné* (1941–69). He made use of Scholastic philosophy's four "causes" (efficient, material, formal, and final) as a means to understand the nature of the church. In the English-speaking world, only volume one, the only one translated, dealing with the church's hierarchy was generally read. For Journet, the church's formal cause, that which definitively makes it what it is and which determines its essence, is not the hierarchy, but the Holy Spirit. The hierarchy, he argued, was the immediate efficient cause.

Journet was well read in the fathers of the church and wrote favorably of the thought of John Henry Newman* and Johann Adam Möhler.* He was a close friend of Jacques Maritain as well as the Dominican philosopher R. Garrigou-Lagrange.* He was also, as early as the 1920s, one of the promoters of modern ecumenism among Catholics. Journet was appointed a member of the preparatory theological commission prior to Vatican II. His thought exercised an indirect but notable influence on sections of the Dogmatic Constitution on the Church (*Lumen gentium*).

Bibliography

A.   *L'Esprit du Protestantisme en Suisse* (Paris, 1925); *L'Union des églises et le christianisme pratique* (Paris, 1927); *L'Eglise du Verbe incarné*, 3 vols. (Paris, 1941, 1951, 1969) [ET: vol. 1 only, *Church of the Word Incarnate*, trans. A. H. C. Downs (New York, 1955)].

B.   LThK³ 5:1020; NCE 17:309–10; for a full listing of Journet's books, see Lucien Méroz, *Le Cardinal Journet, ou La sainte théologie* (Lausanne, 1981) 343–44; Pierre-

Marie Emonet, *Le Cardinal Journet: Portrait intérieur* (Chambray-les-Tours, 1983); Philippe Chenaux, ed., *Charles Journet (1891–1975): Un théologien en son siècle: Actes du colloque de Genève, 1991* (Fribourg, 1992); G. Bedouelle, "L'Histoire comme sagesse dans la pensée de Cardinal Journet," in *Histoire de théologie*, ed. J.-D. Durand (Paris, 1994) 123–35; Dennis M. Doyle, "Journet, Congar, and the Roots of Communion Ecclesiology," ThSt 58 (1997): 461–79.

Michael A. Fahey

JULIAN OF ECLANUM (ca. 380/386, Apulia–ca. 455). Son of bishop Memorius and his wife Juliana; received a good education, married the daughter of the bishop of Beneventum; ca. 416 consecrated bishop of Eclanum in Campania by Innocent I; in the summer of 418 refused, along with eighteen other Italian bishops, to subscribe to the letter of Zosimus (the *Epistula Tractoria*) condemning Pelagianism; deposed and exiled by Zosimus along with the other bishops; appealed to Nestorius* and Theodosius II; condemned by the Council of Ephesus in 431; unsuccessfully attempted reconciliation with the church in 439.

Julian's principal writings, *To Turbantius* and *To Florus*, are preserved in fragments in Augustine's* works written in response to them. In both, Julian presents a strong defense of Pelagianism and accuses the defenders of original sin of being Manichees. He argues that the doctrine of original sin leads its supporters into five errors: the belief that the devil creates new human beings, the condemnation of marriage, the denial that all sins are forgiven in baptism, the accusation that God is unjust, and despair of attaining perfection. Other works of Julian include letters to Count Valerius and Pope Zosimus, as well as scriptural commentaries on Job, the minor prophets, and the Song of Songs, of which only fragments are extant.

Bibliography

A.   *Libri IV ad Turbantium* (*Four Books to Turbantius*), CCSL 88, 340–96, along with his other extant works, except *Libri VIII ad Florum* (*Eight Books to Florus*); extant fragments of the last work are found in Augustine's *Opus imperfectum contra Iulianum* (*Answer to Julian: An Unfinished Work*), CSEL 85 (books 1–3) and PL 45, 1049–1608.

B.   DTC 8:1926–31; LThK³ 5:1076–77; NCE 8:48; ODCC 909; TRE 17:441–43; A. Bruckner, *Julian von Eclanum. Sein Leben und seine Lehre* (Leipzig, 1897); F. Refoulé, "Julien d'Éclane: théologien et philosophe," *RechScRel* 52 (1964): 42–84, 233–47; P. Brown, "Sexuality and Society in the Fifth Century A.D.: Augustine and Julian of Eclanum," in *Tria Corda, Scritti in onore di A. Momigliano*, ed. E. Gabba (Como, 1983), 49–70; A. E. McGrath, "Divine Justice and Divine Equity in the Controversy between Augustine and Julian of Eclanum," *Downside Review* 101 (1983): 312–19.

Roland J. Teske

JUNGMANN, JOSEF ANDREAS (16 November 1889, Sand-in-Taufers in South Tirol [pre–World War I Austria]–26 January 1975, Innsbruck). *Education*: sem., Brixen, 1909–13; doctorate in theology, Univ. of Innsbruck, 1918–23;

habilitation, Munich and Vienna, 1923–25. *Career*: ordained priest, 1913; assistant pastor, Niedervintl and Gossensass, 1913–17; entered Society of Jesus, Lavanttal, 1917; taught pastoral theology, Theologische Fakultät, Univ. of Innsbruck, 1925–39, 1945–63; editor, *Zeitschrift für katholische Theologie*, 1927–39, 1945–63; member, preparatory committee, and *peritus*, Vatican II, 1960–65.

A pastoral theologian and author of nearly 300 books and articles, Josef A. Jungmann, S.J., became the most famous liturgical scholar of the twentieth century because of his widely disseminated two-volume historical study of the Mass, *Missarum Solemnia* (1948). Jungmann was first made aware of the formative importance of the liturgy by Franz J. Dölger and Pius Parsch.* He became a scholar, however, because of the contrast he experienced as a parish priest between the joyful Christianity of St. Paul and the fathers of the church and his own parishioners' practice of the faith as a complex of strict obligations. From then on he directed all his efforts toward a better communication of the central content of the Gospel: the person and work of Jesus Christ.

According to Jungmann's 1925 Habilitationsschrift, *Die Stellung Christi im liturgischen Gebet* (*The Place of Christ in Liturgical Prayer*), the church normally prays to the Father *through* Jesus Christ. However, it began praying in latreutic devotion directly *to* Christ in order to affirm, against Arianism, Christ's full divinity. Although it may overemphasize the anti-Arian reaction, Jungmann's landmark study helps restore appreciation within Christology for the role of Christ's humanity in our salvation.

In *Die lateinischen Bussriten in ihrer geschichtlichen Entwicklung* (1932) Jungmann ratified Poschmann's reversal of the traditional theological judgment that "private" celebration of the sacrament of reconciliation was the original and unbroken practice of the church. In the 1930s, too, he emphasized this communal, over a narrowly hierarchical, understanding of the liturgy in articles that commented on Odo Casel's* theory of *Mysteriengegenwart*. Here, Jungmann argued that the liturgy was more the worship of the locally gathered assembly than it was a sacral mystery-action performed in the name of the universal church. Popular devotions as well as official liturgy are expressions of the same church community so that any distinction between "subjective" and "objective" piety is essentially misleading.

Jungmann's 1936 *Die Frohbotschaft und unsere Glaubensverkündigung* (*The Good News Yesterday and Today*, 1962; rev. ed., *Announcing the Word of God*, 1967) initiated the kerygmatic phase of modern catechetics, emphasizing content over method in all forms of ministry of the Word. Overcoming early ecclesiastical resistance, this work succeeded in creating the consciousness that led eventually to Vatican II's pastoral renewal.

In his 1939 *Die liturgische Feier* (*Liturgical Worship*, 1941; rev. ed., *The Liturgy of the Word*, 1966) Jungmann set forth the basic structure of all liturgical celebrations as: (a) reading, (b) singing, and (c) prayer. However, this comprehensive theory of liturgy as the hearing and possessing of God's word before responding in answering prayer has not had wide acceptance by scholars.

During the Nazi closure of the faculty of theology from 1939 to 1945 Jungmann wrote his *Missarum Solemnia* (*The Mass of the Roman Rite*), the twentieth century's classic study of the Mass. Copious evidence that the Mass developed through the centuries showed his contemporaries that further developments are not only feasible but necessary, thereby creating the climate for Vatican II changes. Jungmann's data also suggested a bipartite structure of the Mass (liturgy of the word and eucharistic liturgy), the importance of the prayers of the faithful, and the secondary status of the Offertory, leading to the reshaped Mass of Paul VI. And his thorough presentation of the interior unity, structure, and major components of the Roman Canon prepared the ground for substantial advances by other scholars in recent years. Most importantly perhaps, *Missarum Solemnia* revealed that one cannot dissociate the Eucharist from the ecclesial community that celebrates it, as theology had done since the Middle Ages. Before being the enactment of Christ's real presence, it is first of all the thanksgiving of the assembled church.

Bibliography

A. *The Place of Christ in Liturgical Prayer*, trans. A. Peeler (New York, 1965); *The Mass of the Roman Rite*, trans. Francis A. Brunner, C.SS.R., 2 vols. (New York, 1950, 1955); *Pastoral Liturgy* (New York, 1962).

B. LThK³ 5:1099–1100; NCE 17:312–13; TRE 17:465–67; Balthasar Fischer and Hans-Bernhard Meyer, S.J., ed., *J. A. Jungmann, Ein Leben für Liturgie und Kerygma* (Innsbruck, 1975); Pierre-Marie Gy, O.P., "Chroniques: L'oeuvre liturgique de Josef Andreas Jungmann (d. 26 January 1975)," *La Maison-Dieu* 121 (1975): 159–65; Johannes Hofinger, S.J., "J. A. Jungmann," *Living Light* 13 (1976): 350–59.

John D. Laurance

JUSTIN MARTYR (d. 165, Rome). Justin, first called "Philosopher and Martyr" by Tertullian*, was the most outstanding Christian apologist of the second century. He was born at Flavia Neapolis (now Nablus) in Palestine of a pagan Greek family. In his search for the truth he passed through several schools of philosophy until he discovered Platonism. An old man then urged him to advance to Christianity, which he embraced as the only trustworthy and useful philosophy. After his conversion Justin founded a school in Rome; Tatian was among his pupils. A trustworthy *martyrium* recounts how Justin and six others were beheaded as Christians at Rome ca. 165. Of his writings two apologies and the *Dialogue with Trypho* survive. The *First Apology* is by far the longer. Justin wrote it ca. 150 or 155 and addressed it to Antoninus Pius. The shorter, first part refutes accusations brought against Christians. The second part describes and defends the Christian religion and includes an extensive proof of the divinity of Christ from Old Testament prophecies and valuable descriptions of baptism and the celebration of the Eucharist. The *Second Apology* may originally have been an appendix to the first. The *Dialogue with Trypho* is the literary recreation of a conversation between Justin and the learned rabbi Tarphon, which took place over two days. After recounting his own journey to Christianity, Justin attempts to show that Jewish ritual law is transitory, that the worship of Christ does not compromise monotheism, and that the Gentiles are called to the church. Justin composed the *Dialogue* after the *First Apology*.

Justin represents the Logos-theology: God's Logos (Word and Reason) emerges, for the purposes of creation and providence, as a divine person subordinate to the Father. He inspires the Greek philosophers and the Hebrew prophets and is incarnate in Christ. Every reasonable being participates in the Logos, and hence in Christ.

Bibliography

A.   *Writings of St. Justin Martyr*, trans. Thomas B. Falls, FC 6 (New York, 1948); *Apologies*, trans. L. W. Barnard, ACW 56 (New York, 1997).

B.   DSAM 8:1640–47; DTC 8:560–87; LThK³ 5:1122–23; NCE 8:94–95; ODCC 915; TRE 17:471–78; E. R. Goodenough, *The Theology of Justin Martyr* (Jena, 1923); W. A. Shotwell, *The Biblical Exegesis of Justin Martyr* (London, 1965); L. W. Barnard, *Justin Martyr: His Life and Thought* (Cambridge, 1967).

Joseph T. Lienhard

K

KARLSTADT, ANDREAS (BODENSTEIN) (ca. 1480, Karlstadt, Germany–
24 December, 1544, Basel, Switzerland). *Education*: B.A., Univ. of Erfurt, 1502;
studied at Univ. of Cologne, 1502–5; M.A., doctor of theology, Univ. of Wittenberg, 1505, 1510; doctor of canon law, doctor of civil law, the Sapienza,
Rome, 1515. *Career*: professor, at times dean, Univ. of Wittenberg, 1510–24;
pastor, Orlamünde, Germany, 1522–24; professor of Hebrew, at times rector,
Univ. of Basel, 1534–44.

Through the influence of Martin Luther,* Karlstadt turned from his scholastic
theology to reject any role for natural ability in the acquisition of merit and to
espouse predestinarianism and Augustine's* teaching that grace alone produces
righteousness. In Luther's absence in 1521 Karlstadt led Wittenberg's reformation. In 1522, restoring the Elector's authority, Luther reversed Karlstadt's
iconoclasm and eucharistic modifications. Karlstadt then instituted independent
reforms in Orlamünde. They included: lay prophecy, worship in homes, and the
elimination of titles and vestments. Images, the Mass, and infant baptism were
rejected. Adult baptism was retained as a sign of repentance. Karlstadt rejected
as detrimental to salvation the doctrine of the sacraments as pledges of forgiveness. He made the same criticism of the claim for Christ's eucharistic presence.
The ascription of forgiveness solely to Christ's death and the reception of the
benefits of his death solely through contemplation were seen as the way to
salvation through experience. Karlstadt considered it irrational to claim Christ's
body could be either in the bread or there and in heaven simultaneously. The
purpose of the Lord's Supper was considered to be in the self-examination
preceding it and in the participants' public witness to their faith.

The idea that doctrines can be received through direct inspiration confirmed
by Scripture moved him in the direction of spiritualism. He borrowed from

mysticism the concept *Gelassenheit*, self-renunciation, to describe the experience of self-negation necessary for regeneration. To attain and maintain righteousness he believed one must have experiences of self-contempt and assurance. Persecution was seen as a spiritual baptism. "Faith rich in love," and "a passionate knowledge of Christ," rather than merely hearing and believing, were declared necessary for justification. He embraced an antinomy: human transformation is solely by grace and human decisions prepare for grace. He condemned Luther for undervaluing scriptural law and teaching forgiveness without adequate doctrines of regeneration and visible righteousness. Contradicting Luther, he tied salvation to actual righteousness in an Augustinian manner. Yet Karlstadt was inconsistent, for at times he rejected the concept of merit with the judgment humans cannot attain true sinless righteousness before death. His denial of sacramental grace contradicted both Augustine and Luther. Against Luther he advocated a form of congregational independence.

Karlstadt eventually backed away from some of his ideas, finding a home in Zurich and Basel. Various elements of his teachings—the memorialist interpretation of the Lord's Supper, believer's baptism, congregational independence, iconoclasm, his use of scriptural law, and the place he gave subjective experience as a channel and confirmation of grace—indirectly influenced the Reformed, Baptist, Puritan, and Pietistic movements.

Bibliography

A. *Karlstadts Schriften aus den Jahren 1523–1525*, 2 parts, ed., Erich Hertzsch (Halle, 1956–57); *Verzeichnis der gedruckten Schriften des Andreas Bodenstein von Karlstadt*, ed. E. Freys and H. Barge (repr. Nieuwkoop, 1965); *Karlstadt's Battle with Luther: Documents in a Liberal Radical Debate*, ed. Ronald J. Sider (Philadelphia, 1978); *The Essential Carlstadt: Fifteen Tracts by Andreas Bodenstein (Carlstadt) from Karlstadt*, ed. and trans. E. J. Furcha (Scottdale, Pa., 1995).

B. ECatt 3:887–89; LThK³ 5:1249–50; NCE 8:132–33; ODCC 288; OEncR 1:178–80; TRE 17:649–57; Gordon Rupp, *Patterns of Reformation* (Philadelphia, 1969); Ronald J. Sider, *Andreas Bodenstein von Karlstadt* (Leiden, 1974); Calvin A. Pater, *Karlstadt as the Father of the Baptist Movements: The Emergence of Lay Protestantism* (Toronto, 1984).

Melvin G. Vance

KEBLE, JOHN (25 April 1792, Fairford, Gloucestershire, England–29 March 1866, Bournemouth, England). *Education*: Corpus Christi Coll., Oxford, 1811. *Career*: fellow, Oriel Coll., Oxford, 1811; tutor, Oriel Coll., Oxford, 1817–23; parish ministry in England, 1823–66, including vicar, Hursley, 1836–66; professor of poetry, Oxford, 1831–41.

Keble was an Anglican priest and a leader of the Oxford Movement in the Church of England. The Oxford Movement defended the Church of England as a divine institution, upheld the doctrine of the apostolic succession, led to renewed interest in liturgy and worship and an appreciation for the mystical and supernatural, expanded ministry to the poor, and revived the religious life. Keble's 14 July 1833 sermon on *National Apostasy* against the proposed suppression of ten Irish bishoprics is generally regarded as the beginning of the Oxford Movement. He contributed several tracts to the series *Tracts for the Times*. After John Henry Newman* left the Church of England, Keble and Edward B. Pusey* contributed to keeping the High Church Movement within the Church of England.

Keble published *The Christian Year* (1827), a collection of poems for the Sundays and holy days of the church year. It was very popular in the nineteenth century and the source of several hymn texts. Keble was also one of the editors of the *Library of the Fathers*, and contributed the translation of St. Irenaeus.* Keble College, Oxford, was founded in his memory in 1870. His life is commemorated in the Episcopal Church calendar of the church year on March 29.

Bibliography

A. *The Christian Year* (Oxford, 1827); *National Apostasy Considered in a Sermon* (Oxford, 1833); *Tracts for the Times by Members of the University of Oxford*, numbers 4, 13, 40, 52, 54, 57, 60, 89 (Oxford, 1833–41); *Sermons, Academical and Occasional* (Oxford, 1847); *Sermons, Occasional and Parochial* (Oxford, 1868).

B. DNB 10:1179–83; NCE 8:142; ODCC 920–21; John T. Coleridge, *A Memoir of the Rev. John Keble* (Oxford, 1868); Georgina Battiscombe, *John Keble, a Study in Limitations* (New York, 1963); *The Oxford Movement*, ed. Eugene R. Fairweather (New York, 1964); John R. Griffin, *John Keble, Saint of Anglicanism* (Macon, Georgia, 1987); A. M. Allchin, *John Keble, Pastor and Theologian* (Winchester, England, 1992).

Robert B. Slocum

KEMPE, MARGERY (ca. 1373, Lynn, Norfolk–ca. 1440, place unknown). The daughter of the mayor of Lynn; married John Kempe in 1393; after bearing him fourteen children, separated from him by mutual consent in order to pursue a form of religious life in the world; made a pilgrimage to the Holy Land and spent six months in Italy in 1414–15 on her way back; visited the shrine at Compostela in 1417–18; returned to Lynn to care for her ailing husband until his death in 1431; traveled in Norway and Danzig in 1433–34. Unable herself to write, dictated to two clerks ca. 1431–38 an account of her travels and mystical experiences in what is the first extant autobiography in English. Until 1934, when a manuscript of her book was found by the Butler-Bowden family, her work was known only by extracts; her book presents an interesting record of the life of a medieval woman. Scholars are divided on whether Kempe was a genuine mystic or a victim of religious mania.

Bibliography

A. *The Book of Margery Kempe*, ed. Sanford B. Meech and Hope E. Allen (New York, 1940); *The Book of Margery Kempe: A New Translation*, trans. Tony D. Triggs (Tunbridge Wells, 1995).

B. DSAM 8:1696–98; NCE 8:149; ODCC 922; Katharine Cholmeley, *Margery Kempe: Genius and Mystic* (New York, 1947); Robert K. Stone, *Middle English Prose*

Style: Margery Kempe and Julian of Norwich (The Hague, 1970); Clarissa W. Atkinson, *Mystic and Pilgrim: The Book and the World of Margery Kempe* (Ithaca, N.Y., 1983); Louise Collis, *Memoirs of a Medieval Woman: The Life and Times of Margery Kempe* (New York, 1983); *Margery Kempe: A Book of Essays*, ed. Sandra J. McEntire (New York, 1992); Margaret Gallyon, *Margery Kempe of Lynn and Medieval England* (Norwich, 1995).

Roland J. Teske

KENRICK, FRANCIS PATRICK (3 December 1796, Dublin, Ireland–8 July 1863, Baltimore, Md.). *Education*: studied at Urban Coll. of the Propaganda, Rome, 1814–21. *Career*: ordained 1821; theology teacher, St. Thomas Sem., Bardstown, Ky., 1821–30; coadjutor and bishop of Philadelphia, 1830–51; archbishop of Baltimore, 1851–63.

Kenrick was the most scholarly and theologically productive of the antebellum nineteenth-century American Catholic bishops. He made three major contributions to the development of an American Catholic theological tradition. First, in the midst of mid-nineteenth-century American Protestant–Catholic theological quarrels, he published a series of pamphlets and books that articulated clearly Catholic Tridentine doctrine on sin and justification, the sacraments, transubstantiation, and especially on papal primacy. His major apologetical work, though, was his *Primacy of the Apostolic See* (1845), which went through numerous subsequent editions and was translated into German. The *Primacy* was Kenrick's attempt to demonstrate with the evidence of biblical, patristic, and medieval sources, which he quoted profusely, the grounds for the prerogative of papal primacy of honor and jurisdiction. His work reflected the Roman, rather than the Gallican, school of historical interpretation of the documents.

Second, Kenrick was from the beginning of his pastoral career in the United States preoccupied with the theological education of the clergy. He soon discovered the paucity of Catholic theological resources and textbooks for clerical training and in the 1830s and 1840s published a four-volume textbook of doctrinal theology and a three-volume textbook on moral theology. Both texts manifested Kenrick's reliance upon Giovanni Perrone's* (1794–1876) theology, a theological tradition that drew on the retrieval of biblical and patristic sources, rather than simply relying upon the scholastic tradition of theology. Kenrick's moral theology took up issues such as slavery that were particularly pertinent to American circumstances. For him slavery was a consequence of original sin, but the institution itself was not essentially sinful. The moral dimension of slavery referred almost exclusively to the moral code of relative rights and duties of masters and slaves.

Third, Kenrick produced from the Vulgate a new English translation of the entire Bible, published in six separate volumes between 1849 and 1860. Although he was open to some modern Protestant critical scholarship and called for more Catholics to become engaged in critical biblical studies and to learn oriental languages, his primary purpose in translating the Bible was to provide a more readable English text than the Douay version and to vindicate the Catholic use of the Vulgate.

Bibliography

A. *Letters of Omega and Omicron on Transubstantiation* (Louisville, Ky., 1828); *Theologiae Dogmaticae tractatus tres*, 4 vols. (Philadelphia, 1834–40); *Theologia Moralis*, 3 vols. (Philadelphia, 1841–43; repr. Baltimore, Md., 1860–61); *The Catholic Doctrine on Justification* (Philadelphia, 1841); *The Primacy of the Apostolic See Vindicated* (Philadelphia, 1845; many subsequent rev. eds.); *A Treatise on Baptism: Also a Treatise on Confirmation*, 2d ed., rev. and corr. (Baltimore, Md., 1852); *The New Testament* (Baltimore, Md., 1862).

B. DAB 10:339–40; DACB, 296–97; DAH, 152–53; DARB 288–89; NCAB 1:485; NCE 8:155–56; NYT 9 July 1863, 4; John Joseph O'Shea, *The Two Kenricks* (Philadelphia, 1904); Hugh J. Nolan, *The Most Reverend Francis Patrick Kenrick* (Washington, D.C., 1948); Joseph D. Brokhage, *Francis Patrick Kenrick's Opinion on Slavery* (Washington, D.C., 1955); Thomas W. Spalding, *The Premier See* (Baltimore, Md., 1989), 154–78; Gerald P. Fogarty, "Kenrick's Translation of the Bible," in *American Catholic Biblical Scholarship* (New York, 1989), 14–34.

Patrick W. Carey

KENRICK, PETER RICHARD (17 August 1806, Dublin, Ireland–4 March 1896, St. Louis, Mo.). *Education*: studied at St. Patrick's Coll. and Sem., Maynooth, Ireland, 1827–32. *Career*: ordained, 1832; chaplain, Carmelite Convent, Dublin, 1832; pastoral work, diocese of Philadelphia, 1833–41; coadjutor, bishop, and archbishop, St. Louis, 1841–95; retired, 1895–96.

Kenrick was significant theologically for his opposition to the doctrine of papal infallibility at the First Vatican Council (1869–70). He was influenced in his early Irish education by a Gallican approach to ecclesiology which emphasized the quasi-autonomy of the national church. In the United States he favored those policies that demonstrated the American character of the Catholic Church in this country and participated actively in the three national Plenary Episcopal Councils of Baltimore in 1852, 1866, and 1884, which set the canonical standards and governing policies for the Catholic Church in the United States.

In 1869 and 1870 Kenrick took an active role at the First Vatican Council, where he became the leading American opponent of the definition of papal infallibility, arguing in his *Concio in Concilio Vaticano habenda et non habita* (Naples, 1870) that the teaching of papal infallibility was a theological opinion, not a definable doctrine, because the evidence from Scripture and tradition was either silent on the issue or opposed to it. Although he eventually accepted the Council's definition of papal infallibility, he never repudiated the arguments of his *Concio* and he refused to make any public statements on his position after returning from the Council.

Bibliography

A. *The Validity of Anglican Ordination* (1841; 2d rev. ed., 1848); ET of *Concio* in "American Prelates in the Vatican Council," ed. Raymond J. Clancy, *Historical Records and Studies* 28 (1937), 93–131.

B. DAB 10:340–41; DACB, 297; DAH, 153; NCAB 13:30; NCE 8:156–57; NYT 5 March 1896, 1; John J. O'Shea, *The Two Kenricks* (Philadelphia, 1904); Samuel J. Miller, "Peter Richard Kenrick: Bishop and Archbishop of St. Louis, 1808–1896," *Records of the American Catholic Historical Society* 84 (1973): 3–163; Gerald P. Fogarty, "Archbishop Peter Kenrick's Submission to Papal Infallibility," *Archivum Historiae Pontificiae* 16 (1978): 205–23.

Patrick W. Carey

KHOMIAKOV, ALEKSEI STEPANOVICH (13 May N.S. [1 May O.S.] 1804, Moscow–October 5, N.S. [23 September O.S.] 1860, near Riazan). *Education*: home tutoring, studied mathematics at Moscow Univ., 1821. *Career*: Society of Wisdom Lovers, Moscow, early 1820s; imperial cavalry guard, St. Petersburg, 1822–25; writer, Paris, 1825–26; literary life in Moscow, 1826–28; resumed military life, war against Turkey, 1828–29; retired from military 1830; writer, Moscow and his estates at Bogucharovo and Lipitzy, 1831–60; trips to England, Germany, and Prague, 1847; founding member, *Russkaia Beseda*, 1856; president, The Society of Friends of Russian Literature, 1859.

Poet, playwright, inventor, philosopher of history, and theologian during the Golden Age of Russian literature, Aleksei Stepanovich Khomiakov was also much engaged in life on his estates, studying medicine and agriculture to help the peasantry. Well read in the Greek Fathers, he was chiefly influenced by the German Romantic and Idealist currents then popular in Russia. Primarily concerned with ecclesiology, he was the most influential Russian Orthodox lay theologian of the nineteenth century.

Along with Ivan Kireevsky, he was a founder of Slavophilism. As against secularist Westernizers, Khomiakov sought to preserve Russia's traditions, especially as lived in the peasant commune. The Orthodox people, not the hierarchy, were the bearers of pure Christianity and were destined to lead other nations into a new Christian era. History showed a clash between two forces, the "Iranian (Aryan) principle" of spiritual and moral freedom (Russia) and the "Cushite principle" of material and logical necessity (the West). The West was fatally flawed by individualism, juridicism, rationalism, and materialism. True progress depends on cooperation and not on competition as in the West.

Dostoyevsky's "Grand Inquisitor" chapter in *Brothers Karamazov* has features negative to Catholicism that point to Khomiakov. Partly educated by a French priest, Khomiakov criticized Catholicism as having politicized Christianity by Roman law and a legalistic hierarchy, thus forcing an exterior unity lacking in interior freedom. Protestantism, building on Catholic rationalism, developed freedom without unity.

The most fruitful of Khomiakov's ideas is his conception of *sobornost*, which he saw as the core of Russia's superiority to other Christian nations. Derived from the word "catholic" in the Creed and likely formed under the influence of J. A. Möhler,* *sobornost* means the combination of freedom and unity of many persons on the basis of their common understanding of truth and their common love of Christ, which is the Holy Spirit. Truth dwells more in *sobornost* than in hierarchy, council, or even Scripture because councils can err and Scripture is from the whole church: complete truth belongs only to the church as a whole. The church is an organic whole spiritualized by Christ Himself, formed by grace and the law of love. Khomiakov rejected the notion of external authority. The universal approval of all believers formed that internalized tradition that is at the heart of Orthodoxy. His followers have insisted that the church, an organism of spiritual life, cannot be defined by the human intellect; it can be known and understood only through an intuitive mystical experience.

His highly interiorized and pneumatic notion of the church has been criticized for being impracticable and antihierarchical. The Russian Church itself would not sanction the publication of his works until 1879, and then only with a cautionary preface.

Khomiakov greatly influenced Russian thinkers Vladimir Soloviev,* Vyacheslav Ivanov, Nicholas Berdiaev,* and Sergei Bulgakov as well as Anglican theologian William Palmer. As prophet of the "people of God" his influence was strongly felt at Vatican II.

Bibliography

A. *Polnoe sobranie sochinenij* [Complete Collected Works, in Russian], 8 vols. (Moscow, 1900); *L'Eglise Latine et le Protestantisme au point de vue de l'Eglise d'Orient* (Lausanne, 1872); *Tserkov Odna* (repr. Moscow, 1991); *The Church Is One* (Seattle, Wash., 1979, and other previous and subsequent English editions); *The Orthodox Doctrine of the Church* (Brussels, 1864).

B. HDOC 184; NCE 8:173–74; ODCC 925–26; N. Berdiaev, *A. S. Khomiakov* (Paris, 1912; repr. Farnborough, UK, 1971); P. K. Christoff, *An Introduction to Nineteenth Century Russian Slavophilism*, vol. 1, *A. S. Xomjakov* (The Hague, 1961); A. S. Gratieux, *A. S. Khomiakov et le mouvement slavophile*, 2 vols. (Paris, 1939); A. Walicki, *The Slavophile Controversy. History of a Conservative Utopia in Nineteenth-Century Russian Thought* (Oxford, 1975); V. Z. Zavitnevitch, *A. S. Khomyakov*, 2 vols. (Kiev, 1902–13), with bibliography.

Raymond T. Gawronski

KIERKEGAARD, SØREN (5 May 1813, Copenhagen, Denmark–4 November 1855, Copenhagen). *Education*: studied philosophy and theology, Univ. of Copenhagen, 1830–40; theological exam, 1840; M.A. thesis, 1841. *Career*: self-described "religious writer," 1841–55.

Kierkegaard was a Danish theologian, philosopher, and social commentator who mounted what was perhaps the most thorough and profound critique of the cultural Protestantism that dominated Denmark and most of northern Europe in the nineteenth century. Unknown outside Denmark during his own lifetime, and unappreciated there, his work was first discovered and celebrated in the larger world only since the first decades of this century by theologians and philosophers as varied as Emmanuel Hirsch, Karl Barth,* Martin Heidegger, Rudolph Bultmann,* and Jean Paul Sartre. Thus, as that Protestant form of European cultural religion increasingly has been called into question in the twentieth century through world wars both hot and cold as well as through the great social changes that have accompanied those events, Kierkegaard has come to be seen as an important resource for both theology and philosophy.

He was born the seventh and last child of a prominent and wealthy Danish businessman and was raised in the center of Copenhagen's cultural and intellectual life. The child of his father's old age, he was in a special way marked by the fervent Lutheranism, the vigor of mind, the material comfort and security, and the struggle with guilt and God that was bequeathed to him and his siblings by the *pater familias*. After a period of hedonism and subsequent reactionary moralism at university, followed by a religious experience to which he often alluded but never described, Kierkegaard took as his life's work the examination of, as he put it, "becoming and being a Christian in Christendom." To that end, he became not a pastor, as was his original intention, but rather a "religious writer," supported by the fortune he inherited at his father's death.

His writings were of four kinds, and they broadly reflect the escalating level of intensity with which he addressed the concerns of his life's work during the fifteen years, 1840–55, that witnessed his literary production. Whatever the genre, the elements of his thought were always the same: paradox, God as absolutely other, truth as subjectivity, and an emphasis upon individual existence. He pursued his theme first by what he called a "method of indirect communication" in which he published a series of pseudonymous books attacking the entrenched Hegelianism of both the church and the ostensibly Christian society of his day. Life is not an inevitable historical process of betterment, he declared in the text, but is rather defined by the individual's "leap" of decision, for every human being is faced with an unavoidable *Either/Or* (1843) of deciding for a life defined either by the aesthetic and the ethical or by Christianity. The aesthetic is marked by flight from commitment, by relativism and hedonism; the ethical bows before the universals of humanity, morality, and religion. In that each tears apart the claim for and the reality of an actual life and thereby falsifies human existence, Kierkegaard argued, both end in despair. Only the decision for Christianity—the "leap" into confession of sin, profession of faith, and following after love—holds together the claims for our lives and the actual reality of those lived lives themselves and thus leads to authentic existence.

Kierkegaard's work received scant attention of substance during the early years of his writing, and he turned, on the one hand, to what he called "edifying discourses" in which he tried to attract the public to his ideas through forms of address that made little or no mention of Christianity and, on the other hand, to a "method of direct communication" in a series of writings under his own name, also to little avail. The last years of his life witnessed his public and overt "attack on Christendom" and the established Church in Denmark. "Christendom," he asserted, "is a conspiracy against the Christianity of the New Testament," for in it Christianity has been "transformed into optimism." It represents, therefore, not the victory but the defeat of the faith. In the course of that attack he clarified all his struggle by reducing it to a single question: "What I have constantly aimed at is to get this problem stated (before God and man, if I may so say): Can one be a Christian without being a disciple?"

Bibliography

A.   *Breve*, 2 vols. (Copenhagen, 1953–); *Papirer*, ed., P. A. Heiburg, V. Kuhn and E. Torsting, 2d ed. with 2 supp. vols., ed. by N. Thulstrup (Copenhagen, 1968–); *Samelde Vaerker*, 15 vols., 2d ed. (Copenhagen, 1920–); *Kierkegaard's Writings*, ed. and trans. H. V. and E. H. Hong, 24 vols. to date (Princeton, N.J., 1978–); *Kierkegaard's Journals and Papers*, ed. and trans. H. V. and E. H. Hong, 7 vols. (Bloomington, Ind., 1967–78).

B.   BBKL 3:1466–69; LThK³ 5:1424–25; NCE 8:174–76; ODCC 926–27; TRE 18: 138–55; Walter Lowrie, *Kierkegaard*, 2 vols. (Gloucester, Mass., 1970); David R. Law, *Kierkegaard as a Negative Theologian* (Oxford, 1993); Gregor Malantschuk, *Kierkegaard's Way to the Truth: An Introduction to the Authorship of Søren Kierkegaard*, trans. M. Michelsen (Montreal,1987); Merold Westphal, *Kierkegaard's Critique of Reason and Society* (Macon, Ga., 1987); Francois LaPointe, *Søren Kierkegaard and His Critics: An International Bibliography of Criticism* (Westport, Conn., 1980).

D. Lyle Dabney

KILWARDBY, ROBERT (ca. 1215, Yorkshire–10 September 1279, Viterbo). *Education*: studied arts at Paris, ca. 1231; M. A., ca. 1237; studied theology at Oxford, after 1245. *Career*: taught in Paris until 1245; entered the Dominican order, probably in England, 1245; master in theology, 1256–61; prior provincial of the English Dominicans, 1261, 1272; archbishop of Canterbury, 1273–78; crowned King Edward I and attended the Council of Lyons, 1274; cardinal bishop of Porto, 1278–79.

Though a Dominican contemporary of Thomas Aquinas* and a student of and commentator on some works of Aristotle, Kilwardby was closer in spirit to the Augustinian tradition and the thought of Bonaventure.* For example, in his *Commentary on the Sentences* he emphasized the vestiges of the Trinity found in creation, maintained the presence of spiritual matter in the angels, and endorsed the Augustinian doctrine of seminal reasons in creation. Kilwardby's condemnation of thirty propositions, on 18 March 1277, followed upon the condemnation of 219 propositions by the bishop of Paris eleven days earlier. It is difficult to grasp the danger to the faith involved in the propositions in grammar and logic. The sixteen propositions in natural philosophy centered on the claim that there is only one substantial form in a human being, namely, the intellective soul, a doctrine that Aquinas had taught. Kilwardby opted for the conservative, so-called "Augustinian" position of a plurality of forms, which in fact stemmed from the Jewish Neoplatonist philosopher, Ibn Gabirol, or Avicebron.

Bibliography

A. *In libros priorum analyticorum* (*Commentary on Aristotle's Prior Analytics*) ca. 1240; attributed to Giles of Rome (Venice, 1516; repr. Frankfurt a. M., 1968); *Logica Sophismata* (*Logical Sophisms*), ca. 1240; *In Priscianum de constructione commentarius* (*Commentary on Priscian's On Construction*), ca. 1240; *In Barbarismum Donati* (*Commentary on Donatus' Barbarism*), ca. 1240; *Sophismata Grammaticalia* (*Grammatical Sophisms*), ca. 1240; *De ortu scientiarum* (*The Rise of the Sciences*), ca. 1250, ed. A. Judy (London and Toronto, 1976); *De natura relationis* (*The Nature of Relation*), ca. 1252–61, ed. L. Schmücher (Brixen, 1980); *De tempore and De spiritu fantastico* (*Time and Imagination*), ca. 1252–61, ed. P. O. Lewry (Oxford and New York, 1987); *Quaestiones in libros sententiarum* (*Questions on the Four Books of the Sentences*), ca. 1256, ed. J. Schneider et al., 4 vols. (Munich, 1985–93); *De necessitate incarnationis* (*The Necessity of the Incarnation*), ca. 1256–61, ed. A. Dondaine, RTAM 8 (1939): 97–100; *Sermo in capite ieiunii* (*Sermon for Ash Wednesday*), ca. 1256–72, ed. E. Sommer-Seckendorff in *Studies in the Life of Robert Kilwardby* (Rome, 1937), 163–76; *Sermo in dominica in passione* (*Sermon for Passion Sunday*), ca. 1256–72, ed. P. O. Lewry, *Archivum Fratrum Praedicatorum* 52 (1982): 89–113; *De XLIII quaestionibus* (*Response to the Questions of John of Vercelli*), 1271, ed. H.-F. Dondaine, ibid. 47 (1977): 5–50.

B. DNB 11:120–22; DTC 8:2354–56; LThK² 8:1340; NCE 12:533–34; ODCC 927–28; M.-D. Chenu, "Le *De spiritu imaginativo* de Robert Kilwarby, O.P. (†1279)," RSPhTh 15 (1926): 507–17; idem, "Les réponses de S. Thomas et de Kilwardby à la consultation de Jean de Verceil (1271)," in *Mélanges Mandonnet* (Paris, 1930), 1:191–222; L. B. Gillon, "L'amour naturel de Dieu d'après Robert Kilwardby," *Angelicum* 29 (1952): 371–79; Ivo Thomas, "Kilwardby on Conversion," *Dominican Studies* 6 (1953): 56–76; L. B. Gillon, "Structure et genèse de la foi d'après Robert Kilwardby," *Revue Thomiste* 55 (1955): 629–36; M. Schmaus, "Augustins psychologische Trinitätserklärung bei Robert Kilwardby, O.P.," in *Sapientiae procerum amore*, ed. T. W. Köhler (Rome, 1974), 149–209; P. O. Lewry, "The Oxford Condemnations of 1277 in Grammar and Logic," in *English Logic and Semantics from the End of the Twelfth Century to the Time of Ockham and Burleigh*, ed. H. A. G. Braakhuis et al. (Nijmegen, 1981), 235–78; idem, "Robert Kilwardby on Meaning: A Parisian Course on the Logica Vetus," in *Sprache und Erkenntnis im Mittelalter*, ed. A. Zimmermann (Berlin and New York, 1981), 1:376–84; idem, "Robert Kilwardby on Imagination: The Reconciliation of Aristotle and Augustine," *Medioevo* 9 (1983): 1–42; idem, "Robert Kilwardby," in *Dictionary of Literary Biography*, vol. 115, *Medieval Philosophers*, ed. J. Hackett (Detroit, Mich., 1992), 257–64.

Roland J. Teske

KLEUTGEN, JOSEPH (9 April 1811, Dortmund, Germany–13 January 1883, Kaltern, Austria). *Education*: classical philology and philosophy, Univ. of Munich, 1831; theology, Univs. of Münster, 1832, and Paderborn, 1833; philosophy and theology, Jesuit house of studies in Fribourg, Switzerland, 1836–40. *Career*: entered the Society of Jesus, Brig, Switzerland, 1834; ordained priest, 1837; professor of moral theology, Jesuit House of Studies, Brig, Switzerland, 1841–

43; staff, Jesuit Curia, Rome; confessor, German Coll., Rome, 1843–47; professor, German Coll., 1847–69; consultor to Congregation of the Index, Rome, 1850–61; helped draft the Constitutions on Faith and on the Church, Vatican I, 1870; prefect of Studies, Gregorian Univ., 1878–79; retirement, 1879–83.

Kleutgen was one of the most influential early-nineteenth-century scholastics. Although German by birth and education, he spent most of his active life in Rome. His influence on the graduates of the German college contributed greatly to the revival of German scholasticism. In company with the Italian Jesuit neo-scholastics, Kleutgen launched a vigorous campaign to make St. Thomas* once again the leading Catholic theologian. Through his writings and his influence on the Papal Curia, Kleutgen helped to bring about the condemnation of several nineteenth-century systems of Catholic theology. Among them were the French and Italian systems of Traditionalism and Ontologism and the German theologies of Günther* and Frohschammer. He also worked for the revival of scholasticism within the Society of Jesus. Vatican I's Constitution on Faith, *Dei Filius*, on whose drafting Kleutgen worked, reflects his own approach to theology through the categories under which unorthodox positions on faith and reason are listed. Whether or not Kleutgen helped to draft Leo XIII's Encyclical *Aeterni Patris* (1878), he considered its endorsement of scholastic theology the vindication of his own life's work. Leo XIII secured his appointment as Prefect of Studies of the Gregorian (1878–79) in order to bring its curriculum into line with the recommendations of *Aeterni Patris*. In 1879, however, the stroke that crippled Kleutgen ended his career.

Kleutgen's extensive knowledge of scholasticism and post-Cartesian philosophy enabled him to correct the erroneous presentation of scholasticism prevalent in the works of modern theologians. It also enabled him to argue that scholastic epistemology and metaphysics could ground a scientific theology more capable of doing justice to the church's teaching on faith, reason, nature, and grace than could the modern theologies based on one or another of the post-Cartesian systems. He did so in his major works *Die Theologie der Vorzeit verteidigt* (*A Defense of Pre-Enlightenment Theology*) and *Die Philosophie der Vorzeit Verteidigt* (*A Defense of Pre-Enlightenment Philosophy*). In *Die Theologie der Vorzeit* Kleutgen corrected the inaccurate presentation of scholasticism in the works of the Bonn theologian Georg Hermes,* the Viennese theologian Anton Günther, and the Freiburg moral theologian Johann Baptist Hirscher, a representative of the Tübingen School who shared its antipathy toward scholasticism. He then criticized their own theologies. Hermes had taken his inspiration from Kant while Günther and Hirscher had taken theirs from post-Kantian idealism. In attacking them, therefore, Kleutgen was arguing against the German project of replacing scholasticism with a contemporary theology built upon German idealism. His objection to that project was twofold. A theology based upon post-Cartesian philosophy could not adequately defend the teachings of the church, and its method was inherently defective. On the contrary, the Aristotelian scientific method of St. Thomas, which the great post-Tridentine scholastics continued to use, could structure the contemporary theology that the church needed. In *Die Philosophie der Vorzeit*, Kleutgen expounded the scholastic epistemology and metaphysics required to ground that theological method.

Kleutgen's philosophy and theology were the work of a brilliant pioneer. The knowledge of the medieval and baroque scholastics revealed in them is remarkable in an author writing before historical research on scholastic texts had begun. Kleutgen's grasp of the crucial distinction between pre-Cartesian and Cartesian reason and of its importance for theology and ethics would be more generally appreciated today than it was in his own lifetime. So would be his understanding of the problems associated with the Cartesian starting point in philosophy. Nevertheless, the significance of Kleutgen's work today is historical rather than systematic. Its focus on an apodictic scientific method bears the mark of the nineteenth century, and historical research has brought to light a complexity and pluralism in medieval and post-Tridentine scholasticism of which a theologian in Kleutgen's time could not have been aware.

Bibliography

A. *Die Theologie der Vorzeit Verteidigt*, 5 vols. (Münster 1853–70; rev. ed. Innsbruck, 1867–74); *Die Philosophie der Vorzeit Verteidigt* (Münster, 1860–63).

B. ChP 2:145–75; DTC 8:2359–60; LThK³ 6:340; NCE 8:212; Sommervogel 4: 1113–16; Franz Lakner, "Kleutgen und die kirchliche Wissenschaft Deutschlands im 19. Jahrhundert," ZKTh 57 (1933): 161–214; Georges van Riet, "Joseph Kleutgen" in *Epistemologie Thomiste* (Louvain, 1946): 69–81; Theo Schäfer, *Die erkenntnis theoretische Kontroverse Kleutgen-Günther* (Padeborn, 1961); Gerald A. McCool, S.J. "Kleutgen's Theological Synthesis" in *Catholic Theology in the Nineteenth Century: The Quest for a Unitary Method* (New York, 1972); reissued under title of *Nineteenth Century Scholasticism* (New York, 1989), same pagination.

Gerald A. McCool

KNOX, JOHN (? 1514 Haddington, East Lothian, Scotland–24 November 1572, Edinburgh). *Education*: studied at Univ. of Glasgow, 1522–?. *Career*: ordained priest, 1536; unknown activity, 1536–40; notary apostolic, diocese of St. Andrews, 1540–46; tutor, 1544–46; galley slave on French ship, 1547–49; licensed preacher, Berwick and Newcastle, 1549–52; preacher, Buckinghamshire, 1553; exiled in Geneva and Dieppe, 1553–59; minister, St. Giles congregation, Edinburgh, 1560–72; travels to England, 1567.

Knox was more a reformer of the Scottish Kirk than he was a systematic theologian, but he had an influence upon ecclesiastical and theological developments in Scotland because of the role he played in shaping the Scots Confession and the Book of Common Order. Knox was ordained a priest and served as a tutor prior to his conversion to Protestantism. As a Protestant reformer, particularly after his return from his Genevan exile in 1559, he established the foundations of the Presbyterian order in Scotland. He also wrote a history of the Reformation in Scotland that served his apologetical purposes.

Bibliography

A. *The Works of Knox*, ed. David Laing, 6 vols. (Edinburgh, 1846–64; New York, 1966); *The First Book of Discipline*, ed. James Cameron (Edinburgh, 1972); *The Second Book of Discipline*, ed. James Kirk (Edinburgh, 1980); *History of the Reformation in Scotland*, ed. W. C. Dickinson, 2 vols. (Edinburgh, 1949); *The Political Writings of Knox*, ed. Marvin A. Breslow (Washington, D.C., and London, 1985).

B. DNB 11:308–328; DTC 8:2361–70; LThK³ 6:360; NCE 8:242; RGG 3:1686; Gordon Donaldson, *The Scottish Reformation* (Cambridge, 1960); Jasper Ridley, *John Knox* (Oxford, 1968); W. Standford Reid, *Trumpeter of God* (Grand Rapids, Mich., 1982).

Patrick W. Carey

KRAUS, FRANZ XAVER (18 September 1840, Trier, Germany–28 December 1901, San Remo, Italy). *Education*: Catholic Sem., Trier, 1858; Ph.D., philosophy, Univ. of Freiburg, 1862; Catholic Sem., Trier, 1862–64; Ph.D., theology, Univ. of Freiburg, 1865. *Career*: private tutor, France, 1860–62; ordained priest, 1864; priest, Platzel, Germany, 1865–72; professor, history of Christian art, Univ. of Strasbourg, 1872–78; professor, church history, Univ. of Freiburg, 1878–1901.

Kraus was a representative of German liberal Catholicism. He wanted to bring Catholic faith and practices into harmony with the demands of German culture at the end of the nineteenth century, to make Catholicism a leading force in the intellectual struggles of the age, and to resolve the practical and theoretical opposition between the church and the state. He called for an end to what he called the ''worldly political and pharisaical aspirations of Ultramontanism.''

Having lived through the *Kulturkampf*, he opposed secular liberalism because he believed it had destroyed the first principle of true liberty by violating the doctrine of ''absolute freedom of conscience and spirit.'' By emphasizing religious over political Catholicism, moreover, Kraus became sympathetic with some of the aims of Catholic Americanists, even though he was much more interested than they were in the struggle for intellectual freedom and scientific investigation within the church.

Bibliography

A. *Ueber das Studium der Theologie sonst und jetzt . . .* (Freiburg im Breisgau, 1890); *Cavour. Die Erhebung Italiens im neunzehnten Jarhhundert* (Mainz, 1902); *Tagebücher*, ed. Hubert Schiel (Cologne, 1957); *Liberal und Integral. Der Briefwechsel zwischen F. X. Kraus und Anton Stöck*, ed. Hubert Schiel (Mainz, 1974).

B. Catholicisme 6:1479–81; KThD 3:241–75; LThK³ 6:596; NCE 8:261; NDB 12: 684–85; ODCC 936; Robert C. Ayers, ''The Americanists and Franz Xaver Kraus: An Historical Analysis of an International Liberal Catholic Combination, 1897–1898,'' Ph.D. diss., Syracuse Univ., 1981.

Patrick W. Carey

KRAUTH, CHARLES PORTERFIELD (17 March 1823, Martensburg, Va.–2 January 1883, Philadelphia, Pa.). *Education*: studied at Pennsylvania [later Gettysburg] Coll., 1834–39, and Theol. Sem., 1839–41. *Career*: pastor, Canton and Baltimore, Md., 1841–47; Shepherdstown, Martinsburg and Winchester, Va., 1847–56; Pittsburgh, 1856–59; Philadelphia, 1859–61; editor in chief, *Lutheran and Missionary Magazine*, 1861–67; professor of Dogmatics, Lutheran Sem., Philadelphia, 1864–83; professor of moral philosophy, Univ. of Pennsylvania, 1867–83; editor in chief, *Lutheran Church Review*, 1882–83.

Krauth was the most influential nineteenth-century theologian and spokesperson for conservative Lutheranism. For nearly twenty years prior to the Civil War, Krauth was a prominent pastor and leader in the General Synod, then the largest body of Lutheran churches in North America.

Slowly but surely he began to reject the theology represented by the General Synod and its leader, Samuel S. Schmucker.* He resisted Schmucker's attempts to ''Americanize'' the Lutheran Church and to move toward some type of union with other Protestant bodies. Krauth was convinced that this position involved a serious compromise and betrayal of Lutheranism's true historical and confessional heritage, and his views prevailed.

At the close of the war Krauth agreed to take part in a movement to form a new body of Lutheran churches called the General Council. The group was organized in 1867. Because of his brilliant scholarship and theological acumen Krauth quickly assumed leadership. He served as president of the General Council for ten years (1870–80), and was the author of nearly all of its position papers and constitutional articles. Krauth's basic theological position was fully presented in his major work, *The Conservative Reformation and Its Theology* (Philadelphia, 1871). A major portion of this book carefully defined the eucharistic doctrine of the ''Real Presence'' as the key mark of a true conservative Lutheranism. As time passed, Krauth advocated a progressively stricter form of conservative policy in the General Council. All the articles of faith contained in the Augsburg Confession were defined as ''fundamental.'' Altar and pulpit fellowship was rigidly restricted. Krauth's conservative theology continues to exert influence among large sections of Lutheranism in the present era.

Bibliography

A. *The Relations of the Lutheran Church to Denominations Around Us* (Philadelphia, 1878); *Theses on the Galesburg Declaration on Pulpit and Altar Fellowship* (Philadelphia, 1877).

B. DAB 10:502–3; NCAB 1:349; NCE 8:262; NYT 3 January 1883, 5; SH 6:381–82; Adolph Spaeth, *Charles Porterfield Krauth*, 2 vols. (New York, 1898; repr. 2 vols. in 1, New York, 1969); Vergilius Ferm, *The Crisis in American Lutheran Theology* (New York, 1927); David A. Gustafson, *Lutherans in Crisis* (Minneapolis, Minn., 1993).

Paul K. Kuenning

KUHN, JOHANNES (20 February 1806, Wäschenbeuren–8 May 1887, Tübingen). *Education*: Latin school, Gmünd, 1818–21; gymnasium, Ellwangen, 1821–24, completed in Rottweil, 1824–25; studied philosophy and theology,

Tübingen, 1825–30. *Career*: ordained priest, 1831; chair of New Testament exegesis, Giesen, 1832–36; professor of biblical exegesis, Tübingen, 1837–38; professor of dogmatics, Tübingen, 1839–87.

Following his Tübingen mentors, Kuhn repudiated rationalism and extreme forms of fideism and traditionism and constructed a theology that combined a historical view of the Scriptures and the development of Christian doctrines with a speculative vision influenced by Idealist philosophical currents. While teaching New Testament exegesis, Kuhn crafted a substantive critique of D. F. Strauss'* *The Life of Jesus Critically Examined* (1835). Granting the confessional character of the New Testament documents did not require discrediting their intention to present a history of Jesus the Christ. He attacked Strauss' claim that the original form of oral tradition, which Strauss claimed was not mythic, and the final mythic narratives about Jesus, which are the unconscious and unintentional creation of the faith of the community (*Volksgeist*), are different in essence. He rejected, moreover, Strauss' contention that the Old Testament provided a key creative source for the mythical rendering of the identity of Jesus of Nazareth, rather than a prophetic confirmation of this identity. Although affirming the value of historical criticism, he argued that Strauss offered an allegorical and naturalistic interpretation of the gospels that reduced every narrative component to the same kind of mythical interpretation and also failed to distinguish the supernatural form and the supernatural content of the New Testament narratives. The gospels need not all be historical for Kuhn, but there must be a genuine historical outline. Strauss failed to appreciate the complex literary character of the gospel traditions that combined historical, didactic, and theological modes of discourse, and his Hegelian assumptions restricted the freedom of God and the free cooperation of human agents in the historical process of a revelatory tradition.

Kuhn struggled with neoscholastic critics. His efforts to articulate the relationship between faith and knowledge, theology and philosophy, were set against the position of neoscholastic Jakob Clemens, who defended the subordination of philosophy to theology. Drawing from Idealist philosophies, Kuhn analyzed the movement from perception to concept in philosophy and positive faith to known faith in theology, without denying the divinely given nature of revelation. The dispute with Constantin von Schäzler, between 1863–66, concerned his efforts to articulate the relations between nature and grace while avoiding the problems of extreme supernaturalism and naturalism.

Kuhn's theology of revelation affirmed the primacy of the Word of God as gospel, which is expressed in the Scriptures and in the living tradition. He qualified J. A. Möhler's* axiom that the church is the ongoing Incarnation. Instead he conceived of the church as an instrument of Christ that stands under the Word of God. The apostolic authority of the gospel is affirmed in and mediated through the church. This faith in the gospel has a history that unfolds through a dialectical process of thought and results in the formation of dogma. In contrast to earlier Tübingen theologians who recognized the *sensus fidei* as an effective presence of the Spirit in the entire community of faith, Kuhn's debate with Strauss over the unconscious generation of myths led him to emphasize the truth of faith secured by the church and its official teaching authority. Kuhn, too, is recognized as an early proponent of "a hierarchy of truths" in matters of Catholic faith.

Bibliography

A. *Das Leben Jesu, wissenschaftlich bearbeitet* (Mainz, 1838; repr. Frankfurt am Main, 1968); *Katholische Dogmatik*, 2 vols. (Tübingen, 1857, 1859; repr. Frankfurt am Main, 1968); *Philosophie und Theologie. Eine Streitschrift* (Tübingen, 1860); *Die christliche Lehre von der göttlichen Gnade* (Tübingen, 1868; repr. Frankfurt am Main, 1968).

B. DTC 8:2377–79; ECatt 7:753–54; LThK³ 6:656–57; NCE 8:265–66; Josef Rupert Geiselmann, *Die lebendige Überlieferung als Norm des christlichen Glaubens. Die apostolische Tradition in der Form der kirchlichen Verkündigung—das Formalprinzip des Katholizismus, dargestellt im Geist der Traditionslehre von John. Ev. Kuhn* (Freiburg, 1959); Hubert Wolf, *Ketzer oder Kirchenlehrer? Der Tübinger Theologe Johannes von Kuhn 1806–1887* (Mainz, 1992); William Madges, *The Core of Christian Faith: D. F. Strauss and His Catholic Critics* (New York, 1987); Karl Josef Mattes, *Die Kontroverse zwischen Johannes v. Kuhn und Konstantin von Schäzler über das Verhältnis von Natur und Gnade* (Freiburg, Switzerland, 1968).

Bradford Hinze

KUYPER, ABRAHAM (29 October 1837, Maassluis, The Netherlands–8 November 1920, The Hague, The Netherlands). *Education*: doctor of theology, Univ. of Leiden, 1855–62. *Career*: minister, Netherlands Reformed Church, 1863–74; editor in chief, *De Standaard*, 1872–76, 1878–1919; *De Heraut*, 1869–72, 1877–1919; elected, Second Chamber of Dutch Parliament, 1874, 1894, 1901, 1908; founder, Free Univ. of Amsterdam, 1880; professor of theology, Free Univ. of Amsterdam, 1880–1908; leader of church renewal and secession, 1886; prime minister of The Netherlands, 1901–5; minister of state in Dutch government, 1908–12; elected, First Chamber of Dutch parliament, 1913.

Kuyper inspired, directed, and personified the revival of Reformed theology and sociopolitical reflection and action in the Netherlands that eventually became labeled as neo-Calvinism. Born into a clerical family in the theologically liberal Dutch national Reformed Church, Kuyper was converted to orthodox Calvinism and became its champion in a multifaceted and influential career that included journalism, church reform, university-level education, and national politics.

Kuyper's neo-Calvinist vision began with the conviction of divine sovereignty over all "spheres" of life—politics, business, labor, education, and the arts as well as church and family. From this primordial principle Kuyper derived four secondary ones: common grace, antithesis, sphere sovereignty, and a distinction between the church as institution and as organism.

For Kuyper, Calvinism was more than a churchly, confessional tradition. It was a *Weltanschauung*, a world and life view, a life system *antithetically* opposed to other life systems such as paganism and, particularly, modernism. The spirit of modernism, captured in the French Revolution's slogan *Ni Dieu, ni maître*, came to expression especially in the political sphere where an idolatry of the state replaced God's ordinances. Kuyper's political ideology was anti-revolutionary as well as antistatist. Divine sovereignty was seen to be exercised *directly* over such sovereign spheres as the school and the family, rather than through the mediation of either the church or the state. This conviction led Kuyper to advocate a principled pluralism that honored both structural as well as religious diversity. One of his major political accomplishments was the legal establishment of a religiously plural education system.

Kuyper's ambition was to inspire conservative Dutch Calvinists to leave behind pietist and sectarian withdrawal from civic, social, and political life and thus to re-Christianize the nation, not through institutional, ecclesiastical privilege but through the voluntary activity of Christians in free churches and distinctly Christian organizations.

Bibliography

A.   *Principles of Sacred Theology*, trans. John Hendrick De Vries (New York, 1898; repr. Grand Rapids, Mich., 1965); *Lectures on Calvinism* (Grand Rapids, Mich., 1931); *The Work of the Holy Spirit*, trans. J. Hendrick De Vries (New York and London, 1900); *The Problem of Poverty*, trans. James W. Skillen (Grand Rapids, Mich., 1991).

B.   LThK³ 6:548; NCE 8:272; ODCC 938; RGG 4:191–92; James D. Bratt, *Dutch Calvinism in Modern America* (Grand Rapids, Mich., 1984); McKendree R. Langley, *The Practice of Political Spirituality: Episodes in the Public Career of Abraham Kuyper* (Jordan Station, Ont., Canada, 1984); Louis Praamsma, *Let Christ Be King: Reflections on the Life and Times of Abraham Kuyper* (Jordan Station, Ont., Canada, 1985); Justus M. Van de Kroef, "Abraham Kuyper and the Rise of Neo-Calvinism in the Netherlands," CH 17 (1948): 316–34.

John Bolt

L

LABERTHONNIÈRE, LUCIEN (5 October 1860, Chazelet dans l'Indre, France–6 October 1932, Paris). *Education*: studied at the Sulpician sem., Bourges, 1886; *baccalauréat*, 1892; *licence* in philosophy, Sorbonne, 1893. *Career*: ordained priest and entered Oratorians, 1886; teacher and administrator, Oratorian schools, 1886–1903; with Maurice Blondel,* coeditor, *Annales de philosophie chrétienne* 1905–13; forbidden to publish by decree from Rome, 1913; lived in Paris, 1913–32.

Laberthonnière's name is inevitably linked with that of Maurice Blondel. Unhappy with the tone of the Catholic apologetics and dogmatic theology of his seminary training, Laberthonnière found in Blondel's *L'action* and his "method of immanence" a mode of philosophical thought ideally suited to working out his own theological insights. The two met in 1894 and became close friends and professional colleagues, active in projects and organizations aimed at bringing French Catholic thought into dialogue with contemporary philosophy, science, and politics.

Laberthonnière never developed his ideas systematically, but his many essays are remarkable for their consistency. His thought may be characterized as "moral dogmatism" or a "metaphysics of charity," characterized by its emphasis on the presence of God as the indwelling of divine love within the human soul and on the interplay of thought and action, faith and reason, mind and will, nature and grace, and the human and the divine. He envisioned an apologetic that allowed for the individual's assimilation and affirmation of truth, including the truths of revelation. Such a moral mode of persuasion would, Laberthonnière argued, display the reasonableness of faith more appropriately than did the neoscholastic emphasis on the authoritative hegemony of reason, detached from the practical exigencies of human life.

Considered a modernist by influential Roman theologians and authorities, La-berthonnière was criticized for making truth subjective and for failing to maintain those distinctions between reason and faith that were considered crucial to Catholic theology. Such criticisms were the apparent basis for the official condemnations.

Laberthonnière at times distinguished between Thomas'* texts and the neo-scholasticism of his opponents, and his own work anticipated an emphasis on the unity of the human person that neo-Thomists such as Joseph Maréchal* would develop. Nonetheless, Laberthonnière strenuously objected to Blondel's growing interest in neo-Thomism; mutual accusations of serious misunderstandings eventually led to the termination of their friendship in 1928. Recent work on Laberthonnière has focused less on his dependence upon Blondel and more on his own originality and creativity.

Bibliography

A.   *Oeuvres de Laberthonnière*, 3 vols. (Paris, 1937); *Le réalisme chrétien, précédé de Essais de philosophie religieuse* (Paris, 1966); *Correspondance philosophique* (Paris, 1961); *Laberthonnière et ses amis* (Paris, 1975); *Dossier Laberthonnière* (Paris, 1983).
B.   ChP 3:364–65; DSAM 9:9–16; LThK³ 6:577; ODCC 940; *Laberthonnière: l'homme et l'œuvre*, ed. Paul Beillevert (Paris, 1972); Gabriel Daly, "Lucien Laberthonnière's 'Critical Mysticism,' " in *Transcendence and Immanence* (Oxford, 1980); Marie-Thérèse Perrin, *La jeunesse de Laberthonnière* (Paris, 1982).

Ann Riggs

LAÍNEZ, DIEGO (1512, Almazán, Spain–19 January 1565, Rome). *Education*: studied Latin, Soria and Sigüenza, 1520s; studied philosophy and some theology, Univ. of Alcalá, 1528–32; M.A., Univ. of Alcalá, 1532; studied at Univ. of Paris, 1533–34. *Career*: ordained priest, 1537; taught theology, Sapienza, Rome, 1537–65; papal theologian, Council of Trent, 1546–47 and 1550–55; general of Jesuits, 1558–65.

Laínez is generally regarded as the most intellectually gifted and the most competent theologian among the first Jesuits. At the Council of Trent he rejected theories of double justification and defended papal rights in the controversy over episcopal jurisdiction. Ignatius Loyola* wanted Laínez to write a theological summa but administrative duties ate up his time and energy. Many considered him *papabilis* at the conclave after Paul IV's death in 1559.

Bibliography

A.   *Jacobii Lainez Disputationes Tridentinae*, ed. H. Grisar, 2 vols. (Innsbruck/New York, 1886).
B.   DTC 8:2449–50; ECatt 7:819–21; LThK³ 6:608–9; NCE 8:326–27; ODCC 943–44; TRE 20:399–404; Joseph H. Fichter, *James Laynez, Jesuit* (St. Louis, Mo., 1944); Feliciano Cereceda, *Diego Lanez en la Europa religiosa de su tiempo, 1512–1565*, 2 vols. (Madrid, 1945–46); Mario Scaduto, *Storia della Compagnia di Gesù. L'epocha di*

Giacomo Lainez 1556–1565, 2 vols. (Rome, 1964–74); John O'Malley, *The First Jesuits* (Cambridge, Mass., 1993).

John Patrick Donnelly

LAMENNAIS, FÉLICITÉ-ROBERT DE (19 June 1782, Saint-Malo, Brittany–27 February 1854, Paris). *Career*: ordained priest, 1816; Catholic writer, 1817–34; editor, *L'Avenir*, 1830–31; socialist writer and advocate, 1834–54.

Lamennais is significant in the history of French Catholic thought for his contributions to traditionalism and his unsuccessful attempts to reconcile Catholicism and modern freedoms. Almost immediately after his ordination to the priesthood, for which he had very little formal education, he promptly wrote the first of the four volumes of his *Essai sur l'indifférence* (1817–23) to great acclaim; it was the book of the moment, of the Restoration. Disillusioned by actual Restoration policies, Lamennais went on to write *De la religion considérée dans ses rapports avec l'ordre politique et civil* (1826). In it he set out to show, in the vein opened by Joseph de Maistre,* that to diminish the authority of the pope was to subject the spiritual power to political power and to undermine the bases of society itself. A court condemned the work.

He also engaged in two projects that would be of the greatest significance for the reviving church of France in the coming decades. At La Chênaie, where he lived, he set up a novitiate to train priests in languages and in the modern natural and social sciences. Among his students were future bishops and founders of orders. And he developed a flair for journalism that went far beyond his other publishing activities. It led him in the course of the 1820s away from the ancien régime ideal to embrace the popular movements for freedom. In his shortlived weekly, *L'avenir* (1830–31), with its celebrated motto, "God and Liberty," he called passionately for freedom of religion and of conscience, freedom of the press, freedom of association, freedom in education, and the separation of church and state. He demanded that the suffrage be democratized and that the highly centralized administration of France be reformed for greater local autonomy.

Such radical proposals did not meet with wide acceptance in the church of France; in a fateful move, Lamennais decided to go to Rome in 1832 and place himself again under the aegis of the pope. But Gregory XVI (1831–46) was not Leo XII (1823–29); the Roman offices found themselves in the unpleasant position of having to repudiate the papacy's foremost champion in the modern world, as gently as possible, but unmistakably; the encyclical *Mirari Vos* condemning his ideas did not mention him by name. He went on to publish the religious-socialist *Paroles d'un croyant* (1834) and *Affaires de Rome* (1836). Thus the pattern of relations between European politics and the Vatican was set for the rest of the century on a collision course. Lamennais' own further life as a religious socialist writer was spent in disillusionment with the church. His attempt to wed the Gospel and the Revolution on a theoretical level was premature and tragic in its consequences.

His enormous influence (without it, as R. Bäumer has noted with a certain understatement, the definition of papal infallibility "would have met greater resistance" at the First Vatican Council) was not simply intellectual. His reasoned "traditionalist" apologetic, though flawed, must not on this account be underestimated in the history of religious thought. His defense against enlightened exaltation of reason pointed out how easily misled an individual's mind is, and hence, upon reflection, how prone to skepticism. The universal consent of mankind (the *sens commun*), on the contrary, can be trusted to communicate certainties given to the human race long ago by God in a primitive revelation together with the gift of language.

Bibliography

A.   *Oeuvres complètes*, 12 vols. (Paris, 1836–37; repr. Frankfurt, 1967); *Oeuvres complètes*, 11 vols., ed. L. Le Guillou (Paris 1981); *Correspondance générale*, 9 vols., ed. L. Le Guillou (Paris, 1971–81).

B.   BBKL 4:1036–45; ChP 1:459–76; LThK³ 6:568–69; NCE 8:347–49; TRE 20: 424–27; Alec Vidler, *Prophecy and Papacy* (New York, 1954); L. Le Guillou, *L'évolution de la pensée religieuse de Lamennais* (Paris, 1966); P. N. Stearns, *Priest and Revolutionary* (New York, 1967); *L'actualité de Lamennais* (Strasbourg, 1981); M. J. Le Guillou and L. Le Guillou, *La condemnation de Lamennais* (Paris, 1982).

Paul Misner

LANFRANC (early 11th century, Pavia–24 May 1089, Canterbury). *Education*: studied at the schools of Bologna. *Career*: master in the cathedral school, Avranches, 1039; entered the monastery at Bec in Normandy, 1042; founded a school at Bec; abbot of a new monastic foundation at Caen, 1063–70; archbishop of Canterbury, 1070–89.

The eleventh century witnessed a turning point in the history of theology, as dialectical processes were introduced into theological enquiry. Although opposition to the use of logic in matters of faith came most often from monastic educators, Lanfranc, who for many years headed the school at the monastery of Bec, embodied a positive acceptance of reason ordered within and under faith. Among Lanfranc's students were Anselm,* his successor at Bec and as archbishop of Canterbury; Ivo of Chartres; and the future Pope Alexander II.

Lanfranc's lasting theological contribution came in the context of the eucharistic debate occasioned by the writings of Berengar of Tours.* It is possible that Lanfranc had studied under Berengar at Tours in the 1030s and thereby developed his appreciation for dialectics. But Lanfranc came to oppose his former master's brand of logical realism once it led him to deny the doctrine of transsubstantiation. Lanfranc wrote one of his most important works, the *Liber de corpore et sanguine Domini adversus Berengarium*, as a refutation of Berengar's teaching. His other theological works include glosses on the Epistles of Paul and on John Cassian's* *Collationes patrum*.

Bibliography

A.   PL 150.

B.   DTC 8:2558–70; LThK³ 6:636; NCE 8:361–62; ODCC 949; TRE 20:434–36; Richard W. Southern, "Lanfranc of Bec and Berengar of Tours," in *Studies in Medieval History Presented to F. M. Powicke*, ed. R. W. Hunt et al. (Oxford, 1948), 27–48; J. de Montclos, *Lanfranc et Bérenger. La controverse eucharistique du XIᵉ siècle* (Louvain, 1971); M. Gibson, *Lanfranc of Bec* (Oxford, 1978).

M. Michèle Mulchahey

LANGTON, STEPHEN, *Doctor nominatissimus* (ca. 1150, Lincolnshire–9 July 1228, Slindon in Sussex). *Education*: studied under Peter Cantor or Peter Comestor, Paris. *Career*: *magister*, Paris, after 1180; cardinal, 1206; archbishop of Canterbury, 1207–28; oversaw the signing of the Magna Carta in June, 1215; participant, Fourth Lateran Council, Rome, 1215; after returning to England in 1218, celebrated the canonization of Hugh of Lincoln and the translation of Thomas Becket.

Langton was a celebrated theologian in his time. He wrote glosses on much of the Bible, and left three theological writings: a short *Summa*, *Quaestiones theologicae*, and a commentary on the *Sentences*, as well as over 500 sermons. Langton divided the Vulgate Bible into chapters, and was the first to cite the Bible in this way. His commentary on the *Sentences* (ca. 1200) was the first to treat the problems raised there independently and with originality. His interests were in moral questions and the doctrine of the sacraments. He treated the definition of "sacrament," and is particularly good on the Eucharist, transsubstantiation, and penance.

Bibliography

A.   Most of his works are unpublished; but see *Der Sentenzenkommentar des Kardinals Stephan Langton*, ed. Artur M. Landgraf (Münster, 1952).

B.   DMA 7:337–38; DSAM 4:1495–1502; DTC, tables generales, 1299; LThK² 9: 1045; NCE 13:699–700; ODCC 950; Frederick M. Powicke, *Stephen Langton* (Oxford, 1928).

Joseph T. Lienhard

LAS CASAS, BARTOLOME DE (1484, Seville, Spain–18 July 1566, Madrid, Spain). *Education*: bachelors in canon law, Univ. of Salamanca, 1498, 1507; licentiate in canon law, Univ. of Valladolid, 1519. *Career*: encomendero in Hispaniola, 1502–14; ordained priest, 1507; Dominican friar, 1522; bishop of Chiapas, 1543–66.

Las Casas, protector of the Indians, was the central figure in the sixteenth century movement for reform of Spain's Encomienda system and Catholic evangelization. In 1498, the son of Pedro de las Casas, a merchant in Columbus' second expedition, interrupted his studies for the priesthood in order to enter five years of service as a provisioner for Spanish authorities in the Indies. During that service, atrocities like those during the Higuey Campaign stirred the social conscience of the young padron. When he returned to Seville in 1506, he committed his life to that of the priest of peace rather than the life of an encomendero.

After completing his baccalaureate studies at Salamanca, he returned to Hispaniola to be the first priest ordained in the New World. Concurrent with his return, Dominicans Pedro de Cordoba and Anton Montesinos arrived and denounced the abuses of the Encomienda system. The prophetic Dominican witness and Las Casas' continued experience of Spanish aggression against the Indians moved the young cleric during a Pentecost sermon (1514) to declare the Encomienda system morally wrong and participation in it a mortal sin.

Between 1515 and 1566, Las Casas was present in word or person in the courts of Spanish kings, European emperors, and Catholic popes. He made theological appeals and moral arguments for a ban on slavery and the abolition of the Encomienda. His remedies for the troubled Indies took the forms of peaceful mediation as in the Spanish confrontation with Cacique Enriquillo and alternative social-economic experiments like the failed Cumana community.

When Las Casas returned to Spain in 1522, he became a Dominican friar. During his retreat into the Dominican discipline of study and prayer, the young friar assessed Indian reality in light of his studies of Scripture, patristics, and theology (especially Aquinas* and Cajetan's* comments on Aquinas). Not long after his return to the Indies (1526), he composed the *History of the Indies*—the historical account of life in the New World from a Mesoamerican perspective. The effectiveness of his memorials, remedies, and histories was manifest in the antislavery law of 1530, the New Laws (governing Spanish colonies) of 1542–43, and the papal encyclical, *Sublimis Deus* (1537), on Catholic evangelization.

Las Casas' greatest contributions to the reform of colonial Catholicism came from his debates with Juan Gines de Sepulveda and from the text *De unico modo* (*The Only Way*). Sepulveda argued that Catholic philosophical theology warranted an aggressive and violent evangelization in the Indies because colonization was a state of justified war—the Conquest was a means for achieving the salvation of the infidel's soul. In *The Only Way*, Las Casas raised the Dominican perspective that sought truth wherever it may be found. He situated his argument for a peaceful, persuasive evangelization in strong creation and incarnational theologies that celebrated the presence and work of grace in the beauty, wisdom, and truth in Indian culture. As Las Casas' theology matured through practice, he concluded that Spain's most effective witness to the Gospel would be the withdrawal of military forces from the Indies, the restitution of all lands to the Indians, and the restoration of Indian culture. Once accomplished, Spain could approach the free Indian peoples in a spirit of cooperation and dialogue—perhaps establishing a commonwealth relationship.

Self-scrutiny was ever the hallmark of Las Casas' life. He recognized a discrimination against African slaves in his argumentation and, consequently, he denounced the enslavement of the African people as a mortal sin.

The enduring historical legacies of Las Casas are his model of a contextual theology and his witness for human rights grounded in a life by communion—an intriguing contrast to the modern perspective on human rights grounded in the life of the isolated autonomous self.

Bibliography

A.   *Obras escogidas*, ed. J. Perez de Tudela, 5 vols. (Madrid, 1957–58); *In Defense of the Indians*, trans. J. Poole (De Kalb, Ill., 1974); *Bartolome de las Casas: The Only Way*, ed. Helen Parish (New York, 1992).

B.   DTC 8:2620–21; LThK³ 6:653–54; NCE 8:394–95; ODCC 952; TRE 20:445–48; M. Fernandez Gemenez, *Bartolome de las Casas*, 2 vols. (Seville, 1953–60); *Bartolome de las Casas in History*, ed. J. Friede and B. Keen (De Kalb, Ill., 1971); L. Hanke, *All Mankind Is One* (De Kalb, Ill., 1974); Gustavo Gutierrez, *Las Casas* (New York, 1993); Helen Rand Parish, *Las Casas as a Bishop: A New Interpretation* (Washington, D.C., 1980).

Dominic P. Scibilia

LA TAILLE, MAURICE DE (30 November 1872, Semblançay, France–23 October 1933, Paris). *Education*: studied at St. Mary's Coll., Canterbury, and Benedictine Coll., Ramsgate, 1880s; humanities, Canterbury, 1892–94; philosophy, Jersey, 1894–97; Ph.L., Sorbonne, 1898; theology, Paris and Lyons, 1898–1902. *Career*: entered Society of Jesus, Canterbury, 1890; ordained priest, Tours, 1901; parish priest, Lancastershire, 1902–4; professor, dogmatic theology, Angers, 1905–14; army chaplain, 1914–18; professor, Gregorian Univ., Rome, 1919–31.

Maurice de la Taille is renowned in Catholic theology for his *magnum opus*, *Mysterium Fidei* (1919), a study of the Mass as a sacrifice. In it La Taille attempts to resolve the theological difficulty that, given the concept of sacrifice, the Mass must somehow involve the killing of a victim. He notes that in any sacrifice, because of God's greatness and goodness, humans make an (1) *offering* of themselves through symbol that necessarily involves an (2) *immolation* of a victim, that is, a death representing the death that results from sin and the reparation owed to God's honor injured by sin. He then argues that in Christ's sacrifice, which according to Catholic tradition is re-presented in the Mass, the Last Supper ritual is the original self-offering and the cross, the immolation on behalf of sinners. However, offering is the essence of sacrifice, and so it is not necessary that a new immolation take place for the Mass to be a sacrifice. Rather, since Christ in his original sacrifice consecrated himself completely to God, his once-and-for-all immolation exists now in effect in himself as the eternally offered victim. The Mass, then, is a true sacrifice and one with the sacrifice of the cross, not because the cross is recalled and symbolized on the altar in the body separate from the blood—although it is, but because in the Mass the same immolated victim, Jesus Christ, is offered.

La Taille broke with the then current theological practice of considering the Mass as sacrifice only in terms of the consecrated sacrament. No longer accepted by theologians today, his theory enjoyed a huge success at the time in great part because of his brilliant reasoning and erudition, though few accepted all of its elements. His published clarifications and responses to objections further developed his theory and were gathered together later into a separate volume.

In 1928 La Taille originated a theology of incarnation, grace, and the beatific vision still widely accepted today, one that explains how God can give his holiness and likeness to human beings without becoming a structure of created being, and one that Karl Rahner* duplicated unknowingly in a 1939 publication—a fact Rahner subsequently acknowledged.

Bibliography

A.   *The Mystery of Faith*, 2 vols. (London, 1940, 1950); *The Mystery of Faith and Human Opinion Contrasted and Defined*, trans. J. J. Schrimpf (London, 1930); *The Hypostatic Union and Created Actuation by Uncreated Act*, trans. Cyril Vollert (West Baden, Ind., 1952).

B.   Catholicisme 6:1890–92; DSAM 9:328; Bernard Leeming, ''A Master Theologian: Father Maurice de la Taille: 1872–1933,''*Month* 163 (1934): 31–40; P. De Letter, ''Created Actuation by the Uncreated Act: Difficulties and Answers,'' ThSt 18 (1957): 60–92.

John D. Laurance

LATIMER, HUGH (1485?, Thurcaston, Leicestershire, England–16 October 1556, Oxford). *Education*: B.A., M.A., B.D., Christ Coll., Cambridge, 1510, 1514, 1524. *Career*: university preacher and chaplain, Cambridge, 1522–35; bishop of Worcester, 1535–39; general preacher and reformer, 1539–56.

Latimer was an English reformer and one of the most influential preachers of the English Reformation during the reigns of Henry VIII and Edward VI. At first he was a defender of Roman Catholic doctrine, an opponent of the New Learning, and for his baccalaureate of theology he delivered a disputation against the teachings of Philipp Melanchthon.* Under the influence of Thomas Bilney, he accepted the Reformation teachings and preached reform throughout the nation. He was ordained priest before 1522, and was one of twelve preachers commissioned to preach anywhere in England. His preaching stressed Protestant doctrines, reform of abuses, and challenges to ecclesiastical authority. On 26 September 1535, he was consecrated bishop of Worcester, and served until he resigned on 1 July 1539 because of his opposition to the Act of Six Articles. On New Year's Day, 1548, Latimer preached his famous sermon ''On the Plough'' at St. Paul's Cross. For the next several years he was a popular court preacher. On the accession of Mary he was arrested and committed to the Tower. He was excommunicated and burned at the stake at Oxford.

Bibliography

A. *Sermons and Remains*, ed. by George E. Corrie, 2 vols. (Cambridge, 1844–45).

B. DNB 11:612–20; LThK³ 6:673; NCE 8:412; ODCC 954–55; RGG 4:238–39; Allan G. Chester, *Hugh Latimer, Apostle to the English* (Philadelphia, 1854).

Donald S. Armentrout

LAUD, WILLIAM (7 October 1573, Reading, England–10 January 1645, London). *Education*: B.A., M.A., B.D., D.D., St. John's Coll., Oxford, 1594, 1598, 1604, 1608. *Career*: chaplain to Earl of Devonshire, 1603–7; vicar, Stanford, Northamptonshire, 1607–10; president, St. John's Coll., Oxford, 1611–21; dean, Gloucester, 1616–21; prebendary, Westminster, 1621; bishop, St. David's, Wales, 1621–26; bishop, Bath, 1626–28; bishop, London, 1628–33; archbishop, Canterbury, 1633–45.

Laud was a leader of the Caroline Divines, those theologians of the seventeenth century who reasserted the catholic principles of the Church of England after the sixteenth-century reformation. Sometimes the Caroline Divines are called Laudians. Under James I and Charles I, he rose rapidly in ecclesiastical office.

Laud was a vigorous opponent of Puritanism and Calvinism. His opposition to Calvinism was so strong that at times he appeared to be an Arminian. As archbishop he was a practical reformer, enforced obedience to the canons of the church, and restored dignity to public worship. He enforced the use of the surplice, kneeling for the reception of communion, and placing the holy table at the east end of the church. The table was railed in. His policies aroused bitter hatred against him, and he was beheaded.

Bibliography

A. *The Works of Archbishop Laud*, ed. William Scott and James Bliss, 7 vols. (Oxford, 1847–60).

B. DNB 11:626–35; LThK³ 6:679–80; NCE 8:529–30; ODCC 957; TRE 20:499–502; Hugh R. Trevor-Roper, *Archbishop Laud, 1573–1645* (London, 1940); E. C. E. Bourne, *The Anglicanism of William Laud* (London, 1946).

Donald S. Armentrout

LAW, WILLIAM (1686, King's Cliffe, Northamptonshire, England–9 April 1761, King's Cliffe, Northamptonshire). *Education*: B.A., M.A., Emmanuel Coll., Cambridge, 1708, 1712. *Career*: ordained priest, 1711; fellow, Emmanuel Coll., 1711; tutor, Putney, 1727–37; writer, King's Cliffe, 1740–61.

Law was a leading eighteenth-century English nonjuror and a controversial, devotional, and spiritual writer. When Queen Anne died in 1714, Law was unable to take the Oath of Allegiance to King George I and the house of Hanover and became a nonjuror. In 1717 he published *Three Letters to the Bishop of Bangor*, which was a refutation of Bishop Benjamin Hoadley's attack on High Church principles, in which he claimed that there is no need for a visible church with its creeds, orders, and discipline. Law insisted that "the Christian Church is an essential part of the divine economy." In 1726 he published *A Practical Treatise on Christian Perfection*, which stressed the imitation of Christ. His major work was *A Serious Call to a Devout and Holy Life*, published in 1728. This was a description of the Christian life as a life of piety and devotion. The first principle of Christianity is an intention to please God in all one's actions. A holy life is devotion to God and a regular method of daily prayer. Both *A Serious Call* and *Christian Perfection* greatly influenced John* and Charles Wesley.

Bibliography

A.   *The Works of William Law*, 9 vols. (London, 1762; repr. ed. G. B. Morgan, 9 vols.; Brockenhurst, 1892–93).

B.   DNB 11:677–81; LThK³ 6:694–95; NCE 8:543; ODCC 959–60; TRE 20:511–14; J. H. Overton, *William Law, Non-Juror and Mystic* (London, 1881).

Donald S. Armentrout

LECLERCQ, JACQUES (3 June 1891, Brussels, Belgium–16 July 1971, Beaufays near Liège, Belgium). *Education*: studied law at the Free Univ. of Brussels and the Catholic Univ., Louvain; doctorate in law, 1911; license and doctorate, Institut Supérieur de Philosophie, Louvain, 1913, 1914; studied at the Grand Sém. de Malines, 1914 with a final year of his seminary training at the Sém. Léon XIII, Louvain. *Career*: ordained priest, 1917; taught Latin at the Coll. Saint-Louis, Brussels 1917–21; professor in the faculty of Philosophy and Letters, Institut Saint-Louis, 1921–38; founder and director, *Cité chrétienne*, 1926–40; member of the Libre Académie of Belgium, 1936; professor, Catholic Univ. of Louvain and canon of Malines, 1938–61; an active collaborator in *La Revue Nouvelle*, 1953–61; director and president, l'École de Sciences Politiques et Sociales, 1950–53; president, La Société d'Études Politiques et Sociales at Louvain, 1953–61; first president of International Conference of Religious Sociology, 1950–53; a book on the understanding of Christian morality (1950) brought Leclercq unjustly under a cloud at the Vatican, but he was exonerated when Paul VI named him a monsignor in 1964; retirement, Hermitage of Caillou Blanc, 1961–71.

Leclercq was a leading Catholic moral philosopher and moral theologian who reacted against the pre–Vatican II manuals of moral theology. He made significant contributions to the meaning of natural law, and he articulated a moral theology informed by love as well as authentic human values. Moreover, Leclercq was a pioneer who, long before it was fashionable, brought the social sciences into effective dialogue with philosophy and theology. An indefatigable worker, Leclercq published prolifically in every possible forum and on a great variety of philosophical, theological, social, and religious issues. He had a special interest in themes relating to marriage and family. From his adolescence Leclercq turned to the gospels, discovering there moral and religious direction.

A number of his works were translated into other languages including English. Leclercq was a tireless letter writer with an intense interest in the philosophical, theological, and social issues of his time.

Bibliography

A.   *Vie interieure* (Tournai, 1947); for a bibliography of his very extensive writings, see Ghislain Morin, *Introduction à l'étude de Jacques Leclercq* (Gembloux, 1973), 63–117.

B.   Catholicisme 7:154–55; DSAM 9:466–68; DTC 2:2930–31; LThK³ 6:735; Pierre Sauvage, *Jacques Leclercq 1891–1971: Un arbre en plen vent* (Paris, 1992).

Keith J. Egan

LEO I, THE GREAT (ca. 400, Volaterra [Volterra], Tuscany?–10 November 461, Rome). *Career*: became archdeacon of Rome under Sixtus III; pope, 440–61; presided through his legates at the Council of Chalcedon, 451; turned away Attila, the "Scourge of God," from Rome, 452; made peace with the Vandal king Genseric, 455.

Leo's written work consists primarily of papal letters, mostly practical in content, which contain clearly expressed expositions of Catholic doctrine, most especially dealing with the two natures of the incarnate Christ and correcting positions of the Eutychians (Monophysites). Other letters respond to questions on ecclesiastical custom, correct abuses, and deal with executive matters.

As pope, Leo insisted on the primacy of the Roman see and the universal responsibility of the bishop of Rome, placing Rome more clearly into a position of centrality. He rejected Chalcedon's canon 28, which gave Constantinople primacy in the Orient, after Rome. All appeals on ecclesiastical matters and those matters that could not be resolved locally were to be referred to Rome. Ecumenical councils and episcopal synods were to have their canons approved by Rome before publication.

Theologically, Leo's writings did not break any new ground but sought to counteract the heterodoxies of the day. Any reasoning of his own had its basis in Scripture and the creeds. Early in life he fought Pelagianism (he insisted on recantation for any Pelagians seeking to return to the church) and Manichaeism and later took on Priscillianism, Nestorianism, and Apollinarianism. His most celebrated theological cause was the upholding of orthodox Christology. In the letters that deal with the Christological language that would be adopted into the formula of the Council of Chalcedon, Leo defined the Incarnation with unprecedented precision. The two famous *Tomes*, Letter 28 to Flavian, bishop of Constantinople, and Letter 165 to Emperor Leo I (which includes a lengthy catena of patristic authorities for the two natures of Christ), argue to the coeternity of the Son, whose Incarnation "in no way minimized his divine and eternal birth, nor did it add thereto. We could not overcome the author of sin and death had not Christ taken on our nature and made it his." He wrote that the Incarnation resulted in the presence of two full natures, human and divine, in one person, without any confusion, each nature performing its own acts in cooperation with the other; "the Word doing what is proper to the Word, and the flesh pursuing what is proper to the flesh." He also affirmed the eternal virginity of Mary.

Bibliography

A.　CPL 1656–61; PL 54–56; CCSL 138–138A; FC 34.

B.　DTC 9:218–301; LThK³ 6:820–22; NCE 8:637–39; ODCC 966–67; TRE 20:737–41; William Halliwell, *The Style of Pope St. Leo the Great* (Washington, D.C., 1939); Trevor Jalland, *The Life and Times of St. Leo the Great* (London, 1941); Philip McShane, *La Romanitas et le Pape Léon le Grand* (Tournai, 1979); Stephan Horn, *Petrou Kathedra. Der Bishof von Rom und die Synoden von Ephesus (449) und Chalcedon* (Paderborn, 1982).

Thomas S. Ferguson

LIBERATORE, MATTEO (14 August 1810, Salerno–18 October 1892, Rome). *Education*: studied in Jesuit house, Naples, 1826–36. *Career*: joined the Jesuits, 1826; professor of philosophy and theology, Jesuit college, Naples, 1837–48; cofounder and staff member, *Civiltà Cattolica*, 1850–92; Archbishop Manning's* theologian, Vatican I, 1869–70; taught philosophy, Roman Coll., 1850–92; adviser to Pope Leo XIII, helped draft *Rerum Novarum*, 1891.

Liberatore learned Thomistic philosophy from some of its few remaining exponents in the early nineteenth century, Domenico Sordi (1790–1880) and Luigi Taparelli d'Azeglio (1793–1862). Although his writings before 1850 are not clearly and declaredly Thomistic, from 1853 he became a champion in the pages of the *Civiltà Cattolica* of Aquinas'* philosophy as the cure for the intellectual chaos of the modern age. Primarily by keen analysis of the trains of thought of his adversaries (idealists, traditionalists, ontologists), he commended the hylemorphic anthropology of body and soul and the abstractive theory of knowledge as alone consistent and adequate. He also retrieved the natural law theory of Thomas, hoping to correct the Enlightenment view of the law of nature.

Bibliography

A.　*Institutiones philosophicae* (originally *Institutiones logicae et metaphysicae*), 2 vols. (Naples, 1840–42); *Della conoscenza intellettuale*, 2 vols. (Rome, 1857–58); *Del composto umano* (Rome, 1862); 2d ed. *Dell'uomo* (Rome, 1874–75); *Carteggio inedito Liberatore-Cornoldi*, ed. G. Mellinato (Vatican City, 1993).

B.　Catholicisme 7:599–600; ChP 2:109–30; NCE 8:713; Sommervogel 4:1774–1803; *Enciclopedia filosofica* (Florence, 1967) 3:1531–32; P. Dezza, ed. *I neotomisti italiani del XIX secolo*, 2 vols. (Milan, 1942); G. Van Riet, *L' épistémologie thomiste* (Louvain, 1946); *L'Enciclica Aeterni Patris: Significato e preparazione* (Vatican City, 1981); G. A. McCool, *Nineteenth-Century Scholasticism* (New York, 1989); F. Dante, *Storia della "Civiltà cattolica" (1850–1891)* (Rome, 1990).

Paul Misner

LIGUORI, ALPHONSUS MARIA DI. *See* ALPHONSUS MARIA DI LIGUORI.

LOISY, ALFRED FIRMIN (28 February 1857, Ambrières, Marnes, in the district of Vitry-le-François, France–1 June 1940, Ceffonds). *Education*: tutored by his parish priest, 1870–71; matriculated at the lycée, Saint-Dizier, 1872–74; at the grand sém., Chalons, 1874–79; higher studies, Institut Catholique, Paris, 1881–84. *Career*: ordained priest, 1879; professor of Hebrew and exegesis, Institut Catholique, Paris, 1881–93; founder, *L'Enseignement biblique*, 1892–93, and *Revue d'histoire et de littérature religieuses*, 1896–1907, 1910–14, 1920–22; chaplain to a Dominican convent, Neuilly, 1893–99; lecturer, École Pratique des Hautes Études, 1900–4; private residence and writing, Garnay, 1904–7, Ceffonds, 1907–9; professor in the history of religion, Coll. de France, 1909–32 and École Pratique des Hautes Études, 1923–27.

Having learned the principles of historical criticism from Ernst Renan, Alfred Loisy became the leading Roman Catholic exegete and theoretician of religion. Some regard his exegetical works, particularly in their deconstructive aspect, as of utmost importance, but Loisy himself regarded his religious interest as primary and as exercised on behalf of his exegetical interest. At the outset of his career, he drafted a potentially lifelong apologetic program on behalf of the Catholic Church, hoping to reform not only the church's biblical teaching but Catholicism's entire intellectual system as well. He gave himself to this program until his rupture with the church. Much of it appeared in various reviews and/or in the first volume of his *Mémoires*, where he referred to it as his *Livre inédit*.

Along with a handful of other Catholic scholars—later defined and condemned by the Vatican as ''modernists''—Loisy realized that the Catholic Church would soon have to engage the new science of historical criticism and its implications for both Scripture and tradition. He understood that this criticism would be as threatening to church teaching as anything since the Copernican revolution and was fully prepared to help the church face the crisis, but not if it meant denying what he regarded as historically reliable facts.

In *L'Évangile et l'Église* (1902), he attempted to refute on strictly historical grounds Harnack's* argument in *Das Wesen des Christentums* that historico-critical studies enabled one to peel back the husk of church tradition to find in the gospels the unchanging essence of Christianity deposited by the historical Christ. Loisy countered that historical studies could never uncover the essence of Christianity because the latter is not a body of final truths committed to verbal transmission but rather the *spirit* of Christ imparted to the church to initiate a religious *movement*. Thus, the church was the legitimate and necessary historical development of Jesus' proclamation of the Kingdom of God as a social reality.

For Loisy development of doctrine implied real change and not simply—as Newman* argued—an accumulation of reformulations to keep pace with changes in culture and language so as by *accidental* change to remain *essentially* the same. The Scriptures are a vehicle of transmission for the spirit of Christ, but they contain no deposit of faith to be explained and developed but never changed. Christian doctrine developed not in Jesus' consciousness but in the church's. Thus, for example, Christ's divinity is a teaching not of Christ but of the church; it existed only in germ in the notion of Jesus as Messiah, Son of God. Jesus was indeed the prophesied Messiah, but his only concern was eschatological: to herald the final judgment and the coming of the Kingdom and to call people to repentance and salvation through himself. When *L'Évangile et l'Église* was condemned as having denied Christ's divinity, Loisy argued in his apologia, *Autour d'un petit livre* (1903), that he had done nothing more than draw out the implications of the simple distinction made by Peter in Acts 2:36, "that God has made both Lord and Christ this same Jesus whom you crucified." Many of Loisy's writings were placed on the *Index*, and he himself was eventually excommunicated as *vitandus* (1908).

To the end of his life Loisy continued to express his rather mystical view that humanity evolves upwards by means of religion, that truth-elements of all religions contribute to this end, and that of all religions, Christianity, particularly in its Roman Catholic embodiment, while not absolute, is the truest presentment of religion. He argued that Roman Catholicism could possibly become the "religion of humanity," but only by a radical transformation because, having refused its servant role, it has tried to dominate thought, history, and politics by imposing as ultimate a form of religion that is but provisional.

Loisy's faith, mystical and chary of attaching personal categories to God, remained firm to the end. He had carved on his gravestone the enigmatic epitaph, "Alfred LOISY / PRÊTRE / . . . Tuam in Votis / tenuit Voluntatem" (He held fast to Your Will in his Intentions).

Bibliography

A. *Les Évangiles synoptiques*, 2 vols. (Amien, 1894, 1896); *The Religion of Israel* (London, 1910); *The Gospel and the Church* (1902; London, 1903); *Mémoires pour servir à l'histoire religieuse de notre temps*, 3 vols. (Paris, 1930–31); *The Birth of the Christian Religion* (1923; London, 1948).

B. ECatt 7:1486–87; LThK³ 6:1041–42; NCE 8:972–73; ODCC 993; TRE 21:453–56; Albert Houtin and Felix Sartiaux, *Alfred Loisy: Sa vie et son oeuvre*, ed. Émile Poulat (Paris, 1960); Henri Bremond, *Une oeuvre clandestine d'Henri Bremond. Sylvain Leblanc (cioè Henri Bremond): Un clerc qui n'a pas trahi, Alfred Loisy d'après ses mémoires. 1931*, ed. Émile Poulat (Rome, 1972); Friedrich Heiler, *Der Vater des katholischen Modernismus, Alfred Loisy (1857–1940)* (Munich, 1947); Émile Poulat, *Histoire, dogme et critique dans la crise moderniste* (Paris, 1979).

David G. Schultenover

LOMBARD, PETER. *See* PETER LOMBARD.

LONERGAN, BERNARD J. F. (17 December 1904, Buckingham, Quebec, Canada–26 November 1984, Pickering, Ontario, Canada). *Education*: philosophy, Heythrop Coll., Oxfordshire, 1926–30; B.A., languages and mathematics, Univ. of London, 1926–30; theology, Gregorian Univ., Rome, 1933–37; doctoral studies in theology, Gregorian Univ., 1938–40. *Career*: entered Jesuits, 1922; teacher of sciences and classics, Montreal, 1930–33; professor of theology, Canadian Jesuit theologates, 1940–53; Gregorian Univ., 1953–65; Regis Coll., To-

ronto, 1965–71, 1972–75; Harvard Div. Sch., 1971–1972; Boston Coll., 1975–
83; retirement, Pickering, Ontario, Canada, 1983–84.

Lonergan's work, like his life, was dedicated to an ever more adequate understanding of both human intelligence and the mysteries of Christian faith. The
topic he chose for his dissertation was Thomas Aquinas'* theory of grace. Setting a pattern for his work, it is a dense and dedicated retrieval of the work of
Thomas Aquinas that is both rigorously historical and systematically relevant to
contemporary issues. First published as four articles in *Theological Studies*
(1941–42) and later as *Grace and Freedom: Operative Grace in the Thought of
St. Thomas Aquinas* (New York, 1971), the dissertation traced the developments
of speculative theology on grace from Augustine* to Aquinas, set out the terms
and relations in his notion of operative and cooperative grace, and presented an
as yet unsurpassed analysis of Aquinas' theory of causation, operation, divine
transcendence, and human liberty. Lonergan was able to disengage the core of
Aquinas' notion of causality and divine providence from the medieval cosmic
hierarchical shell with which it was often expressed. As a result, Lonergan cut
through the enormous difficulties surrounding subsequent theological controversies on grace and freedom. From the voluntarism of Scotus,* through nominalism and the disputes on God's grace and good acts (e.g., the Catholic *de
auxiliis* controversy between Banezians and Molinists), to the Enlightenment
and modern variations on determinism and decisionism, Lonergan indicated how
crucial achievements of Aquinas were ignored.

The intellectual breakthroughs that Aquinas effected were neither understood
adequately by his contemporaries nor communicated through subsequent commentators. Specifically, such terms as ''supernatural,'' ''divine transcendence,''
and ''operation'' are used by Aquinas within a philosophically systematic framework that differentiates their meanings from previous usage. So the ''theorem
of the supernatural'' in Aquinas expresses the mystery of redemption as gifting
humankind with theological virtues and graces natural to God alone and so
absolutely gratuitous and supernatural relative to human nature. The theorem
referred to the entitative disproportion between nature and grace, reason and
faith, good will and agapic love, human honor and merit before God. The subsequent commentators missed the theoretical framework of the theorem and
imagined instead separate realms or planes, one natural and another supernatural.
This led to a host of difficulties characterized by supposed contradictions between the supernatural and the natural, grace and freedom, faith and reason.

This doctoral work convinced Lonergan that the task of historically retrieving
Thomas Aquinas was far more difficult than most modern historians, philosophers, and theologians had envisaged. For what was needed to reach up to the
mind of Aquinas was not simply an historical, philosophical, or theological
reconstruction of Aquinas' work. What was needed for any of these reconstructions to be accurate was a set of profound changes within the historian, philosopher, or theologian doing the reconstructions. From Augustine, Lonergan
learned that Christian conversion to Jesus Christ as Lord involved intellectual

and moral dimensions as well as the religious dimensions. The psychological and phenomenological narratives of Augustine's intellectual conversion to the Truth, moral conversion to Goodness, and religious conversion to God revealed in Christ Jesus (*Confessions* VII–IX) grounded experientially the shift towards theory in Thomas Aquinas. This threefold conversion process of Augustine becomes in Aquinas the fundamental importance of the intellectual, moral, and theological virtues (*Summa Theologiae*, I–II, 55–67; II–II, 1–170). To understand the systematic breakthrough in the theology of Aquinas, Lonergan realized that he had to reach up to the mind of Aquinas by undergoing himself what he would later term "intellectual conversion."

Increasingly Lonergan realized that intellectual conversion had to be made explicit, otherwise the achievements of theology from Augustine to Aquinas would continue to be misunderstood, as in decadent scholasticism and nominalism. In order to retrieve Thomas Aquinas' cognitional theory from the deformations into which it had fallen at the hands of too many so-called Thomists, Lonergan wrote five articles on the notion of *verbum* in Aquinas' thought (*Theological Studies*, 1947–49). These articles were later published as *Verbum: Word and Idea in Aquinas* (Notre Dame, Ind., 1967). This work not only sets out the basic terms and relations operative in the cognitional theory of Aquinas but also shows how those terms and relations are derived from the human experiences of questioning, understanding, and judging. Insight into images generates understanding and this understanding expresses itself in concepts. But human understanding is not content with mere thinking. We want to know what is really true, so questions of truth emerge, and only when we grasp the sufficiency of the evidence do we reach judgment and truth or falsity. In detailed analysis of the texts of Aquinas, as well as attention to our own human acts of understanding, Lonergan shows that what Aquinas terms "the light of active intellect as a created participation in divine light" is in fact our human capacity to raise ever further questions. The human mind is infinite in potency—there is no end to the questions we raise, every answer evokes more questions—while the divine mind is infinite actuality. Just as Augustine saw that our hearts are restless until they rest in God, so for Aquinas our minds are restless until they rest in God. Only through an experiential appropriation of human cognitional operations can one understand how Aquinas' cognitional theory flowers into his systematic presentation of Augustine's psychological analogy of the Trinity.

Lonergan's next major work, *Insight: A Study of Human Understanding* (London, 1957; rev. 1958; Toronto, 1992), transposed the cognitional theory Lonergan had learned from Aquinas into contemporary contexts. The book is an invitation to the reader to appropriate his or her own conscious acts of experiencing, understanding, judging, deciding. The first part sets out insight as activity, showing how attention to acts of understanding enables the reader with Lonergan to correlate methods of the natural and human sciences in such a way as to arrive at an understanding of a coherent and open worldview designated as "emergent probability." The second part builds on the reader's own self-appropriation as a knower, showing how genetic and dialectical methods operate in a cognitionally grounded metaphysics, ethics, and natural theology. Insight demonstrates how human understanding does in fact consist in related and recurrent operations and that failure to attend to and understand those operations has led to the dialectical contradictions in modern cultures, philosophies, and theologies. The program of the book is succinctly stated by Lonergan: "Thoroughly understand what it is to understand, and not only will you understand the broad lines of all there is to be understood, but also you will possess a fixed base, an invariant pattern, opening upon all further developments of understanding" (*Insight*, 1958, xxviii).

Reason and faith, as Lonergan learned from Aquinas, are intrinsically related. From his discoveries in *Insight* Lonergan advanced to *Method in Theology* (New York, 1972; Toronto, 1996) where he shows that his notion of transcendental method can restructure how theology is done. Transcendental method is neither Cartesian nor Kantian, but sets of related and recurrent operations of understanding and acting, yielding cumulative and progressive results. After treating the human good, meaning, and religion, the book develops the notion of functional specialties in theology. There are three types of specialties. (1) Field specialties continually divide and subdivide the fields of data to be investigated, as when biblical, patristic, medieval, reformation fields become genera to be ever further subdivided. (2) Subject specialties classify the results of the investigations in order to teach those results, as when departments are separated into areas such as Hebrew history, early Christian antiquities, Christian theology, or ethics. (3) Functional specialties differentiate the successive stages in the process from data to results. Lonergan distinguishes eight functional specialties, which are sets of methods.

The first set of four deals with theology as indirect discourse, wherein theologians learn from the past. Research methods make available the vast array of data relevant to theology. Interpretation methods uncover what the data, especially written data, mean. Historical methods indicate what is going forward in cultural, institutional, or doctrinal histories. Dialectical methods make explicit the differences between histories, interpretations, and research orientations; and, where such differences are not complementary but contradictory, dialectics seeks to explicate the conflicting value orientations at the root of the contradictory differences.

The last set of four functional specialties shifts theology to direct discourse. The theologian has to develop and take a stand amid the conflicting horizons presented in dialectics. Foundational methods make explicit the intellectual, moral, and religious conversion processes by which theologians genuinely develop. Here we see how Lonergan transposes the basic orientations of Augustine and Aquinas into a contemporary context. The foundations of theology, as sets of scholarly disciplines, are theologians converted intellectually, morally, and religiously. Only through such ongoing conversions can theologians know the realities that the religious texts and traditions express. Only such conversions, especially intellectual conversion as an explicit appropriation of the intellectual operations in theology, can critique the subjectivism so dominant in theology since Schleiermacher without falling into a fideism or fundamentalism. In the light of such foundations, doctrinal methods deal with the religious judgments of fact and value operative within the horizons defined by conversion. Lonergan demonstrates how the development of doctrine from Nicea through the great councils is in fact an orientation of faith towards an ever more systematic intelligence of the faith and, as such, the truth of those doctrines transcend their historical and cultural settings. Systematic methods advance the understandings of the doctrinal truths, while communication methods relate theology to other disciplines in the multiple tasks of communicating the understandings, doctrines, and foundational realities constitutive of theology as direct discourse.

During the final decade of his life Lonergan's major project was a macroeconomic analysis of modern production processes and monetary circulations. This had been an early interest of his and in his final years he continued to refine his *Essay in Circulation Analysis*, which will be published as the fifteenth volume of his *Collected Works*.

Lonergan's writings in whole or in part have been translated into all the European languages as well as several Asian ones. There are ten Lonergan research centers in North America, South America, Europe, Australia, and the Philippines. The Lonergan Research Institute in Toronto is directing the publication of his *Collected Works*, which are being published by the University of Toronto Press in at least twenty-two volumes. There are about 300 dissertations dealing with Lonergan's thought and methods, with more than a third published in whole or in part. Besides workshops dealing with Lonergan in various countries, including several each year at Boston College, there are regular journals devoted to advancing Lonergan's method: *Method: A Journal of Lonergan Studies* and *Lonergan Workshop* as well as the *Lonergan Studies Newsletter* published by the Lonergan Research Institute in Toronto.

Bibliography

A.   *De Deo trino* (Rome, 1964); *De constitutione Christi ontologica et psychologica* (Rome, 1956); *A Second Collection* (Philadelphia, 1974); *A Third Collection* (Mahwah, N.J., 1985); *The Lonergan Reader* (Toronto, 1996); *Collected Works of Bernard Lonergan*, ed. Frederick E. Crowe and Robert M. Doran, 6 vols. to date (Toronto, 1988–).

B.   LThK[3] 6:1046–47; NCE 18:262–64; TRE 21:459–63; David Tracy, *The Achievement of Bernard Lonergan* (New York, 1970); Matthew Lamb, *History, Method, and Theology: A Dialectical Comparison of Whilhelm Dilthey's Critique of Historical Reason and Bernard Lonergan's Meta-methodology* (Missoula, Mont., 1978); Robert Doran, *Psychic Conversion and Theological Foundations: Toward a Reorientation of the Human Sciences* (Chico, Calif., 1981); Frederick E. Crowe, *Method in Theology: An Organon for Our Time* (Milwaukee, Wis., 1980) and *Lonergan* (London, 1992); *Creativity and Method: Essays in Honor of Bernard Lonergan, S.J.*, ed. Matthew Lamb (Milwaukee,

Wis., 1981); Hugo A. Meynell, *The Theology of Bernard Lonergan* (Atlanta, Ga., 1986); *Appropriating the Lonergan Idea*, ed. Michael Vertin (Washington, D.C., 1989).

Matthew Lamb

LOSSKY, VLADIMIR N. (26 May 1903, Göttingen–7 February 1958, Paris). *Education*: studied at Univ. of St. Petersburg, 1919–22; studied in Prague, 1922–24; studied medieval philosophy, Sorbonne, 1924–26. *Career*: lived and wrote in Paris, 1926–58; professor of dogmatic theology, St. Deny's Institute of Orthodox Theol., Paris, 1945–53; retirement, 1953–58.

Lossky was a friend and disciple of Etienne Gilson and also counted among his friends several influential Roman Catholic theologians, including J. Daniélou,* H. De Lubac,* Y. Congar,* and L. Bouyer.* He was the author of some influential books, most notably *The Mystical Theology of the Eastern Church* (1957), which is the type of neopatristic synthesis valued and desired by Georges Florovsky.*

Lossky's emphasis on the *filioque* dispute, so marked in *The Mystical Theology*, has been read by other scholars, Orthodox and Western, both as somewhat exaggerated and as owing as much to Théodore de Régnon's* characterizations of Greek-Latin differences as to Lev Platonovich Karsavine's. His attempt to discover all the differences between Eastern and Western Christianity, and as a result their schism itself, as deriving from this Latin addition to the Nicene-Constantinopolitan Creed is thus surely an overstatement. By the same token, however, he takes the Trinity with utmost seriousness. The integration of dogmatic theology with spirituality and mysticism is something that he insists upon throughout all of his works, and this insistence, together with a style of writing one can only describe as intense, continues to make him an exciting and significant author. Then, too, Lossky is one of the very few modern Orthodox writers with a primary interest in the Medieval Latin West. His work on the knowledge of God in Meister Eckhart,* which he was completing when he died, remains a standard in the field. In spite, then, of his frequently polemical stance and sharp expressions regarding Western Christianity—and one does well to recall that he was often responding to yet more dismissive views of Eastern thought—his work is catholic in its interests, inherently "Western" in its cultural setting, and his interests far broader than those of a narrow polemicist.

Bibliography

A.   *The Mystical Theology of the Eastern Church* (1944; Cambridge, 1957); *The Vision of God*, trans. A. E. Moorhouse (London, 1963); *In the Image and Likeness of God*, trans. J. H. Erickson and T. E. Bird (New York, 1974); *Orthodox Theology: An Introduction*, trans. Ian and Hita Kesarcodi-Watson (New York, 1978); with Leonid Ouspensky, *The Meaning of Icons*, trans. G. E. H. Palmer and E. Kadloubovsky (New York, 1982).

B.   Catholicisme 8:1091–92; DSAM 9:1018–19; LThK³ 6:1061; ODCC 997; S. Tyszkiewicz, "La spiritualité de l'Eglise d'Orient selon Vladimir Lossky," *Gregorianum* 31 (1950): 605–12; George W. Morrel, "Theology of Vladimir Lossky," *Anglican Theological Review* 41 (1959): 35–40; Oliver Clément, *Orient-Occident, deux passiers, Vladimir Lossky, Paul Evdokimov* (Geneva, 1985).

Alexander Golitzin

LUBAC, HENRI DE (20 February 1896, Cambrai (Nord), France–4 September 1991, Paris). *Education*: studied law, Catholic faculty, Lyon, 1912–13; philosophical studies, the Isle of Jersey, 1920–23; theological studies, Hastings, England, 1924–26, and Lyon-Fourvière, 1926–27. *Career*: entered Society of Jesus, Sussex, England, 1913; served in French Army, 1915–19; Jesuit regency, Coll. of Jesuits of Mongré, 1923–24; ordained priest, 1927; professor of fundamental theology, Sch. of Theol., Lyon, 1929–35; professor of theology, Jesuit faculty, Fourvière, 1935–50; cofounder with Jean Daniélou,* *Sources chrétiennes*, 1940; editor, *Recherches de science religieuse*, 1945–50; member, Institut de France (Académie des sciences morales), from 1953; consultor, preparatory theological commission for Vatican II, 1960–62; *peritus*, Vatican II, 1962–65; cardinal, 1983.

De Lubac was a principal advocate of a movement known as the "New Theology." His first major work, *Catholicisme* (Paris, 1938) contained in seminal form the major themes of his theological career. Subtitled *A Study of Dogma in Relation to the Corporate Destiny of Mankind*, it emphasized the communal character of salvation and the solidarity of the human race in its common vocation. His controversial work on the supernatural destiny of the human person, *Surnaturel* (Paris, 1946), challenged the neoscholastic interpretation of Thomas Aquinas* that held the possibility of a purely natural order. De Lubac argued that there was only one destiny for an intellectual creature, the supernatural destiny of the beatific vision. *Corpus Mysticum* (Paris, 1944) retrieved a eucharistic theology grounded in the symbolism of patristic exegesis by showing that the term *corpus mysticum* originally designated the Eucharist. At the time of the eucharistic controversy with Berengar of Tours,* the adjective *mysticum* was dropped with reference to the Eucharist. Two or three centuries later *corpus mysticum* referred to the church. The effect of this change was to divorce the ecclesial body from the eucharistic and historical bodies of Christ.

Such original and fresh examinations of the tradition were consonant with the spirit of the "New Theology," although de Lubac maintained the actual existence of such a "school" of theology to be a myth. The term "New Theology" was first used by Msgr. Pietro Parente in *L'Osservatore Romano* (February, 1942) in reference to two Dominican theologians, M.-D. Chenu* and L. Charlier. Reginald Garrigou-Lagrange,* a neoscholastic theologian, subsequently applied the term to certain theologians associated with the Jesuit faculty at Fourvière in 1946 who were particularly interested in Scripture and patristic literature as theological sources. Jean Daniélou sketched the general orientation of this New Theology in a seminal article, "Les orientations présentes de la pensée religieuse," where he noted the distance that had developed between theology and the pressing concerns of the day, a progressive rupture between exegesis and systematic theology with each discipline developing according to its own method, and a consequent progressive aridity within systematic theology. The new orientation, aimed at a reunification of theology, included a return to Scripture, a return to the Fathers, and a liturgical revival. The controversy surrounding the New Theology tended to set the proponents of scholasticism over against those wishing to return to patristic sources. The controversy ended with Pope Pius XII's encyclical *Humani Generis* (1950), which reiterated the importance of scholasticism, cited the dangers of existentialism, and condemned the concept of progressive evolution as well as the position that God could not create intellectual beings without at the same time ordering and calling them to the beatific vision.

Many of the theologians at Fourvière, and principally de Lubac among them, were thought to be responsible for the errors denounced in the encyclical. Although not cited in *Humani Generis*, de Lubac left his teaching post in the school of theology at Lyon as well as the residence at Fourvière and moved to Paris in 1950. His friend Hans Urs von Balthasar* reports that "his books were banned, removed from the libraries of the Society of Jesus and impounded from the market." De Lubac, however, later said that during those years he was never questioned, did not have a single discussion with Roman authorities, the papal curia, or Society of Jesus about the main issues, nor was he ever told what he was accused of or asked to provide something equivalent to a "retraction" or declaration. In a 1985 interview de Lubac stated that he had good reasons for thinking that Pius XII's concerns did not concern him, noting that *Humani Generis* "borrows a sentence from him to express true doctrine" at the same time that it "avoids all mention of that 'pure nature' that so many established theologians wanted to canonize and accused him of not sufficiently appreciating." Cardinal Gerlier demonstrated his support of de Lubac by refusing to name a successor to his chair and by naming him a member of his theological council. De Lubac's fidelity to and love of the church during this personally trying time found expression in his book *Méditation sur l'Eglise* (Paris, 1953), a work all the more remarkable for the circumstances surrounding its publication. The reversal of his ten years of ostracism resolved slowly and gradually, culminating in the invitation from Pope John XXIII to be a consultor for the preparatory theological commission of the council in 1960. Heinz Neufeld, however, chronicled the lingering suspicion of de Lubac on the part of some at the council.

De Lubac's extensive work numbers about fifty volumes. Especially those on apologetics, revelation, atheism, and the nature of the church enabled him to be an important and valuable influence at the Second Vatican Council. Much of the work he had done previous to the council influenced the *Dogmatic Constitution on Divine Revelation*, the *Dogmatic Constitution on the Church*, and the *Pastoral Constitution on the Church in the Modern World*. For example, he had spoken of the duty of the church to proclaim the gospel to all peoples and to the whole world in *Le fondement théologique des missions* (Paris, 1946), had proposed Mary as "type of the Church" in *Méditation sur l'Eglise* (Paris, 1963) where he also had used the term "mystery of the Church," and had been one of the first to point out its sacramental character. On February 2, 1965 Pope Paul VI cited de Lubac's expression, taken from the titles of the third and fourth sections in Chapter IV of *Méditation*, "The Church makes the Eucharist, but the Eucharist makes the Church" to honor the author of this oft-quoted statement. His work on the relationship between nature and the supernatural had consequences for understanding what it means to be a Christian in the world. Likewise, his work on atheism in *Le drame de l'humanism athée* (Paris, 1945) was important to the *Pastoral Constitution on the Church in the Modern World*. His ideas on the relation of the church with non-Catholic religions in *Catholicisme* and his works on Buddhism partially influenced the *Decree on the Church's Missionary Activity*. Above all, he influenced the *Dogmatic Constitution on Divine Revelation* by means of his work on the spiritual meaning of the Scriptures and the relationship between the Old and New Testament, including a number of articles in the late 1940s on typology, *Histoire et Esprit: L'intelligence de l'Ecriture d'après Origène* (Paris, 1950), and his four-volume *Exégèse médiévale* (Paris, 1959, 1961, 1964), much of which was completed during the council. His nomination as one of the eleven conciliar theologians who concelebrated with Pope Paul VI at the Mass preceding the solemn promulgation of the *Dogmatic Constitution on Revelation* on 18 November 1965 attested to his great influence on that document. After the council he continued his interest in revelation, writing a commentary on the preface and first chapter of *Revelation* and a book entitled *L'Ecriture dans la tradition* (Paris, 1966).

At the direction of the Jesuit father general and the four French provincials, de Lubac wrote five books defending his Jesuit friend, Pierre Teilhard de Chardin.* He clarified and explained his thought, attesting to his faith and deeply Catholic spirit in response to what he considered to be violent and unjust attacks. Although not Teilhard's disciple, he admired him greatly.

After the council, de Lubac was appointed to the International Theological Commission and was a consultor for the Secretariat for Non-Christians as well as for the Secretariat for Non-Believers. When he was appointed cardinal, he requested and received a dispensation from the requirement of being ordained a bishop, arguing that at his age he could not discharge the duties of a bishop properly and therefore would not do justice to the episcopal office.

In 1969 de Lubac wrote about "The Church in Crisis" (*Theology Digest*), criticizing some of the postconciliar theological and ecclesiastical developments. This article and a few other postconciliar writings reflect what some theologians considered a conservative turn in his theological orientation, an ironic twist of events considering that for most of his life he was suspect as a renegade who challenged the dominant theology of the time. His writings, however, show a unity and betray no shifts in theological positions or fundamental convictions. Rather, his conversation partners changed from the preconciliar neoscholastics to the postconciliar reformers like Edward Schillebeeckx, whom he criticized in *Petit catéchèse sur la "nature" et la "grâce"* (Paris, 1980) for his description of the church as the *sacramentum mundi* and for extending Rahner's* concept of an "anonymous" or implicit Christian to an implicit Christianity. In de Lubac's opinion this move reduced the role of the church to the manifestation of a "progressive sanctification" of the world (as a profane reality). De Lubac doubted whether Schillebeeckx adequately distinguished between the sanctification of the world and the technical construction of a new politico-social world. The fundamental issue was how grace was present in the world—within the temporal order by creation or through the Christ event mediated through the church sacramentally. The terms of the conversation had shifted. Schillebeeckx spoke in terms of the relationship between the world and the eschatological Kingdom while de Lubac spoke of the relationship between nature and the supernatural. This shifted the categories from the relationship between grace and nature to the relationship between grace and history. If Schillebeeckx was a fair representative, the fundamental difference between de Lubac and his later interlocutors lies in their theologies of history and the necessity of Christ and the church to mediate grace.

Bibliography

A. *The Splendour of the Church* (New York, 1956); *The Mystery of the Supernatural* (New York, 1967); *The Sources of Revelation* (New York, 1968); *Augustinianism and Modern Theology* (New York, 1969); *Theology in History* (San Francisco, 1996); Edgar Haulotte,"Bibliographie du Père Henri de Lubac," in *L'homme devant Dieu*, vol. 3 (Paris, 1964), 347–56; H. Neufeld and M. Sales, *Bibliographie Henri de Lubac, S. J. (1925–1970)* (Einsiedeln, 1972).

B. LThK³ 6:1074–75; NCE 18:264–66; ODCC 1000–1001; TRE 21:471–73; Hans Urs von Balthasar, *The Theology of Henri de Lubac* (San Francisco, 1991); Karl Heinz Neufeld, "In the Service of the Council: Bishops and Theologians at the Second Vatican Council (for Cardinal Henri de Lubac on His Ninetieth Birthday)," in *Vatican II: Assessment and Perspectives: Twenty-five Years After, 1962–1987*, ed. René Latourelle (New York, 1988), 74–105; Herbert Vorgrimler, "Henri de Lubac," in *Bilan de la théologie du XXᵉ siècle*, ed. Robert Vander Gucht and Herbert Vorgrimler (Paris, 1970), 1: 802–20.

Susan Wood

LUCARIS, CYRIL (13 November 1572, Iraklio, Crete–27 June or 7 July 1638, Constantinople). *Education*: studied at the Univ. of Padua under Paolo Sarpi and Cesare Cremonini, 1594. *Career*: ordained deacon, Alexandria, Egypt, 1594; participant, Council of Brest-Litovsk, 1596; lived and worked as a deacon in Poland, 1594–1600; patriarch of Alexandria, 1601–20; ecumenical patriarch, Constantinople, 1620–38.

Lucaris is known primarily because of his attempts to bring Calvinist thought into the Orthodox tradition. While in Alexandria he had begun a correspondence with Protestant theologians with the intention of undermining the Uniate policies begun by Rome. As a young deacon his involvement in the Council of Brest Litovsk, which created the Uniate Church of the Polish-Lithuanian state, left him embittered with the Roman papacy. During his sojourn in Poland, moreover, he deepened his contacts with Calvinist thought and grew in his acceptance of it. As ecumenical patriarch, he sought diplomatic ties with Moscow, again with the intention of overthrowing the Roman alliance of the Uniate churches in Poland and Lithuania. In the meantime, his contacts with Protestant theologians, continued and deepened through the Dutch embassy at Constantinople, culminated in the *Confession of Faith* he published in Geneva in 1629.

Cyril's *Confession of Faith* clearly set forth a Calvinist theology, including the denial of free will, the doctrine of predestination, the limiting of the sacraments to two, and a negative view of icons. The scandal that ensued led both local Greek churchmen and representatives of the Roman Catholic powers to intrigue with the Sublime Porte against Cyril and resulted in his murder in 1638. His *Confession of Faith* also produced counter-confessional statements from both metropolitan Peter Mogila* of Kiev in 1640 and from Dositheus,* patriarch of Jerusalem, in 1672. Mogila's own *Confession* was approved, with some modifications, at the Synod of Jassy in 1642. Dositheus' *Confession*, wherein he refuted Cyril's doctrine point by point, was approved by the Synod of Bethlehem in 1672.

In both early and recent literature on Lucaris, the question has been repeatedly asked whether he really believed the content of his *Confession of Faith*, since the theology it contains does not match the theology of his homilies and other writings. The position has been advanced that Lucaris wrote the *Confession of Faith* primarily to gather Western military support against Rome and/or the Turks.

Bibliography

A.   *Cyril Lucar, Sermons 1598–1602*, ed Keetje Rozemond (Leiden, 1974); *Confessio Fidei Reverendissimi Domini Cyrille Patriarchae Constantinopolitani nomine et consensu Patriarcharum Alexandrini et Kierosolymitani, aliorumque Ecclesiarum Orientalium Antistitum scripta* (Geneva, 1629).

B.   DTC 9:1003–19; HDOC 208–9; LThK[3] 6:555; NCE 8:1055; ODCC 1001; PRE 11:682–90; Manuel Candal, "La confessión de fe calvinista de Cirilo Lúcaris," *Collectanea theologica: al R. P. Joaquín Salaverri*, ed. A. Temino Salz (Santander, 1960); G. A. Hadjiantoniou, "Cyril Lucaris: the Greek Reformer (1572–1638)," *Reformed and Presbyterian World* 26 (1960): 3–14; Georgios A. Chatzeantoniou, *Protestant Patriarch: The Life of Cyril Lucaris, 1572–1638, Patriarch of Constantinople* (Nashville, Tenn., 1961); Edmund Perret, "Metrophanes Kritopoulos, Kyrilos Loukaris, et Genève (1627–1640)," *Church and Theology*, vol. 2, ed. M. Fougias (1981); Lukas Vischer, "The Legacy of Kyrill Loukaris: A Contribution to the Orthodox-Reformed Dialogue," *Mid-Stream* 25 (1986): 165–83; Constantine Tsirpanlis, "Cyril Loukaris: A Protestant Patriarch or a Pioneer Orthodox Ecumenist?" *The Wisdom of Faith*, ed. H. Thompson (1989); Constantine Tsirpanlis, "Cyril Loukaris' Vision of Unity and Relations with the Western

Churches,'' *Patristic and Byzantine Review* 8 (1989): 85–99; Marianne Carbonnie-Burkard, ''Une liaison gréco-réformée au XVIIe *siècle,''* *Foi et Vie* 89 (1990): 67–77.

Alexander Golitzin

LULL, RAYMOND, Ramon Llull, Raymond Lully; *doctor illuminatus* (1232, Mallorca–1316, Mallorca or Tunis). Catalan poet, philosopher, theologian, missionary, and mystic. Until his conversion in 1263 (as a result of visions of the crucified Christ experienced while writing a cantilena for a beloved woman) he played a prominent role in courtly life. An enthusiastic proponent of the ideals of courtly love, his erotic love embraced more women than his own wife, with whom he had two children. Taking St. Francis of Assisi as his model, he decided to relinquish his worldly life. He destroyed the love songs he had composed, sold his possessions, and undertook pilgrimages. He devoted the remainder of his life entirely to the missions to Jews and, above all, Muslims, referring to himself as a *christianus arabicus*. To prepare himself he first studied theology, philosophy, and Arabic for eighteen years. Although other attempts to win popes for his missionary plans were not as successful, he did succeed in founding (on Mallorca) the first Franciscan monastery where Arabic was taught as part of the training of missionaries to the Muslims. Between 1283 and 1313 he taught in Paris and Montpellier as well as in other cities. In 1291 he went to Tunis, but was soon expelled; nevertheless he returned in 1306 and 1314. Probably in 1295 he joined the third order of the Franciscans. Other places to which his incessant travels brought him were Rome, Anagni, Barcelona, Cyprus, Sicily, Genoa, Pisa, Lyons, and Avignon. He succeeded in convincing the Council of Vienne to establish language courses in Hebrew, Arabic, Greek, and Chaldean.

Lull was a mystic with many facets, including visions and auditions. While meditating on Mount Randa in his homeland, he was inspired with the idea of a ''Great Art'' (first presented in the *Ars compendiosa inveniendi veritatem* [1274], next in the *Ars demonstrativa* [1283–89], then in the *Tree of Knowledge*, and finally in the *Ars brevis* and the *Ars generalis ultima* [1309–16]) with which the whole body of human knowledge was to be systematically categorized in an exhaustive system consisting of tables of principles and rules for their combinations, giving occasion for the claim that Lull was a forerunner of the modern computer. Leibniz was influenced by this idea. Rejecting the crusades (after having supported a crusade at an earlier time), he endeavored to prove the truths of Christian faith with irrefutable arguments (*causae necessariae*) of reason, demanding the assent of all men. This method climaxed in a mystical union (*Ars mystica theologiae et philosophiae*), in which the loving human was inseparably joined to the beloved God (*Arbre de filosofia d'amor*). In spite of adamant rejections of Lullism, especially on the part of ecclesiastical authority, prominent thinkers were influenced by him, notably G. Pico della Mirandola, J. Lefèvre d'Étaples, G. Bruno, and Nicholas of Cusa,* who wrote out in notes still extant excerpts pertaining, among other points, to his idea that there exist three necessary innate principles (''correlatives'') in all substances (*Liber cor-*

relativorum innatorum)—*bonitas*, for example, being thus determined by the three correlatives *bonificativum, bonificabile* and *bonificare*.

Lull wrote over 300 works in Latin, Catalan, Spanish, and Arabic; about 256 works are preserved. His contribution to Catalan literature has been compared with Dante's to Italian. His main writings include *Libre de contemplació en Déu*; *Libre del gentil e dels tres savis*; *Blaquerna* (including *The Book of the Lover and the Beloved* [*Libre d'amic e amat*]); *Fèlix de les meravelles del món*; *Taula general*; *Arbre de ciència*; *Liber Apostrophe*; *Arbre de filosofia d'amor*; *Ars generalis ultima*.

Bibliography

A. *Opera latina*, ed. F. Stegmüller et al. (Palma, 1959–67); *Opera latina*, CCCM 32–39, 75–76, 78 (Turnhout, 1975–); *Selected Works of Raymond Lull (1232–1316)*, ed. and trans. A. Bonner, 2 vols. (Princeton, N.J.., 1985).

B. DSAM 13:171–87; DTC 9:1072–141; LThK² 8:974–76; NCE 8:1074–76; ODCC 990–91; TRE 21:500–506; E. Allison Peers, *Fool of Love: The Life of Ramon Lull* (London, 1946); E. Colomer, *Nikolaus von Kues und Raimund Lull* (Berlin, 1961); Erhard-Wolfram Platzeck, *Raimund Lull. Sein Leben, seine Werke, die Grundlagen seines Denkens* (*Prinzipienlehre*), 2 vols. (Düsseldorf, 1962); J. N. Hillgarth, *Ramon Lull and Lullism in Fourteenth-Century France* (Oxford, 1971); Rudolf Brummer, *Bibliographia Lulliana: Ramon-Llull-Schrifttum 1870–1973* (Hildesheim, 1976); M. Salleras i Corolà, "Bibliographial Llulliana (1974–85)," *Randa* 19 (1986): 153–85; Mark D. Johnston, *The Spiritual Logic of Ramon Llull* (New York, 1987); Dominique de Courcelles, *La parole risquée de Raymond Lulle. Entre judaïsme, christianisme et islam* (Paris, 1993); Mark D. Johnston, *The Evangelical Rhetoric of Ramon Llull: Lay Learning and Piety in the Christian West around 1300* (New York, 1996).

William J. Hoye

LUTHER, MARTIN (10 November 1483, Eisleben, Saxony, Germany–18 February 1546, Eisleben). *Education*: studied at Magdeburg, 1497–98; Eisenach, 1498–1501; Erfurt Univ., 1501–5; bachelor of Bible, Wittenberg Univ., 1509; doctor of theology, Wittenberg Univ., 1511–12. *Career*: novice, Augustinian Hermits, 1505–7; ordained priest, 1507; lecturer in philosophy, Wittenberg Univ., 1508–9; returned to Erfurt, 1509; representative of order in Rome, 1510–11; posted ninety-five theses against sale of indulgences, 31 October 1517; Heidelberg disputation, 1518; Leipzig debate, 1519; burned papal bull (*Exsurge Domine*) threatening excommunication, December, 1520; excommunicated, January, 1521; Diet of Worms, April, 1521; placed under imperial ban, May, 1521; attended Marburg Colloquy, 1529, and Smalcald Conference, 1537; professor of Bible (*lectura in Biblia*), Wittenberg Univ., 1512–46.

No Reformation figure has had a greater impact on theology than the doctor of faith Martin Luther. The intensity of his thought, wrested from his experience of the angry and gracious God, poured into all of his works—60,000 printed pages, 2,013 known sermons, and thirty-five years of lectures as professor of Bible at Wittenberg University. Luther, who admitted he had never opened a

Bible before age twenty, found there the God who died on the cross bearing the sin of the world so that by pure grace divine righteousness might be freely given to sinners through the gift of faith. The formula *sola Scriptura/sola gratia/sola fide*, which has come to be known as the core of Luther's theology, is inadequate to express its depth and breadth, yet it provides a solid framework.

Drawing from Scripture reinforced by Augustine's* anti-Pelagian works, Luther's call for complete reliance on God's mercy rather than on human works for salvation was intended only to reform Pelagian practices that he felt had pervaded the church, evidenced by such things as selling indulgences as an assurance of heavenly reward. Luther had expressed concerns about the proper God/human relationship as early as his first Psalm lectures of 1513, but his proposing theses for debate on the sale of indulgences, 31 October 1517, rapidly accelerated to bitter conflict between Rome and the reformer. At the Leipzig Debate with Johannes Eck,* 1519, Luther incautiously acknowledged that popes and councils could err, whereupon Eck soon left for Rome to provoke heresy charges against Luther. Still hopeful for church renewal, Luther published three major reformational treatises in 1520: *To the Christian Nobility of the German Nation*, *The Babylonian Captivity of the Church*, and *On the Freedom of the Christian Person*. These went beyond criticizing external practices to calling for reform of the church's ecclesiastical structure itself. In response, Luther was excommunicated in January 1521. The following May he was placed under the ban of the empire after he refused to recant at the Diet of Worms in April but instead stood firm on Scripture as his vindication.

For Luther, *Sola Scriptura* is also *solo Christo*. Since the essence of both Old and New Testaments is Christ, the truth of Scripture is in *was Christum treibet* (what promotes Christ) as the soteriological key to scriptural meaning. His belief that Christ as Word speaks in the words of Scripture led Luther to call the church a "mouth house" that must confess and proclaim Christ. Luther's theology lies in the tradition of monastic scriptural reflection that emphasizes *oratio*, *meditatio*, and *tentatio*, that is, prayer, intense study of the texts, and the experience of the cross through temptations (*Anfechtungen*). For the theologian, these are indispensable for recognizing pure doctrine based upon the simplest literal/prophetic sense of the texts. Luther maintained that Scripture interprets itself, adhering to the monastic practice of putting the whole of Scripture to memory so that any text recalls many others for grounding and consistency.

Sola Scriptura does not deny tradition, but tradition must be drawn from Scripture for doctrinal validity. Luther asserted that Scripture has its own grammar and logic, different from the logic of philosophy, as he maintained in his treatise *Against Scholastic Theology*, 1517. The grammar of Scripture rests upon faith in the truthfulness of the Word. God's word of promise is trustworthy since God cannot deceive. Truth is perceived in the logic of faith, in the contradictions and foolishness of the Incarnation and cross—God's manifestation to the world in the humility of Christ, in contradistinction to perspectives of lordship and glory that derive from what seems logical to human understanding.

Law and Gospel are the key to Scripture and must be distinguished. Both are God's Word, but the law has been given to make humans aware of their sinfulness and the anger of a wrathful God whose justice demands perfect righteousness of a fallen people incapable of achieving it. Luther's reflections on Galatians, 1516–38, point to the law as pedagogue, the strict teacher who prepares one for heirship to God's testament of grace. Without the law, the Gospel message of grace eludes because the enormity of sin is not recognized nor the need for repentance. The law condemns, but the Gospel rescues from the power of Satan and heals the wounds of sin because Christ willingly became the curse of our sin and the oath of the law to fulfill it for us. For all who believe, the law is seen in a new light, no longer condemning the believer nor causing him to hate its bondage but, freed of its curse, becoming the law of love and service to others. Luther remarked in his *Freedom of the Christian Person*, 1520: "A Christian is a perfectly free Lord of all, subject to none; a Christian is a perfectly dutiful servant, subject to all."

Sola gratia, salvation purely through God's grace without the works of the law, draws the sinner from death and Satan and gives the inheritance of righteousness that is rightfully Christ's. Human sin and Christ's righteousness are exchanged (*fröhliche Wechsel*) and Christ's righteousness, the righteousness of God, shields the sinner from God's wrath. Thus God reconciles sinners to himself solely through his own gracious trinitarian action. God's gift of faith in Christ allows the individual to stand redeemed before God (*coram Deo*) despite sinfulness that remains, confident because of Christ that God is not angry.

The faith that alone justifies (*sola fide*) is faith in God's promise of forgiveness and salvation, which in eschatological terms is complete through faith, yet still to come in finality on the last day. In this life, the strife between the old and new person continues since the believer is *simul iustus et peccator*, justified and sinner at the same time. Faith draws the believer to Christ, who is object of faith and its subject from whose faith the gift of faith is given. Luther does not teach a process of sanctification in what has come to be known as the third use of the law, but he maintains (cf. *Against Latomus*, 1521) that as faith draws the believer nearer and nearer to Christ, the believer enters into Christ and leaves more and more of the self behind. Although justification is given as passive righteousness, the gift of faith that confirms it is active and dynamic with the activity of the Holy Spirit in the inner person. Luther often used the analogy of the good tree bearing good fruit to describe fruits of faith, not in any sense of salvatory merit but as love and service to the neighbor.

The eschatological stance of the Christian is in the shadow of the cross. In the Heidelberg Disputation, 1518, Luther emphasized his theology of the cross in criticism of a theology of glory that sought to know God through works of reason. To believe in a God who hung from the cross is the essence of a faith that justifies, since the foolishness of the cross strains reasonableness. Luther's Christology is based upon what he perceived as the truth of Scripture about Christ, drawing from Cyril of Alexandria's* formula of *communicatio idioma-*

tum that what is predicated of one nature in Christ is predicated of the other, and vice versa. Luther's Christological two-natures teaching underlies his teaching on the Lord's Supper in which Christ is both bodily and spiritually present in, with, and under the bread and wine. If Christ in his divinity is omnipresent, the same is true for his human nature, which is inseparable from the divine. Luther firmly held to this teaching on the Lord's Supper at the Marburg Colloquy, 1529, against Huldreich Zwingli's* insistence on spiritual presence alone, marking a sharp divergence between Christological perspectives in Lutheran and Reformed beliefs.

Luther's anthropology is based on his Christology that the Christian who is shielded by Christ's righteousness is both justified and sinful at the same time, one predicated of the other, and vice versa. True human freedom is impossible without Christ, since in itself the human will is in bondage to sin and Satan. Luther's *Bondage of the Will* (*De servo arbitrio*), 1525, written in passionate response to Erasmus' *Freedom of the Will* (*De libero arbitrio*), insisted that human beings cannot of themselves turn to God but must be drawn to God by grace from the bondage of the law that condemns and a fallen nature incapable of willing the good. To be able to do "what is in one" in some confidence that God will reward the attempt, as some theologians contemporary to Luther taught, was an impossible fiction in Luther's estimation because "what is in one" was a nature disabled by sin.

Throughout his life, Luther held that the first commandment was the key to understanding the human relationship to God, who created all things from nothing and who recreated the new person from Christ's righteousness rather than from sinful human nature. God's freedom cannot be limited by human efforts because the creature's proper stance is to let God be God. That God chose to manifest his mercy in Christ answers the question of predestination for Luther because he always approaches it from grace revealed in Christ. To cling to Christ who is the enfleshment of the Word of promise puts an end to the terror of damnation that Luther experienced so vividly in his failed attempts to appease an angry God whose wrath would not be moved by the most strenuous obedience to the law. Luther's world was changed by the discovery that the angry, insatiable God of his nightmarish *Anfechtungen* is the same gracious God who died on the cross for him (*pro me*).

In turn, Luther could not keep silent despite excommunication and ban of empire, for he believed the truth of Scripture must be proclaimed for the rescue of souls like himself who were endangered by teaching that encouraged reliance on works for salvation. Grace alone, faith alone, Scripture alone, Christ alone—this was Luther's soteriological sermon to the world.

Bibliography

A.   *Dr. Martin Luthers Werke, kritische Gesammtausgabe (Weimarer Ausgabe)* (Weimar, 1883–); *American Edition of Luther's Works*, ed. Jaroslav Pelikan et al., 56 vols.

(St. Louis, Mo., 1955–); *Dr. Martin Luthers sämmtliche Schriften*, ed. Johann Georg Walch, 24 vols. (Halle, 1740–53; 23 vols., St. Louis, Mo., 1880–1910).

B.   DTC 9:1146–1335; LThK³ 6:1129–39; NCE 8:1085–91; ODCC 1007–10; OEncR 2:461–67; TRE 21:513–94; Paul Althaus, *The Theology of Martin Luther*, trans. Robert C. Schultz (Philadelphia, 1966); Martin Brecht, *Martin Luther*, trans. James L. Schaaf, 3 vols. (Minneapolis, Minn., 1985–93); Kenneth Hagen, *Luther's Approach to Scripture as Seen in His "Commentaries" on Galatians, 1516–1538* (Tübingen, 1993); Gordon E. Rupp, *The Righteousness of God* (London, 1953); Roland Bainton, *Here I Stand: A Life of Martin Luther* (repr. Nashville, Tenn., 1990); Heiko A. Oberman, *Luther: Man between God and Devil*, trans. Eileen Walliser-Schwarzbart (New Haven, Conn., 1986); Bernhard Lohse, *Martin Luther: An Introduction to His Life and Work*, trans. Robert C. Schulz (Philadelphia, 1986).

Joan Skocir

M

McGLYNN, EDWARD (27 September 1837, New York, N.Y.–7 January 1900, Newburgh, N.Y.). *Education*: S.T.D., Urban Coll. of the Propaganda, Rome, 1860. *Career*: pastoral work, diocese of New York, 1860–66; pastor, St. Stephen's Church, New York City, 1866–87; president, Anti-Poverty Society, New York, N.Y., 1887–92; pastor, St. Mary's Church, Newburgh, N.Y., 1894–1900.

McGlynn was a parish priest and noted social reformer in New York City. His excellence in pastoral and theological studies at the Vatican's Urban College earned him the appointment as the first Vice Rector of the new American College (1859). During his years of service to urban parishes populated by Irish immigrants and African-American squatters, he came under the influence of abolitionist and radical reconstructionist priest Thomas Farrell and a collegial group of liberal Catholics known as the Accademia. It was both Farrell's model and McGlynn's service to the urban poor during the Civil War that stirred his reformer's heart.

McGlynn's sacramental social theology matured under pastoral mentor Jeremiah Cummings at St. Stephen's, the city's largest parish located on the Lower East Side. After Cummings' death, McGlynn became the parish pastor, and his service to the poor won public praise from social and religious leaders like Lyman Abbott,* William Llyod Garrison, and Rabbi Stephen Wise. Daily encounters with the life of the poor convinced him that a systemic response to social questions greater than institutional and personal charity was needed. In 1881, McGlynn read Henry George's *Progress and Poverty*, a text he described as the catalyst of his analysis of the use of land and labor.

McGlynn's speech, *The Cross of the New Crusade* (1887), is the definitive statement of his social theological vision. The compelling orator raised a clarion call for Catholics to realize America's providential and humanitarian destiny. Both his pastoral and social investigations of the problems of the day reveal his theological reliance upon Thomas Aquinas.* McGlynn sought to change the American inclination toward a capitalist exploitation of land and labor for the benefit of private interest into the productive social use of land and labor for the realization of a common good.

In 1886, Archbishop Michael A. Corrigan pressed the Vatican to excommunicate McGlynn on the grounds of disobedience to superiors and the suspicion of socialism. McGlynn was excommunicated when he refused to travel to Rome to answer the charges against him. Despite both the ecclesiastical excommunication and his political estrangement from Henry George, McGlynn continued to wage a war on poverty through the Anti-Poverty Society.

In 1892, the persistent lobby of McGlynn's friends moved the papal legate Archbishop Francesco Satolli to review his case. A committee of scholars from the Catholic University of America found his social teachings to be well within the parameters of orthodoxy. In 1892, Pope Leo XIII received McGlynn in Rome and reinstated him to the church and priesthood. McGlynn remained a pastor and advocate for social reform until his death.

Historians identify McGlynn as a Catholic representative of the Social Gospel because of his reference to the principles of the Fatherhood of God and brotherhood of Man. McGlynn's estimation of land and labor—grounded in his reflection of the life of the poor in light of the sacraments, the lectionary, and Catholic theologians—establishes, however, a significant sacramental distinction between nineteenth-century social Catholicism and the Protestant Social Gospel.

Bibliography

A.   "The McGlynn Papers" in the archives of the Archdiocese of New York (Yonkers, N.Y.); "The Cross of the New Crusade" *The Standard* 2 (April, 1887): 2–3.

B.   DAB 7:53–54; DACB 366; DARB 328–29; DCA 687; NCAB 9:242–44; NCE 9: 18–19; NYT 8 January 1900, 1; Stephen Bell, *Rebel, Priest and Prophet* (New York, 1937); Sylvester Malone, *Dr. Edward McGlynn* (New York, 1978); Dominic P. Scibilia, "Edward McGlynn, Thomas McGrady, and Peter C. Yorke: Prophets of American Social Catholicism," Ph.D. diss., Marquette Univ., 1990.

Dominic P. Scibilia

McGRADY, THOMAS (16 June 1863, Lexington, Ky.–26 November 1907, San Francisco, Calif.). *Career*: ordained priest, 1887; pastoral work, diocese of Galveston, 1887–91, diocese of Covington, 1891–1903; lawyer, San Francisco, 1903–7.

McGrady was a priest, lawyer, and fervent activist on behalf of the spiritual and material welfare of the laboring classes. During his pastoral service in Covington he became critically conscious of the social problems in the lives of the mine and railway workers of eastern Kentucky. His parishioners worked and lived in the shadows of mineral moguls like John C. C. Mayo and under the economic constrictions of forfeiture laws and the company town. Economic stresses like the depression of 1893 and the Cincinnati machinist strike in 1901 instigated his intellectual search for a political economy that would respond to the social anguish of the laborer. Like many of the land and labor reformers of the nineteenth century, McGrady examined populist, capitalist, corporatist, and socialist proposals for a just political economy.

Associations with socialists like Eugene Debs and Martha Moore Avery as well as his study of the social thought of German Catholics like bishop von Ketteler fueled his interest in social democratic theories. His published works, especially *The Two Kingdoms* (Cincinnati, 1899) and *Beyond the Black Ocean* (Chicago, 1901), demonstrated his confidence in the ideological sympathies between a Catholic millennialism and the egalitarian and emancipatory themes and policies in social democratic teachings. He delineated a sacramental social theology in which both the church and the state are divinely authorized mediators of God's historical design. Each sphere satisfied the aspirations of the human spirit for loyalty to God and neighbor.

In 1899 *Two Kingdoms* drew ecclesiastical censure. Despite the preponderance of biblical and historical support in his social analysis, his praise of modern thinkers like Ernst Renan troubled bishops Maes (Covington) and Elder (Cincinnati). His superiors instructed him to withdraw the text from publication until its modern proclivities could be remedied. McGrady refused to comply with episcopal instruction. In 1903, at the height of his advocacy for a Catholic social democracy, he left the priesthood.

Even though many socialists and Catholics rejected him after his resignation from the priesthood, McGrady wrote and spoke publicly on behalf of a social democratic political economy informed by a sacramental theology. Until his death in 1907, he believed that institutional autocrats forced him out of the priesthood because he questioned the human (accidental) elements of religion when they overshadowed its divine (essential) elements.

Bibliography

A. *The Mistakes of Ingersoll* (Cincinnati, Ohio, 1898); *Socialism and the Labor Problem* (Bellevue, Ky., 1900); *A Voice from England* (Terre Haute, Ind., 1901); *City of Angels* (Terre Haute, Ind., 1901).

B. Eugene V. Debs, "Obituary of Thomas McGrady," *Christian Socialist* (Chicago) 1 (January 1908):1–4; Toby Terrar, "Catholic Socialism: The Rev. Thomas McGrady," *Dialectical Anthropology* 7 (1983): 209–35; Dominic P. Scibilia, "Thomas McGrady: American Catholic Millennialist, Millennial Social Catholicism," *Records of the American Catholic Historical Society of Philadelphia* 105 (Spring/Summer, 1994): 32–46.

Dominic P. Scibilia

MACHEN, JOHN GRESHAM (28 July 1881, Baltimore, Md.–1 January 1937, Bismarck, N.Dak.). *Education*: B.A. in classics, Johns Hopkins Univ., 1901; graduate study at Johns Hopkins with the renowned American classicist

Basil Gildersleeve, 1901–2; B.D., Princeton Sem., Princeton, N.J., 1902–5; M.A., philosophy, Princeton Univ., 1904; New Testament Fellow, Univs. of Marburg and Göttingen, 1905–6. *Career*: instructor, New Testament, Princeton Sem., 1906–14; ordained, New Brunswick Presbytery, 1914; assistant professor, New Testament literature and exegesis, 1914–29; war service, YMCA, 1918–19; founder, Westminster Sem., Philadelphia, Pa., 1929; professor, New Testament, Westminster Sem., 1929–37; founder, Independent Board for Presbyterian Foreign Missions, 1933; tried and suspended from ministry in the Presbyterian Church in the U.S.A., 1935; founder, Presbyterian Church of America (later named the Orthodox Presbyterian Church), 1936.

Machen was the last major representative of the Princeton Theology in the twentieth century as well as the leading spokesperson for orthodox Protestantism during the fundamentalist/modernist controversy of the 1920s. Although Machen was—and still is—often called a fundamentalist, he did not call himself a fundamentalist because he believed that as a Calvinist he stood in the mainstream of "the historic Christian faith." The "central current of the Church's life," he argued, is that current "which flows down from the Word of God through Augustine* and Calvin,* and which has found noteworthy expression in America in the great tradition represented by Charles Hodge* and Benjamin Breckinridge Warfield* and the other representatives of the 'Princeton School.' "

Although Machen is an historical figure who arouses veneration in some and disdain in others, modern interpreters recognize that he must be regarded as one of the greatest Reformed theologians of the twentieth century for at least two reasons. The first has to do with his conservative contribution to the field of New Testament scholarship. In two major responses to historical-critical attacks upon the integrity of Scripture, Machen championed the cause of orthodoxy by setting forth evidence for the reliability of the New Testament's witness to Christ.

Against those who posited a radical discontinuity between the religion of Jesus and the religion of Paul, Machen penned *The Origin of Paul's Religion* (New York, 1921) to establish that the religion of Paul was at its heart a religion of faith in the Jesus who lived, died, and rose again to redeem his people from their sins. Later, in *The Virgin Birth of Christ* (New York, 1930), Machen demonstrated that traditional supernaturalistic claims better explain the New Testament's witness to Christ than do claims that reject the possibility of the supernatural out of hand. Indeed, Machen demonstrated that the virgin birth is an "integral part" of the gospel, and that it cannot be removed from the New Testament account of Jesus without making the whole account "harder and not easier to accept."

While Machen gained scholarly acclaim for his conservative response to the conclusions of historical-critical scholarship, he is most renown for his devastating critique of theological liberalism's solution to the problem of the relationship between Christianity and culture. In *Christianity and Liberalism* (New York, 1923) Machen argued that the liberal attempt to reconcile Christianity to modern culture by accommodating Christianity to modern culture ultimately reduced the Christian religion to a type of religious practice that is "anti-Christian to the core." Although Machen harbored no contempt for the advocates of theological liberalism, he was convinced that they endorsed a type of religion that is entirely distinct from Christianity. It was this opposition to liberalism, then, that not only led him to resign from Princeton and found Westminster when Princeton's board of directors was reorganized along more liberal lines in 1929, but it was also what led him to found the Orthodox Presbyterian Church in 1936 due to the perceived liberalism of missionaries serving with the Presbyterian Church in the U.S.A.

Bibliography

A. *What is Faith?* (New York, 1925); *The Christian View of Man* (New York, 1937); *What is Christianity and Other Addresses*, ed. Ned B. Stonehouse (Grand Rapids, Mich., 1951).

B. DARB 337–38; NYT 2 January 1937, 11; Ned B. Stonehouse, *J. Gresham Machen: A Biographical Memoir* (Grand Rapids, Mich., 1954); W. Stanford Reid, "J. Gresham Machen," in *Reformed Theology in America*, ed. David F. Wells (Grand Rapids, Mich., 1985); D. G. Hart, *Defending the Faith: J. Gresham Machen and the Crisis of Conservative Protestantism in Modern America* (Baltimore, Md., 1994); David B. Calhoun, *Princeton Seminary*, 2 vols. (Edinburgh, 1994–96).

Paul Helseth

MACINTOSH, DOUGLAS CLYDE (18 February 1877, Breadalbane, Ontario, Canada–6 July 1948, Hamden, Conn.). *Education*: B.A., McMaster Univ., 1903; Ph.D., Univ. of Chicago, 1909; M.A., Yale Univ., 1916. *Career*: minister, Baptist Church, Marthaville, Ontario; instructor in philosophy, McMaster Univ., 1903–4; professor of biblical and systematic theology, Brandon Coll., 1907–9; professor of theology and philosophy of religion, Yale Div. Sch., 1909–42.

Macintosh was a leading American empirical theologian and a proponent of religious realism. He was raised in the revivalistic tradition of the nineteenth century with its emphasis on the experimental basis of Christian faith. A Canadian-born Baptist, he had a conversion experience at the age of ten which gave him the assurance that he was "saved and in no further danger of hellfire." While in college, he became interested in philosophy and this led him away from his earlier evangelical understanding of Christianity. During World War I he served as a chaplain to Canadian forces and as a YMCA worker with American forces. This experience made him a pacifist, and as a result of his pacifist views he was denied United States citizenship.

Macintosh was a theological pragmatist and insisted that theology is an empirical science. He developed his own theory of knowledge, which he called "critical monism," "critical monistic realism," or "critical realistic monism." His realism led him to state that the doctrine of a "primeval divine curse imposed upon a nature because of the Fall of man has passed through the stages of being believed, questioned, denied, and ridiculed, and is now almost forgotten.'' The essence of Christianity is a sort of moral optimism. Macintosh had a deep influence on Reinhold Niebuhr.*

Bibliography

A.   *Theology as an Empirical Science* (New York, 1919); *The Reasonableness of Christianity* (New York, 1925); *Personal Religion* (New York, 1942).

B.   DAB 24:524–26; NCE 9:35; NYT 7 July 1948, 46; Vergilius Ferm, ed. *Contemporary Theology: Theological Biographies*, vol. 1 (New York, 1932).

Donald S. Armentrout

MAISTRE, JOSEPH MARIE, COMTE DE (1 April 1753, Chambéry, Savoy–26 February 1821, Turin, Italy). *Education*: studied law, Turin, 1769–72. *Career*: apprentice legal career, Chambéry, Savoy, 1772–74; entered magistery of Savoy, Chambéry, 1774–88; member of Senate, 1788–92; exiled to Lausanne, 1792–99; regent of Sardinian Kingdom, 1799–1802; Sardinian minister at St. Petersburg, Russia, 1802–17; Régent de la Grande Chancellarie, Turin, 1817–21.

De Maistre was not a theologian, but his political thought and particularly his interpretation of the French Revolution and the eighteenth century in general had a shaping influence upon the rise of nineteenth-century Ultramontanism after his death. A concept of divine providence was at the heart of his understanding of world history and politics. He understood the French Revolution as a divine punishment and as a divinely ordained means for regeneration of church and society. The Revolution was a redemptive event whereby the suffering of the innocent redeems a guilty world.

For de Maistre, the whole of society and all durable institutions had providence and religion as their foundation. The eighteenth-century *philosophes* in general and the French Revolution in particular ruptured that mystical connection between religion and society. De Maistre pinned his hopes for the restoration of this relationship between religion and society on the papacy and its restorative and divinely authoritative powers. He saw the papacy itself as the visible symbol of the survival of the church and society. His high emphasis upon papal authority and infallibility in *Du Pape* (Lyons, 1819) would provide a political as well as a religious justification for the papal role in the world order.

Bibliography

A.   *Oeuvres complètes*, 14 vols. (Lyons, 1884–87); *Considérations sur la France* (Lyons, 1796); *De l'Église gallicane* (Lyons, 1821); *Soirée de St.-Petersbourg, ou Entretiens sur le gouvernement temporel de la Providence* (Lyons, 1821); *Works*, selected and trans. Jack Lively (New York, 1965).

B.   DTC 9:1663–78; LThK[3] 6:1214; NCE 9:89–90; ODCC 467–68; Georges Goyau, *La pensée religieuse de Joseph de Maistre d'après des documents inédites* (Paris, 1921); R. Triomphe, *Joseph de Maistre. Étude sur la vie et sur la doctrine d'un matérialiste mystique* (Geneva, 1968); Richard Lebrun, *Throne and Altar: The Political and Religious Thought of Joseph de Maistre* (Ottawa, 1965); idem, *Joseph de Maistre: An Intellectual Militant* (Kingston, Ontario, 1988); idem, *Maistre Studies* (Lanham, Md., 1988).

Patrick W. Carey

MANNING, HENRY EDWARD (15 July 1808, Copped Hall, Totteridge–14 January 1892, London). *Education*: studied at Harrow School 1822–26; Balliol Coll., Oxford, 1827–30; fellow of Merton Coll., Oxford, 1832; studied at Accademia Ecclesiastica, Rome, 1851–54. *Career*: ordained priest and appointed rector of Lavington, 1833; marriage to Caroline Sargent, 1833; archdeacon of Chichester, 1840; converted to Roman Catholicism, 1851; founder, Oblates of St. Charles, 1857; archbishop of Westminster, 1865–92; cardinal, 1875.

Manning stands out as one of the foremost representatives of Ultramontane ecclesiology. Before he became a champion of both papal infallibility (Vatican Council, 1870) and of papal temporal power, he had been a promising leader in the Church of England and maintained a close association with those in the Oxford Movement. As an Anglican, Manning held principles that revealed a high regard for the autonomous authority of the church, an exalted view of episcopal government and of the ordained clergy, the rejection of lay persons from the internal affairs of the church, and a growing resentment toward the intrusion of the civil power into ecclesiastical affairs.

Manning's deepening sense of the Holy Spirit led him to an understanding of church as the continuation of the Apostolic witness invested with a divine mission not only to preserve and protect what had been passed down through tradition but also invested with an authority to pass judgment on the content and meaning of revelation in all ages.

Manning's Ultramontanism was not simply or even essentially a matter of reactionary politics, but was a type of nineteenth-century populist "Catholicism" that attempted to stem the tide of secularization. Manning's Ultramontanism was of a practical nature. His religious thought was immediately related to the world in which Christians lived. Aside from the historical and theological foundations of the question of papal infallibility, Manning understood the question in terms of the social and political world in which Christians were to carry out their daily lives. For Manning, the issue of infallibility was much more than affirming a dogma of faith; it was a means of conserving Christian belief and Christian society in the midst of social and political upheaval and served to counter certain philosophical assumptions of European Liberalism.

Manning was considered ultraconservative in his Ultramontane policies by prominent liberals and considered a reformer and quasi-socialist in his social justice activity and in his strong identification and association with the working class poor. He was committed to the issue of Catholic education, housing for the poor, the rights of labor, and temperance, to name a few. He was responsible for successfully mediating the London dockworkers strike in 1889 at the age of 81. But Manning will mostly be remembered for his unyielding determination to see the issue of papal infallibility declared a dogma of the Catholic faith at the First Vatican Council.

Bibliography

A.   *The Ground of Faith* (London, 1856); *The Office of the Holy Ghost* (London, 1857); *The Temporal Mission of the Holy Ghost* (London, 1865); *The Eternal Priesthood* (London, 1883).

B.   DNB 12:947–53; LThK³ 6:1283; NCE 9:168–70; ODCC 1028; TRE 22:60–63; Robert Gray, *Cardinal Manning: A Biography* (New York, 1985); V. A. McClelland, *Cardinal Manning: His Public Life and Influence 1865–1892* (London, 1962); David Newsome, *The Convert Cardinals* (London, 1993); E. S. Purcell, *Life of Cardinal Manning*, 2 vols. (New York, 1896).

Barry H. Sargent

MARCELLUS OF ANCYRA (ca. 280–374). Marcellus, bishop of Ancyra in Galatia, was among the earliest and most determined opponents of Arianism but was himself rejected as a heretic. The creedal clause "of whose kingdom there will be no end" is directed against him. The date of his birth is unknown, but he was a bishop by 314. He took part in the Council of Nicaea and thereafter wrote a book against the Arianizing Asterius the Sophist. Eusebius of Caesarea* and many other eastern bishops suspected Marcellus of Sabellianism and deposed him at a synod in Constantinople in 336. Eusebius wrote two refutations of Marcellus: *Against Marcellus* and *On the Ecclesiastical Theology*. In 340, Marcellus was acquitted of heresy and received into communion at Rome; he and Athanasius* became allies there. Their presence among the western bishops at the Council of Sardica in 343 caused the eastern bishops to split off and hold their council at Philippopolis. Marcellus' reputation suffered further when his disciple Photinus lapsed into heretical Adoptionism. Yet a community at Ancyra remained faithful to Marcellus, and they were in communion with Paulinus and his followers at Antioch, probably with Athanasius, and with the West. Basil of Caesarea* and the other Cappadocians met more resistance than they expected to the formula "three hypostases," mostly from parties sympathetic to Marcellus. Of Marcellus' works, his short letter to Julius of Rome (340) survives intact, and many fragments of the work *Against Asterius* survive. Recently half a dozen other works have been attributed to Marcellus, but the attributions remain far from certain.

Marcellus insisted that God must be called one *hypostasis*, one *ousia*, and one *prosôpon*. Perhaps in the tradition of the Apologists' Logos-theology, he speculated that the Son and the Holy Spirit emerged for the purposes of creation, redemption, and sanctification; and (relying on 1 Cor 15:24–28) that at the end they would be reabsorbed into God.

Bibliography

A.   Fragments in GCS Eusebius 4, 2d ed. (Berlin, 1972).

B.   DTC 9:1993–98; ECC 1:522; LThK³ 6:1302–03; NCE 9:191; ODCC 1033; TRE

22:83–89; J. T. Lienhard, ''Marcellus of Ancyra in Modern Research,'' ThSt 43 (1982): 486–503; idem, ''The Arian Controversy: Some Categories Reconsidered,'' ThSt 48 (1987): 415–37.

Joseph T. Lienhard

MARCION (d. ca. 154). Marcion was born in Sinope in Pontus, on the Black Sea. His father was a bishop; Marcion made a fortune in shipping. Ca. 140 he traveled to Rome, joined the church there, and donated a large sum of money to the church. At Rome he came under the influence of the Gnostic teacher Cerdo. In 144 he was excommunicated, and his money was returned to him. Thereupon he founded and organized his own church, which prospered in various cities for over a century. Marcion read the Old Testament and accepted every word of it as literally true. He also read books that were later in the New Testament, especially Paul's letters. He concluded that the God of the Old Testament was an inferior God, the creator of the world, and the God of justice. This God was incompetent, ignorant, fickle, and vengeful. The God of the New Testament, by contrast, was known through a wholly new revelation in Jesus Christ; he was the God of love. Marcion separated creation from redemption and Christianity from its roots in Judaism. He rejected the Old Testament from the church and, by teaching docetism, kept Christ distinct from matter. He believed that only Paul had understood the Gospel: the other apostles had been corrupted by Judaism. But Judaizers had also interpolated Paul's letters. Hence he expurgated Paul's letters and edited the Gospel according to Luke (which he took to be ''Paul's gospel'') to remove Judaizing interpolations. He thereby published the first fixed canon of the New Testament: ten letters of Paul and Luke's gospel. To say that the church established its canon purely in reaction to Marcion is excessive. Among the many works written against Marcion, Tertullian's* is the most thorough and perhaps the best.

Bibliography

A. Tertullian, *Adversus Marcionem*, 2 vols. (Oxford, 1972).

B. DSAM 10:311–21; DTC 9:2009–32; LThK³ 6:1391–93; NCE 9:193–94; ODCC 1033–34; TRE 22:89–101; J. Knox, *Marcion and the New Testament* (Chicago, 1942); E. C. Blackman, *Marcion and His Influence* (London, 1948); A. von Harnack, *Marcion: The Gospel of the Alien God*, trans. John E. Steely and Lyle D. Bierma (Durham, N.C., 1989).

Joseph T. Lienhard

MARÉCHAL, JOSEPH (1 July 1878, Charleroi, Belgium–11 December 1944, Louvain, Belgium). *Education*: novitiate in Society of Jesus, Arlon, Belgium, 1895–97; literary studies at Tronchiennes, Belgium, 1897–98; philosophy at Jesuit House of Studies, Louvain, 1898–1901; Ph. D. studies in biology, Univ. of Louvain, 1901–5; studied theology, Jesuit House of Studies, Louvain, 1905–9; studied ascetical theology, Linz, Austria, 1909–10. *Career*: ordained priest,

1908; superior of refugee Jesuit students, England, 1914–15; professor of philosophy and experimental psychology, Jesuit House of Studies, Louvain, 1919–35; ill health and retirement, 1935–44.

Maréchal was the founder of the movement in philosophy and theology later called Transcendental Thomism. In varying degrees twentieth-century theologians like Henri Bouillard, Henri de Lubac,* Karl Rahner,* and Bernard Lonergan* have been influenced by him. In his five-volume masterpiece, *Le point de depart de la metaphysique*, Maréchal surveyed the history of philosophy and argued that only the dynamic philosophy of Aristotle and Thomas* had been able to unify human knowledge and provide a satisfactory starting point for metaphysics. In St. Thomas' philosophy of man, the dynamic emanation of the faculties from the soul unified human knowledge by subordinating the operation of the sense faculties to the inbuilt drive of the intellect. The intellect's motion toward God's absolute being as its natural end could then refer the cognitional objects, unified through the cooperation of the phantasm and the concept, to God's transcendent, supersensible reality in the affirmation of the judgment. Infinite transcendent being therefore could be known through the *act* of the judgment, even though the cognitional *form* of every object known through abstracted concepts was limited in its content to the finite world of space and time.

Since modern philosophy could neither unify sense and intellect nor provide a satisfactory grounding for metaphysics, it oscillated between a sensist empiricism that denied the possibility of metaphysics and an intellectualist rationalism that tried to justify it through the static forms of its innate ideas. Kant had tried to overcome that dualism by laying bare the a priori conditions of objective knowledge by use of his transcendental method, and he did manage to unify sense and intellect through the a priori forms and categories, which organized the objects of his phenomenal world.

Nevertheless, he remained an idealist, since he had overlooked the indispensable role of the mind's motion toward an end in its preconscious a priori process of unifying its objects. If Kant had noticed that finality, his transcendental method would have led him to a realist metaphysics, grounded in the way in which St. Thomas had justified it. Like St. Thomas, Kant would have made his way into the world of real being by referring the unified objects of his discursive intellect to God's absolute being in a dynamic affirmative act of judgment.

Maréchal pioneered what has become the Transcendental Thomist interpretation of St. Thomas' epistemology. That interpretation, however, remains a controverted one. Relying on it, Maréchal claimed that a Thomist philosopher could set out from an intramental starting point, as Kant had done, and then make his way out to the world of real being through a transcendental reflection of the conditions of possibility for human knowledge. Although other Thomists still contest the validity of that approach and contemporary theologians like Hans Urs von Balthasar* vehemently oppose its use in theology, Maréchalianism, in the theologies of Rahner and Lonergan, remains a vital tradition in twentieth-century Catholic thought.

Bibliography

A. *Etudes sur la psychologie des mystiques*, 2 vols. (Paris, 1938); "Le dynamisme intellectuel dans la connaissance objective," "Au seuil de la metaphysique: Abstraction ou intuition?" "Jugement scholastique concernant la racine de l'agnosticisme Kantien," *Mélanges Joseph Maréchal* 1 (Paris, 1950): 75–101, 102–80, 273–87; *Le Point de depart de la metaphysique: Lesons sur le developpment historique et théorique du problème de la connaissance*, 5 vols. (Paris, 1944–49); *A Maréchal Reader*, ed. Joseph Donceel (New York, 1970).

B. LThK³ 6:1310; NCE 9:198; Georges van Riet, *L'Epistemologie thomiste* (Louvain, 1946), 263; Helen James John, *The Thomist Spectrum* (New York, 1966), 139–49; Etienne Gilson, *Thomistic Realism and the Critique of Knowledge* (San Francisco, 1986), 129–48; Gerald A. McCool, *From Unity to Pluralism: The Internal Evolution of Thomism* (New York, 1989), 87–113.

Gerald A. McCool

MARGERY KEMPE. *See* KEMPE, MARGERY.

MARSILIUS OF PADUA (ca. 1275/80, Padua–ca. 1342, Bavaria). *Education*: baccalaureate degree, Univ. of Padua; intermittently studied medicine, philosophy, theology, Univ. of Paris. *Career*: rector, Univ. of Paris, December 1312–March 1313; perhaps taught at Paris; practiced medicine in Avignon; condemned, 1327; fled to Bavarian court of Emperor Louis III of Bavaria (1314–47), serving as his adviser and spiritual vicar of Rome during imperial invasion of Italy, 1326–28; returned with Louis to Bavaria for the rest of his life, 1329–42.

Marsilius of Padua was a radical conciliarist. Although condemned, his ideas (in his major work, *Defensor pacis* [1324]) found a moderate expression among conciliarists at the General Council of Constance (1414–18). In the first part of *Defensor pacis*, Marsilius presented a theory of civil government based on popular consent; in the second, he applied this theory to the church. The work culminates in a strong apology for the supremacy of a general council as the final authority in ecclesiastical affairs. Marsilius believed that government should be led by an administrator delegated by and responsible to the community. This administrator (in religious terms, the local bishop elected by his congregation; on the widest scale, the pope) was subordinate to the community on whose authority he acted, enforced the laws created by that community, and could be removed. The papacy, therefore, was not a divine institution, but had been established by a general council.

Marsilius also denied temporal authority to all clerics, especially the pope. He reacted against papalist claims of primacy and of jurisdictional supremacy, which had been developing since the reform movement instituted by Gregory VII and were proclaimed perhaps most vociferously by Innocent III. During

Marsilius' own lifetime, Boniface VIII in his battles with Philip IV of France had claimed in *Unam sanctam* (November 1302) that the pope holds both spiritual and temporal authority directly from God, that spiritual authority is above temporal, and that the pope only delegates the exercise of temporal authority to his subordinate, the king. With other imperial publicists, Marsilius argued just the opposite. The church was only one part of the wider community of the state, whose leader could depose the pope. It should enjoy no special privileges, possess no wealth, and exercise no coercive authority. The church's jurisdiction extended only to the internal forum of spirituality and could not be forced upon a member of the faithful.

Bibliography

A.   *Defensor pacis*, ed. C. W. Previté-Orton (Cambridge, 1928); *Marsilius of Padua. The Defender of Peace*, 2, *The Defensor pacis*, trans. Alan Gewirth (New York, 1956).
B.   DTC 12:153–77; LThK³ 6:1416–19; NCE 9:297–98; ODCC 1042–43; TRE 22: 183–90; Ephraim Emerton, *Defensor pacis of Marsiglio of Padua: A Critical Study* (Cambridge, Mass., 1920); Alan Gewirth, *Marsilius of Padua: The Defender of Peace*, 1, *Marsilius of Padua and Medieval Political Philosophy* (New York, 1951); Paul E. Sigmund, "The Influence of Marsilius of Padua on Fifteenth-Century Conciliarism," *Journal of the History of Ideas* 23 (1962): 392–402; Michael Wilks, "Corporation and Representation in the *Defensor pacis*," *Studia Gratiana* 15 (1972): 253–92.

Christopher M. Bellitto

MATHEWS, SHAILER (26 May 1863, Portland, Me.–23 October 1941, Chicago, Ill.). *Education*: B. A., Colby Coll., 1884; B.D., Newton Theol. Inst., 1887; studied in Berlin, 1890–91. *Career*: professor of rhetoric, history, and political economy, Colby Coll., 1887–90, 1891–94; professor of New Testament, 1894–1906, professor of historical and comparative theology, 1906–33, and dean, 1908–33, Chicago Div. Sch.; editor, *The World Today*, 1903–11; editor, *Biblical World*, 1913–20; retirement, 1933–41.

Mathews was a self-professed modernist theologian. By modernist he meant those theologians who relied on the scientific method (particularly the inductive historical method), not on a prescribed set of doctrinal views, in their investigation of the Christian tradition. He saw modernism as an historical phase in the scientific struggle for freedom in thought and belief.

He opposed those dogmatic or confessional Christians in the American religious community whom he believed enforced inherited beliefs and institutions by their appeal to authority (biblical or ecclesiastical). For him traditional Christian doctrines were reflections of the cultural patterns and circumstances that produced them rather than timeless truths. The historical method was essential in reinterpreting those doctrines, in discarding what in them had been outgrown, and in reapplying what was valuable in them to modern conditions. For him the inductive historical method was the only valid means of uncovering and verifying the abiding Christian values that were legitimate for his own day.

Like some nineteenth-century Romantic theologians he believed that religious experience had a priority over doctrine. Salvation, moreover, was something essentially moral. His focus upon the moral dimensions of Christianity was manifested particularly in his historical investigations of Jesus' social teachings and his relations with the social institutions of his day. His emphasis upon the social dimension of Jesus' teachings placed him in the forefront of the social gospel movement in American Christianity, and like other social gospelers he believed Christianity ought to be involved in saving society and the economic order as well as in providing individuals with the motivation they needed for moral living.

Bibliography

A. *The Gospel and the Modern Man* (New York, 1910); *The Faith of Modernism* (New York, 1924); *Jesus on Social Institutions* (New York, 1928, 1971); *The Atonement and the Social Process* (New York, 1930); *The Growth of the Idea of God* (New York, 1931); *Immortality and the Cosmic Process* (Cambridge, Mass., 1933); *New Faith for Old: An Autobiography* (New York, 1936).

B. DAB 23:514–16; DARB 354–56; NCAB 11:74–75; NCE 9:461; NYT 24 October 1941, 23; SH 7:250; *The Process of Religion*, ed. Miles H. Krumbine (New York, 1933; Freeport, N.Y., 1972); Kenneth L. Smith, "Shailer Mathews: Theologian of the Social Process," Ph.D. diss., Duke Univ., 1959; Joseph H. Jackson, *Many But One* (New York, 1964); Charles H. Arnold, *Near the Edge of the Battle* (Chicago, 1966).

Patrick W. Carey

MAURICE, FREDERICK DENISON (29 August 1805, Normanston, Suffolk, England–1 April 1872, London). *Education*: studied at Trinity Coll. and Trinity Hall, Cambridge, 1823–26; Exeter Coll., Oxford, 1830–34. *Career*: writer in London, and editor of *Athenaeum*, 1826–30; ordained priest, 1834; curate, Bubbenhall, Warwickshire, 1834–36; chaplain, Guy's Hospital, London, 1836–46; professor of English literature and history, King's Coll., London, 1840–46; professor of theology, King's Coll., 1846–53; chaplain of Lincoln's Inn, 1846–60; principal, Queen's Coll., London, 1848–54; principal, Coll. for Working Men, London, 1854–60; chaplain, St. Peter's, Vere Street, London, 1860–69; Knightbridge professor of Moral Philosophy, Cambridge, 1866–72; rector, St. Edward's, Cambridge, 1870–72; Cambridge preacher at Whitehall, 1871–72.

Maurice was the father of modern English theology and one of the founders of Christian Socialism. He was the son of a Unitarian minister. His refusal to sign the Thirty-Nine Articles prevented him from getting his degree at Trinity Hall. He became a member of the Church of England and was ordained deacon and priest in 1834. While chaplain at Guy's Hospital, he wrote his most significant book: *The Kingdom of Christ; or Hints to a Quaker concerning the Principle, Constitution and Ordinances of the Catholic Church* (London, 1838). The Catholic Church is the Kingdom of Christ on earth, and the church is both a redeemed and a redeeming community. The church is an essential part of the

Gospel and it is the Body of Christ. There are six signs of a church or a spiritual society. First is baptism, the sacrament of constant union with Christ. This is the fundamental sign of the church and incorporates one into Christ. The Apostles' and the Nicene Creeds are the second sign. The third sign is set forms of worship such as the *Book of Common Prayer*. A good liturgy rescues persons from spiritual individualism. Holy Eucharist is the fourth sign and is the sacrament of Christ's continual presence with His universal family. The fifth sign is the ordained ministry, especially the episcopate, and the sixth sign is the Bible. Maurice's six signs of the church provided the backbone for the Chicago-Lambeth Quadrilateral.

From 1848 until 1854, Maurice was a leader of Christian Socialism. Christian Socialism was the application of Christian principles to social and political problems. He denounced unrestricted competition and stressed the social imperatives of the Gospel. His objective was to change "unsocial Christians and un-Christian socialists." Maurice was one of the sources of concern for social redemption in Anglicanism, which flowed into the Life and Work Movement of the twentieth century. He is the classic example of "Christ the transformer of culture."

Bibliography

A.   *The Epistle to the Hebrews* (London, 1846); *The Religions of the World and Their Relations to Christianity* (Cambridge, 1847); *Theological Essays* (London, 1853).
B.   DNB 13:97–105; ODCC 1059–60; TRE 22:278–81; *The Life of F. D. Maurice, Chiefly Told in His Own Letters*, ed. Frederick Maurice, 2 vols. (London, 1884); C. F. G. Masterman, *Frederick Denison Maurice* (London, 1907); W. Merlin Davies, *An Introduction to F. D. Maurice's Theology* (London, 1964).

Robert B. Slocum

MAXIMUS THE CONFESSOR (580–662). Often considered the last truly prolific thinker among the Greek church fathers, a critical synthesizer of Greek patristic thought, and one of the few genuinely ecumenical theologians of the early Christian era, Maximus the Confessor divided the bulk of his career between his two great devotions: the instruction of monks in spiritual doctrine and ascetic disciplines and the ongoing interpretation of the Orthodox faith and Christology in particular. As a young man, Maximus left an appointment in the Byzantine imperial court and withdrew to monastic life, first in Asia Minor and later (ca. 626) in Carthage with Sophronius, eventually bishop of Jerusalem, as his spiritual father. Already as a young monk, heavily influenced by the legacy of the Cappadocian Fathers, Maximus began work on his theological masterwork, the *Book of Ambiguities*, a commentary on difficult passages from Gregory Nazianzen's* *Orations* and from the corpus of Pseudo-Dionysius the Areopagite.* His other large work, *To Thalassius: On Diverse Difficulties from Holy Scripture*, explored obscure or discrepant texts conveyed to him by a fellow monk seeking their deeper spiritual significance. This work reveals Maximus' critical reappropriation of the hermeneutical theology and methods of his distant predecessors Origen* and Evagrius.

In early and mid-career, Maximus composed other substantial works, some of which, like his *Chapters on Love* and *Chapters on Theology and Economy*, assumed the literary form of scholia or sententiae. Some, like his *Commentary on the Lord's Prayer* or even the *To Thalassius*, defy easy categorization as theological or spiritual works. His *Mystagogia*, a commentary on the liturgy, remains an important source for the history of the Byzantine rite.

Roughly from 641 on, Maximus became increasingly involved in the defense of Chalcedonian Christology in the Monoenergist and Monothelete controversies, which together brought to a head the debate over whether there were properly one or two energies, or wills, in the person of Christ. Maximus emerged a vigorous advocate of the doctrine of two energies and wills: first in 645 in a debate with Pyrrhus, patriarch of Constantinople (the transcript of which we have as the *Disputation with Pyrrhus*); next in 649, at the Lateran Synod in Rome, where Maximus, claiming the support of Greek patristic tradition, joined Pope Martin I in repudiating the Byzantine Empire's officially endorsed Monotheletism. The emperor Constans reacted in 653 by exiling Martin I and subjecting Maximus to a humiliating trial and eventual condemnation as a heretic. The Dyotheletism that he championed was nonetheless vindicated, posthumously, at the Council of Constantinople in 681.

Maximus sketches some definitive outlines of his theology in the earlier set of his *Ambiguities*, where he develops a Christocentric cosmology countering the radically platonized worldview of Origenism. Against the Origenist cosmology, which sets in sequence the creation of the spiritual world, the primordial fall and dispersion of spiritual beings into the corporeal creation, and the final and complete restoration of creation to its original spiritual unity, Maximus posits the cocreation of spiritual and material realms through a singular act of divine will and the preservation of God's unitive purposes within the diversity of creation through the implanted principles (*logoi*) of created nature. The incarnation of the Logos, Jesus Christ, is the true fulfillment of the *logoi* of all creation, the recapitulation of the divine plan for the world. Within the mystery of Christ lie both the redemption of humanity from the legacies of Adam's fall and the advent of the new, eschatological, and ''deified'' humanity of the Second Adam. The projected goal of all creaturely nature is the mystery of deification, but Maximus stops short of categorically affirming a universal restoration; for him the goal of all existents is the reciprocal communion itself between Creator and creatures.

The Incarnation is likewise the real starting point for trinitarian theology. While upholding and developing the apophatic theological tradition of the Cappadocian Fathers and Ps.-Dionysius, wherein the essence of God remains utterly ineffable and incomprehensible, Maximus asserts that the incarnate Logos ''teaches *theologia*'' in the sense of giving creatures access to the mystery of the Tri-Unity and the personal, or hypostatic, vitality of the Godhead. It is the

Son consubstantially related to the Father and the Holy Spirit, and eternally sharing with them a common activity (*energeia*), who assumes flesh in Jesus of Nazareth. As Maximus states more than once, the Father "approves" the Incarnation, the Son "accomplishes" it, the Spirit "cooperates" in it. Through the Incarnation, the Godhead has graciously penetrated the realm of the economy of salvation, whereupon the mystery of the Trinity remains not only a mystery to us but a mystery for us.

According to Maximus' interpretation of the Chalcedonian definition, there is a perfect reciprocity and interpenetration of divine and human natures in Christ's person without annihilating any aspect of his humanity. In the Monothelete controversy, Maximus had occasion to articulate the details of this doctrine of the hypostatic union in Christ. Here, too, he emphasized the perfect consent of Jesus' distinct human will to the will of the Father, a fact paradigmatically demonstrated in Jesus' prayer in Gethsemane ("Not my will, but yours, be done"). Moreover, it is precisely in his historical particularity as a human being—that is, an individual man assumed or "enhypostatized" in the person of the divine Son—that Jesus Christ bears the weight of cosmic salvation and of the re-creation of humanity in the image of God.

According to Maximus, human nature, as a magnificent microcosm of the diversity of spiritual and material creation, was not changed in nature by the Fall of Adam; it was, however, subjected to an aberrant mode (*tropos*) of existence marked by the disintegration of natural human faculties. Humanity has been thrust into the dialectical experience of pleasure and pain; the passible soul has lapsed into a multitude of vicious passions; and the natural will has been preempted by the weakened "gnomic will" (*gnômê*). Only through the reintegrating work of Christ, the New Adam and perfect mediator between God and creation, who pioneers a new mode of human freedom through love, are the natural faculties wholly renewed and transformed, and the proper vocation of humanity itself as mediator within creation restored. Maximus accordingly focuses the Christian's moral and spiritual life on the embodiment of divine love— the cosmic virtue—which, in the context of reintegrated humanity, brings the other virtues to fruition and enables the full realization of human community in the church.

In the end, theology, Christology, soteriology, anthropology, ecclesiology, and ethics all cohere as dimensions of Maximus' one grand vision of the full effects of the Incarnation of Jesus Christ.

Bibliography

A.   CCSG, 7, 10, 16, 22, 23; PG 90–91; *The Ascetic Life* and *Four Centuries on Charity*, trans. P. Sherwood, ACW 21 (Westminster, Md., 1957); *The Life of Our Holy Father Maximus the Confessor*, trans. C. Birchall (Brookline, Mass., 1982); *Selected Writings*, trans. G. Berthold, CWS (Mahwah, N.J., 1985); *Disputation with Pyrrhus*, trans. J. Farrell (South Canaan, Pa., 1990).

B.   DTC 10:448–59; LThK² 7:208–10; NCE 9:514–16; ODCC 1061–62; TRE 22:

298–304; P. Sherwood, *An Annotated Date-List of the Works of Maximus the Confessor* (Rome, 1952); idem, *The Earlier Ambigua of St. Maximus the Confessor and His Refutation of Origenism* (Rome, 1955); H. Urs von Balthasar, *Kosmische Liturgie: Das Weltbild des Maximus' des Bekenners*, 2d ed. (Einsiedeln, 1961); J. M. Garrigues, *Maxime le Confesseur. La charité, avenir divin de l'homme* (Paris, 1976); A. Riou, *Le monde et l'église selon Maxime le Confesseur* (Paris, 1973); F. Heinzer, *Gottes Sohn als Mensch. Die Struktur des Menschseins Christi bei Maximus Confessor* (Fribourg, 1980); *Maxime le Confesseur. Actes du Symposium sur Maxime le Confesseur, Fribourg, 2–5 septembre 1980*, ed. F. Heinzer and C. von Schönborn (Fribourg, 1982); P. Piret, *Le Christ et la Trinité selon Maxime le Confesseur* (Paris, 1983); L. Thunberg, *Man and the Cosmos: The Vision of St. Maximus the Confessor* (Crestwood, N.Y., 1985); P. Blowers, *Exegesis and Spiritual Pedagogy in Maximus the Confessor: An Investigation of the "Quaestiones ad Thalassium"* (Notre Dame, Ind., 1991); idem, "Theology as Integrative, Visionary, Pastoral: The Legacy of Maximus the Confessor," *Pro Ecclesia* 2 (1993): 216–30; A. Nichols, *Byzantine Gospel: Maximus the Confessor in Modern Scholarship* (Edinburgh, 1993); L. Thunberg, *Microcosm and Mediator: The Theological Anthropology of Maximus the Confessor*, 2d ed. (Chicago, 1995); D. Yeago, "Jesus of Nazareth and Cosmic Redemption: The Relevance of Maximus the Confessor," *Modern Theology* 12 (1996): 163–93; A. Louth, *Maximus the Confessor* (New York, 1996).

Paul M. Blowers

MAZZELLA, CAMILLO (10 February 1833, Vitulano, Italy–3 March 1900, Rome). *Education*: studied at Sem., Benevento, 1850–55; studied at Jesuit Sem., Fourvières, Lyons, France, 1860–62. *Career*: ordained priest, 1855; prebendary canon, Vitulano, 1855–57; joined Jesuits, 1857; professor of theology, Jesuit Sem., Fourvières, 1862–67; professor of dogmatic and moral theology, Woodstock Coll., Maryland, 1867–78; chair of dogmatic theology, Roman Coll. (Gregorian Univ.), 1878–1900; cardinal, 1886.

Mazzella is important for neoscholasticism and is included in the so-called Roman School. His formation, however, was not in the Roman College, and he did not come into personal contact with members of the school until 1878 as an associate of Johannes B. Franzelin.* Leo XIII called him to Rome in 1878 and enlisted him in the post–Vatican I papal effort to promote the renewal in scholasticism. Although associated with and influenced by Franzelin, his contribution to the developing treatise on ecclesiology was narrowed to the apologetic concerns occasioned by the truncated constitution "Pastor Aeternus" of the First Council of the Vatican.

Bibliography

A. *De Deo Creante* (Woodstock, Md., 1877); *De Virtutibus Infusis* (Rome, 1884); *De Religione et Ecclesia* (Rome, 1883, 1896); *De Gratia Christi* (Rome, 1896).

B. DTC 10:478; ECatt 8:526–27; LThK² 7:219; NCE 9:523–24; Koch 1187.

William J. Kelly

MEISTER ECKHART. *See* ECKHART, MEISTER.

MELANCHTHON, PHILIPP (16 February 1497, Bretten, Palatine, Germany–19 April 1560, Wittenberg, Saxony, Germany). *Education*: Latin School, Pforzheim, 1508–9; Heidelberg Univ., 1509–12; M. A., Tübingen, 1512–13; bachelor of Bible, Wittenberg Univ., 1519. *Career*: lecturer, Tübingen Univ., 1513–18; professor of Greek, Wittenberg Univ., 1518–60; lecturer in Scripture, Wittenberg Univ., 1519–60; educational organizer of schools throughout Germany, 1519–60; writer of textbooks, scriptural commentaries, systematic theology, *Augsburg Confession*, and studies of the classics, 1513–60.

Melanchthon's role in the German Reformation is often subordinated to the overwhelming presence of Martin Luther,* yet Luther himself had the utmost respect and confidence in his young humanist colleague, his ''son in Christ'' whose logical mind complemented Luther's passionate nature. Melanchthon is more noted for organizing Wittenberg theology into a systematic framework than for originating any of its foundational concepts, yet his active role in expressing the theology and, in so doing, giving it his own accents was influential to future Lutheran thought, most notably seventeenth-century Lutheran neo-scholasticism.

Melanchthon's conciliatory nature tended toward accommodation, especially from 1521 onward, the year he reluctantly became a leader in Wittenberg when Luther was in sanctuary at Wartburg. During that period Melanchthon was unable or unwilling to prevent radical liturgical changes from occurring. In all of his subsequent work, Melanchthon's preference for civility and order became apparent, along with a more pronounced independence of thought. Although at Luther's urging he continued to lecture on Scripture, Melanchthon openly preferred to concentrate on his classics courses. Earlier, he had rejected Aristotle after Luther did so, but in 1521 Melanchthon began writing textbooks that were aimed at popularizing Aristotle.

As a humanist (whose great-uncle was Johannes Reuchlin) Melanchthon's abiding advocacy of education resulted in his being called *Praeceptor Germaniae* for his tireless work in reorganizing curricula for a number of German colleges and secondary schools. His textbooks were used for several generations, and he maintained continuous contacts with Erasmus* and other humanists despite their altercations with Luther.

Melanchthon's *Loci communes* (1521), a dogmatics textbook that was the first systematization of Wittenberg theology, saw at least six revised editions as Melanchthon's doctrinal perspective changed. His earliest edition was his course lectures on Romans (concentrating on sin, law, and grace). By the 1535 edition Melanchthon discussed Trinity and Christology in detail and taught that the human will is a concurrent cause of justification (along with the Spirit and the Word). On the Lord's Supper, the 1535 edition spoke of spiritual reception of Christ and inner communion. This edging toward the Calvinist position created an uproar among Melanchthon's many critics, who also accused him of *synergism* for his justification statements, but Luther ignored the controversy. In his own defense, Melanchthon maintained that Luther privately agreed with him.

After Luther was placed under the ban of the empire in May, 1521, Melanch-thon often attended conferences in Luther's stead. When Charles V called a diet at Augsburg (1530) to try to obtain religious agreement between German prin-cipalities, Melanchthon attended and wrote the *Augsburg Confession* as a state-ment of belief to which German Lutheran princes and cities could witness. Melanchthon avoided polemics in a spirit of peace and confessional unity. He wrote a second version of the *Confession* in 1540 in which he rethought Article X to omit stating that Christ's body and blood are truly present and distributed in the Lord's Supper, only that they are offered *with* the bread and wine. This time Luther strongly disagreed, although not as publicly and vehemently as Melanchthon's growing chorus of critics.

Luther also disagreed with the results of the Regensburg Conference, 1541, in which Catholic and Protestant theologians, including Melanchthon, arrived at doctrinal agreements in the quest for irenic compatibility. The statement offen-sive to both Luther and the pope was on justification, offering a kind of double justification in which justifying faith is effective in works of love.

After Luther's death in 1546, Melanchthon was not readily accepted as his successor at Wittenberg, especially after the Smalkaldic War, 1546, when most Wittenberg theologians moved to Jena to avoid cooperating with Duke Maurice, the new elector imposed on Saxony by the victorious Charles. Melanchthon remained in Wittenberg to attempt conciliation in the hope of preserving the university and church under the *Interim*, which required some return to former Catholic ecclesiastical practices. Although Lutheranism was affirmed for Saxony in the Peace of Augsburg, 1555, Melanchthon could not overcome charges of "turncoat" in the post-*Interim* contentions for theological leadership in Witten-berg.

Crypto-Calvinistic accusations against Melanchthon, questions about adia-phora, and violent polemics by Andreas Osiander* over what he claimed was Luther's mystical understanding of justification, among other problems, troubled the aging scholar. More bitter still, some of Melanchthon's own former students, especially Matthew Flacius,* denounced him. Yet through the controversies, Melanchthon continued to write ecclesiastical guidelines for the developing church and handbooks for its pastors. At his death, his last prayers were for unity in the church.

In our ecumenical age, Philipp Melanchthon, whatever his weaknesses as a standard bearer in the strongly controversialist atmosphere of his time, can be assessed in the light of his lifelong hope for conciliation between the churches. He was a man of our time more so than his own. In that sense, his tireless work for unity is not a betrayal of doctrine but a hope for Christian understanding.

Bibliography

A. *Opera quae supersunt omnia*, ed. K. G. Bretschneider and E. Birdseil, 28 vols. (Brunswick, 1834–60); *Supplementa Melanchthoniana* [adding works omitted from above] (Leipzig, 1910–29); *Selected Works*, ed. R. Stupperich, 7 vols. in 8 (Gütersloh,

1951–75); *Melanchthons Briefwechsel: kritische und kommentierte Gesamtausgabe*, ed. Heinz Scheible, 6 vols. (Stuttgart, 1977); *Loci communes*, trans. C. L. Manschreck (New York, 1965); *Melanchthon and Bucer* (New York, 1969).

B. DTC 10:502–13; LThK² 7:247–49; NCE 9:624; ODCC 1066; OEncR 3:41–45; TRE 22:371–410; Franz Hildebrandt, *Melanchthon: Alien or Ally?* (Cambridge, 1946); Wilhelm Maurer, *Der junge Melanchthon zwischen Humanismus und Reformation*, 2 vols. (Göttingen, 1967–69); Michael Rogness, *Philip Melanchthon: Reformer without Honor* (Minneapolis, Minn., 1969); Robert Stupperich, *Melanchthon*, trans. Robert H. Fischer (Philadelphia, 1965).

Joan Skocir

MERSCH, ÉMILE (30 July 1890, Marche, Belgium–23 May 1940, Lens, Pas de Calais, France). *Education*: entered the Society of Jesus, 1907; philosophical and theological studies, Louvain, 1914–18; ordained priest, 1917; doctoral studies in Louvain, 1918–20. *Career*: philosophy professor at the Facultés Notre Dame de la Paix, Namur, 1920–35; spiritual director, Wépion, 1935; writer and researcher, Louvain, 1936–40.

This Belgian Jesuit ecclesiologist devoted much of his life to researching the history and doctrine regarding the church as the Mystical Body of Christ. His research on the history of this teaching, seen as a prolegomenon to a future systematic study, was undertaken from the years 1920 to 1929 and were published in 1933. He had completed three drafts of the systematic analysis when, fleeing Belgium during the Nazi invasion, he was killed during an air-raid attack in France while caring for the wounded shortly before his fiftieth birthday. His systematic study on the Mystical Body was published posthumously. His writings influenced Pius XII's encyclical *Mystici corporis Christi* (1943) and helped Catholic theology articulate an ecclesiology less focused on institutional aspects and more centered on what came to be known as communion ecclesiology.

Bibliography

A. *The Whole Christ: The Historical Development of the Doctrine of the Mystical Body in Scripture and Tradition*, trans. John R. Kelly (1933; Milwaukee, Wis., 1938); *Le Christ, l'homme et l'univers: Prolégomènes à la théologie du corps mystique* (Paris, 1962); *Morality and the Mystical Body*, trans. Daniel F. Ryan (1937; New York, 1939); *The Theology of the Mystical Body*, trans. Cyril Vollert (1944; St. Louis, Mo., 1951).

B. BBKL 5:1333–34; LThK³ 7:149; NCE 9:693–94; ODCC 1074; Jean Levie, "Le Père Emile Mersch," in E. Mersch, *La théologie du corps mystique* (Brussels, 1944) 1.vii–xxxiii, with bibliography of Mersch's works; Georges Dejaifve, " 'La théologie du corps mystique' du P. Em. Mersch," *Nouvelle revue théologique* 67 (1945): 1016–24; Gregory E. Malanowski "Emile Mersch (1890–1940): Un christocentrisme unifié," *Nouvelle revue théologique* 112 (1990): 44–66; James Arraj, *Mind Aflame: The Theological Vision of One of the World's Greatest Theologians, Emile Mersch* (Chiloquin, Ore., 1994).

Michael A. Fahey

MERTON, THOMAS (31 January 1915, Prades, France–10 December 1968, Outside Bangkok, Thailand). *Education*: studied at Clare Coll., Univ. of Cambridge, 1932–34; B.A., Columbia Univ., 1938; M.A., 1939. *Career*: instructor in English, St. Bonaventure's Univ., Olean, N.Y., 1940–41; entered Cistercian monastery of Our Lady of Gethsemani, 1941; solemnly professed, 1947; ordained priest, 1949; master of scholastics, 1951–55; master of novices, 1955–65; entered hermitage, 1965.

The publication of the autobiographical conversion story *The Seven Storey Mountain* (New York, 1948) made Merton a household name in American Catholicism. A series of autobiographical diary/journals tracked his ever-deepening interest in the intersection of the Christian contemplative life and issues of contemporary culture: *The Sign of Jonas* (New York, 1953); *Conjectures of a Guilty Bystander* (Garden City, N.Y., 1966); and the posthumously published *Asian Journal* (New York, 1973) and *A Vow of Conversation: Journals 1964–66* (New York, 1988).

Merton was not a systematic thinker, but he did write from deep contemplative convictions arguing for a richer appreciation of spirituality that drew on the strengths of Christian monasticism. Works like *Thoughts in Solitude* (New York, 1958) and *New Seeds of Contemplation* (New York, 1961) have proved to be perennial sources for those interested in the spiritual life. Before the Second Vatican Council Merton was already in dialogue with non-Christian religious traditions searching in them for the accumulated mystic wisdom of the world's religions. Such volumes of collected essays like *Mystics and Zen Masters* (New York, 1967) and *Zen and The Birds of Appetite* (New York, 1968) witness to that interest. His conviction was that contemplative persons could reconcile many religious differences at a deep interior level if they were open to the hidden voice of Wisdom in the world.

The continuing popularity of his writings derives from his ability to view the contemporary world from a deep center of prayer in a way that was both sympathetic and critical. He was a pacifist by instinct; a much-published poet and translator; an essayist; but, above all, a monk. His collected essays on the future of the contemplative life, *Contemplation in a World of Action* (Garden City, N.Y., 1968, 1971, 1973), contains both a trenchant critique and an apologia for the monastic tradition of Christianity.

His death in Thailand by accidental electrocution came twenty-seven years to the day of his entrance into the monastery.

Bibliography

A. *Thomas Merton: Spiritual Master*, ed. Lawrence S. Cunningham (Mahwah, N.J., 1992); *The Thomas Merton Reader*, ed. Thomas McDonnell, rev. ed. (New York, 1990). B. DACB 387–88; DARB 362–64; NYT 11 December 1968, 1; *Thomas Merton: A Comprehensive Bibliography*, ed. M. Breit and R. Daggy (New York, 1988); Michael Mott, *The Seven Mountains of Thomas Merton* (Boston, 1987).

Lawrence S. Cunningham

MEYENDORFF (MEJENDORF), JOHN/JEAN (IOANN FEOFILOVI) (2 February 1926, Neuilly-sur-Seine, France–22 July 1992, Montreal, Canada). *Ed-*

ucation: licence-ès-lettres, diplôme d' études supérieures, diplôme de l'école pratique des hautes études, doctorat-ès-letters, Sorbonne, 1949, 1954, 1958; theological training, St. Sergius Orthodox Theol. Institute, 1949. *Career*: ordained priest, 1959; professor of theology, St. Vladimir's Orthodox Theol. Sem., New York, 1959–92; dean of St. Vladimir's, 1984–92; moderator for the World Council of Churches commission on Faith and Order, 1967–75; professor of Byzantine history, Fordham Univ., 1967–92; J. M. Fellow of the National Endowment of the Humanities, 1976–77; acting director of studies in Dumbarton Oaks, Washington, D.C., 1977–78; editor, *The Orthodox Church* and *St. Vladimir's Seminary Quarterly*, 1982–84; retirement, June 1992.

Meyendorff s accomplishments were many. His doctoral dissertation on Gregory Palamas* had to be defended before the entire faculty in theology at the Sorbonne, and while the debate continued for decades in the journal *Istina*, the controversy merely indicated the extent to which Meyendorff's work on Palamas had established the scholarly agenda. Its great accomplishment was to set Palamas firmly within the context of Greek patristic thought and spirituality, whereas before this the fourteenth-century apologist of Byzantine Hesychasm had been treated by Western Christian scholars as a curious and *sui generis* example of medieval Byzantium's intellectual decline. Since Meyendorff's study, however, ''Palamism'' is generally recognized as a faithful witness to the long-standing Eastern Christian emphasis on deification (*theosis*) as the purpose of the divine economy in Christ. Today one might quarrel with the particular strands of traditional Eastern Christian thought that Palamas represented, but what can no longer be denied, thanks to Meyendorff, is the great antiquity of those currents.

While his greatest scholarly contribution was thus revolutionary, it was a revolution in the service of catholic tradition and continuity. In subsequent works dealing with issues in spirituality, sacraments, church history, and ecumenism, Meyendorff contined to display the same careful fidelity to the past of the Orthodox Church and to argue for both its past and present catholicity. Thus, in addressing the complexities of ecumenical rapprochement, one of his abiding concerns, his work is marked by a combination of firm commitment to historical Orthodoxy and a remarkable openness toward Western Christianity, in particular Roman Catholicism. It was perhaps this irenicism, based as it was on his learned devotion to the catholicism of the East, that comprised Meyendorff's most attractive feature. It marked his students for over two generations, and it continues to impress his readers today.

It was not uncommon for Meyendorff to hold two full-time teaching positions while at the same time editing publications, advising the Synod of Bishops, and fulfilling priestly and domestic duties. He wrote technical articles, did his own editing, and spoke fluently in three languages—Russian, French, and English—with little or no accent. He also did simultaneous translations in those languages. Although Meyendorff's reputation came primarily from Byzantine studies, for example serving on the advisory board for the multivolume *Oxford Dictionary* *of Byzantium*, his command of Russian church history qualified him as a Russo-Byzantine scholar. Together with George Florovsky,* he will surely be remembered as one of the greatest Orthodox theologians and ecumenists of the twentieth century.

Bibliography

A. *A Study of Gregory Palamas*, trans. G. Lawrence (London, 1959); *The Orthodox Church: Its Past and Role in the World Today* (New York, 1960); rev. ed., Nicholas Lossky (New York, 1996); *The Primacy of Peter* (London, 1963; repr. New York, 1992); *Christ in Eastern Christian Thought* (Washington D.C. and Cleveland, Ohio, 1969; repr. New York, 1987); *Byzantine Theology* (New York, 1973, and many subsequent eds.); *St. Gregory Palamas and Orthodox Spirituality*, trans. A. Fiske (New York, 1974); *Marriage: An Orthodox Perspective*, 2d rev. ed. (New York, 1975); *Living Tradition: Orthodox Witness in the Contemporary World* (New York, 1978); *The Byzantine Legacy in the Orthodox Church* (New York, 1982); *Catholicity and the Church* (New York, 1983); *Imperial Unity and Christian Divisions: The Church 450–680 A.D.* (New York, 1989); *Byzantium and the Rise of Russia: A Study of Byzantino-Russian Relations in the Fourteenth Century* (New York, 1989); *Rome, Constantinople, Moscow: Historical and Theological Studies* (New York, 1996).

B. HDOC 219–20; "Protopresbyter John Meyendorff. In memoriam," SVTQ 36 (1992/3): 180–82; G. Stricker, "John Meyendorff. In memoriam," *Glaube in der 2. Welt* 20 (1992): 11–14; J. Pelikan, "In Memory of John Meyendorff," in *New Perspectives in Historical Theology: Essays in Memory of John Meyendorff*, ed. B. Nassif (Grand Rapids, Mich., 1996), 7–9; Lewis Shaw, "John Meyendorff and the Heritage of the Russian Theological Tradition," ibid., 10–42.

Alexander Golitzin

MICHEL, VIRGIL GEORGE (26 June 1890, St. Paul, Minn.–26 November 1938, Collegeville, Minn.). *Education*: B.A., Ph.B., M.A., St. John's Univ., Minn., 1909, 1912, 1913; S.T.B., Ph.D., Catholic Univ. of America, Washington, D.C., 1917, 1918; studied at Sant' Anselmo, Rome, 1924; studied at Louvain, 1924–25. *Career*: novice, the Order of St. Benedict, St. John's Abbey, Collegeville, Minn., 1909; teacher and administrator, St. John's Univ., 1918–24; founding editor, *Orate Fratres*, 1926–30, 1936–38; missionary work among the Ojibuay Indians, northern Minn., 1930–33; teacher and administrator, St. John's Univ., 1933–38.

Michel was the foremost spokesman for the liturgical revival in American Catholicism during the early twentieth century. Combining interests in sociology, economics, education, art, and philosophy with his study of liturgy, Michel developed a liturgical movement in the United States that differed significantly from its European Catholic precursor by emphasizing the liturgy's potential for social reform. The liturgy expressed a Christian community of justice as well as faith. For Michel, this meant that a renewal of the social order must be tied to a revival of the liturgy and that a revived concern for the liturgy demanded a corresponding concern for social reconstruction, since the liturgy expressed the divine ideal of communal living and provided the divine means for effectively reforming society.

Michel advanced the connection between liturgy and social reform during the Depression, shortly after the publication of Pius XI's *Quadragesimo Anno* (1931) and after Michel had served a three-year missionary experience (1930–33) among the economically depressed Indians in northern Minnesota. Michel and others established *Orate Fratres* and the Liturgical Press at St. John's to publish liturgical studies and texts and to promote among American Catholics a renewed liturgical sense. His pragmatic and activist-oriented liturgical movement was not a popular movement in American Catholicism, but it did eventually contribute to the renewal of liturgical life and prepared some Americans for the reforms initiated by the Second Vatican Council (1962–65).

Bibliography

A.   *The Critical Principles of Orestes A. Brownson* (Washington, D.C., 1918); *The Liturgical Apostolate* (Collegeville, Minn., 1926); *My Sacrifice and Yours* (Collegeville, Minn., 1926); with Martin B. Hellriegel, *The Liturgical Movement* (Collegeville, Minn., 1930); *Philosophy of Human Conduct* (Minneapolis, Minn., 1936); *The Liturgy of the Church* (New York, 1937); *Christian Social Reconstruction* (Milwaukee, Wis., 1937); *Our Life in Christ* (Collegeville, Minn., 1939); *The Christian in the World* (Collegeville, Minn., 1939).

B.   DAB 22:454–56; DACB 391; DARB 364–65; NCE 9:800–801; NYT 27 November 1938, 48; Emerson Hynes, "The Social Thought of Virgil Michel, O.S.B.," *American Catholic Sociological Review* 1 (December 1940): 172–80; Paul B. Marx, *Virgil Michel and the Liturgical Movement* (Collegeville, Minn., 1957); Jeremy Hall, *The Full Stature of Christ: The Ecclesiology of Dom Virgil Michel* (Collegeville, Minn., 1976); R. W. Franklin and Robert L. Spaeth, *Virgil Michel: American Catholic* (Collegeville, Minn., 1988).

Patrick W. Carey

MOGILA, PETER (21 December 1596, Suceava, Russia–22 December 1646 or 1 January 1647, Kiev). *Education*: studied in Poland and Holland, 1610–20. *Career*: entered Monastery of the Caves, Kiev, 1627; abbot, 1627–33; Metropolitan of Kiev, 1633–46.

As abbot of his monastery, Mogila began a Latin-Polish school, the Academy, that competed with and eventually supplanted Kiev's earlier Slavono-Hellenic brotherhood school. Mogila's school embraced a Jesuit curriculum and was staffed by Jesuits. His consecration as metropolitan was highly irregular, taking place at night in an unlit church. Following this, he was often nominated by Eastern Catholics in the Ukraine to serve as a Western Russian patriarch simultaneously in communion with Constantinope and Rome. Not surprisingly, nothing came of these initiatives.

Mogila is perhaps best known for being the first to give a Confession of Faith to the Orthodox Church in the form of a scholastic argument. In responding to the Calvinist *Confession of Faith* of Cyril Lucaris,* Mogila not only composed his own Confession in Latin, but his document also reflected Roman Catholic theology, including the *Catechismus Romanus* of Peter Canisius. Although Mogila's *Confession* was approved by the Synod of Jassy in 1642 and by the four patriarchates and local councils that joined in the condemnation of Lucaris, it is not considered a primary witness to Orthodox doctrine by the Orthodox today. The *Confession* is, though, perhaps the most important example during this period of the use by Orthodox authorities of Roman Catholic scholastic polemic against Calvinism.

Mogila also printed a liturgical book for priests, an *Euchologian*, together with *The Book of Needs* (*Trebnik*, the priest's book for special services) in which he disregarded many, if not all, the Greek rubrics. He issued a reunion memorandum in 1643 that outlined his plans for unity with Rome but died before he could take any action on it. He is considered the most capable and influential of the seventeenth-century Orthodox churchmen in Poland and Lithuania. Through the efforts of the graduates of his academy at Kiev, his influence spread from the Ukraine throughout Russia, particularly in the following century, when Tsar Peter I went to the Ukraine to find leaders and teachers to effect his reforms of the Russian church. This era in Russian church history is consequently known as the Mogila Epoch.

Bibliography

A.   *Kr(e)st Chr(I)sta Sp(a)s(I)telja* (Kiev, 1632); *Sobranie korotkoi nauki o articulach veri* (Kiev, 1645); *Euchologion seu Rituale a Metropolita Petro Mohyla curatum* (Kiev, 1646); *Fotoperedruk O. Horba a* (Rym, 1988); *M. Syrigos, Orthodoxos homologia pisteos tes katholikes pisteos tes apostolikes ekklesias tes anatolikes* (Amsterdam, 1667); A. Malvy, M. Viller, ed., *La confession orthodoxe de Pierre Moghila*, OC, 39 (Rome, 1927).

B.   DTC 10:2070–76; HDOC 221–22; LThK^2 7:518–19; NCE 9:998–99; ODCC 1099; A. Wenger, "Les influences du rituel de Paul V sur le *Trebnick* de Pierre Moghila," RevScRel, hors série (1956): 477–99; Ernst C. Suttner, "Die rumänische Orthodoxie des 16. und 17. Jahrhunderts in Auseinandersetzung mit der Reformation," *Kirche im Osten* 25(1982): 64–120; Mieczyslaw Olszewiski, "Der Ritus des Sacraments der Busse nach Peter Mogila in seinem historischen Kontext," *Ostkirchliche Studien* 31 (1982): 142–59; Paul Meyendorff, "The Liturgical Reforms of Peter Moghila: A New Look," SVTQ 29 (1985): 101–14; Roman Zuzek, "L'escatologia di Pietro Moghila," *Orientalia Christiana Periodica* 54 (1988): 353–85.

Alexander Golitzin

MÖHLER, JOHANN ADAM (8 May 1796, Igersheim, Germany–12 April 1838, Munich). *Education*: gymnasium, Mergentheim, 1808–12; lyceum in philosophy, Ellwangen, 1813–15; studied theology with J. S. Drey* and J. B. Hirscher, Friederichs-Univ., Ellwangen, 1815–17; Univ. of Tübingen, 1817–18; sem., Rottenburg, 1818–19. *Career*: ordained priest, 1819; assistant pastor, Weilderstadt and Riedlingen, 1819–20; tutored students in Greek, philosophy, and history, Univ. of Tübingen, 1820–22; privatdozent, Univ. of Tübingen, 1822; lectured on church history, patristics, and canon law, Univ. of Tübingen,

1823–35; *professor extraordinarius*, 1826, *professor ordinarius* and doctor of theology, 1832; theological chair, Univ. of Münich, 1835–38.

Möhler's influential writings were in the areas of ecclesiology and comparative symbolics. His first book, *Unity in the Church or The Principle of Catholicism: Presented in the Spirit of the Church Fathers of the First Three Centuries* (1825), espoused a theology of the church, rooted in biblical and patristic thought and fashioned in terms of Romantic subjectivity and organic categories that reflected his indebtedness to J. S. Drey, F. Schelling, F. Schleiermacher,* and A. Neander.* *Unity in the Church* advanced a Spirit-centered ecclesiology. The Holy Spirit is presented as the inner source of the church's mystical and intellectual unity. Doctrinal and institutional forms are the external manifestations of the internal life of the Spirit. Consistent with the Council of Trent, the Bible and tradition are mutually conditioned and provide the outer expressions of the inner living gospel. Ecclesial unity is destroyed by egoism, which motivates heresies and sectarianism, and is a contradiction (*Widerspruch*) of the Catholic faith. Individual diversity offers an antithesis (*Gegensatz*), on the other hand, which is crucial for the vitality of the Catholic faith insofar as it remains in service to the organic church communion and unity. The diocesan bishop, each metropolitan diocese, the episcopacy, and papal primacy reflect the external form of the unity of the body of Christ.

Athanasius the Great and the Church of His Time Especially in the Struggle with Arianism (1827) marks a transition in Möhler's theology. *Unity in the Church* had emphasized the agency of the Spirit and the priority of inner personal and communal identity relative to the outer doctrinal and institutional forms. Beginning with *Athanasius*, Möhler stressed the Incarnation and the outer binding character of doctrinal and institutional forms over their inner source. Athanasius'* struggles against Arianism and Sabellianism are presented not only as a valiant effort from the past, but also as a model for his own day in the struggles against rationalism, pantheism, and especially the contemporary form of Sabellianism identified with the position of Schleiermacher. Following Athanasius' lead, the doctrine of the Incarnation becomes increasingly important for Möhler's theology of the church.

Symbolism: or, Exposition of the Doctrinal Differences Between Catholics and Protestants, as Evidenced by their Symbolical Writings (1832) offered an influential presentation of the doctrinal differences between Catholics and Protestants based on their public creedal confessions, the symbols of faith (e.g., the canons and decrees of Trent and the Lutheran *Book of Concord*). His objective was to identify in a historical and deductive manner "the fundamental and pervading idea" governing the areas of disagreement and to demonstrate their connection in an organic system of thought. Comparative symbolics was to be historically scientific, but not uncommitted. The author's comparative assessment cannot be bracketed, and so symbolics must incorporate apologetic and occasionally polemical arguments. Part I begins with the fundamental issue: the doctrines on theological anthropology (original sin, justification, good works), which is followed by an analysis of sacramental theology and ecclesiology. Each chapter considers the position represented by Catholic dogmas, followed by Lutheran, and then Calvinist and Zwinglian formulas. Part II describes "the smaller Protestant sects"—the Mennonites, Anabaptists, Quakers, Pietists, Methodists, Swedenborgians, Socinians, and Arminians. Möhler commended the objective tradition of the Catholic Church as faithfully articulated by the hierarchy of the church against the subjectivism and egoism of Protestantist doctrine, which was ultimately "without sense and reason." The Catholic Church is hailed as "the continuing incarnation" in history.

Symbolism was widely read and controversial. Among the numerous Protestants and Catholics who published responses, the most significant was written by the Lutheran church historian from the University of Tübingen, Ferdinand Christian Baur,* *Der Gegensatz des Katholicismus und Protestantismus nach den Principien und Hauptdogmen der beiden Lehrbegriffe mit besonderer Rücksicht auf Herrn Dr. Möhler's Symbolik* (1833). Baur repudiated Möhler's contention that Protestantism is subjective and Catholicism is objective and questioned the alleged scientific character of a symbolics that incorporates polemics. Then following Möhler's order—anthropology, sacraments, and church—Baur sought to demonstrate that Möhler had misrepresented Protestant beliefs, and that if properly understood the Protestant position is defensible and consistent with recent doctrinal developments in Protestantism. Möhler responded with *New Investigations of the Doctrinal Differences between Catholics and Protestants, A Defense of My Symbolism against the Critique of Herr Professor Dr. Baur in Tübingen* (1834). Against Baur's argument, Möhler defended his presentation of Protestant beliefs and challenged Baur's own understanding of classical Protestant thought. Moreover, Möhler drove a wedge between classical Protestant theology and the new Protestantism of Schleiermacher in order to repudiate Baur's efforts to show their unity and continuity.

In addition to these books, Möhler contributed numerous essays on a variety of historical topics and contemporary issues, including studies of Anselm,* Jesus and Mohammad, and celibacy.

Bibliography

A. *Unity in the Church or The Principle of Catholicism Presented in the Spirit of the Church Fathers of the First Three Centuries*, ed. Peter C. Erb (1825; Washington, D.C., 1996); *Athanasius der Grosse und die Kirche seiner Zeit, besonders im Kampfe mit dem Arianismus* (Frankfurt am Main, 1973); *Symbolism: or, Exposition of the Doctrinal Differences between Catholics and Protestants, as Evidenced by their Symbolical Writings*, trans. James Burton Robertson (London, 1843, and many subsequent eds.); *Neue Untersuchungen der Lehrgegensätze zwischen den Katholiken und Protestanten: Eine Vertheidigung meiner Symbolik gegen die Kritik des Herrn Professors Dr. Baur in Tübingen* (repr. of 1834 ed. Frankfurt am Main, 1969).

B. DSAM 10:1446–48; DTC 10:2048–63; LThK² 7:521–22; NCE 9:1004–5; ODCC 1099–1100; TRE 23:140–43; Joseph Rupert Geiselmann, *Lebendiger Glaube aus geheiligter Überlieferung: Der Grundgedanke der Theologie Johann Adam Möhlers und der katholischen Tübinger Schule*, 2d ed. (Freiburg, 1966); Harald Wagner, *Die eine Kirche und die viele Kirchen: Ekklesiologie und Symbolik beim jungen Möhler* (Munich, 1977); Joseph Fitzer, *Moehler and Baur in Controversy, 1832–38: Romantic-Idealist Assessment of the Reformation and Counter-Reformation* (Tallahassee, Fla., 1974).

Bradford Hinze

MOLINA, LUIS DE (September, 1535, Cuenca, Spain–12 October, 1600, Madrid). *Education*: studied jurisprudence, Salamanca, 1551–52; philosophy, Alcalá, 1552–53; studied philosophy and theology, Coimbra, Portugal, 1554–58, and Évora, Portugal, 1558–62. *Career*: entered the Jesuits, Alcalá, 1553; taught philosophy, Coimbra, 1563–67, and theology, Évora, 1568–88; retired to write, 1588–1600; taught moral theology, Jesuit coll., Madrid, 1600.

Active in the fields of moral theology, international law, and ethics of economics, Molina distinguished himself most as leader of the Jesuit school in the acrimonious sixteenth-century debate between the Jesuits and the Dominicans over grace and free will. The ingenious and controversial theology that he fathered bears the name "Molinism."

The key work in which Molina expounded his ideas on grace and free will was his *Concordia liberi arbitrii cum gratiae donis* ("The Harmony of Free Will with the Gifts of Grace," published in Lisbon, 1588). The Molinists took their cue from the Jesuit founder, St. Ignatius Loyola,* who wrote in the *Spiritual Exercises* that his followers should not speak of faith and grace "in such a way that works and free will receive any harm or be held for nothing" (Rule 17). To ensure freedom of the will under grace, Molina appealed to the divine *scientia media* ("middle knowledge"), a novel category first devised, most likely, by himself. It was so called because it stands midway between God's knowledge of all actually existent beings, past, present, and future, and his knowledge of purely possible beings. Its mid-position is evident in that it is a knowledge of beings or states of being that certainly *would* exist if given conditions were fulfilled (e.g. John would certainly perform this virtuous deed *if* God gave him the grace). For these conditional beings the term *futurabilia*, "futurables," was coined.

Applied to the question of grace and free will, the *scientia media* operates as follows. In any given order of futurables the help bestowed by God for the performance of salutary acts is indifferent (i.e., it allows the will to determine itself). Thus freedom is preserved under grace. Further, as the assent of the will is the factor rendering indifferent grace effective, there is, in this system, no ontological difference between sufficient and efficient grace. Surveying the endless number of orders of futurables presenting themselves as candidates for creation, each with its own set of outcomes, God chooses for creation, and actually creates, that order alone which corresponds most perfectly to his inscrutable designs. In thus conferring existence on one order alone, God maintains his absolute sovereignty, and Pelagianism and semi-Pelagianism in the operation of the human will are avoided.

Molina and his system were soon under attack as "Pelagian" from the Dominican school led by Domingo Báñez. In 1594 the case was referred to Rome, but no definitive decision was ever reached. Today the entire controversy is regarded by theologians as of historical interest only, as both systems are considered too anthropomorphic.

Bibliography

A. *Concordia liberi arbitrii cum gratiae donis*, ed. J. Rabineck (Madrid, 1953); *Commentaria in primam Divi Thomae partem*, 2 vols. (Cuenca, 1592); *De iustitia et iure*, 6 vols. (Cuenca, 1595–1609); *On Divine Foreknowledge*, trans. A. J. Fredosso (Ithaca, N.Y., 1988).

B. BBKL 6:43–44; *Catholicisme* 9:492–98; LThK² 7:526–27, 527–30; NCE 9:1010–11, 1011–13; ODCC 1100; OEncR 3:71–72; TRE 23:199–203; Gerard Smith, *Freedom in Molina* (Chicago, 1966).

David Coffey

MOSHEIM, JOHANN LORENZ VON (9 October 1694, Lübeck, Germany–9 September 1755, Göttingen, Germany). *Education*: studied at Univ. of Kiel, 1715–23. *Career*: professor of theology, Univ. of Helmstedt, 1723–47; supervisor of educational systems, Kingdom of Hannover, 1747–55; chancellor and professor of theology, Univ. of Göttingen, 1747–55.

Mosheim was the leading church historian of the early Enlightenment and was known for his tireless industry and critical ability. He translated and commented on Ralph Cudworth's *Intellectual System of the Universe* (1733). His *Elementa theologiae dogmaticae* (1758) made a distinction between religion and theology. As his *Versuch einer unparteischen . . . Ketzergeschichte* (1746–48) shows, he considered "heretic" a neutral term, although he sharply criticized the Quakers. In the practice of preaching, he encouraged the use of ancient rhetorical models. A meditator between Lutheran orthodoxy, Pietism, and the early Enlightenment, he worked to replace confessional polemics with nonpartisan objectivity. His "pragmatic method" in church history emphasized causality and recognized facts.

His chief work, *Institutiones historiae ecclesiasticae Novi Testamenti* (Helmstedt, 1755) helped lay the foundation for nineteenth-century church history.

Bibliography

A. *An Ecclesiastical History, Ancient and Modern* (London, 1841, and many subsequent editions).

B. LThK² 7:656–57; NCE 10:15; ODCC 1119; RGG 4:1157–58; TRE 23:365–67; John Stroup, *The Struggle for Identity in the Clerical Estate* (Leiden, 1984), 51–81; E. P. Meijering, "Mosheim on the Philosophy of Church Fathers," *Nederlands Archief voor Kirkgeschiedenis* 56 (1975): 67–83.

Oliver K. Olson

MUHLENBERG, WILLIAM AUGUSTUS (16 September 1796, Philadelphia–8 April 1877, New York City). *Education*: B. A., Univ. of Pennsylvania,

1815; read theology with bishop William White of Pennsylvania and the Rev. Jackson Kemper, 1815–18. *Career*: curate, Christ Church, Philadelphia, 1817–20; rector, Lancaster, Pa., 1820–26; founder and headmaster, Flushing Institute, Flushing, N.Y., 1828–46; professor, St. Paul's Coll., N.Y., 1837–46; rector, Church of the Holy Communion, New York, 1846–58; founder (with Anne Ayres), Sisterhood of the Holy Communion, 1852; founder and pastor, St. Luke's Hospital, New York City, 1857–77.

Muhlenberg, an Episcopal priest and evangelical catholic, is best known as the drafter of the "Muhlenberg Memorial." It was presented to the House of Bishops at the General Convention of the Episcopal Church in 1853. The Memorial reflected Muhlenberg's ecumenical vision of a catholic and reformed church for all Christians. The Memorial urged that Episcopal bishops should ordain qualified Protestant clergy who accepted the basic teachings of the Episcopal Church. The Memorial affirmed the traditional teaching of the Episcopal Church concerning the creeds, the Eucharist, and episcopal ordination. Clergy ordained in accordance with the Memorial would continue to serve in their own denominations. Muhlenberg thus envisioned what would become a comprehensive Protestant church with apostolic succession. The Memorial also called for the Episcopal Church to relax "somewhat the rigidity of her liturgical services." Although the Memorial was never approved, the deliberations of a study commission concerning it were published as *Memorial Papers* (1857). The Memorial is considered to have exerted significant influence on subsequent ecumenism and liturgical reform in the Episcopal Church and the Anglican Communion. It is considered to be the precursor of the Commission on Church Unity of the House of Bishops (1856) and the Chicago-Lambeth Quadrilateral (1886–88). Muhlenberg also founded a monthly church journal, *The Evangelical Catholic* (1851–53), which reflected his vision for ecumenical union of Protestant churches. Muhlenberg and Anne Ayres formed the Sisterhood of the Holy Communion in 1852. Ayres was the first American in the Anglican tradition to take monastic vows. Muhlenberg's life is commemorated in the Episcopal Church calendar year on April 8.

Bibliography

A. *Memorial of Sundry Presbyters of the Protestant Episcopal Church, Presented to the House of Bishops* (Philadelphia, 1853); *An Exposition of the Memorial of Sundry Presbyters* (New York, 1854); *What the Memorialists Want* (New York, 1856); *Evangelical Catholic Papers*, comp. Anne Ayres, 2 vols. (New York, 1875–77).

B. DAB 13:313–14; DARB 381–82; NCAB 9:199; NYT 9 April 1877, 5; SH 8:51; Anne Ayres, *The Life and Work of William Augustus Muhlenberg* (New York, 1880); Paul A. W. Wallace, *The Muhlenbergs of Pennsylvania* (Philadelphia, 1950); Alvin W. Skardon, *Church Leader in the Cities: William Augustus Muhlenberg* (Philadelphia, 1971).

                                                                                Robert B. Slocum

MUNGER, THEODORE THORNTON (5 March 1830, Bainbridge, N.Y.–11 January 1910, New Haven, Conn.). *Education*: B. A., Yale Coll., 1851; B.D.,

Yale Div. Sch., 1855; studied at Andover Sem., 1855. *Career*: minister, Dorchester, Mass., 1856–60; Haverhill, Mass., 1864–69; Providence, R.I., 1869–71; Lawrence, Mass., 1871–75; San Jose, Calif., 1875–77; North Adams, Mass., 1877–85; United Congregational Church, New Haven, Conn., 1885–1900; retirement, 1900–1910.

Munger was a representative of American Protestant liberalism in the second half of the nineteenth century. As a pastor-theologian he followed and popularized Horace Bushnell's* theology. Like Bushnell, he emphasized Christian life over doctrine, creeds, and ecclesiastical polity. For him doctrinal statements were symbolic constructions of a life-force that could not be captured in language, creeds, or formal ecclesiastical statements.

Munger continued Bushnell's inclusive and comprehensive approach to Christianity; stressed intellectual and ecclesiastical freedom in the search for religious truth, the catholicity of Christianity, and its openness to all systems of divinity; criticized the rigidity and intolerance of exclusionary denominationalism; and saw theology as more akin to poetry than to science. His published works tended to emphasize the freedom of faith and the intellectual search for meaning.

Bibliography

A.   *The Freedom of Faith* (Boston, 1883); *The Appeal of Life* (Boston, 1887); *Character through Inspiration* (Boston, 1897); *Horace Bushnell: Preacher and Theologian* (Boston, 1899); *Essays for the Day* (Boston, 1904).

B.   DAB 13:327–28; DARB, 385–86; NCAB 31:339–40; NYT 12 January 1910, 9; SH 8:53; Benjamin W. Bacon, *Theodore Thornton Munger: New England Minister* (New Haven, Conn., 1913).

Patrick W. Carey

MÜNTZER, THOMAS (c. 1490, Stolberg, Germany–25 May 1525, Heldrungen, Germany). *Education*: enrolled at Leipzig Univ., 1507; Univ. of Frankfurt on the Oder, 1512. *Career*: ordained priest, Braunschweig, c. 1514; pastoral positions, Halle and the nunnery in Froshe, 1516–20; preacher, Zwickau, 1520–21; writer and preacher in Prague and Erfurt, 1521–23; preacher in Allstedt, 1523–24; preacher and leader, German Peasant Revolt, Mühlhausen, 1524–25.

Müntzer was the first radical reformer of the newly born Protestant reformation. Not much is known of him prior to 1520. Thereafter, it soon became evident that he was a popular preacher and a voracious reader with a keen intellect. His theological writings, while confined to short treatises and letters, were both innovative and perceptive. Müntzer began his career as a disciple of Martin Luther,* but gave greater value to the tradition of mysticism and held to the view that revelation was not totally confined to the past or to the Scriptures but was available in present-day spiritual encounters, including dreams and visions. Müntzer's liturgical revisions and his translation of the Mass into German, much of it finely done and of lasting value, preceeded Luther's reforms by several years.

By the time Müntzer took up his parish duties in Allstedt in 1523, he had become Luther's most articulate critic and outright antagonist. This schism with his former mentor was fomented in large part by the social and political unrest then surging throughout the German provinces, which erupted in the Peasant Wars of 1524–25. These events became the central focus of Müntzer's life. His theological views were admirably suited to speak to the current situation in a direct and revolutionary manner. Müntzer rejected the traditional doctrine of the church, accepted by Luther, that all rebellion against legally constituted government was forbidden. He was the first Protestant reformer to articulate clearly a biblical theology that affirmed the ultimate right of the people actively to resist an unyielding tyranny.

In keeping with these convictions he became personally involved in the uprisings. After first attempting to serve as a mediator, he took up an active leadership role with the Peasant forces. Following a rout of their troops near Frankenhausen on May 15, 1525, Müntzer was captured and under torture forced to recant. A few days later he was convicted of heresy and sedition, and beheaded. The nonviolent aspects of Müntzer's theology exerted a major influence on some of the early leaders of the Anabaptist movement.

Bibliography

A. *Schriften und Briefe*, ed. Günther Franz and Paul Kirn, *Quellen und Forschungen zur Reformation-geschichte* 33 (Gütersloh, 1968); "Sermon Before the Princes," in *Spiritualist and Anabaptist Writers* (Philadelphia, 1957).

B. LThK² 7:689–90; NCE 10:79–80; ODCC 1125; OEncR 3:99–102; TRE 23:414–36; Gordon Rupp, *Patterns of Reformation* (Philadelphia, 1969); James M. Stayer, *Anabaptists and the Sword* (Lawrence Kan., 1972); Eric Gritsch, *Thomas Müntzer, a Tragedy of Errors* (Minneapolis, Minn., 1989).

Paul K. Kuenning

MURRAY, JOHN COURTNEY (12 September 1904, New York, N.Y.–16 August 1967, New York, N.Y.). *Education*: B.A., M.A., Boston Coll., 1926, 1927; S.T.L., Woodstock Sem., Md., 1934; S.T.D., Gregorian Univ., Rome, 1937. *Career*: ordained, 1933; instructor, Ateneo de Manila, Phillippines, 1927–30; professor of theology, Woodstock Sem., 1937–67; editor, *Theological Studies*, 1941–67; associate editor, *America*, 1945–46; advisor, Second Vatican Council, 1963–65.

Murray was the principal twentieth-century American Catholic theoretician on religious liberty. His views on religious liberty not only gave American Catholics a systematic way of looking at their political experience but also influenced the official Catholic teaching at the Second Vatican Council. The issue of religious liberty and the American experience of separation of church and state gradually arose as central theological and political problems for Murray in the immediate post–World War II era. Religious liberty evolved as a problem for two very different reasons. On the one hand, during the war Murray saw the necessity of intercreedal political and social cooperation to meet the national and international crises created by the war. Before Catholics could cooperate with other Christians and Jews in addressing issues of justice and peace, however, they had to overcome Protestant and Jewish suspicions about the supposed Catholic designs on the world order. These suspicions arose because of an official Catholic teaching on the confessional nature of the state. In this teaching, articulated by modern popes and by John A. Ryan* in the United States, union and harmony between the Catholic Church and the state was the ideal institutional relationship; religious liberty was at best a constitutional historical expedient that could be allowed because it provided for the church's freedom in society.

On the other hand, after the 1947 and 1948 Supreme Court decisions on religious freedom, Murray believed that there was an increasingly secularist interpretation of the first amendment that relegated religion to the sacristry or to the "private" sphere of individual conscience, thereby making religious perspectives totally irrelevant to political and social processes. These postwar circumstances made it necessary, he believed, for a new investigation of the Catholic teaching on religious liberty that would enable Catholics to cooperate with others in the social and political arena and to provide legitimate grounds for the influence of religion upon the issues of justice and peace in society.

In the course of a number of systematic-historical studies published after 1948, Murray developed the view that the constitutional provisions for religious liberty that had developed in the Western world for the past two centuries were consistent with an evolving Catholic teaching on the dignity and freedom of the human person. Catholics should accept the constitutional developments not simply on the grounds of historical expediency and beneficial historical experience but also on the moral ground that they provided for social peace and harmony among peoples—that is, they fulfilled the state's ultimate purpose for existence. The state's function was to protect freedom, not to enforce or secure religious belief or ecclesiastical goals. Such a view, he argued, provided for the church's freedom as well as that of the individual. Such a view of the state's role, moreover, was consistent with all that the church had struggled to achieve in its own past declarations. For him there was no such thing as an ideal relationship between church and state.

Murray's position was contrary to the prevailing view at the Vatican and at the Catholic University of America where the theologian Joseph Fenton* challenged Murray's orthodoxy. In the mid-1950s, Rome and Murray's Jesuit superiors silenced him on the issue, but his position was eventually vindicated at the Second Vatican Council, where he became a primary contributor to the Council's *Declaration on Religious Liberty* (*Dignitatis Humanae*, 1965).

Bibliography

A.   With Edward S. Corwin, *Religion and the State; the Supreme Court as National School Board* (Durham, N.C., 1949); with Walter Mills, *Foreign Policy and the Free Society* (New York, 1958); *We Hold These Truths* (New York, 1960); *The Problem of*

God: Yesterday and Today (New Haven, Conn., 1964); *The Problem of Religious Freedom* (Westminster, Md., 1965); articles in ThSt, 1941–67.

B.   DACB 413; DARB 386–87; DCA 785–86; NYT 17 August 1967, 37; *Religious Freedom 1965–1975: A Symposium on an Historical Document*, ed. Walter J. Burghardt (New York, 1977); Thomas T. Love, *John Courtney Murray's Contemporary Church–State Theory* (Garden City, N.Y., 1965); Donald E. Pelotte, *John Courtney Murray: Theologian in Conflict* (New York, 1975); J. Leon Hooper, *The Ethics of Discourse: The Social Philosophy of John Courtney Murray* (Washington, D.C., 1986); Thomas Hughson, *The Believer as Citizen: John Courtney Murray in a New Context* (New York, 1993).

Patrick W. Carey

N

NEANDER, JOHANN AUGUST WILHELM, born David Mendel (17 January 1789, Göttingen, Germany–14 July 1850, Berlin, Germany). *Education*: studied at gymnasium, Hamburg, 1805, 1809–11; Univ. of Halle, 1806, 1807–9; Univ. of Göttingen, 1806–7; habilitation, Univ. of Heidelberg, 1811. *Career*: instructor, gymnasium, Hamburg, 1809–11; professor, Univ. of Heidelberg, 1812–13; professor, Univ. of Berlin, 1813–50.

An influential German historian of the Romantic period, Neander was known for his biographical portrayal of church history, which emphasized the providential working of Christ. The history of the church is the process by which the ideal life of Christ becomes concrete in individuals. As a student of both Plato and Schleiermacher,* Neander's historiography was, in part, a reaction to the "pragmatic school" of J. G. Plank, which abandoned the supernatural in favor of a more psychological approach. Rejecting all forms of Hegelianism as well as rigid orthodoxy, Neander had a high estimate of Schelling's idealism. In America, his historiography had a notable influence on the Mercersburg theology of John W. Nevin* and Philip Schaff.*

Bibliography

A. *General History of the Christian Religion and Church*, trans. Joseph Torey, 6 vols. (Boston, 1881); *Lectures on the History of Christian Dogmas*, ed. J. L. Jacobi, 2 vols. (London, 1858).

B. LThK² 7:856; NCE 10:289; ODCC 1135; RGG 4:1388–89; SH 8:95–97; TRE 24:238–42; Philip Schaff, *Saint Augustin, Melanchthon, Neander* (New York, 1888); Frank Kaufman, *Foundations of Modern Church History* (New York, 1992); Kurt-Victor Selge, *August Neander* (Göttingen, 1989).

William DiPuccio

NESTORIUS (ca. 381–ca. 451). Theodosius II chose Nestorius, an Antiochene monk, to fill the see of Constantinople in 428. Shortly thereafter Nestorius distinguished himself as a preacher and proclaimed himself an ardent defender of orthodoxy. He opposed the use of the title *Theotokos* (''God-bearer'') for the Virgin Mary, since he found it difficult to reconcile with his own understanding of Christ, which was deeply influenced by Theodore of Mopsuestia.* Both men thought that to predicate human experiences of the Logos led either to Arianism or to Apollinarianism. Nestorius found himself opposed by Cyril of Alexandria,* who accused him of affirming two separate sons in Christ. In 430, a Roman synod condemned Nestorius' teachings. In June 431, the Council of Ephesus, led by Cyril, deposed Nestorius and anathematized his teachings. Nestorius was sent back to his monastery at Antioch and in 436 was exiled to Egypt. There he wrote the *Liber Heracleides* in which he tried to clarify his thought and show its orthodoxy.

Scholars generally agree that Nestorius did not intend to teach a double-son Christology, or Adoptionism. Nevertheless, disagreement exists among scholars over the orthodoxy of Nestorius' Christology, especially in relation to the later Christological definition at Chalcedon. Some sympathetic scholars have suggested that Nestorius' Christology was in the end vindicated by Chalcedon. Recently, more skeptical scholars have questioned whether Nestorius was really comfortable with the notion of a substantial unity in Christ that understands the divine Son as fully immanent in history together with all the limitations and afflictions that go along with it.

Nestorius sought to uphold the distinctive integrity of the divine and human reality of Christ and the oneness of Christ, but these intentions were hampered by an inability to distinguish clearly nature from person. His habit of referring to the humanity of Christ as the ''man Jesus'' and the divinity of Christ as ''the Logos'' inevitably invited charges of dualism. Nestorius opposed explaining the oneness of Christ as ''hypostatic'' because he thought it made the Incarnation a matter of necessity and involved confounding the divine and human realities in Christ. For Nestorius, a voluntary union cannot be a natural or hypostatic union. Instead, he preferred describing the oneness of Christ as a perfect conjunction or as an association by grace (*synapheia kat' eudokian*) based upon God's love. But Nestorius' account of the single subjectivity of Christ was highly complex, difficult to understand, and easy to misrepresent. Nestorius had great difficulties, even as late as the *Liber Heracleides*, with the communication of idioms because it made the divine Logos the final bearer and subject of the suffering of the God-man. These sorts of difficulties led the opponents of Nestorius to charge that his Christology failed to articulate correctly the faith of the church, especially as it was expressed at Nicaea and in the liturgy.

Bibliography

A.   ACO, *Concilium universale Ephesinum*, ed. Eduard Schwartz (Berlin and Leipzig, 1927–30), 1:1–5; *The Bazaar of Heracleides*, ed. G. R. Driver and L. Hodgson (Oxford, 1925).

B. DTC 11:76–157; LThK² 7:888–89; NCE 10:348; ODB 2:1460; ODCC 1138–39; TRE 24:276–86; André de Halleux, "Nestorius: histoire et doctrine," *Irénikon* 66 (1993): 38–51, 163–78; John A. McGuckin, "The Christology of Nestorius," in idem, *St. Cyril of Alexandria: The Christological Controversy* (New York, 1994), 126–74; Lawrence J. Welch, *Christology and Eucharist in the Thought of Cyril of Alexandria* (San Francisco, 1994).

Lawrence J. Welch

NEVIN, JOHN WILLIAMSON (20 February 1803, near Shippensburg, Pa.– 6 June 1886, Lancaster, Pa.). *Education*: B.A., Union Coll., Schenectady, N.Y., 1821; graduated Princeton Theol. Sem., Princeton, N.J., 1826; D.D. Jefferson Coll., Canonsburg, Pa., 1840; LL.D. Union Coll., 1873. *Career*: instructor of oriental and biblical literature, Princeton Theol. Sem., 1826–28; ordained Presbyterian minister, Carlisle, Pa., 1828; professor of biblical literature, Western Theol. Sem., Pittsburgh, Pa., 1830–40; editor, *The Friend* (Pittsburgh), 1833– 35; professor of theology and biblical literature, Theol. Sem. of the German Reformed Church, Mercersburg, Pa., 1840–51; president, Marshall Coll., Mercersburg, Pa., 1841–53; founding editor, *The Mercersburg Review*, 1849–52; professor of history and aesthetics, Franklin and Marshall Coll., Lancaster, Pa., 1861–66; president, Franklin and Marshall Coll., 1866–76; retirement, 1876–86.

Nevin was a leading critic of American religion and the chief architect of "Mercersburg theology." As a prominent advocate of Reformed, eucharistic theology, his sacramental and Romantic tendencies were also evident in his emphasis upon the organic nature of the church and its connection to the Incarnation. Despite his erudition, Nevin's theology was, at bottom, an expression of his deeply felt Scotch-Presbyterian piety. His system was not simply a reaction to the excesses of contemporary revivalism, but an attempt to synthesize Anglo-American thinking with aspects of German theology and idealism. Mercersburg theology was, nonetheless, a liturgical and confessional theology ruled by the orthodox spirit of the Heidelberg Catechism and the Apostles' Creed.

The theological center of Nevin's thought was the Incarnation, which was not just a theological paradigm but a cosmic archetype that defined and governed the organic relationship between the spiritual (or ideal) and the world of time and space. Every created thing, Nevin maintained, existed under a twofold aspect: the *ideal* (which is universal, eternal, and necessary) and the *actual* (which is particular, temporal, and contingent). All of creation, therefore, was a sacrament that dynamically embodied (i.e., actualized or externalized) the spiritual or ideal powers from which it originated.

Through Christ's incarnation, death, and resurrection, the fallen order of nature and humanity was taken up and transformed into a new creation by his redemptive power. This life-power is concretely and dynamically embodied in the *church*, the *sacraments*, and the *Scriptures*. The *church*, according to Nevin, is not a voluntary society of individual believers as most Americans maintained, but an organic whole, historically and supernaturally united to the incarnate Christ. Consequently, he vehemently opposed the proliferation of religious sects, arguing, instead, for historical catholicity.

The *sacraments* of the church involve "a real rending of the heavens—the canopy that separates the world of nature from the world of grace." While opposing transubstantiation on the one side and symbolic memorialism on the other, Nevin insisted that Christ is actually present (body and spirit) in the transaction of the Lord's Supper. Despite his many antagonists, he convincingly demonstrated that his view of the "mystical presence" was, in fact, the historic Reformed position.

But, Nevin came to realize, in ever-increasing degrees, that the *Scriptures* are also sacramental. In his later writings on sacred hermeneutics, the Bible is, for him, nothing less than the Incarnation of the life of Christ (i.e., the Logos) in human thought and language. It is the medium through which we enter into communion with the powers of heaven by faith. Ever wary of sectarian interpretations and false authority, however, he never wavered from his belief in the Apostles' Creed as the only hermeneutical lens of scriptural interpretation and theological reflection.

Recently, Nevin's critique of American culture and theology has become a source of interest to historians seeking to understand the foundations of American society. Throughout most of his life, Nevin engaged a sustained polemic against cultural materialism, religious skepticism, and individualism. The only remedy for these evils, in his view, was a Christian idealism rooted in the Incarnation and classic creedal theology.

Bibliography

A. *Antichrist, or the Spirit of Sect and Schism* (New York, 1848); *The Anxious Bench* (Chambersburg, Pa., 1846); *The Mercersburg Review*, 1849–53, 1855–59, 1861, 1867, 1871–80, 1882–83; *The Mystical Presence and Other Writings on the Eucharist*, ed. Bard Thompson and George H. Bricker (Philadelphia, 1966); *The Mercersburg Theology*, ed. James H. Nichols (New York, 1966).

B. DAB 13:442–43; DARB 390–91; NCAB 5:256; SH 8:130; Theodore Appel, *The Life and Work of John Williamson Nevin* (Philadelphia, 1889); James H. Nichols, *Romanticism in American Theology: Nevin and Schaff at Mercersburg* (Chicago, 1961); William DiPuccio, *The Interior Sense of Scripture: The Sacred Hermeneutics of John W. Nevin* (Macon, Ga., 1997); Sam Hamstra, Jr. and Arie J. Griffioen, eds., *Reformed Confessionalism in Nineteenth-Century America: Essays on the Thought of John Williamson Nevin* (Lanham, Md., 1995).

William DiPuccio

NEWMAN, JOHN HENRY (21 February 1801, London, England–11 August 1890, Birmingham, England). *Education*: Trinity Coll., Oxford, 1817–22; fellowship Oriel Coll., Oxford, 1822; read theology with Charles Lloyd, Christ Church, 1822–25; studied theology, Coll. of Propaganda, Rome, 1846–47. *Career*: ordained Anglican priest, 1825; curate, St. Clements, 1825–26; tutor, Oriel Coll., 1826–32; vicar, St. Mary the Virgin Church, Oxford, 1828–41; residence at Littlemore, 1841–46; editor, *British Critic*, 1838; entered Catholic Church, 1845; resided in old Oscoff Coll., 1846–48; ordained Catholic priest, 1847;

founder and member, Oratory of St. Philip Neri, Birmingham, 1849–90; rector, Roman Catholic Univ., Dublin, 1852–58; editor, *The Rambler*, 1858; cardinal-deacon, 1879.

Newman was a leading exponent of the Oxford Movement, a convert to Catholicism, and a creative theologian whose works on doctrinal development and religious knowledge have had a long-lasting impact on modern Catholic theology. He was a lifelong student of the church fathers and the primitive church. This study and his association with Hurrell Froude, John Keble,* Edward Pusey,* and others occasioned the beginning of the Oxford Movement. The nineteenth century was for the church a struggle between rationalism and fideism. Newman addressed this struggle in the *Parochial and Plain Sermons* (1834–42), which he preached between 1826 and 1845 in Saint Mary the Virgin Church. These sermons remain a classic exposition of the relation of faith to reason in Christian life. In these years also he formulated what he meant by liberalism and set himself firmly against its influences on culture and church. From his study of the Fathers, the writing of *The Arians of the Fourth Century* (1833), and the publication of the *Tracts for the Times* (1833–41), he discovered the principle of development. His *Essay on the Development of Christian Doctrine* (1845) was intended to give him some intellectual and reasonable—not merely emotional—ground for changing his religious commitment from the Anglican to the Roman Catholic communion. The *Essay* had a far wider effect than its author intended, for it has contributed a theory of development of Christian doctrine that has marked contemporary theological thinking. Without completing the *Essay*, he decided that Rome had a better claim to be the modern development from the original and primitive Christian Church. In 1845, after much soul-searching in a retreat at Littlemore, he requested to be received into the Roman Catholic communion through the good offices of Blessed Dominic Barberi, C.P.

The following forty-five years demonstrated energy for the Catholic cause. The foundation of the Oratory in England, the efforts in Ireland to found the Catholic University of Great Britain, the stress of the Achilli trial, establishing the school attached to the Oratory, the discourses to Anglicans, the work with the *Rambler*, the correspondence, the spiritual direction, and the inspiration he gave to the Catholic laity, the growing friendship with his bishop Ullathorne, the complex relationship with Cardinal Wiseman and later with Cardinal Manning,* the attentive following of the acts of the First Council of the Vatican, the explanation of the theology of papal infallibility to Gladstone and to all England through his 1875 *Letter to the Duke of Norfolk*—all testify to a productive life. He did experience the fluctuation of success and frustration in his Catholic life. Some of this was due to a mutual lack of sympathy between his theological approach and that of the prevailing neoscholastic style. With the haunting *Dream of Gerontius* (1865) he seemed ready to surrender his activity and seek peace in obscurity, but the publication of the *Apologia* in 1864 gave him a new lease on life.

In 1870 he published his *Essay in Aid of a Grammar of Assent*, a fat little book that treated a subject that had been on his mind for years and that was ten years in the composition. Its contribution was an awakening to a new mode in Christian apologetics. Finally, his elevation to the status of cardinal-deacon in 1879 was for him a seal of approval both of his person and of his teachings that he did not always experience in his earlier years. Although annoyed by bouts of illness during his long life, he was gifted with resilience.

As a priest of the Anglican communion he was among the leaders of the Oxford Movement, and later as a priest and eventual cardinal-deacon of the Roman Catholic communion he helped guide fellow Catholics in English public life. His writings were wrung from him to meet the demands of a given occasion. The results, however, were magnificent English prose productions—sermons, controversies, historical essays, and expressions of his speculative thought. His efforts at poetry were less successful, but they contributed some lasting works in devotional and religious literature. His *Apologia pro Vita Sua* (1864) is his best-known work and it has become a classic in the genre of spiritual and intellectual autobiography. He anticipated much of the intellectual struggle of the present Christian community and is said to have been a "presence" at the Second Council of the Vatican (1963–65) by reason of the number of times his works were cited. He has become a model of Christian holiness and learning that has attracted many to his cause. International societies of the "Friends of Newman" are working with the Birmingham Oratory to promote his cause as confessor and doctor. He has been declared "Venerable."

Bibliography

A.   *Letters and Diaries*, ed. Charles Stephen Dessain et al., 31 vols. (London, New York, 1961–); *Sermons, 1824–1845*, 2 vols. to date (Oxford, New York, 1991–); *Apologia pro Vita Sua*, ed. Martin J. Svaglic (Oxford, 1967); *An Essay on the Development of Doctrine*, ed. J. M. Cameron (Baltimore, Md., 1973); *An Essay on the Development of Christian Doctrine*, ed. Charles Frederick Harrold (New York, 1949); *An Essay in Aid of a Grammar of Assent*, ed. Ian T. Ker (Oxford, 1985); *Fifteen Sermons Preached before the University of Oxford between A.D. 1826 and 1843* (London, 1918).

B.   DNB 14:340–51; DTC 11:327–98; LThK² 7:932–36; NCE 10:412–19; ODCC 1141–42; TRE 24:416–22; Sheridan Gilley, *Newman and His Age* (London, 1990); Ian T. Ker, *John Henry Newman: A Biography* (Oxford, New York, 1988); Meriol Trevor, *Newman*, 2 vols. (London, 1962); Wilfrid Philip Ward, *The Life of John Henry Cardinal Newman*, 2 vols. (London and New York, 1927); Johannes Artz, *Newman-Lexikon* (Mainz, 1975); Vincent Blehl, *John Henry Cardinal Newman, 1801–1890: Founder of the English Oratories: Positio super Virtutibus*, 2 vols. (Birmingham, 1989); Nicholas Lash, *Newman on Development* (Shepherdstown, W.Va., 1975); Paul Misner, *Papacy and Development: Newman and the Primacy of the Pope* (Leiden, 1976); D. H. Newsome, *The Convert Cardinals: John Henry Newman and Henry Edward Manning* (London, 1993).

William J. Kelly

NICHOLAS OF CUSA, Nicolaus Cusanus, N. Treverensis, N. Kryfts or Krebs (1401, Kues on the Moselle River–11 August 1464, Todi, Umbria). *Education*:

studied in Heidelberg, 1416–17; doctorate in canon law, Padua, 1423; studied philosophy and theology, Cologne, where he was influenced by the Albertist Heymeric de Campo, who introduced him to the thought of Raymond Lull,* 1425; discovery of Tacitus' *Annales* I-VI and comedies of Plautus earned him the respect of the Italian humanists of his day. *Career:* Twice he rejected the offer of a chair in law at Louvain. He gained public attention by his participation at the Council of Basel in 1432, in particular through his ecclesiastical study *De concordantia catholica*, which is a defense of conciliarism (he later turned to the defense of papalism) and in which he taught that "since all are by nature free, every governance, whether it consists in a written law or living law in the person of a prince, can only come from the agreement and consent of the subjects." He was also engaged in the discussions with the Hussites on the chalice for the laity. In 1437–38, returning from a papal legation to Constantinople, he had his crucial insight into the divine infinity and learned ignorance, which is documented in his best-known work, *De docta ignorantia*. In 1449 he was made cardinal and in 1450 prince-bishop of Brixen (Bressanone) in South Tirol. Before taking up residence in Brixen, he made extensive reform journeys as papal legate throughout the German-speaking countries. His attempts at reform within his own diocese occasioned such adamant opposition among the nobility that he ultimately abandoned Brixen in 1458. He spent his remaining years in Italy, active in ecclesiastical politics and writing until his death. His body is buried in his titular church of St. Peter in Chains. His heart and the larger portion of his library are still kept in the home for the elderly poor that he founded in Kues.

Nicholas understood his own theological work as a "hunt for wisdom" (*De venatione sapientiae*). Although his primary interest was directed to theological problems, he also treated scientific and mathematical questions. Historians have taken note of his doctrines that the universe is infinite and that the earth is not its center and is itself in motion. Nicholas, who considered mathematics essential to doing theology, even devoted publications to mathematical problems. Nevertheless, for him all human knowledge of the real world remains "conjectural" (*De coniecturis*).

Cusanus attempted to come to terms, both institutionally and theoretically, with the relationship of Christianity to other world religions, especially Islam. In his work *On the Peace of Faith* he developed a solution based on the principle "one religion in a variety of rites."

In his abstract dialectical thinking he relied upon symbols (*De beryllo, De ludo globi, De visione dei*) and the creation of innovative divine names to which he devoted individual books. An indication of why he has been regarded as "the first modern thinker" (Ernst Cassirer) can be seen in his explicit refusal to be led by authority. Nonetheless, Cusanus studied past thinkers (especially those in the Neoplatonic tradition) assiduously and made substantial use of them (often attested to by excerpts, notes, and glosses in his own hand).

One of the divine names developed by him is the "absolutely *maximum*." In accordance with his idea of the *coincidentia oppositorum*, which represents a leitmotiv throughout his work, *maximum* is to be understood in such a way that the absolutely *maximum* coincides with the absolutely *minimum*. Other divine names, to which he devoted individual books, are the *non-aliud*, the *possest*, and *posse ipsum*.

In his teaching on God as absolute Oneness it becomes evident to what extent Cusanus' thought depends upon and, nonetheless, innovatively differs from traditional Neoplatonism, claiming to transcend not only reason and intellect, but also even the notion of divine Unity. As the enfoldment (*complicatio*) of everything, God is the Unity of all opposites, the *coincidentia oppositorum*. Creation is an unfolding (*explicatio*) of what exists enfolded (*implicatio*) in the divine Unity. Human knowledge (*mens viva Dei imago*) is an analogous unfolding of the human spirit (*vis assimilativa* as opposed to God's *vis entificativa*). Thus, Nicholas called man a "human god," a "second god," a "god manqué" (*deus occasionatus*). The role of sense experience was given a nominalistic interpretation by Cusanus, who described it as an awakening of attention out of a sleep. Since there is nothing outside of God, Cusanus referred to God as the "notother." Mystical theology, as the culmination of Cusanus' thought, represents the leap over the "wall of paradise," which embodies the principle of noncontradiction and defines the limits of human knowledge. "No one," he wrote, "can see God mystically unless in the darkness of the coincidence." This is "learned ignorance" (*docta ignorantia*), or what he also called "sacred ignorance." One enters the darkness, abandoning reason and intellect and even one's self, transcending the *via positiva* and the *via negativa* as well, attaining the coincidence of impossibility and necessity. These abstract thoughts, far from being an experience of God or an affective union with him, were developed by Cusanus in the form of an interpretation of Pseudo-Dionysius the Areopagite's* *Mystical Theology.*

Bibliography

A. *Nicolai de Cusa opera omnia*, 19 vols. to date (Hamburg, 1932–); *Schriften des Nikolaus von Kues in deutscher Übersetzung, editio minor*; Latin-German edition, usually with extensive notes (Hamburg, 1932–).

B. DTC 11:601–12; LThK² 7:988–91; NCE 10:449–52; ODCC 1149–50; TRE 24: 554–64; "Special Issue: Nicholas of Cusa," ed. Louis Dupré, *American Catholic Philosophical Quarterly* 64 (1990); *Nicholas of Cusa: In Search of God and Wisdom*, ed. Gerald Christianson and Thomas M. Izbicki (New York, 1991; this and the following volume include extensive bibliographies of English translations and secondary literature); *Nicholas of Cusa on Christ and the Church*, ed. idem (New York, 1996); Jasper Hopkins, *Nicholas of Cusa on Wisdom and Knowledge* (Minneapolis, Minn., 1996).

                                                                    William J. Hoye

NICHOLAS OF LYRA (ca. 1270, Lyra, Normandy–October, 1349, Paris). *Education*: took Franciscan habit at the house of Verneuil, 1300; studied theology in Paris. *Career*: regent master in theology at Paris, 1309; elected minister of the province of Paris, 1319; began *Literal Postill on the Whole Bible*, 1322; presented *Literal Postill* to Pope John XXII, 1331; elected provincial minister of Burgundy, 1325; founded college for Burgundian students at the Univ. of Paris, 1330; participated in convocation at Vincennes to discuss Pope John XXII's position on the beatific vision, 1333; wrote *Moral Commentary on the Whole Bible*, 1333–39.

Nicholas of Lyra was the most prolific and influential biblical exegete of the late Middle Ages and, it has been argued, the greatest biblical commentator since Jerome.* His reputation was securely established with the production of his *Postilla Literalis* on the Bible, a running commentary on both Testaments. The *Postilla* was the first biblical commentary to be printed (*Glossae seu Postillae perpetuae in universa Biblia*, Rome, 1471–72). In some printed editions, his commentaries are accompanied by the *Additiones* of Paul of Burgos (d. 1435) and the *Replicae* of Matthew Doering (d. 1469). In 1339 Lyra completed his *Postilla moralis* (which was often printed with the *Postilla literalis*), a shorter commentary that emphasized the moral and mystical meanings of the text and was intended as a practical handbook for preachers and teachers.

Unlike most contemporary Christian exegetes, Lyra was able to read at least some Hebrew, and he knew the Talmud, the midrash, and the works of the medieval Jewish exegete Rashi (d. 1105), who influenced him deeply. He had also read the Jewish philosopher Maimonides. Nonetheless, Lyra engaged in Jewish–Christian polemic and wrote two tracts in which he criticized Jewish practice and belief. Lyra also wrote nearly 300 sermons, a commentary on the *Sentences* of Peter Lombard,* and other minor works on the Eucharist, the beatific vision, and Franciscan poverty.

His great hermeneutical innovation was his teaching on the "double literal sense" (*duplex sensus literalis*), which held that citations from the Hebrew scriptures found in the New Testament had two literal meanings. The first and more perfect meaning referred to Christ, the second and less perfect to pre-Christian history.

Lyra's influence was enormous. Over 200 manuscripts of his *Postilla Literalis* exist. Since the late fifteenth century, it has been printed 176 times. It ranks, along with the *Glossa Ordinaria* and the *Sentences* of Peter Lombard, as one of the most influential theological works of the Middle Ages. Moreover, some of his commentaries influenced Luther,* at least indirectly, an influence immortalized in a famous late-medieval couplet: "Si Lyra non lyrasset, Lutherus non saltasset" ("Had Lyra not lyred, Luther would not have danced"). Lyra shared with Luther a revulsion for what he took to be the overallegorization of the Bible and an emphasis on the plain, clear sense of the biblical text, an exegetical emphasis that has caused him to be known as "the clear and plain doctor."

Bibliography

A. *Biblia sacra, cum glossis, interlineari et ordinaria, Nicolai Lyrani postilla, ac moralitatibus, Burgensis additionibus, et Thoringi replicis* (Venice, 1588); *Oratio ad Honorem S. Francisci* (Paris, 1641); *Tractatulus contra quendam Judaeum* (Antwerp, 1634).

B. DSAM 11:291–92; DTC 9:1410–22; LThK² 7:992–93; NCE 10:453–54; ODCC 1151; TRE 24:564–66; H. Hailperin, *Rashi and the Christian Scholars* (Pittsburgh, Pa., 1963); J. Preus, *From Shadow to Promise* (Cambridge, Mass., 1969); idem, *Nicholas of Lyra: the Senses of Scripture* (Leiden, 1997).

Kevin Madigan

NICODEMUS OF THE HOLY MOUNTAIN, born Nicholas Kallivourtsis (ca. 1749, Aegean Island of Naxos—14 July 1809, Mt. Athos). *Career:* secretary to metropolitan of Naxos, 1770–75; monk of Mt. Athos, 1775–1809.

Nicodemus came early into contact with exiled members of the *kollyvades* movement, scholar monks whose advocacy of patristic scholarship and liturgical renewal had generated controversy at the monastic center of Mt. Athos sufficient to compel the departure of many of them for different points in Ottoman Greece. After a period of study at Smyrna and five years serving as secretary to the metropolitan of Naxos, the young Nicholas went himself to Athos in 1775 where he was tonsured monk and received the name Nicodemus. There, too, he began the engagement with the editing, translation, and commentary on spiritual texts from the fourth century through the Counter-Reformation that would occupy him until his death.

Two publications in particular illustrate the breadth of his interests. In 1782, and in collaboration with bishop Macarius of Corinth, he published at Venice the five volume collection of the *Philokalia*, a compendium of ascetical and mystical texts from the fifth through the fifteenth centuries. This has with some justice been called the most important publication in the Orthodox Christian world of the past two centuries. Sometime later, Nicodemus published annotated translations of Lorenzo Scupoli's *Unseen Warfare* and the *Spiritual Exercises* of Pinamonti. Other works and translations included commentaries on Scripture, on the liturgical year (the *Kyriakodromion*), an abriged, four-volume collection of saints' lives (*Synaxarion*), the works of Symeon the New Theologian* (d. 1022), and, perhaps most importantly in addition to the *Philokalia*, his massive collection and commentary on canon law in the *Rudder* (*Pedalion*).

Nicodemus' contributions to the recovery of traditional Orthodox spirituality and renascence of patristic studies were enormous and remain both in effect and justly celebrated. He and Paisii Velichkovsky* were instrumental in the revival of Orthodox monastic life in the nineteenth and twentieth centuries. Less noted, though perhaps as important, and certainly more problematical, was his articulation of ecclesiology in the course of his commentaries in the *Rudder*. Confronted with the pressures of Western Christian—especially Roman Catholic— missions in the Ottoman Empire, the Ecumenical Patriarchate had, in 1755, unilaterally declared the baptism of all non-Orthodox Christians invalid. All other Christians who sought entry into the Orthodox Church were to be received by baptism. Nicodemus was the most important Greek theologian to accept this view and lend it reasoned support. His commentary takes the views of Cyprian of Carthage* (d. 258 A.D.) as providing the norms of patristic ecclesiology. In order to reconcile Cyprian's absolute nonrecognition of sacraments outside the church's visible communion with the later, far milder and more nuanced practices of reception in the Byzantine and post-Byzantine church, Nicodemus elaborated a theology of "sacramental economy" which held that the one true church has the authority "to make valid what is invalid"—that is, that it can accord retroactive effectiveness to sacramental action (here, baptism), administered outside the Orthodox Church. The theory was a novelty, in spite of Nicodemus' assertion that it represented the patristic consensus, but it has come to hold sway among many contemporary Orthodox theologians, particularly in the Greek-speaking world, and has just as often been advertised by Western Christian scholars as the traditional Orthodox position (e.g., Y. Congar* and A. de Halleux). It also poses what is perhaps the single most pressing internal problem confronting Orthodox theologians involved in ecumenical dialogue.

Bibliography

A. *Philokalia ton hieron neptikon*, 5 vols. (Athens, 1957), ET: *The Philokalia: The Complete Text Compiled by St. Nikodemus of the Holy Mountain and St. Makarios of Corinth*, trans. K. T. Ware, P. Sherrard, and G. E. H. Palmer, 4 vols. to date (London: 1980–); *Pedalion tes noetes neos tes mias hagias katholikes kai apostolikes ton orthodoxon ekklesias, etoi apantes hoi hieroi and theioi kanones* (Thessaloniki, 1991), ET: *The Rudder, or: All the Sacred and Divine Canons*, trans. D. Cummings (Chicago, 1957); *Nicodemus of the Holy Mountain: A Handbook of Spiritual Counsel*, trans. Peter A. Chamberas (New York, 1989).

B. DSAM 11:234–50; DTC 11:486–90; ECatt 1:454; HDOC 237–38; NCE 10:458–59; ODCC 1152; Constantine Cavarnos, *St. Nicodemus the Hagiorite* (Belmont, Mass., 1974); George Bebis, "Introduction," *Nicodemus of the Holy Mountain: A Handbook of Spiritual Counsel*, 5–65; John H. Erickson, "On the Cusp of Modernity: The Canonical Hermeneutic of St. Nicodemus the Hagiorite," SVTQ 42 (1998): 45–66.

Alexander Golitzin

NICODEMUS OF MT. ATHOS. *See* NICODEMUS OF THE HOLY MOUNTAIN.

NICOLAS DE CLAMANGES (ca. 1363/64, Clamanges–1437, Paris). *Education*: master of arts, bachelor of theology, Univ. of Paris, 1380, by 1394. *Career*: composed Univ. of Paris' official letters, ca. 1394–97; secretary to Avignon pope Benedict XIII, 1397–98, 1403–8; taught arts, Univ. of Paris, ca. 1381–97, 1423–37.

Known primarily as a literary humanist, Clamanges advocated personal religious reform during the Great Schism. Because of politics and his own disposition, he spent 1398–1403 and 1408–23 in self-imposed exile. From quiet retreats, he sent his plans for reform to influential correspondents (Pierre d'Ailly,* Jean Gerson,* Charles VI of France, Benedict XIII, and others) for implementation. His personal reform program did not invert the top-down plans prevalent at the Council of Constance but offered an inside-out model. Clamanges drew on patristic and humanistic reform ideas, the predominant spiritual milieu of the *Devotio Moderna* and pious exercises imitating Christ's life. Personal reform was cultivated by purgation, humility, and eremitical solitude. Institutional reform radiated out from this personal reform. All clerics (pope, diocesan bishops, parish priests) who had undergone personal reform had to root out simony and worldliness, reform scholastic education, and refocus on pastoral care throughout the institutional church.

Bibliography

A.   *Opera omnia*, ed. J. Lydius, 3 vols. (Leiden, 1613; repr. Farnborough, 1967); *Le Traité de la ruine de l'Église de Nicholas de Clamanges et la traduction française de 1564*, ed. Alfred Coville (Paris, 1936).
B.   DTC 11:597–600; LThK² 7:983–84; NCE 10:448–49; TRE 24:546–49; Ezio Ornato, *Jean Muret et ses amis, Nicolas de Clamanges et Jean de Montreuil* (Geneva, 1969); François Bérier, "La figure du clerc dans le '*De studio theologico*' de Nicolas de Clamanges," *Travaux de linguistique et de littérature* 21 (1983): 81–103.

Christopher M. Bellitto

NIEBUHR, HELMUT RICHARD (3 September 1894, Wright City, Mo.–5 July 1962, Rowe, Mass.). *Education*: graduated from Elmhurst Coll., Elmhurst, Ill., 1912; graduated, Eden Theol. Sem., St. Louis, Mo., 1915; M.A., (German) Washington Univ., St. Louis, Mo., 1917; B.D., Yale Div. Sch., New Haven, Conn., 1923; Ph.D. (religion), Yale Univ., 1924; studied in Berlin and Marburg, 1930. *Career*: pastor, Walnut Park Evangelical Church, St. Louis, Mo., 1916–18; instructor (theology and ethics), Eden Theol. Sem., 1919–22, dean, 1927–31; pastor, First Church of Christ (Congregational), Clinton, Conn., 1922–24; president, Elmhurst Coll., 1924–27; faculty (theology and ethics), Yale Div. Sch., 1931–62.

Niebuhr was the preeminent Protestant theologian and social ethicist in mid-twentieth century America. In addition to contributions in theology and ethics, Niebuhr produced ground-breaking studies on the sociology and history of American religion. During the early 1930s Niebuhr affiliated himself with the neo-orthodox movement. In America, neo-orthodox theologians stressed divine transcendence, human depravity, and cultural resistance over against a liberal theological creed that emphasized divine immanence, confidence in human nature, and a sympathetic stance toward secular culture. Nevertheless, Niebuhr always distanced himself from certain forms of neo-orthodoxy, criticizing crisis theology's lack of a sufficient social ethic and maintaining that God's sovereignty does not preclude but rather entails God's activity and immanence in the world. Moreover, during the 1950s Niebuhr dissociated himself from the later forms of neo-orthodoxy. Thus, Niebuhr's true theological lineage is best seen in a group of theologians whose affirmations of the divine sovereignty deeply influenced his thought: Augustine,* Calvin,* and Jonathan Edwards.* Niebuhr's legacy continues through the work of several distinguished theologians for whom he was a mentor during their doctoral studies at Yale. These former students include Hans Frei, James Gustafson, Gordon Kaufman, and Paul Ramsey.

The dominant motif in Niebuhr's thought was the sovereignty of God. During the 1930s Niebuhr came to a personal conviction of God's sovereignty, which profoundly affected his life and thought. The fundamental insights of this conviction were of the reality of God and the trustworthiness of being itself. Niebuhr's movement away from liberalism was a movement away from the belief that value could be defined apart from God to the conviction that value and being are inseparable in God. Hereafter, Niebuhr spoke of God as always active in the world as the structure of things, the ground of all being, the source of all meaning, and the rock against which humans beat in vain when they try to impose their wishes contrary to the will of God.

Radical monotheism was the prime theological formulation of Niebuhr's conviction of the sovereignty of God. God in radical monotheism is the One beyond the many, who is the principle of being as well as the principle of value. Two implications follow from radical monotheism. First, since only the One is truly absolute, all other claimants to the status of absolute are relativized. Second, although all beings except the One are relativized, they are also sanctified because they are called forth and valued by the One. Hence the two mottoes of radical monotheism: "I am the Lord thy God; thou shalt have no other gods before me," and "Whatever is, is good."

However, Niebuhr's fundamental conviction of God's sovereignty found theological formulation not only in the abstract language of being but also in the biblical language of the God who acts. For Niebuhr, God is the Creator, Governor, and Redeemer. In all things, God's activity is manifest as the power of the Creator, the order of the Governor, and the goodness and mercy of the Redeemer. Yet, God does not act alternatively in one moment as Creator and in another as Redeemer, but rather is simultaneously present and active in all things as Creator, Governor, and Redeemer.

Inextricably connected with Niebuhr's understanding of God was his analysis of the structure of human faith. Fundamentally, faith is trust in and fidelity to a reality that is construed as the source of value and the object of loyalty. All of human life is characterized by some form of faith. However, our natural forms of faith are perverted by the placing of trust and loyalty in finite centers of value. At heart this misplaced trust and loyalty is sin, which results in the fragmentation of our personal and social existence. Only in radical monotheism does faith find its proper object, which allows one to act as an integrated self. Therefore, all human life involves a continuous process of *metanoia*, wherein one's trust and loyalty are reoriented away from finite value-centers and toward God. Radical monotheistic faith is trust in God, who is the ground of all being, and loyalty to God's cause, which is reverence for all being.

Niebuhr died without completing a systematic treatise on Christian ethics. In *Christ and Culture* he had updated Troeltsch's* threefold typology of Christian attitudes toward culture (i.e. church, sect, and mysticism) by developing a five-fold typology (i.e. opposition, agreement, synthesist, dualist, and conversionist). The posthumously published *The Responsible Self* might have served as the prologue to a projected work that would have included sections on "The Principles of Christian Action," and "Christian Responsibility in the Common Life." In *The Responsible Self* Niebuhr offered a phenomenological analysis of moral experience based upon the image of "man-the-answerer" who seeks fitting responses to what is happening. While the ethics of responsibility articulated in *The Responsible Self* was intended to illuminate moral experience generally, it was also thoroughly informed by Niebuhr's radical monotheism. Indeed, responsibility affirms that God is acting in all actions upon us. Therefore, we ought to respond to all actions upon us as we would respond to the action of God.

Bibliography

A.   *The Social Sources of Denominationalism* (New York, 1929); *The Kingdom of God in America* (New York, 1937); *The Meaning of Revelation* (New York, 1951); *Christ and Culture* (New York, 1951); *Radical Monotheism and Western Culture, with Supplementary Essays* (New York, 1960).

B.   DARB 392–94; NCAB 47:64–65; NCE 10:462; NYT 6 July 1962, 25; *Faith and Ethics: The Theology of H. Richard Niebuhr*, ed. Paul Ramsey (New York, 1957); Libertus A. Hoedemaker, *The Theology of H. Richard Niebuhr* (Philadelphia, 1970); *The Legacy of H. Richard Niebuhr*, ed. Ronald F. Thiemann (Minneapolis, Minn., 1991).

Joseph Pagano

NIEBUHR, (KARL PAUL) REINHOLD (21 June 1892, Wright City, Mo.–1 June 1971, Stockbridge, Mass.). *Education*: studied at Elmhurst Coll., Elmhurst, Ill., 1907–10; Eden Theol. Sem., Wellston, Mo., 1910–13; B.D., M.A., Yale Div. Sch., New Haven, Conn., 1914, 1915. *Career*: interim pastor, St. John's German Evangelical Synod Church, Lincoln, Ill., 1913; pastor, Bethel Evangelical Church, Detroit, Mich. 1915–28; executive secretary, Synod War Welfare Council, 1917; professor of Christian ethics, Union Theol. Sem., New York, N.Y., 1928–60; cofounder, Fellowship of Socialist Christians, 1930–31; U.S. Senatorial candidate, Socialist Party, 1931; founder and editor in chief, *Radical Religion*, 1934–45; delivered Gifford Lectures, Edinburgh, Scotland, 1939; cofounder and editor, *Christianity and Crisis*, 1941; cofounder and spokesman, Union for Democratic Action, 1941; retirement, 1960–71.

Niebuhr was the preeminent U.S. Christian ethicist of the mid-twentieth century. His thirteen years in the pastorate and over thirty-two in seminary teaching were stamped by passionate engagement with the affairs of his day. Niebuhr was a public intellectual, a prolific and sought-after lecturer, political commentator, and editorialist. He delivered the prestigious Gifford lectures (1939), appeared on the cover of *Newsweek* magazine (1948), and was called "the greatest living political philosopher of America" by political scientist Hans Morgenthau (1961).

Niebuhr's scholarly publications appeared amid four decades of political activity, travel, lecturing, teaching, and journalistic writing. Indebted to the social gospel movement, Niebuhr's social ethics contested both naively optimistic forms of religious liberalism and cynical, amoral *Realpolitik*. Early socialist leanings later gave way to advocacy for American-style democracy.

"Christian realism" denotes Niebuhr's distinctive political, moral, and theological vantagepoint on social ethics. *Political* realism is "the disposition to take all factors in a social and political situation, which offer resistance to established norms, into account, particularly the factors of self-interest and power." Niebuhr's theocentric *moral* realism rejects epistemological relativism or agnosticism concerning good and evil. Grounding these is a *theological* realism shaped by a "biblical faith" that illumines the human situation and provides social analysis and action its firmest possible footing. Christian realism attends to the "gap between the biblical vision of God's rule and the realities" of society, and attempts to provide a "vision and direction" for historical engagement.

Niebuhr's Gifford lectures, *The Nature and Destiny of Man* (1941–43), represent his sustained effort to clarify the theological underpinnings of his mature thought. He elaborates a religious anthropology that underscores the tension between humans' capacities for self-transcendence and their creaturely limitations. Humanity is a dialectical synthesis of nature and spirit, necessity and freedom. Biblical faith discerns the original law of human existence as "love, the harmonious relation of life to life in obedience to the divine center and source of life."

Sin's root is humanity's refusal to address responsibly its potentials and limits. Christian teaching on the Fall illumines "a tragic reality about human life": Humans respond to existential anxiety by abusing freedom and grasping after the infinite value and power belonging to God alone. Sin conspiring with finitude produces estrangement from self, God, and others. As the natural "will to live" degenerates into the sinful "will to power," coercion, conflict, and division enter history. Whether self-isolating or dominating, the will to power, the primary form of pride, involves the ego in injustice. "It seeks a security beyond the limits of human finiteness, and this inordinate ambition arouses fears and enmities which the world of pure nature, with its competing impulses of survival, does not know."

The contention that sin uniquely infects social life is a hallmark of Niebuhr's political realism. "A sharp distinction must be drawn between the moral and social behavior of individuals and of social groups;" "this distinction justifies and necessitates political policies which a purely individualistic ethic must always find embarrassing." Groups compound individual egotism exponentially by harnessing even personal altruism in service of collective selfishness, yet are incapable of moral self-transcendence. The political sphere remains, distinctly, "a realm of sin." Ironically, dominative power, a primary instrument of social sin, is also the primary weapon against it.

Niebuhr's political theory depicts society as a dynamic, tension-filled field; "a vast series of encounters between human selves and their interests." Tolerable harmonies require "setting force, as the instrument of order, against force as the instrument of anarchy." Order is social structure's first aim, tyranny a constant threat.

State power checks anarchy and promotes cohesion by providing a unifying center. To prevent exploitation, however, government authority must be offset by other, decentralized positions of strength. Niebuhr's often-cited theory of the balance of power embraces the premise that "the domination of one life by another is avoided most successfully by an equilibrium of powers and vitalities, so that weakness does not invite enslavement by the strong." A dynamic balance of power restrains government's oppressive tendencies; government protects competing centers of vitality from chaos. These strategies deflect, but do not reduce, collective egoism. One can never eliminate "the potential contradiction to brotherhood implicit in the political instruments of brotherhood," but no moral or social advance can redeem society from its dependence upon them.

Niebuhr's interpretation of the doctrine of redemption focuses on God's power "above" history as forgiveness and perceives God's work "within" history principally in the freely accepted weakness of Jesus, the Suffering Servant. The cross reveals the significance yet impotence of pure goodness in history. Jesus' teachings on self-sacrifice are directly relevant only to individuals. God's Kingdom and intrahistorical possibilities are related dialectically; Jesus' perfect love ethic, an "impossible possibility," stands over every concrete approximation of justice as ideal and judgment. Social justice entails "regulative principles" of liberty and equality. But such principles cannot delineate actions or policies; frequently their requirements conflict. Christian realist justice-seeking thus requires a pragmatic moral style tempered by dispositions of contrition and humility, fruit of the awareness that sin taints every historical effort.

Bibliography

A. *Moral Man and Immoral Society* (New York, 1932); *An Interpretation of Christian Ethics* (New York, 1937); *The Nature and Destiny of Man*, 2 vols. (New York: 1941, 1943); *Christian Realism and Political Problems* (New York: 1953).

B. DARB 394–95; NCAB G:468–69; NYT 2 June 1971, 1; Richard W. Fox, *Reinhold Niebuhr: A Biography* (New York, 1985); Harlan Beckley, *Passion for Justice* (Louisville, Ky., 1992); Robin W. Lovin, *Reinhold Niebuhr and Christian Realism* (London, 1995).

Christine Firer Hinze

NOVATIAN (third century). Novatian was the first Roman theologian to write in Latin. He is first mentioned ca. 250 as a respected presbyter of the church at

Rome. In 250–51, when the bishop's office was vacant, he drafted letters in the name of the college of presbyters there. The bishop Cornelius, elected in March of 251, treated those who fell in the persecution of Decius mildly. Novatian thereupon had himself ordained bishop and gathered a group of rigorists around himself. He was excommunicated by a synod at Rome and ended his life as a schismatic and a heretic. His church spread throughout the West and East and perdured until the sixth century. Despite his schism, his theological works are orthodox.

His main work is *On the Trinity*, written before 251. He defends God the Creator as one, and the Son as true God and true man, against Marcion,* Docetists, Adoptionists, and Modalists. He mentions the Holy Spirit only briefly. *On Jewish Foods* shows that Christians are not bound to Jewish dietary laws. *On Spectacles* urges Christians not to attend pagan shows. *On the Good of Modesty* encourages virginity, chastity, and fidelity in marriage. Two letters from Novatian to Cyprian* are preserved among Cyprian's letters.

Novatian's *On the Trinity*, sometimes called the first great Latin contribution to theology from Rome, is typical of pre-Nicene theology. He never uses the word "trinity," or calls the Holy Spirit "God" or "person." The book is mainly concerned with demonstrating the Son's divinity and the unity of Father and Son. Novatian based the work on the Roman Creed and presented it as an explication of the rule of faith.

Bibliography

A. CCSL 4 (Turnhout, 1972); *Novatian: The Writings*, trans. Russel J. De Simone, FC 67 (Washington, D.C., 1974).

B. DSAM 11:479–83; DTC 11:816–49; EEC 2:604; NCE 10:534–35; ODCC 1165; TRE 24:678–82; H. J. Vogt, *Coetus Sanctorum. Der Kirchenbegriff des Novatian und die Geschichte seiner Sonderkirche* (Bonn, 1968).

Joseph T. Lienhard

NYGREN, ANDERS (15 November 1890, Göteborg, Sweden—20 October 1978, Lund). *Education*: studied at Univ. of Lund, 1912; Ph.D., Univ. of Lund, 1921. *Career*: ordained, 1912; assistant professor, philosophy of religion, Univ. of Lund, 1921–24; professor of systematic theology, Univ. of Lund, 1924–49; bishop of Lund, 1949–58; president, Lutheran World Federation, 1947–52.

Nygren was the Lund theologian who developed the method of "motif research." Being a student at Lund, he experienced the influence of Nathan Söderblom* and Einar Billing* only indirectly. As faculty colleagues, Gustaf Aulén* and Nygren were mutually stimulating, and the younger man enthusiastically adopted and adapted the periodization of *Christus Victor* for his own purposes.

He began as a philosopher of religion and remained concerned with epistemology. Since theology is a science about the faith, he concluded that its questions are best answered historically. Hence, he focused on the *patterns* in

Christianity. In his classic *Agape and Eros*, he uses Aulén's luminaries, Irenaeus* (with Marcion* as his foil) and Luther,* to demonstrate that "love" (rather than "lust" or "law") is the central Christian motif. The question of motif, however, misses Aulén's (and Wingren's*) thrust; so it is odd that his concept quickly came to define "Lundensian theology."

Motif research, apart from a welter of Swedish dissertations, has had little influence; more significantly, Nygren ignores the technique in his useful and theologically vigorous commentary on Romans and returns to the philosophical issue in a treatise on methodology he wrote during his retirement. His analytical work was original; others have imitated the technique without exhilarating results.

By identifying love as the characteristic motif of the Christian faith, Nygren opens himself to the charge of distorting the Christian tradition in three ways: (1) he flattens the complexities and denies the tensions in Christian revelation, failing to preserve the paradoxes his historic lights (Irenaeus and Luther) insisted upon; (2) he transforms theology into ideas with a history, thus preventing reflection on the Bible as a word that addresses one in the present; (3) he makes the New Testament and Christ the starting point for Christian theology, transcendentalizing a faith that is intended for life within creation.

He was active in the pre–World War II World Conferences on Faith and Order (1927, 1937) and in the World Council of Churches after its formation (1948). He was elected first president of the Lutheran World Federation when that confessional body was organized in Lund (1947). As bishop, he served the Church of Sweden faithfully and encouraged others' scholarship; in his retirement, as in his career, he was constantly active as writer, speaker, and adviser, domestically and ecumenically.

Bibliography

A. *Agape and Eros*, 2 vols. (1932, 1939; rev., Philadelphia, 1953); *Commentary on Romans* (Philadelphia, 1949); *Essence of Christianity* (London, 1960); *The Significance of the Bible for the Church* (Philadelphia, 1963); *Meaning and Method: Prolegomena to a Scientific Philosophy of Religion and a Scientific Theology* (London, 1972); ed. *This Is the Church* (Philadelphia, 1952); "Intellectual Autobiography," in *Philosophy and Theology of Anders Nygren*, ed. Charles W. Kegley (Carbondale, Ill., 1970), 3–29.

B. TRE 24:711–15; Edgar M. Carlson, *The Reinterpretation of Luther* (Philadelphia, 1948); Bernard Erling, *Nature and History* (Lund, 1960); idem, "Swedish Theology from Nygren to Wingren," *Religion in Life* 30 (1960–61): 196–208; Nels R. S. Ferré, *Swedish Contributions to Modern Theology* (New York, 1939); Gustaf Wingren, *Theology in Conflict* (London, 1958).

David T. Priestley

O

OCCAM, WILLIAM. *See* WILLIAM OF OCKHAM.

OCKHAM. *See* WILLIAM OF OCKHAM.

OECOLAMPADIUS [HUSZGEN], JOHANNES (1482, Weinsberg–24 November 1531, Basel). *Education*: studied law at Bologna, theology at Heidelberg, Tübingen, and Basel, 1500–10. *Career*: cathedral preacher, Basel, 1515; entered Briggitine monastery near Augsburg, 1520; pastor, Basel, 1522–31.

Oecolampadius ("'lantern," a reference to his commitment to humanistic studies) was a Swiss reformer who helped institute evangelical reforms in Basel and Bern in the 1520s. Early in his career he became part of the humanist circle of Melanchthon* and Reuchlin and helped Erasmus* complete the annotations to his Greek edition of the New Testament. Although Oecolampadius seemed in favor of the Reformation, in 1520 he surprised his friends by entering a monastery, where he studied the church fathers and Luther.* He became a pastor in Basel in 1522, and, openly embracing the Reformation, helped that city to achieve unity in its commitment to reforms. He was also instrumental in the move of Bern to a Reformed position. Never an original or influential theologian, Oecolampadius defended Zwingli's* interpretation of the Eucharist throughout his career, most notably at the Marburg Colloquy of 1529, and labored to establish a Reformed ecclesiastical order in Basel. In poor health for much of his life, he died just weeks after Zwingli's death in 1531.

Bibliography

A. Ernst Staehlin, *Briefe und Akten zum Leben (tm)kolampads: Zum vierhundertjährringen Jubiläum der Basler Reformation*, 2 vols. (Leipzig, 1927); idem, *Das theologische*

Lebenswerk Johannes Oekolampads (1939; repr. New York, 1971); idem, *Ökolampad-Bibliographie*, 2d ed. (Nieuwkoop, 1963).

B. DTC 11:947–51; LThK² 7:1125–26; NCE 10:648; ODCC 1175; OEncR 3:169–71; RGG 4:1567–68; TRE 25:29–36; Karl Hammer, "Der Reformator Oekolampad, 1482–1531," in *Reformiertes Erbe*, ed. Heiko Oberman (Zurich, 1992), 1:157–70.

Anthony D. DiStefano

OLIVI, PETER JOHN (1247/48, Serignan, France–1298, Narbonne). *Education*: entered the Franciscan order at the Franciscan convent in Béziers, 1260; studied at Paris in 1260s and early 1270s. *Career*: served as lector in the Franciscan convents at Montpellier and Narbonne; aided a papal commission in the composition of the bull *Exiit qui seminat*, 1279; began writing biblical commentaries, 1279–82; censured by a commission of seven Parisian scholars for some philosophical, theological, and disciplinary opinions, 1283; works banned; defended himself, 1285–87; rehabilitated at general chapter of Montpellier, 1287; appointed lector at convent of Santa Croce, Florence, 1287; appointed lector at Montpellier, 1289; wrote his last work, a commentary on the Apocalypse, 1297.

An original philosopher and theologian, a prolific biblical commentator, and a courageous reformer, Peter Olivi ranks as one of the most interesting and accomplished—and least well-understood—thinkers of the high Middle Ages. Almost altogether ignored until the twentieth century, he is now recognized as a figure of versatile talent and original opinion: an innovative economic thinker, an early exponent of nominalism, the first to express a doctrine of papal infallibility, and an opponent of the idea that marriage was a sacrament in the true sense of the term.

Olivi is best known for his disciplinary and apocalyptic views. He was a vigorous defender of the idea that the Franciscan implied in his vow a promise to bind himself not only to renunciation of property but to the strictest possible use of material goods (*usus pauper*). This position did much to split the order into two distinct wings in the late thirteenth century. Meanwhile, in his Apocalypse commentary and in other biblical commentaries as well, Olivi, basing his views on the works of Joachim of Fiore* (ca. 1135–1202), announced that the third great age (*status*) of salvation history had been inaugurated by Francis and his followers. More daringly, he insisted that the beginning of this era was marked by resistance to these "spiritual men" by an unholy, carnal alliance of ecclesiastical leaders and thinkers, an alliance that would eventually involve the papacy—a prophecy that seemed eerily fulfilled in the actions of John XXII in the fourteenth century.

When Olivi died in 1298, the minister general of the order, John of Murrovalle, renewed persecution of the Spiritual wing of the order, and Olivi's writings were again placed under ban. At this point, Olivi's followers began to accept Olivi's apocalyptic views as inspired prophecy, the church as the great harlot of Babylon, and Olivi himself as an actor in the apocalyptic drama. Olivi's tomb soon became a popular pilgrimage site. In 1312 the Council of Vienne condemned views that were traceable to Olivi's writings. Six years later, Pope John XXII launched an investigation that finally resulted in the condemnation, in 1326, of Olivi's Apocalypse commentary and probably of several of his other writings. Despite being banned often, Olivi's writings remained influential in Franciscan circles for about another century.

Bibliography

A.   Most of Olivi's writings are unedited and untranslated; see, however, *Quaestiones in Secundum Librum Sententiarum*, ed. B. Jansen, 3 vols. (Quaracchi, 1922–26); *Lectura super Apocalypsim*, ed. in W. Lewis, "Peter John Olivi: Prophet of the Year 2000," diss. Tübingen, 1976; *Olivi's Rule Commentary*, ed. D. Flood (Wiesbaden, 1972); *De Usu Paupere: The Quaestio and the Tractatus*, ed. D. Burr (Florence, 1992).

B.   DSAM 11:751–62; DTC 11:982–91; LThK² 7:1149–50; NCE 11:219–20; ODCC 1183; TRE 25:239–42; David Burr, *The Persecution of Peter Olivi* (Philadelphia, 1976); idem, *Olivi and Franciscan Poverty* (Philadelphia, 1989); idem, *Olivi's Peaceable Kingdom: A Reading of the Apocalypse Commentary* (Philadelphia, 1993).

Kevin Madigan

ORIGEN (ca. 185–ca. 253). Origen was reared in Alexandria. His parents were Christians, evidently wealthy enough to afford him a splendid education in standard Hellenistic curriculum: the study of Greek literature along with mathematics and astronomy. They also saw to it that he was taught from the Christian Scriptures and, given his phenomenal mastery of the Bible as an adult, we may well believe reports that he displayed precocious understanding of it as a child. Around 203 Origen's father died during a persecution under Septimius Severus, who attempted to stem the spread of the church by targeting converts and catechists. The accompanying confiscation of his father's estate left Origen responsible for his family, which he was able to support by the respected occupation of a *grammateus*, a teacher of Greek literature.

With the patronage of a wealthy Christian woman, he was able to further his own studies, learning philosophy from Ammonius Saccas, a noted Platonist who also taught Origen's younger pagan contemporary, Plotinus. By his own testimony, Origen was also exposed during this period to Gnostic teaching, which he opposed as contrary to the church's rule of faith. Although, curiously, he does not say so in any of his extant writings, we have strong reason to presume that, during his youth, he also studied under Clement of Alexandria,* whose theological writings adumbrate many themes that Origen would develop more fully and systematically. Although the Jewish presence in Alexandria seems to have been weak in Origen's time, he became familiar there with the works of Philo, to which Clement probably introduced him, and sought help with Hebrew and insights from Jewish exegetical traditions from at least one Jewish teacher.

Some years after his father's death, Origen appears to have undergone a conversion to a rigorously ascetic life. Abandoning his occupation as a *grammateus* along with his books of Greek literature, he devoted himself entirely to the study and teaching of the Bible, imperiling his own life by serving as a catechist. It seems that Origen's youthful ascetic enthusiasm led him to follow what he then took to be a counsel of self-castration in Mt 19:12, an act and an interpretation that he later regretted. Origen matured as a Christian teacher at a time when the role of the lay teacher in the Alexandrian Christian community was challenged by the increasing authority of Bishop Demetrius over the teaching of the church. Origen, himself, while submitting to the church's rule of faith and always open to informed criticism, considered his ability as a teacher to be a divinely be-stowed charism and a talent he was obligated to employ. Another wealthy lay patron, Ambrosius, whom Origen's teaching had won away from Gnosticism, encouraged and enabled Origen to begin his phenomenal career as a writer by furnishing him with a staff of copyists and calligraphers to transcribe notes from his lectures and turn them into books. As his fame spread even to the imperial family (no longer hostile to Christianity) his position with Bishop Demetrius became increasingly untenable.

In 231 Origen left Alexandria permanently for Caesarea, where he had been ordained a presbyter by Bishop Theoctistus. In Caesarea he continued to publish, becoming one of the most prolific authors of antiquity, had the opportunity to preach as well as to teach, and was involved on at least two occasions in ex-amining bishops for heresy. Unlike Alexandria, Caesarea had a flourishing Jew-ish community with which Origen had extensive, if touchy, intellectual relations. He died around 253 as a result of injuries sustained in 251 under torture during the Decian persecution.

Because he wrote so much and because he was condemned as a heretic after his death, only a relatively small part of Origen's oeuvre survives, often only in Latin translations. Even so, far more remains to us from him than any other author before the fourth century. Origen's works fell into four distinct categories: learned books (*tomoi*), homilies, dialogues, and letters. Most of the books are multivolume scriptural commentaries, usually expounding a single biblical book verse by verse, but occasionally treating selected passages. We possess some whole volumes of his commentaries on John and Matthew in the original Greek and parts or abridgments of his commentaries on the Song of Songs, Matthew, and Romans in Latin translations. Other commentaries, including his massive works on Genesis and the Psalms, survive only in disconnected fragments, if at all. Other books were occasional treatises: eight volumes *Against Celsus* (*Contra Celsum*), four volumes *On First Principles* (*De Principiis, Peri Archôn*), *On Prayer, Exhortation to Martyrdom*, and *On the Passover*. As an apology for Christianity, the *Contra Celsum* can only be compared to Augustine's *City of God*, which it far excels in erudition and in the seriousness of its engagement with the classical intellectual tradition. Twenty homilies on Jeremiah and one of 1 Samuel survive in Greek, and 184 more on various books (all from the Old Testament except for a series on Luke) in Latin translations. These consti-tute our only significant window on preaching in the pre-Constantinian church. One dialogue, the *Dialogue with Heracleides*, survives, as do a handful of let-ters. His single most massive work, the *Hexapla*, a word-for-word comparison of the various Greek translations of the Old Testament, also survives only in fragments. All of these works, including the treatises occasioned by particular issues, testify to a life absorbed in the study of Scripture.

Origen's critical appropriation of the various intellectual traditions to which his rich education exposed him marks him as one of the great synthetic geniuses of the western tradition. He had the best philosophical training of any Christian author in antiquity, and he had learned from Philo and Clement of Alexandria how to relate philosophy to the Bible through a symbolic interpretation of biblical language. His training as a *grammateus* equipped him with highly sophisticated skills for the establishment and interpretation of texts that he also applied to the Bible. His skill as a biblical interpreter, particularly of the Pauline epistles, is now being appreciated. Origen believed that the rigorous exercise of the intellect in the study of the Bible provided a means, along with prayer and good works, for the progressive personal transformation of the soul. Biblical study was therefore the heart of his scholarship, and his theology had no larger goal than putting biblical study into an overall context.

In this effort he was anticipated by the Gnostic theologians of the second century, notably Valentinus, Basilides, and Marcion.* They, nonetheless, called the integrity of the Bible into question by denying the identity of the God and Father of Jesus Christ with the God of the Old Testament who created the world and gave the Law to Moses. Valentinus also seemed to call into question human moral responsibility by claiming that rational beings are saved by nature. The need to oppose them stimulated him to develop a full and coherent system based on the rule of faith. He expounded this system in *On First Principles*, the first work of systematic theology per se in the Christian tradition. *On First Principles* is a complex book that sets forth the church's rule of faith as Origen understood it in its introduction, where he claims that the Apostles had passed on this rule of faith, not with the intention of making it the last word, but fully expecting that more intelligent Christians, inspired by the Holy Spirit, would seek out the underlying connections between the individual doctrines they passed on to the church.

On First Principles does not encompass all of Christian theology (there is, notably, no discussion of the church or of the sacraments, both of which Origen did discuss elsewhere in his works) but deals with those aspects of theology that Origen identified as most vital for the attainment of spiritual perfection; these are, by his account (*On First Principles* 4, 2, 7) the doctrines of God, of the nature and work of Christ, of the nature of rational creatures and their fall and redemption, of the world and why it exists, and of the nature of evil. In addition to these Origen deals with free choice of the will and biblical interpretation. In his exposition of the doctrine of God, Origen argues that God (the Father) is one and utterly simple and, hence, incorporeal. God's Son or Word, having his own individual existence (*hypostasis*) mediates between the simple unity of God and the complex multiplicity of the cosmos. Various aspects (Greek: *epinoiai*) of the Son meet the needs of rational beings on every level of distance from God. A third divine hypostasis, the Holy Spirit, inspires and sanctifies those rational beings that have become children by adoption through the Son. Although they receive their being from the Father, the ultimate source of all existence, the Son and Holy Spirit did not come into existence in time and so are coeternal with the Father. This doctrine of eternal generation is Origen's signal contribution to the doctrine of the Trinity as it developed in the fourth century.

At a lower level of being are created rational beings (*logikoi*), which were created to know and enjoy God. Almost all of these beings, however, have fallen to some degree or another from their original unity with God. The material world was created by God as a means whereby these rational beings, now called souls (*psychai*) because of their having cooled (*psychesthai*) from their original ardor for God, will freely choose to return to him. In Origen's thought God's providence extends the divine plan of salvation (*oikonomia*) to each individual rational being, arranging circumstances so that it will repent of its sinful state of alienation. In this process, more advanced rational beings assist those less advanced. These include the angels, who do not require material bodies; the stars, clothed in ethereal bodies and witnessing by their ordered movements to the divine order; and human spiritual teachers. Adverse powers, the demons, who have fallen too far for material bodies to be helpful, oppose the soul's progress. One rational being, the soul of Christ, did not fall at all but, by its steadfast devotion, became utterly united with the Logos. The preexistent soul of Christ became the means whereby the Logos was united, in the Incarnation, with a full human being in such a way that the properties of his divinity became those of his humanity, and vice versa. Origen's understanding of the Incarnation thus also foreshadowed later dogmatic developments. Origen's eschatology involved the return of created order to a state like that which it had had originally, with all rational creatures united to God. He expected that this process would take many successive world-ages.

Origen's influence on many aspects of Christian thought was immense. He provided much of the intellectual foundation for later Christian dogma and was the father of serious Christian biblical study in all of its aspects, from the establishment of the text itself to its interpretation. His understanding of human life as an opportunity for transformation into the image of God was also highly influential in the development of Christian spirituality, inspiring such important early monastic figures as Antony of Egypt and Evagrius Ponticus.* In addition, Origen, by virtue of his dedication, intelligence, and ability to appropriate new ideas critically, still provides a model for Christian scholarship.

Bibliography

A. PG 11–17; critical editions in GCS and SC; *On First Principles*, trans. G. W. Butterworth (London, 1937); *Contra Celsum*, trans. Henry Chadwick, rev. ed. (Cambridge, 1965); *Homilies on Genesis and Exodus* and *Commentary on the Gospel According to John*, trans. Ronald A. Heine, FC 71, 80 and 89; *Homilies on Leviticus*, trans.

Gary Wayne Barker, FC 83; *Homilies on Luke*, trans. Joseph T. Lienhard, FC 94; *On Prayer*, trans. John J. O'Meara, ACW 19; *Commentary on the Song of Songs*, trans. R. P. Lawson, ACW 26; *Treatise on the Passover and Dialogue with Heracleides*, trans. Robert J. Daly, ACW 54.

B. DTC 11:1489–565, 1565–88; EEC 2:619–23; LThK² 7:1230–35; NCE 10:767–74; ODCC 1193–95; TRE 25:397–420; Hal Koch, *Pronoia und Paideusis: Studien über Origenes und sein Verhältnis zum Platonismus* (Berlin, 1932); Marguerite Harl, *Origène et la fonction révélatrice du Verbe incarné* (Paris, 1958); Henri Crouzel, *Bibliographie critique d'Origène; Supplément I; Supplément II* (The Hague, 1971, 1982, 1996); Pierre Nautin, *Origène: sa vie et son œuvre* (Paris, 1977); Joseph Wilson Trigg, *Origen: The Bible and Philosophy in the Third-century Church* (Atlanta, 1983); Bernhard Neuschäfer, *Origenes als Philologe* (Basel, 1987); Henri Crouzel, *Origen* (San Francisco, 1989).

Joseph W. Trigg

OSIANDER, ANDREAS (19 December, 1498, Franconia–17 October, 1552, Königsberg). *Education*: studied at Univ. of Ingolstadt, 1515. *Career*: ordained priest, Eichstätt, 1520; preacher, St. Lorenz Church, Nuremberg, 1522; joined Lutheran movement, 1522; representative at Marburg Colloquy, 1529; representative at Diet of Augsburg, 1530; signatory of Schmalkald Articles, 1537; present at the religious discussions in Hagenau and Worms, 1540–41; professor of theology, Königsberg, 1549–52.

Having studied at the University of Ingolstadt, and influenced by the humanist movement, Osiander later undertook a revision of the Vulgate Bible and a harmony of the gospels. He learned both Hebrew and Aramaic, studied Cabbalism, and by 1520 taught Hebrew at a Nuremberg monastery. A prominent Lutheran pastor at Nuremberg, Osiander held some doctrines at odds with fellow reformers: principally his doctrine of essential righteousness.

Osiander proposed that Christ, dwelling in the elect through faith according to his divinity, actually becomes the believer's righteousness, while the forgiveness of sins merited by Christ is the preparation and cause of God's conferring of the gift of righteousness, which is God himself. Osiander had put aside the forensic concept of justification (viz., the imputation of the merits of Christ in favor of an infusion of the divine nature of Christ). Hence, justification was not simply an act by which God declares the person just, but an act by which one is actually made just. For Osiander, righteousness was, therefore, more than the forgiveness of sins; for sins are covered by the essential righteousness of Christ dwelling with the believer by faith. Justification by faith is not abandoned, but radically altered, as it is no longer simply an appeal to the merits of Christ but that which unites the believer with Christ's divine nature.

His opponents argued that the righteousness of faith is the forgiveness of sins through the obedience of Christ which, through faith alone by grace, is imputed as righteousness to all believers. And while they upheld the mystical union between Christ and believers engrafted into Christ's body and sharing in his righteousness, they condemned Osiander for rejecting this spiritual bond in favor of an inappropriate mixture of the divine and human essences. Osiander had confused God's free acceptance of the sinner with God's gift of regeneration. Indeed, it was feared that Osiander had minimized the sacrificial aspect of justification, the mediatorial role of Christ, since his position too closely resembled the scholastic doctrine of infused grace rather than grace as the favor of God. The Lutherans formally rejected Osiander's doctrine in the 1577 Formula of Concord.

Bibliography

A. *Bibliographia Osiandrica: Bibliographie der gedrucken Schriften Andreas Osiander. Ä, 1496–1552*, ed. Gottfried Seebass (Nieuwkoop, 1971); *Gesamtausgabe*, vols. 1–6, ed. Gerhard Müller, vols. 7–10, ed. Gottfried Seebass (Gütersloh, 1975–95).

B.   LThK² 7:1261–63; NCE 10:806–7; ODCC 1200; OEncR 3:183–85; RGG 4:1730–31; TRE 25:507–15; Emanuel Hirsch, *Die Theologie des Andreas Osiander und ihre geschichtlichen Voraussetzungen* (Göttingen, 1919); Gottfried Seebass, *Das reformatorische Werk des Andreas Osiander*, Enzelarbeiten aus der Kirchengeschichte Bayerns, 44 (Nuremberg, 1967); Martin Stupperich, *Osiander in Preussen, 1549–1552* (Berlin, 1973).

Ian Christopher Levy

P

PAISII. *See* VELICHKOVSKY, PAISII.

PALAMAS, GREGORY (1296/97, Constantinople–14 September 1359, Thessalonica). *Education*: Palamas was born into the Byzantine nobility and raised in the circle of the imperial court. He broke off his studies upon completion of his secondary education, which grounded him in Aristotelian thought, and embraced the monastic life on Mt. Athos, following the discipline of prayer brought there by Gregory of Sinai. *Career*: Palamas became famous because of his championship in the 1330s of the Athonite hermits and, with them, of the tradition of Eastern Christian ascetics on the possibility of seeing God in this life, against charges of heresy brought by Barlaam of Calabria. In responding to Barlaam's accusations of ''Messalianism'' against the monks, Palamas wrote his greatest work, *The Triads in Defense of the Holy Hesychasts*, in which he assembled scriptural and patristic evidence for deification, arguing that the same claims his contemporaries were making to direct experience of God were already present in the authorities of the past and, further, were evidence for a distinction in God between the divine essence and the divine activities or energies. Palamas' *Triads* followed the *Hagioritic Tome*, which he wrote in 1340/41, and which the monks signed. It was this work that opened an intense debate within the Orthodox Church, which lasted for more than a decade. The debate culminated in Palamas' official vindication at local councils held at Constantinople in 1341, 1347, and 1351, where the distinction between essence and energy he had advanced was accepted as the official teaching of the Orthodox Church.

Palamas' life was not limited by his doctrinal struggles. He was elected archbishop of Thessalonica in 1347, where his pastorate was marked by the challenges of civic strife. Much of his corpus comprises sermons from this last period of his life. His notes and reflections on a year (1350–51) in Turkish captivity provide an interesting and surprisingly irenic analysis of relations between Muslims and Christians. He was likewise involved in discussions with Western Christians, where he again avoided fierce partisanship. About ten years after his death in 1369, his lifelong disciple, the patriarch Philotheos of Constantinople, saw to Palamas' canonization. He is commemorated in the Orthodox Church on the second Sunday of Great Lent.

Bibliography

A. PG 150–151; *Défense des saints hésychastes*, ed. and trans. John Meyendorff (Louvain, 1959); *Syngrammata*, ed. Boris Bobrinskoy, John Meyendorff, and P. Chrestou, 4 vols. (Thessalonica, 1962–88); *The Triads*, trans. Nicholas Gendle (New York, 1983).

B. DSAM 12:81–107; DTC 11:1735–76; LThK³ 4:1008–10; NCE 10:872–74; ODCC 713; TRE 14:200–206; John Meyendorff, *A Study of Gregory Palamas*, trans. J. Lawrence (Aylesbury, 1974); Ioannes Anastasiou, ''The Social Teaching of Saint Gregory Palamas,'' GOTR 32 (1987): 179–90; David Coffey, ''The Palamite Doctrine of God: A New Perspective,'' SVTQ 32 (1988): 329–58; Gerry Russo, ''Rahner and Palamas: A Unity of Grace,'' ibid. 157–80; George C. Papdemetriou, ''The Human Body according to Saint Gregory Palamas,'' GOTR 34 (1989): 1–9; Hannu Kamppuri, ''Theosis in der Theologie des Gregorios Palamas,'' *Luther und Theosis*, ed. S. Peura and A. Raunio (Erlangen, 1990), 49–60; Jacques Lison, ''L'energie des trois hypostases divines selon Grégoire Palamas,'' *Science et Esprit* 44 (1992): 67–77; Thomas Anastos, ''Gregory Palamas' Radicalization of the Essence, Energies, and Hypostasis Model of God,'' GOTR 38 (1993): 335–49; A. N. Williams, ''Light from Byzantium: The Significance of Palamas' Doctrine of Theosis,'' *Pro Ecclesia* 3 (1994): 483–96.

Alexander Golitzin

PALEY, WILLIAM (July 1743, Peterborough, England–25 May 1805, Lincoln, England). *Education*: B.A., Christ Coll., Cambridge, 1763. *Career*: curate, Greenwich, 1763–66; fellow, Christ Coll., 1766–75; rector, Musgrave, Cumberland, 1775–76; vicar, Dalston, 1776–77; vicar, Appleby, 1777–82; prebendary, Carlisle, 1780–82; archdeacon, Carlisle, 1782–85; chancellor, Carlisle, 1785–94; prebendary, St. Paul's cathedral, London, 1794–1805; subdean, Lincoln, 1795–1805.

Paley has been called the father of the early orthodox party of the late eighteenth and early nineteenth century. While he had a strong leaning toward a naturalistic understanding of religion, he held firmly to a supernatural revelation in the Bible, and he taught the validity of the Thirty-Nine Articles. In the tradition of Joseph Butler,* Paley was a ''rational supranaturalist'' and was convinced that he could prove by rational argument that the Deists, who denied the supranatural, were wrong. He taught that reason forces human beings to posit the supernatural. Paley popularized the argument that the complexity of creation points to a creator, just as a watch requires that there be a watchmaker. From a watch we infer a maker; so from the wonderful adaptation of the human body, the eye, the hand, the muscles, we infer an almighty designer. In his last major work, *Natural Theology* (1802), he presented the eighteenth-century argument from design for the existence of God in its classic form: ''There cannot be design without a designer.'' This wonderfully complex world could not have been the result of blind, unthinking chance. In *Natural Theology*, Paley successfully established the reasonableness and probability of a theistic understanding of the universe.

The argument from design proved the existence of God, who made the divine will the rule of human action and has revealed that will to the world. Paley taught that actions are to be judged by their consequences. His ethical position was a severe utilitarianism, and his canon was ''Whatever is expedient is right.'' His central ethical teaching was ''Virtue is the doing of good to mankind, in obedience to the will of God, and for the sake of everlasting happiness.'' He contended that the will of God, and consequent moral obligations, can be learned by an inquiry into the natural consequences of human action as well as from the revealed declarations of the Bible.

Another thesis Paley developed was that of the evidences of Christianity. He argued that the truth of Christianity can be affirmed because ''there is clear proof that the apostles and their successors underwent the greatest hardships rather than give up the Gospel and cease to obey its precepts.'' Furthermore, revelation is confirmed by miracles, since miracles are a work of power that only God can do. Stated simply, miracles confirm the truth of divine revelation.

Bibliography

A.   *The Works of William Paley*, ed. Alexander Chalmers, 5 vols. (London, 1819).

B.   DNB 15:101–7; NCE 10:925; ODCC 1210; RGG 5:31–32; SH 8:320–21; Martin L. Clarke, *Paley: Evidences for the Man* (London, 1974); D. L. LeMahieu, *The Mind of William Paley: A Philosopher and His Age* (Lincoln, Neb., 1976).

Donald S. Armentrout

PALMER, PHOEBE WORRALL (18 December 1807, New York, N.Y.–2 November 1874, New York, N.Y.). *Career*: lay Methodist evangelist, 1837–74; editor, *Guide to Holiness*, 1862–74.

As a spiritual consultant, revivalist lay itinerant, editor of the *Guide to Holiness*, and author of books on the spiritual life, Palmer became one of the foremost women theologians of mid-nineteenth century America. Her theology of Christian holiness emphasized entire sanctification and anticipated the holiness movement of the late nineteenth century.

Palmer viewed entire sanctification as a process that involved three progressive steps. First was a fundamental conversion to Christ and a consecration of the self to God. Second was a trusting belief in God's biblical promise to sanctify, a belief in the possibility of an entire sanctification of the human person. Third was the bearing witness to the power of sanctification in all things, leading to revivalist activity and humanitarian and social reform movements. The primary emphasis in her theology, however, was always placed upon the inner experience of holiness and union with God.

Bibliography

A.   *The Way of Holiness* (New York, 1845); *Present to My Christian Friend: Entire Devotion to God* (New York, 1845; London, 1853); *Faith and its Effects* (New York, 1846); *Incidental Illustrations of the Economy of Salvation: Its Doctrines and Duties* (New York, 1855); *Promise of the Father* (Boston, 1859); *Pioneer Experiences: The Gift of Power Received by Faith* (New York, 1867).

B.   DARB 416–17; DCA 860–61; NAW 3:12–14; Richard Wheatley, *The Life and Letters of Mrs. Phoebe Palmer* (New York, 1876); C. E. White, *The Beauty of Holiness: Phoebe Palmer as Theologian, Revivalist, Feminist, and Humanitarian* (Grand Rapids, Mich., 1986); H. B. Raser, *Phoebe Palmer: Her Life and Thought* (Lewiston, N.Y., 1987).

Patrick W. Carey

PARKER, MATTHEW (6 August 1504, Norwich, England–17 May 1575, London). *Education*: studied at St. Mary's Hostel, Cambridge Univ.; B.A., M.A., B.D., D.D., Corpus Christi Coll., Cambridge Univ., 1527, 1528, 1535, 1537. *Career*: ordained 1527; chaplain to Anne Boleyn, 1535–36; dean, Coll. of St. John the Baptist, Stoke-by-Clare, Suffolk, 1535–47; rector, Ashen (Ashdon), 1542–44; master and vice-chancellor, Corpus Christi Coll., 1544–52; dean, Lincoln Cathedral, 1552–53; archbishop of Canterbury, 1559–75.

Parker was the first archbishop of Canterbury under Queen Elizabeth and was responsible for enacting and enforcing the Elizabethan Settlement. While at Cambridge he belonged to a group called the "Cambridge Reformers," who helped to bring the Reformation to England. At first Parker was attracted to the teachings of Martin Luther* but then moved away from Luther as he studied more deeply the patristic literature. He supported the publication of *The Institute of a Christian Man* (1537), known as the *Bishops' Book*, which was a commentary on the Ten Articles. The Ten Articles were Henry VIII's greatest concessions to the Protestants. Martin Bucer,* the reformer at Strasbourg, was Regius professor of divinity at Cambridge, 1549–1551, and had a great influence on Parker. Bucer represented a moderating position between Ulrich Zwingli* and Martin Luther.

Parker's primacy as archbishop of Canterbury was one of the most important in the history of the English church. He had to work between the extremes of the Marian party, which wanted to restore the Church of England to Roman obedience and medieval theology, and the extreme reforming party, at first called "precisianists," and then Puritans, who wanted to aggressively reform the Church of England with regard to ceremonial and theology. Parker's great success was to steer the Church of England between these two extremes, and it has been suggested that in so doing he orginated the *via media*, which is the primary characteristic of Anglicanism. He was evangelical but conservative, and catholic but reformed. He applied the broad principles of the Reformation to the Church of England without betraying the catholicity of the church.

Under Parker's leadership, the "42 Articles" were revised and issued in 1563, and published in 1571 as the "39 Articles." He supervised the translation of the "Bishops' Bible," which was published in 1568 and which superceded Tyndale's translation and the "Geneva Bible" of 1560. It remained the official English version until the publication of the Authorized Version in 1611.

Bibliography

A.   *Correspondence of Matthew Parker . . . Comprising Letters Written by and to Him, from A.D. 1535, to His Death, A.D. 1575*, ed. John Bruce and Thomas T. Perowne (Cambridge, 1853).

B.   DNB 15:254–64; LThK² 8:105–6; NCE 10:1023–24; ODCC 1222; RGG 5:114–15; SH 8:358–59; John Strype, *The Life and Acts of Matthew Parker*, 3 vols. (Oxford, 1821); W. M. Kennedy, *Archbishop Parker* (London, 1908); Victor John Knight Brook, *A Life of Archbishop Parker* (Oxford, 1962).

Donald S. Armentrout

PARKER, THEODORE (24 August 1810, Lexington, Mass.–10 May 1860, Florence, Italy). *Education*: studied at Harvard Coll., 1830–34; Harvard Div. Sch., 1834–37; honorary M.A., Harvard, 1840. *Career*: taught grammar school in and around Boston, 1827–32; editor, *Scriptural Interpreter*, 1835–37; ordained Unitarian minister, 1837; pastor, Second Church of West Roxbury, Mass., 1837–47; minister, Boston's Twenty-Eighth Congregational Society, Boston, 1847–59; editor, *Massachusetts Quarterly Review*, 1848–51.

Parker battled conservative Unitarianism his whole career and articulated a faith which led to political activism. While at Harvard, he read voraciously, especially Kant, Hegel, Schelling, Fichte, Jacobi, and Schleiermacher.* Like Emerson,* he broke with Unitarianism's orthodoxy, which was driven by Lockean epistemology and Enlightenment anthropology. He championed instead a religion based on the theology of Schleiermacher. On 19 May 1841, in a landmark sermon, "The Transient and Permanent in Christianity," he publicly sided with the liberal "Transcendentalists" against the conservative Unitarians. He developed three major points: the separation of form and content in absolute religion, the anthropology and Christology of consciousness, and reform of the church, which implies the reform of society. For Parker, social reform meant the abolition of slavery, equal rights for women and the poor, and free public education.

In his major theological work, *A Discourse on Matters Pertaining to Religion*, he defined absolute religion as perfect obedience to the law of God and the service of God by normal use, development, and discipline of all human attributes. More than Emerson and many other Transcendentalists, he stressed service to the underclasses. Love of neighbor, or charity, as a natural consequence to the love of God, led him to political activism.

Rooted in self-consciousness, religious sensibility and morality are developmental processes for Parker because he believed that self-consciousness itself is developmental. Religious sensibility and morality are found in every act of cognition because the human self-consciousness is tacitly aware of its finitude and utter dependence upon the infinite or absolute consciousness. This sense of utter dependence engenders piety and worship. The essence of absolute religion is the awareness that one is absolutely dependent on a mysterious "Other" who has caused one's being. The urge to worship this Other and deal morally with other finite creatures distinguishes the human being from all other finite beings and is the essence of religion.

For Parker, absolute religion mandates social change because love for God necessarily demands practical love for humanity; the total development of one's individual attributes demands that persons afford others the same opportunities that they have had. Thus, slavery, repression of women and the poor, and lack of opportunity due to poor education were immoral. Parker considered republican, industrial democracy the most advanced and best form of civil polity that the human race had found to date.

Bibliography

A.   *The Collected Works of Theodore Parker*, ed. Frances Power Cobbe, 14 vols. (London, 1863–71); *The Works of Theodore Parker, Centenary Edition*, 15 vols. (Boston, 1907–13).

B.   DAB 14:238–41; DARB 420–21; NCAB 2:377–78; NCE 10:1024; SH 8:359–61; O. B. Frothingham, *Theodore Parker: A Biography* (Boston, 1876); John Weiss, *Life and Correspondence of Theodore Parker*, 2 vols. (New York, 1864); John E. Dirks, *The Critical Theology of Theodore Parker* (New York, 1948).

John P. Fitzgibbons

PARSCH, PIUS, born Johann (18 May 1884, Olmütz, Moravia–11 March 1954, Klosterneuburg, Austria). *Education*: sem., Klosterneuburg, 1904–8; theology doctorate, Vienna, 1912. *Career*: entered Augustinian Canons, Klosterneuburg, 1904; ordained priest, 1905; chair in pastoral theology, Klosterneuburg, 1913–15, 1918–38; founder and first editor, *Bibel und Liturgie*, 1926; retirement, 1938–54.

A pastoral theologian and major figure in the liturgical movement, Parsch learned love for the church's liturgy from Guéranger's* *L'Année liturgique* and Wolter's *Psallite Sapienter*. Dismayed by the laity's ignorance of the liturgy, Parsch devoted his life to fostering popular liturgical understanding and participation. He reinstituted ancient liturgical practices, such as daily Lauds and Mass facing the people, and inaugurated a dialogue Mass with congregational singing of the propers, Kyrie, Sanctus and Agnus Dei (*"Betsingmesse"*). He also published pastoral liturgical writings of all sorts, including his widely influential commentary on the church year, *Das Jahr des Heiles* (1929). In everything

Parsch presented the Bible and the liturgy as complementary manifestations of the one mystery of Christ.

Parsch's writings are valuable today, not so much for their scholarship that shared the archaistic tendency of his time to value ancient forms simply because of their age, but for their ability to instill love of the liturgy and their pastoral spirit of encouraging experimentation to promote greater liturgical participation.

Bibliography

A. *The Liturgy of the Mass,* trans. Frederic Eckhoff (St. Louis, Mo., 1936); *The Church's Year of Grace*, trans. Daniel Coogan, Jr., 5 vols. (Collegeville, Minn., 1953–59).

B. LThK² 8:111; NCE 10:1040; Charles Rauch, ''Pius Parsch (1884–1954),'' *La Maison-Dieu*, 40 bis (1954): 150–56; Norbert Höslinger and Theodor Maas-Ewerd, ed., *Mit sanfter Zähigkeit* (Klosterneuburg, 1979).

John D. Laurance

PASCAL, BLAISE (19 June 1623, Clermont, France–19 August 1662, Paris). *Education*: studied under the exclusive direction of his father, Etienne Pascal, a noted mathematician and physicist. *Career*: first published work in mathematics, *Essai sur coniques*, 1641; invention, elaboration, and marketing of first calculating machine, 1643–47; publication of preliminary researches on the vacuum, 1647; publication of a treatise on the equilibrium of liquids, 1648; more research on the vacuum published, 1651; three treatises in physics and mathematics written (published posthumously); materials gathered for an *apologie* for the Christian religion, 1656–62 (published posthumously in 1670 as the *Pensées*); publication of the *Provincial Letters*, 1656–57; a treatise on divine grace and another on the elements of geometry written (published posthumously); publication of a treatise on the cycloid, 1658; inauguration of public transport in Paris, 1662.

Pascal, one of the grand figures of France's *grand siècle*, contributed substantially to both the religious and intellectual achievements of the seventeenth century. His pioneer research in mathematics and theoretical physics earned him the plaudits of savants all over Europe. But his fertile mind also concentrated upon the solution of practical problems of continuing significance, as witness his invention of the first calculating machine and, on the very eve of his death, his successful scheme to provide mass transport in a large city. And in the course of his work he became, perhaps unconsciously, one of the creators of modern French prose.

As a religious thinker, Pascal can offer no particular originality. He was a product rather of the great revival in French Catholicism that was itself part of the continent-wide revival of religion associated with the Reformation and the Counter-Reformation. One strand of this heightened spiritual awareness in both public and private life was that set of doctrinal and moral attitudes called Jansenism—after the Flemish theologian and bishop, Cornelius Jansen* (d. 1638), who claimed to follow the genuine teaching of St. Augustine.* The Jansenist creed rested upon a sharp distrust of the role of human freedom in the process of justification, and its code imposed a collection of extremely austere norms of conduct. Although Jansenism was condemned first by the French hierarchy and the Sorbonne, and then by a series of papal pronouncements, its influence perdured and spread within the Catholic community over the succeeding three centuries.

Pascal underwent his "first conversion" to Jansenist principles in 1647. This experience, largely an intellectual one, was immeasurably intensified seven years later by what he himself called "the night of fire"—a searing confrontation with "the God of Abraham, Isaac, and Jacob, not the God of the philosophers and scholars, the God of Jesus Christ." From this time onward Pascal devoted himself to the defense of Jansenism—most notably in *The Provincial Letters*, a savagely witty assault upon the Jansenists' powerful enemies, the French Jesuits—and to the elaboration of his own inner spirituality. This latter activity resulted in several treatises on grace and conversion, and most particularly in the accumulation of materials intended to produce a methodical apologetic for the Christian religion. Published only after his death, these fragments came to form one of the greatest of all spiritual testaments, the *Pensées*.

Bibliography

A.   *Oeuvres*, ed. Jacques Chevalier (Paris, 1954, 1965); *Pensées* (London, 1966); *The Provincial Letters* (London, 1967).

B.   DSAM 12:279–91; DTC 11:2074–2203; LThK² 8:125–26; NCE 10:1046–48; ODCC 1224–25; RGG 5:132–34; TRE 26:37–43; Fortunat Strowski, *Pascal et son temps*, 3 vols. (Paris, 1922); Albert Béguin, *Pascal* (Paris, 1952); Henri Gouhier, *Blaise Pascal. Commentaires* (Paris, 1962); Buford Norman, *Portraits of Thought: Knowledge, Methods, and Styles in Pascal* (Columbus, Ohio, 1988); Marvin R. O'Connell, *Blaise Pascal: Reasons of the Heart* (Grand Rapids, Mich., 1997).

Marvin R. O'Connell

PASCHASIUS RADBERTUS (ca. 790, Soissons–ca. 859). Educated in Soissons, Radbertus entered the abbey of Corbie under abbot Adalard (cousin of Charlemagne, d. 826), and was elected abbot 843–44. He represented the monastery at the councils of Paris (847) and Quierzy (849), resigning as abbot in 851 to live and study for a time at Saint-Riquier, though he soon returned to Corbie. He is perhaps best remembered for his work *On the Body and Blood of the Lord*, the first systematic treatment of the Eucharist. It defends a strong doctrine of the Real Presence. The Body of Christ, present "in truth" and not "in figure," is identical to Christ's historical body. Ratramnus,* his fellow monk at Corbie, opposed this position.

Radbertus' Marian works are important in the history of the dogmas of the Virgin Birth and the Assumption. Radbertus' work is rooted in an excellent acquaintance with the Fathers, as exemplified in his commentaries on Matthew and on Lamentations. The latter balances remarkably both literal and spiritual senses.

Bibliography

A. *De benedictionibus patriarcharum*, CCCM 96; *De corpore et sanguine Domini*, CCCM 16; *De partu virginis; De assumptione . . . virginis*, CCCM 56C; *Expositio in lamentationes Hieremiae*, CCCM 85; *Expositio in Matheo*, CCCM 56–56B; PL 120.

B. LThK³ 7:1411–12; NCE 10:1050; ODCC 1227–28; SH 9:380–81; Max Manitius, *Geschichte der lateinischen Literatur des Mittelalters*, 2d ed. 1:401–11 (Munich, 1911); Henri Peltier, *Pascase Radbert abbé de Corbie* (Amiens, 1938); G. Gliozzo, *La dottrina della conversione eucaristica in Pascasio Radberto et Ratramno* (Palermo, 1945); H. Weisweiler, "Paschasius Radbertus als Vermittler des Gedankengutes der karolingischen Renaissance in den Matthäuskommentaren des Kreises um Anselm von Laon," *Scholastik* 35 (1960) 363–402, 503–36; G. Mathon, "Pascase Radbert et . . . l'humanisme carolingien," in Corbie: Abbaye Royale, 135–55 (Lille, 1963); David Ganz, *Corbie in the Carolingian Renaissance* (Sigmaringen, 1990).

John C. Cavadini

PASSAGLIA, CARLO (2 or 9 May 1812, Lucca, Tuscany, Italy–12 March 1887, Turin, Piedmont, Italy). *Education*: studied philosophy and theology, Roman Coll., 1827–37. *Career*: entered Jesuits, 1827; prefect of studies, Germanicum, Rome, 1840–44; professor of dogmatic theology, Roman Coll., 1845–57, Sapienza, Rome, 1858–59; dismissed from Jesuits, 1859; member, papal commission on the Italian question, 1860; exiled to Turin, 1861–87; deputy to Parliament, 1864.

Passaglia was a minor but early exponent of the renewal of scholastic philosophy and theology and was a participant on the liberal side of the so-called Italian question. He encouraged Joseph Kleutgen* to bring Jesuit scholastic philosophy and theology into line with modern German thought, particularly Kant and Hegel. He encountered opposition both to his teaching style and to his proposed renewal of the scholastic method, but during his years at the Roman College he had great influence on future theologians—Schrader, Franzelin,* Manning,* Denzinger,* Scheeben.* With Clemens Schrader's collaboration, he published a treatise on the nature of the church (1853) in which he departed from a strict scholastic approach, using patristic sources, Petavius,* and Thomassin.

After his dismissal from the Jesuits, Passaglia became involved in the Italian question. By 1861, he sided with the liberal Italian cause, opposed Pope Pius IX on the Papal States and the unification of Italy, and while in Turin he edited political journals espousing the liberal cause. After a series of publications and acts of disobedience to the pope, he was suspended from his clerical functions. In 1868 he sought reconciliation with the church, writing a positive essay on the encyclical *Aeterni Patris* of Leo XIII, and shortly before his death he made a public retractation of his faults and errors and submitted this to Cardinal Alimonda of Turin.

Bibliography

A. *De Immaculato Deiparae Virginis Conceptu* (Naples, 1855); *De Ecclesia Christi* (Regensburg, 1853).

B. DTC 11:2207–10; LThK² 8:133; NCE 10:1051–52; Sommervogel, 6:332–36.

William J. Kelly

PECKHAM, JOHN, or Pecham (ca. 1225, Patcham–1292, Canterbury). *Education*: studied probably at Lewes; studied arts, Univ. of Paris; transferred to Oxford where he joined the Franciscan order ca. 1250; studied theology, Paris, ca. 1259. *Career*: master in theology, Paris, 1269; held the Franciscan chair in theology, 1269–71; defended his order against attacks from secular masters; returned to Oxford, 1272; provincial of the English Franciscans, 1275–77; lectured in theology at the papal court (*lector sacri palatii*), 1277–79; archbishop of Canterbury, 1279–92; actively worked for ecclesiastical reform, fighting against various abuses and improving the training of the clergy.

In his theological outlook Peckham was a proponent of the Augustinian or Franciscan tradition. He was most likely inspired by Bonaventure's* Lenten sermons in the 1260s to oppose the dangers of the more radical Aristotelian thought that he encountered in Paris. He was strongly opposed to Thomas Aquinas'* teaching that there is only one substantial form in a human being; later, as archbishop of Canterbury, he even wanted that position condemned as heretical. He himself held that there are several degrees of forms—vegetative, sensitive, and rational—united in each human being. Following Augustine,* he defended the need for divine illumination in human intellectual knowledge to guarantee its necessity and certitude. His scientific interests led him to write a treatise on optics, which was influenced by Roger Bacon* and has continued to attract the interest of contemporary scholars. Though Peckham did not disapprove of the use of philosophy in theology and even adopted some Aristotelian language, he strongly opposed the sort of Aristotelian thought taught by the Dominicans, in favor of the Augustinian thought of his brother Franciscans such as Alexander of Hales* and Bonaventure. Points that Peckham held most insistently against the new Aristotelianism were the need for divine illumination, the unity of the powers of the soul with its essence, and the doctrine of seminal reasons. Though he granted to each human being an agent intellect, he also held that there was one higher agent intellect, namely, God, the light of minds. In that way he steered a middle path between Avicenna's position, which held that the tenth or agent intelligence was the source of human knowledge, and Aquinas' view, which made the agent intellect simply a part of the human soul. On this point, however, he found Avicenna preferable to Aquinas, but Augustine the best of all. Along with his interest in the Fathers, Peckham pursued various scientific inquiries, wrote commentaries on several books of the Bible, defended the poverty of his order, and was a gifted poet.

Bibliography

A. *Registrum epistolarum Johannis Peckham*, ed. Charles T. Martin (London, 1882–85); *Tractatus tres de paupertate*, ed. Charles L. Kingsford et al. (Aberdeen, 1910; repr. Farnborough, 1969); *Quaestiones de anima*, ed. H. Spettmann (Münster, 1918); *Summa de esse et essentia*, ed. F. Delorme in *Studi Francescani* 14 (1928): 1–18; *Quodlibet Romanum*, ed. idem (Rome, 1938); *Tractatus de anima*, ed. G. Melani (Florence, 1948); *John Pecham and the Science of Optics: Perspectiva communis*, ed. and trans. David C. Lindberg (Madison, Wis., 1970); *Tractatus de perspectiva*, ed. idem (St. Bonaventure, N.Y., 1972); *Quodlibeta quatuor*, ed. G. J. Etzkorn and F. Delorme (Grottaferrata, 1989); *Questions Concerning the Eternity of the World*, ed. and trans. Vincent G. Potter (New York, 1993).

B. DNB 15:635–42; DSAM 8:645–49; DTC 12:100–140; LThK³ 5:956–57; NCE 7: 1065; ODCC 1246–47; Hieronymus Spettmann, *Die Psychologie des Johannes Pecham* (Münster, 1919); André Callebut, "Jean Peckham O.F.M. et l'augustinisme," *Archivum Franciscanum Historicum* 18 (1925): 441–72; Theodore Crowley, "John Peckham O.F.M., Archbishop of Canterbury, versus the New Aristotelianism," *Bulletin of the John Rylands Library* 33 (1950/51): 242–55; Decima Douie, *Archbishop Pecham* (Oxford, 1952); Ignatius Brady, "John Peckham and the Background of Aquinas' *De aeternitate mundi*," in *St. Thomas Aquinas, 1274–1974: Commemorative Studies*, ed. B. Smalley et al. (Toronto, 1974), 2:141–78; Antoine Dondaine, "Le Quodlibet de Jean Pecham *De natali* dans la tradition manuscrite thomiste," in *Studies Honoring Charles Ignatius Brady, Friar Minor*, ed. R. Almagno (St. Bonaventure, N.Y., 1976), 199–218; Antonio Pérez Estévez, "Voluntad y Poder en los Quodlibetos de Juan Pecham," in *Les philosophies morales et politiques au Moyen Age*, ed. B. Carlos Bazán et al. (New York, 1995), 2:787–96.

Roland J. Teske

PELAGIUS (ca. 360, probably Britain–after 421, perhaps Palestine). Pelagius lived at Rome, perhaps as early as 380, where he won a considerable following through his ascetical life and moral teaching, especially among the aristocracy; gained his outspoken disciple Caelestius ca. 390 and came into contact ca. 399 with Rufinus the Syrian, who is sometimes regarded as the true founder of Pelagianism; ca. 402 publicly attacked the concept of grace he found in a line from Augustine's* *Confessions*; in Rome wrote a commentary on the letters of Paul and probably *On Nature* (*De natura*); fled Italy before the Goths in 409; passed through Carthage in 411; arrived in Palestine soon after, where he wrote the *Letter for Demetrias* and his *Defense of Free Choice* (*Pro libero arbitrio*); tried for heresy in summer of 415 at a synod in Jerusalem and in December of that year at Diospolis, where twelve bishops declared him Catholic; excommunicated by Pope Innocent in January of 417 under the influence of African bishops; returned to Rome where he was acquitted of heresy by Pope Zosimus in September of 417; definitively condemned in the spring of 418 by the Council of Carthage, by a rescript of the emperor Honorius, and soon after by the *Epistula Tractoria* of Zosimus; left Rome, probably for the East, where he died at an unknown date.

Pelagius' own teaching involved stern moral exhortations to a life of sinlessness and sanctity for which God had given human beings the means in creating them with free choice and in giving them the Mosaic Law and the teaching and example of Jesus. The grace of God was for Pelagius equivalent to the nature with which human beings are born, the teaching which God has provided, and the forgiveness of sins. Since the authenticity of many of the extant works ascribed to Pelagius is questioned and since many of his works are preserved only in fragments cited by his opponents, principally Augustine, it is difficult to know what he personally held as opposed to what he was accused of holding, and there is a strong contemporary tendency to view his teaching simply as a defense of human freedom and assertion of personal responsibility in the face of any kind of determinism. The propositions condemned by the synod of Carthage in 411 and brought as charges against Pelagius at Diospolis in 415 represent the core of Pelagian doctrine: (1) Adam was created mortal, so that he would have died whether he sinned or not; (2) the sin of Adam harmed him alone and not the human race; (3) the Law leads to the kingdom just as the Gospel does; (4) before the coming of Christ there were human beings without sin; (5) newly born infants are in the same state in which Adam was before his transgression; (6) the whole human race does not die through the death or transgression of Adam, nor does the whole human race rise through the resurrection of Christ.

Bibliography

A.   PLS 1, 1110–570; Alexander Souter, *Texts and Studies* (Cambridge, 1922–31), 5, 1–3; B. R. Rees, *The Letters of Pelagius and his Followers* (Woodbridge, N.Y., 1991); R. Evans, *Four Letters of Pelagius* (New York, 1968); Theodore de Bruyn, *Pelagius' Commentary on St. Paul's Epistle to the Romans* (New York, 1993).

B.   DSAM 13:2889–942; DTC 12:675–715; LThK² 8:246–49; NCE 11:58–60; ODCC 1248–49; TRE 26:176–85; G. de Plinval, *Pélage: ses écrits, sa vie et sa reforme* (Lausanne, 1943); Gerald Bonner, *Augustine and Modern Research on Pelagianism* (Villanova, Pa., 1972); B. R. Rees, *Pelagius: A Reluctant Heretic* (Woodbridge, N.Y., 1988); Gerald Bonner, "Augustine and Pelagianism," *Augustinian Studies* 23 (1992): 33–51; 24 (1994): 27–47.

Roland J. Teske

PERRONE, JOHN (GIOVANNI) (11 March 1794, Chieri, near Turin, Italy– 28 August 1876, Rome). *Education*: sem. theological studies, Turin, 1810–14; doctorate in theology, Turin, 1815. *Career*: entered Jesuits, 1815; professor of theology, Orvieto, 1817–24; professor of dogmatic theology, Roman Coll., 1824–48, 1853–76; residence in England, 1848–51; professor of theology, Ferrara, 1851–53; rector, Roman Coll., 1853–55.

Perrone was a dogmatic theologian and a prominent member of the so-called neoscholastic Roman School. His multivolume *Praelectiones Theologicae* (1835) was the basis of the theological formation of generations of seminarians at the Propaganda, at the Roman College, and, by reason of their thirty-four editions and translations, at many other seminaries throughout the world. He was both teacher and mentor of Passaglia,* Franzelin,* and Schrader. In 1846 when Newman* was attending lectures in theology in preparation for ordination to the Roman Catholic priesthood, he judged Perrone to be a superior dogmatic theologian but an ineffective apologist. Perrone seems to have been influenced by J. A. Möhler* in his reflections on both tradition and ecclesiology. In spite of the emphasis they gave to patristics and positive theology, however, neither Perrone nor Passaglia were very open to Newman's *Essay on the Development of Doctrine* (1845).

In addition to being a theological educator, Perrone was a theological resource person for three popes: Leo XII, Gregory XVI, and Pius IX—particularly in the polemics with rationalism (Hermes*), indifferentism (Lammenais*), and fideism (Bautain). He was also a consultor for many Roman congregations. After the departure of Passaglia and Schrader from the Roman College he helped prepare for the definition of the Immaculate Conception of the Blessed Virgin Mary. In 1869 he was appointed to a theological commission with Franzelin, Schrader, and Pecci [brother of Leo XIII] to prepare the schemata for the First Council of the Vatican. He was perceived as less brilliant than Passaglia and less solid than Franzelin; nevertheless, his theological method was clear, concise, and precise, and his more than forty major publications had an impact upon seminary education throughout the Catholic world. He modestly and successfully avoided the cardinal's red hat that Pope Pius IX wished to confer on him and lived out his days as prefect of studies in the Roman College.

Bibliography

A. *Praelectiones Theologicae*, 9 vols. (Rome: 1835, 1842); *De Romani Pontificis Infallibilitate*; *Index Alphabeticus Analyticus Rerum Quae in Universa Theologia P. Joannis Perrone Continentur, Praecedenti Synopsi Historica Theologiae Ejusdem Auctoris* (Turin, 1868).

B.   DTC 12:1255–56; Hurter 5:1496–98; Koch 1399–1400; LThK² 8:282; NCE 11: 146; ODCC, 1257; Sommervogel 6:558–71; John Henry Cardinal Newman, *Letters and Diaries* (London, 1961), 11:351–52; 12:437; 23:451.

William J. Kelly

PÉTAU, DENIS. *See* PETAVIUS, DIONYSIUS.

PETAVIUS, DIONYSIUS, Denis Pétau (21 August 1583, Orléans–11 December 1652, Paris). *Education*: M.A., Paris, 1599; studied theology, Sorbonne, 1604–7, and Univ. of Pont-à-Mousson, 1607–9. *Career*: lecturer in philosophy, Bourges, 1602–4; entered Jesuits, 1605; ordained priest, 1610; professor of rhetoric, Reims and La Flèche, 1611–21; professor of positive theology, Coll. de Clermont, Paris, 1621–44; librarian, Clermont, 1644–52.

Petavius was an anti-Jansenist Jesuit humanist and theologian who examined church doctrines and practices historically. Competent in ancient languages he became a significant collector and editor of ancient theological and ecclesiastical manuscripts, prepared a work on the chronology of world history, and argued against the rigidity and lack of historical basis for the Jansenist Antoine Arnauld's* *De la fréquente communion* (1644). His own historical analysis of the church's practices of public penance and preparation for communion demonstrated that the Jansenist position was unfounded in the tradition.

Petavius' major contribution to theology was in the area of the history of doctrine. Like the Dominican Melchior Cano* and Jesuit Juan Maldonatus (1533–83) before him, Petavius traced ecclesiastical doctrines to their genetic origins in Scripture and tradition. In his major theological work on doctrine, his unfinished *de theologicis dogmatibus*, he illustrated each doctrine by its historical development. Although he did not depart entirely from the scholastic method with its emphasis upon philosophical thought, he did criticize an overdependence upon philosophical categories in scholastic theology and tried to modify the scholastic approach by explicating the historical sources of the church's doctrine. His own dogmatic theology was written in response to both the Protestant reformers, who appealed to Scripture as the rule of faith, and the Jansenists, who claimed that the primitive purity of doctrine had been corrupted in the church's history. Like Cano and others influenced by the humanist tradition, he did not write a history of dogma or theology, but he supported a return to the sources of doctrine to demonstrate what had been believed in the church—in opposition to reformers and Jansenists alike.

Petavius did not establish a school of thought, but his historical methodology would be taken up again in French Catholicism by the Oratorian Richard Simon* at the end of the seventeenth and beginning of the eighteenth century, by Théodore de Régnon* in the nineteenth, and Jules Lebreton and Jean Daniélou* (to mention a few) in the twentieth century.

Bibliography

A. *Opus de Doctrina Temporum*, 2 vols. (Paris, 1627); *Opus de Theologicis Dogmatibus*, 4 vols. (Paris, 1644, 1650); 6 vols. (Antwerp, 1700); 8 vols. (Paris, 1865–67); *De la pénitence publique et de la préparation à la communion* (Paris, 1644).

B. DTC 12:1313–37; ECatt 9:1281–83; LThK² 8:314; NCE 11:199–200; ODCC 1260; Sommervogel 6:588–616; J. C. Vital Chatelain, *Le P. Denis Petau d'Orléans, Jésuite: Sa vie et ses oeuvres* (Paris, 1884); P. Galtier, "Petau et la préface de son De Trinitate," RechScRel (1932): 472–76; L. Karrer, *Die historisch-positive Methode des Theologen Dionysius Petavius* (Munich, 1970); Michael Hofmann, *Theologie, Dogma und Dogmenentwicklung im theologischen Werk Denis Petau's* (Bern, 1976).

Patrick W. Carey

PETER ABELARD. *See* ABELARD, PETER.

PETER AUREOLI, *Doctor facundus, Doctor ingeniosus* (ca. 1280, near Gourdon, Aquitaine–1322, Aix-en-Provence). *Education*: studied in Paris by 1304, possibly under John Duns Scotus.* *Career*: entered the Franciscan order; taught at Bologna, Toulouse, and Paris; provincial of the Franciscans of the province of Aquitaine, ca. 1320; bishop of Aix-en-Provence, 1321–22.

Peter's works include two commentaries on the first book of the *Sentences*, a treatise on poverty, an unfinished treatise on the principles of nature, a treatise on the conception of the Blessed Virgin Mary, and a compendium of the literal meaning of all of Scripture. He is famous for his defense of the Immaculate Conception of Mary. In philosophy he taught that every form is essentially the act of matter and cannot exist or be conceived apart from matter. Since the Council of Vienne (1311–12) had just decreed that the human rational soul is the form of the body, Peter was faced with a problem. His understanding of form made the immortality of such a soul impossible to understand and also seemed to eliminate the possibility of any intellectual knowledge. Peter evaded this difficulty by arguing that the council may oblige one to accept its teaching, though one is not obliged to understand it—anymore than one is obliged to understand the Trinity.

Bibliography

A.   *Commentariorum in primum librum sententiarum* (Rome, 1596–1605; repr. St. Bonaventure, N.Y., 1953).

B.   DTC 12:1810–81; LThK² 8:350; NCE 11:210–11; TRE 26:283–85; Raymundus Dreiling, *Der Konzeptualismus in der Universalienlehre des Franziskanererzbischofs Petrus Aureoli* (Münster, 1913); Paul Vignaux, *Justification et prédestination au XIV⁴ siècle. Duns Scot, Pierre d'Auriole, Guillaume d'Occam, Grégoire de Rimini* (Paris, 1934); Rainulf Schmucker, *Propositio per se nota: Gottesbeweis und ihr Verhältnis nach Petrus Aureoli* (Werl, 1941); Calvin Normore, ''Petrus Aureoli and His Contemporaries on Future Contingents and Excluded Middle,'' *Synthese* 96 (1993): 83–92; Dominik Perler, ''What Am I Thinking About? Duns Scotus and Peter Aureol on Intentional Objects,'' *Vivarium* 32 (1994): 72–89.

Roland J. Teske

PETER DAMIAN (ca. 1007, Ravenna–1071, monastery of S. Maria, Faenza). *Education*: tradition recalls abandonment by parents; his older brother, Damian, sponsored Peter's education. *Career*: while teaching in Ravenna, he was ordained to the priesthood; entered the hermitage of the Holy Cross at Fonte Avellana, 1035; elected prior, 1043; began a process of reform, beginning with monks and hermits; synthesized the rules of Benedict and Romuald; turning his attention to the clergy, fought rampant simony and nicolaitism (clerical marriage); cardinal-bishop of Ostia, 1057–71; papal emissary to France and Germany; declared a doctor of the church in 1828.

Peter Damian wrote in polished Latin style a number of works: letters, sermons, opuscula, dogmatic works, prayers and poems. In addition to reform topics, he wrote on church-state relations. He presented the preeminence of the church over the state, and Rome's spiritual authority over all the sees of Christendom. His theological writing is practical in nature rather than theoretical, more anecdotal than methodical. Spiritual works stress the process of *conversio* and *confessio*, the latter especially important, as well as the importance of religious vows, which he calls a "second baptism."

Bibliography

A. PL 144–145; *Die Briefe des Petrus Damiani*, ed. Kurt Reindel (Munich, 1983); *Sancti Petri Damiani Sermones*, ed. Giovanni Lucchesi (Turnholt, 1983).

B. DSAM 12:1551–73; LThK² 8:358–60; NCE 11:214–15; ODCC 1265; TRE 26: 294–96; Owen Blum, *St. Peter Damian: His Teaching on the Spiritual Life* (Washington, D.C., 1947); Irven Resnick, *Divine Power and Possibility in St. Peter Damian's "De divina omnipotentia"* (New York, 1992).

Thomas S. Ferguson

PETER JOHN OLIVI. *See* OLIVI, PETER JOHN.

PETER LOMBARD (ca. 1095, Lombardy–1160, Paris). *Education*: educated largely in France; attended the cathedral school at Rheims as Bernard of Clairvaux's* protégé; Bernard recommended Peter to the prior of St. Victor in Paris in order that he might continue his education with the Victorines, ca. 1134–36. *Career*: respected teacher and writer, Paris, by 1140s; joined the community of canons at the cathedral of Notre Dame and began to teach there, by 1145; participated as an expert at the Council of Rheims, convoked to consider the controversial teachings of Gilbert of Poitiers (La Porée)* and presided over by Pope Eugene III, 1148; Peter is generally thought to have traveled to Rome in the suite of bishop Theobald of Paris late in 1154, and there encountered the *De fide orthodoxa* of St. John Damascene in the recent translation of Burgundio of Pisa; bishop of Paris, 1159–60.

Peter Lombard wrote one of the most influential textbooks in the whole history of theology, the *Libri quattuor Sententiarum*, or *Four Books of Sentences*, which earned him the nickname "Master of the *Sentences*." Other authentic works include commentaries on the Psalms and on the epistles of Paul (together known as the *Magna glossatura*), and more than thirty sermons.

The *Commentarius in Psalmos* is Peter's earliest known work, completed before 1138. Herbert of Bosham, one of the Lombard's English students and later secretary to Thomas Becket, reports that Peter began the work, which he intended solely for his own spiritual edification, shortly after arriving in France. Many years later Peter lectured from his Psalms commentary in the schools, at the same time correcting it for publication, probably in the mid-1150s. The *Commentarius* displays little interest in theological science and is largely derivative in its exegesis, depending heavily upon the earlier glosses of Anselm of Laon* and Gilbert of Poitiers.

The Lombard's next surviving major work is his commentary on Paul, known as the *Collectanea in epistolas sancti Pauli*. Two separate redactions of the *Collectanea* were produced. The original was composed between 1139 and

1141; the second version revealing the deepening of Peter's thought after his exposure to the writings of John of Damascus* between 1155 and 1158. While it is unclear whether he initially intended his Pauline exegesis for the classroom, the updating of the *Collectanea* was probably occasioned by Peter's decision to use it alongside his *Sentences* for a cycle of lectures. The two works exhibit a notable methodological kinship: the technique for handling conflicting sources that would find its mature expression in the *Sentences* first evolved as Peter addressed the doctrinal issues raised by his reading of Paul.

The celebrated *Four Books of Sentences* represents a summary of the course in theology that the Lombard taught at Paris for over twenty years. Its final written form can be dated with precision to 1155–57. Peter's easy familiarity with the doctrine of John of Damascus, evident when he reformulates his own trinitarian theology, places the work securely after Peter's encounter with the *De fide orthodoxa* in 1154. As a *terminus ante quem*, Peter is known to have lectured from his text in the academic year 1157–58; a final version was put into circulation almost immediately thereafter.

In the *Sentences* Peter Lombard attempts to present a comprehensive treatment of the whole of Christian doctrine. Following Augustine's* traditional division of doctrine into "things" and "signs," Peter begins in Book I by considering the divine essence and the Trinity; in Book II he focuses upon creation and the Fall; in Book III upon the Incarnation, Redemption, Christ's virtues, and Christian virtues in general; and in Book IV he brings his discussion to a close by considering the sacraments, as the visible signs of grace, and eschatology. Peter's procedure throughout is to present the authoritative opinions or *sententiae* of time-revered writers relevant to each topic and then to reconcile any apparent conflicts through reasoned analysis. His sources include the Bible itself, Augustine, John Damascene, Hilary,* Ivo of Chartres, the *Glossa ordinaria* on the Bible, Abelard,* Gratian, and Hugh of St. Victor,* as well as Peter's own glosses.

The genius of the *Sentences* lies in its organic unity, its clear plan, and—despite Peter's declared intention to furnish a collection of patristic texts so thorough as to render recourse to the originals unnecessary—its relative brevity. The Lombard was also attentive to his students' interest in dialectics. These qualities made it an ideal textbook, and the mark of its success as such can be seen in its soon becoming the object of commentaries in its own right. Early in the thirteenth century master Alexander of Hales* introduced the *Sentences* as a set text for his lectures at the university of Paris, and soon every aspirant to the mastership in theology was required to spend two years expounding it. The classroom time devoted to the *Sentences* came to rival that given to the Bible, and some thinkers, including Roger Bacon,* voiced concern over the trend. But the *Sentences* would remain a standard text in the university theology curriculum well into the sixteenth century.

Lombard's text is not without shortcomings, however. There is little philosophy employed in its argumentation, which at times leads to a lack of precision in terminology. Nor is Peter's method of reconciling divergent opinions unassailable: although, like Abelard, he recognizes the layered meanings of words, all too often he will simply juxtapose texts or offer a so-called "benign exposition" of sources too well respected to be criticized harshly. And despite his reputation for sound doctrine generally, Peter did espouse a few opinions that gave rise to considerable debate. He was implicated in the error of Christological nihilism, which posited that Christ, insofar as he is human, has no substantial reality. After his death, Peter was also accused by some of holding an erroneous view of trinitarian procession and of arguing that the divine essence is not identical with the three Persons; his teaching was, however, upheld by the Fourth Lateran Council (1215).

Criticisms aside, the acknowledgment that Peter Lombard had seized the theological initiative was well nigh universal in the later twelfth and early thirteenth centuries. In the 1240s Vincent of Beauvais* observed that Peter's works were already classics "publicly taught in the schools" everywhere. Early in the fourteenth century Dante Alighieri still respected the "Master of the *Sentences*" enough to place him in the Heaven of the Sun, together with the other theologian saints (*Paradiso* 10:107–8).

Bibliography

A.   PL 171, 191, 192; *Sententiae in IV libris distinctae*, 3d rev. ed. Ignatius C. Brady, 2 vols. (Grottaferrata, 1971–81).

B.   DSAM 12:1604–12; DTC 12:1941–2019; LThK² 8:367–69; NCE 11:221–22; ODCC 1266–67; TRE 26:297–303; Friedrich Stegmüller, *Repertorium commentariorum in Sententias Petri Lombardi*, 2 vols. (Würzburg, 1947); Ignatius C. Brady, "Peter Lombard: Canon of Notre Dame," RTAM 32 (1965): 277–95; Marcia L. Colish, *Peter Lombard*, 2 vols. (Leiden, 1994).

M. Michèle Mulchahey

PETER MARTYR. *See* VERMIGLI, PETER MARTYR.

PHILARET. *See* DROZDOV, FILARET.

PIERRE D'AILLY. *See* D'AILLY, PIERRE.

POLE, REGINALD (3 March 1500, Stourton Castle, Staffordshire–17 November 1558, London). *Education*: B.A., Magdalen Coll., Oxford, 1515; studied at Rome, Padua, and Venice, 1519–27. *Career*: residence in England, 1527–32; cardinal, 1536; member, Roman Reform Commission, 1536; papal legate to Spain, 1539; governor of Viterbo, 1541; papal legate, presider at Council of Trent, 1545; ordained, 1555; archbishop of Canterbury, 1555–58.

Pole was a humanist and ecclesiastical reformer whose conciliatory views on justification were not accepted by the Roman Church and the Council of Trent. In 1527, after his education on the Continent, Pole returned to England where his opposition to King Henry VIII's divorce of Catherine of Aragon forced him to leave England in 1532. When Henry later sought his opinion on the divorce, Pole wrote a strong defense of the papacy (*Pro ecclesiasticae unitatis defensione*, Rome, 1537), which attacked both Henry's divorce and his claim to royal supremacy over the English church.

Pope Paul III made Pole a cardinal in 1536 and appointed him to the famous reform commission with cardinals Gasparo Contarini* and Gianpietro Carafa (later Paul IV) and others who produced the famous *Consilium de emendanda ecclesia*, which attacked many abuses in the church. Paul III implemented the suggested reforms only cautiously, largely because they threatened papal finances. The next year the pope sent him as legate to England during the Pilgrimage of Grace, but by the time Pole reached Paris in April 1537, Henry had crushed the Pilgrimage and Pole returned to Rome. Henry had Pole declared a traitor, hired agents to assassinate him, executed his brother, and imprisoned and beheaded his pious mother.

As governor of Viterbo, Pole gathered around him a circle of *spirituali* friends (Vittoria Colonna, Pietro Carnesecchi, Marcantonio Flaminio) who shared his views about theology and church reform. Pole and his friends developed a theology of double justification, one inherent, one imputed, which came close to the views of Cardinals Contarini and Seripando* and had affinities to Luther's teachings. The Council of Trent would later reject double justification.

As archbishop of Canterbury, Pole tried unsuccessfully to restore Catholicism in England. He also urged Mary Tudor to moderate her persecution of Protestants, but this only increased the suspicions of the new pope, Paul IV, who summoned him to Rome to face heresy charges.

Bibliography

A. *Epistolae Reginaldi Poli . . . et aliorum ad ipsum*, ed. A. M. Quirini, 5 vols. (Brescia, 1744–1757); *Pole's Defense of the Unity of the Church*, ed. and trans. J. G. Dwyer (Westminster, Md., 1965); *Nuovi documenti su Vittoria Colonna e Reginald Pole*, ed. S. M. Pagano and C. Ranieri (Vatican City, 1989).

B. DNB 16:35–46; DTC 12:2413–16; NCE 11:487–88; ODCC 1305; OEncR 3:288–89; TRE 26:755–58; Wilhelm Schenk, *Reginald Pole, Cardinal of England* (London, 1950); Dermot Fenlon, *Heresy and Obedience in Tridentine Italy: Cardinal Pole and the Counter Reformation* (Cambridge, 1972); Paolo Simoncelli, *Il caso Reginald Pole: eresia e santità nelle polemiche religiose del Cinquecento* (Rome, 1977).

John Patrick Donnelly

PROSPER, TIRO, OF AQUITAINE (ca. 390–ca. 455). A native of Aquitaine, probably from the Gallo-Roman aristocracy, Prosper benefited from an excellent education; his literary output spans the genres of letters, verse, theological tractates, and historical chronicles. He first appears ca. 426 on the fringes of the monastic milieu at Marseilles. As the semi-Pelagian controversies over Augustine's* doctrine of grace erupted, Prosper and his associate Hilary* became ardent defenders of Augustine, who sent them the works *De praedestinatione sanctorum* and *De dono perseverantiae*. As the controversy died down, Prosper moved to Rome, where he became an adviser to Leo I.

Prosper succeeded in writing theology as poetry in his *De ingratis carmen*, written ca. 429–30, in which he articulates an Augustinian response to Pelagian and semi-Pelagian teaching. A number of prose theological works from the years 431–33 expound the same teaching. His time in Rome saw the production of a few other works, notably the *De vocatione omnium gentium*, treating the salvation of the heathen, and a *Liber sententiarum* from Augustine's writings. Prosper's florilegia transmitted Augustinianism to the Middle Ages and also modified it, softening Augustine's insistence on absolute divine predestination.

Bibliography

A. PL 51, 77–202; *The Call of All Nations*, trans. P. De Letter, ACW 14 (Westminster, Md., 1952); *Carmen de ingratis*, trans. Charles Huegelmeyer (Washington, D.C., 1962); *Defense of St. Augustine*, trans. idem, ACW 32 (Westminster, Md., 1963).

B. DSAM 12:2446–56; DTC 13:846–50; LThK² 8:811–12; NCE 11:878; ODCC 1338; TRE 27:525–26; Rebecca Weaver, *Divine Grace and Human Agency: A Study of the Semi-Pelagian Controversy* (Macon, Ga., 1996).

Thomas A. Smith

PRZYWARA, ERICH (12 October 1889, Kattowitz, Germany–28 September 1972, Munich). *Education*: studied philosophy and theology, Jesuit sem., Valkenburg, Holland, 1910–13, 1917–21. *Career*: entered Jesuits, Exaten, Holland, 1908; prefect of music, Jesuit coll., Stella Matutina, Feldkirchen, Holland, 1914–17; ordained priest, 1922; Jesuit writers' community, *Stimmen der Zeit*, Munich, 1922–72.

Przywara became known as a major spokesman in Germany for the Catholic viewpoint and its philosophy in relation to Protestantism and many modern intellectual and cultural movements. His original approaches in neoscholasticism and Jesuit spirituality inspired fellow Jesuits Karl Rahner* and Hans Urs von Balthasar.* His poetry and inspirational works appealed to everyday believers. After the Second World War, though handicapped by illness, he continued to publish on mainly spiritual and biblical subjects.

His interests ranged from philosophers and theologians (especially Augustine,* Thomas Aquinas,* Kant, Kierkegaard,* Newman,* Max Scheler) to literature, poetry, and spirituality. In fact, throughout all his work there is an attempt to discern a polar "balance in tension" that begins in the concrete world of human culture and culminates in a final "tension" between the world and God as "ever greater." As a Jesuit preacher and writer, he is a faithful son of St. Ignatius,* intent on service of God's majesty. For him this means demonstrating philosophically how God is present in all things and discerning this presence in ongoing writers and trends. Thus, an early work, *Gottgeheimnis der Welt* (1923, *The Mystery of God in the World*) was originally lectures for Catholic teachers and consisted of a philosophical and spiritual analysis of contemporary cultural movements. Later, in dialogue with Protestant theologians such as Karl Barth,* he defended the analogy of being against the Reformation's dialectical or "tragic" thought.

His major contribution to Catholic philosophy is undoubtedly his work on the analogy of being. Although using neoscholastic language, he refused to be confined by neoscholastic technicalities and effectively demonstrated the broader implications or "dynamic" of analogy. His outpouring of articles and books effectively demonstrated that the philosophical issues were alive in the "concreteness" of this world. His other contribution was to the field of spirituality, especially Ignatian spirituality (cf. *Deus Semper Maior: Theologie der Exerzitien*). Among lengthy elaborations of the anthropological basis and (frequently fanciful) scriptural resonances that he finds in the text of the *Spiritual Exercises*, we find genial insights into their structure and meaning.

Bibliography

A. *Schriften*, 3 vols. (Einsiedeln, 1962); *Religionsbegründung: Max Scheler–J. H. Newman* (Freiburg, 1923); *Deus Semper Maior: Theologie der Exerzitien*, 2 vols. (Munich, 1964); *Logos* (Dusseldorf, 1964).

B. TRE 27:607–10; J. Teran-Dutari, *Christentum und Metaphysik* (Munich, 1973); James Zeitz, *Spirituality and Analogia Entis according to Erich Przywara* (Washington, D.C., 1982); Leo Zimny, *Erich Przywara: Sein Schriftum 1912–1962* (Einsiedeln, 1963).

James Zeitz

PSEUDO-DIONYSIUS. *See* DIONYSIUS AREOPAGITA.

PUSEY, EDWARD BOUVERIE (22 August 1800, Berkshire, England–16 September 1882, Berkshire, England). *Education*: B.A., M.A., Christ Church Coll., Oxford, 1822, 1825. *Career*: Fellow, Oriel Coll., Oxford, 1824; Regius professor of Hebrew, Oxford, 1828–82; canon, Christ Church, Oxford, 1828–82.

Pusey, an Anglican priest, was one of the three leaders of the Oxford Movement, along with John Henry Newman* and John Keble.* Pusey was the acknowledged leader of the Oxford Movement after Newman joined the Roman Catholic Church. Pusey and Keble contributed to keeping the movement within the Church of England. Pusey's influence on the Oxford Movement was so strong that the movement was also known as "Puseyism." The Oxford Movement was also known as the Tractarian Movement because of the series *Tracts for the Times*, which began to appear in 1833. Pusey wrote eight of the ninety tracts in this series, including *Thoughts on the Benefits of the System of Fasting* (Tract 18) and *Scriptural Views of Holy Baptism* (Tracts 67, 68, and 69). He was a patristic scholar, and with Keble and Newman he edited *A Library of the Fathers of the Holy Catholic Church* (1838–85) and was solely responsible for the first volume of this series, *Augustine's Confessions* (1838). The editors hoped that this series would make the teaching of the Fathers of the undivided Christian

Church available to the English people, thereby demonstrating the Anglican Church's roots in Scripture and catholic tradition.

Pusey was a noted preacher. Controversy over his preaching on the Eucharist focused attention on the doctrine of the Real Presence. The revival of private confession in the Anglican communion has also been dated from a university sermon by Pusey. In his three-part *Eirenicon* (1865, 1869, 1870), Pusey urged that the Church of England and the Roman Catholic Church were separated by late medieval abuses and corruptions rather than disagreements over essential doctrine. In 1845 he established the Sisterhood of the Holy Cross, the first Anglican sisterhood since the Reformation.

Bibliography

A. *An Historical Enquiry into the Probable Causes of the Rationalist Character Lately Predominant in the Theology of Germany*, 2 vols. (London, 1828); *Tracts for the Times by Members of the University of Oxford*, nos. 18, 66–70, 77, 81, 6 vols. (Oxford, 1833–41); *Nine Sermons Preached before the University of Oxford* (Oxford, 1865); *Eirenicon, Parts I, II, III* (Oxford, 1865, 1869, 1870).

B. DNB 16:496–504; DTC 13:1363–1425; LThK² 8:905–6; NCE 11:1051–52; ODCC 1351–52; Henry P. Liddon, *Life of Edward Bouverie Pusey*, 4 vols. (London, 1893–97), with list of Pusey's writings, 4:395–446; Augustus B. Donaldson, *Five Great Oxford Leaders* (London, 1900); C. C. Grafton, *Pusey and the Church Revival* (Milwaukee, Wis., 1902); George W. E. Russell, *Dr. Pusey* (London, 1907); *The Oxford Movement*, ed. Eugene R. Fairweather (New York, 1964); D. Forrester, *Young Doctor Pusey: A Study in Development* (London, 1989).

Robert B. Slocum

Q

QUESNEL, PASQUIER (14 July 1634, Paris–2 December 1719, Amsterdam). *Education*: philosophy and theology, Sorbonne, 1650s. *Career*: joined Cong. of Oratory, 1657; ordained priest, 1659; taught the young, Maison d'Institution, Paris, 1660–66, 1670–78; resided in Brussels, Belgium, 1684–1703; imprisoned, Mechlin, Belgium, 1703; resided in Amsterdam, 1703–19.

After the death of Antoine Arnauld* (1694), Quesnel became the leading popular purveyor of Jansenist principles. Like some other French Jansenists, he tried to retrieve biblical and patristic sources for the renewal of Catholic life and piety in France. In 1672 he wrote *Abrégé de la morale de l'Évangile*, which emphasized the close study of Scripture in developing true devotion. Later that text, which was intended for the youth he was teaching, was developed in his famous *Le Nouveau Testament en français, avec des réflexions morales sur chaque verset* (Paris, 1687–92), usually called *Réflexions morales*. That text, his numerous defenses of Jansenist positions, and his scholarly edition of the works of St. Leo, works whose footnotes demonstrated clearly Quesnel's Gallican theories, were condemned by the archbishop of Paris, cardinal L. A. de Noailles, and by Pope Clement XI in 1708 and by the papal bull *Unigenitus* in 1713.

Quesnel asserted the absolute necessity and irresistibility of the grace of the Redeemer, maintaining that fallen human nature had been so vitiated that it was, without grace, free only to do evil. For him, moreover, all human volitions and actions arose from two loves: the love of God (charity), which referred everything to God as the source and end of all human activity, and the love of self and of the world, which was itself evil because it did not refer everything to God. From this perspective all human volitions and actions, even human repentance and attrition, that did not flow from the perfect love of God were useless and in fact sinful themselves.

From these ideas of grace Quesnel built up his notions about the church, which he considered primarily an invisible body of the elect and the just. This purified and holy church, moreover, had all the powers of the apostolic church, but in the exercise of those powers, like the power of excommunication, the hierarchy could act only with the presumed consent of the whole body.

Quesnel defended his controversial theological positions throughout the 1680s and in 1684 he refused to subscribe to an anti-Jansenist formula prepared by his religious superiors in the Congregation of the Oratory. In 1684, after his refusal, he left the Oratory and went to Brussels to join his fellow Jansenist Antoine Arnauld. Like Arnauld and Jansen, Quesnel believed his views on grace were consistent with Augustinian thought.

Bibliography

A.   *Mémoires domestiques pour servir à l'histoire de l'Oratoire*, ed. A. M. P. Ingold, 5 vols. (Paris, 1902–11), 4:424–93 for list of Quesnel's writings.

B.   DTC 13:1460–1535; LThK² 8:935–36; NCE 12:21–22; ODCC 1356–57; Albert LeRoy, *Un Janséniste en exil* (Paris, 1900); J. A. G. Tans, *Pasquier Quesnel et les Pays-Bas* (Amsterdam, 1960).

Patrick W. Carey

R

RABANUS MAURUS (ca. 780, Mainz–4 February 856, Mainz). *Education*: entered the monastery at Fulda, perhaps in 788 as a child oblate; educated in Fulda and Tours. *Career*: ordained priest, 814; teacher and master of the monastic school at Fulda; elected abbot of Fulda, 822; resigned as abbot, 842; ordained archbishop of Mainz, 847.

Rabanus was a student of Alcuin's* and spread the influence of the Carolingian renaissance; he is sometimes called the Preceptor of Germany. While a teacher at Fulda, Rabanus built up the library and school there. Under Rabanus, Fulda also became a center for the production of literature in Old High German. As abbot, Rabanus oversaw more than 600 monks at Fulda and other abbeys. He resigned from his office as abbot for political reasons. As archbishop of Mainz, the most influential German see of its day, he worked effectively as pastor. Rabanus was known among his contemporaries especially for his biblical commentaries. He drew on Augustine,* Jerome,* Gregory the Great,* and Bede,* either citing or paraphrasing their works. He considered the historical sense of the biblical books but also added allegorical interpretations. His practical work *On the Education of Clerics* enjoyed widespread popularity. Rabanus may be the author of the hymn used at Pentecost, *Veni creator Spiritus*. He also took part in the controversy over predestination with Gottschalk and Hincmar of Rheims.*

Bibliography

A. CCCM 44; PL 107–12.
B. DTC 13:1601–20; TRE 15:606–10; Helmut Spelsberg, *Hrabanus Maurus: Bibliographie* (Fulda, 1984).

Joseph T. Lienhard

RADBERTUS. *See* PASCHASIUS RADBERTUS.

RAHNER, HUGO KARL ERICH (5 May 1900, Pfullendorf/Baden, Germany–21 December, 1968, Munich, Germany). *Education*: studied philosophy, Valkenburg, Holland, and Innsbruck, 1920–23; studied theology, Innsbruck, 1926–30; doctorate in theology, Innsbruck, 1931; studied history with F. J. Dölger and W. Levinson, Bonn, 1931–34; doctorate in philosophy, Innsbruck, 1934. *Career*: entered Jesuits, 1919; ordained priest, 1929; university lecturer for early church history, patrology, and the history of dogma, Innsbruck, 1935–38, 1945–62; exile in Sitten/Wallis, Switzerland (collaborator with the *Eranos* conferences), 1938–45; dean of the theology faculty, Innsbruck, 1945–49; rector of the Univ. of Innsbruck, 1949–50; rector of *Collegium Canisianum*, 1950–56; retirement with Jesuits, Munich, 1964–68.

Rahner and liturgist Josef Jungmann* sought to provide for their students a "kerygmatic theology" (i.e., a theology that could be preached). For Rahner theology was not only a science but also and essentially the message of salvation. To this end Hugo published *A Theology of Proclamation* in 1939. It emphasized that a knowledge of the Scriptures and of patristic theology was indispensable for a kerygmatic revival. Hugo's brother, Karl,* agreed that scholastic theology did not adequately prepare students for pastoral ministry. Karl felt that "the strictest theology, that most passionately devoted to reality alone and ever on the alert for new questions, the most scientific theology, is itself in the long run the most kerygmatic" (*Theological Investigations* I, 7). Both Hugo and Karl Rahner agreed that academic theology was not an end in itself but existed to serve the church's life of faith and its mission to preach God's word. Thus, for them, true theology is always a *theologia cordis*, a theology of the heart.

The central theme in Hugo Rahner's theology was the ecclesiology of the Fathers of the church, or more generally, the mystery of salvation as presented in the rich symbolic language of the church fathers. He discovered that the writings of the church fathers contained profound truths clothed in images, symbols, and allegories. He hoped that by reintroducing the symbolic theology of the Fathers he could help make dogmatic theology more vibrant and free it from its apologetic and juridical language and categories. He devoted his life to studying and teaching patristic theology.

Rahner also had a special love for the "father" of the Society of Jesus, Ignatius of Loyola.* Beginning in 1935 he wrote a number of articles about Ignatius and in 1947 he published a book, *Ignatius The Theologian*, in which he studied the evolution of Ignatian spirituality. Hugo Rahner, a true son of Ignatius of Loyola, analyzed the lesser known side of Ignatius, as mystic and theologian.

Bibliography

A. *Symbole der Kirche* (Salzburg, 1964); *A Theology of Proclamation* (N.Y., 1968); *Ignatius the Theologian* (San Francisco, 1990).

B. NCE 16:373–74; Karl H. Neufeld, "Unter Bruedern," in *Wagnis Theologie* (Freiburg, 1979), 341–54; Herbert Vorgrimler, *Understanding Karl Rahner* (New York, 1986); William V. Dych, *Karl Rahner* (Collegeville, Minn., 1992); Karl H. Neufeld, *Die Brueder Rahner* (Freiburg, 1994).

Melvin Michalski

RAHNER, KARL (5 March 1904, Freiburg in Breisgau, Germany–30 March 1984, Innsbruck, Austria). *Education*: Jesuit formation in Ignatian spirituality and philosophy, Austria, 1922–25, and Germany, 1925–27, and in theology in Holland, 1929–33; graduate studies in philosophy, Freiburg, 1934–36, with four semesters in Martin Heidegger's seminar; habilitation, Innsbruck, 1937. *Career*: entered the Jesuit novitiate, 1922; taught Latin, 1928; ordained priest, 1932; taught dogmatics at Innsbruck until the Jesuits were expelled by the Nazis, 1937–39; pastoral work, Vienna, 1939–44, and the Bavarian village, Mariakirchen, 1944–45; taught theology, Pullach, 1945–48, and Innsbruck, 1948–64; peritus, Vatican Council II, 1962–65; succeeded Romano Guardini* in the chair for Christianity and the Philosophy of Religion, Munich, 1964–67; professor of dogmatic theology, Münster, 1967–71; International Theological Commission, 1969–74; retirement, frequently engaged in preaching, giving retreats, lectures, talks, and media interviews, Munich, 1971–81, and Innsbruck, 1981–84. Editor: *Lexikon für Theologie und Kirche*, *Sacramentum Mundi*, *Questiones Disputatae*, *Kleines theologisches Wörterbuch*, *Handbuch der Pastoraltheologie*, and *Christlicher Glaube in moderner Gesellschaft*; member of the editorial committee of *Concilium* and of influential academic societies concerned with ecumenism, with the relation between science and religion, and with dialogue between Christians and Marxists.

Rahner's creative appropriation of diverse theological and philosophical sources (including Ignatian spirituality, Thomas Aquinas,* Kant, Hegel, Maréchal,* Rousselot,* and Heidegger) provided an innovative conceptual framework for retrieving Catholic doctrine and the neoscholastic theology of the previous generation and established his reputation as one of the most influential systematic theologians in the Vatican II era. His probing essays responded to the broad range of topics most at issue for Catholics from the 1940s to the 1980s. The earliest of these helped prepare for the council. The later ones provided rich resources for both academic and pastoral theology. He was influential in German-speaking countries through his teaching, lectures, editorial labors, and membership in learned societies. His thought had broader impact because of his involvement in international publications like *Concilium*, his role as a peritus at the Second Vatican Council, the extensive dissemination of his work (1,651 publications, 4,744 counting reprints and translations), his impact on the foreign students who attended his classes and later became influential in their own countries, and the positive reception of his contributions by many Protestant thinkers. In the English-speaking world, for example, George Lindbeck, a Lutheran, ranked him with Barth* and Tillich*; John Macquarrie, an Anglican, added that of these Rahner's theology was the most helpful.

At the heart of Rahner's thought is a coherent vision of the world as the profoundly mysterious arena of God's self-communication in Jesus and the Spirit. Rahner, however, never elaborated this as a systematic theology worked out in progressive volumes. The philosophical underpinnings were presented in his first two books: *Spirit in the World* and *Hearer of the Word*. The details of the theological scheme emerged over the years in lectures, talks, and articles, the most important of which were published in his *Theological Investigations* (23 vols.). Despite their erudition and nuance, these reflections were not primarily concerned with contributing to specialized theological scholarship, although many certainly did that. Most had a broadly pastoral concern to explore ways of recovering the meaning of Christian doctrine and Catholic teaching in an intellectually plausible and contemporary idiom. This was the case in early reflections that focused on the preoccupations of Catholic dogmatic teaching and piety, in later essays contributing to issues that were being raised at Vatican II regarding the nature of the church and its relation to the modern world, and in the publications of his last years, which wrestled with pluralism, the historicity of the church and theology, ecumenism, and the notion of a "world church" no longer dominated by Western culture and peoples. Although Rahner's "transcendental Thomism" provided the philosophical categories for fleshing out this understanding, his positions were deeply rooted in the Ignatian spirituality of seeking God in all things, sacramental piety, devotion to Jesus, and Catholic doctrine. He distilled essential elements of this vision in *Foundations of Christian Faith*, his attempt to offer a "first level" account that would be accessible to readers without specialized theological training. Notwithstanding the pastoral thrust of these works, the style of writing and argument makes for notoriously demanding reading. Rahner was much more successful in articulating his theological vision without the difficult conceptual apparatus in his sermons, prayers, meditations, and numerous interviews, particularly those that he gave towards the end of his career. The most important of these have been collected in: *Prayers for a Lifetime*, *Karl Rahner in Dialogue*, *Faith in a Wintry Season*, and *I Remember*.

As a doctoral candidate, Rahner worked out the basic lines of his philosophical perspective in a metaphysical reflection on the possibility of knowing God. This groundbreaking retrieval of Thomas Aquinas in light of modern philosophical currents (particularly Kant and Heidegger) was rejected by his dissertation director but published in 1939 as *Geist in Welt*. Rahner argued that we can know of God by attending to the movement of our knowing itself towards its objects. Reflection on this reveals that our thinking always reaches beyond its immediate objects towards a further horizon. Hence, the movement of our knowing, and the ultimate goal towards which it reaches, can be grasped only indirectly (or "transcendentally") as our thinking turns back on itself. Rahner identified the elusive and final "term" of this dynamism with God and contended that the same movement towards God is entailed in freedom and love. By conceiving God, who always exceeds our reach, as the horizon presupposed in the movement of knowing, freedom, and love, Rahner provided a way for talking and thinking about God as "mysterious," that is to say, as a reality who is known, but only reflexively and indirectly—and perhaps not even consciously—as the ever-receding horizon of the human spirit. For Rahner, we are "spirits" (oriented and able to know God) only through our being "in the world." Conversely, as humans, we are in the world in a spiritual way—in a way that either is moving towards and affirming God or is denying and closing itself to God. Knowledge of God always has a distinctly analogical character and logic because it necessarily entails reference to God as mystery while at the same time this reference is mediated through an unavoidable "turning" to objectifiable realities.

In *Hearer of the Word*, originally lectures given at Salzburg in the summer of 1937, Rahner developed his "transcendental arguments" further to explain why God must be thought of as personal, even though not a finite person, and as one whose self could be revealed further in the human realm of history and language if God so chose. As the ones who either encounter or miss this possible self-revelation, we are hearers of either God's "word" or silence.

Subsequent reflections on the theology of symbol and the doctrine of the Incarnation, which drew creatively from sacramental, trinitarian, Thomistic, and Ignatian themes, provided Rahner with a way of explaining how we might conceive God speaking such a "word." A person's words of love do more than tell about a relationship to another. Genuine expressions of love, though in a certain sense realities distinct from the person who offers them, are nevertheless also truly *self*-communications to the beloved. Rahner's notion of Jesus as God's "realsymbol" proposed this sort of analogy for conceiving how Jesus' very humanity could be God's *self*-expression in history and how the church and sacraments could mediate that event to subsequent generations. This paradigm also helped Rahner explain an essential feature of the symbolic-like causality involved in God's relationship with the world. Self-expressions between persons have a history. The communication of one to another in love begins before it is fully and explicitly expressed. Love causes the gestures towards the other, even though the love is not fully concretized until it is expressed in those words or deeds. Rahner suggests that, in a similar way, God's self-communication (uncreated grace) is operative in human history from the moment of creation through the work of the Holy Spirit even though it is only in Jesus' life and death on the cross that the grounds for this possibility are definitively and explicitly concretized in history. Early in his career Rahner suggested that this dynamic could be thought of as giving a kind of supernatural possibility (or "existential") to human existence; this would preserve the distinction between grace and nature while also accounting for humankind's openness for God. This emphasis on "uncreated grace," a revolutionary move in Catholic theology at the time, would also open groundbreaking possibilities for ecumenical dialogue with Lutherans and Orthodox Christians. Further refinements of this paradigm enabled Rahner to elaborate his seminal vision of humanity, and even of creation itself, as mediums of God's loving and absolutely free revelation and gift of self. This distinctly incarnational (and in later works more clearly pneumatological) center of gravity guided his subtle explorations of the dialectic at the heart of so many crucial theological issues and grounded his innovative and sometimes controversial proposals for understanding the relationships between faith and reason, theology and anthropology, the immanent and economic Trinity, ascending and descending Christology, transcendental and historical revelation, love of neighbor and love of God, unchangeable and changeable truths of faith, and unity and pluralism in the church.

God, so conceived in Rahner's theological investigations, is not one being among others, but the holy mystery and fullness of all that it is "to be" who is revealed in Jesus and operative in history through the Holy Spirit. Given the interconnectedness of human history and God's participation in it through Jesus and the Spirit, something of God, this ineffable and trinitarian fullness of Being-as-such, is anticipated whenever we know, choose, or love a specific being, particularly our neighbor in need. Conversely, God is rejected to some extent in every refusal of truth, freedom, and love. In these cases, since the affirmation or denial is of a particular being and not necessarily directly cognizant of God or Jesus, it is quite possible that the true nature of the "fundamental option" implicitly taken toward God's self-communication (at the tacit or transcendental level) might be hidden or even denied (at the explicit or categorical level) by the person taking it. In either case, however, a stance towards God and Jesus is taken in the turning of a person's mind and heart towards realities of the world. Rahner suggested that a fundamentally affirmative option could be characterized as a kind of "anonymous Christianity," although he admitted that the phrase itself could be misunderstood. In later works he explored the notion of a "searching Christology"—a Christology "from below" that offered a more historically immanent explanation for the Catholic confession of God's universal salvific will.

There is an immense body of secondary literature either directly assessing Rahner's significance, responding to the more controversial proposals, or constructively attempting to exploit his insights. The bibliography maintained at Professor Albert Raffelt's Freiburg web site numbered 2,074 citations in July 1998.

Bibliography

A. Extensive up-to-date bibliographies of primary and secondary literature are available at the Karl Rahner Society web site (http://www.theo.mu.edu/krs/); *Spirit in the World* (New York, 1994); *Hearer of the Word*, trans. Joseph Donceel (New York, 1994), much more reliable than the earlier translation entitled *Hearers of the Word*; *Theological Investigations*, 23 vols. (London, Baltimore, Md., and New York, 1961–92); *Foundations of Christian Faith* (New York, 1978); *Karl Rahner in Dialogue: Conversations and Interviews 1965–1982* (New York, 1986); *Prayers for a Lifetime* (New York, 1984); *I*

Remember (New York, 1985); *Faith in a Wintry Season: Conversations and Interviews with Karl Rahner in the Last Years of His Life* (New York, 1991).

B. NCE 18:411–13; ODCC 1362; TRE 28:111–17; *Theology and Discovery*, ed. William J. Kelly (Milwaukee, Wis., 1980); *A World of Grace*, ed. Leo J. O'Donovan (Washington, D.C., 1995); idem, "A Journey into Time: The Legacy of Karl Rahner's Last Years," ThSt 46 (1985): 621–44; Herbert Vorgrimler, *Understanding Karl Rahner* (New York, 1986); William V. Dych, *Karl Rahner* (London, 1992).

Robert Masson

RATRAMNUS OF CORBIE (d. ca. 870). Ratramnus entered the monastery of Corbie sometime after 825. We know very little about his life apart from the history of his writings. His first and most famous work, *De corpore et sanguine Domini*, written at the request of Charles the Bald, takes a position opposed to the intense "realism" of Paschasius Radbertus,* but it is not itself a merely "symbolic" doctrine of the Eucharist. Theologians involved in later eucharistic controversies were perhaps too ready to claim these theologians in support of their own positions, and so (e.g.) Radbertus looks "Catholic" to us in opposition to Ratramnus as "Protestant." Rather, both should be seen as attempting to develop a vocabulary adequate for the interpretation of patristic teaching on the Eucharist (especially the appropriate use of *veritas* and *figura*), and neither should be judged using the more technical vocabulary of later ages. Ratramnus's *De praedestinatione* was also written at the request of Charles the Bald (part one, 849; part two, 850) during the continuing debate over predestination after the condemnation of Gottschalk (spring 849). Ratramnus was sympathetic to Gottschalk and defended an Augustinian doctrine that was not, however, as extreme as Gottschalk's. Ratramnus's last work, written in 868, the *Contra Graecorum opposita*, defends the *filioque* and also certain western practices such as clerical celibacy. We hear no more of Ratramnus after the publication of this work.

Bibliography

A. PL 121: includes *Contra Graecorum opposita* (PL 121.223–346), *De praedestinatione* (PL 121.11–80); *Epistula de Cynocephalis* (PL 121.1153–56; also MGH *Epistolae* 6), and *De propinquorum conjugiis* (MGH *Epistolae* 6); *De anima*, ed. André Wilmart, *Revue bénédictine* 43 (1931): 207–23; *Liber de anima ad Odonem Bellouacensem*, ed. C. Lambot, Analecta mediaevalia namurcensia 2 (Namur, 1952); *De nativitate Christi*, ed. I. M. Canal (Rome, 1968); *De corpore et sanguine Domini: texte original et notice bibliographique*, ed. J. N. Bakhuizen van den Brink (Amsterdam, 1974); Timothy R. Roberts, "A Translation and Critical Edition of Ratramnus of Corbie's *De Praedestinatione Dei*," Ph.D. diss. University of Missouri, 1977; I. Tolomio, *L'Anima dell'uomo: trattati sull' anima dal V al IX secolo* (Milan, 1979); *De infantibus incaute oppressis*, ed. G. Schmitz, *Deutsches Archiv für Erforschung des Mittelalters* 38 (1982): 363–87.

B. BBKL 7:1382–85; LThK² 8:1001–1002; NCE 12:93–94; ODCC 1367–68; John F. Fahey, *The Eucharistic Teaching of Ratramn of Corbie* (Mundelein, Ill., 1951); Jean-

Paul Bouhot, *Ratramne de Corbie* (Paris, 1976); David Ganz, *Corbie in the Carolingian Renaissance* (Sigmaringen, 1990).

John C. Cavadini

RAUSCHENBUSCH, WALTER (4 October 1861, Rochester, N.Y.–25 July 1918, Rochester, N.Y.). *Education*: graduated Rochester Free Academy, 1879; Evangelisches Gymnasium, Gütersloh, Germany, 1879–83; B.A., Univ. of Rochester, 1883–85; Rochester Theol. Sem., Rochester, N.Y., 1883–86; studied at Berlin, Kiel, and Marburg, 1891–92, 1907–8. *Career*: pastor, Louisville, Ky., summers 1884–85; pastor, Second German Baptist Church, New York City, 1886–97; founding editor, *For the Right*, 1889–91; editor, *Der Jugend Herold*, 1892–96; founding member, Brotherhood of the Kingdom, 1892; professor of New Testament, German department, Rochester Theol. Sem., 1897–1902; professor of church history, Rochester Theol. Sem., 1902–18.

Rauschenbusch was the leading exponent and theologian of the social gospel in America. His social thought can be traced to fourain influences: pietism, sectarianism, liberalism, and transformationism. The theologian who exerted the greatest influence on him was Albrecht Ritschl.* Rauschenbusch drew on these influences in a free and original way, never slavishly following any one pattern.

During his pastorate in New York City, Rauschenbusch was confronted by the social problems brought on by industrialization, urbanization, and the exploitation of labor. Finding that the pietistic heritage in which he had been reared was inadequate for dealing with the social concerns confronting him, he sought to combine his evangelical concern for individuals and his social vision of a redeemed society, striving for a synthesis of the religious and the social-ethical. He found the unifying element in his conception of the kingdom of God. For him the doctrine of the kingdom of God was the most essential dogma of the Christian faith, for it contained the lost social ideal of Christendom. The kingdom of God is humanity organized according to the will of God. It implies the progressive reign of love in human affairs. While it is divine in its origin, progress, and consummation, it was to be realized in history. The kingdom is always present as well as future and therefore is always calling for immediate action. It must embrace all of life, including social institutions. Since institutions can incorporate evil within their makeup, they need to be redeemed, even as individuals need to be redeemed. This redemption would come through the progressive transformation of all human affairs by the thought and spirit of Christ. Jesus thus stood at the center of the kingdom. As the incarnation of a new type of human life, he was the inaugurator of a new humanity. By virtue of his personality he became the initiator of the kingdom. While Rauschenbusch taught that there could only be an approximation of a perfect social order within history, he felt that such a vastly improved social order was within reach.

In his writings Rauschenbusch stressed the doctrine of sin. Defining sin as selfishness, he believed that the individual rarely sins against God alone. There is a social dimension to sin. It was the vision of the kingdom of God that brought this social dimension of sin into focus. The sins of individuals are incorporated into the life of social institutions. These then take on a life of their own as superpersonal forces of evil. These superpersonal forces of evil, taken together, comprise the kingdom of evil. It is against this kingdom of evil that the kingdom of God is locked in a struggle. The struggle is won as the social institutions are saved by restructuring them through democratic, solidaristic, socialistic principles. Equal rights must replace special privilege; the public good must take priority over personal gain; cooperation and association must replace competition.

Rauschenbusch had a thoroughly instrumental conception of the church. It was a means to an end and was always subordinate to the kingdom of God. He depicted the church as being the social factor in salvation.

Though deeply influenced by liberal scholarship and at times deeply critical of the individualistic pietism that was part of his heritage and personal makeup, Rauschenbusch always cherished the personal aspects of his faith. His aim was to add a social dimension to the gospel, not to displace the personal experience of faith. Generally characterized as an evangelical liberal, he exemplified a personally profound Christianity throughout his life.

Bibliography

A. *Christianity and the Social Crisis* (New York, 1907); *Christianizing the Social Order* (New York, 1912); *The Social Principles of Jesus* (New York, 1916); *A Theology for the Social Gospel* (New York, 1917).

B. DAB 15:392–93; DARB 447–48; NCAB 19:193; NCE 12:94; SH 9:405; Dores R. Sharpe, *Walter Rauschenbusch* (New York, 1942); Vernon P. Bodein, *The Social Gospel of Walter Rauschenbusch and Its Relation to Religious Education* (New Haven, Conn., 1944); Paul M. Minus, *Walter Rauschenbusch: American Reformer* (New York, 1988); Donovan E. Smucker, *The Origins of Walter Rauschenbusch's Social Ethics* (Montreal, Kingston, London, Buffalo, 1994).

Heinz D. Rossol

RAYMOND LULL. *See* LULL, RAYMOND.

RÉGNON, THÉODORE DE (11 October 1831, St. Herblain, Loire Inferieure, France–26 December 1893, Paris). *Education*: studied philosophy, Coll. de Brugelette, Belgium, 1848–51; studied theology, Laval, 1864–68. *Career*: entered Jesuits, 1852; taught physics, Ecole Sainte-Geneviève, 1855–64, 1869–80; theological research, Paris, 1880–93.

De Régnon is perhaps the most influential and yet least known of modern Catholic historians of doctrine. His influence comes from the widespread acceptance of his account of the character of Augustinian and Cappadocian trinitarian theologies. His anonymity is due to the fact that particularly in English language scholarship his account of these theologies has been promulgated but used without credit. De Régnon contributed substantially to the French Jesuit tradition of the history of doctrine, which began with Denis Petau* and which continued in the twentieth century with Jules Lebreton and Jean Daniélou.*

De Régnon began his academic career teaching mathematics, chemistry, and physics but in his mature years turned to theology. His earliest work in theology is on the controversy between Bañez* and Molina*; he published a major study of their moral theologies in 1883, wrote several journal articles on these figures, and participated in a scholarly debate with H. Gayraud, O.P., on their theologies, which was published in the journal *Science catholique*. De Régnon's next major work of scholarship was a treatment of the notion of causality in the writings of Albert the Great* and Thomas Aquinas.* His most important contribution to theology, however, must be considered his massive study of the theology of the Trinity, the *Études de théologie positive sur la sainte Trinité* (Paris, 1892/98).

His *Études* argued that the classical doctrine of the Trinity developed in two stages. In the first stage reflection on the Trinity proceeds from the diversity of persons to the unity of the nature. This trinitarian theology is especially Greek and expressed in its most definitive form in the writings of the Cappadocians. In the second stage, reflection proceeds from the unity of nature. This trinitarian theology is especially Latin and expressed in its fundamental form in the writings of Augustine.* The first form of trinitarian theology de Régnon identifies as the "patristic" doctrine of the Trinity; the second form he identifies as the "scholastic" doctrine of the Trinity. This judgment by de Régnon on the two fundamental models of trinitarian theology has been taken for granted as the basis for most twentieth-century western trinitarian theology: there have been arguments over which model is "better" but little argument over the accuracy of or basis for de Régnon's judgment.

Bibliography

A.   *Bañes et Molina. Histoire, doctrines critique, métaphyisque* (Paris, 1883); *La métaphysique des causes d'après saint Thomas et Albert le Grand* (Paris, 1886; 2d ed. 1906).
B.   DTC 13:2121–25; LThK[2] 8:1101–2; Sommervogel 6:1602–3; Michel René Barnes, "De Régnon Reconsidered," *Augustinian Studies* 26:2 (1995): 51–79; idem, "The Use of Augustine in Contemporary Trinitarian Theology," ThSt 56 (1995): 237–51; M. J. Le Guillou, "Rèflexions sur la theologie trinitaire à propos de quelques livres anciens et rècents," *Istina* 17 (1972): 457–64; André de Halleux, "Personalisme ou essentialisme trinitaire chez les Peres cappadociens? Une mauvaise controverse," *Revue thèologique de Louvain*, 17 (1986): 129–55, 265–92; Jules Lebreton, *Histoire du dogme de la Trinité des origines à saint Augustin* (Paris, 1910); Vladimir Lossky, *Essai sur la théologie mystique de l'église d'orient* (Paris, 1944); H. Paissac, *Théologie du Verbe: Saint Augustin et Saint Thomas* (Paris, 1951).

Michel René Barnes

RICHARD OF ST. VICTOR (?, Scotland–10 March 1173, Paris). Little is known of Richard's early life; entered the abbey of St. Victor in Paris in the early 1150s at a young age; became subprior in 1159 and held the office of prior from 1162 until his death, for most of the time under the abbot Ernisius, whose rule proved to be such a disaster that he was finally removed by the pope in 1171. A second-generation figure at the abbey of St. Victor following upon Hugh of St. Victor,* who died in 1141 well before Richard's arrival, Richard became the best representative of Victorine spirituality in the latter half of the twelfth century. Coming just prior to the influx of the translated works of Greek and Islamic thinkers that was to lead to the rise of scholasticism, Richard lacked the philosophical tools that would effect the transformation of theology in the first half of the thirteenth century, and he was limited in his theological method to the best that was available in his day, namely, grammatical analysis and dialectical precision.

His writings include *Liber de Verbo incarnato*, *De statu interioris hominis*, *Adnotationes mysticae in psalmos*, *De quatuor gradibus charitatis*, *Liber exceptionum*, and some one hundred sermons. His two best-known works are *The Twelve Patriarchs*, also known as *Benjamin minor*, and *The Mystical Ark*, also known as *Benjamin major*. Both works present allegorical interpretations of various biblical figures.

The *Benjamin minor*, for example, which aims to prepare the mind and body for contemplation by helping one to achieve the requisite peace and quiet, takes the birth of each of Jacob's sons as a stage in spiritual development. Thus, the seven sons of Leah are the virtues, Reuben being fear of the Lord, Simeon contriteness of heart, Levi hope of forgiveness, and so on. In the second half of the work a similar process of allegorical personification is applied to the gospel narrative of the transfiguration. The *Benjamin major*, which deals with the grace of contemplation, provides a brilliant analysis of the six kinds of contemplation, each with its many subdivisions. The first is in imagination and according to imagination alone; the second in imagination, but according to reason; the third is formed in reason, but according to imagination; the fourth formed in reason and according to reason; the fifth is above reason, but not beyond reason; the sixth is above reason and seems to be beyond reason. Though the works were written for the monks of St. Victor, Richard's approach to the theme of contemplation has a more universal application.

Richard's *De trinitate*, a work in speculative theology, aims to discover in the manner of Anselm of Canterbury* necessary reasons for the oneness and threeness in God, though these reasons do not involve the strong sense of necessity that the term conveys to modern ears. In fact, Richard devotes a good part of the work to an explanation of the Athanasian Creed, which the monks recited daily. Richard found it necessary to criticize the distinctions introduced into the Trinity by Gilbert of La Porrée;* he also saw need to improve upon the Boethian definition of person by emphasizing the incommunicable existence (*existentia incommunicabilis*) of each of the persons, despite the oneness of their essence. Central to Richard's theology of the Trinity is the supreme goodness and love of God the Father, which, he claimed, cannot remain alone in itself, but must move out to another person of equal dignity, the Son, while the Father and the Son must, in turn, have a third person, the Holy Spirit, as the object of their love. Thus he shows that love requires at least two persons, but demands three for its perfection. Richard's influence upon later theologians was due more to the excellence of his mystical theology than to the prowess of his speculative thought.

Bibliography

A.   *Opera omnia*, PL 196; *De Trinitate*, ed. Jean Ribaillier (Paris, 1958); *Liber exceptionum*, ed. Jean Chatillon (Paris, 1958); *Selected Writings on Contemplation*, trans. Clare Kirchberger (New York, 1957); *The Twelve Patriarchs; The Mystical Ark; Book Three of The Trinity*, trans. Grover A. Zinn (New York, 1979).

B.   DSAM 13:593–654; DTC 13:2669–75; LThK² 8:1292; NCE 12:483–84; ODCC 1396–97; PRE 16:749–54; G. Dumeige, *Richard de Saint-Victor et l'idée chrétienne de l'amour* (Paris, 1952); George Walker, "Richard of St. Victor: An Early Scottish Theologian?" *Scottish Journal of Theology* 11 (1958): 37–52; J. Bligh, "Richard of St. Victor's De trinitate: Augustinian or Abelardian?" *Heythrop Journal* 1 (1960): 118–39; Gaston Salet, "Les chemins de Dieu d'après Richard de Saint-Victor," in *L'homme devant Dieu*, ed. J. Guillet et al. (Paris, 1963), 2:73–88; Jean Châtillon, "Contemplation, action, et prédication d'après un sermon inédit de Richard de Saint-Victor en l'honneur de saint Grégoire-le-Grand," ibid. 89–98; Robert Javelet, "Sens et réalité ultime selon Richard de Saint-Victor," *Journal of Ultimate Reality and Meaning* 6 (1983): 221–43.

Roland J. Teske

RITSCHL, ALBRECHT BENJAMIN (25 March 1822, Berlin, Prussia–20 March 1889, Göttingen, Germany). *Education*: studied at the Univ. of Bonn, 1839–41, and the Univ. of Halle, 1841–43; Univs. of Heidelberg and Tübingen, 1845–46; licentiate in theology, Bonn, 1846. *Career*: professor, Univ. of Bonn, 1846–64; Univ. of Göttingen, 1864–89; prorector of the Univ. of Göttingen, 1876–77 and 1886–87; editor, *Zeitschrift für Kirchengeschichte*, 1876–89.

Ritschl was the leading Protestant theologian in Germany during the 1870s and 1880s. His contributions to New Testament studies, historical theology, and systematic theology helped move Protestant theology from speculative idealism to a more sociological-historical understanding of the church. His many students included Karl Holl, J. Wilhelm Herrmann,* Ernst Troeltsch,* and Adolf von Harnack.*

Ritschl's father, a pastor and the general superintendent of the churches in Pomerania, supported the Prussian Union of the Reformed and Lutheran Churches. Albrecht likewise advocated a united Protestantism. He opposed (and was opposed by) neoconfessionalists, pietists, and rationalists. For support he appealed to the Reformers, especially the "young Luther,"* rather than post-Reformation orthodoxy. This appeal helped spark a "Luther renaissance" which profoundly shaped German theology for nearly a century.

During the 1840s Ferdinand Christian Baur* was Ritschl's chief mentor. From him he learned the significance of detailed historical study and a comprehensive view of the church's past. Ritschl's research gradually convinced him, however, that Baur had overemphasized the importance of ideological conflict in the early church. Early Christians, Ritschl argued in the 1857 edition of *Die Entstehung der altkatholischen Kirche*, evidenced sociological/contextual diversity but were united by an "apostolic consciousness." This same consciousness found expression in the New Testament and remained normative for Christianity.

Ritschl regarded deterministic materialism to be a contemporary danger. Religion, he emphasized, offers divine support for the freedom of the human spirit in the face of those societal and natural forces over which individuals have little control. Because he thought speculative theism obscured the distinction between freedom and unfreedom, he criticized its influence on Christian theology and objected to the attributes classically ascribed to God. God was better characterized as "loving Will." Rejecting the possibility of a disinterested knowledge of God, Ritschl thought theology always reflected the value judgments of the community of faith from which it emerges.

Ritschl endeavored to rehabilitate the doctrine of justification, understanding it not so much in juridical as in interpersonal categories. Justification was straightforwardly God's act, aimed not at placating divine wrath but at overcoming the estrangement of humans by means of the forgiveness of sin.

The object of God's love is the organic community, the church. Membership gives access to revelation and to the saving influence of Jesus—an influence that transforms distrust into trust and disobedience into obedience. This emphasis on the community distinguished Ritschl's thought from the individualism of some pietist and of much rationalist thought.

Anxious to overcome the dichotomy between belief and moral behavior, he utilized the concept of the Kingdom of God as the unifying goal of both God's justifying action and the human response to grace. For Ritschl, God's selfhood was not at rest behind actions but evident in revelation and redemption. Likewise, human faith was not passive but expressed actively: toward God in humility, patience, and prayer and toward others in love—in an ethical vocation aimed at the Kingdom of God.

After World War I, neo-orthodox theologians tended to dismiss Ritschl. Since the 1960s he has come to be recognized as a perceptive historical theologian and the progenitor of several important tendencies that have deeply affected twentieth-century theology—including even the neo-orthodoxy of his critics.

Bibliography

A. *Die christliche Lehre von der Rechtfertigung und Versöhnung*, 3 vols., 3d ed. (Bonn, 1889); ET of vol. 1, *A Critical History of the Christian Doctrine of Justification and Reconciliation* (Edinburgh, 1872); ET of vol. 3, *The Christian Doctrine of Justification and Reconciliation: The Positive Development of the Doctrine* (Edinburgh, 1900, and Clifton, N.J., 1966); *Three Essays*, ed. Philip Hefner (Philadelphia, 1972), which contains the Prolegomena to *The History of Pietism* (1880), *Theology and Metaphysics* (1881), and *Instruction in the Christian Religion* (1886); *Geschichte des Pietismus*, 3 vols. (Bonn, 1880–86); *Gesammelte Aufsätze*, ed. Otto Ritschl, 2 vols. (Freiburg i. B. and Leipzig, 1893, 1896).

B.   LThK² 8:1324–25; NCE 12:522–23; ODCC 1400–1401; PRE 17:22–34; RGG 5: 1114–17; Otto Ritschl, *Albrecht Ritschls Leben*, 2 vols. (Freiburg i. B., 1892, 1896); James Richmond, *Ritschl: A Reappraisal* (London, 1978); David Lotz, *Ritschl and Luther: A Fresh Perspective on Albrecht Ritschl's Theology in the Light of His Luther Study* (Nashville, Tenn., 1974); Darrell Jodock et al., *Ritschl in Retrospect: History, Community, and Science* (Minneapolis, Minn., 1995).

Darrell Jodock

ROBERT GROSSETESTE. *See* GROSSETESTE, ROBERT.

ROBERT KILWARDBY. *See* KILWARDBY, ROBERT.

ROBERT OF MELUN (end of 11th century, England–1167, Hereford, England). *Education*: studied perhaps in Oxford, and then in Paris. *Career*: succeeded Abelard as master at Mont Ste. Geneviève, probably not for long; directed a school at Melun, at that time an important see and host to the king and court at certain times of the year; at King Henry II's command, returned to England in 1160; ordained priest, Oxford, 1163; bishop of Hereford, 1163–67.

Robert wrote three major works: *Questiones de divina pagina*, which treats material similar to that in Abelard's* *Sic et non* but proposes solutions to the apparent paradoxes; *Questiones de epistolis Pauli*; and *Sententiae*.

During his teaching career in Paris, Robert entered into several of the day's controversies, criticizing Abelard's teachings on original sin and Christology, Gilbert de la Porrée's* on the Trinity, and Peter Lombard's,* which stated that the power to sin came from God. His *Sententiae* addressed the discourses of the time and, though widely used, never became as popular as the work of the same name by Peter Lombard. His works treat the Incarnation, the Trinity, divine omnipotence, free will, and the nature of original sin. Robert's writing style set a standard for scholasticism and influenced such thirteenth-century masters as Albert the Great,* Bonaventure,* and Thomas Aquinas.*

Bibliography

A.   *Oeuvres de Robert de Melun*, ed. Raymond Martin, 4 vols. (Louvain, 1932–52).
B.   DTC 13:2751–53; LThK² 8:1341; NCE 11:533–34; ODCC 1402; F. Anders, *Die Christologie des Robert von Melun* (Paderborn, 1927).

Thomas S. Ferguson

ROGER BACON. *See* BACON, ROGER.

ROSMINI-SERBATI, ANTONIO (24 March 1797, Rovereto, Italy–1 July 1855, Stresa, Italy). *Education*: after studies in the public academy at Rovereto, he read theology at Padua, although his deserved reputation as a polymath was gained principally through unremitting private study and research; study and research at Rovereto and Milan, 1821–28. *Career*: ordained priest, 1821; founded the Institute of Charity, a religious congregation (which he governed until his death), 1828; published major works in philosophy, theology and sociology, 1830–55; parish priest, Rovereto, 1833–34; mission to Rome on behalf of the Piedmontese government and its projected concordat with the Holy See, 1848; accompanied Pius IX into exile at Gaeta, 1848–49; retired to Stresa, 1849–55.

Rosmini, a devout Catholic whose cause for beatification is now in hand at the Congregation for Saints, Rome, was undoubtedly the most controversial figure in nineteenth-century Italian theology. His philosophical starting point is the idea of being, the objective, universal, necessary, but indeterminate light of reason. Through its divine characteristics, this innate idea, although expressing only the possibility of things, not their reality, furnishes human nature with its dignity as the image of God and, philosophically speaking, answers the subjectivism of Kant and the German Idealists. It is the foundation of obligation in the moral field, the basis of all human right(s) and the bond of unity within the universal society of humankind. On the other hand, Christian regeneration finds its roots in being which, seen no longer solely in its possibility but perceived in its reality through the deiform and triniform grace of baptism, frees human beings (persons) from original sin, raises them to share in the divine nature, and makes them members of the church, which is "the society of mankind raised to a supernatural level."

Rosmini's vital devotion to the church and the essence of his ecclesiology are presented in his *Delle cinque piaghe della santa Chiesa [On The Five Wounds of Holy Church]*, a work that, although placed on the *Index of Forbidden Books* (1849), exerted considerable influence on Italian and other bishops during Vatican II. During his lifetime, all Rosmini's extant works were submitted to examination by the Congregation of the Index and declared free from error by the decree *Dimittantur* (1854). Forty propositions, some taken from works already examined, some from posthumous works, were condemned by the Holy Office decree *Post Obiturn* (1887) but without any explicit accompanying theological "note."

Bibliography

A. *Opere edite e inedite di Antonio Rosmini, edizione critica*, 30 of 80 vols. to date (Rome-Stresa, 1974–); *The Origin of Thought* (Durham, N.C., 1987); *The Five Wounds of the Church* (Leominster, Mass., 1987); *The Constitutions of the Society of Charity* (Durham, N.C., 1988); *Conscience* (Durham, N.C., 1989); *Certainty* (Durham, N.C., 1992); *The Philosophy of Politics*, 2 vols. (Durham, N.C., 1994); *The Philosophy of Right*, 6 vols. (Durham, N.C., 1993–96).

B. ECatt 10:1359–71; LThK² 9:54–55; NCE 12:677–79; ODCC 1419; Claude Leetham, *Rosmini, Priest and Philosopher* (New York, 1982); Denis Cleary, *Antonio Rosmini: Introduction to his Life and Teaching* (Durham, N.C., 1992).

Denis Cleary

ROUSSELOT, PIERRE (29 December 1878, Nantes, France–25 April 1915, Eparges, France). *Education*: licentiate in classical languages and licentiate in modern languages, Sorbonne, 1899; studied philosophy, French Jesuit House of Studies, Jersey, England, 1900–1903; studied theology, French Jesuit House of Studies, Hastings, England, 1905–9; Ph.D., Sorbonne, 1908. *Career*: entered Jesuits, Canterbury, 1895; teacher of classics to younger Jesuits, 1903–5; ordained priest, 1908; professor of dogmatic theology, Institut Catholique, Paris, 1909–14; mobilized, 1914, and killed in action, 1915.

Rousselot was one of the most original Thomist theologians in the first half of the twentieth century. His brief career coincided with the modernist crisis, during which Blondel's* philosophy and apologetics of immanence and Bergson's process metaphysics were very popular. To younger Catholics, Blondel and Bergson seemed to provide the philosophy that the church required to counter the impersonal positivism and the deductive conceptual idealist systems prevalent in France's universities. Older scholastic theologians, on the other hand, feared that these philosophies, far from countering modernism, could lend support to it. By conceding no more than a practical value to the concept, Bergsonism undermined the speculative truth of the church's dogmatic formulas; and, relying as it did upon the subjective love of the human will rather than the objective knowledge of the intellect, Blondel's apologetics ignored the need for the objectively verifiable signs and miracles to ground a valid apologetics and justify the reasonableness of the act of faith.

Rousselot, on the other hand, believed that modern philosophy and Thomism could profit from their contact with each other. In his two Sorbonne theses, *The Intellectualism of St. Thomas* and *The Problem of Love in the Middle Ages*, and in a set of review articles, Rousselot rediscovered a philosophy of knowledge, love, life, participation, and connaturality in the text of St. Thomas that revolutionized the historical interpretation of Thomisitic philosophy and showed that it was not the static rationalism that it was often thought to be. For St. Thomas, the highest form of knowledge was not the concept. It was the preconceptual insight of the *intellectus*, an immediate grasp of the singular under the influence of love. This was the knowledge that God and angels had of themselves and others, and it was the knowledge that we would have of God and ourselves in the Beatific Vision.

In 1910 Rousselot applied this philosophy to the theology of faith. His article *The Eyes of Faith* linked together St. Thomas' philosophy of *intellectus* or "insight," the role of human nature's natural love of God in St. Thomas' theory of knowledge, and the place of dynamic connaturality in St. Thomas' account of our grasp of truth. Through that synthesis Rousselot could show how the act of faith could be at once supernatural, free, and reasonable. That was possible because the act of faith was not a conclusion reached through conceptual reasoning. It was an act of insight through which a concrete human subject, under the influence of love and connaturality, grasped a truth of faith in a specific fact that, for him, had become a clue to its veracity.

Rousselot was killed almost before his career got under way. Nevertheless, his influence on Thomists for the rest of the century has been very great. Maréchalian and Lonerganian Thomism owe a great deal to him.

Bibliography

A. *The Intellectualism of St. Thomas* (New York, 1935); *Pour l'histoire du problème de l'amour au moyen-âge* (Munster, 1908); "Les yeux de la foi," RechScRel 1 (1910): 241–59, 444–75; ET, *The Eyes of Faith* (New York, 1990)

B. DTC 14:134–38; ECatt 10:1416; LThK² 9:76–77; NCE 12:692; Georges van Riet, *L'Epistemologie Thomiste* (Louvain, 1946), 301–13; Roger Aubert, *Le problème de l'acte de foi* (Louvain, 1958), 452–511; John M. McDermott, *Love and Understanding: The Relation of Will and Intellect in Rousselot's Christological Vision* (Rome, 1983); Gerald A. McCool, *From Unity to Pluralism: The Internal Evolution of Thomism* (New York, 1989), 39–80; idem, The Neo-Thomists, (Milwaukee, Wis., 1994), 97–116.

Gerald A. McCool

RUPERT OF DEUTZ (ca. 1075, in or near Liège, Belgium–4 March 1129, Deutz). *Education*: studied the liberal arts as oblate in the abbey of St. Lawrence, Liège, 1082. *Career*: professed as a monk of St. Lawrence, 1091; exiled at priory of Evergnicourt in France, 1092–95; experienced visions, 1105–8; ordained, 1108; participated in debates with schoolmasters, 1113–16; trial and exile to Siegburg because of teachings on simony, 1116–17; returned to Liège and debated masters at Laon on predestinarianism, 1117; appointed abbot of Deutz, 1120–29.

Rupert was a leading defender of the Benedictine tradition against attacks by canons regular; however, his greatest influence was confined to the German Empire. He criticized the failure of schoolmasters to apply dialectic to the study of Holy Scripture. Rupert developed a trinitarian theology of history. He applied allegorical exegesis to the Apocalypse, Eucharist, and predestination, and was among the first to interpret the *Song of Songs* as Christ's love for the Virgin. Rupert was a zealous supporter of papal reform, suffering several exiles, and resisted ordination from a simoniac bishop.

Bibliography

A. *Opera Omnia*, PL 167–170; CCCM 7, 9, 21–24, 26, 29; MGH, Geistesgeschichte 5; MGH, *Libelli de Lite* 3.

B. DSAM 13:1126–33; DTC 14:169–205; LThK² 9:102–6; NCE 12:723; ODCC 1424–25; PRE 17:229–43; Egid Beitz, *Rupertus von Deutz: Seine Werke und die bildende Kunst* (Cologne, 1930); Mariano Magrassi, *Teologia e storia nel pensiero di Ruperto di Deutz* (Rome, 1959); Maximo Peinador, "El comentario de Ruperto de Deutz al Cantar de los cantares," *Marianum* 31 (1969): 1–58; Rhabanus Haacke, "Nachlese zur Überlieferung Ruperts von Deutz,'' *Deutsches Archiv* 26 (1970): 528–40; Bernard McGinn, *Visions of the End* (New York, 1979); John H. Van Engen, *Rupert of Deutz* (Berkeley, Calif., 1983).

Daniel Marcel La Corte

RUYSBROECK, JAN VAN (1293, Ruisbroek, Brabant–2 December 1381, Groenendaal, Brabant). Left home at eleven to live under the guidance of his priest-uncle, a canon of St. Gudeles in Brussels; ordained priest, 1317; withdrew in March 1349 with two canons to a hermitage at Groenendaal where they became a community of canons regular with Ruysbroeck as prior; composed there all but the first of his writings, *The Spiritual Espousals*, which is also his masterpiece. In it and *The Book of the Twelve Beguines*, both commentaries on Mt 25:6, Ruysbroeck describes the coming of the divine bridegroom to meet the soul with his gifts, and the correlative going forth of the soul to meet her God. Ruysbroeck's mysticism recalls that of Saint Bernard* and of Richard of St. Victor* for whom, as for him, mystical experience was a foretaste of the beatific vision. Others of his notable works include *The Kingdom of Lovers*, *The Tabernacle*, *The Little Book of Enlightenment*, and *The Book of the Sparkling Stone*, also known as *The Treatise of the Perfection of the Sons of God*.

Bibliography

A.   *Werken*, 4 vols., rev. ed. (Tielt, 1944–48); *The Spiritual Espousals and Other Works*, trans. James A. Wiseman (New York, 1985).

B.   DSAM 8:659–97; DTC 14:408–20; NCE 12:763–65; ODCC 1430; PRE 17:267–73; Joseph Kuckhoff, *Johannes von Ruysbroeck der Wunderbare, 1293–1381. Einführung in sein Leben; Auswahl aus seinen Werken* (Munich, 1938); Bernhard Fraling, *Der Mensch vor dem Geheimnis Gottes. Untersuchungen zur christlichen Lehre des Jan van Ruusbroec* (Würzburg, 1967); *Jan van Ruusbroec: The Sources, Content and Sequels of His Mysticism*, ed. P. Mommaers and N. de Paepe (Louvain, 1984); Louis Dupré, *The Common Life: The Origins of Trinitarian Mysticism and Its Development by Jan Ruusbroec* (New York, 1984); Paul Verdeyen, *Ruusbroec and His Mysticism*, trans. Andre Lefevere (Collegeville, Minn., 1994).

Roland J. Teske

RYAN, JOHN AUGUSTINE (28 May 1869, Dakota County, Minn.–16 September 1945, St. Paul, Minn.). *Education*: studied at St. Thomas (St. Paul) Sem., St. Paul, Minn., 1887–92, 1892–98; S.T.L., S.T.D., The Catholic Univ. of America, 1900, 1906. *Career*: ordained priest, 1898; professor of moral theology, St. Paul Sem., 1902–15; professor of political science and theology, The Catholic Univ. of America, 1915–39; founder and editor, *Catholic Charities Review*, 1917–21; director, Social Action Department of the National Catholic Welfare (Council) Conference, 1919–45; lecturer in social ethics, National Catholic School of Social Service and Trinity Coll., 1921–39; member, Industrial Appeals Board of the National Recovery Administration, 1934–35.

Ryan was the leading American Catholic social theorist during the first half of the twentieth century. During his early studies, he discovered in Pope Leo XIII's 1891 encyclical on the condition of labor, *Rerum Novarum*, an authoritative religious approbation for his growing interest in industrial ethics. Pius XI's *Quadragesimo Anno* and the policies of the New Deal also provided Ryan's life of "social doctrine in action" both spiritual and political vindication.

Ryan's dissertation, published in 1906 as *A Living Wage*, and his 1916 book, *Distributive Justice*, detail his vision of economic justice and social reform. Drawing on neoscholastic Catholic philosophy, social scientific data, and common experience, Ryan deftly joined appeals to universal religio-moral principles with wily analysis of concrete economic circumstances and political dynamics. As director of the Social Action Department of the National Catholic Welfare Conference and during a multifaceted career as academic, author, ecclesial administrator, political commentator, and policy advocate, Ryan pioneered a still-influential style of Catholic Church engagement in U.S. public life.

As a public intellectual and Catholic social philosopher, Ryan's appeal and associations cut across typical Catholic boundaries of the day. Critics like Virgil Michel* deplored Ryan's lack of theological substance; radio priest Charles Coughlin castigated his progressive politics with the epithet, "Right Reverend Spokesman for the New Deal." In fact, Ryan's Catholic natural law perspective maintained firm theological moorings and direct links to papal social teaching. Economy, he judged, has a distinctly moral purpose and, indirectly, a religious one: to ensure material conditions for a decent livelihood conducive to persons' developing their God-given capacities and fulfilling their temporal and spiritual destinies. Ryan's priestly vocation fired his efforts to assure workers' right to economic opportunities to "live decently, as human beings in the image and likeness of God." Human dignity, religiously grounded, is the linchpin of his social agenda.

Ryan's economic ethics affirms that God has created the world for the sustenance of all His creatures; thus, a just economic system must assure fair access to all. Rights and duties of workers, employers, and capitalists spring from this imperative and are framed by religious injunctions against greed and the idolatry of material success. Ryan's theological anthropology led him to distinguish false from true understandings of human welfare and to specify minimum and maximum standards of living.

Ryan's agenda for economic justice had two main goals: a universal family living wage for workers and the establishment of industrial democracy, whereby workers would share in management, profits, and ownership. These were to be attained by social reform legislation, by a more powerful and participative status for workers in industry, and by the promotion of a strong, interdependent multigroup economic order. The latter, occupational group system—a scheme for reestablishing organic group relations among workers in various fields, and between worker's associations in cooperation with owners and capitalists—echoed that promoted by Pius XI in *Quadragesimo Anno*.

Ryan envisaged two concrete methods for advancing reform, methods his life exemplified. The first, "moral suasion," appeals to the hearts and consciences of individuals; the second, "social effort," involves associations such as labor unions and the state. Ryan warned against false consciousness that enthralls many, even "good Christians" to the foreign and inhumane ethical standards of the competitive marketplace. Combatting this is a task for molders of public opinion; but no societal change is possible without concerted, organized effort, especially in the modern era, when "social relations have become so numerous and so complex."

Bibliography

A. *A Living Wage* (New York, 1906); *Distributive Justice* (New York, 1916; 1927; 1942); *A Better Economic Order* (New York, 1935); *Social Reconstruction* (New York, 1920); *Declining Liberty and Other Papers* (New York, 1927); *Social Doctrine in Action* (New York, 1941).

B. DAB 23:679–82; DARB 464–65; NCAB C:190; NCE 12:767; NYT 17 September 1945, 19; Francis L. Broderick, *Right Reverend New Dealer: John A. Ryan* (New York, 1963); Charles E. Curran, *American Catholic Social Ethics* (Notre Dame, Ind., 1983); Joseph M. McShane, *Sufficiently Radical: Catholicism, Progressivism, and the Bishops' Program of 1919* (Washington, D.C., 1986); Harlan Beckley, *Passion for Justice* (Louisville, Ky., 1992).

Christine Firer Hinze

S

SADOLETO, JACOPO (12 July 1477, Modena–18 October 1547, Rome). *Education*: classical languages, Modena and Rome, 1498–1504. *Career*: poet and humanist, Rome, 1504–11; ordained priest, 1511; Apostolic Secretariate, Rome, 1513; bishop of Carpentras, 1517–47; cardinal, 1536.

Among his humanist tracts the most important was *On Educating Boys* (1530), which was frequently reprinted. Despite his excellence as a scholar of Latin and Greek letters, Sadoleto lacked depth as a theologian. His 1535 commentary on Paul's Epistle to the Romans tried to defend Catholic teaching against Luther,* but his treatment of justification had such a Pelagian flavor that both the Sorbonne and the papacy banned it. Despite that, Paul III recalled him to Rome to serve with Gasparo Contarini* on the commission that drew up the famous *Consilium de emendanda ecclesia*. He encouraged Paul III to convoke an ecumenical council that would work toward reforming the church and healing the schism north of the Alps. Sadoleto's conciliatory correspondence with German Protestants such as Philipp Melanchthon* only roused the ire of militant German Catholics. His famous 1539 *Letter to the Senate and People of Geneva* encouraging them to return to Catholicism backfired, for John Calvin* wrote a crushing theological reply that paved the way for Calvin's return to Geneva from Strasbourg.

Bibliography

A.   *Jacopi Sadoleti . . . opera quae extant omnia*, 4 vols. (repr. Ridgeway, N.J., 1964).
B.   LThK² 9:209–10; NCE 12:846; ODCC 1439; RGG 5:1278–79; Richard M. Douglas, *Jacopo Sadoleto, 1477–1547: Humanist and Reformer* (Cambridge, 1959).

John Patrick Donnelly

SAILER, JOHN MICHAEL (17 November 1751, Aresing, Upper Bavaria–20 May 1832, Regensburg). *Education*: studied philosophy, Univ. of Ingolstadt,

1770–75. *Career*: entered Jesuits, 1770; ordained diocesan priest, 1775; professor of dogmatic theology, Univ. of Ingolstadt, 1780; professor of ethics and pastoral theology, Univ. of Dillingen, Bavaria, 1784–94; pastoral work, 1794–99; professor of pastoral theology, Ingolstadt, 1799–1800; Univ. of Landshut, Bavaria, 1800–1821; cathedral canon, Regensburg, 1821; auxiliary and bishop of Regensburg, 1822–29.

Sailer is acknowledged as a leading German Catholic theologian of his day. He was hailed as a pioneer, even founder, in the study of pastoral theology—catechetics, religious pedagogy, homiletics—and was remembered as an effective teacher who influenced a number of noteworthy theologians and public figures. His literary remains are extensive and address a wide variety of fields, including philosophy of religion, moral theology, mystical theology, and pastoral theology. Sailer's works need to be placed in the context of post-Tridentine theology and the German Aufklärung and Romanticism. His theology offered an alternative to the post-Tridentine emphasis on the hierarchial and juridical nature of the visible church and the moralistic character of Enlightenment thought. His view of the church accentuated the importance of each individual's spiritual experience. Moreover, he accentuated the role of the imagination and the affections in the spiritual life, moral decision making, religious pedagogy, and preaching. In contrast to the scholastic methods found in the post-Tridentine period, Sailer marshaled his theological arguments drawing heavily from the Scriptures and the church fathers.

Sailer's early writing shows the influence of his teacher, Benedict Stattler (1728–97), who adhered to the philosophy of Christian Wolff* and G. W. Leibniz and advanced a eudaimonistic approach to ethics and theology: happiness is the purpose of creation and provides the prism for understanding law, affectivity, and human acts. Sailer broke away from this approach after his encounter with the epistemological and ethical theories of Immanuel Kant, but also because of his previous experience in the spiritual exercises of Saint Ignatius* and his increasing knowledge of the mystical traditions of the baroque period.

His emphasis on experience (*Erlebnis*), imagination, and the affections is evident in his widely read book on prayer, *Vollständiges Lese— und Gebetbuch für katholische Christen*, and in his works on moral theology, *Glückseligkeitslehre aus Vernunftgründen* (2 parts, 1787–91) and *Handbuch der christlichen Moral, zunächst für künftige katholische Seelsorger und dann für jeden gebildeten Christen* (3 vols., 1817). His writings on a variety of topics in pastoral theology (preaching, religious pedagogy, liturgy) are contained in *Vorlesungen aus der Pastoraltheologie* (3 vols., 1788–89) and in *Der katholische Seelsorger in gegenwärtiger Zeit* (2 parts, 1819–23).

Bibliography

A. *Johann Michael Sailers sämtliche Werke*, ed. Joseph Widmer, 41 vols. (Sulzbach, 1830–41, vol. 41 in 1855).

B. DTC 14:749–54; LThK² 9:214–15; NCE 12:851–52; Joseph Rupert Geiselmann, *Von lebendiger Religiosität zum Leben der Kirche: Johann Michael Sailers Verständnis der Kirche geistesgeschichtlich gedeutet* (Stuttgart, 1952); *Johann Michael Sailer und seine Zeit*, eds. George Schwaiger and Paul Mai, Beiträge zur Geschichte des Bistums Regensburg (Regensburg, 1982); Georg Schwaiger, *Johann Michael Sailer: Der bayerische Kirchenvater* (Munich, Zürich, 1982); Bertram Meier, *Die Kirche der wahren Christen: Johann Michael Sailers Kirchenvertändnis zwischen Unmittelbarkeit und Vermittlung*, Münchener kirchenhistorische Studien, Band 4 (Stuttgart, Berlin, Cologne, 1990).

Bradford Hinze

SCHAFF, PHILIP (1 January 1819, Chur, Switzerland–20 October 1893, New York, N.Y.). *Education*: studied at gymnasium, Stuttgart, Germany, 1835–37; Univ. of Tübingen, Germany, 1837–39; Univ. of Halle, Germany, 1839–40; licentiate in theology, Univ. of Berlin, Germany, 1841. *Career*: lecturer (privatdozent), Univ. of Berlin, 1842–44; ordained Reformed minister, Elberfeld, Germany, 1844; professor of church history and biblical literature, Theol. Sem. of the German Reformed Church, Mercersburg, Pa., 1844–63; heresy triai and acquittal, York, Pa., 1845; founding editor, *Der Deutsche Kirchenfreund*, 1848–53; corresponding secretary, New York Sabbath Committee, 1864–70; executive officer, American branch of the Evangelical Alliance, 1867–93; professor of theology, symbolics, biblical literature, and church history, Union Theol. Sem., New York, N.Y., 1870–93; president, American Committee on Bible Revision, 1872–84; founder and president, American Society of Church History, New York, N.Y., 1888–93.

Schaff was perhaps the most prominent and prolific church historian and ecumenist of nineteenth-century America. Despite the astounding number of books and articles that he published over his fifty-year career, the blueprint for much of his thought is contained in his first American work, *The Principle of Protestantism* (Chambersburg, Pa., 1845). Influenced by German idealism, Schaff viewed church history as the progressive manifestation of Christ's life in the world. This process of organic development, however, does not advance along a straight line, but (owing to the presence of sin) moves dialectically from one age to the next. So every era exhibits some extremity, which then gives birth to an opposing but legitimate reaction.

Consequently, though Schaff decried the authoritarian excesses of medieval Catholicism, to the alarm of many of his American counterparts, he regarded the Reformation as "the legitimate offspring, the greatest act of the Catholic Church." He looked forward to the final reunion of Christendom in which the sectarian extremes of Protestantism (exemplified by American religion) would give way to an organically united Reformed Catholicism. His orthodox, but irenic, historical and biblical scholarship, as well as his international ecumenical activities, were all undertaken with this end in mind.

Bibliography

A. *America: Sketch of the Political, Social and Religious Character of the United States of North America*, ed. Perry Miller (Cambridge, Mass., 1961); *History of the*

Christian Church, completed by David Schaff, 8 vols. (6 vols. New York, 1882–92; repr. Grand Rapids, Mich., 1985); *Theological Propaedeutic: A General Introduction to the Study of Theology* (New York, 1892); *Philip Schaff: Historian and Ambassador of the Universal Church*, ed. Klaus Penzel (Macon, Ga., 1991); *Reformed and Catholic: Selected Historical and Theological Writings of Philip Schaff*, ed. Charles Yrigoyen, Jr. and George H. Bricker (Pittsburgh, Pa., 1979).

B.   DAB 16:417–18; DARB 470–72; NCAB 3:76–77; NYT 21 October 1893, 2; SH 10:223–25; Stephen R. Graham, *Cosmos in the Chaos: Philip Schaff's Interpretation of Nineteenth-Century American Religion* (Grand Rapids, Mich., 1995); David S. Schaff, *The Life of Philip Schaff* (New York, 1897); George H. Shriver, *Philip Schaff: Christian Scholar and Ecumenical Prophet* (Macon, Ga., 1987); James H. Nichols, *Romanticism in American Theology: Nevin and Schaff at Mercersburg* (Chicago, 1961).

William DiPuccio

SCHEEBEN, MATTHIAS JOSEPH (1 March 1835, Meckenheim, Germany– 21 July 1888, Cologne). *Education*: studied theology under Jesuits of the "Roman School," Passaglia, Franzelin, Schrader, Cercia at the Collegium Germanicum et Hungaricum, Gregorian Univ., Rome, 1852–59. *Career*: ordained priest, Rome, 1858; rector of the Ursuline Sisters' church and religion instructor in their convent-school, Münstereifel, 1859; professor of theology, Cologne sem., 1860–88; editor, *Das ökumenische Concil vom 1869*, 1869–82 (title changed to *Periodische Blätter* in 1872); director, *Katholischer Hausfreund* magazine, 1860–66; founding editor, *Kölner Pastoralblatt*; author, 1860–88.

Scheeben was one of the outstanding Catholic theologians of the nineteenth century. His uncommon method combined a Petavian positive theology of the church fathers with Thomist principles of speculative theology. Focus on the supernatural characterized his dogmatic theology of the Trinity, Christ, Redemption, indwelling Spirit, church, Mary, Eucharist, grace, and eschatology. He defended Catholic faith, Vatican I, and papal infallibility against nineteenth-century liberalism. He recognized the theological significance of the laity. Pastoral concern for the spiritual and theological formation of believers animated even his most speculative reflections. Respect for an affective dynamic in faith, love for God, suffused his expositions of the truths of faith with a spirit of reverence. Much of his writing—critiques of rationalism and liberalism aside—has a prayerful quality often called mystical.

Systematic emphasis on the supernatural, however, did not produce a fideist dogmatics. Convinced about the congruence of philosophy and theology, a student of Cyril of Alexandria* and Thomas Aquinas,* Scheeben had a scientific (i.e. truths of faith ordered and unified) idea of theology. Harmony between faith and reason was a methodological principle. Nonetheless, some have linked him to the Romantic movement and vitalism because he situated theological reflection within an individual and an ecclesial "life" of faith that was expressed in practice. Indeed, reference to the living of faith characterized each theme later considered as the key to his theology—the supernatural as such, the Trinity, a mission proper to the Holy Spirit, divinization, theological epistemology.

He considered theology essential to living the faith and to spiritual progress. His hope was that his works would contribute to the theological understanding of clergy and laity beyond the circle of professional theologians. The objective was not only a deepening grasp of truth held in faith but movement toward God through Christ in the Spirit. An orientation to what amounted to renewal, a theological method synthesizing patristic with scholastic insight, a trinitarian perspective, a nonjuridical ecclesiology centered in the liturgy of the Eucharist, a developed pneumatology, and a theology of the laity permit his contribution to be read also in reference to specific themes and to the overall purpose of Vatican II.

Bibliography

A. *Gesammelte Schriften*, ed. Josef Hofer et al., 8 vols. (Freiburg im Breisgau, 1941–67); *The Mysteries of Christianity*, trans. Cyril Vollert (St. Louis, Mo., 1946); *Nature and Grace*, trans. Cyril Vollert (St. Louis, Mo., 1954).

B. DSAM 14:404–8; DTC 14:1270–74; ECatt 11:33–34; KThD 2:386–408; LThK² 9:376–79; NCE 12:1122; ODCC 1461; John Courtney Murray, "Matthias Joseph Scheeben's Doctrine on Supernatural, Divine Faith: A Critical Exposition" (1937), in *Matthias Scheeben on Faith: The Doctoral Dissertation of John Courtney Murray*, ed. D. Thomas Hughson (Lewiston, 1987); *Wegbereiter heutiger Theologie: Matthias Scheeben* (Graz, 1976); Karl-Heinz Minz, *Pleroma Trinitatis: die Trinitätstheologie bei Matthias Joseph Scheeben* (Frankfurt am Main, 1982); *M. J. Scheeben: teologo cattolico d'ispirazione tomista*, in *Studi tomisti* 33 (Rome, 1988); Wolfgang W. Müller, *Die Gnade Christi: Eine geschichtlich-systematische Darstellung der Gnadentheorie M. J. Scheebens und ihrer Wirkungsgeschichte* (St. Ottilien, 1994); Ivo Muser, *Das mariologische Prinzip "gottesbräutliche Mutterschaft" und das Verständnis der Kirche bei M. J. Scheeben* (Rome, 1995); Andrzej Napiorkowsi, *Schrift, Tradition, Kirche: Glaubensquelle in Matthias Joseph Scheebens theologischer Erkenntnislehre* (Frankfurt am Main, 1996).

                                                                D. Thomas Hughson

SCHELL, HERMAN (28 February 1850, Freiburg im Breisgau–31 May 1906, Würzburg). *Education*: Catholic sem. training, Univ. in Freiburg, 1868–70, Würzburg, 1870–72; studied theology, Gregorian Univ., Rome, 1879–81. *Career*: ordained priest, 1873; professor of apologetics, history of Christian art and archaeology, and philosophy of religion, Univ. of Würzburg, 1884–1906; rector, Univ. of Würzburg, 1896–97.

Schell is most closely associated with German *Reformkatholizismus*. Using the method of "immanence apologetics," he tried to demonstrate the catholicity of the Roman Catholic tradition and its relevance to modern culture by bringing neoscholasticism into dialogue with the best elements of late-nineteenth-century German thought. Influenced primarily by J. E. Kuhn,* Jakob Sengler, Franz Brentano, and Domenico Palmieri, Schell learned the content of Roman Catholic neoscholasticism but rejected its ideology. Sengler and Brentano worked with him on his first doctoral dissertation, Palmieri in Rome on his second, completed in 1883 and accepted at Tübingen for his "promotion" in theology. On 15

December 1898, Rome placed his most recent four works on the *Index* as suspected of "modernism"—faulted for his dynamic concept of God as *causa sui*, for minimizing the pains of hell, for erroneous conceptions of freedom, and for exalting reason's power to penetrate the mystery of the Trinity. Schell submitted and then published two works critical of liberal Protestant thought. Rome's censure meant that the work of this most creative German Catholic theologian of his day is now too little known.

Bibliography

A. *Die Einheit des Seelenlebens nach Aristotles* (Freiburg, 1873); *Das Wirken des dreieinigen Gottes* (Mainz, 1885); *Katholische Dogmatik*, 3 vols. in 4 (Paderborn, 1889–93); *Gott und Geist*, 2 vols. (Paderborn, 1883, 1886); *Der Katholizismus als Princip des Fortschritts* (Würzburg, 1897); *Die neue Zeit und der alte Glaube* (Würzburg, 1898).

B. DTC 14:1275–77; ECatt 11:37–39; LThK² 9:384–85; NCE 12:1124; RGG 5: 1395–96; Vincent Berning, *Das Denken Herman Schells* (Essen, 1964); *Gott, Geist und Welt: Herman Schell als Philosoph und Theologe* (Munich, 1978); *Systematisches Philosophieren* (Paderborn, 1984); George E. Griener, *Ernst Troeltsch and Herman Schell: Christianity and the World Religions* (Frankfurt, 1990).

David G. Schultenover

SCHLEIERMACHER, FRIEDRICH DANIEL ERNST (21 November 1768, Breslau–12 February 1834, Berlin). *Education*: Stadtschule, Ples, 1780–83; Pädagogicum der Brüderunität, Niesky, 1783–85; Theologishes Seminar der Brüderunität, Barby, 1785–87; Univ. of Halle, 1787–90; first theology exam., 1790; second exam., 1794. *Career*: private tutor, 1790–93; assistant pastor of Reformed Church, Landsberg/Warthe, 1794–96; pastor of Charité Hospital, Berlin, 1796–1802; pastor of Reformed Church, Stolp, 1802–3; professor and Universitätsprediger, Halle, 1804–7; preacher at the Dreifaltigkeitskirche, Berlin, 1809–34; member of founding commission and professor, Univ. of Berlin, 1810–34; first dean of the theological faculty, Berlin, 1810–34; secretary of the Berlin Academy of Sciences, 1814–34; rector of the Univ. of Berlin, 1815–34; translator of Plato's works, 1805–28.

German polymath: at once a theologian, pastor, ecclesiastical administrator, philosopher, educator, patriot, and man of letters. Widely acknowledged to be the "father of modern theology," his work decisively influenced the direction and often anticipated the results of the development of subsequent Protestant—and now Catholic—liberal theology in the nineteenth and twentieth centuries. In his life and thought the three streams that combined to form theological liberalism—Pietism, Romanticism, and Idealism—first flowed together in an original and unique confluence that was to dominate the whole of the theology of the modern period by establishing the categories and terms of the debate for both proponents and opponents alike.

Schleiermacher was born into the home of a Reformed chaplain of the Prussian army and was stamped religiously by the piety of the Moravian schools of his childhood and intellectually by the Enlightenment philosophy taught him at Halle as a young man. While yet an obscure pastor in the Prussian capital, he published his epochal *Über Die Religion. Reden an die Gebildeten unter ihren Verächtern* (1799), which was strongly influenced by the Romanticism he encountered in the literary circles of Berlin society. The book was both an apologetic and a work of highly original constructive theology that redefined the traditional understanding of the field. In it he defended religion against the contemptuous attacks of its Enlightenment critics and the growing disdain of the social classes they influenced. He argued that its opponents as well as its defenders had dismissed religion only by fundamentally misconstruing its true nature. True religion is in the first place, he claimed, neither a matter of metaphysics and dogma (as in Protestant orthodoxy), nor of natural science and philosophy (as in Enlightenment rationalism), nor even of private and public morality (as with Kant)—though each of these has a subordinate and coordinate role to play. Religion is rather, he maintained, at root a matter of "piety," a unique and distinct "intuition" or "feeling" defined as "a sense and taste for the Infinite" that goes before and underlies all abstract thought, empirical experience, and ethical compulsion. Such intuition or feeling, therefore, is the "original thing" and not a "third thing" alongside knowing and doing. Indeed, it is precisely that original and most basic human act that opens the pious individual to the universe and establishes that individual in his or her concrete, finite existence in encounter with the Infinite. Thus, he wrote, "The contemplation of the pious is the immediate consciousness of the universal existence of all finite things in and through the Infinite, and of all temporal things in and through the Eternal." With that "immediate consciousness" he claimed to have identified the unique aspect of human reality that is the provenance of religion alone. And now understood as reflection on that immediate consciousness, he thought to establish theology anew as a distinct field of scientific inquiry to be differentiated from both philosophy and the natural sciences by its unique object. Although published anonymously for fear of public derision, the response of many theologians and much of the educated public was enthusiastic approbation. They recognized in his proposal a positive advance beyond the categories of eighteenth-century orthodoxy and Enlightenment naturalism as well as an opportunity to lay renewed claim to the status of an objective science on behalf of theology alongside the other emergent sciences in the modern university.

As a result, Schleiermacher soon received an appointment to the theological faculty at Halle. There he lectured not only on various topics in theology but also on philosophy and hermeneutics. The latter represented an area of groundbreaking research and pointed to his growing interest in the Enlightenment's reformulation of the question of the historical origins of Christianity in Jesus and how Christ relates to those who live centuries later. Those concerns came to fullest expression in a brief work entitled *Die Weihnachtsfeier* (1805), a text reminiscent of Plato's dialogues. There he describes a gathering of a group of friends on Christmas Eve and recounts their conversation about the meaning of the season and the biblical story of Christ's birth. By means of this literary device, Schleiermacher produces a condensed and pointed narrative that clarifies his understanding of religion's essence and theologically advances this concept beyond the form it had taken earlier in the *Reden* by rooting it in the historical particularity of the person of Jesus Christ. First, to distinguish what he has identified as the true nature of religion from Schelling's speculative metaphysical notion of "intellectual intuition," he dispenses with all his earlier talk of "intuition" and will speak now only of "feeling." He distances himself thereby from any notion of the active, productive functioning of the rational capacity of the human ego in Idealist philosophy and makes clear that the feeling that concerns him is essentially a passive receptivity to the consciousness of communion with absolute unity and totality that is granted to humanity by religion alone, an immediate consciousness of human being as being in God, in which an individual's free acts are but reflections of his or her finite particularity being freely determined by the Infinite. Second, Schleiermacher then goes on to relate that clarified account of feeling to Jesus himself. Employing the reductionist historical-critical assertions of one of the participants in the conversation as a foil (i.e., that we have little reliable historical knowledge about Jesus and what we have indicates he was more akin to the Jewish prophet, John the Baptist, than to the Christian apostle, Paul of Tarsus), Schleiermacher insists that although we have limited historical knowledge of Christ, to focus on that alone is to miss the true significance of the season and the birth entirely. Much more to the point, he claims, is to begin with religious consciousness. Humanity lives in the disharmony and estrangement of the separation of spirit and flesh and thus desperately needs redemption. That redemption is known in the immediate consciousness of the Infinite and Eternal in the temporal and finite that true religion brings. That consciousness itself, however, is not eternal or infinite; it has a point of origin in space and time, both in terms of an individual life and the life of the human community as a whole. The point at which that immediate consciousness first entered history was, he argues, "the birth of a divine child," Jesus the Redeemer, the very reason for the celebration of Christmas. The season marks the emergence of the one who was perfectly conscious of the Infinite in the finite, of the Eternal in the temporal, in the midst of a confused and conflicted world of opposing realities, of becoming, of duplicity, and of distortion. "In the first bud of the new life we see at the same time its finest blossom, its highest perfection," he writes. As such, Jesus the Redeemer, according to Schleiermacher, embodied the archetype of the idea of true humanity, perfect consciousness of God and self, and communicated that to all who came after him. He sums that up it the biblical text that would become his ever repeated refrain: Jn 1:14, "And the Word became flesh and lived among us, and we have seen his glory, the glory as the Father's only Son, full of grace and truth." In the combination of those two elements, revelation in Jesus Christ the Redeemer and the subsequent pious perception and reception of that emergent consciousness, we have, he argues, the true understanding of Christmas and the true essence of Christianity.

In 1806 Halle was conquered by Napoleon's army and the university was closed. Schleiermacher, who actively opposed the French and just as aggressively advocated the Prussian cause, was eventually forced to return to Berlin where he became involved with both a reorganization of the Evangelical Church in Prussia and with the plans of Friedrich Wilhelm III to establish a new university in the capital to serve as an intellectual center for a renewed Prussian state. There he spent the rest of his life. He became a professor at the founding of the university in 1810, was the first dean of the theological faculty, and became the university rector in 1815. There also he developed his understanding of theology as a systematic enterprise. In 1811 he published his *Kurze Darstellung des theologischen Studiums*, in which he laid out a new conception of the organization of a theological faculty and theological pedagogy. He then proceeded to lecture on every area in the discipline, with the exception of the Old Testament. It was, however, the appearance of his magisterial work on systematics, *Der christliche Glaube* (1821–22), that marked the high point of his theological efforts. He took as the task of systematic theology the rigorous interrogation of that religious consciousness bequeathed to the Christian community by Jesus of Nazareth—among the many varieties of such consciousness in human history, the highest, he argued—in order to gain understanding of the transcendent reality that is its ultimate ground. Thus, although formally the immediate object of his theology's investigation is a distinct form of finite and temporal human consciousness (i.e., piety), materially the ultimate subject of the inquiry is to be the Infinite and the Eternal (i.e., God). It is only the former, Christologically determined, that gives access to the latter. For this reason Schleiermacher maintains that in his understanding of dogmatics, "everything is related to the redemption accomplished by Jesus of Nazareth." The book begins with a further clarification of the definition of the essence of piety as "the consciousness of being absolutely dependent, or, which is the same thing, of being in relation with God." It then proceeds to give an account of all the traditional topics of Western systematic theology, beginning with God in relation to the world and ending with the Trinity. Each step seeks to illustrate his programmatic claim that "Christian doctrines are accounts of the Christian religious affections set forth in speech."

Bibliography

A. *Friedrich Daniel Ernst Schleiermacher: Kritische Gesamtausgabe*, ed. H.-J. Birkner, G. Ebeling, H. Fischer, H. Kimmerle, and K.-V. Selige, 17 vols. to date (Berlin, 1980–); *On Religion. Speeches to Its Cultured Despisers*, trans. J. Oman (New York, 1958); *Christmas Eve. Dialogue on the Incarnation*, trans. T. N. Tice (Richmond, Va., 1967); *Brief Outline of the Study of Theology*, trans. T. N. Tice (Atlanta, Ga., 1977); *The Life of Jesus*, ed. J. C. Verheyden, trans. S. M. Gilmour (Philadelphia, 1975); *Hermeneutics: The Handwritten Manuscripts*, ed. H. Kimmerle, trans. J. Duke and J. Forstman (Missoula, Mont., 1977); *The Christian Faith*, ed. H. R. Mackintosh and J. S. Stewart (Edinburgh, 1976); *On the Glaubenslehre. Two Letters to Dr. Lücke*, trans. J. Duke and F. Fiorenza (Chico, Calif., 1981); *Dialectic, or, The Art of Doing Philosophy: A Study Edition of the 1811 Notes*, trans. T. N. Tice (Atlanta: Ga., 1996).

B.   BBKL 9:253–70; EKL 4:71–81; LThK³ 2:768–69; NCE 12:1136–37; ODCC 209–10; Karl Barth, *The Theology of Schleiermacher: Lectures at Göttingen 1923–1924* (Edinburgh, 1982); Wilfried Brandt, *Der Heilige Geist und die Kirche bei Schleiermacher*, (Zurich, 1968); B. A. Garrish, *A Prince of the Church: Schleiermacher and the Beginnings of Modern Theology* (Philadelphia, 1984); R. R. Niebuhr, *Schleiermacher on Christ and Religion* (London, 1965); Martin Redeker, *Schleiermacher: Life and Thought*, trans. J. Wallhausser (Philadelphia, 1973).

D. Lyle Dabney

SCHMAUS, MICHAEL (17 July 1897, Oberbaar, Bavaria–8 December, 1993, Gauting, Bavaria). *Education*: Dr. theol., Univ. of Munich, 1924. *Career*: ordained priest, 1922; lecturer, Philosophische-theologische Hochschule und Seminar, Freising, 1924–29; lecturer, Univ. of Munich, 1928–29; professor of dogmatic theology, German Univ. in Prague, 1929–33; Univ. of Münster, 1933–46; Univ. of Munich, 1946–1965; rector, Univ. of Munich, 1951–52; domestic prelate, 1952; founder, Grabmann Institute for Research of Medieval Theology and Philosophy, 1954; consultor and peritus, Second Vatican Council, 1960–65; professor emeritus, 1965; visiting professor, Univ. of Chicago, 1966–67; supernumerary prothonotary apostolic, 1984; active retirement, 1965–93.

In his early training at the hands of Martin Grabmann, Schmaus learned well the method of historical theology. Consequently his work is marked not only by a concern for historical accuracy and attention to detail but by a strong sense of the relativity of theological statements. His published articles, over 140 in number, reveal a predilection for historical subjects. At the same time, his scope was universalist. His major works, the *Katholische Dogmatik* and *Der Glaube der Kirche*, were both accounts of the whole of Catholic systematic theology. The principal interest of Schmaus as a theologian lies in the creative tension here revealed between meticulous attention to detail and concern to realize in systematic fashion a vision of the whole of theology. With his devotion to tradition, Schmaus was no theological innovator. His was the theology of neo-scholasticism, but at his hands it was translated into a theology of interpersonal relations placed at the service of the proclamation of the Gospel.

The *Dogmatik* began as a work of three volumes. By the sixth edition it had grown to eight volumes, and it went through a further nine editions and was translated into other European languages. It bears comparison with Barth's* *De Kirchliche Dogmatik*, with which it was roughly contemporaneous. Inspired by the same pastoral zeal, it was written in clear and passionate German, though it lacked the originality of Barth. Schmaus' respect for history ensured that Scripture as a source was treated more scientifically than was usual in Catholic manuals, but at the same time his strong theological sense precluded every hint of positivism. Among Catholic manuals the *Dogmatik* was outstanding for its rigor, its thoroughness, and its accessibility, not to mention its overriding sense of the unbroken continuity of the Catholic tradition. After the Council, Schmaus felt the need to produce a new *Dogmatik* taking into account its insights and concerns. Hence *Der Glaube der Kirche*, in two volumes, which had a clear Christological focus, involved the believer and his/her subjectivity in the theology of revelation and faith, and manifested both a commitment to ecumenism and a positive assessment of the non-Christian religions.

Bibliography

A. *Die psychologische Trinitätslehre des hl. Augustinus* (Münster, 1927); *Der Liber Propugnatorius des Thomas Anglicus and die Lehrunterschiede zwischen Thomas von Aquin und Duns Scotus* (Münster, 1930); *Katholische Dogmatik*, 8 vols. (Munich, 1938–64); *Der Glaube der Kirche—Handbuch katholischer Dogmatik*, 2 vols. (Munich, 1969–70).

B. *Wahrheit und Verkündigung—Michael Schmaus zum 70. Geburtstag*, ed. Leo Scheffczyk, Werner Dettloff and Richard Heinzmann (Munich, 1967); Obituary, in *Münchener theologische Zeitschrift* 45 (1994): 113–27; Heinz Hürten, *Deutsche Katholiken, 1918–1945* (Paderborn, 1992).

David Coffey

SCHMEMANN, ALEXANDER (13 September 1921, Estonia, Russia–13 December 1983, Crestwood, N.Y.). *Education*: theological studies at St. Sergius Orthodox Theol. Institute, Paris, 1940–45. *Career*: instructor of Byzantine church history, St. Sergius, 1945–51; ordained priest, 1946; professor of church history and liturgical theology, St. Vladimir's Theol. Sem., N.Y., 1951–83; dean of the sem., 1962–83; Orthodox observer, Second Vatican Council, 1962–65.

Schmemann played a vital role in making St. Vladimir's Theological Seminary a center of liturgical and eucharistic revival. He was influenced by the church historian A. V. Kartashev, by the eucharistic theology of Nikolai Afanassieff,* and by the *théologie nouvelle* of Jean Daniélou* and Louis Bouyer.*

As a writer, teacher, and speaker Schmemann's genius lay less in the realm of formal scholarship (for which he always expressed a certain impatience) than in the forcefully charismatic presentation and, to be sure, personal synthesis of materials from the teachers of his youth (e.g., Kartashev, Afanassieff, and Fr. Sergei Bulgakov), together with the contributions of liturgical scholars such as A. Baumstark and O. Casel,* and of scholars of comparative religion, notably of his friend and correspondent Mircea Eliade.

The mind of the church, Schmemann held, is revealed in its liturgical worship. This did not mean for him simply that the *lex orandi* is a source of dogmatic formulae, or even the primary source. It meant more, specifically that in the church's liturgy the experience of Christ and of the world transfigured in Him is both presupposed and illustrated, revealed. By reflecting on the sequence of the services, the hymnody and its ordering, one acquires a proper sense of "theology," which for Schmemann always meant primarily doxology, the revelation and praise of God's Kingdom present among and through the worshiping community. His sense of beauty was thus very sharp, and this appeared in a second great love that he frequently referred to and saw as a corroboration of his vision: the great poetry of Russia and Western Europe. Both the liturgy and the poets, he felt, carried on in their particular ways the act of Christ. Both reconcile God and cosmos. Both break down the false barriers between sacred and profane, barriers which Schmemann summed up under the heading of "secularism," and for which he reserved his most impassioned condemnations.

Bibliography

A.   *The Historical Road of Eastern Orthodoxy* (New York, 1963, rev. ed. New York, 1977); *Introduction to Liturgical Theology*, trans. A. E. Moorhouse (London, 1966); *For the Life of the World: Sacraments and Orthodoxy* (rev. ed. New York, 1973); *Of Water and the Spirit* (New York, 1974); *Church, World, and Mission: Reflections on Orthodoxy in the West* (New York, 1979); *The Eucharist* (New York, 1987); *Liturgy and Tradition: Theological Reflections of Alexander Schmemann*, ed. Thomas Fisch (New York, 1990).

B.   HDOC 291; NYT 14 December 1983, B5; Paul Garrett, "Fr. Alexander Schmemann: A Chronological Bibliography (Excluding Book Reviews)," SVTQ 28 (1984): 11–26; John Meyendorff, "Father Alexander Schmemann, Dean, 1962–1983," SVTQ 28 (1984): 3–65; W. Jardine Grisbrooke, "An Orthodox Approach to Liturgical Theology: The Work of Alexander Schmemann," *Studia Liturgica* 23 (1993): 140–57; Michael Plekon, "Alexander Schmemann: Father and Teacher of the Church," *Pro Ecclesia* 3 (1994): 275–88; Vigen Guroian, "An Orthodox View of Orthodoxy and Heresy: An Appreciation of Fr. Alexander Schmemann," *Pro Ecclesia* 4 (1995): 79–91.

Alexander Golitzin

SCHMUCKER, SAMUEL SIMON (28 February 1799, Hagerstown, Md.–26 July 1873, Gettysburg, Pa.). *Education*: Univ. of Pennsylvania, 1814–17; Princeton Sem., 1818–20. *Career*: pastor in and around New Market, Va., 1820–26; professor of theology and administrator of the Lutheran Sem., Gettysburg, Pa., 1826–64; retirement, 1864–73.

For two decades during the second quarter of the nineteenth century (1825–45) Samuel S. Schmucker was the unrivaled theological leader of the huge majority of Lutherans in the United States. Shortly before he was ordained in 1820 he helped form the first consolidation of Lutheran synodical groups, called the General Synod. He was the author of all the major documents that guided the General Synod's polity and served as its president from 1828 to 1845. Schmucker was the prime mover in the organization of a Lutheran Seminary (1826) and later a college (1832) located at Gettysburg, Pa.. He was appointed as the seminary's first professor of theology and served in this capacity for nearly forty years (1826–64). His textbook, *Elements of a Popular Theology* (1834), was regarded as the standard of Lutheran theology in North America.

Schmucker's theological orientation was grounded in the traditions of German Lutheran Pietism. Like his Pietist predecessors, he was a strong defender of the basic teachings of Lutheranism, contained in the Augsburg Confession. At the same time he was a staunch advocate of inter-Protestant unity. His *Fraternal Appeal* (1838) envisioned a confederation of Protestant denominations based on a common confession of fundamental Christian doctrines. Schmucker's theology also exhibited a strong social concern. He was a leader and advocate of many of the moral reforms of his day, especially the abolition of slavery. He believed in relating and adapting Lutheranism's heritage to the American scene.

By the late 1840s Schmucker's "American Lutheranism" was increasingly challenged by the rising tide of a more conservative, confessional, and sectarian Lutheranism. For the rest of his life he fought an aggressive but losing battle against this movement. The culminating point in this struggle came in 1855, when a pamphlet in which he called for revisions in the Augsburg Confession met with an overwhelming rejection. Coming at the heighth of the controversy over slavery, it is possible that Schmucker's avid abolitionism may have added to the completeness of this repudiation. After an abortive attempt to begin impeachment proceedings against him, Schmucker resigned from his position at Gettysburg Seminary in 1864. His last years were spent in writing and working for the cause of Christian unity.

Bibliography

A.   *Elements of a Popular Theology* (New York, 1834, and many subsequent editions); *Fraternal Appeal*, ed. Frederick Wentz (Philadelphia, 1965); *American Lutheranism Vindicated* (Baltimore, Md., 1856).

B.   DAB 16:443–44; DARB 475–76; NCAB 5:100–101; NCE 12:1139–40; SH 10: 254; Paul Anstadt, *Life and Times of Rev. Samuel S. Schmucker* (York, Pa., 1896); Abdel Ross Wentz, *Pioneer in Christian Unity* (Philadelphia, 1967); Paul P. Kuenning, *The Rise and Fall of American Lutheran Pietism* (Macon, Ga., 1988).

Paul K. Kuenning

SCHWEITZER, ALBERT (14 January 1875, Kaisersberg, Alsace–4 September 1965, Lamberènè, French Congo). *Education*: studied organ, Paris; studied music, Berlin; Dr. phil., diss. on Kant, Berlin, 1899; Dr. theol., diss. On the Lord's Supper, Berlin, 1900; habilitation, Strasbourg, 1902; studied medicine, M.D., Strasbourg, 1905–12. *Career*: privatdozent, Strasbourg, 1902; professor of theology, Strasbourg, 1912; medical missionary to the French Congo, 1913–65; recipient of numerous awards, including the Goethe Prize from the city of Frankfurt, 1928, and the Nobel Peace Prize, 1955.

A German theologian, philosopher, musicologist, and medical missionary whose career began in the academic halls and church cathedrals of Europe and ended in the jungle clearings and village hospitals of equatorial Africa. The son of a Protestant pastor, Schweitzer early on evinced interest in two issues that were to absorb him throughout his career. The first was the question of the historical Jesus. In his monumental study of 1906, *Vom Reimarus zu Wrede*, he surveyed the nineteenth-century *Leben Jesu* research. The Jesus of history, he argued, was very different from the idealistic or romantic figure that research depicted. The real Jesus came proclaiming the imminent arrival of the eschatological kingdom and called people to repentance in the expectation of that new order. That kingdom, however, failed to appear, and Jesus then attempted to bring it about through an act of self-sacrifice. Thus the historical Jesus is the Jesus of what Schweitzer called "consequent eschatology." Following the tragic death of Jesus, Schweitzer argued, a form of "deeschatologized" theology arose, seen above all in the writings of John and Paul.

The second issue that concerned Schweitzer was social ethics. Here his chief writing was *Kultur und Ethik* (1923), in which he began to develop his philosophy of "reverence for life," a veneration of all that brings about and fosters life and a commitment to the preservation of every living thing. His own life in the Congo as a medical missionary can be seen as a concrete expression of that philosophy.

Bibliography

A.   *Civilization and Ethics*, trans. C. T. Campion, 3d ed., rev. C. E. B. Russell (London, 1946); *Letters: 1905–1965*, ed. H. W. Bahr, trans. J. Neugroschel (New York, 1992); *Memoirs of Childhood and Youth*, trans. C. T. Campion (New York, 1949); *The Mysticism of Paul the Apostle*, trans. W. Montgomery (New York, 1968); *Out of My Life and Thought: An Autobiography*, trans. C. T. Campion (New York, 1949); *The Psychiatric Study of Jesus: Exposition and Criticism*, trans. and C. R. Joy (Boston, 1948); *The Quest of the Historical Jesus: A Critical Study of its Progress from Reimarus to Wrede*, trans. W. Montgomery (New York, 1948).

B.   BBKL 9:1195–1200; EKL 5:553–55; ODCC 1469–70; E. N. Mozley, *The Theology of Albert Schweitzer for Christian Inquirers* (London, 1950); Jackson Lee Ice, *Schweitzer: Prophet of Radical Theology* (Philadelphia, 1971); James Brabazon, *Albert Schweitzer: A Biography* (New York, 1975); Nancy Snell Griffith, *Albert Schweitzer: An International Bibliography* (Boston, 1981).

D. Lyle Dabney

SCHWENCKFELD, CASPAR VON (1489, Ossig Estate, Silesia–10 December 1561, Ulm, Germany). *Education*: studied at Univ. of Cologne, 1505; the Viadrina, Frankfurt on the Oder, 1507. *Career*: courtier, c.1511–29; church reformer, Lower Silesia, 1518–29; leader of conventicles, 1529–61.

After establishing a Lutheran reformation in Lower Silesia Schwenckfeld began to oppose infant baptism and the traditional doctrine of the Eucharist. Through what he regarded as revelations he came to believe that the freedom of will and regeneration, which he felt the preaching of justification by faith was not producing, could be restored through spiritually feeding on the flesh of Christ. His movement "temporarily" replaced the Eucharist with a service based on John 6 of recollecting the spiritual experience of feeding on Christ. Paradoxically, though denying real presence in the physical elements, he held he was unworthy of the outward sacrament. Adopting the concept of substance, he held that Christ's substantially divine flesh transforms believers substantially.

When his reform was outlawed, Schwenckfeld was briefly welcomed in Strasbourg before he had to go into hiding. Reformation and Anabaptist writers attacked his doctrine of an invisible church within all churches, his rejection of church establishment and discipline, his doctrine of an outer and an inner word, and his denial of the humanity of Christ. He wrote critiques of Anabaptist legalism, the lack of charity of the magisterial reformers, and contemporary deviations from trinitarianism. The Schwenckfelder Church and, indirectly, the Friends inherited his individualistic spiritualism and concern for loyalty to Scripture and tradition.

Bibliography

A. *Corpus Schwenckfeldianorum*, 19 vols. (Leipzig, 1907–65).

B. DTC 14:1586–91; LThK² 9:546; NCE 12:1189; ODCC 1470; OEncR 4:21–23; PRE 18:72–81; RGG 5:1620–23; Paul Maier, *Caspar Schwenckfeld on the Person and Work of Christ* (Assen, 1959); Hans-Jürgen Goertz, ed. *Profiles of Radical Reformers* (Kitchener, Ont., and Scottdale, Pa., 1982); Robert Emmet McLaughlin, *Caspar Schwenckfeld, Reluctant Radical* (New Haven, Conn., 1986); George Huntston Williams, *The Radical Reformation*, 3d ed. (Kirksville, Mo., 1992).

Melvin G. Vance

SCOTUS. *See* DUNS SCOTUS, JOHN.

SEGUNDO, JUAN LUIS (31 October 1925, Montevideo, Uruguay–17 January 1996, Montevideo). *Education*: entered the Society of Jesus, 1941; studied philosophy, San Miguel, Argentina, 1946–48; studied theology, Facultés St. Albert de Louvain, Belgium, 1953–56; ordained priest 1955; doctoral studies (Doc. ès lettres), Univ. of Paris, 1958–63. *Career*: director of Peter Faber Center of Social Studies, Montevideo, 1964–75; visiting professor at Harvard, Chicago, Regis Coll. (Toronto), Birmingham, and São Paulo.

Segundo is recognized as one of the founders of Latin American liberation theology. His publication *Función de la Iglesia en la realidad rioplatense* (1962) is one of the pioneering works addressing the need for the church and theology in Latin America to reflect a fundamental option for the poor. Through his association with the Peter Faber Center in Montevideo he organized a series of lectures and retreats for lay Christians that inspired production of a theological series called *Teologia abierta para el laico adulto* (1968–72), translated into English as a five-volume work, *A Theology for Artisans of a New Humanity*. These volumes manifest the initial influence of French theology and literature on his thinking. In 1976 he published a methodological study on how theology itself needs to purify its attachments to various hidden ideologies. Despite extensive lecturing and teaching outside of Latin America, he also produced five volumes in a series called *Hombre de hoy ante Jesus de Nazaret*, published in the United States as *Jesus of Nazareth, Yesterday and Today*. In these studies a deeper inculturation with the Latin American context is notably present. After cardinal Joseph Ratzinger of the Congregation for the Doctrine of the Faith published in 1984 an instruction that was highly negative of liberation theology, Segundo produced a strong refutation of the Congregation's assessment and method, *Theology and the Church* (1985). Until his death he remained active in writing on theological method and hermeneutics.

Bibliography

A.   *Existencialismo, filosofia y poesia: Ensayo de sintesis* (Buenos Aires, 1948); *Berdiaeff: Une réflexion chrétienne sur la personne* (Paris, 1963); *A Theology for Artisans of a New Humanity*, vol. 1: *The Community Called Church*; vol. 2: *Grace and the Human Condition*; vol. 3: *Our Idea of God*; vol. 4: *The Sacraments Today*; vol. 5: *Evolution and Guilt* (Maryknoll, N.Y., 1973–74); *The Liberation of Theology* (Maryknoll, N.Y., 1976); *The Hidden Motives of Pastoral Action* (Maryknoll, N.Y., 1978); *Jesus of Nazareth, Yesterday and Today*, vol. 1: *Faith and Ideologies*; vol. 2: *The Historical Jesus of the Synoptics*; vol. 3: *The Humanist Christology of Paul*; vol. 4: *The Christ of the Ignatian Exercises*; vol. 5: *An Evolutionary Approach to Jesus of Nazareth* (Maryknoll, N.Y., 1984–88); *Theology and the Church: A Response to Cardinal Joseph Ratzinger and a Warning to the Whole Church* (Minneapolis, Minn., and London, 1985; San Francisco, 1987); *The Liberation of Dogma* (Maryknoll, N.Y., 1992).

B.   Alfred T. Hennelly, *Theologies in Conflict: The Challenge of Juan Luis Segundo* (Maryknoll, N.Y., 1979); Teofilo Cabestrero, "A Conversation with Juan Luis Segundo," in *Faith: Conversations with Contemporary Theologians* (Maryknoll, N.Y., 1980) 172–80; Theresa Lowe Ching, *Efficacious Love: Its Meaning and Function in the Theology of Juan Luis Segundo* (Lanham, Md., 1989); Marsha Aileen Hewitt, *From Theology to Social Theory: Juan Luis Segundo and the Theology of Liberation* (New York, 1990); Frances Stefano, *The Absolute Value of Human Action in the Theology of Juan Luis Segundo* (Lanham, Md., 1992).

Michael A. Fahey

SEMLER, JOHANN SALOMO (18 December 1725, Saalfeld, Thuringia–14 March 1791, Halle, Saxony). *Education*: Univ. of Halle. *Career*: taught Arabic in the gymnasium at Coburg and edited the Coburg *Staats-und Gelehrtenzeitung*, 1750; taught history and Latin poetry, Altdorf, 1751; professor of Theology, Halle, 1752–91.

Semler was raised in an atmosphere of Pietism, but rejected it because of the nonacademic spirit associated with the movement in his hometown. He came under the influence of rationalism while attending the University of Halle where he was drawn to the teaching of S. J. Baumgarten. He retained a deep personal piety but turned his intellect to the scientific investigation of religion, history, and doctrine.

Semler was among the first German theologians to apply the historical-critical approach to the canon of Scripture and the development of Christian doctrine. His work gave impetus to the critical study of both the Old and New Testaments. He distinguished between private faith or the individual's personal religious convictions and public religion of the organized church regulated by the state. He rejected the idea of natural religion and claimed that Christianity was based on divine revelation. He reacted strongly to the radical rationalism of Reimarus and Lessing, answering the *Wolfenbüttel Fragments* with sharp polemics. He made a distinction, however, between Holy Scripture and the Word of God. Revelation is to be found in the Bible, but not everything in the Bible is divine revelation. The truths of Scripture are conditioned by the circumstances under which the individual books of the Bible were written. He saw a difference between Jewish national religion and the universal religion of Christianity and between Jewish Christianity and the Christianity of Paul.

Semler was a prolific author. Approximately 150 of his writings were published during his lifetime. Toward the end of his life his literary interests turned to subjects like freemasonry, mystical theosophy, natural science, and alchemy.

Bibliography

A. *Historiae Ecclesiasticae Selecta Capita*, 3 vols. (Halle, 1767–69); *Abhandlung von freier Untersuchung des Kanon*, 4 vols. (Halle, 1771–75); *Comentarii Historici de Antiquo Christianorum Statu*, 2 vols. (Halle, 1771–72); *Versuch eines fruchtbaren Auszugs der Kirchengeschichte*, 3 vols. (Halle, 1773–81).

B. LThK² 9:657; NCE 13:78–79; ODCC 1481–82; Heinrich Hoffmann, *Die Theologie Semlers* (Leipzig, 1905); F. Huber, *Johann Salomo Semler, seine Bedeutung für die Theologie* (Berlin, 1906); Albert Schweitzer, *The Quest of the Historical Jesus* (New York, 1910; repr. New York, 1968); W. G. Kümmel, *The New Testament: The History of the Investigation of Its Problems* (Nashville, Tenn., 1972), 62–69; Helmut Thielecke, *Modern Faith and Thought* (Grand Rapids, Mich., 1990), 140–56.

John M. Brenner

SERIPANDO, GIROLAMO (6 October 1493, Troia, Apulia–17 March 1563, Trent). *Education*: studied Greek and logic, Naples, 1507–10; studied Greek, Hebrew, philosophy, and theology, Augustinian *studium generale*, Rome, 1510–13. *Career*: ordained priest, 1513; secretary of Augustinians, 1514–17; teacher, Siena and Naples, 1517–19; director of studies, Augustinian *studium*, Naples, 1523–39; general, Augustinians, 1539–51; archbishop of Salerno, 1554–63; cardinal, 1561.

Seripando's most important work as a theologian was preparing preliminary drafts for the theologians to discuss at the first phase of the Council of Trent. His position on justification was strongly influenced by St. Augustine,* stressing grace, not works: "works can be called merits but they should also be called gifts." Like cardinals Reginald Pole* and Gasparo Contarini,* he argued for a double justice—an inherent and insufficient justice acquired by works and the justice of Christ imputed to believers. His draft was radically revised. In the debate among the theologians only six sided with Seripando, while thirty-one, led by Diego Laínez,* preferred a single inherent justification for sinners. His drafts on merit and the sacraments (notably the Mass as a sacrifice and communion under one species) were more successful, but he failed to persuade the council to subordinate tradition to Scripture.

A stroke in 1551 forced him to resign during his third term as general, but he recovered rapidly and was elected archbishop of Salerno in 1554. During the pontificate of Paul IV (1555–59) Seripando was out of favor, but in 1561 Pius IV named him a cardinal and made him legate to the reassembled Council at Trent, where he had the difficult task of mediating between the French and Spanish bishops and the more conservative Italians led by Cardinal Ludovico Simonetta over questions of church reform. It was in the midst of these struggles that he died.

In his lifetime Seripando published only a funeral oration for Charles V. Later his expositions of Galatians, Romans, the Lord's Prayer, and the creeds were printed.

Bibliography

A.   Many of Seripando's papers are printed in *Concilium Tridentinum. Diariorum, actorum, epistularum, tractatuum. Nova collectio*, 17 vols. to date (Freiburg, 1950–).

B.   DSAM 14:655–61; DTC 14:1923–40; NCE 13:115; ODCC 1486–87; OEncR 4: 47–48; Hubert Jedin, *Papal Legate at the Council of Trent: Cardinal Seripando* (St. Louis, Mo., 1947); Anselm Forster, *Gesetz und Evangelium bei Girolamo Seripando* (Paderborn, 1963).

John Patrick Donnelly

SERVETUS, MICHAEL (1509/1511, Villanueva, Spain–27 October 1533, Geneva, Switzerland). *Education*: Univ. of Toulouse, 1528–29; mathematics, Univ. of Calvi, 1532; medicine, Univ. of Paris, 1536–38. *Career*: editor and corrector, Treschsel Publishing, Lyons, France, 1533–40; author, editor and doctor of medicine, Vienne, France, 1540–53.

Servetus was the best-known antitrinitarian heretic of the sixteenth century. Condemned by Catholic authorities in French Vienne, he was burned at the stake by Protestant Reformers in Geneva. Although remembered for his theological views, he also made contributions to medicine and geography.

Early contact with Jews and Moors stirred skepticism about the Trinity. Doubts were confirmed when he studied Scripture and found the orthodox doctrine absent. He developed a theology of progressive divine modalism set against an apoclayptic backdrop. God battled Satan by revealing his righteousness in a variety of names: El Shaddai, Elohim, Father, Son, and Spirit. The Son was not human, but the perfect representative of the divine character who revealed the way to deification through the sacraments. Following the death of the Son, the Spirit guided people in the battle against the final Antichrist, Rome.

Bibliography

A.   *De Trinitatis erroribus libri septem* (Frankfurt a. M., 1965); *Christianismi restitutio and Other Writings*, trans. Charles D. O'Malley (Birmingham, Ala., 1989).

B.   DSAM 14:672–79; DTC 14:1967–72; ECatt 11:408–9; LThK² 9:694; NCE 13: 131; ODCC 1487–88; OEncR 4:48–49; Roland H. Bainton, *Hunted Heretic: The Life and Death of Michael Servetus (1511–1553)* (Boston, 1953); Jerome Friedman, *Michael*

Servetus: A Case Study in Total Heresy (Geneva, 1978); Gordon A. Kinder, *Michael Servetus* (Strasbourg, 1989).

Matthew Brandt

SHEED, FRANCIS JOSEPH (20 March 1897, Sydney, New South Wales, Australia–20 November 1981, Jersey City, N.J.). *Education*: B.A., LL.B., Sydney Univ., 1917, 1926. *Career*: master, Catholic Evidence Guild, London, England, 1922–23, 1927–28, and 1935–36; cofounder (with his wife, Maisie Ward) and president of Sheed and Ward, London, England, 1926–73, and New York, 1933–73; active retirement, 1973–81.

Sheed contributed to the teaching mission of the church by showing how Catholic theology is effective in communicating the Christian faith. As a street-corner speaker with the Catholic Evidence Guild, Sheed developed a method of theological exposition formed by three insights derived from a single experience: that apologetic proofs of doctrine, like those found in the manuals, had no impact on members of the crowd. Sheed's first discovery was that, if a doctrine's meaning and importance were explained, then its intrinsic truth and goodness could attract the listener and possibly stimulate the reception, or reactivation, of faith. For Sheed, theology was the means of explanation. Secondly, Sheed learned that members of a theologically illiterate audience could not understand Catholic teaching about God, man, and their reunion in Christ until they grasped the concepts of spirit, God's conserving action, and supernatural life. Sheed's own comprehension of these doctrines and concepts was based on the thought of St. Thomas Aquinas.* And third, although theological exposition could present the meaning of Christian doctrine, it was insufficient in communicating a sense of doctrine's reality. Sheed's solution was to coordinate the testimony of theology with that of the Gospels, so that the realness of Christ would affirm the realness of revealed truth. Encouraged by his speaking experience, Sheed believed that a method of exposition with these components would improve religious instruction in Catholic schools, which he faulted for doing little to prevent ignorance of and apathy toward Christ.

Sheed considered the Catholic publishing house of Sheed and Ward to be an extension of his evangelizing work with the Guild. As a publisher, he brought the Catholic theology of England, Continental Europe, and the United States to a worldwide audience. His career also gave him the opportunity to write theology books designed for the laity that reflected his background as a lay street preacher.

Bibliography

A. *A Map of Life* (New York, 1933); *Catholic Evidence Training Outlines* (New York, 1934); *Communism and Man* (New York, 1938); *Theology and Sanity* (New York, 1946); *Society and Sanity* (New York, 1953); *Theology for Beginners* (New York, 1957); *To Know Christ Jesus* (New York, 1962); *God and the Human Condition, Volume I: God and the Human Mind* (New York, 1966); *Is It the Same Church?* (Dayton, Ohio,

1968); *Genesis Regained* (New York, 1969); *What Difference Does Jesus Make?* (New York, 1971); *The Church and I* (New York, 1974); *Christ in Eclipse* (Kansas City, 1978); *The Instructed Heart* (Huntington, Ind., 1979); *The Holy Spirit in Action* (Ann Arbor, Mich., 1981).

B.   DACB 526; NCE 18:473–74; NYT 21 November 1981, 19; Wilfrid Sheed, *Frank and Maisie: A Memoir with Parents* (New York, 1985); James McLucas, "Frank Sheed: Apologist," Ph.D. diss., Pontifical Univ. of St. Thomas, Rome, 1991.

Christopher M. Carr

SHEPARD, THOMAS (5 November 1605, Towcester, England–25 August 1649, Boston). *Education:* B.A., M.A., Emmanuel Coll., Cambridge, England, 1623, 1627. *Career:* ordained priest, Church of England, 1627; minister, Earles-Colne, Essex, 1627–30; silenced by Archbishop William Laud, 1630; tutor and chaplain, Yorkshire, 1630–32; in Newcastle, 1632–34; emigrated to Boston, 1635; pastor, Cambridge, Mass., 1636–49; cofounder, Harvard Coll., 1636.

Shepard was a Puritan pastor-theologian who helped shape the pastoral and theological orientation of New England. Like William Perkins, William Ames,* John Cotton,* and other Puritan theologians, he developed a covenantal view of the relationship between God and the human person that stressed divine initiative and the obligation of consent in faith. His covenant theology, as his ecclesial experiences in New England, tried to avoid the antinomian emphasis upon justification by grace through faith without the law as well as the Arminian emphasis upon freedom of the will in the process of salvation.

Although Shepard followed the Synod of Dort's emphasis upon divine sovereignty and predestination, he was preoccupied with discovering and testing the stages and signs of personal conversion. Like William Perkins, he tried to develop a morphology of conversion, setting out the preparatory stages of the experiences of legal fear, self-conviction of sin, humiliation, and then moving in progressive stages toward further degrees of conviction and real conversion—ultimately ending with a sense of genuine sorrow for sin and a reception of the grace of justification and sanctification that led to obedience to the divine will. Shepard's tests for religious conversion became useful in determing membership in the local church covenant, which was intended to be a close visible approximation of the covenant of grace.

In Massachusetts he took part in the 1637 synod that condemned Anne Hutchinson's antinomianism and was instrumental in the Cambridge Convention that developed a Congregational plan for church government.

Bibliography

A.   *The Works of Thomas Shepard*, ed. John A. Albro, 3 vols. (Boston, 1853; New York, 1967); *The Sincere Convert* (London, 1641); *The Sound Beleever. Or, a Treatise of Evangelical Conversion* (London, 1645); *A Treatise of Ineffectual Hearing the Word* (London, 1652); *The Church Membership of Children and Their Right to Baptisme* (Cambridge, 1663); *The Parable of the Ten Virgins* (London, 1660); *God's Plot: The Paradoxes of Puritan Piety. Being the Autobiography and Journal of Thomas Shepard*, ed.

Michael McGiffert (Amherst, Mass., 1972); *God's Plot: Puritan Spirituality in Thomas Shepard's Cambridge*, ed. Michael McGiffert (Amherst, 1994); *Thomas Shepard's Confessions*, ed. George Selement and Bruce Wolley (Boston, 1981).

B.   DAB 17:75–76; DCA 1082–83; DNB 18:50–51; Samuel Eliot Morison, "Master Thomas Shepard," in *Builders of the Bay Colony* (Boston, 1930); Karl Arthur Olsson, "Theology and Rhetoric in the Writings of Thomas Shepard," Ph.D. diss., Univ. of Chicago, 1948; Thomas Werge, *Thomas Shepard* (Boston, 1987).

Patrick W. Carey

SIGER OF BRABANT (ca. 1249, Brabant [in modern Belgium]–1284, Orvieto, Italy). Together with Boethius of Dacia,* Siger of Brabant is famous as the leader of a group of philosophers at the University of Paris in the later thirteenth century who have been variously labelled by scholars as "integral," "radical," or "unorthodox Aristotelians," or owing to their interest in the doctrine of the Arab philosopher Averroës, as "Latin Averroïsts."

As a young man Siger was a canon at the cathedral of St. Paul in Liège. By the 1260s he was teaching philosophy in the faculty of arts at the University of Paris; by 1266 he had become a *cause célèbre* in the schools. At issue was Siger's spirited adherence to Aristotelian teaching as seen through the interpretive medium of Averroës. Siger represented himself as a philosopher in search of the authentic thought of Aristotle who would follow the consequences of Aristotle's writings to their logical conclusions—regardless of the implications for Christian orthodoxy. As a result, Siger early in his career espoused a number of theologically questionable opinions, including the doctrine of the eternality of the world and the doctrine of the unicity of the human intellect, or monopsychism—that is, the belief in the existence of a single intelligence common to all men.

For such views Siger was assailed by the theologians of the university. In both 1267 and 1268 the Franciscan Bonaventure lashed out at the intellectual audacity of certain members of the Parisian arts faculty; he never mentions Siger by name but catalogs a number of heterodox teachings found in Siger's writings. Thomas Aquinas* entered the fray upon his return to Paris in 1269, penning his masterly refutation of the Averroïst doctrine of monopsychism, the *De unitate intellectus contra Averroïstas*, in 1270. In the same year the theology faculty convinced the bishop of Paris, Étienne Tempier, to issue a formal condemnation of some teachings emanating from the arts faculty. He condemned thirteen articles, touching not only the doctrines of the eternality of the world and monopsychism per se, but several others that flowed from them: the mortality of the individual soul once the individuality of the intellect is denied; determinism of the will; and the negation of divine providence in a world seen to operate according to strict causal necessity.

Siger submitted to the authorities, pleading that his intention had never been to oppose orthodox Christian doctrine but rather to expose the implications of a pure Aristotelianism. He took pains in subsequent writings, such as his *Ques-*

tiones in Metaphysicam (1272–73), to make it clear that he was merely setting out the views of the philosophers he studied, not making any claims for their validity. In fact, he later declared that the arguments adduced by Aristotle and Averroës to prove the eternality of the world and the existence of the single intellect were not actually demonstrative at all. In the *De anima intellectiva* (ca. 1273) Siger confessed he no longer knew what the correct position in the debate over the nature of the human intellect was; within another few years he repudiated the Averroïstic doctrine as incoherent.

Nonetheless, the Paris theologians continued their campaign against the arts faculty, issuing stern directives in both 1272 and 1276. Some masters were accused of veiling their opinions behind a so-called doctrine of "double truth," by which they could claim to teach the conclusions derived from philosophy while maintaining that the contrary might be true according to revelation. Whether Siger ever appealed to the doctrine in his defense is doubtful. But under suspicion still, he fled to Italy to lay his case before a papal tribunal. When he was cited to appear before the inquisitor of France in November, 1276 to answer the charge of heresy, Siger was no longer in the country. In January Pope John XXI asked Bishop Tempier to review the situation in Paris. Tempier's response came in March 1277 in the form of a new, more extensive condemnation, which now banned the teaching of 219 propositions, including the doctrine of "double truth."

This second condemnation ended Siger's career. He would ultimately be acquitted of heresy by Pope Nicholas III but was placed under house arrest to prevent his ever teaching publicly again. He was stabbed to death by his own secretary while still under arrest in Orvieto, around 1284. An enigma while he lived, Siger and the true nature of his intellectual posture remain the object of scholarly debate 700 years after his death.

Bibliography

A.   *Quaestiones in Tertium De Anima, De Anima Intellectiva, De Aeternitate Mundi,* ed. Bernard Bazán (Louvain, 1972); *Quaestiones in Metaphysicam,* ed. William Dunphy and Armand Maurer, 2 vols. (Louvain, 1981–83).

B.   DTC 14:2041–52; LThK² 9:746–47; NCE 14:204–5; ODCC 1499–15000; Edward Mahoney, "Saint Thomas and Siger of Brabant Revisited," *Review of Metaphysics* 27 (1974): 531–53; Fernand van Steenberghen, *Matre Siger de Brabant* (Louvain and Paris, 1977); Armand Maurer, *Medieval Philosophy,* 2d ed. (Toronto, 1982), 194–207.

M. Michèle Mulchahey

SIMON, RICHARD (13 May 1638, Dieppe, France–11 April 1712, Dieppe). *Education*: studied at the Oratorian Coll. of Dieppe, 1656–57; Jesuit Coll., Rouen, 1657–58; Sorbonne, 1659–61. *Career*: entered and reentered the French Oratory, 1658, 1662; professor at Coll. de Juilly, 1663–64; la maison de la rue Saint-Honoré, Paris, 1664–78; ordained priest, 1670; removed from French Oratory, 1679; retired to parish in Bolleville, 1679–88; lived and wrote in Rouen, Dieppe, Paris, 1689–1712; retired to Dieppe, 1712.

Simon was an early Catholic exponent and advocate of biblical criticism. His first and probably most important work in biblical criticism was his *Histoire critique du Vieux Testament* (Paris, 1678) which, among other things, questioned the Mosaic authorship of the Pentateuch. Because of his use of historical criticism and because he questioned the Mosaic authorship, he has at times been called a "Spinoza Catholic." His own concerns, however, were not those of Spinoza or the rationalists. He used the historical critical method not to question the revealed tradition but to help preserve it in its purity. His *Histoire critique* outlined critical methods necessary for examining various versions of the Bible, establishing accurate biblical texts, and interpreting them within the milieu in which they were written. His critical approach, however, came under severe attack shortly after his book was published and he was removed from the French Oratorians.

Simon was also an anti-Augustinian whose historical criticisms of the Western theological tradition made him a *persona non grata* especially among Gallicans and Jansenists. His *L'histoire critique des principaux commentateurs du Nouveau Testament* (Rotterdam, 1693; Frankfurt am Main, 1969) criticized the excessive reliance of Western, and particularly French, Christianity upon an Augustinianism that had obscured some significant elements of the church's tradition, and had distorted in particular the church's tradition on predestination, grace, and free will. He examined the history of biblical commentaries and argued that Augustinian presuppositions were operative in the commentary tradition in the West.

Simon's work was not an attack upon tradition but a call for theologians in the West to return to the Fathers, to the church's tradition prior to the distortions of the scholastic method. But such a return meant an abandonment of the Augustinianism that had captured the theology of the West. He maintained that the Greek Fathers had a very different view of predestination, original sin, and free will than did the Augustinian tradition and that the earlier Greek tradition represented the common consent of the ancient church. The Greek emphasis on the freedom of the will had been eclipsed in the West because many in the West had identified Augustine* with the tradition, and to do that was to ignore all science and all critical exegesis. Among a number of other criticisms of the Western tradition—doctrinal, liturgical, and ecclesiastical—Simon criticized what has been called the illegitimate character of Augustinianism in theology.

Simon did not create a school of theology, primarily because he was assaulted on all sides: by Jacques Bossuet* and other Gallicans, the Jansenists, and the scholastic tradition that continued on after the Council of Trent. His was a lonely voice of criticism and reform, but few within seventeenth-century France found his criticisms valid or comfortable.

Bibliography

A. *Histoire critique du texte du Nouveau Testament où l'on établit la vérité des actes sur lesquels la religion chrétienne est fondée* (Paris, 1689); *Nouvelles observations sur le texte et les versions du Nouveau Testament* (Paris, 1695; Frankfurt am Main, 1973).

B. DTC 14:2094–118; LThK² 9:773–74; NCE 13:226; ODCC 1503–4; Henri Margival, *Essai sur Richard Simon et la critique biblique au XVIIème siècle* (Paris, 1900); Jean Steinmann, *Richard Simon et les origines de l'exégèse biblique* (Paris, 1960); Heinrich Fries and Georg Kretschmar, *Klassiker der Theologie*, vol. 2, *Von Richard Simon bis Dietrich Bonhoeffer* (Munich, 1981); Patric Ranson, *Richard Simon ou du charactère illégitime de l'augustinisme en théologie* (Lausanne, 1990).

Patrick W. Carey

SIMONS, MENNO (1496, Witmarsum, The Netherlands–31 January 1561, Wüstenfeld, Germany) *Education*: Bolsward monastery school, The Netherlands, 1520s. *Career*: priest, 1524–36; leader of conventicles, fugitive, and writer, 1536–61.

Following the killing of his Münsterite brother, Simons made public his objections to infant baptism and Christ's bodily presence in the Eucharist and was rebaptized and reordained by the Anabaptists. In regathering and reforming the persecuted Anabaptists after the Münster debacle he argued against apocalyptic violence, self-defense, and concealment of faith, and for public nonconformity, the legitimacy of civil government (provided it used nonlethal means), the divinity of Christ, and trinitarian teaching. He rejected Luther's* doctrines of justification by faith, predestination, and bondage of the will. Simons believed that Christ's death removed original sin and that salvation was gained by an experience of grace that replaced fear of God's judgment with love. With spiritual resurrection come visible fruits in a holy life. Christians, however, remain susceptible to temptation and unforgivable apostasy. They depend upon the true church, which maintains its purity through recognizing the authority of the Bible, baptizing only those who have experienced grace and using the ban to remove those who commit sins. Simons' communal-centered piety focused on the Lord's Supper as an observance of a unity possible only among the regenerated. Such unity was sustained by common sharing in Christ's sinless, heavenly originated flesh. This Christology appears to derive from Caspar Schwenckfeld* through Melchior Hoffman. Simons' commitment to nonresistance has been maintained by Mennonite Churches. His doctrine of free will indirectly influenced Arminianism.

Bibliography

A. *The Complete Writings of Menno Simons*, ed. John C. Wenger (Scottdale, Pa., 1956).

B. LThK² 7:274–76; NCE 9:653–54; OEncR 3:55–56; RGG 4:855–58; *The Mennonite Encyclopedia* 3:577–84; George H. Williams, *The Radical Reformation* (Philadelphia, 1962); J. R. Loeschen, *The Divine Community: Trinity, Church, and Ethics in*

Reformation Theologies (Kirksville, Mo., 1981); *Dutch Dissenters: A Critical Companion to Their History and Ideas*, ed. Irvin B. Horst (Leiden, 1986).

Melvin G. Vance

SLATTERY, JOHN RICHARD (16 July 1851, New York, N.Y.–6 March 1926, New York, N.Y.). *Education*: St. Charles Coll., Ellicott City, Md., 1868–70; Columbia Coll. Law School, 1871–73; attended sem. of St. Joseph Foreign Missionary Society of Mill Hill, England, 1873–77. *Career*: ordained priest, 1877; provincial of American Mission of the Mill Hill Fathers, 1878–82; founder and director, Mill Hill mission, Richmond, Va., 1883–87; rector of St. Joseph's Sem., 1888–93; superior, St. Joseph Society of the Sacred Heart (independent American Josephite society), 1893–1903; retired as superior of the Josephites, 1903; left the priesthood, 1906; independent journalist and author, 1883–1910.

As a Roman Catholic priest, Slattery was a tireless promoter of missions to African-Americans and a staunch advocate of the education and training of African-American priests and missionaries. He began his priestly career as a missionary of the English Mill Hill Fathers but grew disillusioned with their relative lack of attention to the missions in the United States. Accordingly, he initiated a move to form an independent American branch of the Josephites, to which he was named first superior under the jurisdiction of Cardinal Gibbons of Baltimore. Under Slattery's leadership the American Josephites opened a new seminary in 1893 and founded churches, schools, mission posts, orphanages, and industrial institutes in the South to serve African-Americans, including St. Joseph's Catechetical College in Montgomery, Alabama, in 1902. Slattery also encouraged women religious who evangelized African-Americans; he was the first ecclesiastical superior of the Mission Helpers of the Sacred Heart.

In 1884, a year he described as "a turning point in my life," Slattery discovered "the modernist canon." On the evolution of species, he read Darwin, Huxley, and St. George Jackson Mivart, the English Catholic biologist who was an early formulator of "theistic evolution." On the higher criticism of the Bible, he read the European Catholic modernist Alfred Loisy,* among others. On the historical development of Catholic doctrine, the espiscopacy, and the papacy, he read Duchesne,* Harnack,* and Döllinger.* Slattery began to correspond with Americanist Catholics sympathetic to this body of thought.

The cumulative effect of this period of intellectual ferment was to convince Slattery that the modern Roman Catholic Church was an autocratic and corrupt institution, captive to narrow European political and ideological interests. If the findings of modern science and historical and biblical criticism were acknowledged, he wrote, they would undermine "Rome's supremacy" over the state. He accused the hierarchy of racism (not entirely absent from Slattery's own writings) and authoritarianism, a combination that condemned the African-American missions to failure, he felt. After leaving the church as a self-professed modernist, Slattery denounced the "Jesuitism" of the institution and castigated the "Italian hatred of democracy" that stood behind the *Syllabus of Errors* and other papal documents that are, he wrote, "the charters and by-laws of the [Roman Catholic] theocracy."

Bibliography

A.   "Biographie de J. R. Slattery," 2 vols., 1906 [handwritten manuscript] in Papier Houtin, Bibliothèque Nationale, Paris. Ouevre, Tome IV; "The Negro Race: Their Condition, Present, and Future," *Catholic World* 59 (November 1893): 219–31; "A Catholic College for Negro Catechists," *Catholic World* 70 (October 1899): 1–12; "How My Priesthood Dropped from Me," *New York Independent* 61 (6 September 1906): 565–71; "The Workings of Modernism," *American Journal of Theology* 13 (October 1909).

B.   NYT 15 June 1927, 48; Jamie Theresa Phelps, "The Mission Ecclesiology of John R. Slattery: A Study of the African-American Mission of the Catholic Church in the Nineteenth Century," Ph.D. diss., Catholic Univ. of America, 1989; William L. Portier, "John R. Slattery's Vision for the Evangelization of American Blacks," *U. S. Catholic Historian* 5 (1986): 19–45; William L. Portier, "Modernism in the United States: The Case of John R. Slattery (1851–1926)," in *Varieties of Modernism*, eds. Ronald Burke, Gary Lease, and George Gilmore (Mobile, Ala., 1986).

R. Scott Appleby

SMITH, JOSEPH, JR. (23 December 1805, Sharon, Vt.–27 June 1844, Carthage, Ill.). *Career*: backwoods farmer and treasure-seeker at Palmyra, N.Y., until 1830; Mormon prophet-founder; leader from 1832 and President of the Church of Jesus Christ of Latter-Day Saints, 1830–44.

Smith's theology evolved radically from the Christocentric modalism of the *Book of Mormon* (1830), to binitarianism (*Lectures on Faith*, 1835), to a trans-Christian system of man's "exaltation" (1842–44), expressed in the couplet, "as man is, God once was; as God is, man may become." God is a deified Man; man's deification depends on the Mormon sacraments, which after 1842 incorporated Masonic rites. "Celestial Marriage" allows deified couples to conceive spirit offspring who will experience mortality, achieve Godhood, and repeat the cycle. Several Mormon denominations differ over which of Smith's revelations were "divine." The Utah-based Church of Jesus Christ of Latter-day Saints perpetuates the last, polytheistic phase of Smith's theology.

Bibliography

A.   *The Book of Mormon, Doctrine and Covenants*, and *Pearl of Great Price* (Salt Lake City, Utah, 1982); *An American Prophet's Record: The Diaries and Journals of Joseph Smith*, ed. Scott H. Faulring (Salt Lake City, Utah, 1989); *Lectures on Faith* (Independence, Mo., 1988); *Teachings of the Prophet Joseph Smith*, ed. Joseph Fielding Smith (Salt Lake City, Utah, 1977).

B.   DAB 17:310–12; DARB 497–98; NCAB 16:1–3; NCE 13:304–5; SH 8:9–10; Fawn M. Brodie, *No Man Knows My History: The Life of Joseph Smith*, 2d ed. (New York, 1971); Donna Hill, *Joseph Smith: The First Mormon* (Garden City, N.Y., 1977).

R. Ben Madison

SOCINUS, FAUSTUS—SOZZINI, FAUSTO (5 December 1539, Siena, Italy–3 March 1604, Cracow, Poland). *Education*: Accademia degli Intronati, beginning in 1557. *Career*: merchant, Lyon, France, 1561–63; the service of Isabella de Medici, Florence, Italy, 1563–74; writer, Basel, Switzerland, 1574–79; adviser to Count Báthory, Kolozsvár, Transylvania, 1579–80; theological publicist, Cracow, Poland, 1580–1604.

Socinus was an antitrinitarian. He argued for the natural mortality of all humans from creation and denied the immortality of the soul. He regarded eternal life as possible only through God's gracious and miraculous gift. His attack on what he regarded as the irrationality of the satisfaction theory became an impetus to many later reevaluations of the significance of the death of Christ. He defended the authority of the Scripture on the basis of its miracles, especially the resurrection of Christ. His thought developed from early attacks on trinitarian concepts to a highly developed reconceptualization of theology around the figure of Christ. He opposed the doctrine of nonadorantism which regarded prayer to Christ as idolatry. He taught that Christ was not the preexistent Son but a human who through receiving divine qualities became divine by office. The resurrection of Christ became the center of his soteriology. He held that Christ had ascended into heaven before his earthly ministry to receive the final, more gracious and merciful version of the divine law. He saw the significance of Christ's death as making possible an adoring trust in Christ as the resurrected King, helper, and guide to righteousness. He defended the necessity of Christian pacifism. He defined the celebration of the Lord's Supper as the testimony of the members of the church to their unity in Jesus Christ. Though he was not admitted to the Polish Brethren because of his objections to the external rite of baptism, he wrote theological works at their behest. His thought was accepted by one body of that movement after his death and expressed in the Racovian Catechism, which he had helped draft. Socinianism became influential in the English-speaking world.

Bibliography

A. "The Latin Racovian Catechism" in *The Polish Brethren*, part 1, trans. and ed. George H. Williams (Missoula, Mont., 1980); *Faust Socin*, trans. Jean-Pierre Osier (Paris, 1996).

B. DTC 14:2326–34; LThK² 9:928–31; NCE 13:397–98; ODCC 1512–13; Zbigniew Ogonowski, "Faustus Socinus, 1539–1604," in *Shapers of Religious Traditions in Germany, Switzerland, and Poland, 1560–1600*, ed. Jill Raitt (New Haven, Conn., 1981); George H. Williams, *The Radical Reformation*, 3d ed. (Kirksville, Mo., 1992).

Melvin G. Vance

SÖDERBLOM, NATHAN (15 January 1866, Tröno, Sweden–12 July 1931, Uppsala). *Education*: Univ. of Uppsala, 1886, 1892; Univ. of Paris, 1901. *Career*: ordained, 1893; chaplain to Swedish delegation and pastor to Swedish congregation, Paris, and seamen in Dunkirk, Calais, and Bologna, 1894–1901; professor of theology, Univ. of Uppsala, 1901–14 (concurrently, visiting professor at Univ. of Leipzig, 1912–14); archbishop of Uppsala, 1914–31; convener of First Universal Christian Conference on Life and Work, Stockholm, 1925; Nobel Peace Prize, 1930; Gifford Lectures, Univ. of Edinburgh, 1931.

Söderblom was a fountainhead for twentieth-century Swedish theology and an active participant in the modern ecumenical movement. His father (a pastor in the Church of Sweden) and his mother embodied both the piety and missionary concern of the nineteenth-century "evangelical awakening" in Sweden and the high regard of the Swedish Church for Luther and the Reformation.

During his university years, he attended one of the early Student Volunteer Movement conferences (1890) at Northfield, Mass., which prompted the diary entry: "Lord, give me humility and wisdom to serve the great cause of the free unity of Thy Church." It also forged a lifelong friendship with John R. Mott, the indefatigable ecumenist. While in Paris as a student and pastor, he observed at an assembly in Erfurt how Germany's "Innere Mission" linked Christian social endeavor with the idea of Christian unity. He was actively involved in the Constantinople conference (1911) of the World Student Christian Federation (organized 1895 in Lund, Sweden); that landmark conference brought Eastern Orthodoxy into continuing relations with Western Protestantism and into his own ecumenical vision. His career reflects the ideals and the personal relationships that coalesced in the 1910 World Missionary Conference, Edinburgh.

Söderblom was among those who faced the early challenges of biblical criticism and of comparative religions. But, like Einar Billing,* his faculty colleague at the University of Uppsala, he came to believe that proper critical study of the Bible could have only positive benefits. His graduate studies at the University of Paris in Iranian religions convinced him that comparative study demonstrates the distinctiveness of Christianity rather than reducing it to just another instance of human religiosity.

Söderblom and Billing were also interested in Martin Luther* as the one who recovered primitive Christianity from the accretions of the centuries. Early in his teaching career he wrote a major monograph on Luther. Söderblom was also concerned with the question of the church. From his parents, he had a passion for the vitality of the Church of Sweden and from his ecumenical involvements, a vision for the church catholic.

These themes (the uniqueness of Christianity, the critical investigation of the biblical faith, Luther as the benchmark recoverer and expositor of apostolic Christianity, and the church as God's institution in the world) were the seeds of the later Lundensian theology of Aulén,* Nygren,* and Wingren.* Söderblom's twelve-year academic career influenced other figures in less obvious ways. His greatest direct impact domestically and internationally, however, was as primate of the Church of Sweden.

In May 1914 amidst the threat of war in Europe, Söderblom was elevated as bishop of Uppsala. Throughout that conflict, he tried to unite the continental churches in a concerted campaign for peace, for conciliation rather than conflict. Only churchmen of the "neutral" countries subscribed to the "Appeal for Peace and Christian Fellowship" he wrote just after his elevation. He persisted, however, and was a driving force in the formation and later work of the "World Alliance for Promoting International Friendship through the Churches." The Nobel Peace Prize in 1930 was his reward for these efforts.

In the post–World War I years, his ecumenical and social interests continued. Full intercommunion between the Church of Sweden and the Church of England was reached in 1922. The Universal Christian Conference on Life and Work (August 1925) was the Swedish scholar-archbishop's crowning achievement. United Christian practical action was a too pressing demand to be delayed until consensus on faith, order, and liturgy is reached. Söderblom sometimes appeared naive about the weight of faith and order in interchurch harmony, but he was too astute a thinker and diplomat to ignore the fundamental seriousness of doctrinal questions. Age and declining health forced him to restrict his energies to his episcopal responsibilities at home in the years following.

As archbishop, he spearheaded worship renewal; in his role as "father in God," he authored numerous devotional and catechetical works and faithfully administered the Church of Sweden. At the time of his death, he was engaged in preparing the Gifford Lectures for Edinburgh University for 1931; *The Living God* integrates his persistent academic and ecclesiastical themes.

Bibliography

A. *Christian Fellowship* (Chicago, 1923); *The Living God* (New York, 1933); *Das Werden des Gottesglaubens* (Leipzig, 1916); *Mystery of the Cross* (1929; Milwaukee, Wis., 1933); *Nature of Revelation* (1903; ET 1934; rev. ed. Philadelphia, 1966).

B. LThK² 9:844–45; NCE 13:411–12; ODCC 1513–14; RGG 6:115–16; Yngve Brillioth, "Biographical Introduction" in Söderblom's *Living God*; Charles J. Curtis, *Nathan Soderblom: Theologian of Revelation* (Chicago, 1966); Hugh G. G. Herklots, *Nathan Soderblom, Apostle of Christian Unity* (London, 1948); *Nathan Soderblom, A Prophet of Christian Unity*, ed. Peter Katz (London, 1949); B. Sundkler, *Nathan Soderblom: His Life and Work* (Lund, 1968).

David T. Priestley

SOLOVIEV, VLADIMIR SERGEEVICH (28 January NS [Jan. 16 OS] 1853, Moscow–13 August NS [July 31 OS] 1900, Uzkoe, near Moscow). *Education*: Univ. of Moscow, 1869–73; M.A., Univ. of Moscow, 1874; student, theological faculty of Moscow, 1873–74; studied mysticism and theosophy, London, 1875; Ph.D., Univ. of Moscow, 1880. *Career*: trip to London, Egypt, 1875–76; teaching, Univ. of Moscow, 1876; member Ministry of Public Instruction, 1877–81; lecturer, St. Petersburg, 1877–78; retired from teaching, 1881; traveled in Croatia, conversations with Bishop Strossmayer, 1886–88; lectured in Paris on the Russian Church, 1887; communion in Catholic Church, 1896.

Learned in patristic and Gnostic literature as well as modern philosophy, Soloviev was the first great Russian systematic philosopher. Mystically inclined, he lived like a wandering pilgrim, visiting Optina Monastery with Dostoyevsky who, it is said, took Soloviev as model for Alyosha in *The Brothers Karamazov*.

Dubbed the "Russian Newman" because of his broad erudition, Soloviev's desire was to restore inner unity to the intellectual world. There are three levels of "integral knowledge": the empirical, the metaphysical, and the spiritual/mystical. They must be brought into an aesthetic synthesis by intuitive contemplation. Theology and science are joined with philosophy (theosophy), which includes mysticism. All are then related to creativity and moral practice (theurgy and theocracy).

God is the "total oneness" (*Vseedinstvo*) within which are the three hypostases, unified in the organism that is Christ and manifested in Sophia, the divine matter. After the Incarnation all evolves towards the "God man." "Godmanhood" (*Bogochelovechestvo*) means the raising of the individual man to identification with Christ. His twelve lectures on Godmanhood in St. Petersburg, 1877–78, were attended by Dostoyevsky and Tolstoy, among others.

Soloviev's teaching on Sophia (of whom he had visions) is rather obscure. A perfect being, coeternal with God, she is the eternal feminine. Sophia is the beauty of the transfigured world, the church, the Bride of the Logos while associated with the Mother of the Incarnate God.

The "world-soul," bearer of evolution that began with creation, is the medium of Sophia's realization, the final unity of the world process: humanity become one divine-human organism in Christ.

Christianity's uniqueness lies in Christ's person: His resurrection is the true Christian novelty. Spiritualized matter, as in the Eucharist, is a central concern of Soloviev's.

The church is a divine/human society, mirroring the natures of Christ. The East, ascetical and otherworldly, has preserved the divine element in religion; the West, the human. There is need for a synthesis. Soloviev advocated an understanding between Russian Orthodoxy and Roman Catholicism, even collaboration between tsar and pope. Neither Slavophile nor westernizer, he held that each nation has a unique vocation.

Having received communion in the Catholic Church, Soloviev yet received his final sacraments from an Orthodox priest, causing ongoing dispute concerning his church membership. Soloviev himself held that the church was already mystically one.

Because the telos of the universe is Christ, morality must be dynamic. He developed a theology of sexuality, speculating that God divided to unite by love. Eros and asceticism are intimately linked. Virginity is the ultimate—eschatalogical—goal of sexual life in which the spiritual man can be born of the carnal.

In later years, Soloviev grew apocalyptic and pessimistic. Powerless in a world united under Antichrist, divided Christians will come together under an earthly head, the pope, as symbol of unity.

He greatly inspired the Russian religious and artistic renaissance of the twentieth century, especially P. Florensky and S. Bulgakov. Soloviev's disciple Vyacheslav Ivanov coined the expression, the "two lungs" of the church.

Bibliography

A.   Collected works in Russian, 9 vols. (St. Petersburg, 1901–7; 2d ed. 10 vols. 1911–14); collected works in German, 8 vols. (Munich, 1953–79); *A Solovyov Anthology*, ed. S. L. Frank (London, 1950); *Russia and the Universal Church* (London, 1948); *The Meaning of Love* (New York, 1985).

B.   DSAM 14:1024–33; ECatt 11:945–46; HDOC 304–5; LThK² 9:869–70; NCE 13: 423–24; ODCC 1517–18; B. M. d'Herbigny, *Vladimir Soloviev. A Russian Newman* (London, 1934); E. Munzer, *Solovyev, Prophet of Russian–Western Unity* (London, 1956); Hans Urs von Balthasar, "Vladimir Soloviev" in *The Glory of the Lord*, vol. 3, *Lay Styles* (San Francisco, 1986); Martin George, *Mystische und religiöse Erfahrung im Denken Vladimir Solov'evs* (Göttingen, 1988); Jonathan Sutton, *The Religious Philosophy of Vladimir Solovyov: Towards a Reassessment* (New York, 1988).

Raymond T. Gawronski

SOZZINI, FAUSTO. *See* SOCINUS, FAUSTUS.

SPENER, PHILIPP JAKOB (13 January 1635, Rappoltsweiler, Upper Alsace–5 February 1705, Berlin, Germany). *Education*: studied theology at Univ. of Strasbourg, 1651–59; traveled and studied in Switzerland, France and Germany, 1659–61; doctoral studies, Univ. of Strasbourg, 1661–66. *Career*: preacher and superintendent of Lutheran Churches, Frankfurt-am-Main, 1666–86; chaplain at Saxon Court, Dresden, 1686–91; pastor, St. Nicholas Church, Berlin, 1691–1705.

Spener was the father of what has since been called the classical form of German Lutheran Pietism. He provided this movement with its fundamental theological foundations and was by far the most influential figure in its rapid rise and development during the latter half of the seventeenth century. Spener was more interested in practical piety than in doctrine. Though undoubtedly influenced to some extent by mystical and Reformed thought, Spener's theology never strayed far from Luther's* Catechism or the Lutheran Confessions. Yet he revised or expanded these doctrines in such fashion that they appeared to be departures from orthodoxy. As a result, charges of heresy were brought against him by church authorities a number of times, but they were never upheld.

Spener began his reforms by the encouragement of lay religion. In Frankfurt he initiated a series of informal "house meetings" at which the laity gathered to discuss devotional readings, the Sunday sermons, or biblical passages. Called *collegia pietatis*, these gatherings became a central feature of Lutheran Pietism.

Spener was a prolific writer, but the essentials of his theology and proposed reforms were contained in one of his earliest works, *Pia Desideria* (1675). The book begins with a scathing attack upon the moral laxity and absence of true spirituality within the Lutheran Church and concludes with a detailed description of specific reforms. Between these sections Spener outlines the unique and most influential aspect of his theology. He is optimistic about the future of the church and looks for "better times to come." This hope is grounded in various biblical promises, but the people of God must act as the divine instruments. Here, Spener's views fall into the category of a vague post-millennialism. This aspect of his theology helped spawn an intensity of ethical endeavor and missionary fervor that Lutheranism had never before experienced. While Spener's Pietism contained a definite element of withdrawal from the pleasures and enjoyments of the world, it was also motivated by a deep social concern and dedicated to the improvement of society.

Bibliography

A.   *Pia Desideria*, ed. and trans. Theodore Tappert (Philadelphia, 1964); *The Spiritual Priesthood*, trans. A. G. Voigt (Philadelphia, 1917); *Der neue Mensch*, ed. Hans-Georg Feller (Stuttgart, 1966); *Theologische Bedencken* (Halle, 1712).

B.   DSAM 14:1121–24; DTC 12:2084–89; LThK² 9:959; NCE 13:562; ODCC 1528–29; PRE 18:609–22; RGG 6:238–39; K. James Stein, *Philipp Jakob Spener, Pietist Patriarch* (Chicago, 1986); Johannes Wallmann, *Philipp Jakob Spener und die Anfänge des Pietismus* (Tübingen, 1970); Dale Brown, *Understanding Pietism* (Grand Rapids, Mich., 1978).

                                                                                            Paul K. Kuenning

STANILOAE, DUMITRU (16 December 1903, Vladeni, Transylvania–5 November 1993 Bucharest). *Education*: studied at the faculty of theology at Cernauti, Bukovina, 1922–27; doctorate in theology, 1928; traveled and studied languages in Athens, Munich, Paris, and Belgrade, 1927–29. *Career*: professor of dogmatics, sem. of Sibiu, 1929; ordained priest, 1929; at Sibiu began his intensive studies of Orthodox theology and spirituality, chiefly through his editing, translation, and monograph on the *Triads* of Gregory Palamas;* editor, *Telegraphul Roman*, 1934–44, to which he contributed nearly four hundred articles to the discussion of issues absorbing Romanian intellectual life of the period, particularly those touching on the national identity and its Orthodox inheritance; professor of Christian spirituality, faculty of theology at Bucharest, 1945–93; imprisoned, 1958–63.

Staniloae devoted the first twenty-five years of his academic life to his translation, editing, and commentary on the Greek *Philokalia*, a collection whose original five volumes he expanded into twelve, together with other translations of patristic works, all of them thickly annotated. The last twenty years of his life, under circumstances less constrained, saw him devoting his efforts to a labor of synthesis that resulted in the massive pair of trilogies on systematics and ethics, *Orthodox Dogmatic Theology* (1978) and *Orthodox Moral Theology* (1981–86). The first has recently been translated into German (third volume in 1994), and volume one to date into English (*The Experience of God*, 1994). Further works followed, including *The Immortal Image of God* (1987) and *Jesus Christ, the Light of the World and Deification of Man* (1993), among others. The complete bibliography of Fr. Dumitru's works—as compiled by G. Anghelescu for the *Gedenkschrift*, edited by I. I. Ica, Jr., *Persona si Comuniune* (Sibiu, 1993)—lists eight hundred titles.

In volume alone, this enormous output is comparable to the works of K. Barth,* or of H. von Balthasar* and K. Rahner,* in the Protestant and Catholic West. Staniloae's importance for twentieth- and twenty-first century theology in the Orthodox world, and for the ecumenical exchange, also promises comparison with the Western giants. The title of his memorial volume, *Person and Communion*, is a kind of summary of his thought. It embraces the elements he understood as central in the ancient works he had devoted his earlier years to translating and commenting. Those elements, listed as four by K. T. Ware in the latter's introduction to *The Experience of God*, include: love and personal communion, the Trinity as plenitude of that communion, the simultaneous transcendence and immanence of God, and cosmic transfiguration. This is, of course, equally a summary of the ruling themes of the great Eastern fathers, from Gregory of Nyssa* through Cyril of Alexandria* to Maximus the Confessor,* Symeon the New Theologian,* and Gregory Palamas,* and it is no accident that these are the church fathers, together with Dionysius Areopagita,* who are cited most frequently in Staniloae's works. He is most comparable among twentieth-century Orthodox theologians to Fr. Georges Florovsky.* His work embodies what Florovsky looked for in a "neopatristic synthesis," but Staniloae arrived at his vision independently of the Russian emigré theologian. They think along parallel lines. His own investigation of the ascetical and mystical tradition, particularly through that inheritance from Paisii Velichkovsky* which was still at work in Rumanian monasticism, began with his dissatisfaction with the school theology he had been obliged to absorb as a seminarian and then repeat as a seminary professor. His oeuvre, given particularly the recent translations into Western languages (with more to come), will surely increase in importance in the coming years and decades.

Bibliography

A.   *Dieu est amour*, trans. D. Nesser (Geneva, 1980); *Theology and the Church*, trans. R. Barringer (Crestwood, N.Y., 1980); *Prière de Jésus et expérience de Saint Esprit* (Paris, 1981); *Prayer and Holiness: The Icon of Man Renewed in God* (Oxford, 1982); *Ose comprendre que je t'aime* (Paris, 1983); *Orthodoxe Dogmatik*, trans. H. Pitters (Zurich-Einsiedeln-Köln, 1985, 1990, 1995); *The Experience of God*, trans. I. Ionita and R. Barringer (Brookline, Mass., 1993); "The Orthodox Conception of Tradition and the Development of Doctrine," *Sobornost* 5 (1969): 662–73; "The Foundation of Christian Responsibility in the World: The Dialogue of God and Man," *Studies Supplementary to Sobornost* 2 (London, 1971): 53–73; "Jesus Christ, Incarnate Logos of God, Source of Freedom and Unity," *Ecumenical Review* 26 (1974): 403–12; "The Role of the Holy Spirit in the Theology and Life of the Orthodox Church," *Diakonia* 9 (1974): 343–66; "Der dreieinige Gott und die Einheit der Menschheit," *Evangelische Theologie* 41 (1981): 439–50; "Le Saint Esprit dans la théologie byzantine et dans la reflexion orthodoxe contemporaine," in *Credo Spirtum Sanctum* (Vatican, 1983), 661–79.

B.   HDOC 311; A. Plamadeala, "Some Lines on Professor Staniloae's Theology,"

The Altar (London, 1970): 24–29; Ioan Bria, "A Look at Contemporary Romanian Dogmatic Theology," *Sobornost* 6 (1972): 230–336; Istvan Juhasz, "Dumitru Staniloae's Ecumenical Studies as an Aspect of the Orthodox-Protestant Dialogue," *Journal of Ecumenical Studies* 16 (1979): 747–64; D. Nesser, "Le monde, don de Dieu, réponse de l'homme: aspects de la pensée de Père D. Staniloae," *Revue théologique et philosophique* 112 (1980): 130–50; R. Robertson, *Contemporary Rumanian Orthodox Ecclesiology. The Contribution of Dumitru Staniloae and His Younger Contemporaries* (Rome, 1988); *Persona si Comuniune, Prinos de Cinstre: Preotului, Professor, Academician Dumitru Staniloae (1903–1993)*, ed. I. I. Ica Jr. (Sibiu, 1993).

Alexander Golitzin

STAPLETON, THOMAS (July 1535, Henfield, Sussex, England–12 October 1598, Louvain, Belgium). *Education*: B.A., New Coll., Oxford, 1556; M.A., Oxford, 1556; doctorate in theology, Douai, 1571. *Career*: ordained priest, 1558; prebend, Chichester Cathedral, 1558; professor of theology, Douai, 1569–85; rector of Univ. of Douai, 1574–75; Regius professor of Scripture, Louvain, 1590–98.

Stapleton was the leading English Catholic theologian of the Elizabethan era. Most of his writings had a polemical edge; his main opponents were John Calvin,* Theodore Beza,* and their English disciples William Whitaker and John Jewel.* His major work was his three-volume *Antidota apostolica contra nostri temporis haereses* (Antwerp, 1595–98). He also wrote on justification and the authority of the church in scriptural questions. Most of his works were written in Latin, but his English translation of Bede's* *Ecclesiastical History of the English People*, his biography of Thomas More, and a tract defending Philip II against Elizabeth I all witness his continuing concern for his homeland. His pastoral interests are evident in a catechetical work on the seven deadly sins (Lyons, 1599) and a collection of material for sermons on the Sunday gospels (Lyons, 1598, frequently reprinted).

Bibliography

A. *Opera quae exstant omnia*, 4 vols. (Paris, 1620); *Universa justificationis doctrina hodie controversa* (Paris, 1582).
B. DNB 18:988–91; DTC 14:2566–67; LThK² 9:1019–20; NCE 13:643–44; ODCC 1537; Marvin R. O'Connell, *Thomas Stapleton and the Counter Reformation* (New Haven, Conn., 1964); Michael Seybold, *Glaube und Rechtfertigung bei Thomas Stapleton* (Paderborn, 1967).

John Patrick Donnelly

STAUDENMAIER, FRANZ ANTON (11 September 1800, Donzdorf–19 January 1856, Freiburg im Breisgau). *Education*: Latin School, Gmünd, 1815–17; gymnasium, Ellwangen, 1818–22; studied Catholic theology with J. S. Drey,* J. A. Möhler,* J. B. Hirscher, Tübingen 1822–26; sem., Rottenburg, 1826–27. *Career*: ordained priest, 1827; pastoral ministry, 1827–28; tutor in theology,

Tübingen, 1828–30; chair of theology, Giesen, 1830–37; professor of theology, Univ. of Freiburg, 1837–55.

Although Staudenmaier never taught at Tübingen, his work represents the Tübingen tradition of theology associated with the legacy of his mentors Drey, Möhler, and Hirscher. He reacted against the spiritual and intellectual deficiencies of the Aufklärung and the supranaturalism of the older Protestant Tübingen faculty and forged an alternative by developing a trinitarian understanding of the human person, nature, and human history. In 1834 he published a book presenting John Scotus Erigena* as a pivotal contributor to the scientific method of medieval theology. That same year he published *Encyclopedia of the Theological Sciences as a System of all Theology*, which set forth his own Idealist approach to the scientific nature of theology, its divisions, and aims. He is among the most important Catholic interpreters and critics of Hegel's philosophical system. Acknowledging the importance of Hegel's views of science and the historical character of reality and *Geist*, he criticized the close identification of faith and thought, theology and philosophy in the Hegelian system and the risks of an organic understanding of reality for the Christian view of revelation and creation. These concerns culminated in his indictments against Hegel for pantheism, extreme pneumaticism, and Sabellianism. He also offered a substantive critical evaluation of Schleiermacher's* *Glaubenslehre*. His four-volume dogmatics appeared between 1844 and 1852, and the final part addressed church-state issues in the German context.

Bibliography

A. *Enzyklopädie der theologischen Wissenschaften als System der gesamten Theologie* (Mainz, 1834; 2d ed. 1840; Frankfurt am Main, 1968); *Der Pragmatismus der Geistesgaben oder das Wirken des göttlichen Geistes im Menschen und in der Menschheit* (Tübingen, 1835; Frankfurt am Main, 1975); *Darstellung und Kritik des Hegelschen Systems. Aus dem Standpunkte der christlichen Philosophie* (Mainz, 1844; Frankfurt am Main, 1966); *Die christliche Dogmatik*, 4 vols. (Mainz, 1844–52; Frankfurt am Main, 1967).

B. DTC 14:2579–80; LThK² 9:1024; A. Burkhart, *Der Mensch—Gottes Ebenbild und Gleichnis: Ein Beitrag zur dogmatischen Anthropologie* (Freiburg, 1962); Peter Hünermann, *Trinitarische Anthropologie bei Franz Anton Staudenmaier* (Freiburg, 1962); Philipp Weindel, *Das Verhältnis von Glauben und Wissen in der Theologie Franz Anton Staudenmaiers. Eine Auseinandersetzung katholischer Theologie mit Hegelschem Idealismus* (Düsseldorf, 1940); Cyril O'Regan, ''Hegel as Roman Catholic Opportunity and Challenge in the Nineteenth Century: The Emblematic Case of Franz Anton Staudenmaier (1800–1856)'' (forthcoming).

Bradford Hinze

STEPHEN LANGTON. *See* LANGTON, STEPHEN.

STEPHEN OF TOURNAI (18 February 1128, Orléans–9 or 12 September 1203, Tournai). *Education*: studied letters at Orléans, and law at Bologna; studied theology at Chartres. *Career*: canon, St.-Euverte, Orléans, ca. 1155; abbot at St.-Euverte, 1167; abbot of Ste.-Geneviève, Paris, 1176; bishop of Tournai, 1191/92–1203.

Stephen was a theologian and a canonist. The *Decretum Gratiani* had recently been established as the basic text of canon law at Bologna. Stephen composed glosses on the *Decretum* and a *Summa* on parts 1 and 2 of it, as well as letters. His principal interests were the history of the church and of canon law. But he also showed zeal for the reform of the church and for ecclesiastical discipline. He defended strict norms of life for monks and canons, and he was known for preaching to the laity in the vernacular.

Bibliography

A.   PL 211, 309–580; *Die Summa des Stephanus Tornacensis über das Decretum Gratiani*, ed. J. F. von Schulte (Giessen, 1891); new edition of the letters by Jules Desilve (Paris, 1893).

B.   DDC 5:487–92; DHGE 15:1274–78; DMA 11, 481; DSAM 4:1526–27; NCE 13: 701; PRE 19:5–6; Joseph Warichez, *Étienne de Tournai et son temps, 1128–1203* (Tournai, 1936).

Joseph T. Lienhard

STOJKOVIC, JOHN. *See* JOHN OF RAGUSA.

STRAUSS, DAVID FRIEDRICH (29 January 1808, Ludwigsburg, Württemberg–8 February 1874, Ludwigsburg, Württemberg). *Education*: seminary studies, Blaubeuren, 1821–25; studied philosophy and theology, Univ. of Tübingen, 1825–31; Berlin, 1831–32. *Career*: tutor, Tübingen, 1832–35; instructor, Ludwigsburg, 1835; author, 1835–74.

Strauss studied under F. C. Baur,* Friedrich Schleiermacher,* and Georg Hegel. He was only twenty-seven years old when he published his monumental *Das Leben Jesu*. The storm of controversy that arose after the publication of this work effectively ended his academic career. He was released from his position at Tübingen, taught for a short time at Ludwigsburg, and was appointed to the University of Zurich. Opposition led to his dismissal from Zurich before he began his duties. Barred from an academic position, he supported himself through his literary endeavors.

Das Leben Jesu began the quest for the historical Jesus and the controversy over what historical inferences can be drawn from the gospels. Strauss denied the historicity of the gospel accounts. He challenged both the orthodox and the rationalists by applying the myth theory to the gospels. He claimed that the Christian community created the mythical Christ from the background of the Old Testament messianic prophecies, Jesus' belief in his own messiahship, and stories arising from the spiritual longings of the community. Strauss did not accuse the writers of deliberate error or fraud but believed that their work was the result of unconscious invention and reflection on religious ideas and spiritual truths. Nearly every subsequent study of the life of Jesus has had to take Strauss' work into account.

In his *Die christliche Glaubenslehre* (1840–41) Strauss' historical presentation of Christian doctrines cast doubt on their validity. In *Der alte und der neue Glaube* (1872) he rejected the belief in immortality and a personal God. By the end of his life he had turned his back on historic Christianity and had become a materialist and pantheist.

For a time Strauss turned from theology to the writing of biographies of historical proponents of freedom of thought, including Ulrich von Hutten and Hermann Samuel Reimarus. He later authored a study of Voltaire. Strauss was a nationalist who opposed the revolutionary tendencies of the democratic movements in Germany and was a supporter of German unification under Bismarck.

Bibliography

A. *Gesammelte Schriften*, ed. E. Zeller, 12 vols. (Bonn, 1876–78); *Ulrich von Hutten, His Life and Times*, trans. G. Sturge (London, 1874); *The Life of Jesus Critically Examined*, ed. with notes and intro., Peter C. Hodgson (Philadelphia, 1972); *In Defense of My "Life of Jesus" against the Hegelians*, trans. and intro., Marilyn C. Massey (Hamden, Conn., 1983); *The Christ of Faith and the Jesus of History: A Critique of Schleiermacher's The Life of Jesus*, trans. and ed. with intro., Leander E. Keck (Philadelphia, 1977).

B. BBKL 11:27–32; LThK² 9:1108–9; NCE 13:732; ODCC 1547; Albert Schweitzer, *The Quest of the Historical Jesus: A Critical Study of Its Progress from Reimarus to Wrede*, trans. William Montgomery (London, 1911); Horton Harris, *David Friedrich Strauss and His Theology* (Cambridge, 1973); William J. Brazil, *The Young Hegelians* (New Haven, Conn., 1970).

John M. Brenner

STRINGFELLOW, WILLIAM (26 April, 1929 Cranston, R.I.–2 March 1985, Providence, R.I.). *Education*: A.B., Bates Coll., 1949; London Sch. of Economics, 1950; LL.B., Harvard Law Sch., 1956. *Career*: private legal practice in Harlem, 1957–60; in New York City, 1961–85; and in Rhode Island, 1971–85; member, Faith and Order Commission, World Council of Churches, 1960–83.

Stringfellow was an Episcopal layman and an attorney who defended the legal rights of poor black people. He was identified with activist causes and brought a theological perspective to the fight against racism, the war in Viet Nam, and other social ills. After moving to Block Island (New Shoreham), Rhode Island, he was charged with harboring Daniel Berrigan as a fugitive. Berrigan, a Jesuit priest, was arrested at Stringfellow's home after being convicted for burning draft records to protest American involvement in the war in Viet Nam. The charges against Stringfellow, and Anthony Towne, who lived with Stringfellow, were eventually dismissed. Stringfellow perceived the powers and principalities of death to be at work in the social evils of his day and in the idolatries of contemporary culture. In *The Politics of Spirituality* (Philadelphia, 1984), he urged that intercession and eucharistic praise are especially suited to political resistance.

Bibliography

A. *Free in Obedience* (New York, 1964); *Dissenter in a Great Society* (New York, 1966); *Count It All Joy* (Grand Rapids, Mich., 1967); *A Second Birthday* (Garden City, N.Y., 1970); *An Ethic for Christians and Other Aliens in a Strange Land* (Waco, Tex., 1973); *Instead of Death, New and Expanded Edition* (New York, 1976); *Conscience and Obedience* (Waco, Tex., 1977); *A Simplicity of Faith: My Experience of Mourning* (Nashville, Tenn., 1982).

B. *Radical Christian and Exemplary Lawyer*, ed. Andrew McThenia (Grand Rapids, Mich., 1995); *A Keeper of the Word*, ed. Bill Wylie-Kellermann (Grand Rapids, Mich., 1994); Robert B. Slocum, ''William Stringfellow and the Christian Witness Against Death,'' *Anglican Theological Review* (1995): 173–86; idem, ed. *Prophet of Justice, Prophet of Life* (New York, 1997).

Robert B. Slocum

STUCKENBERG, JOHN HENRY WILBURN (6 January 1835, Bramsche, near Osnabrück, Kingdom of Hanover–28 May 1903, London, England). *Education*: Wittenberg Coll., Springfield, Ohio, 1852–58; Univ. of Halle, Germany, 1859–61; Univs. of Göttingen, Berlin, and Tübingen, Germany, 1865–66. *Career*: pastor, Davenport, Iowa, 1858–59, Erie, Pa., 1861–62, 1863–65; U. S. Army chaplaincy (at battles of Antietam, Fredericksburg, Chancellorsville, and Gettysburg), 1862–73; professor, Wittenberg Coll., Springfield, Ohio, 1873–80; associate editor, *Homiletic Review*, 1884–97; pastor of the American (Protestant) church, Berlin, Germany, 1880–94; private scholar and public lecturer, Harvard Coll., Cambridge, Mass., and Marietta Coll., Marietta, Ohio, and in Berlin, Paris and London, 1895–1903.

Among fin de siècle American Lutheran church figures, Stuckenberg stood out as an innovator in the new science of sociology and developed a theological position that was congenial with the emerging ''social gospel'' movement. Stuckenberg was a ''Christian realist'' who accepted as authentic only those forms of Christianity that made a difference in favor of progressive public policy, social cohesion, and lasting reform. Doctrinal orthodoxy, worship, and personal piety, while foundational to the Christian mission, were not the final criteria for distinguishing between authentic and counterfeit or defective forms of the church.

In *Christian Sociology* (New York, 1880), Stuckenberg employs the Lutheran dichotomy of ''true church'' and ''visible church'' in his theological analysis of society. All humanity is called by God in Jesus Christ to be what the church in its authentic form actually is (i.e., the community of human beings reconciled with God and living in just and peaceful relation with one another). It is toward this organic goal that all human history is tending. In Stuckenberg's eschaton, all class distinctions will vanish and all inequities will be righted. The true church is the microcosm and paradigm of a truly humane society. Only where the social relations found in the New Testament actually obtain in society will a pragmatically workable and ethically defensible system of private, political, and economic life be found. The person and work of Jesus Christ, as paradigm of authentic humanity in both his teaching and his person, is the cardinal principle of any authentic social system. In *The Age and the Church* (Hartford, Conn., 1893), Stuckenberg asserted that liberal Protestantism alone possessed the principles of progress, adaptation, and reform adequate to Christianity's future survival.

Bibliography

A. *The Final Science, or, Spiritual Materialism, Being a Strict Application of the Most Approved Modern Scientific Principles to the Solution of the Deepest Problems of the Age* (New York and London, 1885); *The Social Problem* (York, Pa., 1897); *Introduction to the Study of Sociology* (New York, 1898); *Sociology, the Science of Human Society* (New York and London, 1903).

B. *The Encyclopedia of the Lutheran Church*, 3:2271; John Oluf Evjen, *The Life of J. H. W. Stuckenberg, Theologian—Philosopher—Sociologist—Friend of Humanity* (Minneapolis, Minn., 1938); Mark Granquist, "J. H. W. Stuckenberg and Lutheranism in America," in *Essays and Proceedings of the Lutheran Historical Conference, Ft. Wayne, 1996*, ed. David J. Wartluft (Philadelphia, forthcoming); August R. Suelflow and Clifford E. Nelson, "Following the Frontier, 1840–1875," in *The Lutherans in North America*, ed. Clifford E. Nelson (Philadelphia, 1975), 147–50.

Guy C. Carter

SUÁREZ, FRANCIS (5 January 1548, Granada, Spain–25 September 1617, Lisbon, Portugal). *Education*: studied canon law, Salamanca, 1564; studied philosophy and theology, Salamanca, 1565–71. *Career*: entered the Society of Jesus, 1564; ordained priest 1572; professor of philosophy, Ávila and Segovia, 1571–74; professor of theology, Ávila, Segovia, Valladolid, 1574–80; Roman Coll., Rome, 1580–85; Alcalá, 1585–93; Salamanca, 1593–97; and Coimbra, 1597–1615.

Suárez is probably the most renowned of the late Renaissance scholastic philosopher-theologians. Although he was primarily a theologian, his scholarly work has had a significant influence on classical modern philosophers. Descartes learned philosophy from Suarezian manuals at the Jesuit school of La Flèche and later read the *Disputationes* himself. Leibniz claims that he read the *Disputationes* as easily as one reads a novel. Both Schopenhauer and Christian Wolff* respected the *Disputationes* as a compendium of the best of scholastic metaphysical thought. Early modern political thought also bears the marks of Suárez's legal analysis. Grotius* and Hobbes especially have expressed fascination with Suárez's analyses of international law and the distinction between *lex* (law) and *jus* (right).

The *Disputationes* holds the place of honor as the first systematic treatment of metaphysics after Aristotle. Until Suárez wrote this work, metaphysics as a study had been exclusively commentary on Aristotle. Since Suárez had a keen sense that theologians must have a firm foundation in metaphysical thought before studying theology, in the *Disputationes* he reordered the Aristotelian treatment in order to display the logical relationships among metaphysical concepts. In several key notions Suarez departed from Thomas Aquinas* and the early Thomists. Suárez denied the real distinction between essence and existence; he reworked the theory of relations; and he placed great emphasis on the unity of finite being.

The *De Legibus* as a work of legal philosophy arose out of the controversies surrounding the place of the monarch in civil society, the burgeoning commerce among people of various nations, and the notion of God as supreme legislator. In light of these concerns Suárez redefined the notions of law (*lex*) and right (*jus*). Beginning with a discussion of the inadequacy of Thomas Aquinas' definition of law, Suarez redefined law as "a common, just, and stable precept which has been sufficiently promulgated." He then defined right as "a certain moral power possessed by everyone, either over one's own property or with respect to what is due to oneself." These two notions provide the foundations for lengthy discussions of morality and law, the place of the monarch in society, and equal rights.

Bibliography

A.   *Opera Omnia*, ed. Charles Breton, 26 vols. (Paris, 1856–77, and 2 vols. of indices, 1878); *Disputationes Metaphysicae*, ed. S. Rabade Romeo et al., 7 vols. (Madrid, 1960–66); *De Legibus et Legislatore Deo*, ed. L. Pereña et al. 8 vols., *Corpus Hispanorum de Pace*, vols. 11–17, 21–22 (Madrid, 1971–); *De Deo uno et trino* (Burgos, 1962); *De Opere Sex Dierum* (Brussels, 1859).

B.   DTC 14:2638–728; LThK² 9:1129–32; NCE 13:751–54; ODCC 1550–51; OEncR 4:123–24; Joseph M. Fichter, *Man of Spain: Suarez* (New York, 1940); Leon Mahieu, *François Suarez: sa philosophie et les rapports qu'elle a avec sa théologie* (Paris, 1921); R. de Scoraille, *François Suarez de la Compagnie de Jésus*, 2 vols. (Paris, 1911).

Jack Treloar

SULLIVAN, WILLIAM LAURENCE (15 November 1872, East Braintree, Mass.–5 October 1935, Germantown, Pa.). *Education*: studied at Boston Coll., 1891–92; B. Phil., St. John's Sem., Brighton, Mass., 1896; S.T.B., S.T.L., Catholic Univ. of America, 1899, 1900. *Career*: ordained Paulist priest, 1899; mission preacher, Tenn., 1900–1902; professor of theology, St. Thomas Coll., Catholic Univ. of America, 1902–7; mission preacher, Chicago, 1907–8; assistant pastor, Austin, Tex., 1908–9; resigned from Paulists, 1909; independent writer and teacher, 1909–12; admitted to Unitarian ministry, Schenectady, N.Y., 1912; associate and pastor, All Souls' Unitarian Church, New York City, 1913–22; mission preacher, Unitarian Laymen's League, 1922–24; pastor, St. Louis, Mo., 1924–28, and Germantown, Pa., 1929–35.

The most outspoken of the handful of American Catholic modernists, Sullivan's apologetic concerns led him to biblical study. He struggled, especially in the area of Christology, to reconcile the results of critical scholarship with traditional faith. His publications after 1907 voiced Sullivan's near-Puritanical moral revulsion at both Vatican suppression of modernists and acquiescence in it by the clergy. After 1911, as a Unitarian, he worked to combine the "mystical depth" of Catholicism with the "rational modern freedom" of Unitarianism.

Bibliography

A.   Unpublished papers, Andover Harvard Library, Cambridge, Mass.; *Letters to His Holiness Pope Pius X. By a Modernist* (Chicago, 1910); *The Priest: A Tale of Modernism in New England* (Boston, 1911); *From the Gospels to the Creeds: Studies in the Early History of the Christian Church* (Boston, 1919); *Under Orders, The Autobiography of William Laurence Sullivan* (Boston, 1944).

B.   NYT 7 October 1935, 15; R. Scott Appleby, *"Church and Age Unite!" The Modernist Impulse in American Catholicism* (Notre Dame, Ind., 1992); John Ratté, *Three Modernists* (London, 1967).

William L. Portier

SWEDENBORG, EMANUEL (29 January 1688, Stockholm, Sweden–29 March 1772, London, England). *Education*: graduated from the Univ. of Uppsala, Sweden, 1709. *Career*: assessor for the Swedish Board of Mines, 1715–47; author of various treatises on the natural sciences as well as philosophy and theology, 1747–72.

Swedenborg was the son of a wealthy Lutheran bishop. The young aristocrat traveled extensively on the Continent, striving to develop a comprehensive philosophy of nature. He also employed modern scientific methods in his ongoing effort to describe the seat of the soul. Swedenborg's eclectic studies moved him beyond traditional dichotomies. He came to view the cosmos as a mystical reality, containing an exact "doctrine of correspondence" between phenomenon and spirit.

Between 1743 and 1745 a spiritual crisis overtook Swedenborg. He believed he had become an eschatological event, perfectly inspired. He abandoned non-spiritual writing and concentrated upon unorthodox biblical exegesis and gnostic speculations. During this seer/shamanistic phase, Swedenborg experienced visions, premonitions, and physical manifestations, which he portrayed as messages from the Lord. His radical anthropocentrism denied the doctrine of the divinity of Christ and the need for redemption. Swedenborg saw his "Heavenly Doctrines" as the true meaning of the Scriptures.

In America, Swedenborg attracted active followers and sympathizers of both liberal and sectarian tendencies. His antidogmatism, stressing new unitive combinations, appealed to opponents of evangelical certitudes. In *Representative Men*, Emerson* portrayed Swedenborg as the last great Father of the church.

Bibliography

A.   *Worship and Love of God* (1745; New York, 1969); *Heaven and Hell* (1758; New York, 1971); *Arcana Coelestia* (1749–56; New York, 1870–73); *The True Christian Religion* (1771; New York, 1970).

B.   DTC 14:2874–75; LThK² 9:1199–1200; NCE 13:833–34; ODCC 1563–64; RGG

6:535–36; Inge Jonsson, *Emanuel Swedenborg* (New York, 1971); George Trobridge, *Swedenborg: Life and Teaching* (New York, 1955).

Terrence Crowe

SYMEON THE NEW THEOLOGIAN (949, Galatia [Paphlagonia]–12 March 1022, near Constantinople). Born to an aristocratic family in the Byzantine provinces, Symeon spent his youth and early manhood at the imperial court in Constantinople. Moved by a vision in his early twenties and encouraged by the counsel and example of his spiritual father, Symeon the Pious, a monk at the Studion monastery, he eventually embraced monastic life at age twenty-seven. Two years later he was elected abbot of the monastery of St. Mamas, where he served until compelled by the imperial chancery and patriarchal court to retire in 1005. In 1009 he was exiled to the opposite shores of the Bosphorus at Chrysopolis, where he died thirteen years later after having assembled a second monastic community around himself. He was canonized a saint in 1054, thanks largely to the influence of his disciple, editor and biographer, Nicetas Stethatos.

Symeon was clearly a controversial figure, both during his life and thereafter. His works effectively disappeared for two hundred years following the death of Nicetas (ca. 1090), only to emerge again with increased prominence during the Hesychast revival of the fourteenth and fifteenth centuries. The republication of his writings has also marked both of the two great revivals of Greek monasticism that followed the end of the Byzantine era, the renewal associated with Nicodemus of the Holy Mountain* and the *Philokalia* in the late eighteenth century and the recent awakening of Mt. Athos during the last three decades of the twentieth century.

The reason for both the controversy and the attraction lies in the extraordinary quality of Symeon's witness. His sobriquet, the New Theologian, was likely coined by his enemies in order to underline the novelty and suspicion of heresy that they discerned in him. There is no doubt that Symeon's claim to have experienced the ''substantial light'' of the Trinity was new, though not so much for the idea of the *visio gloriae* in this life, for which there was ample precedent in Eastern Christian ascetic literature, as for his use of the first person singular—''I have seen''—which broke with ancient precedent going back to St. Paul in 2 Cor 12:2ff. Nor was Symeon shy about claiming the mantle of prophetic authority, often to the consternation of the Constantinopolitan hierarchy. He felt he had been set apart by God to preach what he felt was the heart of the Gospel, that through Christ in the Holy Spirit humanity has been called to participate in the very life of the godhead. Here, too, the content of his message was nothing new. It was the Eastern Christian soteriology of deification (*theosis*) whose formulation dates back at least to Irenaeus* of Lyons, if not before. Nothing that Symeon said was in itself unusual. The content of his writings, his theological and mystical vocabulary, is no more nor less than that of the Eastern Church as expressed in the first seven Ecumenical Councils, in the liturgy, and in the literature of the Fathers. What thrilled—or shocked—his listeners lay in his delivery, his personal testimony and unflagging, even ferocious insistence that the demands and promises of Scripture and tradition are not theory, not abstract or distant truth, but immanent, alive, and, even within the confines of this present life, transfiguring. Hence his assertion, frequently repeated, that the great age of the Apostles is not a distant past but, once again, a present possibility and vocation.

Symeon's followers and admirers thus welcomed the phrase New Theologian, which they understood as witnessing to one who they felt had received, like the saints of old, a "word" from the living God and who had thus spoken in their own days with the *auctoritas* of the prophets and apostles. It is thus surely no accident that three hundred years later Gregory Palamas* would open his defense of the Hesychasts of Mt. Athos by equating the ascetic holy men of his and past generations with the prophets of Israel. Just as the latter had seen and declared the coming of the Messiah and Day of the Lord, so the former see and announce the glory of the world to come.

Bibliography

A.   *Symeon the New Theologian: The Discourses*, trans. C. J. de Catanzaro (New York, 1980); *Symeon the New Theologian: The Practical and Theological Chapters and the Three Theological Discourses*, trans. P. McGuckin (Kalamazoo, Mich., 1982); *Hymns of Divine Love*, trans. G. Maloney (Denville, N.J., n.d.); *St. Symeon the New Theologian on the Mystical Life: The Ethical Discourses*, 2 vols., trans. A. Golitzin (Crestwood, New York, 1995, 1996).

B.   DMA 11:553; DTC 14:2941–56; HDOC 313; LThK² 9:12–5–6; NCE 13:875–76; ODB 3:1987; ODCC 1500–1501; K. Holl, *Enthusiasmus und Bussgewalt beim griechischen Mönchtum: eine Studie zum Symeon dem neuen Theologen* (Leipzig, 1898); I. Hausherr, *Vie de Syméon le nouveau théologien* (Rome, 1928); W. Völker, *Praxis und Theoria bei Symeon dem neuen Theologen: ein Beitrag zur.byzantinischen Mystik* (Wiesbaden, 1974); B. Fraigneau-Julien, *Les sens spirituels et la vision de Dieu chez Syméon le nouveau théologien* (Paris, 1985); B. Krivocheine, *In the Light of Christ: St. Symeon the New Theologian*, trans. A. Gythiel (Crestwood, New York, 1985); H. J. M. Turner, *St. Symeon the New Theologian and Spiritual Fatherhood* (Leiden, 1990); A. Hatzopoulos, *Two Outstanding Cases in Byzantine Spirituality: The Macarian Homilies and Symeon the New Theologian* (Thessalonica, 1991); A. Golitzin; "Hierarchy versus Anarchy? Dionysius Areopagita, Symeon the New Theologian, Nicetas Stethatos, and Their Common Roots in Ascetical Tradition," SVTQ 38 (1994): 131–79; idem, *St. Symeon the New Theologian on the Mystical Life*, vol. 3: *Life, Times, and Theology* (Crestwood, New York, 1997); J. A. McGuckin, "The Luminous Vision in Eleventh Century Byzantium: Interpreting the Biblical and Theological Paradigms of St. Symeon the New Theologian," in *Work and Workshop at the Theotokos Evergetes 1050–1200*, ed. M. Muller and B. Kirby(Belfast, 1997), 90–123.

Alexander Golitzin

T

TANQUEREY, ADOLPHE-ALFRED (1 May 1854, Blainville, Manche, France–21 February 1932, Aix-en-Provence). *Education*: Coll. of Saint-Lô, Manche, 1867–72; major sem., Coutances, 1873; Saint-Sulpice, Paris, 1875; doctorate in theology, Angelicum, Rome, 1876–78. *Career*: ordained priest, 1878; entered the Society of Saint-Sulpice, 1878; professor of philosophy, Nantes, 1878–79; professor of dogmatic theology, moral theology, and canon law, sem., Rodez, 1879–87; St. Mary's Sem., Baltimore, Md., 1887–95; vice president, St. Mary's Sem., 1896–1902; professor of theology, Saint-Sulpice Sem., Paris, 1902–5; spiritual director and writer, Sem., Issy-le-Moulineaux, 1907–26; superior of the Sulpician Solitude (novitiate), Issy, 1915–26; retired to the major sem., Aix-en-Provence, 1927–32.

Tanquerey is one of the best and best-known Roman Catholic authors in the tradition of scholastic manual theology. Early in his career he taught dogmatic theology, first in France, then in the United States, where he authored several Latin volumes on the subject. Because of their comprehensive treatment, scholarly content, clarity of organization, and fine literary style, these texts quickly established themselves among the most widely used in seminaries around the world for half a century. Basing himself on the Fathers of the church and following Thomas Aquinas* and Alphonsus Ligouri,* his expressed intention was to deemphasize controversial points in favor of the best of the received tradition. Indeed, his restraint earned him the reproach of not being a sufficiently rigorous Thomist—Bruno de Solages dubbed him *doctor conciliator*. However, Tanquerey was not a slave to the tradition; his pastoral concern led him creatively to elaborate on the practical application of speculative truths to daily living.

In the latter part of his career, Tanquerey made his most memorable mark on the theological landscape as a pioneer in the science of ascetical and mystical

Christian theology. He was convinced that authentic Christian spiritual life is founded on dogmatic truth; thus his treatises on the spiritual life, still considered classics, always began with the dogmatic principles of Christian belief before proceeding to the nature and practice of the spiritual life. His weighty *Précis de théologie ascétique et mystique* (translated into at least ten languages) explains in clear yet scientific terms the classical "three ways" of the spiritual life (purgative, illuminative, and unitive) experienced by committed practitioners of prayer. But in this field as well, Tanquerey's pastoral concern led him to adapt for busy priests and lay people his more scholarly teaching without over-simplifying it—thus his *Les dogmes générateurs de la piété* and *La divinisation de la souffrance*, as well as numerous articles in journals, specialized dictionaries, and small popular works. His substantial output, marked by solid and balanced theology as well as by a clear and concrete style, has introduced countless seekers around the world to the riches of the Christian spiritual life.

Bibliography

A. *Synopsis theologiae dogmaticae specialis*, 2 vols. (Baltimore, Md., 1894), abridged as *Brevior synopsis theologiae dogmaticae* (New York, 1911), ET: *A Manual of Dogmatic Theology* (New York, 1959); *Synopsis theologiae dogmaticae fundamentalis* (Baltimore, Md., 1896); *Synopsis theologiae moralis et pastoralis*, 2 vols. (Baltimore, Md., 1902), abridged as *Brevior synopsis theologiae moralis et pastoralis* (Rome, 1911); *The Spiritual Life* (1923; Tournai, 1930); *Les dogmes générateurs de la piété* (Paris, 1926) and *La divinisation de la souffrance* (Paris, 1931), combined in ET: *Doctrine and Devotion* (Tournai, 1933); *Pour ma vie intérieure*, with Jean Gautier (Paris, 1927).

B. DSAM 15:25–27; DTC 15:47–48; ECatt 11:1733–34; LThK² 9:1290; NCE 13: 934; Paul H. Hallett, "My Friends the Manualists," *Homiletic and Pastoral Review* 83 (October 1982): 20–23.

David G. Schultenover

TATIAN THE ASSYRIAN (ca. 120, "the land of the Assyrians"–after 170, Antioch). *Education*: Hellenistic rhetorical and philosophical education at an unknown location; much traveling; Christian convert in Rome 150/65, pupil of Justin Martyr.* *Career*: student and associate of Justin Martyr; debate with Cynic philosopher Crescens in Rome; composition in the West of anti-Hellenistic *Discourse to the Greeks*; gains disciple, Rhodo; departure for Mesopotamia to found a school and Christian group later identified with Encratites; authorship of the *Diatessaron* or Gospel harmony.

Known through his one extant work, the *Discourse*, and through alleged translations of his *Diatessaron*, Tatian was subject to much attack on the part of later authors (Irenaeus,* Tertullian,* Clement,* Hippolytus,* Origen,* Eusebius,* Epiphanius) for his radical asceticism and tampering with the biblical text. A productive author (viz., the lost *On Animals, Perfection according to the Savior, Problems* [of Scripture]), Tatian's apology for Christianity consisted in savaging Greek culture for moral enormities (gross sexual license, civic entertainments, use of *pharmaka*, all demonic in origin) and praising Christian theology and behavior. Borrowing a Jewish theme, he claimed the greater antiquity for Christianity and promoted its monotheism. The Logos created the world, but the Fall of the first parents resulted in the hegemony of the diabolic until the Incarnation and its promise of bodily resurrection. A radical interpreter of Paul, Tatian taught the incompatibility of marriage with the imitation of Christ, the New Adam; likewise wine was forbidden to his followers. Like the Gnostics he may have dissociated the High God from the Creator God.

Bibliography

A. *Tatiani Oratio ad Graecos*, ed. Eduard Schwartz, TU 4, 1 (Leipzig, 1888); A. Puech, *Recherches sur le Discours aux Grecs de Tatien, suivies d'une traduction française du Discours, avec notes* (Paris, 1903); *Tatian: Oratio ad Graecos and Fragments*, ed. and trans. Molly Whittaker (Oxford, 1982); *St. Ephrem's Commentary on Tatian's Diatessaron; An English Translation of Chester Beatty Syriac Ms. 709*, trans. Carmel McCarthy (Oxford, 1993).

B. DTC 15:59–66; LThK² 9:1305; ODCC 1579; Robert M. Grant, "The Heresy of Tatian," JTS n.s. 5 (1954): 62–68; Tietje Baarda, "Tatian's Theological Method," HTR 51 (1958): 123–28; G. F. Hawthorne, "Tatian and His Discourse to the Greeks," HTR 57 (1964): 161–68; Gilles Quispel, *Tatian and the Gospel of Thomas* (Leiden, 1975); Tietje Baarda, *Essays on the Diatessaron* (Kampen, 1994); William L. Petersen, *Tatian's Diatessaron: Its Creation, Dissemination, Significance, and History in Scholarship* (Leiden, 1994).

Robin Darling Young

TAYLOR, NATHANIEL WILLIAM (23 June 1786, New Milford, Conn.–10 March 1858, New Haven, Conn.). *Education*: graduated from Yale Coll., 1807; read theology under Timothy Dwight, New Haven, Conn., 1808–12. *Career*: pastor, First Congregational Church, New Haven, Conn., 1812–22; professor of didactic Theology, Yale Div. Sch., 1822–57.

Taylor was the primary spokesman for the New Haven (i.e., Yale) school of theology in the early nineteenth century. His theology represented a bridge between the inherited Reformed orthodoxy of the eighteenth century and the liberal Protestant theology of the middle- and late nineteenth century. To some extent he constructed a new Reformed theology that met the democratic élan of early nineteenth-century America, responded to the Unitarian attacks upon the so-called "immorality" of predestinarian Calvinism, modified the rigors of the New Divinity views of sin and the moral government of God, and established a theological justification for an early nineteenth-century Protestant revivalism.

The moral government of God was the controlling idea in Taylor's theology. Like Joseph Bellamy* and other New Divinity Men, Taylor rejected the traditional substitutionary theory of the Atonement and replaced it with the moral government theory of the Atonement. According to this view, Christ's death was necessary to prove that God hated sin and insisted that his rule be maintained. Unlike the substitutionary view, the moral view placed more stress upon God's law and authority than on his honor. Unlike the New Divinity Men, however, Taylor insisted that a truly moral government implies free moral agency and that the divine governor rules the minds of these free agents by motives and not by force. Rule, law, and authority implied the assent of the governed.

Within his own understanding of the moral government of God, Taylor developed his characteristic contribution to the emergence of a new kind of Reformed theology in nineteenth century America. He tried to reconcile the doctrine of natural depravity, which he inherited from the eighteenth-century Calvinists, with the democratic and Unitarian emphasis on free will and individual decision. Unlike early nineteenth-century Unitarians, however, he insisted upon the universality and inevitability of sin. Moral depravity, he insisted, is "by nature," not "in nature" as traditional Calvinists held. For him this meant that depravity consisted in a voluntary act, an act of nature, and not a necessary result of being human. Sin was in the sinning. Sin was simultaneously a certain and a free act because human nature was such (i.e., having free will) that it was certain that human beings would sin, even though they had the power to the contrary. Such was their nature that they would sin and only sin in all the appropriate circumstances of their being—but they did so freely and not by necessity nor because of the environmental circumstances of their lives. In *Man, a Free Agent without the Aids of Divine Grace* (New Haven, Conn., 1818), Taylor first articulated this view when he wrote that "the human mind never did and never can conceive of any other principle on which blame can be attached to any being but this: that he will not do what he *can* do."

Although Taylor held to a doctrine of predestination he believed that human beings were free because they felt themselves to be free even though a sovereign God from the foundation of the world had foreknowledge of their ultimate destinations.

The emphasis upon free will was also evident in his doctrine of conversion and regeneration in which he invoked the idea of a moral governor who appeals to free human beings to repent and believe. They have the ability to respond freely when invited by God to do so. This emphasis upon moral freedom became a linchpin in the theology that governed the Protestant revivalist movement during much of the nineteenth century. Although Taylor acknowledged that regeneration was accomplished through the work of the Holy Spirit and grace, it was not clear how he reconciled grace and freedom in the human being's movement toward conversion and regeneration; he merely asserted that the sinner acted through the Spirit, but he never demonstrated how this could be so.

Bibliography

A. *Essays on the Means of Regeneration* (New Haven, Conn., 1829); *Practical Sermons*, ed. Noah Porter (New York, 1858); *Essays . . . upon Select Topics in Revealed Theology* (New York, 1859); *Lectures on the Moral Government of God*, 2 vols. (New York, 1859).

B.   DAB 18:338–39; DARB, 542–43; NCAB 7:187; NCE 13:953–54; SH 11:285; S. E. Mead, *Nathaniel William Taylor, 1786–1858: A Connecticut Liberal* (Chicago, 1942).

Patrick W. Carey

TEILHARD DE CHARDIN, MARIE-JOSEPH PIERRE (1 May, 1881, Sarcenat, France–10 April, 1955, New York, N.Y.). *Education*: studied philosophy at Maison St. Louis on Isle of Jersey, 1902–5; theology at Hastings, England, 1908–12; studies in geology, Sorbonne, 1912–14, 1919–22. *Career*: entered Jesuit novitiate, Aix-en-Provence, 1899; professor of physics and chemistry, Coll. de la Sainte Famille, Cairo, 1905–8; ordained priest, 1911; professor of geology, Institut Catholique, Paris, 1920–25; lived mostly in China working on the geology of Asia and early human remains in China, 1923–46; lived in Paris, 1946–51; lived in New York to work with the Viking (Wenner-Gren) Foundation, which sponsored his trips to South Africa and Rhodesia to study early human fossils, 1951–55.

As a young seminarian, Teilhard told of two attractions dividing his allegiance: one was for the transcendent and personal God that he knew through revelation, and the other was for the immanent and impersonal matter that he knew through science. But on studying each he saw them coming into conjunction: By his study of science (geology/evolution) he saw the impersonal world of matter rising in forms of increasing complexity. As life proceeded through fish, reptiles, and mammals to hominids it also showed an increasing consciousness. The first human appeared when the rising consciousness became reflexive; the human individual was "evolution conscious of itself." By Teilhard's study of the Revelation (especially the "cosmic" texts of St. Paul) he learned that the transcendent God had descended into the lowest parts of the earth so that rising from there He might fill all things (Eph 4:10). Accordingly, he saw Christ forming his Body by drawing all things to himself to become the one "in whom all things hold together" (Col 1:17). Thus the conjunction of the two stars: by the descent of God and the rising of matter the personal God (as soul) would permeate the impersonal cosmos (as body) to form the Body of Christ: Teilhard would speak of Christ having a mystical Body (believers) and a cosmic Body (the cosmos).

In today's world Teilhard saw scientific, social, and political developments leading to a single world order as though forming a single organism with a single developing mind, the "noosphere." Others had spoken of the earth as an organism of sorts with its increasingly interrelated forms of life, but Teilhard (again appealing to St. Paul) went further and saw the earth gradually acquiring a single divine Soul, the "Omega Point." Thus the progress and increasing interrelationship of nations and the social and economic development of nations were seen as part of the work by which Christ was building his Body and gathering all things to himself. Teilhard developed an appropriate spirituality concerning human work in building the earth. He urged that we realize that evolution is sacred and see our "secular" activities contributing to the Divine

Pleroma. His call for a united humanity spoke to many nonbelieving humanists. But Teilhard insisted that the single soul of humanity must also be Divine so that humanity might escape the cosmic death of entropy. Intent on bringing hope to the world, he wrote on both human growth and human diminishments. Teilhard argued the Kingdom of Christ is ultimately beyond this world, so the earth itself needs to go through death to reach its final fulfillment in God. By the Eucharist as Body of Christ the development of the earth is consecrated by God and received by us; by the Eucharist as Blood of Christ the pain and setbacks of the earth are consecrated by God and received by us.

In 1925 Teilhard was required to submit to a rigid censorship of his religious/philosophic writing, so that most of his works were published by friends only after his death (now collected in thirteen volumes); there were no restrictions on his scientific writings (now collected in ten volumes). He developed an immense popular following in the 1960s and 1970s; the Vatican gave him a positive recognition in June 1981.

Bibliography

A.   *Oeuvres*, 13 vols. (Paris, 1956–76); *L'oeuvre scientifique*, 10 vols. (Olten/Freiburg im Breisgau, 1971); *The Phenomenon of Man*, trans. Bernard Wall (New York, 1959); *The Divine Milieu*, trans. unidentified (New York, 1960); *The Heart of Matter*, trans. Rene Hague (New York, 1979).

B.   LThK² 9:1341–42; NCE 13:977–78; ODCC 1582; Christopher F. Mooney, *Teilhard de Chardin and the Mystery of Christ* (New York, 1964); Thomas M. King, *Teilhard's Mysticism of Knowing* (New York, 1981); idem, *Teilhard de Chardin* (Wilmington, Del., 1988); Henri de Lubac, *The Religion of Teilhard de Chardin* (New York, 1967); Mary Lukas and Ellen Lukas, *Teilhard* (New York, 1977); Joseph M. McCarty, *Pierre Teilhard de Chardin: A Comprehensive Bibliography* (New York, 1981).

Thomas M. King

TEMPLE, WILLIAM (15 October 1881, Exeter, Devonshire, England–26 October 1944, Westgate-on-Sea, Kent, England). *Education*: studied at Balliol Coll., Oxford, first class, classical moderations, 1902; first class, *Literae Humaniores*, 1904. *Career*: fellow, Queen's Coll., Oxford, 1904–10; headmaster, Repton, 1910–14; rector, St. James' Church, Piccadilly, 1914–19; canon, Westminster, 1919–21; bishop, Manchester, 1921–29; archbishop, York, 1929–42; archbishop, Canterbury, 1942–44.

Temple was the ninety-third archbishop of Canterbury, a leading twentieth-century English theologian in the tradition of Christian Socialism, and a major ecumenical leader. He has been described as "the most significant Anglican churchman of the first half of the twentieth century." At the center of his theology, faith, and philosophy was the Incarnation of God in Jesus Christ. He wrote: "The whole of my theology is an attempt to understand and verify the words, 'He that hath seen me hath seen the Father.' " He believed that the church is the result of the Incarnation and the continuance of its principle. The task of the church is to win the world for the Kingdom of God. Temple was a national leader and world figure in the ecumenical movement. He was chairman of the Archbishops' Commission on Christian Doctrine, which published *Doctrine in the Church of England* (1938).

Bibliography

A.   *Mens Creatrix* (London, 1917); *Christus Veritas* (New York, 1924); *Nature, Man and God* (London, 1934); *Readings in St. John's Gospel* (London, 1939); *Christianity and Social Order* (London, 1942).

B.   DNB [1941–50], 869–73; NCE 13:994; ODCC 1586; *William Temple and His Message*, ed. A. E. Baker (New York, 1946); F. A. Iremonger, *William Temple* (London, 1948); Joseph Fletcher, *William Temple, Twentieth-Century Theologian* (New York, 1963).

Donald S. Armentrout

TERESA OF ÁVILA (28 March 1515, Ávila, Spain–4 October 1582, Alba de Tormes, Spain). *Education*: attended convent boarding school of Our Lady of Grace, Ávila, 1531–32. *Career*: entered Carmelite Monastery of the Incarnation, Ávila, 1535; founder of seventeen monasteries for women, Spain, 1562–82; beatified 1614; canonized 1622; declared first woman doctor of the church, 27 September 1970; feast 15 October.

Of Jewish ancestry, Doña Teresa de Ahumada y Cepeda, after her first foundation, called herself Teresa of Jesus. Perhaps the best-known mystic in the Roman Catholic tradition, Teresa had a gift for describing her mystical experiences clearly and tellingly. While she lacked training in writing and theology, she wrote about her experiences of the divine in a way that made her mystical experiences paradigmatic for Christian theology. Her corpus of writings comprises the *Book of Her Life*, *The Way of Perfection*, her acknowledged classic *The Interior Castle*, the much neglected *The Book of Her Foundations*, various minor writings, and her numerous lively letters.

Without theological education, Teresa consulted, concerning her experiences and writings, professional theologians like the Dominican Domingo Báñez,* and she sought advice from those whose holiness she admired like John of the Cross,* the Franciscan Peter of Alcantara, and the Jesuit Francis Borgia.

Teresa emphasized the absolute and special gift character of the mystical life as described in the fourth to the seventh dwelling places of *The Interior Castle*; she taught that love of neighbor is the test of mystical experience, and she found that the humanity of Christ was the *locus* of her experience of the divine. As a reformer of the contemplative life, she found her inspiration in the Carmelite hermits who lived on Mount Carmel in the thirteenth century. For her, the key to a successful Carmelite reform was to arrange for monasteries small enough for the sake of solitude and large enough to support the community. This solitude within community is the essence of the "primitive" Carmelite Rule, which Teresa professed to retrieve. Through John of the Cross and others, Teresa fostered the reform of the Carmelite men. In 1593 the Discalced Carmelites became a separate order.

Bibliography

A. *The Collected Works of St. Teresa of Avila*, trans. Kieran Kavanaugh and Otilio Rodriguez, 3 vols. (Washington, D.C., 1976, 1980, 1985).
B. DSAM 15:611–58; NCE 13:1013–16; ODCC 1589–90; Rowan Williams, *Teresa of Avila* (Harrisburg, Pa., 1991).

Keith J. Egan

TERTULLIAN (ca. 160, Carthage—after 220, Carthage). *Education*: well educated in rhetoric, Greek, and Latin, he was a jurist by training and profession. *Career*: in *On Illustrious Men* Jerome* states that after his conversion he was ordained a presbyter, but this and other details reported by Jerome are uncertain.

The first known Christian author to write in Latin, Tertullian exercised noteworthy influence not only in his own lifetime but also in subsequent centuries. His apologetic works include *To the Heathens*, *On the Testimony of the Soul*, *To Scapula*, *Against the Jews*, and the *Apology*, which is his most important work. Christians are hated and persecuted out of ignorance. Against the accusations of pagans Tertullian insisted that Christians do not sacrifice children. Christians share all things in common except their wives. Christians are not atheists but worship the one true God. He also wrote dogmatic and polemical works. *The Prescription of Heretics* contains his brief but famous tirade against pagan philosophy. His longest work, *Against Marcion*, is written in the form of a court case against Marcion* in five books in which he emphasized Christ as the Messiah as well as the continuity between the Old and New Testaments. Tertullian also wrote *Against Hermogenes*, *Against the Valentinians*, *Scorpiace*, *On the Flesh of Christ*, *On the Resurrection of the Dead*, and *On the Soul*, all against various forms of Gnosticism. He affirms the physical resurrection of the body. In *On the Soul* Tertullian subscribes to traducianism, the teaching that the soul comes to be at the same time as the body through generation, making it a corporeal substance. *On Baptism* is the earliest work on the subject and its contribution to sacramental theology is significant. Water and blood flowing from the side of Christ are symbolic of baptism and Eucharist, the two great sacraments of the church. *Against Praxeas* presents his teaching on the Trinity against Praxeas, a modalist and Patripassian who made no distinction between the Father, the Son, and the Holy Spirit. His practical and ascetic works include *To the Martyrs* and *On Flight in Persecution*, concerning martyrdom and persecution. *On the Crown* deals with the problem of Christians' serving in the Roman military. For Tertullian the wearing of a military wreath is incompatible with Christianity, just as the swearing of a military oath is incompatible with the baptismal vow. *On Idolatry* addresses the same problem and goes on to condemn all forms of painting and sculpture. Several treatises criticize various aspects of pagan culture existing in contemporary society. *On the Shows* condemns public games. *On the Dress of Women* prohibits women from wearing cosmetics and jewelry. It also demands that virgins be veiled, as does *On the Veiling of Virgins*. Several treatises (*Exhortation to Chastity, On Monogamy*, and *To His Wife*) deal with remarriage, which Tertullian rejects even after the death of a spouse. *To His Wife* urges his own wife to remain a widow after his death. *On Repentance*, written before his Montanist period, treats of both pre-baptismal penance for catechumens and ecclesiastical penance allowed once in the case of a serious sin. Other practical works include *On Prayer, On Patience, On Fasting, On Modesty*, and *On the Pallium*. Some have attributed the *Passion of Saints Perpetua and Felicity* to him because of its African origin and Montanist characteristics, but this is not at all certain.

Tertullian gradually drifted into Montanism, ultimately becoming its spokesman in North Africa and its most important theologian. In works written toward the end of his life, Tertullian emphasizes many Montanist themes. Flight in times of persecution was not permitted. A spouse must not remarry after the death of a partner. Virginity and fasting were encouraged. Serious sins such as idolatry, fornication, and murder could be pardoned by no one. Tertullian's brand of Montanism was so distinctive in North Africa that Augustine* (*On Heresies* 86) called it Tertullianism.

Bibliography

A.   CPL 1–36; PL 1–2; PLS 1, 29–32; CSEL 20, 47, 69, 70, 76; CCSL 1–2; ANF 3–4; ACW 10, 40; FC 10, 40; *Apology and On Spectacles*, LCL (Cambridge, Mass., 1931); *Adversus Marcionem*, ed. Ernest Evans, 2 vols. (Oxford, 1972).

B.   DTC 15:130–71; LThK² 9:1370–74; NCE 13:1019–22; ODCC 1591–92; Adhemar d'Alès, *La théologie de Tertullien* (Paris, 1905; repr. Paris, 1974); Dimitri Michaélidès, "*Sacramentum*" *chez Tertullien* (Paris, 1970); Timothy D. Barnes, *Tertullian: A Historical and Literary Study* (Oxford, 1971); Robert D. Sider, *Ancient Rhetoric and the Art of Tertullian* (London, 1971); Gosta Claesson, *Index Tertullianeus*, 3 vols. (Paris, 1974–75); Douglas Powell, "Tertullianists and Cataphrygians," VC 29 (1975): 33–54; Gerald Lewis Bray, *Holiness and the Will of God: Perspectives on the Theology of Tertullian* (London, 1979); Robert D. Sider, "Approaches to Tertullian: A Study of Recent Scholarship," *Second Century* 2 (1982): 228–60; Heinrich Steiner, *Das Verhältnis Tertullians zur antiken Paideia* (St. Ottilien, 1989); Cecil M. Robeck, *Prophecy in Carthage: Perpetua, Tertullian, and Cyprian* (Cleveland, Ohio, 1992); Cahal B. Daly, *Tertullian the Puritan and His Influence: An Essay in Historical Theology* (Dublin, 1993); since 1976 *Revue des Etudes Augustiniennes* publishes an annual *Chronica Tertullianea*, which was expanded and renamed *Chronica Tertullianea et Cyprianea* in 1986.

Kenneth B. Steinhauser

THEODORE OF MOPSUESTIA (350, Antioch, Syria–428, Mopsuestia, Cilicia). *Education*: probably studied with John Chrysostom* at the rhetorical school of Libanius in Antioch; monk with him in monastic school of Diodore and Karterios outside city. *Career*: ordained priest, 383; bishop of Mopsuestia, 392–428.

Theodore was condemned posthumously at Council of Constantinople (553) for "nestorianizing," dyophysite Christology. He was the author of many theological discourses and commentaries, most surviving in Syriac alone. Of the former, his major writings are *On the Incarnation* (lost); *Catechetical Homilies*; *Dispute with the Macedonians* (lost); *The Assumer and the Assumed* (lost); *Against [Persian] Magic* (lost); *Against the Defenders of Original Sin* [in the theology of Augustine*] (lost). Of the latter, the most important are commentaries on the books of the Pentateuch, Pss, Prophets, Jb, Eccl; also Mt, Lk, Jn, Acts, and the epistles of Paul. Of these, all are lost save the *Commentary on Minor Prophets* (Greek), *John* (Syriac), fragments of the Psalms commentary (Greek), and a Latin translation of the work on the minor epistles of Paul, with fragments on the major epistles.

Like Diodore, Theodore was principally a biblical exegete, who stressed the narrative, rhetorical, and historical aspects of Scripture. He used typology sparingly and avoided allegory, gravitating toward a contextual understanding of Scripture. He understood the OT to refer to the Jewish religion and the NT to a new covenant and age inaugurated by the Incarnation.

Theodore's ill repute, his condemnation, and the destruction of most of his works in their native Greek stem from his Christology, which stresses the distinction between the divine and human natures (*physeis*) of Christ. Christ is one person, one Son, one Lord, the man assumed and the Son of God, united *kat' eudokian* (by the good pleasure, or grace) of God. Adopted and simplified by Nestorius,* Theodore's Christology provoked scathing polemics by Cyril of Alexandria.* For the Syriac-speaking church of Persia he became simply *Mepasqanna* ("the interpreter") and one of the "Three Doctors"; hence the preservation of some of his works in the Syriac language. Their retrieval in the early twentieth century led to revived scholarly interest in him and the School of Antioch.

Bibliography

A. *Theodori episcopi Mopsuesteni in epistulas B. Pauli commentarii*, ed. H. B. Swete, 2 vols. (Cambridge, 1880–82); *Commentary of Theodore of Mopsuestia on the Nicene Creed*, ed. and trans. Alphonse Mingana (Cambridge, 1932); *Commentary of Theodore of Mopsuestia on the Lord's Prayer and on the Sacraments of Baptism and the Eucharist*, ed. and trans. idem (Cambridge, 1933); *Le Commentaire de Théodore de Mopsueste sur les Psaumes*, ed. R. Devreesse (Vatican City, 1933); *Commentarius in XII prophetas*, ed. H. N. von Sprenger (Göttingen, 1977).

B. DTC 15:235–79; LThK² 10:42–44; NCE 14:18–19; ODCC 1598–99; R. Devreesse, *Essai sur Théodore de Mopsueste* (Vatican City, 1948); F. A. Sullivan, *The Christology of Theodore of Mopsuestia* (Rome, 1956); R. A. Greer, *Theodore of Mopsuestia, Exegete and Theologian* (London, 1961); R. A. Norris, *Manhood and Christ: A Study in the Christology of Theodore of Mopsuestia* (Oxford, 1963); D. Z. Zaharopoulos, *Theo-*

dore of Mopsuestia and the Bible: A Study of His Old Testament Exegesis (New York, 1989).

                                                                    Robin Darling Young

THEODORE OF STUDIOS (759, Constantinople–826). *Career*: he entered the monastic life under the influence of his uncle, Plato, ca. 780; ordained priest, 787; replaced Plato as abbot of Saccudium, 794. Because he opposed the second marriage of Constantine VI, his monastery was disbanded and he was exiled. The next year, however, Constantine's mother, Irene, deposed her son, and Theodore and his monks could return. In 798 he and most of his community moved to the monastery of Studios in Constantinople, which was almost deserted. The number of monks quickly grew to several hundred, and Theodore's energy and teachings soon made Studios the leading monastery of the East. The Studite rule, elaborated by Theodore's disciples, became the norm for many Byzantine and Slavic cenobitic communities. In a controversy under Nicephorus I (802–66) Theodore was again banished and appealed unsuccessfully to Pope Leo III of Rome (795–816). In 813 the new emperor, Leo V, revived the iconoclastic policies of Constantine V, and Theodore was again exiled. Leo's successor Michael (820) was less intolerant but still would not permit the veneration of images in Constantinople, so Theodore remained outside the capital. His many writings include the *Long Catechesis* and the *Short Catechesis*, instructions addressed to monks, an *Exposition of the Liturgy of the Presanctified*, spiritual orations, and polemical works against the Iconoclasts.

One of Theodore's principal theological achievements is his defense of icons. The iconoclasts, adopting a Platonizing view, saw the human nature of Christ as equivalent to humanity in general, and thus to an abstraction, and argued that such an abstraction could not be depicted in art. Theodore adopted a more Aristotelian view, and asserted that "humanity" exists only in human beings, "only in Peter and Paul," he wrote. Iconoclasts held that Christ, in virtue of the hypostatic union, was indescribable; but for Theodore, an indescribable Christ is an incorporeal Christ. For Theodore, moreover, the icon can only be the image of Christ's hypostasis; an image of a nature is inconceivable. Thus the icon of Christ is an image of the incarnate Logos.

Theodore also developed a rigorous ideology of monasticism. In general, higher clergy were iconoclasts, while monks were iconodules. Theodore stressed the eschatological witness of monasticism but rejected the spiritual individualism of the early Christian hermits. He organized Studios around the liturgy, work, obedience, and poverty. He also wanted the monks to be involved in the affairs of the city. The monks, for example, opposed Emperor Constantine VI's second marriage (in 795) as adulterous, while the patriarchs tolerated it with an appeal to *oikonomia*, adaptation. In the course of his struggles, Theodore came into conflict with his own patriarchs, but found support in Popes Leo III (795–816) and Paschal I (817–824).

Bibliography

A. PG 99 (incomplete).

B. DSAM 15:401–14; DTC 15:287–98; LThK² 10:45–46; NCE 14:19–20; ODCC
1599–1600; Alice Gardner, *Theodore of Studium: His Life and Times* (London, 1905);
Daniele Stiernan, "Teodoro Studita," *Bibliotheca Sanctorum* 12 (1969): 265–70.

Joseph T. Lienhard

THEODULF OF ORLÉANS (ca. 760–821). Visigothic by birth, Theodulf entered the service of Charlemagne ca. 780 and was bishop of Orléans from 798.
Nicknamed Pindar by Alcuin* to celebrate his poetic accomplishments (including the hymn "Gloria, laus, et honor"), Theodulf also became one of the foremost theologians of the age, revising the Latin Bible, writing treatises on the
filioque and on baptism, and producing two collections of canons. Most significantly, as Ann Freeman has demonstrated, Theodulf, not Alcuin, is the author
of the *Libri Carolini*, commissioned by Charlemagne to refute the iconodulism
of Nicaea II. Theodulf's canons demonstrate that he was as dedicated a pastor
and administrator as he was a theologian. Suspected of participating in Bernard
of Italy's revolt against Louis the Pious, Theodulf was deposed in 818 and exiled
to Angers.

Bibliography

A. PL 105:191–380; MGH, *Poetae latini aevi carolini* 1:437–581; *Libri Carolini* at
MGH *Concilia* vol. 2, *Supplementum*; canons in MGH *Capitula episcoporum* 1:73–184.

B. BBKL 11:1003–8; LThK² 10:52–53; NCE 14:28; ODCC 1603; SH 11:327–28;
H. Liebeschütz, "Theodulf of Orléans . . ." in *Fritz Saxl: A Volume of Memorial Essays*,
ed. D. J. Gordon, 77–92 (London, 1957); Bonifatius Fischer, "Bibeltext und Bibelreform
unter Karl dem Grossen," in *Karl der Grosse: Lebenswerk und Nachleben*, 2. *Das geist-
ige Leben*, ed. Bernhard Bischoff, 156–216 (Düsseldorf, 1966); A. Freeman, "Further
Studies in the *Libri Carolini*," *Speculum* 46 (1971): 597–612; Elisabeth Dahlhaus-Berg,
*Nova antiquitas et antiqua novitas: typologische Exegese und isidorianisches Geschichts-
bild bei Theodulf von Orleans* (Böhlau, 1975); P. Meyvaert, "The Authorship of the
Libri Carolini . . ." *Revue bénédictine* 89 (1979): 29–57; Peter Godman, *Poets and Em-
perors* (Oxford, 1987); Lawrence Nees, *A Tainted Mantle: Hercules and the Classical
Tradition at the Carolingian Court* (Philadelphia, 1991); A. Freeman, "Scripture and
Images in the Libri Carolini," in *Testo e immagine nell' alto medioevo*, ed. G. Tabacco,
1:163–95 (Spoleto, 1994).

John C. Cavadini

THÉRÈSE OF LISIEUX (2 January 1873, Alençon, France–30 September
1897, Lisieux). *Education*: Benedictine Abbey Sch., Lisieux, 1881–84. *Career*:
entered Discalced Carmelite Convent, Lisieux, 1888; acting mistress of novices,
1893–97.

The Carmelite nun, Thérèse of the Child Jesus and the Holy Face, called
herself the "Little Flower" in her widely read *Histoire d'une âme* (1898; *Story
of a Soul*) and has been known as the "Little Flower" by subsequent generations

of Catholics, distinguishing her from Teresa of Ávila. In the Catholic Church Thérèse has been recognized, according to Pope John Paul II, as "one of the great masters of the spiritual life in our times." She was a teacher of the spiritual life more than a systematic theologian and on the basis of her spirituality of divine love Pope John Paul II declared her a doctor of the church on 19 October 1997, one of three women to have received that title (the other two being Catherine of Siena* and Teresa of Ávila*).

Thérèse wrote very little and published nothing during her lifetime. Her posthumously published spiritual autobiography (*Histoire*), however, was distributed to other Carmelite nuns and within fifteen years after her death it became a classic spiritual text of what she called the "little way." Over 200,000 copies were sold within the first fifteen years of its publication and more than a million since then. The text hit a responsive cord in Catholic spirituality of the first half of the twentieth century.

Thérèse's doctrine of the "little way" (found in *Histoire*) was the "way of spiritual childhood, the way of trust and total surrender." Thérèse's life as well as her teachings reflected most emphatically upon those biblical passages that revealed divine love to the little ones (e.g., Mt 18:3–4; Mk 10:14–15; Prov 9: 4; Wis 6:7; Is 66:12–13; Ps 118:130). She emphasized that the little way was not just a series of acts or works of love, but a demand upon one's whole being to live in the grace of divine mercy and love. To be perfect was not a matter of extraordinary penances or heroic deeds, nor even of little acts of self-sacrifice, as much as it was a condition of the soul filled with divine grace and totally open to God's will in the very ordinary things of everyday life. "Perfection consists in doing His [God's] will, in being what He wills us to be."

Thérèse's life and her simple spirituality quickly came to the notice of the Catholic hierarchy and she became a model of twentieth-century sanctity, being beatified in 1923 and canonized on 17 May 1935. Hans Urs von Balthasar* called her one of two nineteenth-century saints (the other being the Curé d'Ars) whose life and doctrine came together to interpret the revelation of God and to give personal witness to it in the church.

Bibliography

A. *Oeuvres complètes* (Paris, 1992); *Story of a Soul. The Autobiography of St. Therese of Lisieux*, trans. John Clarke (Washington, D.C., 1976); *General Correspondence*, vol. 1: 1877–90; vol. 2: 1890–97, trans. John Clarke (Washington, D.C., 1982, 1988); *Poems of St. Therese of Lisieux*, trans. Alan Bancroft (London, 1996).

B. BBKL 11:1090–94; LThK² 10:102–4; NCE 14:77–78; ODCC 1590; André Combes, *Introduction à la spiritualité de sainte Thérèse de l'Enfant-Jésus* (Paris, 1946); M. M. Philipon, *Sainte Thérèse de Lisieux* (Paris, 1946); Mgr. Paulot, *Le message doctrinal de sainte Thérèse de l'Enfant-Jesus à lumière de saint Paul* (Paris, 1934); P. T. Rohrbach, *The Search for St. Therese* (Garden City, New York, 1961); Hans Urs von Balthasar, *Two Sisters in the Spirit: Thérèse of Lisieux and Elizabeth of the Trinity*, trans. Donald Nichols, Anne Elizabeth Englund, and Dennis Martin (1970; San Francisco, 1992); Conrad de Meester, ed., *Saint Thérèse of Lisieux: Her Life, Times, and Teaching* (Washington, D.C., 1997); John Paul II, " 'Divini Amoris Scientia.' Apostolic Letter: St. Therese, Doctor of the Church," *Origins* 27 (November 20, 1997): 390–96.

Patrick W. Carey

THOMAS AQUINAS (1224/26–7 March 1274, Cisterian Abbey of Fassanova). *Education*: educated at the Benedictine monastery of Monte Cassino and the Univ. of Naples, where he encountered the philosophy of Aristotle, which subsequently became a major source of philosophical inspiration to him; studied under St. Albert the Great* in Cologne and Paris, after 1243. *Career*: he entered the Dominican order of friars, 1242 or 1243; professor at the Univ. of Paris, 1256–59, ca. 1269–72; taught at Orvieto and Rome, where he was assigned to establish a house of studies in 1265; taught at the priory of San Domenico, Naples, 1272–73; set out to attend the second Council of Lyons (1274) but became seriously ill on the way and died.

Aquinas was first and foremost a Christian theologian. His greatest achievement, the *Summa Theologiae*, is written on the presumption that God exists and that the Christian religion is true. The same can be said of his second major work, the *Summa contra Gentiles*. But much of Aquinas' writings are devoted to what are recognizably purely philosophical topics, ones that Aquinas discusses in a way that is recognizably purely philosophical, among which are his early works *De ente et essentia* and *De principiis naturae* and his many commentaries on the writings of Aristotle. Aquinas has often been treated as if he were a theologian, as opposed to a philosopher, and as a philosopher, as opposed to a theologian. But he is best described as a philosophical theologian. He assumes the truth of many theological judgments, but he often discusses them as open to public philosophical scrutiny. Like many medieval theology teachers, he presented his theology with an eye not just on Scripture and the authority of Christian tradition but also on what follows from what, what is per se reasonable to believe (without recourse to Christian revelation), and what it makes sense to say in general.

One way of viewing Aquinas' teaching is to see it as defending what is usually called an *exitus-reditus* picture of reality. God, says Aquinas, is "the beginning and end of all things." Creatures derive from God (*exitus*), who is therefore their first efficient cause (that which accounts for their being there). But God is also the final cause of creatures, that to which they aim, tend, or return (*reditus*), that which contains the perfection or goal of all created things. According to Aquinas, everything comes from God and is geared to him. God accounts for there being anything other than God, and he is what is aimed at by anything moving towards its perfection. Aristotle says that everything aims for its good. Aquinas says that any created good derives from God, who contains all the perfections found in creatures. Insofar as a creature moves to its perfection, Aquinas goes on to argue, the creature is tending to what is to be found in God. As Father, Son, and Spirit, Aquinas adds, God is the special goal of rational individuals, for these can share in what God is by nature.

Aquinas is sometimes reported as teaching that someone who claims rationally to believe in the existence of God must be able to prove that God exists. But this is not what Aquinas teaches. He says that people can have a rational belief in the existence of God without being able to prove God's existence. And he holds that, apart from the question of God's existence, people may be rational in believing what they cannot prove. Following Aristotle, he maintains that people may rationally believe indemonstrable principles of logic. He also maintains that one may rationally believe what a teacher imparts to one, even though one is in no position to demonstrate the truth of what the teacher has told one. He does, however, contend that belief in God's existence is one for which good philosophical reasons can be given. This is clear from *Summa Theologiae*, Ia, 2, 2, *Summa contra Gentiles*, I, 9, and elsewhere. According to Aquinas, "we can demonstrate . . . that God exists" and that God can be made known as we "proceed through demonstrative arguments" (*Summa contra Gentiles, I, 9*). "Demonstrative arguments" here means what it does for Aristotle—that is, arguments using premises that are knowable to anyone and entail a given conclusion on pain of contradiction.

Aquinas denies that proof of God's existence is given by arguing that "God does not exist" is a contradiction. So he rejects the suggestion, commonly associated with St. Anselm,* that the existence of God can be demonstrated from the absurdity of denying that God exists. He also rejects the view that human beings are naturally capable of perceiving or experiencing God as they perceive or experience the things with which they are normally acquainted. According to Aquinas, our perception and seeing of things is based on sensory experience. Since God is not a physical object, Aquinas concludes that there can be no natural perception or seeing of God on the part of human beings. He does not deny that people might have a knowledge of God without the medium of physical objects. In talking of life after death, he says that people can have a vision of God that is nothing like knowing a physical object. But he denies that human beings in this world have a direct and unmediated knowledge of God. On his account, our knowledge of God starts from what we know of the world in which we live. According to him, we can know that God exists because the world in which we find ourselves cannot account for itself.

Aquinas considers whether we can prove that God exists in many places in his writings. But his best-known arguments for the existence of God come in *Summa Theologiae*, Ia, 2, 3 (the "Five Ways"). His thinking in this text is clearly indebted to earlier authors, especially Aristotle, Maimonides, Avicenna, and Averroes. And it would be foolish to suggest that the reasoning of the Five Ways can be quickly summarized in a way that does them justice. In general, though, each begins by drawing attention to some general feature of things known to us on the basis of experience (change, efficient causality, generation and perishing, degrees of perfection, orderedness in nature). It is then suggested that none of these features can be accounted for in ordinary, mundane terms, that we must move to a level of explanation that transcends any with which we are familiar. According to the Five Ways, questions we can raise with respect to what we encounter in day-to-day life raise further questions, the answer to which can only be thought of as lying beyond what we encounter.

Aquinas is often described as someone who first tries to prove the existence of God and then tries to show that God has various attributes. But, though this description can be partly defended, it is also misleading. For Aquinas holds that the attributes we ascribe to God are not, in reality, anything distinct from God. According to Aquinas, God is good, perfect, knowledgeable, powerful, and eternal. But he does not think that, for example, "the goodness of God" signifies anything other than God himself. In the thinking of Aquinas, God does not have attributes or properties. God is his attributes or properties. Aquinas also maintains that, though we speak of God and ascribe certain attributes to God, there is a serious sense in which we do not know what God is. Aquinas' teaching on our natural knowledge of God is exceedingly apophatic. "The divine substance," he says, "surpasses every form that our intellect reaches. Thus we are unable to apprehend it by knowing what it is" (*Summa contra Gentiles*, I, 14).

Central to Aquinas' thinking is the notion that any reality at all derives from God. Among other things, this leads him to the insistence that free human actions are caused by God. He frequently alludes to arguments suggesting that people cannot be free under God's providence (cf. *De Malo*, 6). He replies to such argments by insisting that the reality of providence (which means the reality of God working in all things as first cause and sustainer) is not incompatible with human freedom. People, he thinks, have freedom. Yet God, for Aquinas, really does act in everything. And since "everything" includes human free actions, Aquinas concludes that God works in them as much as in anything else. In *Summa Theologiae*, Ia 2ae, 109, 3, for example, he says: "People are in charge of their acts, including those of willing and of not willing, because of the deliberative activity of reason, which can be turned to one side or the other. But that someone should deliberate or not deliberate, supposing that one were in charge of this too, would have to come about by a preceding deliberation. And since this may not proceed to infinity, one would finally have to reach the point at which a person's free decision is moved by some external principle superior to the human mind, namely by God, as Aristotle himself demonstrated. Thus the minds even of healthy people are not so much in charge of their acts as not to need to be moved by God." According to Aquinas, what is incompatible with human free will is "necessity of coercion" or the effect of violence, as when something acts on one and "applies force to the point where one cannot act otherwise" (*Summa Theologiae*, Ia, 82, 1). Aquinas' position is that to be free means not to be under the influence of some other creature, it is to be independent of other bits of the universe; it is not and could not mean to be independent of God.

Aquinas' philosophy of the human person is much indebted to Aristotle. Therefore, he rejects a dualistic account of people of the kind found in the writings of Plato or Descartes. People, for Aquinas, are essentially bodily. They are human animals with a range of sensory and intellectual powers and capacities. Aquinas believed that human beings have souls that can survive the death of their bodies. But human souls are not, for Aquinas, human individuals. For Aquinas, my human soul is something that subsists. And it does so because I have an intellectual life that cannot be reduced to what is simply bodily. It does not subsist as something with its own life apart from me, any more than my left hand does, or my right eye. Both of these can be spoken of as things, but they are really parts of me. We do not say "my left hand feels" or "my right eye sees"; rather we say "I feel with my left hand" and "I see with my right eye." And Aquinas thinks that something similar should be said about my soul. I have a human soul because I have intellect and will. But it is not my soul that understands and wills. I do. One might put this by saying that my soul is not I. And Aquinas says exactly this in his commentary on St. Paul's first letter to the Corinthians.

As a disciple of Aristotle, Aquinas holds that there are philosophical grounds on which to base an account of human action, including an account of what human action should consist in. But where Aristotle will say that the proper goal of human action is *eudaimonia*, Aquinas will say that it is *beatitudo*. According to Aquinas, people are destined for union with God, and much that he writes is intended to explain what this means and how it is achieved. His presiding view is that by grace people can be raised to a share in God's knowledge and love grounded in the Incarnation of Christ. This view, impossible to do justice to in brief compass, is the theme of the second and third parts of the *Summa Theologiae* as well as of other writings. In developing it, Aquinas provides a vast range of sophisticated argument drawing on biblical, patristic, and philosophical texts. An especially interesting feature of his discussion is the way in which he sustains a rigorous insistence on both the unknowability of God and the intimate union between God and the Christian faithful.

Bibliography

A. The most authoritative study in English of Aquinas' works is I. T. Eschmann, "A Catalogue of St. Thomas' Works: Bibliographical Notes," in E. Gilson, *The Christian Philosophy of St. Thomas Aquinas* (see below), supplemented by "A Brief Catalogue of Authentic Works" in J. Weisheipl, *Friar Thomas D'Aquino* (see below). The definitive text of Aquinas' writings is being published by the Leonine Commission, established by Pope Leo XIII in 1880, which has already produced editions of Aquinas' most important works. Publication before the Leonine edition include *Opera Omnia* (Parma, 1852–73, the Parma Edition), and *Opera Omnia* (Paris, 1871–82, the Vivès Edition).

B. DTC 15:618–751; LThK² 10:119–34; NCE 14:102–15; ODCC 1614–17; Vernon J. Bourke, *Thomistic Bibliography: 1920–1940* (St. Louis, Mo., 1945); P. Mandonnet and J. Destrez, *Bibliographie Thomiste*, rev. 2d ed. M.-D. Chenu (Paris, 1960); Terry L. Miethe and V. J. Bourke, *Thomistic Bibliography, 1940–1978* (Westport, Conn., and London, 1980); Richard Ingardia, *Thomas Aquinas: International Bibliography 1977–1990* (Bowling Green, Ky., 1993); Étienne Gilson, *The Christian Philosophy of St. Thomas Aquinas* (London, 1957); M.-D. Chenu, *Towards Understanding Saint Thomas*, trans. A. M. Landry and D. Hughes (Chicago, 1964); James A. Weisheipl, *Friar Thomas D'Aquino* (Oxford, 1974; corrected ed. Washington, D.C., 1983); Leo J. Elders, *The Philosophical Theology of St. Thomas Aquinas* (New York, 1990); Brian Davies, *The Thought of Thomas Aquinas* (New York, 1992); Thomas F. O'Meara, *Thomas Aquinas, Theologian* (Notre Dame, Ind., 1997).

Brian Davies

THOMAS BRADWARDINE. *See* BRADWARDINE, THOMAS.

TILLICH, PAUL (20 August 1886, Starzeddel, Germany [now in Poland]–20 October 1965, Chicago). *Education*: gymnasium, Berlin; Univ. of Berlin, 1904; Tübingen, 1905; Halle, 1906–9; Dr. phil., Univ. of Breslau, 1910; habilitation, Univ. of Halle, 1915. *Career*: pastor, Lichtenrade, 1909, and Berlin, 1912; military chaplain, 1914; privatdozent, Berlin, 1919–24; professor of theology, Marburg, 1924–25; professor of theology and philosophy, Dresden and Leipzig, 1925–29; professor of philosophy and sociology, Frankfurt am Main, 1929–33; professor, Union Theol. Sem., N.Y., 1933–55; member of "Self-Help for German Refugees," 1936–37; lecturer for Voice of America, 1942–44; elected chairman of the Council for a Democratic Germany, 1944; Univ. professor, Harvard Univ., 1955–62; John Nuveen professor of theology, Univ. of Chicago, 1962–65.

Tillich was a German-American theologian and philosopher who was one of the most influential thinkers of his generation. Born into the home of a conservative Lutheran pastor, later superintendent in the Prussian church, Tillich was shaped early on by nineteenth-century idealism, especially that of Friedrich Wilhelm von Schelling, and the theology of Martin Kähler, who made of Luther's* doctrine of justification a systematic principle for all dogmatics. His service in World War I as a military chaplain, during which he experienced the horrors of Verdun, had a profound impact upon his intellectual development. In that event Tillich, like many of his contemporaries, perceived the end of the comfortable bourgeois world of modern Europe as well as of the self-assured and optimistic theology that was its religious counterpart. Returning to Berlin after the war, he took up cultural analysis and criticism, becoming one of the leaders of the "Kairos-circle," which called for the establishment of socialism in Germany. He also associated himself for a time with Karl Barth,* Friedrich Gogarten,* and others in the early "theology of crisis."

His repudiation of Protestant liberalism and, to an even greater extent, his championing of socialism earned him the suspicion of many within and without the church and contributed to his difficulty in finding a satisfactory position on a theological faculty. Failing despite his strenuous efforts to secure a call to Berlin and elsewhere, he reluctantly accepted a chair in philosophy and sociology at Frankfurt in 1929 and found himself on the margins of establishment theology. But there he continued to explore the interface—the "boundary," he called it—between theology and various expressions of contemporary culture, from expressionist art to Freudian psychology, as he joined in the postwar German search for a way out of the ruins of the old world and toward a more viable future. At the rise of National Socialism and the failure of German conservatives to respond effectively, Tillich wrote *Die sozialistische Entscheidung* (1933), offering a compelling argument that religious socialism's prophetic critique of culture was the only adequate answer to the crisis that he and his contemporaries faced. The result was that in April of 1933 he was the first Protestant theologian that the Nazis deprived of a university position when they came to power. Simultaneously he received an invitation from Union Theological Seminary in New York to serve as guest lecturer for the 1933–34 academic year. He immediately accepted, thus taking the first steps to what would eventually become permanent emigration to the United States.

His first years at Union were difficult because outside the German refugee community he was not well known and his English was very poor. Gradually, however, he found a place there and spent the next twenty-two years on that faculty, establishing a worldwide reputation in the process. The high point of his teaching in New York was the appearance of the first volume of his *Systematic Theology* in 1951. The two subsequent volumes appeared in 1957, after he had been appointed to the prestigious position of University Professor at Harvard, and in 1963, when he had taken a position in Chicago to work with the historian of religion Mircea Eliade.

In his volumes on systematics Tillich articulated the rationale that informed the whole of his theology throughout his career. He developed what he called a method of correlation, which he intended as a form of theology that mediated between the errors of nineteenth-century Protestant liberalism, which assumed a direct continuity between anthropology and theology, and the errors of the Neo-Orthodox theology of Karl Barth, which asserted an absolute discontinuity between the Word of God addressed to humanity in Jesus Christ and the human word about God. Tillich claimed that theology was rightly about its business only when it sought to correlate the questions being asked by a culture at a given time and the answers that are offered in the Christian tradition. Thus, he sought to develop a consciously apologetic theology that addressed a concrete social and historical context.

Early in his career he had said that "Theologie ist Angriff," theology is "attack" or "offense," and all of his work can be seen as a theological effort to close with whatever stood before him in whatever cultural situation he found himself. He sought to relate Protestant theology to idealist philosophy in the first two decades of this century, to cultural criticism in the 1920s and 1930s, with existentialism in the 1940s and 1950s, and with other religious traditions in the early 1960s. As such, he represented a unique and cogent approach to Christian theology in the twentieth century and many believe for the twenty-first century as well.

Bibliography

A. *Main Works/Hauptwerke*, ed. C. H. Ratschow, vols. 1–6 (New York and Berlin,1987–); *Systematic Theology*, 3 vols. (Chicago, 1951, 1957, 1963).

B. BBKL 12:85–123; EKL 5:614–17; LThK² 10:194–96; NCE 16:454–55; ODCC 1622; RGG 6:900–901; W. Pauck and M. Pauck, *Paul Tillich, His Life and Thought*, vol. 1 (New York, 1976); John Powell Clayton, *The Concept of Correlation: Paul Tillich and the Possibility of a Mediating Theology* (New York and Berlin, 1980); *The Theology of Paul Tillich*, ed. Charles W. Kegley (New York, 1982); *The Thought of Paul Tillich*, eds. J. L. Adams, W. Pauck, and R. L. Shinn (San Francisco, 1985); Alexander C. Irwin, *Eros Towards the World: Paul Tillich and the Theology of the Erotic* (Minneapolis, Minn., 1991); *Paul Tillich: A New Catholic Assessment*, ed. Monica Hellwig (Collegeville, Minn., 1994).

D. Lyle Dabney

TILLOTSON, JOHN (? October, 1630, Halifax, England–22 November, 1694, Whitehall). *Education*: Clare Hall, Cambridge, 1647–57; M.A., 1654. *Career*: tutor and chaplain for Prideux Hall, 1656–57; ordained, 1660 or 1661; curate to Thomas Hacket, Cheshunt, 1661–63; rector, Kedington, Suffolk, 1663–64; preacher, Lincoln's Inn, 1663–91; Tuesday lecturer, St. Lawrence Jewry, 1664–91; chaplain, Charles II, 1666; second prebend, Canterbury, 1670–72; dean, Canterbury, 1672–75; prebend, Ealdland, 1675; prebend, Oxgate, 1676–77; dean of St. Paul's, 1689–91; archbishop of Canterbury, 1691–94.

Tillotson was a latitudinarian Anglican divine who wanted to include in the Church of England all Protestant denominations except the Unitarians. He opposed the Athanasian Creed and supported a Zwinglian view of the Eucharist and an enlightened and reasonable form of Christianity that emphasized the comprehensive unity that did exist within the Protestant communion. Although he stressed the role of reason in religion, he was not a rationalist or a precursor of deism as some deists and later rationalists saw him. He believed the design of Christianity was to reinforce nature, but he also held that it was "not unreasonable to believe some things which are incomprehensible by our reason."

Tillotson upheld the supernatural character of the Scripture and believed that reason ought to be used in its interpretation, but he also believed that the best guide to understanding the Scripture, besides Scripture itself, was the accumulated wisdom of the community, especially the wisdom of the earliest days of the believing community. For him, moreover, the Incarnation and the central mysteries of Christianity ought to provide the hermeneutical tool by which the whole of Scripture was to be interpreted.

Although Tillotson was a latitudinarian rather than a rationalist, his periodic unguarded and unconditioned statements on the relation of Christianity to the religion of nature gave some eighteenth-century rationalists grounds for seeing in his thought a prologue to their own positions. Hume, for example, used and expanded Tillotson's arguments against transubstantiation to argue against all miracles. Although Hume and others distorted Tillotson's positions, they saw a rationalist trajectory in his thought that was indeed there.

Bibliography

A. *The Works of the Most Reverend Doctor Tillotson*, ed. Ralph Barker, 3 vols. (London, 1728, 1735); *Four Lectures on the Socinian Controversy* (London, 1693); *Tillotson's Sermons*, ed. G. W. Weldon (London, 1886); *The Golden Book of Tillotson*, ed. James Moffatt (London, 1926).

B. DNB 19: 872–78; ODCC 1622–23; L. G. Locke, *Tillotson* (Copenhagen, 1954); J. O'Higgins, "Archbishop Tillotson, Religion of Nature," JTS 24 (April 1973): 123–42; Geoffrey Scarre, "Tillotson and Hume on Miracles," *Downside Review* 110 (January 1992): 45–65; Gerard Reedy, "Interpreting Tillotson," HTR 86 (January 1993): 81–103; Peter Anthony Selo, "John Tillotson, Archbishop of Canterbury, 1630–1694: A Study in Anglican Ideology," Ph.D. diss. Univ. of Delaware, 1970.

Patrick W. Carey

TINDAL, MATTHEW (1653?, Beer Ferrers, England–16 August 1733, London). *Education*: studied at Lincoln Coll., Oxford: B.A., B.C.L., D.C.L., Exeter Coll., Oxford, 1676, 1679, 1685. *Career*: fellow, All Souls' Coll., Oxford, 1678–1733.

Tindal was one of the leading English Deists. Deism flourished from Lord Herbert of Cherbury (d. 1648) until David Hume (d. 1776), and Tindal was one of its major figures during its middle period of maturity. It arose during the reign of Charles I (1625–48), flourished during the period of the Revolution until 1688, and declined toward the close of the reign of George II (1727–60).

Tindal was raised in the Church of England, but during the reign of James II (1685–88) he became for a period of time a Roman Catholic. In 1688 he became alert to the "absurdities of popery" and returned to the Church of England.

Tindal's major publication was *Christianity as Old as the Creation. Or the Gospel a Republication of the Religion of Nature* (1730), which soon became known as the "Bible of Deism," or the "Deist Bible." The thesis of the book is that reasonable living, which leads to happiness in life, is religion and leads to the morally good. God's infinite goodness desires that all persons should arrive at the knowledge of true religion. This true or perfect religion must grant its truth equally to all persons at all times. Christianity is the only true and perfect religion, thus it must have been made for all human beings from the beginning of time. "Christianity is as old as the creation." Christianity introduced nothing new, but is simply the republication or the restoration of the religion of nature. Religion is essentially a reasonable way of living. The criterion of true religion is the universality of natural religion. The Christian religion is the natural religion, and Christianity can have no doctrines that differ from this natural or reasonable religion. The purpose of the Gospel is not to bring some kind of redemption or a new revelation, but to show that there is a universal natural law that is the basis and content of all religion. If Christianity claims to teach more than is contained in natural religion, then those additions are superstition and the corruption of true religion. Anything that is obscure or above reason in so-called revelation is superstitious and worthless. Miracles are unnecessary and are an insult to the perfect workmanship of the Creator God. Doctrines such as the Fall, original sin, and the Atonement must be discarded. The end of religion is morality, for true religion is a constant disposition to do all the good we can.

Bibliography

A.   *The Rights of the Christian Church Asserted* (London, 1706); *A Defence of the Rights of the Christian Church* (London, 1709).

B.   DNB 19:883–85; HERE 4:535–37; LThK² 10:201; ODCC 1624; E. Curll, *Memoir of the Life and Writings of Matthew Tyndal* (London, 1733); A. C. McGiffert, *Protestant Thought before Kant* (London, 1911); Leslie Stephen, *History of English Thought in the Eighteenth Century* (New York, 1881).

Donald S. Armentrout

TOLAND, JOHN (30 November 1670, Inishowen, Derry, Ireland–11 March 1721, Putney, England). *Education*: studied, Univ. of Glasgow, 1687–90; studied divinity under Frederick Spanheim, Leiden, 1692–94; Oxford, 1694–95. *Career*: converted from Catholicism to Protestantism, 1686; editor, pamphleteer, writer, and seeker of patronage, 1696–1721.

Toland was one of the most influential Deists. His books and pamphlets contributed much to eighteenth-century debates on the relation of reason to revelation and to discussions of the authenticity and genuineness of the New Testament books. He was important for Christian theology in the eighteenth century because he raised a number of significant critical issues that forced some Christian theologians to provide a rational justification for supernatural revelation and for Christian faith.

In what was perhaps his most important work, *Christianity not Mysterious* (London, 1696), he argued for the sufficiency of reason in understanding God and his revelation. For him the so-called mysteries of Christianity were nothing more than the machinations of priestcraft and the historical result of Christian borrowings from pagan religions.

In subsequent published works Toland cast doubt upon the authenticity of the New Testament, criticized High Churchmen and Jacobites, wrote on the Ebionites, provided a series of natural explanations for biblical miracles, and prepared a liturgy in mock imitation of Christian worship.

Bibliography

A.   *An Historical Account of the Life and Writings of the Late Eminently Famous Mr. John Toland* (London, 1722); *The Miscellaneous Works of Mr. John Toland, Now First Published from His Original Manuscripts*, 2 vols. (London, 1926, 1947); *The Theological and Philological Works of the Late Mr. John Toland* (London, 1932); *The Life of John Milton* (London, 1698, 1972).

B. DNB 19:918–22; LThK² 10:234; ODCC 1628; RGG 6:931–32; SH 11:459; Stephen H. Daniel, *John Toland: His Method, Manners and Mind* (Montreal, McGill, 1984); Robert Rees Evans, *Pantheisticon: The Career of John Toland* (New York, 1991); Gerard Reedy, "Socinians, John Toland, and the Anglican Rationalists," HTR 70 (July-October 1977): 285–304; Robert E. Sullivan, *John Toland and the Deist Controversy: A Study in Adaptations* (Cambridge, Mass., 1982).

Patrick W. Carey

TORREY, REUBEN ARCHER (28 January 1856, Hoboken, N.J.–26 October 1928, Montrose, Pa.). *Education*: studied at Walnut Hill, Geneva, N.Y., 1866–70; B.A., Yale Univ., New Haven, Conn., 1871–75; B.D., Yale Div. Sch., 1875–78; studied at Leipzig and Erlangen, Germany, 1882. *Career*: Congregational Minister, Garrettsville, Ohio, 1878–82; minister, Open Door Congregational Church, Minneapolis, Minn., 1883–86; minister, People's Church, Minneapolis, Minn., 1886–89; superintendent, Moody Bible Institute, Chicago, Ill., 1889–1908; itinerant evangelist, 1908–11; dean and teacher, Bible Institute of Los Angeles (BIOLA), Los Angeles, Calif., 1911–24; director, Bible Conference Center, Montrose, Pa., 1924–28.

Torrey was a principal architect of American fundamentalism during the late nineteenth and early twentieth centuries. During his time at Yale University, Torrey came under the influence of Scottish Common Sense Realism, a philosophy that attacked skepticism by appealing to both the reasonableness and the availability of immutable truths. Torrey's confidence in the power of observation and objective fact was buttressed by his acceptance of Francis Bacon's empiricism, which also stressed observation over speculation and which was the basis for the inductive method, where facts were deliberately limited and imaginative leaps were discouraged. Common Sense Realism and Baconian method gave Torrey a sense of certainty, buttressed by his unflinching belief in the absolute inerrancy of the Bible, which he regarded as a perfect evidential instrument whose various books shed light on one another and anchored the believer in truth. Torrey's apologetic style stressed intellect over emotion, and he represented a voice of assurance that appealed to many evangelicals confused by the accelerating rate of social change.

Many of these believed that Torrey had inherited the evangelistic mantle of Dwight L. Moody, especially after his highly publicized world revival tour of 1901–5. In all, Torrey preached to over fifteen million persons between 1901 and 1911. Through a combination of writings, teachings, and direct preachings, Torrey became a leading controversialist. In 1910, he became a contributor to and an editor of *The Fundamentals*, a series of essays mailed free of charge to Protestant ministers that espoused conservative Christianity, the integrity of the Bible, and the truth of traditional doctrines. During his tenure at BIOLA, Torrey became entrenched in campaigns against tobacco, alcohol, and liberal tendencies in the churches. His extreme propositionalism and uncompromising stance on matters of private deportment were interpreted by many as inflexibility. By the

1920s, Torrey was often seen as out of touch with his times and his revival appeal dwindled.

Bibliography

A.   *What the Bible Teaches* (New York, 1898); *The Power of Prayer and the Prayer of Power* (New York, 1924); *The Fundamental Doctrines of the Christian Faith* (New York, 1918); *The Return of the Lord Jesus* (Los Angeles, 1913).

B.   DARB 556–57; NCAB 21:428; NYT 27 October 1928, 19; SH 11:467; George M. Marsden, *Fundamentalism and American Culture; The Shaping of Twentieth Century Evangelicalism: 1870–1925* (New York, 1980); Ernest R. Sandeen, *The Roots of Fundamentalism: British and American Millennarianism, 1800–1930* (Chicago, 1970); Kermit L. Staggers, ''Reuben A. Torrey: American Fundamentalist, 1856–1928,'' Ph.D. diss., Claremont Graduate School, 1986.

Terrence Crowe

TROELTSCH, ERNST (17 February 1865, Augsburg–1 February 1923, Berlin). *Education*: gymnasium, Augsburg; Univ. of Erlangen, 1884; Berlin, 1885; Göttingen, 1886, Lic. theol., 1888. *Career*: privatdozent, Göttingen, 1890; professor of systematic theology, Bonn, 1892; professor of theology and philosophy, Heidelberg, 1894–1913; professor of philosophy, Berlin 1914–23; member of the German Reichstag, 1921.

Troeltsch was a German theologian, philosopher, and sociologist. Born into the bourgeois home of a prominent physician in Augsburg, Troeltsch took as his central concern the emerging crisis of values, which he—along with many others in the last quarter of the nineteenth century—perceived as undermining European Christendom. Convinced of the centrality of the role played by Christianity in Western history in the development of the notion of individual freedom, its highest value in his estimation, he undertook a wide-ranging investigation of the relationship between church and culture in an effort to lay a new foundation for the ethical norms of Christianity as a defense against what he saw as the modern threats to such freedom: technology, capitalism, and governmental bureaucratization. Thus, he sought to identify and ground a set of common ethical values associated with the notion of freedom that could serve as a basis for an increasingly fractured society.

Troeltsch began his career as a representative of Protestant liberal theology, shaped by the theology of Schleiermacher* and Ritschl* as well as by the philosophy of the neo-Kantians. His first major publication, *Vernunft und Offenbarung bei J. Gerhard und Melanchthon* (1892), was an analysis of Protestant orthodoxy in which he argued that while the roots of such theology were to be found in a medieval supernaturalism that deformed the idea of Christianity, its normative character was found in its rightly joining the notion of natural law with stoic and biblical conceptions to produce a rational, future-oriented Reformation theology that facilitated the emergence of modernity. Soon, however, under the influence of the writings of the history of religions school, as well as those of Karl Marx and Max Weber, his thought turned increasingly in the direction of historicism. This led him to take up the question of *Die Absolutheit des Christentums* (1902) in which he dismissed the answer of Protestant orthodoxy as well as the supernaturalist and Hegelian solutions in favor of a strict historical analysis allowing only for claims of historical probability and employing the principles of analogy and correlation. Echoing Schleiermacher and Ritschl, Troeltsch argued that religion was an a priori domain of immediate God-consciousness in which fundamental human values are rooted. He then proceeded to demonstrate by way of a history of religions analysis, as well as a matter of personal predilection, that Christianity was the highest expression of that God-consciousness. Toward the end of his life, he revisited this question and came to severely limit that latter claim by reducing its extent from the universal to the merely European.

Besides writing a great number of historical and systematic articles touching on various aspects of theology, he also published an important collection of papers under the title *Soziallehren der christlichen Kirchen und Gruppen* (1912). There, he sought to demonstrate that the original unitary idea of Christianity had come to fragmented, historical expression in the form of church, sect, and mysticism under the pressure of concrete social conditions. In his last years, Troeltsch abandoned theology for philosophy and cultural/historical studies, which evidence a final and radical historicist turn.

Bibliography

A. *Kritische Gesamtausgabe*, ed. F. W. Graf (Berlin, 1998–); *The Absoluteness of Christianity and the History of Religions*, trans. David Reid (Richmond, Va., 1971); *The Christian Faith: Based on Lectures Delivered at the University of Heidelburg in 1912 and 1913*, ed. G. V. le Fort, trans. G. E. Paul (Minneapolis, Minn., 1991); *Protestantism and Progress: The Significance of Protestantism for the Rise of the Modern World* (Minneapolis, Minn., 1986); *The Social Teaching of the Christian Churches*, trans. O. Wyon (Chicago, 1981).

B. BBKL 12:497–562; EKL 5:621–23; LThK² 10:372; NCE 14:313–14; ODCC 1643–44; RGG 6:1044–47; Robert J. Rubanowice, *Crisis in Consciousness: The Thought of Ernst Tröltsch* (Tallahassee, Fla., 1982); Waller E. Wyman, *The Concept of Glaubenslehre: Ernst Tröltsch and the Theological Heritage of Schleiermacher* (Chico, Calif., 1983); Sarah Coakley, *Christ Without Absolutes: A Study of the Christology of Ernst Tröltsch* (Oxford, 1988); Bryce Gayhart, *The Ethics of Ernst Tröltsch: A Commitment to Relevancy* (Lewiston, N.Y., 1990); Hans-Georg Drescher, *Ernst Tröltsch: His Life and Work* (London, 1992).

D. Lyle Dabney

TURRETIN, FRANÇOIS (17 October 1623, Geneva, Switzerland–28 September 1687, Geneva). *Education*: studied Reformed theology at Geneva, 1640–44, Leyden, 1644, Utrecht, Paris, 1645–46, Saumur 1646–48, and philosophy with the Catholic Pierre Gassendi, Paris, 1645–46. *Career*: pastor of Italian congregation, Geneva, 1648–87; interim pastor, Lyon, 1652; professor of theology, Academy of Geneva, 1653–87; pastor of French congregation, 1653–87.

Perhaps the most eminent Reformed theologian of his century, Turretin published a number of disputations, the most important of which are *De Satisfactione Christi disputationes* (1666) and *De necessaria secessione nostra ab Ecclesia Romana et impossibili cum ea syncretismo* (apparently completed by 1661; published in 1687). With J. H. Heidegger and others, moreover, he contributed to the composition of the Helvetic Consensus Formula (1675). His primary literary contribution, however, was his three-volume *Institutio Theologiae Elencticae*, which appeared in 1679, 1682, and 1685.

Turretin's *Institutio* culminates the development of Reformed scholasticism (his son Jean-Alphonse would begin dismantling it). The *Institutio* had a widespread and enduring use as a textbook, most notably at Princeton Seminary from 1812 until the publication of Charles Hodge's* *Systematic Theology* (1872–73). Throughout the *Institutio*, the Roman Catholics, the Socinians, and the Remonstrants provide the primary opponents, along with the Lutherans, Anabaptists, and others. Within the Reformed tradition, he defended the Canons of Dordt against the universal grace and conditional election of the Remonstrants and against the hypothetical universalism of the school of Saumur. Turretin represents both infralapsarian Reformed orthodoxy and federal theology, with its Covenants of Redemption, Works, and Grace.

The *Institutio*'s "elenctic" format characterizes it as polemical. In scholastic fashion, it rigorously "disputes" about "questions." Turretin defends Scripture as God's verbally inspired word, as the supreme authority for the church, subordinating rational argument. He warns against conjecture and insists that theology is more "practical" than "theoretical." His arguments sometimes include extensive scriptural exegesis. Scripture may err on minor historical matters (*Institutes of Elenctic Theology*, Topic I, question V, paragraph 12). Reminiscent of John Calvin's* *Institutes*, Turretin's ecclesiological section is the longest, indicating the continued prominence of Reformation ecclesiastical disputes.

Bibliography

A. *Francisci Turrettini Opera*, 4 vols. (Edinburgh, 1847); *Institutes of Elenctic Theology*, trans. James T. Dennison, 3 vols. (Phillipsburg, N.J., 1992–97); *The Atonement of Christ*, trans. James R. Willson (New York, 1859; repr. Grand Rapids, Mich., 1978).

B. NCE 14:348; RGG 6:1089–90; SH 12:43; Paul Timothy Jensen, "Calvin and Turretin: A Comparison of Their Soteriologies," Ph.D. diss., Univ. of Virginia, 1988; Gerrit Keizer, *François Turrettini: Sa vie et ses oeuvres et le consensus* (Lausanne, 1900); Timothy R. Phillips, "Francis Turretin's Idea of Theology and Its Bearing upon His Doctrine of Scripture," Ph.D. diss., Vanderbilt Univ., 1986; Stephen R. Spencer, "Reformed Scholasticism in Medieval Perspective: Thomas Aquinas and Francois Turrettini on the Incarnation," Ph.D. diss., Michigan State Univ., 1988.

Stephen R. Spencer

TYCONIUS (ca. 330–ca. 390). An enigmatic figure, Tyconius was a Donatist theologian highly respected by Augustine.* Though excommunicated by a Donatist council in 380, he never joined the Catholic Church. Augustine ironically praises him for writing well against the Donatists. Gennadius in *On Illustrious Men* reports that Tyconius wrote four works. Two polemical works, *De bello intestino* and *Expositiones diversarum causarum*, are lost. His *Book of Rules*, a handbook of seven hermeneutical rules, has been preserved in its entirety. Tyconius' exegesis is spiritual and his theology ecclesial, directed specifically toward dealing with the rift between Donatists and Catholics in contemporary North Africa. His *Commentary on the Apocalypse* exists in two fragments located in Turin and Budapest. It may be partially reconstructed on the basis of citations by various patristic and medieval authors, particularly Beatus of Liébana. Tyconius' influence on Augustine was profound; Augustine's idea of the two kingdoms may have originated from Tyconius' second rule concerning the bipartite body of the Lord.

Bibliography

A.   CPL 709–10; *The Book of Rules of Tyconius*, ed. F. C. Burkitt (Cambridge, 1894; repr. Nendeln, 1967); *Tyconius: The Book of Rules*, trans. William S. Babcock (Atlanta, Ga., 1989); *The Turin Fragments of Tyconius' Commentary on Revelation*, ed. Francesco Lo Bue (Cambridge, 1963).

B.   LThK² 10:180–81; ODCC 1648–49; William S. Babcock, "Augustine and Tyconius: A Study of the Latin Appropriation of Paul," StPatr 17 (1982): 1209–15; Kenneth B. Steinhauser, *The Apocalypse Commentary of Tyconius: A History of Its Reception and Influence* (New York, 1987); Pamela Bright, *The Book of Rules of Tyconius: Its Purpose and Inner Logic* (Notre Dame, Ind., 1988); Paula Fredriksen, "Tyconius and Augustine on the Apocalypse," in *The Apocalypse in the Middle Ages*, ed. Richard K. Emmerson and Bernard McGinn (Ithaca, N.Y., 1992), 20–37; Kenneth B. Steinhauser, "Tyconius: Was He Greek?" StPatr 27 (1993): 394–99.

Kenneth B. Steinhauser

TYRRELL, GEORGE (6 February 1861, Dublin–15 July 1909, Storrington, Sussex, England). *Education*: studied at Rathmines Sch., Dublin, 1869–77; Middleton Coll., County Cork, 1873; matriculated at Trinity Coll., Dublin, 1878; entered Jesuit novitiate, Manresa House, Roehampton, England, 1880–82; studied neoscholastic philosophy, St. Mary's Hall, Stonyhurst, England, 1882–85; studied theology, St. Bruno's Coll., North Wales, 1885–93. *Career*: converted to Catholicism, 1879; entered Jesuits, 1880; ordained priest, 1891; chair of philosophy at the Jesuit seminary, St. Mary's Hall, Stonyhurst, 1894–96; literary staff of *The Month* at Jesuit headquarters in central London, 1896–1900; censored by Rome and exiled to a mission house at Richmond-in-Swaledale, 1900–1906; dismissed from Jesuits, 1906; excommunicated, 1907; continued writing from various private residences, 1907–9.

Schooled in a thought-world different from that of his Jesuit confreres, Tyrrell was unprepared to accept the Ultramontanist ecclesiology and rationalist, neoscholastic apologetics of the post–Vatican I church. Two Jesuit professors steered him in a direction more congenial to the English thought-world: Thomas Rigby toward Thomas Aquinas* rather than his inferior commentators and Joseph Rickaby toward Newman.* Aquinas provided Tyrrell a model of theological *aggiornamento*, while Newman provided an experience-based psychology of religion along with an inductive, historical method that contrasted and often conflicted with the aprioristic, ahistorical, deductive method of neoscholasticism. Newman's *Grammar of Assent*, Tyrrell said, occasioned "a profound revolution in my way of thinking."

Attracted by Tyrrell's spiritual writings, Baron Friedrich von Hügel* befriended Tyrrell and introduced him to a host of continental scholars. Most influential were Loisy,* Laberthonnière,* Bergson, Blondel,* Dilthey, Schweitzer,* Troeltsch,* and Weiss.

Tyrrell's most characteristic thesis—expressed in his seminal essay, "The Relation of Theology to Devotion" (1899) and redolent of Matthew Arnold* and Loisy—is that religion is concerned primarily with life and conduct and arises first from experience and only derivatively from doctrine. Tyrrell decried Vatican "theologism"—that is, the attempt to impose on the church the rationalist scholastic system with its substitution of abstractions for a living belief and its presentation of mysteries as rigidly ascertained facts rather than as increasing assurances of a knowledge that grows as life grows. He began to see the "deposit of faith" less as a "form of sound words" and more as "a Spirit, or a Principle, or an Idea"—two notions reconcilable by distinguishing revelation and theology as "generically different orders of Truth and Knowledge" and by denying development to revelation and dogma but giving it to theology.

In his posthumous *Christianity at the Cross-Roads* (London, 1910), Tyrrell went distinctly beyond Newman's conception of doctrinal development with its assumed identity between the "idea" of Christ and Christianity and the "idea" of Roman Catholicism; he argued that the categories of apocalyptic and eschatology had carried the "idea" or "Spirit of Christ" unaltered from age to age. This "Spirit" distinguishes Christianity from religions that follow a teacher or prophet. "Jesus Himself was the great sacrament and effectual symbol of the Divine Life and Spirit . . . a personal influence, fashioning the soul to its own divine nature." Creeds and doctrines are the creation of the collective religious experience of Christians and are protective of that experience. The purpose of "the church's teaching-office is simply to guard the Apostolic Revelation identically for all ages." Thus "her dogmatic decisions possess a protective but not a scientific or philosophical infallibility."

Tyrrell was the foremost English Catholic "modernist." His thought, always suspect, foreshadowed the theology of Vatican II. He was excommunicated not for doctrinal deviance but for sharply criticizing Pius X's *Pascendi dominici gregis* (1907) in the London *Times*.

Bibliography

A. *The Church and the Future* (London, 1903); *Lex Orandi* (London, 1903); *Through Scylla and Charybdis* (London, 1907); *Autobiography*, vol. 1 of *Autobiography and Life of George Tyrrell*, ed. M. D. Petre, 2 vols. (London, 1912).

B.   DNB, 1901–11, 542–45; LThK² 10:426–27; NCE 14:356–57; ODCC 1649–50; Maude Dominica Petre, *Autobiography and Life of George Tyrrell*, 2 vols. (London, 1912); Nicholas Sagovsky, *'On God's Side': A Life of George Tyrrell* (Oxford, 1990); David G. Schultenover, *George Tyrrell: In Search of Catholicism* (Shepherdstown, W.Va., 1981); Marvin R. O'Connell, *Critics on Trial* (Washington, D.C., 1994).

David G. Schultenover

U

UBERTINO OF CASALE (1259, Casale–after 1328, place unknown). A leader of the Spiritual Franciscans; studied and taught at Paris; entered the Franciscan order, 1273; returned to Italy in 1283; came under the influence of Spiritual Franciscans and Joachimites, particularly John of Parma and Peter John Olivi*; was denounced and summoned to Rome by Benedict XI in 1304, and suspended; withdrew to La Verna; later served as a papal legate and consultant; transferred to the Benedictines, 1317. After teaching at Paris, Ubertino began (in 1289) preaching against Conventual Franciscans. In a sermon against the ''church of the flesh,'' he acknowledged the priesthood and the sacraments but denied the validity of the election of Boniface VIII and his successors. In 1305 he composed the *Arbor vitae crucifixae Jesu*, the life of the Word from the eternal generation to the Last Judgment in five books. Books 2 to 4 are a harmonized life of Jesus. The book fosters devotion to Christ, but contains apocalyptic ideas on the church and society and invective against Boniface VIII and Benedict XI. Ubertino also wrote on the controversy on poverty among the Franciscans.

Bibliography

A. *Arbor vitae crucifixae Jesu* (Venice, 1485, repr. ed. Charles T. Davis, Turin, 1961).

B. DMA 12:235–36; DSAM 16:3–15; DTC 15:2021–34; LThK² 10:440–41; NCE 14:360–61; ODCC 1651; Johann Ch. Huck, *Ubertin von Casale und dessen Ideenkreis* (Freiburg i. Br., 1903); Ernst Knoth, *Ubertino von Casale. Ein Beitrag zur Geschichte der Franziskaner an der Wende des 13. und 14. Jahrhunderts* (Marburg, 1903).

Joseph T. Lienhard

V

VELICHKOVSKY, PAISII (2 December 1722, Poltava, Ukraine–15 November, 1794, Sekul, Moldavia). *Education*: studied at Kievan Academy, 1740s. *Career*: joined Mt. Athos Monastery, 1746–63; founder, religious communities in Moldavia at Dragomirna, Kedul, Niamets, 1763–94.

Paisii was a Ukrainian ascetical and spiritual teacher, translator, and founder of his own religious communities. While on Athos, he began collecting and checking Slavic translations of ascetical works. An exacting and painstaking translator, he continued his work after resettlement in the Niamets monastery in Moldavia, which as a result soon became a literary and theological center concerned with spiritual enlightenment and intellectual construction.

Paisii's translation and the publication in St. Petersburg in 1793 of the *Dobrotoliubye* (*Philokalia*) raises the interesting question of his relationship to his younger contemporary, Nicodemus of the Holy Mountain.* Both men published similar, but not identical collections of ancient texts on prayer and the ascetic life. Yet they never met, nor do they appear to have been in correspondence. The question so far unaddressed by modern scholars lies in the degree of their mutual dependence, if any. If there is no reciprocal influence, then the Slavic and Greek publications they edited would testify to the prior existence of similar collections and thus to the continuity of the ancient Hesychast tradition that both men sought to reinvigorate.

Paisii has the reputation of being a great Ukrainian ascetic and spiritual teacher and is credited with being the creator of a unique spiritual tradition, both in the Slavic and in the Romanian Orthodox worlds. In fact, originality was the very last thing he sought to foster and continuity what he devoutly hoped to embody. His writing depended upon the literary style of Nilus Sorsky (d. 1503) and he continued Sorsky's interrupted work. Paisii's disciples focused on translations from Greek and carried on the master's work in both Romania and Russia. In the latter country, they were largely responsible for the extraordinary monastic renewal of the nineteenth and early twentieth centuries and in particular for the reinvigoration of the great monasteries of Valaam, Sarov, and Optina, thus contributing as well to the appearance of such notable ascetic saints as Seraphim of Sarov, Herman of Alaska, and the Optina Elders. The Paisii movement also served as a catalyst for the return to traditional ascetical sources among certain notable Russian Slavophiles (e.g., A. Khomiakov* and A. Kireevsky), and one may point as well to the indirect influences of the Paisian revival on such novelists as F. M. Dostoyevsky and N. Leskov.

In Romanian Moldavia Paisii founded monasteries at Dragomirna, Sekul, and Niamets, using the fourteenth-century rule of Byzantine monasticism. In the biography of his contemporary, Nicodemus of Mount Athos, it is related that the number of monks under the spiritual direction of the Ukrainian elder surpassed a thousand.

Bibliography

A.   *Dobrotoljubie* (Moscow, 1884–1905); *Ob umnoj ili vnutrennej molitve. Sotinaija blazhennogo startsa, skhimonakha i arkhimandrita Paisii Velichkovskogo* (Moscow, 1902); *Philocalie Slavonne de Paissy Velichkovsky*, in series *Monuments de la culture mondiale* (Bucharest, 1990); *Autobiografia di uno Staret*, trans. Fratelli Contremplativi di Gesù (Abbazia di Praglia, 1988); "How We Must Always Wage War against Three Enemies: Instruction for the Tonsure to the Monastic Order," trans. *Epiphany* 9 (1989): 45–50.

B.   HDOC 333–34; NCE 14:593; ODCC 1685; RGG 6:1252; M. Schwarz, "Un réformateur du monachisme orthodoxe au XVIIIe siècle: Paisius Velickovskij," *Irénikon* 11 (1934): 561–72; Metrophanes [Mytrofan], Schema Monk, *Blessed Paisius Velichkovsky. The Life and Ascetic Labors of Our Father, Elder Paisius, Archimandrite of the Holy Moldavian Monasteries of Niamets and Sekoul. Optina Version*, trans. St. Hermann of Alaska Brotherhood, vol. 1 (Platina, Calif., 1976); Cuthbert Hainsworth, *Staretz Paisy Velichkovsky (1722–1794). Doctrine of Spiritual Guidance* (Rome, 1976); Sergei Chetverikov, *Staretz Paissy Velichkovsky*, trans. V. Lickwar and A. Lisenko (Belmont, Mass., 1980); *The Life of Paisij Velykovskj*, trans. J. M. E. Featherstone (Cambridge, Mass., 1989); E. Vladimirova, "St. Paisy Velichkovsky [sermon]," *Journal of the Moscow Patriarchate* 11 (1989): 40.

Alexander Golitzin

VERMIGLI, PETER MARTYR (8 September 1499, Florence–12 November 1562, Zurich). *Education*: studied philosophy and theology, Padua, 1518–26; studied Hebrew, Bologna, 1539–41. *Career*: entered Augustinian Canons, Fiesole, 1514; taught and preached in several north Italian cities, 1526–39; reforming abbot at Spoleto and Naples and prior at Lucca, 1533–42; Protestant reformer, Zurich, Strasbourg, and England, 1542–56; professor of Hebrew, Zurich, 1556–62.

Peter Martyr was an Augustinian canon who was influenced by the humanist and reforming movements in early sixteenth-century Italy. After 1542 he left the Augustinians and became a Protestant reformer whose written treatises had a significant impact on the Reformation. When Paul III set up the Roman Inquisition in 1542, Vermigli fled to Zurich but quickly moved to Strasbourg where he lectured on the Pentateuch, 1542–48, and came under Martin Bucer's* influence. In 1547 the Schmalkaldic War in Germany drove Vermigli to England, where he assisted Archbishop Thomas Cranmer* in revising English canon law. Cranmer secured for him the Regius Professorship of Theology at Oxford, where he lectured on First Corinthians and Romans and held a public disputation on the Eucharist that was later printed by the government of Edward VI.

The accession of Queen Mary in 1553 forced Vermigli to return to Strasbourg, where he lectured on Judges and Aristotle's *Ethics*. His teaching on the Eucharist, which fell between the positions of Zwingli* and Calvin,* alienated many Strasbourg Lutheran pastors. In 1556 Vermigli assumed the chair of Hebrew at Zurich where he lectured on the books of Samuel and Kings.

Peter Martyr's lectures and writings combined clarity, careful organization, and great erudition in both the scholastic and humanist traditions. Roughly half of his lectures and writings were printed in his lifetime, the rest posthumously. He wrote thirteen major works—among them eight on Scripture and four polemical works (three on the Eucharist, one against clerical celibacy). Vermigli also wrote a catechism and twenty-four minor works, many published posthumously. His biblical commentaries were peppered with systematic tracts on doctrinal and moral questions; these Robert Masson gathered into the massive *Loci communes* of 1576, whose fourteen editions (including an English translation in 1583) rivaled the influence of Calvin's *Institutes* in the period 1575–1625.

Bibliography

A. *Loci communes* (London, 1576); *The Life, Letters and Eucharistic Writings of Peter Martyr*, ed. J. C. McLelland and G. E. Duffield (Abingdon, Oxford, 1989); *A Bibliography of the Works of Peter Martyr Vermigli*, ed. J. P. Donnelly and R. M. Kingdon (Kirksville, Mo., 1990); *Early Writings: Creed, Scripture, Church*, ed. J. C. McLelland (Kirksville, Mo., 1994); *Dialogue on the Two Natures in Christ*, ed. J. P. Donnelly (Kirksville, Mo., 1995).

B.   DTC 15:2693–94; LThK[2] 10:717–18; ODCC 1267; OEncR 4:229–31; RGG 6: 1361–62; J. C. McLelland, *The Visible Words of God: An Exposition of the Sacramental Theology of Peter Martyr Vermigli* (Edinburgh, 1957); Philip McNair, *Peter Martyr in Italy: An Anatomy of Apostasy* (Oxford, 1967); M. W. Anderson, *Peter Martyr Vermigli, A Reformer in Exile (1542–1562)* (Nieukoop, 1975); J. P. Donnelly, *Calvinism and Scholasticism in Vermigli's Doctrine of Man and Grace* (Leiden, 1976); J. C. McLelland, ed. *Peter Martyr Vermigli and Italian Reform* (Waterloo, Ontario, 1980).

John Patrick Donnelly

VINCENT OF BEAUVAIS (ca. 1190, probably Beauvais–1264, Paris). Studied at Saint-Jacques and entered the Dominican order in Paris ca. 1220; assigned to the priory of Beauvais, where he conceived the idea of compiling an immense encyclopedic work that would sum up all of human knowledge. His *Greater Mirror* (*Speculum majus*), which is still regarded as the greatest encyclopedic work until modern times, was divided into three parts: on nature (*Naturale*), history (*Historiale*), and doctrine (*Doctrinale*); a part on morals (*Morale*), drawn largely on the work of Aquinas,* was added in the following century. The part on nature dealt with the six days of creation, the elements and their properties, the Fall and redemption, the sacraments, and the virtues; the historical part covered the whole of history from the creation until 1254; and the doctrinal part summarized what was known of the liberal, mechanical, and practical arts. He was appointed lector to the court of Louis IX ca. 1250, where in 1260–61 he wrote a pedagogical treatise, "On the Education of Children of the Nobility" (*De eruditione filiorum nobilium*).

Bibliography

A.   *Speculum majus* (*Bibliotheca mundi. Speculum quadruplex: naturale, doctrinale, morale, historiale*), 4 vols. (Douai, 1624; repr. Graz, 1964–65); *De morali principis institutione*, ed. Robert J. Schneider, CCCM 137 (Turnhout, 1995).

B.   DTC 15:3026–33; LThK² 10:798; NCE 14:679–80; ODCC 1699; Astrik L. Gabriel, *The Educational Ideas of Vincent of Beauvais* (Notre Dame, Ind., 1956); Joseph M. McCarthy, *Humanistic Emphases in the Educational Thought of Vincent of Beauvais* (Leiden, 1976); Serge Lusignan, *Préface au Speculum maius de Vincent de Beauvais: Réfraction et diffraction* (Montreal, 1979); Rosemary B. Tobin, *Vincent of Beauvais' "De eruditione filiorum nobilium": The Education of Women* (New York, 1984); *Vincent de Beauvais: Intentions et réceptions d'une oeuvre encyclopédique au Moyen Age* (Saint-Laurent and Paris, 1990).

Roland J. Teske

VINCENT OF LÉRINS (d. before 450). Though Vincent is the most famous of the writers of the island monastery of Lérins, little is known of his life. Writing under the pseudonym Peregrinus (the pilgrim), Vincent wrote a *Commonitorium* (aid to memory), described by Gennadius (*De vir. ill.* 64) as a "very powerful dissertation" against heresy. This was Vincent's best-known and most influential work, for in it he developed criteria for discerning the authenticity of Christian tradition. In the second chapter of the *Commonitorium* he produces his famous canon: to believe in the true Catholic faith "we must hold what has been believed everywhere, always, and by all." Among these three criteria, antiquity has pride of place, and must be appealed to in cases where universality is lacking. The *Commonitorium* clearly depends on Tertullian's* *De praescriptione haereticorum*. Vincent may have written two other works: the *Obiectiones Vincentianae*, not extant but referred to by Prosper of Aquitaine,* and the *Excerpta*, a patchwork of anti-Nestorian texts taken from Augustine's* writings. Some controversy exists about Vincent's attitude toward Augustine, since some texts in the *Commonitorium* could reveal anti-Augustinian sentiment. From the sixteenth century until the nineteenth, Vincent was admired among both Protestants and Catholics seeking criteria for normative doctrine.

Bibliography

A.   *Commonitorium*, ed. R. Demeulenaere, CCSL 64; *Commonitories*, trans. Rudolph E. Morris, FC 7 (New York, 1949).

B.   DTC 15:2045–55; LThK² 10:800–801; NCE 14:681–82; ODCC 1699–1700; William O'Connor, ''Saint Vincent of Lérins and Saint Augustine,'' *Doctor Communis* 16 (1963): 123–257.

Thomas A. Smith

VON HARNACK. *See* HARNACK, ADOLF VON.

VON HÜGEL. *See* HÜGEL, BARON FRIEDRICH VON.

W

WALTER OF ST. VICTOR (early twelfth century–ca. 1190). Nothing is known of Walter's early life and education. *Career*: prior of St. Victor, 1173–90; took part in the controversy surrounding Peter Lombard's* Christology and identified Lombard, along with Gilbert de la Porrée,* Abelard,* and Peter of Poitiers, as "four minotaurs" bent upon devouring the Christian faith.

Walter made no original contribution to the theological thought of the twelfth century. He exhibited zeal in defending orthodoxy, but his orthodox theological source for attacks on the four theologians is an anonymous work, *Apologia pro Verbo Incarnato*. His attacks were placed into an extended diatribe against heresies, *Contra quattuor labyrinthos Franciae*, each of the four labyrinths containing one of the four minotaurs. Even though well intentioned, Walter attacked the rationalism that was a danger in dialectics and in the process went on to attack human reason, which places him outside the mainstream of contemporary and later developments in scholastic thought.

Bibliography

A. Thirty of Walter of St. Victor's sermons have been preserved in manuscript, but have not been edited.

B. LThK² 20:949; NCE 14:791; ODCC 1718; R. F. Studeny, "Walter of St.-Victor and the *Apologia de Verbo Incarnato*," *Gregorianum* 18 (1937): 579–85.

Thomas S. Ferguson

WALTHER, CARL FERDINAND WILHELM (25 October 1811, Langenchursdorf, Saxony–7 May 1887, St. Louis, Mo.). *Education*: graduated from the gymnasium in Schneeburg, 1829; graduated from Univ. of Leipzig, 1833. *Career*: private tutor, 1834–36; ordained Lutheran minister, 1837; minister,

Braeunsdorf, Germany, 1837–38; minister, Dresden, 1839; minister, Johannesberg, Mo., 1839–41; minister, Trinity Church, St. Louis, Mo., 1841–87; founding editor, *Der Lutheraner*, 1844–87; president, Missouri Synod, 1847–50, 1864–78; professor, Concordia Sem., St. Louis, 1850–87; founding editor, *Lehre und Wehre*, 1855–87; first president, Synodical Conference, 1872.

Walther was the foremost confessional Lutheran theologian in America in the nineteenth century. His theology was based on the verbally inspired and inerrant Scriptures. He insisted on strict adherence to the Lutheran confessions as contained in the Book of Concord (1580). Following Luther,* he focused on God's grace and forgiveness through the atoning sacrifice of Jesus. Salvation comes only through faith in Jesus. The Holy Spirit works faith through the gospel in word and sacrament. Walther also emphasized the importance of the Lutheran distinction between law and gospel in preaching and teaching.

Reacting to his rationalistic training, he joined a Pietistic group during his university years but found no real spiritual comfort. During a six-month convalescence he eagerly read his father's set of Luther's works. He came under the influence of pastor Martin Stephan and became part of the resurgence of Lutheran orthodoxy. He emigrated to America with Stephan and a number of others, settling in Perry County, Missouri. Walther became the acknowledged leader of the group after Stephan was deposed because of charges of immorality.

The removal of Stephan caused serious doubts among the immigrants about their religious undertaking in Missouri. In the Altenburg Debate (1841) Walther reassured them that the church existed in their midst. Although the church is essentially invisible, it is present wherever the Gospel is proclaimed and the sacraments administered. A group of Christians has the right to call pastors and to depose them for doctrinal aberrations or immorality. In later disputes he rejected hierarchical views of the ministry, insisting on the congregation's right to call. This divine call conferred the ministerial office rather than ordination. He defended a congregational form of church government.

In the American Lutheran election controversy Walther rejected election *intuitu fidei* and double predestination. The cause of election is God's grace. Faith is the result of election, not the cause of it. He maintained divine monergism in conversion.

Bibliography

A.   *Selected Writings of C. F. W. Walther*, ed. August Sueflow, 6 vols. (St. Louis, Mo., 1981); *The Proper Distinction Between Law and Gospel*, trans. William Dau (St. Louis, Mo., 1928); *Essays for the Church*, 2 vols. (St. Louis, Mo., 1992); *Church and Ministry*, trans. J. T. Mueller (St. Louis, Mo., 1987); *Walther's Pastorale*, trans. John Drickamer (New Haven, Mo., 1995).

B.   DAB 19:402–3; DARB 578–79; NCAB 26:118–19; NCE 14:793; SH 12:259; William Polack, *The Story of C. F. W. Walther* (St. Louis, Mo., 1935); Lewis Spitz, *The*

Life of C. F. W. Walther (St. Louis, Mo., 1961); *C. F. W. Walther: The American Luther*, ed. Arthur Drevlow, John Drickamer, and Glenn Reichwald (Mankato, Minn., 1987).

John M. Brenner

WARD, WILFRID PHILIP (2 January 1856, Ware, Hertfordshire, England–9 April 1916, Hampstead [London]). *Education*: studied at Downside Abbey, Bath, 1868–69; St. Edmund's Coll., Ware, 1869–74; Catholic Univ. Coll., Kensington, 1874–76; Gregorian Univ., 1877–78; Ushaw Coll., Durham, 1878–81. *Career*: writer mainly of Catholic apologetics and biography, and editor of the *Dublin Review*, 1906–16; cofounder with Arthur Balfour, Synthetic Society.

Ward was intellectually gifted but a desultory student. Out of a need to please his father, William George Ward, he drifted from one academic possibility to another and, although passionately interested in music, never pursued it as a career. In 1881, a year before his father died—leaving him independently wealthy—he showed his father some earlier essays on the interplay between faith and desire; his father was elated, the essays soon appeared in book form, and the course of Wilfrid's life was set. After publishing several more volumes of apologetics, he hit upon the field of biography, where he would exercise his most original talent.

His brief study in Rome thwarted all inclination toward Ultramontanism. Much influenced by Newman,* Ward sought a renewed Catholic apologetics for genuine dialogue with the modern world. During the modernist crisis he attempted to mediate between Ultramontanism on the one hand—attributing past magisterial rigidity to the ''state of siege'' prevailing in Catholicism since the Reformation—and liberalism and modernism on the other. Neither side was pleased. Cardinal secretary of state Merry del Val considered Ward's work ''very insidious.'' Most disinterested observers, however, think he largely succeeded, and his *Dublin Review* found many devoted readers, even among non-Catholics.

Bibliography

A. *The Wish to Believe* (London, 1884); *William George Ward and the Oxford Movement* (London, 1889); *William George Ward and the Catholic Revival* (London, 1893); *The Life and Times of Cardinal Wiseman*, 2 vols. (London, 1897); *Problems and Persons* (London, 1903); *The Life of John Henry Cardinal Newman*, 2 vols. (London, 1912); *Last Lectures* (London, 1916); Mary Jo Weaver, ''A Bibliography of the Published Works of Wilfrid Ward,'' *Heythrop Journal* 20 (1979): 399–420.

B. DNB, 1912–21, 552–53; NCE 809; ODCC 1721; *Times* (London) 10 April 1916; Maisie Ward, *The Wilfrid Wards and the Transition*, 2 vols. (London, 1934–37); Nadia M. Lahutsky, ''Wilfrid Ward, English Catholicism, and the Modernist Controversy, 1890–1912,'' Ph.D. diss., Vanderbilt Univ., 1984.

David G. Schultenover

WARD, WILLIAM GEORGE (21 March 1812, London–6 July 1882 Hampstead [London]). *Education*: studied at Winchester Coll., 1823–29; Oxford Univ. as commoner of Christ Church, 1830; scholar at Lincoln, 1833; fellow, Balliol Coll., 1834. *Career*: lectureship and tutor, Balliol, 1834–41; ordained priest, 1840; resigned fellowship at Oxford, 1845; lecturer in moral philosophy and professor of dogmatic theology, St. Edmund's Coll., Ware, Hertfordshire, 1851, 1852–58; managed family property and editor of the *Dublin Review*, 1863–78; founder, the Metaphysical Society, 1869; independent writer, 1858–80.

A charming man of keen intellectual abilities, Ward early on excelled in mathematics and philosophy. At Balliol he distinguished himself as a debater principally against his friend Archibald Campbell Tait, later archbishop of Canterbury. A strong opponent of both the narrow dogmatism of low church evangelicalism and the liberalism of Richard Whately and Thomas Arnold, he gravitated increasingly to the Oxford Movement and the views of Hurrell Froude and John Henry Newman.* That influence led to his conversion to Roman Catholicism in 1845. Lacking Newman's historical and theological depth, however, Ward leaped to conclusions that Newman could not support and became, according to his own rationalist bent, a radical Ultramontane, supporting a narrow understanding of papal infallibility. In 1854 Pope Pius IX rewarded him with a Ph.D.

Bibliography

A.   *The Ideal of a Christian Church* (Oxford, 1844); *On Nature and Grace* (London, 1859); *De Infallibilitatis Extensione* (London, 1869); *Essays on the Church's Doctrinal Authority* (London, 1880); *Essays on the Philosophy of Theism* (London, 1884).
B.   DNB 20:801–5; LThK² 10:956; NCE 809–10; ODCC 1721; Wilfrid P. Ward, *William George Ward and the Oxford Movement* (London, 1889); idem, *William George Ward and the Catholic Revival* (London, 1893); Maisie Ward, *The Wilfrid Wards and the Transition*, 2 vols. (New York, 1934–37); K. Theodore Hoppen, "W. G. Ward and Liberal Catholicism," JEH 23 (October 1972): 323–44.

David G. Schultenover

WARFIELD, BENJAMIN BRECKINRIDGE (5 November 1851, Lexington, Ky.–16 February 1921, Princeton, N.J.). *Education*: Coll. of New Jersey, 1868–71; Princeton Sem., Princeton, N.J., 1873–76; Univ. of Leipzig, 1876–77. *Career*: editor, *Farmer's Home Journal*, 1872–73; clergy supply in Ohio and Ky., 1875–76; assistant pastor, First Church, Baltimore, Md., 1877–78; instructor, professor, New Testament literature and exegesis, Western Sem., 1878–87; ordained evangelist, Ebenezer Presbytery, 1879; professor, didactic and polemic theology, Princeton Sem., 1887–1921; coeditor, *The Presbyterian Review*, 1888–89; editor, *The Presbyterian and Reformed Review*, 1890–1903.

Warfield was professor of theology at Princeton Seminary during the rise of theological liberalism in the late nineteenth and early twentieth centuries. Against liberalism's repeated attempts to reduce the Christian religion to a natural phenomenon by bending Scripture "into some sort of conciliation" with "the latest pronouncements of philosophy or science or criticism," Warfield championed the supernatural character of Christianity and insisted that the Bible rather than the "provisional findings" of modern scholarship is the objective rule of faith and practice. Although Warfield recognized that progress is made in theology by building upon the established doctrinal constructions of the past, he insisted that the naturalism of the modern era necessitated the perfection of an existing system of truth rather than the construction of a wholly new one. As such, he was content to expound and defend the doctrines of Reformed orthodoxy and to challenge those who "give up the substance . . . of Christianity" by looking at the teachings of God's Word "from the standpoint of the world's [naturalistic] speculations."

While modern historiography recognizes that Warfield was one of the greatest Reformed apologists of the twentieth century, many interpreters insist that the rationalistic tendency of the Princeton Theology reached its zenith in his apologetical response to the subjectivism of the age. Warfield's effort to ground faith in objective truth owes more to an endorsement of Scottish Common Sense Realism than it does to the Reformed tradition, they suggest, because it manifests a profound indifference to the moral nature of religious epistemology. Whereas Warfield certainly affirmed that saving faith is "a form of conviction, and is, therefore, necessarily grounded in evidence," he also insisted that faith is "a moral act and the gift of God." The charge of rationalism is without foundation, therefore, because Warfield recognized that there is more to a saving apprehension of the gospel than the rational appropriation of objective truth. Indeed, since he recognized that the act of faith involves a movement of the regenerated soul, he acknowledged that "It is God and God alone who saves, and that in every element of the saving process."

Bibliography

A. *Faith and Life* (New York, 1916); *The Works of Benjamin B. Warfield*, 10 vols. (New York, 1927–32); *Selected Shorter Writings of Benjamin B. Warfield*, ed. John E. Meeter, 2 vols. (Nutley, N.J., 1970–73).

B. DAB 19:453–54; DARB 581–82; NCAB 20:59; NCE 14:810–11; NYT 18 February 1921, 11; SH 12:273; Andrew Hoffecker, *Piety and the Princeton Theologians* (Phillipsburg, N.J., 1981); Andrew Hoffecker, "Benjamin B. Warfield," in *Reformed Theology in America*, ed. David Wells (Grand Rapids, Mich., 1985); David Calhoun, *Princeton Seminary*, 2 vols. (Edinburgh, 1994–96).

Paul Helseth

WEIGEL, GUSTAVE (15 January 1906, Buffalo, N.Y.–3 January 1964, New York, N.Y.). *Education*: Woodstock Coll., Md., 1926–34; doctorate in theology, Pontifical Gregorian Univ., Rome, 1935–37. *Career*: faculty of The Catholic Univ. of Chile, Santiago, 1937–48; professor of ecclesiology and fundamental theology, Woodstock Coll., Md., 1949–64; consultant for Protestant theology,

Theological Studies, 1948–64; consultor, Vatican Secretariat for Promoting Christian Unity, 1960–62; member of the U.S. bishops' press panel and the principal interpreter for the English-speaking Protestants attending Vatican II, 1962–64.

Weigel was one of the first theologians in the United States to seek to understand and dialogue with Protestant theology and theologians. He was arguably the most popular U.S. ecumenist in the 1950s and early 1960s. His conversations with theologians and church leaders of other religious communities helped to prepare the way for Vatican II in the United States.

As a theologian Weigel was at once a traditionalist and a reformer. This lifelong spirit he expressed in a 1934 diary entry: "I am making the Spiritual Exercises of St. Ignatius* on the basis that they leave the soul in freedom. . . . I use my own ideas in these meditations. . . . I know that the ways taught me years ago are impossible. I shall trust the Spirit." Through his life he struggled with the problem of the surrender of his will to authority while preserving his treasured liberty intact.

Weigel's theology of the church was, in most respects, quite traditional except for his emphasis on the church as mystery. He stressed that the Roman Catholic Church, as the Mystical Body of Christ, was a divinely instituted society and that the truth of that claim could best be demonstrated by the moral miracle of the church's united and effective existence in the world. Yet his warm, open personality allowed him to transcend the strictures and structures of his thought and training as he entered into conversation with the major religious thinkers and leaders of his time.

From 1954 on, Weigel became a supreme activist in behalf of ecumenism. Speaking and writing extensively, his ecumenical style was based upon his remarkable memory and his magnetic personality. Ecumenism for him was, above all else, a conversation between differing brothers, leading to a type of unity that only God could give to the church.

Weigel mentioned four approaches to ecclesial unity. Compromise: through give-and-take, a common basis is agreed upon and all melt into one church. Comprehension: certain basic principles are accepted but interpreted differently by various churches. Conversion: all churches disband and join one remaining church. All of these Weigel found wanting. He preferred the path of convergence in which the churches, gathered in conversation, would move closer and closer to one another. It was this coming together, not the achievement of unity, that was the true purpose of human efforts toward Christian unity.

His final contributions centered around the Second Vatican Council (1962–65). He participated minimally in the preparatory work of the Secretariat for Promoting Christian Unity. During the first two sessions his ecumenical spirit bore great fruit as he served as the interpreter for the English-speaking separated brethren. He also made stellar presentations at the U.S. bishops' press panel.

In his attitudes toward Vatican II, Weigel wavered from initial pessimism prior to the council to optimism after the first session due to the pastoral spirit of John XXIII. But then, at the close of session two, he became pessimistic, tired and disenchanted, feeling that the curial-style leadership of Paul VI was stifling progress.

Bibliography

A. *A Catholic Primer on the Ecumenical Movement* (Westminster, Md., 1957); *A Survey of Protestant Theology in Our Day* (Westminster, Md., 1954); *Catholic Theology in Dialogue* (New York, 1961); *The Modern God: Faith in a Secular Culture* (New York, 1963); with Robert McAfee Brown, *An American Dialogue. A Protestant Looks at Catholicism and a Catholic Looks at Protestantism* (Garden City N.Y., 1960); "Contemporaneous Protestantism and Paul Tillich," ThSt 11 (June, 1950): 177–202; "Ecumenism and the Catholic," *Thought* 30 (Spring, 1955): 5–17; "Catholic and Protestant Theologies in Outline," *American Scholar* 25 (Summer, 1956): 307–16; "Protestant Theological Positions Today," ThSt 11 (December, 1950): 547–66; "Protestantism as a Catholic Concern," ThSt 16 (June, 1955): 214–32; "Recent Protestant Theology," ThSt 14 (December, 1953): 568–94; "The Historical Background of the Encyclical *Humani Generis*," ThSt 12 (June, 1951): 208–30; "The Theological Significance of Paul Tillich," *Gregorianum* 36 (1956): 34–54; "Theology and Freedom," *Thought* 35 (Summer, 1960): 165–78.

B. DARB 587–88; NCE 14, 843–44; NYT 4 January 1964, 1; Patrick W. Collins, *Gustave Weigel: A Pioneer of Reform* (Collegeville, Minn., 1992); *One of a Kind: Essays in Tribute to Gustave Weigel* (Wilkes-Barre, Pa., 1967).

Patrick W. Collins

WESLEY, JOHN (17 June 1703, Epworth, England–21 March 1791, London). *Education*: Charterhouse Public School, 1714–20; B.A., M.A., Christ Church, Oxford Univ., 1724, 1727. *Career*: ordained deacon in the Church of England, 1725; ordained priest, 1728; fellow, Lincoln College, Oxford Univ., 1726–51; missionary to North America, 1735–37; evangelist, 1739–91; founder of Methodism.

English priest, scholar, missionary, and evangelist whose participation in the eighteenth-century evangelical revival in the British Isles led to the founding of Methodism. He was the fifteenth child of Samuel and Susanna Wesley, both of whom had come from leading Puritan families but had joined the Church of England in their youth, with Samuel becoming a priest. They were well-educated and strong-minded individuals, and the family ethos was one of vigorous will and passionate opinion in a context of discipline, scholarship, and piety.

Those characteristics were amply illustrated as he decided to follow his father in the priesthood while at Oxford. He gave himself to a regime of spiritual discipline that he believed accorded with such a decision. As part of that discipline, he began a personal journal, which he was to continue virtually uninterrupted for the rest of his life. That journal—and his many surviving letters of the period—depict a process of gradually deepening devotion and slowly mounting frustration as he sought to conform his life to the piety and morality he thought consistent with Christian discipline. Despite his most strenuous efforts—at times bordering on the pathological—he could not achieve that goal. Thus, his years at Oxford were marked by contradiction. Outwardly, he was a very successful young scholar, elected to a prestigious fellowship at Lincoln College and becoming one of the most popular preachers at the university church; yet inwardly, he struggled to realize an ideal that eluded him. The context of his spiritual efforts at Oxford was the ''Holy Club,'' a name given by critics, but one that Wesley characteristically embraced. They were a group of like-minded students who under his leadership engaged in prayer, mutual confession and exhortation, discussion of edifying literature, and the visitation of the sick and imprisoned. They were also derisively referred to as ''Methodists.''

In some disillusionment he traveled to Georgia in 1735 to serve as priest to the English colonists and missionary to the indigenous tribes. In seeking the salvation of others he hoped to achieve his own, as he frankly wrote at the time. The trip was in many ways disastrous: terrible storms made for a terrifying Atlantic crossing; he got on badly with both the governor and the colonists; he had little success with the native peoples; and he suffered public humiliation due to a foolish and unsuccessful love affair. But as the ship threatened to go down on the journey out, he observed Moravian missionary families face death with a quiet assurance of faith that made him profoundly conscious of his own terrorized lack of the same. When he returned to England in 1738 he sought out the Moravians and, with one of their own, organized the Fetter Lane Society in London. For Wesley, that endeavor came to a culmination in May of that year, when, as he listened to the public reading of Luther's preface to his commentary on Galatians, he experienced a deep sense of God's personal love for him and interpreted it as a expression of the reformer's doctrine of justification by faith. Soon thereafter, in his next—and last—university sermon at Oxford, he declared that salvation by faith was the fundamental issue facing England.

He was soon unwelcome in the pulpits of the Church of England. At the urging of others who were already involved in the evangelical revival then reaching the British Isles, he took up the practice of preaching in the open air to the common people. The results were extraordinary. Hundreds and thousands of working and lower-middle-class men and women were drawn into ''bands'' of Christian discipleship organized by Wesley as he traveled through England, Scotland, Ireland, and Wales. Ultimately, the movement escaped the shores of Great Britain and was brought to other countries as well. In order to provide leadership for this burgeoning ''Methodist connection,'' including the vast amount of social work it performed in the areas of education, health, and the like, Wesley appointed, trained, and kept under his personal discipline an ever growing cadre of preachers. Despite his determined efforts, the Anglicans never recognized those preachers or allowed the Methodists any place within the established church. At his death, the Methodists formed a church body separate from the Church of England.

Wesley, it has been said, was a serious but not a systematic theologian. His theology is best understood as an effort to hold together the two concerns that were central to his own spiritual biography: first, a deep conviction that Christian faith demanded an active program of personal discipline and social service through which spiritual progress was realized; and second, an equally profound belief that such faith was the utterly free and gracious gift of God. It was and is the struggle to reconcile those two themes—so often at odds in the Western tradition—and find a form of theological discourse that could express them together, a struggle carried out in practical debate with Catholic and Calvinist and Lutheran and Independent that gave his thought its dynamic in his day and continues to do so even in ours.

Bibliography

A. *The Works of John Wesley* (The Bicentennial Edition), ed. Frank Baker, 26 vols. to date (Nashville, Tenn., 1984–); *Wesley's Works* (London, 1872); *John Wesley,* ed. Albert C. Outler (New York, 1964).

B. BBKL 13:914–76; DNB 20:1214–29; LThK² 10:1064; NCE 14:878–79; ODCC 1727–28; SH 12:307–10; Henry D. Rack, *Reasonable Enthusiast: John Wesley and the Rise of Methodism,* 2d ed. (Nashville, Tenn., 1993); Richard P. Heitzenrater, *The Elusive Mr. Wesley,* 2 vols. (Nashville, Tenn., 1984); idem, *Wesley and the People Called Methodists* (Nashville, Tenn., 1995); Randy Maddox, *Responsible Grace: John Wesley's Practical Theology* (Nashville, Tenn., 1994); Manfred Marquardt, *John Wesley's Social Ethics: Praxis and Principles,* trans. J. E. Steely and W. S. Gunter (Nashville, Tenn., 1992).

D. Lyle Dabney

WHITEFIELD, GEORGE (27 December 1714, Gloucester, England–30 September 1770, Newburyport, Mass.). *Education*: B.A., Pembroke Coll., Oxford Univ., 1736. *Career*: itinerant preacher in England and the American colonies, 1736–70.

Whitefield was more an eighteenth-century evangelist than a theologian, but he had an impact on the theological orientation of the century by his emphasis upon the necessity of grace, Christian experience, and the inner subjective union with Christ—issues that permeated his sermons. He also helped to revolutionize the art of preaching by his extemporaneous homilies, which he gave in court-houses, barns, and open fields in both England and the American colonies. Such pastoral and evangelical tactics won him a host of admirers and a variety of critics. The critics focused upon the almost exclusive emotional appeal of the sermons and his harsh criticisms of the standing or parochial clergy, whom he particularly assaulted with the charge of being unconverted. The dramatic and sensational appeal of his sermons, however, also attracted large crowds and created numerous clerical imitators of his style.

Bibliography

A. *A Journal and a Continuation of the Reverend Mr. Whitefield's Journal,* 7 vols. (London, 1739–43); *The Works of the Reverend George Whitefield,* 6 vols. (London,

1771–72); *Fifteen Sermons* (Philadelphia, 1794); *Eighteen Sermons* (Newburyport, Mass., 1797).

B.   AAP 5:94–108; DAB 20:124–29; DARB 600–602; NCAB 5:384–85; NCE 14: 895–96; SH 12:341–42; Edward Ninde, *George Whitefield* (New York, 1924); Stuart C. Henry, *George Whitefield: Wayfaring Witness* (Nashville, Tenn., 1954); John Pollock, *George Whitefield and the Great Awakening* (Garden City, N.Y., 1972); Harry S. Stout, *The Divine Dramatist: George Whitefield and the Rise of Modern Evangelicalism* (Grand Rapids, Mich., 1991).

Patrick W. Carey

WILBERFORCE, ROBERT ISAAC (19 December 1802, Clapham–3 February 1857, Albano, Italy). *Education*: B.A., Oriel Coll., Oxford, 1824. *Career*: fellow, Oriel Coll., 1826–28; ordained priest, Church of England, 1828; tutor, Oriel Coll., 1828–32; vicar, East Farleigh, Kent, 1832–40; vicar, Burton Agnes, Yorkshire, 1840–41; archdeacon, East Riding, 1841–54.

Wilberforce was a leading theologian of the Tractarian movement and has been described as "the greatest philosophical theologian of the Tractarians." He was tutor with Richard Hurrell Froude and John Henry Newman.* In 1843, he became a close friend of Henry Edward Manning.* His four major books are *The Doctrine of the Incarnation of Our Lord Jesus Christ* (London, 1848), *The Doctrine of Holy Baptism* (London, 1849), *The Doctrine of the Holy Eucharist* (Philadelphia, 1853), and *Principles of Church Authority* (London, 1854). Partly under the influence of Manning, who joined the Roman Catholic Church in 1851, Wilberforce was received into the Roman Catholic Church on 1 November 1854. Wilberforce entered the Accademia Ecclesiastica in Rome in 1855 and died while studying for the Catholic priesthood.

Wilberforce was an ecumenical theologian. He studied Friedrich Schleiermacher* and was influenced by the Mercersburg theology of John Williamson Nevin* and Philip Schaff.* His *Doctrine of the Incarnation* is the major synthesis of Tractarian teaching. He stresses the Incarnation as the fundamental and distinctive doctrine of Christianity and taught that Christ is present with people in the church, which is His Mystical Body. A person's union with Christ is realized by union with the church.

Bibliography

A.   With Samuel Wilberforce, *The Life of William Wilberforce*, 5 vols. (London, 1838).

B.   DNB 21:201–4; ODCC 1740; Thomas Robert Artz, "One in the Body of Christ: Robert Isaac Wilberforce and the Theology of Concorporation," Ph.D. diss., Boston Coll., 1985.

Robert B. Slocum

WILLIAM OF AUVERGNE (ca. 1180, Aurillac, Auvergne–30 March 1249, Paris). *Career*: master in theology, Univ. of Paris, by 1223; canon of the cathedral of Notre Dame in 1223; bishop of Paris, 1228–49.

Before and after his consecration as bishop, William wrote his massive *Magisterium divinale et sapientiale*, which includes *De trinitate, De universo creaturarum, De anima, Cur Deus homo, De fide et legibus, De sacramentis,* and *De virtutibus et moribus.* He also fostered the presence of the Dominicans and Franciscans at the University of Paris and was advisor to the young Louis IX.

William of Auvergne, or of Paris, was the first systematic theologian of the thirteenth century to take into serious account the philosophy that had poured into the Latin West for over half a century. He was especially influenced by Avicenna, whose metaphysics and psychology he adopted to a large extent. For instance, he refers to God with the Avicennian expressions "the First" and "being necessary through itself," appeals to Avicenna's "floating man" thought-experiment, and argues for a single generation within the Trinity on Avicennian principles. On the other hand, he opposed Avicenna on many points. He followed Ibn Gabirol in his emphasis upon the divine will, insisting upon the divine freedom and denying an eternal and necessary creation and the cascade of intelligences emanating from the First. William anticipated Thomas Aquinas* in maintaining a real distinction between being and essence in created things. In his *De universo* William argues against many errors of his time, for example—the Cathar dualism rampant in southern France, the Avicennian doctrine of an agent intelligence, and the Platonic claim that true beings are found only in the archetypal world.

Bibliography

A.   *Opera Omnia*, 2 vols. (Orléans and Paris, 1674; repr. Frankfurt a. M., 1963); *De trinitate: An Edition of the Latin Text with an Introduction*, ed. Bruno Switalski (Toronto, 1976); *William of Auvergne: The Trinity or the First Principle*, trans. Roland J. Teske and Francis C. Wade (Milwaukee, Wis., 1989); *William of Auvergne: The Immortality of the Soul*, trans. Roland J. Teske (Milwaukee, Wis., 1991).

B.   DTC 16:1967–76; LThK² 10:1127–28; NCE 14:921; ODCC 1743; Amato Masnovo, *Da Guglielmo d'Auvergne a S. Tommaso d'Aquino*, 3 vols. (Milan, 1946); Étienne Gilson, "La notion d'existence chez Guillaume d'Auvergne," *Archives d'histoire doctrinale et littéraire du moyen âge* 21 (1946): 55–91; Steven P. Marrone, *William of Auvergne and Robert Grosseteste: New Ideas of Truth in the Early Thirteenth Century* (Princeton, N.J., 1983); Gabriel Jüssen, "Wilhelm von Auvergne und die Transformation der scholastischen Philosophie im 13. Jahrhundert," *Philosophie im Mittelalter: Entwicklungslinien und Paradigmen*, ed. Jan P. Beckmann et al. (Hamburg, 1987), 141–64; Roland J. Teske, "William of Auvergne," *Dictionary of Literary Biography*, vol. 115, *Medieval Philosophers*, ed. J. Hackett (Detroit, Mich., 1992), 344–53.

Roland J. Teske

WILLIAM OF AUXERRE (d. 1231). A master of theology at the University of Paris during the first quarter of the thirteenth century, William of Auxerre belongs to the generation of scholars who first grappled with the recently recovered philosophical writings of Aristotle. Under the impress of Aristotelian natural philosophy, they developed a new vehicle for expressing their sense of the interconnectedness of all aspects of theology: the comprehensive summary or *summa* of theology. William of Auxerre's *Summa aurea* (ca. 1215–25) is considered by some to be the prototype of the classic *summa* of the thirteenth century in which every element of Christian revelation is systematically explored according to the principles of human knowledge. Thus conceived, theology, from this point in its history, increasingly assumes the forms and procedures of Aristotelian *scientia*. William of Auxerre is important for raising the question whether theology is, in fact, a science in the Aristotelian sense of the term—that is, a discipline that proceeds to its conclusions by means of a priori deduction from first principles. William argues that, for the believer, the truths of faith are like the *per se nota* (the self-evident first principles) of other sciences because faith affords sure, evident knowledge. Both the structure and the premises of the *Summa aurea* therefore mark a significant moment in medieval theology. When, in 1231, Pope Gregory IX decreed that Aristotle's works of natural philosophy were not to be used at the University of Paris until they had been examined and expurgated, William of Auxerre was one of three theology masters commissioned to undertake the assessment of the prohibited books. The committee never reported, however, perhaps owing to William's death that same year.

Bibliography

A. *Summa aurea Magistri Guillelmi Altissiodorensis*, ed. Jean Ribaillier, Spicilegium Bonaventurianum 16–20 (Rome, 1980–87).

B. DTC 16:1976; LThK² 10:1128–29; NCE 14:921–22; ODCC 1743; Jules A. St. Pierre, "The Theological Thought of William of Auxerre: An Introductory Bibliography," RTAM 33 (1966): 147–55; A. Vanneste, "Nature et grâce dans la théologie de Guillaume d'Auxerre et de Guillaume d'Auvergne," EThL 53 (1977): 83–106.

M. Michèle Mulchahey

WILLIAM OF OCCAM. *See* WILLIAM OF OCKHAM.

WILLIAM OF OCKHAM (c. 1285, Ockham, a village in county Surrey, southwest of London–10 April 1347, Munich). *Education*: joined the Franciscans before the age of fourteen and quite likely studied philosophy at the friars' school in London; studied theology and as a bachelor of the *Sentences*, commented on Lombard's* work, Oxford, 1317–19. Because of the long line of Franciscan candidates before him, he never became a presiding Master at Oxford. His fame was thus achieved under the title *Venerable Inceptor*, although some records refer to him as the *Invincible Doctor* or the *Singular Doctor*. *Career*: his chief academic work was done between 1319 and 1324 at the Franciscan house of studies in London, where he had close association with Walter Chatton (a chief opponent) and Adam Wodeham (a frequent follower); revised his *Commentary on Book I of Lombard's Sentences*, which is called the *Scriptum* or *Written Commentary*, in contrast to the *Reportationes* or *Quaestiones* that are the records of his Oxford lectures on Books II-IV of the *Sentences*; wrote expositions on Porphyry's *Isagoge* and on Aristotle's *Categories*, *On Interpreta-*

tion, and *Sophistical Refutations*; his theological treatises, such as *De sacramento altaris*, and his well-organized *Summa logicae* also date from this period at London, which ended in 1323–24 with the disputation of his *Quodlibets* and the crafting of his final philosophical work, the *Questions on the Physics*; called to Avignon in 1324 by Pope John XXII to answer charges against him contained in the *Libellus* or *Pamphlet against the Teaching of William of Ockham* drawn up by John Lutterell, the chancellor of Oxford who was deposed two years earlier. The commission appointed to investigate the propositions presented fifty-one of them as worthy of censure, but no formal condemnation was ever made by the pope. On 26 May 1328, Ockham fled with Michael of Cesena and Bonagratia de Bergamo, the general minister and vicar of the Franciscans, to Pisa. There, they sought the protection of Louis of Bavaria, emperor of the Holy Roman Empire. Two years later they journeyed with Louis to Munich, where for the next seventeen years Ockham wrote on the proper extent of papal power. Although he continually expressed a willingness to submit to what he called the legitimate authorities of the church and the Franciscan order, he died unrepentant on 10 April 1347 in Munich, where he was buried in the Franciscan church.

William of Ockham has been portrayed in modern times as an innovator, a nominalist, and the leading figure of the *via moderna*. Since the recent critical edition of his works, however, and the studies it has spurred, more tempered judgments of the innovative character of his work have been passed. As a better knowledge of his sources has developed, the influences of earlier writers and contemporaries (John Duns Scotus,* Walter Burleigh, Hervaeus Natalis, Henry of Harclay, William of Alnwick, William of Nottingham, Richard of Conington, Robert Cowton, John of Reading, Peter Aureoli,* and others) on his thought have become more visible. One ruling principle of his philosophy and theology is his famous "Razor" (i.e., the principle of parsimony: "Beings should not be multiplied without necessity"). In philosophy, for example, he speaks of substances and certain inhering qualities, such as whiteness, as realities, while other qualities, such as curvedness and straightness, and the other categories (such as quantity, relation), are names—that is, concepts or words (*Opera Philosophica*, I, 20ss.). The latter categories, he argues, do not require an extra reality beyond substances and real qualities. Curvedness is not an inhering real quality but can be explained more economically by local motion (i.e., when the ends of something are bent up or down, and are thus closer to one another, then the substance is curved), not by a curvedness inhering in it (*OP* II, 283s.). Similarly, "twin" is not a real distinct characteristic that inheres in each member of a set of twins. Two individuals are twins because they come from the same mother at approximately the same time (*OP* II, 241s.). Likewise, when different objects (e.g., men) are similar, there does not exist in them a special quality, "similarity," beyond the quality that makes them similar. If, for instance, they are both white, they are similar in whiteness, but do not have a distinct characteristic "similarity" inhering in them (*OP* II, 245s.). In parallel ways in theology, due to Ockham's denial that quantity is a reality distinct from substances and real accidents, his discussions of the Eucharist (e.g., in *De quantitate* and *De corpore Christi*) vary significantly from those authors who take a more realist view of the categories. For example, in speaking of transubstantiation, Ockham says that we are forced to admit that the substance of the bread is transubstantiated into the quantity of the body of Christ (*Opera Theologica* X, 79). The sacraments of the New Law, likewise, do not, according to him, have an inherent power in them that of itself causes grace, so that by their very nature they would produce grace. It is God who gives grace, using the sacraments as necessary instruments that He has freely chosen to channel this gift (*OT* VII, 12ss.). Similarly, "creation" and "conservation" signify the same reality. If they differ, it is not because they express different realities. Rather, they express the same reality, but also express two different forms of negation. "Conservation" signifies what "creation" signifies and also indicates that the reality did not just come into existence, but rather already existed. "Creation," on the other hand, signifies the same reality but as not having existed previously and now existing (*OT* V, 60ss.).

Another ruling principle for Ockham is the distinction between God's absolute and ordained power. Although there is in God only one power that actually creates (i.e., God's ordained power, which causes the created order chosen by the divine will), still, God could have chosen other orders that creation might have followed. The collection of all possible worlds—ones the making of which would not include a contradiction—is the domain of God's absolute power. This distinction in effect stresses the contingency of the chosen order. Absolutely speaking, grace is not necessary for salvation, according to Ockham; but in the de facto contingent order established by God's ordained will, it is required (*OT* III, 471s.). Although Christian theologians, who hold that God freely created the world, must admit a distinction of two powers, its use in Ockham's case underscored the contingency of the natural order and at times it tended to stress other orders that could have been at the expense of the created order that is. God could have produced the world from eternity, because eternal creation includes no contradiction (*OT* VIII, 59ss.). He also could increase charity or grace infinitely, since whatever finite charity exists, there is no contradiction in admitting that a greater one may exist (*OT* III, 546ss.). Likewise, beyond every creature that exists, God could produce another species of creature that is even higher, since every type of creature that exists is finite in its perfection and no contradiction is involved in admitting another more noble species (*OT* IV, 650ss.). In his effort to stress the contingency of creation, Ockham led some followers to give a priority of the possible over the actual.

Further conclusions based on the distinction between God's absolute and ordained power at times became more startling. Ockham admitted that God can be hated meritoriously by a created will. For one man could command another to hate God, and there is no contradiction involved in such a command being carried out. Since God, however, can do whatever does not involve a contradiction, and as a first cause can do whatever a second cause can do, then God can command the same thing that a creature commands. Now, whenever a man does what God commands he does something worthy of merit, so it follows that God can be hated in a meritorious way by a creature (*OT* V, 353).

Some of Ockham's positions seem less startling if we put them in the context of the authors with whom he was arguing. In philosophy, his theory of universals, and all that flows from it, becomes less stunning if we read his positions in relation to the excessive realistic positions defended by contemporaries like Walter Burleigh and Walter Chatton. In theology, Ockham's theories of grace and merit appear more moderate and have greater plausibility when studied in the light of Peter Aureoli's more Pelagian-leaning positions. Although these contexts do not excuse Ockham for faulty philosophical and theological positions, they do show some of his declarations as necessary correctives.

Furthermore, some of Ockham's startling statements are due to the fact that he aims at a highly technical use of language. He claims, for example, that the Trinity may be known by a philosopher, because God may be known by a philosopher. Ockham does not mean that a philosopher as philosopher may come to know that God is triune. He simply means that the God whom the philosopher knows is triune. In other words, if a philosopher knows the true God, he knows the triune God—without knowing that God is triune; in fact, Ockham claims, it would be an error to claim that he knows that God is triune (*OT* I, 456ss.). Ockham's *Summa logicae* is effectively a codebook that invites us to examine philosophical and theological statements to determine more precisely the exact realities they signify. In effect, it helps rid the mind of all the imagined realities that imprecise language might suggest. This, for Ockham, is one of the main tasks of the philosopher and theologian.

Bibliography

A.   *Guillelmi de Ockham Opera Philosophica et Theologica ad fidem codicum manuscriptorum edita*, ed. Gedeon Gál et al., 17 vols. (St. Bonaventure, N.Y., 1967–88); *Guillelmi de Ockham Opera Politica*, ed. Jeffrey G. Sikes and H. S. Offler, 3 vols. (Manchester, 1956–74); *The De sacramento altaris*, ed. and trans. T. Bruce Birch (Burlington, Iowa, 1962); *William of Ockham: Predestination, Foreknowledge, and Future Contingents*, trans. Marilyn McCord Adams and Norman Kretzmann (Indianapolis, Ind., 1983); *Quodlibets*, trans. Alfred J. Freddoso and Francis E. Kelley, 2 vols. (New Haven, Conn., and London, 1991); *William of Ockham: A Letter to the Friars Minor and Other Writings*, ed. A. Stephen McGrade and John Kilcullen (Cambridge, New York, and Melbourne, 1995); *Treatise on the Principles of Theology*, trans. Julian Davies (St. Bonaventure, N.Y., 1998). A number of philosophical works and selections from his whole corpus have been translated into English (and other languages). For a complete list of them, see *Ockham-Bibliographie 1900–1990*.

B.   BBKL 6:1090–93; LthK² 10:1142–45; NCE 14:932–35; ODCC 1745–46; TRE 25:6–18; Richard Cross, "Nominalism and Christology of William of Ockham," RTAM 58 (1991): 126–56; Alfred J. Freddoso, "Ontological Reductionism and Faith versus Reason," *Faith and Philosophy* 8 (1991): 317–39; John Kilcullen, "Ockham and Infallibility," *Journal of Religious History* 16 (1991): 387–409; Ignacio Miralbell-Guerin,

"Omnipotencia divina y logicismo critico en Ockham," in *El hombre: Immanencia y trascendencia* (Pamplona, 1991) 2, 945–58; *Ockham-Bibliographie 1900–1990*, ed. Jan P. Beckmann (Hamburg, 1992); Claude Panaccio, "Intuition, abstraction, et langage mental dans la théorie occamiste de la connaissance," *Revue de métaphysique et de morale* 97 (1992): 61–81; Matthias Kaufmann, *Begriffe, Sätze, Dinge: Referenz und Wahrheit bei Wilhelm von Ockham* (Leiden, 1994); Jan P. Beckmann, *Wilhelm von Ockham* (Munich, 1995); Oliver Leffler, *Wilhelm von Ockham: Die sprachphilosophischen Grundlagen seines Denkens* (Werl/Westfalen, 1995); Volker Leppin, *Geglaubte Wahrheit: Das Theologieverständnis Wilhelms von Ockham* (Göttingen, 1995); Angelo Pelligrini, *Statuto epistemologico della teologia secundo Guglielmo di Occam* (Florence, 1995); Armand Maurer, *The Philosophy of William of Ockham in the Light of Its Principles* (Toronto, 1998).

Stephen F. Brown

WILLIAM OF ST. THIERRY (1085, Liège, Belgium–8 September 1148, Signy, France). *Education*: studied at Rheims; after entering the Benedictine monastery of St. Nicaise, he studied Scripture and the Fathers, 1113. *Career*: elected abbot of St. Thierry, ca. 1119; wrote *On the Nature and Dignity of Love*, *On Contemplating God*, and *Meditations* (1119–21); retired to the Cistercian monastery at Signy, France, ca. 1135, where he produced his *Expostition on the Song of Songs*, *Mirror of Faith*, and *Enigma of Faith* (1140–44); wrote the *Golden Letter* and *Life of Bernard* (1145–48).

William was an excellent administrator and spiritual adviser. His writings are considered classics of Western spirituality and his influence extended over the leading authorities of his age. His scholarship was especially linked with Bernard of Clairvaux,* a close friend. William's writings center on the trinitarian theology of the soul's image and likeness to God and the ascent of the soul to contemplative union with God through degrees of love.

Bibliography

A. *Guillelmi a Sancto Theodorico Opera omnia*, ed. Paul Verdeyen, CCCM 86 (Turnhout, 1989); *The Works of William of St. Thierry*, 4 vols. (Kalamazoo, Mich., 1971–80).

B. DTC 16:1891–92; LThK² 10:1150–52; NCE 14:938–39; ODCC 1746–47; E. Rozanne Elder, "The Way of Ascent: The Meaning of Love in the Thought of William of St. Thierry," *Studies in Medieval Culture*, ed. J. R. Sommerfeldt (Kalamazoo, Mich., 1964), 1:39–47; David Bell, *The Image and Likeness: The Augustinian Spirituality of William of St. Thierry* (Kalamazoo, Mich., 1984); Colloque international d'histoire monastique, *William, Abbot of Saint Thierry: A Colloquium at the Abbey of Saint Thierry*, trans. Jerry Carfantan (Kalamazoo, 1987); Paul Verdeyen, *La théologie mystique de Guillaume de Saint-Thierry* (Paris, 1990).

Daniel Marcel La Corte

WILLIAMS, DANIEL DAY (12 September 1910, Denver, Colo.–3 December 1973, New York, N.Y.). *Education*: B.A., Univ. of Denver, 1931; M.A., Univ.

of Chicago, 1933; B.D. Chicago Theol. Sem., 1934; Ph.D., Columbia Univ., 1940. *Career*: ordained Congregational Church, 1936; pastor, Colorado Springs, Colo., 1936–38; instructor in religion, Colorado Coll., 1938–39; professor of Christian theology, Univ. of Chicago, 1939–54; professor, Union Theol. Sem., New York, N.Y., 1954–73; delegate, World Council of Churches, 1971–73.

Williams' theology mediated between Protestant liberalism and neo-orthodoxy. He was educated within the context of American Protestant liberalism but was one of the mid-twentieth-century American Protestant liberals who were open to the neo-orthodox criticisms of liberalism and who was himself critical of the excessive optimism and utopianism of the nineteenth-century liberal tradition that he inherited. Nevertheless, like a few other liberals, he used the categories of modern science and especially the categories of the process philosophers Alfred North Whitehead and Charles Hartshorne in his attempts to make the Christian tradition intelligible and relevant to the modern world. He asserted that the starting point of the theological task was faith, but faith as it engaged the spirit of the times in which it stood.

As a thoroughgoing or hardcore Whiteheadean, Williams rejected the classical Christian conception of an immutable, impassible, and absolute God. He opted instead for a God who genuinely suffered and who entered into real relations with creatures and saved them because he suffered with them. For him, as for other Protestant process theologians, the ultimate theological question was soteriological, and for him that meant a theology of divine love—divine love manifested in divine suffering on the cross. As a process theologian he discovered human hope in God's grace, which he saw working in human beings and in the world. In this sense, he accepted liberalism's most basic premise of divine immanence. Williams' process theology, his emphasis upon divine immanence, and his focus upon the salvific dimension of divine love were most clearly evident in his *The Spirit and the Forms of Love* (New York, 1968).

Bibliography

A. *The Andover Liberals, a Study in American Theology* (New York, 1941); *God's Grace and Man's Hope* (New York, 1949); *What Present Day Theologians Are Thinking* (New York, 1952; London, 1953); "Moral Obligation in Process Philosophy," in *Alfred North Whitehead, Essays on His Philosophy*, ed. George L. Kline (Englewood Cliffs, N.J., 1963), 189–95; *Essays in Process Theology*, ed. P. Lefevre (Chicago, 1985); Jean C. Lambert, "Daniel Day Williams, 1910–1973: A Bibliography," *Union Seminary Quarterly Review* 30 (Winter–Summer, 1975): 217–29.

B. NYT 4 December 1973, 3; Charles Harvey Arnold, *Near the Edge of Battle: A Short History of the Divinity School and the "Chicago School of Theology" 1866–1966* (Chicago, 1966), 90–97; "Festschrift in Honor of Daniel Day Williams," *Union Seminary Quarterly Review* 30 (Winter–Summer, 1975); William David Eisenhower, "The Theology of Daniel Day Williams in Context," Ph.D. diss, Union Theol. Sem., Richmond, Va., 1985; L. Steven Sadler, "A Theological Construct for Worship Drawn from the Process Theologies of Daniel Day Williams and W. Norman Pittenger,'' Ph.D. diss., Baylor Univ., 1990.

Patrick W. Carey

WILLIAMS, ROGER (1603, London, England–March 1683, Providence, R.I.). *Education*: B.A., Pembroke Coll., Cambridge Univ., 1627; studied at Cambridge Univ., 1627–29. *Career*: Anglican chaplain to William Masham family, Essex, 1629–30; minister, Plymouth colony, 1631–33; minister, Salem, Mass., 1634–35; banished from Mass., 1635; founder and resident, Providence (later R.I.), 1636–83; travels to England for R.I. charter, 1643–44; second trip to England, 1651–54; governor, R.I., 1654–57.

Williams was a religious thinker more than a systematic theologian, but he contributed to the modern development of religious liberty by emphasizing the soul's liberty in its relationship with God and its freedom from all external coercion, whether from the church or the state. Educated under the auspices of English Puritans at Cambridge, Williams passed through several distinct phases in his theological development, from separatist Puritan to Baptist and to independent Christian with no affliation to any Christian denomination.

Three interrelated questions were the central focus of his life's work: what power properly belonged to the civil government? what power ought to be exercised by ecclesiastical government? and what liberty belonged to the individual conscience and to those who sincerely sought after the truth? These questions were opened up in rather unsystematic fashion in his first major publication, *The Bloudy Tenent of Persecution, for cause of Conscience* (London, 1644). He used historical experience, biblical mandates, and reason to argue for the soul's God-given freedom and right to meet God in ways that it perceived to be true.

He asserted that the Christian Church since the time of Constantine had either been in captivity to the state or had dominated the state. In the early seventeenth century, he believed it was time to separate the church from the state, returning it to the ancient order that prevailed in early Christianity before Constantine.

Williams established Providence, Rhode Island, in 1636, and there he built the colony with a larger amount of religious tolerance and liberty than had previously existed in Europe. In Providence he became a member of a Baptist Church but left that church in 1639 because by then his intense millennialism had convinced him that it was impossible to restore primitive Christianity (or the New Testament Church) without the return of the New Testament Christ. In the meantime, he awaited that return living a Christian life without identification with any religious denomination because, in his view, all had fallen short of the primitive ideal.

Bibliography

A. *The Hireling Ministry None of Christs* (London, 1652); *George Fox Digg'd out of His Burrowes* (Boston, 1676); *Experiments of Spiritual Life and Health*, ed. Winthrop S. Hudson (Philadelphia, 1951); *The Complete Writings of Roger Williams*, 7 vols. (New

York, 1963); *Correspondence of Roger Williams*, ed. Glenn W. LaFantasie (Hanover, N.H., 1988).

B.   AAP 6:8–21; DAB 20:286–89; DARB 611–12; NCAB 10:4–6; NCE 14:944; SH 12:369–71; Samuel H. Brockunier, *The Irrepressible Democrat: Roger Williams* (New York, 1940); Perry Miller, *Roger Williams* (Indianapolis, Ind., 1953; New York, 1962); Edmund S. Morgan, *Roger Williams: The Church and the State* (New York, 1967); John Garrett, *Roger Williams: Witness Beyond Christendom* (New York, 1970); Wallace Coyle, *Roger Williams: A Reference Guide* (Boston, 1977); W. Clark Gilpin, *The Millenarian Piety of Roger Williams* (Chicago, 1979); Edwin S. Gaustad, *Liberty of Conscience: Roger Williams in America* (Grand Rapids, Mich., 1991).

Patrick W. Carey

WINGREN, GUSTAF (29 November 1910, Tryserum, Sweden–). *Education*: Univ. of Lund, 1939, 1942; *Career*: visiting professor, Univ. of Basel, 1947; Univ. of Göttingen, 1950; professor of theology, Univ. of Lund, 1951–79; member, Faith and Order Commission, World Council of Churches; active retirement, 1979–.

Wingren was the third of the Lundensian theologians, more like Gustaf Aulén* (and Einar Billing*) than like his teacher Anders Nygren.* He accepted Aulén's judgment that Irenaeus* and Luther* were the epochal interpreters of the apostolic message. His first thesis (unpublished) contrasted Irenaeus and Marcion* (Nygren's antagonists in *Agape and Eros*) on the doctrine of Creation; his doctoral dissertation examined Luther's view of the Christian's calling as a creation mandate. The third of his historical theology monographs investigated Irenaeus' doctrine of the Incarnation; it analyzed how the church father resisted the prevalent gnosticism by expounding how fully the Redeemer entered what was truly His own creation.

As he explains himself in his theological autobiography, *Creation and Gospel* (New York, 1979), delivered in lectures to a Canadian audience at the time of his retirement, the doctrine of Creation is foundational in his thought; in this he aligns himself with Aulén and against Nygren. He deliberately challenged Nygren, Barth,* and Bultmann* in *Theology in Conflict* (1954, ET: London, 1958) for ignoring the first article of the creed. Because they (though in different ways) take the Christological second article as their starting point, Wingren argues here and in other places, they are unable to view creation positively; revelation and salvation for them can be only invasions from beyond, without analogy or preparation in the material world. Nygren was offended by this critique, which had already begun during Wingren's student years; Barth was puzzled that he so wilfully misunderstood him (*Church Dogmatics* CD IV, 3, 1:260f).

The hallmark of Wingren's thought is the consistency with which he has made the first article the starting point for his theological reflections. Preaching (not a theological concern, historically, in Sweden), he argues in *The Living Word* (Philadelphia, 1960, 1965), presupposes a creature designed to hear and, therefore, needy of the word of God. In *Creation and Law* (1958, ET: London,

1961) and *Gospel and Church* (1960, ET: London, 1964), he takes up Aulén's task of constructive theology, constantly appealing to the suitability of the created for relationship with the Creator through the Redeemer by the Spirit.

Since retirement in 1979, he has been an active writer and speaker on academic topics and themes relevant to the Church of Sweden and the life of the Christian in Sweden. A mature monograph on Irenaeus, *Människan och kristen* (1983), and his autobiography, *Mina fem universitet: Minnen* (1991), remain untranslated.

In Europe, Wingren has a substantial reputation. His writings appeared in German even more often than in English. He was active in the Lutheran World Federation and in the World Council of Churches. He has been a major interpreter of modern Swedish theology to the international academic community. In the 1990s, none of the Lund faculty is "Lundensian" in the Aulén-Nygren-Wingren sense; nevertheless, that influence certainly persists in Sweden. The Aulén-Wingren appeal to Irenaeus and Luther will continue to attract attention. Wingren's contribution to Lundensian (and Christian) theology is his distinctive appeal to make the first article the baseline for Christian theological analysis.

Bibliography

A. *Luther on Vocation* (1942; ET: Philadelphia, 1957; repr. St. Louis, Mo., 1988); *Man and the Incarnation* (1947; ET: Philadelphia, 1959); "The Doctrine of Creation: Not an Appendix but the First Article," *Word and World* 4 (1984): 353–71.

B. Bernard Erling, "Swedish Theology from Nygren to Wingren," *Religion in Life* 30 (1960–61): 196–208; S. Paul Schilling, "Gustaf Wingren" in *Contemporary Continental Theologians* (Nashville, Tenn., 1966), 161–82; Mary C. Vance-Welsh, "Gustaf Wingren: Creation Faith and Its Call for Full Incarnation," *Currents in Theology and Mission* 19 (1992): 259–66.

David T. Priestley

WITZEL, GEORGE (1501, Vacha, Rhön–16 February 1573, Mainz). *Education*: clerical studies at Univ. of Erfurt, 1516–19; Univ. of Wittenberg, 1520. *Career*: ordained priest, 1521; Protestant reformer, 1525–31; pastorates in Vacha, Fulda, Neimegk, Eisenach, 1522–30; returned to Catholicism, 1531; preacher, writer and church reformer in Eisleben, Dresden, Berlin, Fulda, Mainz, 1532–73.

Witzel was an ecclesiastical reformer who spent six years as a Protestant before returning to the Catholic Church. His ideas for the reform of the church came from his study of the Fathers, Vincent of Lerins,* the *Devotio Moderna*, and Erasmus.* His *Gesprächbüchlein* (Little Book of Dialogues) took both Lutherans and Roman Catholics to task for intransigent positions. At a conference at Leipzig (1539), Witzel and Martin Bucer* jointly wrote a formula for a German accord based on early church practices rather than medieval developments. Although the formula was widely circulated in Germany, it was rejected by the Catholic Church as too Protestant.

Bibliography

A. *Die Schriften Georg Witzels*, ed. G. Richter (Fulda, 1913).

B. DTC 15:3577–82; LThK² 10:1205–6; NCE 14:984–85; OEncR 4:287–88; RGG 6:1787–88; John P. Dolan, *The Influence of Erasmus, Witzel, and Cassander in the Church Ordinances of the United Duchees of Cleve during the Middle Decades of the 16th Century* (Münster, 1957); J. J. von Döllinger, *Die Reformation*, vol. 1 (Ratisbon, 1846), 26–125; Hubert Jedin, *A History of the Council of Trent* (London, 1957), 1:361ff; Barbara Henze, *Aus Liebe zur Kirche Reform: die Bemühungen Georg Witzels (1501–1573)* (Munster, 1995).

Joan Skocir

WOLFF, CHRISTIAN (24 January 1679, Breslau, Silesia–9 April 1754, Halle, Prussia). *Education*: studied at the gymnasium in Breslau and the Univ. of Jena; M.A., Univ. of Leipzig, 1703. *Career*: private tutor in philosophy, Leipzig, 1703–7; professor of mathmatics (then physics and various branches of philosophy), Halle, 1707–23; professor at Univ. of Marburg, 1723–40; vice chancellor, Univ. of Halle, 1740–43, chancellor, 1743–54.

Wolff was the most influential philosopher of his day in Germany. Not an original thinker, he was strongly influenced by Leibniz and also Descartes. He systematized and popularized Enlightenment thought and established German philosophical terminology. He was a prolific writer, authoring works on a wide variety of subjects.

He demonstrated the existence of God with variations of the ontological, cosmological, and teleological arguments. Although he did not deny the possibility of revelation or miracles, his emphasis on natural religion and his claim that revelation cannot contradict reason minimized their importance.

He was banished from the University of Halle in 1723 because of the opposition of the Pietists. His reappointment in 1740 by Frederick the Great marked the triumph of rationalism in Germany.

Bibliography

A. *Gesammelte Werke*, photographically reproduced with introduction by J. Ecole and H. W. Arndt, 20 vols. (Hildesheim, 1962); *The Preliminary Discourse on Philosophy in General*, trans. Richard A. Blackwell (Indianapolis, Ind., 1963).

B. LThK² 10:1214; NCE 14:985–87; ODCC 1759–60; RGG 6:1801–2; *Encyclopedia of Philosophy* 8:340–44; W. Arnsperger, *Christian Wolff's Verhältniss zu Leibniz* (Heidelberg, 1897); Lewis White Beck, *Early German Philosophy: Kant and His Predecessors*, (Cambridge, Mass., 1969); Emil Utitz, *Christian Wolff* (Halle, 1929); Thomas P. Saine, *The Problem of Being Modern: or the German Pursuit of Enlightenment from Leibnitz to the French Revolution* (Detroit, Mich., 1997).

John M. Brenner

WYCLIF, JOHN (ca. 1335/38, Yorkshire–31 December 1384, Lutterworth, Leicestershire). *Education*: B.A., M.A., B.Th., D.Th., Oxford Univ. by 1356, by 1360; by 1369; by 1372. *Career*: master of Balliol Coll., 1360–61; warden of Canterbury Coll., 1365–67; rector of Fillingham, 1361–68; rector of Ludg-ershall, 1368–74; rector of Lutterworth, 1374–84.

One of the most prolific writers of the late Middle Ages, John Wyclif was at once schoolman and reformer. Having written extensively in philosophy before taking his doctorate in 1372, Wyclif devoted his efforts to theological matters from that time forward. He completed a commentary on the entire Bible and produced often massive works on the nature of the church, on the Bible, on civil and ecclesiastical dominion, and on the Eucharist. Wyclif taught a meta-physical realism owing much to the older Platonic tradition of Augustine,* An-selm,* and Grosseteste.* A sharp critic of nominalism, Wyclif proposed a hierarchy of universals, the greatest of which is the primary exemplar and first cause existing within the divine intellect.

Very concerned with church corruption, Wyclif held that nobody rightfully exercised dominion if not in a state of grace, and that clergy, if acting unjustly, could be deprived of their temporalities by secular authorities. The church com-prised the predestined, whose only head was Christ, while those foreknown to be damned possessed no legitimate jurisdiction. The Bible, a manifestation of eternal truth and possessing a sacred logic, was wholly authoritative. Though maintaining the infallibility of Scripture, Wyclif acknowledged its subtleties of language and signification, often turning to the church fathers for exegetical guidance.

When, by 1380, Wyclif had repudiated the scholastic doctrine of transsub-stantiation, asserting instead the substantial remnance of elements, though still affirming the true, spiritual presence of Christ, he was condemned and lost much of his support among the nobility and fellow scholastics. Leaving Oxford by the end of 1381, he retired to Lutterworth where he continued to write sermons and polemical works. He died in 1384 still in communion with the church, though in 1428 his body was burned and the ashes cast into the river Swift.

Bibliography

A. *De veritate sacrae scripturae*, ed. R. Buddensieg, 3 vols. (London, 1905–7; repr. New York, 1966); *De ecclesia*, ed. J. Loserth (London, 1886; repr. New York, 1966); *De eucharistia tractatus maior*, ed. idem (London, 1892; repr. New York, 1966); *De civili dominio*, ed. idem, 3 vols. (London, 1902; repr. New York, 1966); *Tractatus de universalibus*, ed. I. J. Mueller (Oxford, 1985), trans. A. Kenny, *On Universals* (Oxford, 1985).

B. DTC 15:3585–614; LThK² 10:1278–81; NCE 14:1050–52; ODCC 1769–70; Got-thard Lechler, *Johann von Wicliff und die Vorgeschichte der Reformation*, 2 vols. (Leip-zig, 1873); trans. P. Lorimer, *John Wycliffe and His English Precursors* (London, 1884); Herbert B. Workman, *John Wyclif: A Study of the English Medieval Church*, 2 vols. (Oxford, 1926); J. A. Robson, *Wyclif and the Oxford Schools* (Cambridge, 1961); An-thony Kenny, *Wyclif* (New York, 1985); *Wyclif in His Times*, ed. Anthony Kenny (Ox-ford, 1986).

Ian Christopher Levy

X

XAVIER, FRANCIS. *See* FRANCIS XAVIER.

XIMÉNES DE CISNEROS, FRANCISCO (Jiménez) (1436, Torrelaguna, Spain–8 November 1517, Roa, Spain). *Education*: studied law and theology, Univs. of Alcalá and Salamanca, 1450s; studied at Rome under Italian humanists, 1459–66. *Career*: imprisoned in Spain, 1473–79; chaplain, diocese of Siquenza, 1480–84; entered the Franciscans, Toledo, 1484; confessor to Queen Isabella, 1492; archbishop of Toledo and primate of Castile, 1495–1517; cardinal, 1507.

Although deeply conservative, Ximénes was the founder of the humanist University of Alcalá (1508) and funded the great Compultensian Polyglot Bible. On the death of King Ferdinand in 1516 Ximénes was regent; he died on the way to meet the new ruler, Charles V. He was not a theologian himself. Ironically, he fostered a broader range of scholastic theology in Spain and encouraged humanism at the same time that he was strengthening the Inquisition. Some have even seen his encouragement of mental prayer as a prelude to the *alumbrado* movement. His reform of the clergy and religious orders made Spain less receptive of Protestant ideas after his death. He was largely responsible for the 1499 Spanish decree that required Muslims to convert or leave Spain. In 1509, moreover, he led a crusade expedition against Oran.

Bibliography

A. *Cartas del cardenal . . . Cisneros* (Madrid, 1867).
B. LThK² 10:1285–87; NCE 14:1062–64; ODCC 1771; OEncR 2:345–46; RGG 6:

1854; Tarsicio de Azcona, *La elección y reforma del episcopado español en tiempo de los Reyes Católicos* (Madrid, 1960); L. Fernández de Retuna, *Cisneros y su siglo*, 2 vols. (Madrid, 1929–30).

John Patrick Donnelly

Z

ZABARELLA, FRANCISCUS (1360, Padua–26 September 1417, Constance). *Education*: studied law at Bologna, 1378–83; received doctorate in both laws at Florence, 1385. *Career*: taught at Florence, 1385–90 and Padua, 1390–1410; bishop of Florence, 1410; cardinal, 1411.

Zabarella was one of the most influential legal minds of his generation; dozens of students from all over Europe studied with him. His ideas were passed on to later generations (e.g., Cusa,* Cesarini, Panormitanus) through his extensive commentaries on both the Gregorian and Clementine decretals; but his most famous work is probably his *De scismate* (1403–8). Zabarella applied medieval corporation theory, the implications of the idea of the church as the Body of Christ, to the crisis of his age, when that church was hopelessly divided between two and then three obediences, each claiming to be the followers of the true and valid pope. Applying many of the accepted phrases from the earlier canonistic tradition (e.g., "quod omnes tangit," "nisi devius a fide"), Zabarella argued that the Body of Christ, the community of the faithful, which could not err nor fail, was indeed the *Ecclesia Romana* to which Christ had promised his presence for all time. Hence, this body in itself held the ultimate authority and so could act to preserve its existence as "one, holy." Therefore, any authority held by any individual, in any office in the church, could only be authority delegated to it by the community, and the one holding authority was thus answerable to that community, not as lord of the community but as minister for the body, which was Christ. As a conciliarist, Zabarella's view was that the church elected a person as the pope who held divine authority to serve for the good of the believing community, and hence that community could remove him if and when he acted against this mandate. The agent with the authority to depose the pope was the general council, which represented the whole body of the faithful and so could exercise its authority. Zabarella was active in the negotiations that led to the Council of Constance and then in its sessions down to his death just weeks before the election of Pope Martin V, which brought an end to the Western Schism.

Bibliography

B.   DMA 12:735; NCE 14:1101; ODCC 1776; PRE 18:339–41; Gregorio Piaia, "La fondazione filosofica della teoria conciliare in Francesco Zabarella," in *Scienza e Filosofia all' Università di Padova nel Quattrocento*, ed. Antonino Poppi (Padua, 1983), 431–61; Dieter Girgensohn, "Franciscus Zabarella aus Padua," *Zeitschrift der Savigny— Stiftung für Rechtsgeschichte. Kanonistische Abteilung* 110 (1993): 232–77; Thomas E. Morrissey's articles cited in Ansgar Frenken, "Die Erforschung des Konstanzer Konzils 1414–1418," AHC 25 (1993): 466.

Thomas E. Morrissey

ZAHM, JOHN AUGUSTINE (14 June 1851, New Lexington, Ohio–10 November, 1921, Munich, Germany). *Education*: B.A., Univ. of Notre Dame, 1871; studied at Notre Dame Sem., Ind, 1871–75. *Career*: ordained priest, 1875; professor of chemistry and physics, Univ. of Notre Dame, 1875–92; visiting lecturer in N.Y., Wis., Calif., Belgium, and Switzerland, 1893–97; United States provincial of the Congregation of the Holy Cross, 1889–1905; explorer and author, 1906–21.

Zahm was one of the first American Catholic intellectuals to offer a rigorous apology for the Catholic Church as a friend to modern science. Between 1892 and 1898, he published widely (his works were translated into French, Italian, and Spanish) on the sympathetic relationship between modern science and Catholic teachings. In his most noteworthy work, *Evolution and Dogma* (Chicago, 1896), Zahm opposed an unscientific, literal approach to a Catholic reading of the biblical account of creation. He encouraged natural scientists and theologians to avoid the intellectual traps of special creationism and naturalistic evolutionism. In publications like *The American Catholic Quarterly Review* and *The American Ecclesiastical Review*, Zahm challenged material evolutionists like Cornell University President Andrew White with a theistic theory of evolution.

Both American and European liberal Catholics welcomed Zahm's compelling arguments for a rapprochement between Catholic teachings and modern scientific insights. Even though Pope Leo XIII awarded Zahm a Doctor of Philosophy in Rome (1895), conservative American and European Catholics pressured the Vatican to judge Zahm's ideas far too "advanced" in the areas of natural science and theology to be consistent with church dogma. Zahm ceased the publication of his scientific works after 1898 because of the opposition to them.

Bibliography

A.   *Catholic Science and Catholic Scientists* (Philadelphia, 1893); *Bible, Science and Faith* (Baltimore, Md., 1894); *Science and the Church* (Chicago, 1896).
B.   DAB 20:641–42; DACB 609–10; DARB 635–36; NCAB 9:274; NCE 14:1109;

NYT 12 November 1921, 13; Ralph E. Weber, *Notre Dame's John Zahm* (Notre Dame, Ind., 1961).

Dominic P. Scibilia

ZIGLIARA, TOMASSO MARIA (29 October 1833, Bonifacio in Corsica–10 May 1893, Rome, Italy). *Education*: studied philosophy and theology, Perugia, 1840s; studied in Rome, 1851–56. *Career*: entered Dominicans, Rome, 1851; ordained priest, 1856; professor of philosophy and theology, Rome and Corbara in Corsica, 1856–60, Viterbo, 1861–70; professor of theology, Coll. of St. Thomas (Minerva), Rome, 1870–93; cardinal, 1879.

Zigliara was an acknowledged leader in the revival of Thomistic philosophy and theology. His lifelong reflections on St. Thomas'* teachings on nature and supernature qualified him as a chief opponent of the traditionalism of Casimir Ubaghs and the ontologism of Rosmini-Serbati.* He was named editor in chief of the newly proposed Leonine edition of the *Summa Theologiae* and served on several papal commissions, aiding Pope Leo XIII in the composition of several encyclicals, among others *Aeterni Patris* (1879). He was also prefect of the Sacred Congregation on Historical Studies and helped to open up the Vatican archives to scholars.

Bibliography

A. *Summa Philosophica in Usum Scholarum*, 3 vols. (Rome, 1876); *Propaedeutica ad Sacram Theologiam seu Tractatus de Ordine Supernaturali* (Rome, 1880).

B. DTC 15:3692–94; ECatt 12:1797–98; LThK[2] 10:1370; NCE 14:1120; Antonio Iodice, "La spiritualità dell'anima umana nei neotomisti Tommaso Zigliara, Matteo Liberatore e Vincenzo Remer," *Atti del IX Congresso tomistico internazionale*, ed. A. Piolanti (Vatican City, 1991); Marco Giammarino, "Alle origine del neo-tomismo: il cardinal Tommaso Zigliara (1833–1893) nelle sue opere filosofiche e nell'epistolario," *Tomismo e neotomismo*, ed. Henri Fret, et al. (Pistoia, Italy, 1975).

William J. Kelly

ZINZENDORF, NIKOLAUS LUDWIG VON (26 May 1700, Dresden, Saxony–9 May 1760, Herrnhut, Saxony). *Education*: attended the Paedagogium, Halle, 1710–16; studied law, Univ. of Wittenberg, 1716–19. *Career*: king's councilor, court of Augustus the Strong, King of Saxony, 1721–27; ordained Lutheran minister, 1734; consecrated Moravian bishop, 1737; banished from Saxony, visited Moravian settlements and missions, 1736–47; promoted Moravianism in Saxony and England, 1747–60.

Zinzendorf was influenced by eighteenth-century Lutheran Pietism. Philipp Spener* (1635–1705) was his godfather and he studied under August Hermann Francke* (1663–1727) at Halle. True to his pietistic heritage he was not a systematic theologian. For him religion was a matter of feeling rather than reasoning. He departed from much of Pietism, however, by emphasizing the joy and confidence of the Christian life rather than penitential struggles and conversion.

Having given the Moravians refuge on his estate, Zinzendorf felt an obligation for their welfare. He became the leader of the group and did much to mold the theological outlook of this renewed Moravianism.

Zinzendorf was original and even daring in his theological expression. Although his theology was Christocentric, he went beyond Luther.* For him the person of the Savior was not only the Redeemer of the world, but the Creator and Preserver almost to the exclusion of the Father. Zinzendorf emphasized the *slaughtered* Lamb and the necessity of identifying psychologically with the Savior in his suffering. In this way a person appropriates the benefits of Christ's work. He departed from orthodox expression in speaking of the Trinity in terms of the divine Father, Mother, and Son. He referred to the church not only as the bride of Christ, but also as the daughter-in-law of the Father and the Holy Ghost Mother.

He tried to break down denominational barriers because he saw the church as bound together by common salvation, obedience, and joy, rather than common confession of theological truths. His hopes of bringing various denominations together met with disappointment and often increased discord. Because he instilled a strong missionary zeal in his followers, Moravian missions were planted in many parts of the world.

He was a prolific hymn writer. Some of his hymns have become Christian favorites, most have been forgotten, and many are characterized by an extreme sentimentalism.

Bibliography

A.   *Hauptschriften*, ed. Erich Beyreuther and Gerhard Meyer, 6 vols. (Hildesheim, 1962–63); *Ergänzungsbände zu den Hauptschriften*, ed. Erich Beyreuther and Gerhard Meyer, 12 vols. (Hildsheim, 1964–72); *Nine Public Lectures on Important Subjects in Religion*, ed. and trans. George W. Forell (Iowa City, Iowa, 1973).

B.   DTC 15:3695–704; NCE 14:1122; ODCC 1781–82; PRE 21:679–703; RGG 6: 1913–16; Augustus G. Spangenberg, *Leben des Herrn Nicolaus Ludwig Grafen und Herrn von Zinzendorf und Pottendorf*, 3 vols. (Barby, Germany, 1772–75) abridged and trans. Samuel Jackson, *The Life of Nicholaus Lewis, Count Zinzendorf* (London, 1838); A. J. Lewis, *Zinzendorf the Ecumenical Pioneer* (London, 1962); John R. Weinlick, *Count Zinzendorf* (Nashville, Tenn., 1956); F. Ernest Stoeffler, *German Pietism during the Eighteenth Century* (Leiden, 1973).

John M. Brenner

ZWINGLI, ULRICH or HULDREICH (1 January 1484, Wildhaus, Toggenburg District, Switzerland–11 October 1531, Canton of Zug, Switzerland). *Education*: studied at Univ. of Vienna, 1498–99, 1501–2; B.A., M.A., Univ. of Basel, 1504, 1506. *Career*: ordained priest, 1506; pastor, Glarus, 1506–16; military chaplain to Swiss mercenaries in papal service, 1513, 1515; pastor, Einsiedeln, 1516–18; Leutpriester (people's priest), Grossmünster, Zurich, 1519–31; resigned priesthood, 1522, and reemployed in same position by city council as evangelical pastor, 1522–31.

Zwingli and Switzerland are closely joined, both in his patriotism and his doctrinal emphasis on faith that transforms the believer into a concerned member of the community. His early association with humanists at the University of Basel and especially his admiration for Erasmus'* *Enchiridion* and *Novum Instrumentum* helped shape Zwingli's Reformed perspective of Christian life and total reliance on Scripture. At the same time, the tradition of self-governance in Zurich, in which the city council often decided upon religious as well as civic matters, gave a distinct community character to the Swiss Reformation in Zurich. Zwingli's liturgical changes reflect this community aspect, since the bread and wine were passed from person to person in the assembly in a horizontal theology that placed emphasis on Christ's spiritual presence in the faithful rather than in the sacramental elements.

The Swiss Reformation can be dated from Zwingli's call to the Grossmünster in December 1518, whereupon he immediately began preaching from the entire Bible rather than from prescribed pericopes. Scripture as absolute authority and guide for the Christian was proclaimed in Zwingli's *Of the Clarity and Certainty of the Word of God* (1522). He considered that the Old and New Testaments formed one whole, inspired by the Holy Spirit, with no possibility for error or disagreement since obscurities are clarified by referring to other texts and the Holy Spirit enlightens the humble and searching soul.

Zwingli's calls for reform accelerated in Zurich with the general support of the city council. His published sermon, "Of freedom of choice in the selection of food," 1522, marked the beginning of many written works critical of the church's practices. In response to external criticisms of Zwingli, the Zurich city council asked him to defend his positions, which he did with sixty-seven theses presented to 600 assembled civic and religious authorities, January and October 1523. The debates touched upon reverence for images, married clergy, intercessions, the meaning of church, papal authority, purgatory, and the Mass as sacrifice. The Council accepted Zwingli's positions and initiated an orderly removal of images from Zurich churches, a gradual beginning of cooperative efforts by city and church for reform.

In his conception of church as civic and religious community, Zwingli eagerly accepted Philip of Hesse's invitation to Reformers to a colloquy at Marburg, 1529, in the hope of presenting a united religious and political front to Charles V. The Reformers agreed or compromised on fourteen of fifteen points, including justification by faith and scriptural authority, but parted ways in the essential matter of Christ's presence in the eucharistic elements that also reflected upon Christology itself. In this, Zwingli followed a spiritual understanding of Christ's presence in the Eucharist because he is physically present at the right hand of the Father. For Zwingli *edere est credere*—that is, to eat the consecrated elements in faith is to make Christ spiritually present to the heart. Because Zwingl's position could not be reconciled with Luther's* theology of real presence, which was central to Luther's Christology, the attempt at unity failed.

Berne, Basle, St. Gall, and Schaffhausen agreed to the Zurich reforms after

1528, but the five Forest Cantons resisted despite evangelization efforts and a blockade. They unexpectedly attacked Zurich at Kappel, where Zwingli was killed in full battle armor as a citizen/soldier.

Bibliography

A. *Huldreich Zwinglis sämtliche Werke*, 14 vols., *Corpus Reformatorum*, ed. Emil Egil et al. (Leipzig, Berlin, 1905–); *Selected Works of Huldreich Zwingli*, ed. Samuel M. Jackson (Philadelphia, 1901); *Zwingli and Bullinger*, vol. 24. of LCC, ed. G. W. Bromiley (Philadelphia, 1953); *Zwinglis Hauptschriften*, vols. 1–4, 7, 9–11, ed. Fritz Blanke et al. (Zurich, 1940–); *Selected Writings of Huldrych Zwingli*, trans. E. J. Furcha and H. Wayne Pipkin, 2 vols. (Allison Park, Pa., 1984).

B. DTC 15:3716–44; ECatt 12:1836–40; LThK² 10:1114–18; NCE 14:1141–42; ODCC 1783–84; OEncR 4:320–23; PRE 21:774–815; RGG 6:1952–69; Jacques Courvoisier, *Zwingli: A Reformed Theologian* (Richmond, Va., 1963); Oskar Farner, *Zwingli, the Reformer, His Life and Work*, trans. D. G. Sear (New York, 1952); H. Wayne Pipkin, *A Zwingli Bibliography* (Pittsburgh, 1972); G. R. Potter, *Zwingli* (Cambridge, 1984); W. P. Stephens, *The Theology of Huldrych Zwingli* (Oxford, 1986).

Joan Skocir

SELECTED BIBLIOGRAPHY

Adam, Alfred. *Lehrbuch der Dogmengeschichte*. 2 vols. Gütersloh: G. Mohn's, 1965, 1968.

Aulén, Gustaf. *Christus Victor: An Historical Study of the Three Main Types of the Idea of Atonement*. 1931, 1967. Trans. A. G. Hebert. New York: Macmillan, 1969.

Baur, Ferdinand Christian. *Lehrbuch der christlichen Dogmengeschichte*. 1867. Repr. Darmstadt: Wissenschaftliche Buchgesellschaft, 1968.

Bosc, Jean. *La foi chrétienne: Accords et divergences des églises*. Paris: Presses Universitaires de France, 1965.

Bouyer, Louis. *The Word, Church, and Sacraments in Protestantism and Catholicism*. Trans. A. V. Littledale. 1961. Repr. New York: Desclée, 1981.

Burkill, T. Alee. *The Evolution of Christian Thought*. Ithaca, N.Y.: Cornell University Press, 1971.

Campenhausen, Hans Freiherr von. *The Formation of the Christian Bible*. Trans. J. A. Baker. Philadelphia: Fortress, 1972.

C.E.R.I.T., Strasbourg. *Les Chrétiens et leurs doctrines*. Paris: Desclée, 1987.

Chenu, Marie-Dominique. *La théologie comme science au XIIIᵉ siècle*. Paris: Librairie philosophique J. Vrin, 1957.

Congar, Yves. *A History of Theology*. Trans. Hunter Guthrie. Garden City, N.Y.: Doubleday, 1968.

Copleston, Frederick Charles. *A History of Philosophy*. 9 vols. Westminster, Md.: Newman, 1946–75.

Cunliffe-Jones, Hubert, ed. *A History of Christian Doctrine*. Edinburgh: T. and T. Clark, 1978.

Di Berardino, Angelo, and Basil Studer, eds. *History of Theology*. Vol. 1, *The Patristic Period*; Vol. 3, *The Renaissance*. Trans. Matthew J. O'Connell. Collegeville, Minn: Liturgical Press, 1997–.

Drumm, Joachim. *Doxologie und Dogma: Die Bedeutung der Doxologie für die Wied-*

ergewinnung theologischer Rede in der evangelischen Theologie. Paderborn: Ferdinand Schöningh, 1991.

Fisher, George Park. *History of Christian Doctrine.* 1901. Repr. New York: AMS Press, 1976.

Geiselmann, Josef Rupert. *The Meaning of Tradition.* Trans. W. J. O'Hara. Freiburg: Herder, 1966.

Gonzalez, Justo L. *Christian Thought Revisited: Three Types of Theology.* Nashville, Tenn.: Abingdon, 1989.

———. *A History of Christian Thought.* 3 vols. 1975. Rev. ed. Nashville, Tenn.: Abingdon, 1987.

Grabmann, Martin. *Die Geschichte der katholischen Theologie seit dem Ausgang der Väterzeit.* Repr. Darmstadt: Wissenschaftliche Buchgesellschaft, 1983.

Grillmeier, Aloys. *Christ in Christian Tradition.* 2 vols. in several parts. Trans. John Bowden et al. Atlanta, Ga.: John Knox, 1975–.

Hägglund, Bengt. *History of Theology.* Trans. Gene J. Lund. St. Louis, Mo.: Concordia, 1968.

Hanson, R. P. C. *The Search for the Christian Doctrine of God: The Arian Controversy, 318–381.* Edinburgh: T. and T. Clark, 1988.

Harnack, Adolf von. *History of Dogma.* Trans. Neil Buchanan from 3rd ed. in 4 vols. Repr. New York: Dover, 1961.

Heick, Otto Wilhelm. *A History of Christian Thought.* 2 vols. Philadelphia: Fortress, 1965–66.

Herr, William A. *Catholic Thinkers in the Clear: Giants of Catholic Thought from Augustine to Rahner.* Chicago: Thomas More, 1985.

Hödl, Ludwig. *Welt-Wissen und Gottes-Glaube in Geschichte und Gegenwart: Festgabe für Ludwig Hödl zu seinem 65. Geburtstag.* St. Ottilien: EOS Verlag, 1990.

Jedin, Hubert. *Ecumenical Councils of the Catholic Church: An Historical Outline.* Trans. Ernest Graf. New York: Herder and Herder, 1960.

Kelly, J. N. D. *Early Christian Creeds.* 3d ed. London: Longmans, 1972.

———. *Early Christian Doctrines.* San Francisco: Harper and Row, 1978.

Lohse, Bernhard. *A Short History of Christian Doctrine.* Trans. F. Ernest Stoeffler. 1966. Repr. Philadelphia: Fortress, 1978.

Löser, Werner, et al. *Dogmengeschichte und katholische Theologie.* Würzburg: Echter, 1985.

Macy, Gary. *The Banquet's Wisdom: A Short History of the Theologies of the Lord's Supper.* New York: Paulist, 1992.

McGiffert, Arthur Cushman. *A History of Christian Thought.* 2 vols. 1932. Repr. New York: C. Scribner's Sons, 1953.

McGrath, Alister E. *The Genesis of Doctrine: A Study in the Foundations of Doctrinal Criticism.* Oxford: B. Blackwell, 1990.

Meyendorff, John. *Christ in Eastern Christian Thought.* Washington, D.C.: Corpus Books, 1969.

Neander, Augustus. *Lectures on the History of Christian Dogmas.* 2 vols. Trans. J. E. Ryland. London: H. G. Bohn, 1858.

Neve, Juergen Ludwig. *A History of Christian Thought.* 2 vols. 1946. Repr. Philadelphia: Fortress, 1965–66.

Newman, John Henry. *An Essay on the Development of Christian Doctrine.* 1845. Rev. ed. 1878. Repr. Notre Dame, Ind.: University of Notre Dame Press, 1989.

Nichols, Aidan. *The Shape of Catholic Theology: An Introduction to Its Sources, Principles, and History*. Collegeville, Minn.: Liturgical Press, 1991.

Otten, Bernard John. *A Manual of the History of Dogmas*. 2 vols. St. Louis, Mo.: B. Herder, 1917–18.

Peerman, Dean G., and Martin E. Marty, eds. *A Handbook of Christian Theologians*. 1965. Rev. ed. Nashville, Tenn.: Abingdon, 1984.

Pelikan, Jaroslav. *From Luther to Kierkegaard: A Study in the History of Theology*. 1950. Repr. St. Louis, Mo.: Concordia, 1963.

————. *The Christian Tradition: A History of the Development of Doctrine*. 5 vols. Chicago: University of Chicago Press, 1971–89.

Placher, William C. *A History of Christian Theology*. Philadelphia: Westminster, 1983.

Prestige, G. L. *God in Patristic Thought*. 2d ed. London: S. P. C. K., 1952.

Robinson, James McConkey. *Theology as History*. New York: Harper and Row, 1967.

Ruckert, Hanns. *Vorträge und Aufsätze zur historischen Theologie*. Tübingen: Mohr, 1972.

Seeberg, Reinhold. *Text-book of the History of Doctrines*. Trans. Charles E. Hay. Repr. Grand Rapids, Mich.: Baker, 1977.

Shedd, William Greenough Thayer. *A History of Christian Doctrine*. 3d ed. New York: Scribner, Armstrong, 1872.

Strauss, David Friedrich. *Die christliche Glaubenslehre in ihrer geschichtlichen Entwicklung und im Kampfe mit der modernen Wissenschaft*. 1840. Repr. Frankfurt/Main: Minerva, 1984.

Tillich, Paul. *A History of Christian Thought*. 2d ed. rev. New York: Harper and Row, 1968.

Tixeront, Joseph. *History of Dogmas*. Trans. H. L. B. 3 vols. St. Louis, Mo.: B. Herder, 1910–16.

Toon, Peter. *The Development of Doctrine in the Church*. Grand Rapids, Mich.: Eerdmans, 1979.

Troeltsch, Ernst. *The Social Teachings of the Christian Churches*. Trans. Olive Wyon. 2 vols. 1931. Repr. Louisville, Ky.: Westminster, 1992.

Urban, Linwood. *A Short History of Christian Thought*. New York: Oxford, 1986.

Weber, Otto. *Foundations of Dogmatics*. Trans. Darrell L. Guder. 2 vols. Grand Rapids, Mich.: Eerdmans, 1981–83.

Wegman, Herman A. J. *Christian Worship in East and West: A Study Guide to Liturgical History*. Trans. G. W. Lathrop. New York: Pueblo, 1985.

INDEX

Note: **bold** numbers indicate biographical entries.

CONTRIBUTORS

R. SCOTT APPLEBY, University of Notre Dame, Notre Dame, Ind.: John Richard Slattery.

DONALD S. ARMENTROUT, University of the South, Sewanee, Tenn.: William Dwight Peter Bliss; Joseph Butler; Thomas Cranmer; Richard Hooker; John Jewel; Hugh Latimer; William Laud; William Law; Douglas Clyde Macintosh; William Paley; Matthew Parker; William Temple; Matthew Tindal.

JEFFREY W. BARBEAU, Port Washington, Wis.: Samuel Taylor Coleridge.

MICHEL RENÉ BARNES, Marquette University, Milwaukee, Wis.: Athanasius of Alexandria; Didymus the Blind; Eusebius of Nicomedia; Ignatius of Antioch; Théodore de Régnon.

CHRISTOPHER M. BELLITTO, St. Joseph's Seminary, Yonkers, N.Y.: Pierre D'Ailly; Jean Gerson; Marsilius of Padua; Nicolas de Clamanges.

PAUL M. BLOWERS, Emmanuel School of Religion, Johnson City, Tenn.: Gregory of Nyssa; Maximus the Confessor.

JOHN BOLT, Calvin College, Grand Rapids, Mich.: Herman Bavinck; Abraham Kuyper.

MATTHEW BRANDT, St. Paul, Minn.: Balthasar Hubmaier; Michael Servetus.

PETER W. BREITSCH, Williamsville, N.Y.: Gabriel Biel; Thomas Bradwardine; Gregory of Rimini.

JOHN M. BRENNER, Mequon, Wis.: Ferdinand Christian Baur; Johann Salamo Semler; David Friedrich Strauss; Carl Ferdinand Wilhelm Walther; Christian Wolff; Nikolaus Ludwig von Zinzendorf.

STEPHEN F. BROWN, Boston College, Chestnut Hill, Mass.: John Duns Scotus; William of Ockham.

PATRICK W. CAREY, Marquette University, Milwaukee, Wis.: Lyman Abbott; Alphonsus Maria di Liguori; William Ames; Antoine Arnauld; Cesar Baronius; Joseph Bellamy; Jacob Boehme; Thomas Joseph Bouquillon; Orestes Augustus Brownson; Melchior Cano; William Ellery Channing; William Chillingworth; Mary Baker Eddy; Jonathan Edwards; Jonathan Edwards, Jr.; Ralph Waldo Emerson; Nathaniel Emmons; Joseph Clifford Fenton; Charles Grandison Finney; George Fox; Francis de Sales; [Hyacinthe] Giacinto Sigismundo Gerdil; Georg Hermes; Augustine Francis Hewit; Samuel Hopkins; Francis Patrick Kenrick; Peter Richard Kenrick; John Knox; Franz Xaver Kraus; Joseph Marie de Maistre; Shailer Mathews; Virgil George Michel; Theodore Thornton Munger; John Courtney Murray; Phoebe Worrall Palmer; Dionysius Petavius; Pasquier Quesnel; Thomas Shepard; Richard Simon; Nathaniel William Taylor; Thérèse of Lisieux; John Tillotson; John Toland; George Whitefield; Daniel Day Williams; Roger Williams.

CHRISTOPHER M. CARR, Wellesley, Mass.: Francis Joseph Sheed.

GUY C. CARTER, St. Peter's College, Jersey City, N.J.: Paul August William Hermann Althaus; Dietrich Bonhoeffer; Friedrich Gogarten; John Henry W. Stuckenberg.

JOHN C. CAVADINI, University of Notre Dame, Notre Dame, Ind.: Alcuin; John Scotus Erigena; Gottschalk of Orbais; Paschasius Radbertus; Ratramnus of Corbie; Theodulf of Orléans.

DENIS CLEARY, Durham, England: Vincenzo Gioberti; Antonio Rosmini-Serbati.

DAVID COFFEY, Marquette University, Milwaukee, Wis.: Domingo Báñez; Luis de Molina; Michael Schmaus.

PATRICK W. COLLINS, Douglas, Mich: Gustave Weigel.

RICHARD F. COSTIGAN, Loyola University, Chicago, Ill.: Charles-Rene Billuart; Jacques-Benigne Bossuet; Rene-François de Chateaubriand; Johann Nikolaus von Hontheim [Febronius].

EWERT COUSINS, Fordham University, Bronx, N.Y.: Bonaventure.

J. KEVIN COYLE, Saint Paul University, Ottawa, Canada: Augustine of Hippo.

TERRENCE CROWE, Milwaukee, Wis.: Edward Bellamy; Edward John Carnell; William Henry Channing; John Cotton; Harry Emerson Fosdick; Emanuel Swedenborg; Rueben Archer Torrey.

LAWRENCE S. CUNNINGHAM, University of Notre Dame, Notre Dame, Ind.: Thomas Merton.

D. LYLE DABNEY, Marquette University, Milwaukee, Wis.: Rudolf Bultmann; Oscar Cullmann; Adolf von Harnack; Wilhelm Herrmann; Søren Kierkegaard; Friedrich Schleiermacher; Albert Schweitzer; Paul Tillich; Ernst Troeltsch; John Wesley.

BRIAN DAVIES, Fordham University, Bronx, N.Y.: Anselm of Bec and Canterbury; Catherine of Siena; Thomas Aquinas.

WILLIAM DiPUCCIO, Munroe Falls, Ohio: Johann August Wilhelm Neander; John Williamson Nevin; Philip Schaff.

ANTHONY D. DiSTEFANO, Mesa, Ariz.: Martin Bucer; Heinrich Bullinger; John Oecolampadius [Huszgen].

JOHN PATRICK DONNELLY, Marquette University, Milwaukee, Wis.: Robert Bellarmine; Thomas de Vio Cajetan; Gasparo Contarini; Desiderius Erasmus; Francis Xavier; Ignatius of Loyola; John of St. Thomas; Diego Laínez; Reginald Pole; Jacopo Sadoleto; Girolamo Seripando; Thomas Stapleton; Peter Martyr Vermigli; Francisco Ximénes de Cisneros.

KEITH J. EGAN, St. Mary's College, South Bend, Ind.: Louis Jean Bouyer; John of the Cross; Jacques Leclercq; Teresa of Ávila.

MICHAEL A. FAHEY, Marquette University, Milwaukee, Wis.: Augustin Bea; Marie-Dominique Chenu; Charles Journet; Émile Mersch; Juan Luis Segundo.

PAUL J. FEDWICK, University of St. Michael's College, Toronto, Canada: Basil the Great of Caesarea.

RONALD J. FEENSTRA, Calvin Theological Seminary, Grand Rapids, Mich.: Karl Barth; John Calvin.

THOMAS S. FERGUSON, Manhattan College, Bronx, N.Y.: Alan of Lille; Anicius Manlius Serverinus Boethius; Fulgentius of Ruspe; Gregory I, the Great; Hugh of St. Victor; Isidore of Seville; Leo I, the Great; Peter Damian; Robert of Melun; Walter of St. Victor.

JOHN P. FITZGIBBONS, Omaha, Neb.: Theodore Parker.

RAYMOND T. GAWRONSKI, Marquette University, Milwaukee, Wis.: Hans Urs von Balthasar; Nikolas Aleksandrovich Berdiaev; Aleksei Stepanovich Khomiakov; Vladimir Sergeevich Soloviev.

CLYDE GLASS, Calgary, Alberta, Canada: François Fénélon; Madame Jeanne Guyon.

ALEXANDER GOLITZIN, Marquette University, Milwaukee, Wis.: Nikolas N. Afanassieff; Dionysius Areopagita; Dositheus of Jerusalem; Filaret Drozdov; Georges V. Florovsky; John of Damascus; Vladimir Lossky; Cyril Lucaris; John Meyendorff; Peter Mogila; Nicodemus of the Holy Mountain; Gregory Palamas; Alexander Schmemann; Dumitru Staniloae; Symeon the New Theologian; Paisii Velichkovsky.

DAVID HADDORFF, St. John's University, Jamaica, N.Y.: Horace Bushnell.

PAUL HELSETH, Minnetonka, Minn.: Archibald Alexander; Charles Hodge; John Gresham Machen; Benjamin Breckinridge Warfield.

I. JOHN HESSELINK, Western Theological Seminary, Holland, Mich.: H. Emil Brunner.

BRADFORD HINZE, Marquette University, Milwaukee, Wis.: Johann Sebastian von

Drey; Johannes Kuhn; Johann Adam Möhler; John Michael Sailer; Franz Anton Staudenmaier.

CHRISTINE FIRER HINZE, Marquette University, Milwaukee, Wis.: (Karl Paul) Reinhold Niebuhr; John Augustine Ryan.

WILLIAM J. HOYE, University of Münster, Germany: Albert the Great; Alexander of Hales; Thomas Hooker; Raymond Lull; Nicholas of Cusa.

KEITH HUEY, Valparaiso, Ind.: Alexander Campbell.

D. THOMAS HUGHSON, Marquette University, Milwaukee, Wis.: Matthias Joseph Scheeben.

DARRELL JODOCK, Muhlenberg College, Allentown, Pa.: Albert Benjamin Ritschl.

WILLIAM J. KELLY, Marquette University, Milwaukee, Wis.: Johann Baptist Franzelin; Camillo Mazzella; John Henry Newman; Carlo Passaglia; John (Giovanni) Perrone; Tomasso Maria Zigliara.

THOMAS M. KING, Georgetown University, Washington, D.C.: Marie-Joseph Pierre Teilhard de Chardin.

ROBERT A. KRIEG, University of Notre Dame, Notre Dame, Ind.: Karl Adam; Romano Guardini.

PAUL K. KUENNING, Milwaukee, Wis.: Johann Arndt; Augustus Hermann Francke; Charles Porterfield Krauth; Thomas Müntzer; Samuel Simon Schmucker; Philipp Jakob Spener.

DANIEL MARCEL LA CORTE, Kalamazoo, Mich.: Anselm of Havelberg; Bernard of Clairvaux; John of Salisbury; Rupert of Deutz; William of St. Thierry.

MATTHEW LAMB, Boston College, Chestnut Hill, Mass.: Bernard J. F. Lonergan.

JOHN D. LAURANCE, Marquette University, Milwaukee, Wis.: Odo Casel; Gregory Dix; Prosper Louis Pascal Guéranger; Josef Andreas Jungmann; Maurice de la Taille; Pius Parsch.

MEL LAWRENZ, Elmbrook Christian Study Center, Brookfield, Wis.: John Chrysostom.

JAMES LeGRYS, New York, N.Y.: Maurice Blondel.

IAN CHRISTOPHER LEVY, Milwaukee, Wis.: Berengarius of Tours; Robert Grosseteste; Jan Hus; Andreas Osiander; John Wyclif.

JOSEPH T. LIENHARD, Fordham University, Bronx, N.Y.: Bede the Venerable; Clement of Rome; Henry (Heinrich) Heimbuche of Langenstein; Hermas; Hincmar of Rheims; Hippolytus of Rome; Humbert of Romans; John of Brevicoxa; Justin Martyr; Stephen Langton; Marcellus of Ancyra; Marcion; Novatian; Rabanus Maurus; Stephen of Tournai; Theodore of Studios; Ubertino of Casale.

GERALD A. McCOOL, Fordham University, Bronx, N.Y.: Reginald Garrigou-Lagrange; Joseph Kleutgen; Joseph Maréchal; Pierre Rousselot.

KEVIN MADIGAN, Catholic Theological Union, Chicago, Ill.: Joachim of Fiore; Nicholas of Lyra; Peter John Olivi.

R. BEN MADISON, Milwaukee, Wis.: Joseph Smith, Jr.

MARK S. MASSA, Fordham University, Bronx, N.Y.: Charles Augustus Briggs; William Adams Brown; William Newton Clarke.

ROBERT MASSON, Marquette University, Milwaukee, Wis.: Karl Rahner.

MELVIN MICHALSKI, St. Francis Seminary, Milwaukee, Wis.: Hugo Karl Erich Rahner.

PAUL MISNER, Marquette University, Milwaukee, Wis.: Franz Xaver von Baader; Michael Baius (de Bay); Heinrich Joseph Denzinger; Johannes Joseph Ignaz von Döllinger; Anton Günther; Fredrich Heiler; Cornelius Jansenius (Jansen); Félicité-Robert de Lamennais; Matteo Liberatore.

THOMAS E. MORRISSEY, State University of New York at Fredonia: James of Viterbo; John (Quidort) of Paris; John de Pouilly; John of Ragusa; Franciscus Zabarella.

M. MICHÈLE MULCHAHEY, University of Victoria, B.C., Canada: Anselm of Laon; Hugh of St.-Cher; Lanfranc; Peter Lombard; Siger of Brabant; William of Auxerre.

FREDERICK W. NORRIS, Emmanuel School of Religion, Johnson City, Tenn.: Gregory of Nazianzus.

RICHARD A. NORRIS, Union Theological Seminary (emeritus), New York, N.Y.: Irenaeus.

MARVIN R. O'CONNELL, University of Notre Dame, Notre Dame, Ind.: Blaise Pascal.

OLIVER K. OLSON, Minneapolis, Minn: Martin Chemnitz; Matthias Flacius; Johann Gerhard; Johann Lorenz von Mosheim.

JOSEPH PAGANO, Chicago, Ill.: Helmut Richard Niebuhr.

TROY PFLIBSEN, Hawkeye, Iowa: Theodore Beza; Johannes Bugenhagen.

WILLIAM L. PORTIER, Mt. St. Mary's College, Emmitsburg, Md.: Isaac Thomas Hecker; William Laurence Sullivan.

DAVID T. PRIESTLEY, Edmonton Baptist Seminary, Alberta, Canada: Gustaf Aulén; Einar Billing; Anders Nygren; Nathan Soderblom; Gustaf Wingren.

ANN RIGGS, Milwaukee, Wis.: Lucien Laberthonnière.

R. DAVID RIGHTMIRE, Asbury College, Wilmore, Ky.: Jacobus Arminius; William Booth; Franciscus Gomarius.

HEINZ D. ROSSOL, Holliswood, N.Y.: Walter Rauschenbusch.

BARRY H. SARGENT, Milwaukee, Wis.: Henry Edward Manning.

DAVID G. SCHULTENOVER, Creighton University, Omaha, Neb.: Louis Billot; Louis-

Marie-Olivier Duchesne; Baron Friedrich von Hügel; Alfred Firmin Loisy; Herman Schell; Adolphe-Alfred Tanquerey; George Tyrrell; William George Ward; Wilfrid Philip Ward.

DOMINIC P. SCIBILIA, New York, N.Y.: Solomon Washington Gladden; Bartolome de Las Casas; Edward McGlynn; Thomas McGrady; John Augustine Zahm.

DONALD SINNEMA, Trinity Christian College, Palos Heights, Ill.: Hugo Grotius.

JOAN SKOCIR, Milwaukee, Wis.: Johann Eck; Conrad Grebel; Jacob Hutter; Martin Luther; Philipp Melanchthon; Georg Witzel; Ulrich Zwingli.

ROBERT B. SLOCUM, Lake Geneva, Wis.: Lancelot Andrewes; William Porcher Dubose; Charles Gore; Francis Joseph Hall; John Henry Hobart; William Reed Huntington; John Keble; Frederick Denison Maurice; William Augustus Muhlenberg; Edward Bouverie Pusey; William Stringfellow; Robert Isaac Wilberforce.

THOMAS A. SMITH, Loyola University, New Orleans, La.: Faustus of Riez; John Cassian; Prosper, Tiro, of Aquitaine; Vincent of Lérins.

STEPHEN R. SPENCER, Dallas Theological Seminary, Dallas, Tex.: François Turretin.

KELLEY McCARTHY SPOERL, St. Anselm College, Manchester, N.H.: Apollinarius of Laodicea; Arius; Clement of Alexandria; Cyril of Jerusalem; Eusebius of Caesarea.

KENNETH B. STEINHAUSER, Saint Louis University, St. Louis, Mo.: Cyprian of Carthage; Tertullian; Tyconius.

ROLAND J. TESKE, Marquette University, Milwaukee, Wis.: Antoninus of Florence; Roger Bacon; Bernard of Tours; John Capreolus; Dionysius (Denis) the Carthusian; Durandus of St. Pourçain; Meister Eckhart; Gilbert of La Porrée; Giles of Rome; Geert de Groote; Henry of Ghent; Hervé of Nedellec; Julian of Eclanum; Margery Kempe; Robert Kilwardby; John Peckham; Pelagius; Peter Aureoli; Richard of St. Victor; Jan Van Ruysbroeck; Vincent of Beauvais; William of Auvergne.

JACK TRELOAR, Marquette University, Milwaukee, Wis.: Francis Suárez.

JOSEPH W. TRIGG, La Plata, Md.: Origen.

MELVIN G. VANCE, Sussex, Wis.: Johannes Brenz; Hans Denck; Sebastian Franck; Andreas (Bodenstein) Karlstadt; Caspar von Schwenckfeld; Menno Simons; Faustus Socinus.

LAWRENCE J. WELCH, Kenrick School of Theology, St. Louis, Mo.: Cyril of Alexandria; Nestorius.

DANIEL H. WILLIAMS, Loyola University, Chicago, Ill.: Ambrose of Milan; Hilary of Poitiers; Jerome.

SUSAN WOOD, St. John's University, Collegeville, Minn: Yves Marie-Joseph Congar; Jean Daniélou; Henri de Lubac.

ROBIN DARLING YOUNG, The Catholic University of America, Washington, D.C.: Ephrem the Syrian; Evagrius of Pontus; Tatian the Assyrian; Theodore of Mopsuestia.

JAMES ZEITZ, Our Lady of the Lake University, San Antonio, Tex.: Erich Przywara.

WANDA ZEMLER-CIZEWSKI, Marquette University, Milwaukee, Wis.: Peter Abelard; Hildegard of Bingen.

ISBN 0-313-29649-9

90000>

EAN

9 780313 296499

HARDCOVER BAR CODE